Standard Normal Distribution

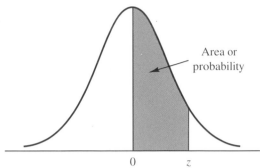

Area or probability

Entries in the table give the area under the curve between the mean and z standard deviations above the mean. For example, for $z = 1.25$ the area under the curve between the mean and z is .3944.

z	.00	.01	.02	.03	.04	.05	.06	.07	.08	.09
.0	.0000	.0040	.0080	.0120	.0160	.0199	.0239	.0279	.0319	.0359
.1	.0398	.0438	.0478	.0517	.0557	.0596	.0636	.0675	.0714	.0753
.2	.0793	.0832	.0871	.0910	.0948	.0987	.1026	.1064	.1103	.1141
.3	.1179	.1217	.1255	.1293	.1331	.1368	.1406	.1443	.1480	.1517
.4	.1554	.1591	.1628	.1664	.1700	.1736	.1772	.1808	.1844	.1879
.5	.1915	.1950	.1985	.2019	.2054	.2088	.2123	.2157	.2190	.2224
.6	.2257	.2291	.2324	.2357	.2389	.2422	.2454	.2486	.2518	.2549
.7	.2580	.2612	.2642	.2673	.2704	.2734	.2764	.2794	.2823	.2852
.8	.2881	.2910	.2939	.2967	.2995	.3023	.3051	.3078	.3106	.3133
.9	.3159	.3186	.3212	.3238	.3264	.3289	.3315	.3340	.3365	.3389
1.0	.3413	.3438	.3461	.3485	.3508	.3531	.3554	.3577	.3599	.3621
1.1	.3643	.3665	.3686	.3708	.3729	.3749	.3770	.3790	.3810	.3830
1.2	.3849	.3869	.3888	.3907	.3925	.3944	.3962	.3980	.3997	.4015
1.3	.4032	.4049	.4066	.4082	.4099	.4115	.4131	.4147	.4162	.4177
1.4	.4192	.4207	.4222	.4236	.4251	.4265	.4279	.4292	.4306	.4319
1.5	.4332	.4345	.4357	.4370	.4382	.4394	.4406	.4418	.4429	.4441
1.6	.4452	.4463	.4474	.4484	.4495	.4505	.4515	.4525	.4535	.4545
1.7	.4554	.4564	.4573	.4582	.4591	.4599	.4608	.4616	.4625	.4633
1.8	.4641	.4649	.4656	.4664	.4671	.4678	.4686	.4693	.4699	.4706
1.9	.4713	.4719	.4726	.4732	.4738	.4744	.4750	.4756	.4761	.4767
2.0	.4772	.4778	.4783	.4788	.4793	.4798	.4803	.4808	.4812	.4817
2.1	.4821	.4826	.4830	.4834	.4838	.4842	.4846	.4850	.4854	.4857
2.2	.4861	.4864	.4868	.4871	.4875	.4878	.4881	.4884	.4887	.4890
2.3	.4893	.4896	.4898	.4901	.4904	.4906	.4909	.4911	.4913	.4916
2.4	.4918	.4920	.4922	.4925	.4927	.4929	.4931	.4932	.4934	.4936
2.5	.4938	.4940	.4941	.4943	.4945	.4946	.4948	.4949	.4951	.4952
2.6	.4953	.4955	.4956	.4957	.4959	.4960	.4961	.4962	.4963	.4964
2.7	.4965	.4966	.4967	.4968	.4969	.4970	.4971	.4972	.4973	.4974
2.8	.4974	.4975	.4976	.4977	.4977	.4978	.4979	.4979	.4980	.4981
2.9	.4981	.4982	.4982	.4983	.4984	.4984	.4985	.4985	.4986	.4986
3.0	.4986	.4987	.4987	.4988	.4988	.4989	.4989	.4989	.4990	.4990

SECOND EDITION

ESSENTIALS OF STATISTICS FOR BUSINESS AND ECONOMICS

David R. Anderson
University of Cincinnati

Dennis J. Sweeney
University of Cincinnati

Thomas A. Williams
Rochester Institute of Technology

South-Western College Publishing
an International Thomson Publishing company I(T)P®

Cincinnati · Albany · Boston · Detroit · Johannesburg · London · Madrid · Melbourne · Mexico City
New York · Pacific Grove · San Francisco · Scottsdale · Singapore · Tokyo · Toronto

To: Marcia, Cherri, and Robbie

Publisher: Dave Shaut
Acquisitions Editor: Charles E. McCormick, Jr.
Senior Developmental Editor: Alice C. Denny
Marketing Manager: Joseph A. Sabatino
Production Editor: Deanna R. Quinn
Media and Technology Editor: Kevin von Gillern
Media Production Editor: Robin K. Browning
Manufacturing Coordinator: Dana Began Schwartz
Internal Design: Michael H. Stratton
Cover Design: Michael H. Stratton
Cover Photographer: Mark Tomalty/Masterfile
Production House and Compositor: BookMasters, Inc.
Printer: World Color Book Services

Printed in the United States of America
1 2 3 4 5 6 7 8 9 10

International Thomson Publishing Europe
Berkshire House
168-173 High Holborn
London, WC1V7AA, United Kingdom

Nelson ITP, Australia
102 Dodds Street
South Melbourne
Victoria 3205 Australia

Nelson Canada
1120 Birchmount Road
Scarborough, Ontario
Canada M1K 5G4

International Thomson Publishing Southern Africa
Building 18, Constantia Square
138 Sixteenth Road, P.O. Box 2459
Halfway House, 1685 South Africa

International Thomson Editores
Seneca, 53
Colonia Polanco
11560 Mèxico D.F. Mèxico

International Thomson Publishing Asia
60 Alberta Street #15-01
Albert Complex
Singapore 189969

International Thomson Publishing Japan
Hirakawa-cho Kyowa Building, 3F
2-2-1 Hirakawa-cho, Chiyoda-ku
Tokyo 102, Japan

Library of Congress Cataloging-in-Publication Data

Anderson, David Ray
    Essentials of statistics for business and economics / David R.
  Anderson, Dennis J. Sweeney, Thomas A. Williams. — 2nd ed.
      p. cm.
    Includes bibliographical references and index.
    ISBN 0-324-00328-5 (package : hc. : alk. paper) — ISBN
  0-324-00332-3 (book only : alk. paper)
      1. Social sciences—Statistical methods.   2. Commercial
  statistics.   3. Economics—Statistical methods.   4. Statistics—
  Problems, exercises, etc.   I. Sweeney, Dennis J.   II. Williams,
  Thomas Arthur.   III. Title.
  HA29.A587   2000
  519.5—dc21   99-27531

CONTENTS IN BRIEF

CONTENTS

Contents

The purpose of *Essentials of Statistics for Business and Economics, 2e* is to give students, primarily in the fields of business administration and economics, a conceptual introduction to the field of statistics and its many applications. The text is applications oriented and written with the needs of the nonmathematician in mind; the mathematical prerequisite is knowledge of algebra.

Applications of data analysis and statistical methodology are an integral part of the organization and presentation of the text material. The discussion and development of each technique is presented in an application setting, with the statistical results providing insights to decisions and solutions to problems.

Although the book is applications oriented, we have taken care to provide sound methodological development and to use notation that is generally accepted for the topic being covered. Hence, students will find that this text provides good preparation for the study of more advanced material. A revised and updated bibliography to guide further study is included as an appendix.

CHANGES IN THE SECOND EDITION

We appreciate the acceptance of and positive response to the first edition of *Essentials of Statistics for Business and Economics*. Accordingly, in making modifications for this new edition, we have maintained the presentation style and readability of the previous edition. The significant changes in the new edition are summarized here.

New Examples and Exercises Based on Real Data

We have added 180 new exercises and several new examples that are based on real data and recent reference sources of statistical information. Using the Census Bureau, *The Wall Street Journal, USA Today, Fortune, Barron's,* and a variety of other sources, we have drawn on actual studies to develop explanations and to create exercises that demonstrate many uses of statistics in business and economics. We believe that the use of real data helps generate more student interest in the material and enables the student to learn about both the statistical methodology and its application.

New Case Problems

We have added 6 new case problems to this edition, bringing the total number of case problems in the text to 15. The new case problems appear in the chapters on descriptive statistics, probability, hypothesis testing, comparisons involving means, comparisons involving proportions, and regression analysis. The case problems provide students with the opportunity to analyze somewhat larger data sets and prepare managerial reports that are based on the results of the analysis.

New Statistics in Practice

To emphasize how companies use statistics, each chapter begins with an application supplied by a practitioner. These chapter openings briefly describe an organization and a problem in which the statistical methodology introduced in the chapter has been applied. We have added two new Statistics in Practice to this edition: Small Fry Design (Chapter 3) and Citibank (Chapter 5). Procter & Gamble, Polaroid, Monsanto, Mead, Dow Chemical and Colgate-Palmolive have provided additional Statistics in Practice vignettes.

Annotations

Annotations that highlight key points and provide additional insights for the student are a new feature of this edition. These annotations, which appear in the margins, are designed to provide emphasis and enhance understanding of the terms and concepts being presented in the text.

MINITAB and Microsoft® Excel Spreadsheet Appendixes

Optional MINITAB and Excel Spreadsheet appendixes appear at the end of most chapters. Each appendix provides step-by-step procedures that make it easy for students to use MINITAB or Excel to conduct the statistical analysis present in the chapter. All appendixes have been updated for the latest versions of MINITAB and Excel. New appendixes have been added for dotplots, stem-and-leaf displays, crosstabulations, box plots, hypothesis testing, two population studies, tests of independence and quality control charts.

Data Files Accompany the Text

Over 100 data files are now available and are packaged with the text. The data files are available in both MINITAB and Excel formats. Data files for all case problems, as well as for larger data sets in exercises are included.

Content Revisions

The following list summarizes selected content revisions for this edition.

- The use of the Internet to obtain statistical information (Chapter 1)
- The uniform discrete probability distribution (Chapter 5)
- The hypergeometric distribution (Chapter 5)
- Data set for EAI population added and sampling error defined (Chapter 7)
- New text example for proportion and sample size determination (Chapter 8)
- Simplification of the material and use of MSTR and MSE notations in analysis of variance (Chapter 10)
- Computer output and the computation of p-values for Chi-square tests (Chapter 11)
- The use and interpretation of control charts provided by MINITAB (Chapter 13)

FEATURES AND PEDAGOGY

We have continued many of the features that appeared in the first edition. Some of the important ones follow.

Methods Exercises and Applications Exercises

The end-of-section exercises are split into two parts, "Methods" and "Applications." The Methods exercises require students to use the formulas and make the necessary computations. The Applications exercises require students to use the chapter material in real-world situations. Thus, students focus on the computational "nuts and bolts" and then move on to the subtleties of statistical applications and interpretation.

Self-test Exercises

Certain exercises are identified as self-test exercises. Completely worked-out solutions for these exercises are provided in an appendix at the end of the book. Students can attempt the self-test exercises and immediately check the solutions to evaluate their understanding of the concepts presented in the chapter.

Notes & Comments

At the end of many sections, we provide "Notes & Comments" designed to give the student additional insights about the statistical methodology and its application. "Notes & Comments" include warnings about limitations of the methodology, recommendations for application, brief descriptions of additional technical considerations, and other matters.

ANCILLARY TEACHING AND LEARNING MATERIALS

Two ancillaries are available to students either through their bookstore or for direct purchase through the on-line catalog at **www.swcollege.com**.

- Prepared by Mohammad Ahmadi of the University of Tennessee-Chattanooga, the Work Book (ISBN: 0-324-00331-5) provides the student with significant supplementary study materials. It contains an outline, review, list of formulas in each chapter, sample exercises with step-by-step solutions, exercises with answers, and a series of self-test questions with answers.
- A new student ancillary is *An Excel Companion for Business Statistics* (ISBN: 0-538-89088-6) by David Eldredge of Murray State College. This manual provides step-by-step instructions for using Microsoft® Excel 97 to solve many of the problems included in an introductory business statistics course.

The following instructor support materials are available to adopters from the ITP Academic Resource Center at 800-423-0563 or through **www.swcollege.com:**

- **Solutions Manual** The *Solutions Manual* (ISBN: 0-324-00330-7), prepared by the authors, includes solutions for all problems in the text. At the request of the instructor, the Solutions Manual can be packaged with the text for student purchase
- **Instructor's Resource Kit on CD-ROM** (ISBN: 0-324-00329-3) All instructor ancillaries are now provided on a single CD-ROM. Included in this convenient format are:
  - **Instructor's Manual** The *Instructor's Manual* also prepared by the authors, contains solutions to all case problems presented in the text.
  - **PowerPoint™ Presentation Slides** Prepared by John Loucks of St. Edward's University, the presentation slides contain a teaching outline that incorporates graphics to help instructors create even more stimulating lectures. The PowerPoint 97 slides may be adapted using PowerPoint software to facilitate classroom use.
  - **Test Bank and Thomson Learning Testing Tools™** Prepared also by Mohammad Ahmadi, the Test Bank includes true/false, multiple choice, short answer questions, and problems for each chapter. Testing Tools computerized testing software allows instructors to create, edit, store and print exams.

ACKNOWLEDGMENTS

We would like to acknowledge the work of our reviewers who provided comments and suggestions of ways to continue to improve our text. Thanks to:

Mike Bourke, Houston Baptist University

Robert Carver, Stonehill College

Tom Dahlstrom, Eastern College

Alan Humphrey, University of Rhode Island

Ann Hussein, Philadelphia College of Textiles and Science

Don Marx, University of Alaska, Anchorage

Tom McCullough, University of California - Berkeley

Mitchell Muesham, Sam Houston State University

Alan Olinsky, Bryant College

Harold Rahmlow, St. Joseph's University

David Tufte, University of New Orleans

Jack Vaughn, University of Texas-El Paso

We would like to recognize the following individuals who have helped us in the past and continue to influence our writing.

Peter Bryant, University of Colorado,

Terri L. Byczkowski, University of Cincinnati

Ying Chien, University of Scranton

Robert Cochran, University of Wyoming

David W. Cravens, Texas Christian University

Ronald Ehresman, Baldwin-Wallace College

Nicholas Farnum, California State University-Fullerton

Michael Ford, Rochester Institute of Technology

Phil Fry, Boise State University

Paul Guy, California State University-Chico

Ben Isselhardt, Rochester Institute of Technology

Jeffery Jarrett, University of Rhode Island

Barry Kadets, Bryant College

David Krueger, St. Cloud State University

Martin S. Levy, University of Cincinnati

Ka-sing Man, Georgetown University

Mario Miranda, The Ohio State University

Richard O'Connell, Miami University of Ohio

Tom Pray, Rochester Institute of Technology

Tom Ryan, Case Western Reserve University

Bill Seaver, University of Tennessee

Ari Wijetunga, Morehead State University

J. E. Willis, Louisiana State University

Mustafa Yilmaz, Northeastern University

A special thanks is owed to our associates from business and industry who supplied the "Statistics in Practice" features. We recognize them individually by a credit line in each of the articles. In addition, we acknowledge the cooperation of Minitab, Inc., in permitting the use of MINITAB statistical software in this text. Finally, we are also indebted to our acquisitions editor Charles McCormick, Jr., our senior developmental editor Alice Denny, our production editor Deanna Quinn, our marketing manager Joe Sabatino and others at South-Western College Publishing for the editorial counsel and support during the preparation of this text.

David R. Anderson
Dennis J. Sweeney
Thomas A. Williams

David R. Anderson.   David R. Anderson is Professor of Quantitative Analysis in the College of Business Administration at the University of Cincinnati. Born in Grand Forks, North Dakota, he earned his B.S., M.S., and Ph.D. degrees from Purdue University. Professor Anderson has served as Head of the Department of Quantitative Analysis and Operations Management and as Associate Dean of the College of Business Administration. In addition, he was the coordinator of the College's first Executive Program.

At the University of Cincinnati, Professor Anderson has taught introductory statistics for business students as well as graduate-level courses in regression analysis, multivariate analysis, and management science. He has also taught statistical courses at the Department of Labor in Washington, D.C. He has been honored with nominations and awards for excellence in teaching and excellence in service to student organizations.

Professor Anderson has coauthored eight textbooks in the areas of statistics, management science, linear programming, and production and operations management. He is an active consultant in the field of sampling and statistical methods.

Dennis J. Sweeney.   Dennis J. Sweeney is Professor of Quantitative Analysis and Director of the Center for Productivity Improvement at the University of Cincinnati. Born in Des Moines, Iowa, he earned a B.S.B.A. degree from Drake University and his M.B.A. and D.B.A. degrees from Indiana University where he was an NDEA Fellow. During 1978–79, Professor Sweeney worked in the management science group at Procter & Gamble; during 1981–82, he was a visiting professor at Duke University. Professor Sweeney served as Head of the Department of Quantitative Analysis and as Associate Dean of the College of Business Administration at the University of Cincinnati.

Professor Sweeney has published more than 30 articles and monographs in the area of management science and statistics. The National Science Foundation, IBM, Procter & Gamble, Federated Department Stores, Kroger, and Cincinnati Gas & Electric have funded his research, which has been published in *Management Science, Operations Research, Mathematical Programming, Decision Sciences,* and other journals.

Professor Sweeney has coauthored eight textbooks in the areas of statistics, management science, linear programming, and production and operations management.

Thomas A. Williams.   Thomas A. Williams is Professor of Management Science in the College of Business at Rochester Institute of Technology. Born in Elmira, New York, he earned his B.S. degree at Clarkson University. He did his graduate work at Rensselaer Polytechnic Institute, where he received his M.S. and Ph.D. degrees.

Before joining the College of Business at RIT, Professor Williams served for seven years as a faculty member in the College of Business Administration at the University of Cincinnati, where he developed the undergraduate program in Information Systems and served as its coordinator. At RIT he was the first chairman of the Decision Sciences Department. He teaches courses in management science and statistics, as well as graduate courses in regression and decision analysis.

Professor Williams has coauthored nine textbooks in the areas of management science, statistics, production and operations management, and mathematics. He has been a consultant for numerous *Fortune* 500 companies and has worked on projects ranging from the use of data analysis to the development of large-scale regression models.

I

DATA AND STATISTICS

CONTENTS

BUSINESS WEEK*
New York, New York

With a global circulation of more than 1,000,000, *Business Week* is the most widely read business magazine in the world. More than 200 dedicated reporters and editors in 26 bureaus worldwide deliver a variety of articles of interest to the business and economic community. Along with feature articles on current topics, the magazine contains regular sections on International Business, Economic Analysis, Information Processing, and Science & Technology. Information in the feature articles and the regular sections help readers stay abreast of current developments and assess the impact of those developments on business and economic conditions.

Most issues of *Business Week* provide an in-depth report on a topic of current interest. Often, the in-depth reports contain statistical facts and summaries that help the reader understand the business and/or economic information. For instance, the February 2, 1998, issue contained a report on mutual funds; the April 20, 1998, issue contained a report on executive compensation; and the July 13, 1998, issue contained a report on the *Business Week* Global 1000 companies. In addition, the weekly *Business Week* Index contains statistics about the state of the economy including production indexes, stock prices, real estate loan values, and interest rates.

Business Week also uses statistics and statistical information to help manage its own business. For example, an annual survey of subscribers helps the company learn about subscriber demographics, reading habits, likely purchases, lifestyles, and so

*The authors are indebted to Charlene Trentham, Research Manager at *Business Week*, for providing this Statistics in Practice.

Business Week uses business and economic statistics in many of its articles.© SWCP/Carry Benbow.

on. *Business Week* managers use the statistical summaries from the survey to provide better services to subscribers and advertisers. For instance, the most recent North American subscriber survey indicated that 90% of *Business Week* subscribers have a personal computer at home and that 64% of *Business Week* subscribers are involved with computer purchases at work. Such statistics alert *Business Week* managers to subscriber interest in articles about new developments in computers. The results of the survey are also made available to potential advertisers. The high percentage of subscribers using personal computers at home and the high percentage of subscribers involved with computer purchases at work would be an incentive for a computer manufacturer to consider advertising in *Business Week*.

In this chapter, we discuss the types of data that are available for statistical analysis and describe how the data are obtained. We introduce descriptive statistics and statistical inference as ways of converting data into meaningful and easily interpreted statistical information.

Frequently, we see the following kinds of statements in newspaper and magazine articles:

- The median cost for the one-day rental of an intermediate-size automobile is $58 (*USA Today,* October 16, 1998).
- The major airline with the best on-time record was TWA with 83.5% of flights arriving on-time (*U.S. Department of Transportation,* August 1998).
- Volkswagon and its luxury Audi division sold an average of 22,440 cars per month from January to September 1998 (*Barron's,* November 9, 1998).
- The Dow Jones Industrial Average topped 10,000 for the first time closing at 10,006 (*The Wall Street Journal,* March 30, 1999).
- Stock funds account for 37% of investors' portfolios (*The American Association of Individual Investor's Journal,* November 1997).
- The average price of a ticket to a major league baseball game during the 1998 season was $11.98 (*USA Today,* November 11, 1998).

The numerical facts in the preceding statements ($58, 83.5%, 22,440, 10,006, 37%, $11.98) are called statistics. Thus, in everyday usage, the term "statistics" refers to numerical facts. However, the field, or subject, of statistics involves much more than numerical facts. In a broad sense, *statistics* is the art and science of collecting, analyzing, presenting, and interpreting data. Particularly in business and economics, a major reason for collecting, analyzing, presenting, and interpreting data is to give managers and decision makers a better understanding of the business and economic environment and thus enable them to make more informed and better decisions. In this text, we emphasize the use of statistics for business and economic decision making.

Chapter 1 begins with some illustrations of the application of statistics in business and economics. A discussion of how data are acquired and used follows. The use of data in developing descriptive statistics and in making statistical inferences is described in Sections 1.4 and 1.5.

1.1   APPLICATIONS IN BUSINESS AND ECONOMICS

In today's global business and economic environment, vast amounts of statistical information are available. The most successful managers and decision makers are the ones who can understand the information and use it effectively. In this section, we provide examples that illustrate some of the uses of statistics in business and economics.

Accounting

Public accounting firms use statistical sampling procedures when conducting audits for their clients. For instance, suppose an accounting firm wants to determine whether the amount of accounts receivable shown on a client's balance sheet fairly represents the actual amount of accounts receivable. Usually the number of individual accounts receivable is so large that reviewing and validating every account would be too time-consuming and expensive. The common practice in such situations is for the audit staff to select a subset of the accounts called a sample. After reviewing the accuracy of the sampled accounts, the auditors draw a conclusion as to whether the accounts receivable amount shown on the client's balance sheet is acceptable.

Finance

Financial advisors use a variety of statistical information to guide their investment recommendations. In the case of stocks, the advisors review a variety of financial data including price/earnings ratios and dividend yields. By comparing the information for an individual stock with information about the stock market averages, a financial advisor can begin to draw a conclusion as to whether an individual stock is over- or undervalued. For example, *Barron's* (November 9, 1998) reported that the average price/earnings ratio for the 30 stocks in the Dow Jones Industrial Average was 22.0. Philip Morris had a price/earnings ratio of 16.9. In this case, the statistical information on price/earnings ratios showed that Philip Morris had a lower price in comparison to its earnings than the average for the Dow Jones stocks. Therefore, a financial advisor might have concluded that Philip Morris was currently underpriced. This and other information about Philip Morris would help the advisor make buy, sell, or hold recommendations for the stock.

Marketing

Electronic scanners at retail checkout counters are being used to collect data for a variety of marketing research applications. For example, data suppliers such as A. C. Nielsen and Information Resources, Inc., purchase point-of-sale scanner data from grocery stores, process the data, and then sell statistical summaries of the data to manufacturers. Manufacturers spent an average of $387,325 per product category to obtain this type of scanner data (Scanner Data User Survey, Mercer Management Consulting, Inc., April 1997). Manufacturers also purchase data and statistical summaries on promotional activities such as special pricing and the use of in-store displays. Brand managers can review the scanner statistics and the promotional activity statistics to gain a better understanding of the relationship between promotional activities and sales. Such analyses are helpful in establishing future marketing strategies for the various products.

Production

With today's emphasis on quality, quality control is an important application of statistics in production. A variety of statistical quality control charts are used to monitor the output of a production process. In particular, an x-bar chart is used to monitor the average output. Suppose, for example, that a machine is being used to fill containers with 12 ounces of a well-known soft drink. Periodically, a sample of containers is selected and the average number of ounces in the sample containers is computed. This average, or x-bar value, is plotted on an x-bar chart. A plotted value above the chart's upper control limit indicates overfilling, and a plotted value below the chart's lower control limit indicates underfilling. The process is termed "in control" and allowed to continue as long as the plotted x-bar values are between the chart's upper and lower control limits. Properly interpreted, an x-bar chart can help determine when adjustments are necessary to correct a production process.

Economics

Economists are frequently asked to provide forecasts about the future of the economy or some aspect of it. They use a variety of statistical information in making such forecasts. For instance, in forecasting inflation rates, economists use statistical information on such indicators as the Producer Price Index, the unemployment rate, and manufacturing capacity utilization. Often these statistical indicators are entered into computerized forecasting models that predict inflation rates.

Applications of statistics such as those described in this section are an integral part of this text. Such examples provide an overview of the breadth of statistical applications. To supplement these examples, we have asked practitioners in the fields of business and economics to provide chapter-opening Statistics in Practice articles that introduce the material covered in each chapter. The Statistics in Practice applications show the importance of statistics in a wide variety of decision-making situations.

1.2   DATA

Data are the facts and figures that are collected, analyzed, and summarized for presentation and interpretation. Together, the data collected in a particular study are referred to as the *data set* for the study. Table 1.1 shows a data set containing financial information for 25 companies, taken from the Stock Investor Pro database.

Elements, Variables, and Observations

The *elements* are the entities on which data are collected. For the data set in Table 1.1, each company is an element. With 25 companies, there are 25 elements in the data set.

Company

Table 1.1	A DATA SET CONTAINING FINANCIAL INFORMATION FOR 25 COMPANIES				
Company	Exchange	Ticker Symbol	Annual Sales ($ millions)	Share Price ($)	Price/ Earnings Ratio
Award Software	OTC	AWRD	15.7	11.500	22.5
Chesapeake Energy	NYSE	CHK	255.3	7.880	12.7
Craig Corporation	NYSE	CRG	29.4	17.000	7.5
Edisto Resources	AMEX	EDT	254.6	9.688	6.0
Franklin Elect. Pbls.	NYSE	FEP	88.7	12.880	15.7
Gentia Software	OTC	GNTIY	27.7	5.750	27.4
Giant Group	NYSE	GPO	7.2	6.563	2.1
Hot Topic	OTC	HOTT	48.3	15.750	27.2
Hudson General	AMEX	HGC	30.2	39.750	11.2
ICU Medical	OTC	ICUI	26.5	8.500	15.7
Jackpot Enterprises	NYSE	J	90.6	10.875	17.0
Kentek Information	OTC	KNTK	60.5	9.500	11.4
Larscom, Inc.	OTC	LARS	71.1	10.313	24.6
Lumisys, Inc.	OTC	LUMI	23.7	7.375	14.2
Maynard Oil	OTC	MOIL	38.2	10.750	4.8
Mechanical Dynamics	OTC	MDII	26.0	6.688	17.1
Metrika Systems	AMEX	MKA	67.2	15.250	15.7
National Home Health	OTC	NHHC	34.9	5.130	7.7
National Tech Team	OTC	TEAM	78.1	10.875	32.0
OrCad	OTC	OCAD	21.9	11.375	18.3
OroAmerica	OTC	OROA	164.8	5.125	16.0
Overland Data	OTC	OVRL	66.5	7.000	13.5
PIA Merchandising	OTC	PIAM	123.1	7.500	28.8
Plenum Publishing	OTC	PLEN	52.5	44.000	10.7
Premier Research	OTC	PRWW	16.5	8.250	28.4

Source: *Stock Investor Pro,* American Association of Individual Investors, August 31, 1997.

A *variable* is a characteristic of interest for the elements. The data set in Table 1.1 has the following five variables:

- *Exchange:* Where the company's stock is traded—NYSE (New York Stock Exchange), AMEX (American Stock Exchange), and OTC (over the counter).
- *Ticker Symbol:* The abbreviation used to identify the company on the exchange listing.
- *Annual Sales:* Total sales for the most recent 12 months in millions of dollars.
- *Share Price:* Market price per share for the company's stock.
- *Price/Earnings Ratio:* Market price per share divided by the most recent 12 months' earnings per share.

Data are obtained by collecting measurements on each variable for every element in the study. The set of measurements collected for a particular element is called an *observation*. Referring to Table 1.1, we see that the first element (Award Software) provides the observation OTC, AWRD, 15.7, 11.500, 22.5. With 25 elements, there are 25 observations; with five variables for each observation, there are 125 data values in the data set.

Qualitative and Quantitative Data

The statistical analysis that is appropriate for a particular variable depends on whether the data for the variable are qualitative or quantitative. *Qualitative data* are labels or names used to identify an attribute of each element. For example, referring to the data set in Table 1.1, we see that the data values for the exchange variable (NYSE, AMEX, and OTC) are labels used to identify where the stocks are traded. Hence, the data are qualitative and exchange is referred to as a *qualitative variable*. Ticker symbol is also a qualitative variable, with the data values AWRD, CHK, CRG, and so on being the labels used to identify the corresponding company.

Quantitative data indicate either how much or how many. For example, the data values for annual sales in Table 1.1 are quantitative, with the values 15.7, 255.3, 29.4, and so on indicating how many millions of dollars of sales the company had during the most recent 12-month period. Since the data are quantitative, annual sales is referred to as a *quantitative variable*. Share price and price/earnings ratio are also quantitative variables.

Quantitative data are always numeric, but qualitative data may be *either numeric or nonnumeric*. For example, to facilitate data collection and prepare the data for easy entry into a computer database, we might decide to use numeric codes for exchange, letting 1 denote a stock traded on the New York Stock Exchange, 2 denote a stock traded on the American Stock Exchange, and 3 denote a stock traded over the counter. In this case, the numeric values are the labels or codes used to identify where the stock is traded. The data are qualitative and exchange is a qualitative variable even though the data are shown as numeric values. Social security numbers such as 310-22-7924 consist of numeric values. However, social security numbers are qualitative because the data are actually labels that identify particular individuals. Automobile license plates such as CWX802 and product part codes such as A132 are qualitative data, with the combined numeric and nonnumeric entries being the labels used to identify the particular automobile or particular part.

For purposes of statistical analysis, the important distinguishing difference between qualitative and quantitative data is that *ordinary arithmetic operations are meaningful only with quantitative data.* For example, with quantitative data, the data values can be added together and then divided by the number of data values to compute the average value for the data. This average is meaningful and usually easily interpreted. However, when qualitative data are recorded as numeric values, such arithmetic operations provide meaningless results.

Cross-Sectional and Time Series Data

For purposes of statistical analysis, distinguishing between cross-sectional data and time series data is important. *Cross-sectional data* are data collected at the same or approximately the same point in time. The data in Table 1.1 are cross-sectional because they describe the five variables for the 25 companies at the same point in time. *Time series data* are data collected over several time periods. For example, Figure 1.1 is a graph of installment credit as a percent of disposable income. It shows that installment credit had grown from just over 20% of disposable income at the beginning of 1996 to 21% by mid-year 1997. Most of the statistical methods presented in this text apply to cross-sectional data.

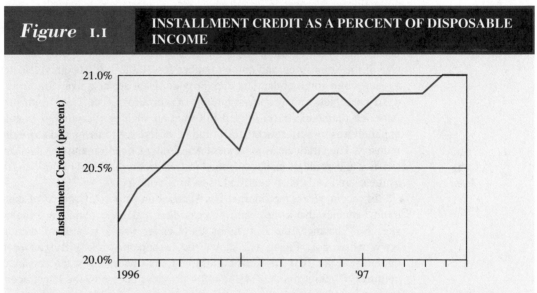

Figure 1.1   INSTALLMENT CREDIT AS A PERCENT OF DISPOSABLE INCOME

Source: Reprinted from the August 4, 1997 issue of *Fortune* by special permission; copyright 1997, Time Inc.

NOTES and Comments

An observation is the set of measurements obtained for each element in a data set. Hence, the number of observations is always the same as the number of elements. The number of measurements obtained on each element is equal to the number of variables. Hence, the total number of data values in a data set is the number of elements multiplied by the number of variables.

1.3   DATA SOURCES

Data can be collected from existing sources or obtained through surveys and experimental studies designed to obtain new data.

Existing Sources

In some cases, data needed for a particular application may already exist within a firm or organization. All companies maintain a variety of databases about their employees, customers, and business operations. Data on employee salaries, ages, and years of service can usually be obtained from internal personnel records. Data on sales, advertising expenditures, distribution costs, inventory levels, and production quantities are generally available from other internal record-keeping systems. Most companies also maintain detailed data about their customers. Table 1.2 shows some of the data commonly available from the internal information sources of most companies.

Substantial amounts of business and economic data are available from organizations that specialize in collecting and maintaining data. Companies obtain access to these external data sources through leasing arrangements or by purchase. Dun & Bradstreet and Dow Jones & Company are two firms that provide extensive business database services to clients. A. C. Nielsen and Information Resources, Inc., have built $100-million businesses collecting and processing retail checkout-counter scanner data that they sell to product manufacturers.

Government agencies are another important source of existing data. For instance, the U.S. Department of Labor maintains considerable data on employment rates, wage rates, size of the labor force, and union membership. Table 1.3 lists other selected governmental agencies and some of the data they provide. Data are also available from a variety of industry associations and special interest organizations. The Travel Industry Association of America maintains travel-related information such as the number of tourists and travel expenditures by state. Such data would be of interest to firms and individuals in the travel industry. The Graduate Management Admission Council maintains data on student characteristics and graduate management education programs. Most of the data from sources such as these are available to qualified users at a modest cost.

In recent years, the Internet has become an important source of data. Most government agencies that collect and process data make the results available through a web site. For instance, the Bureau of the Census has a wealth of data at its web site, www.census.gov. Figure 1.2 shows the homepage for the Bureau of the Census. By clicking on the **Just For Fun** button, you can obtain maps and census data for all U.S. counties. Clicking on the **News** button provides access to the latest economic indicators such as housing starts, etc.

Table 1.2	EXAMPLES OF DATA AVAILABLE FROM INTERNAL COMPANY RECORDS
Source	**Some of the Data Typically Available**
Employee records	Name, address, social security number, salary, number of vacation days, number of sick days, and bonus
Production records	Part or product number, quantity produced, direct labor cost, and materials cost
Inventory records	Part or product number, number of units on hand, reorder level, economic order quantity, and discount schedule
Sales records	Product number, sales volume, sales volume by region, and sales volume by customer type
Credit records	Customer name, address, phone number, credit limit, and accounts receivable balance
Customer profile	Age, gender, income level, household size, address, and preferences

Table 1.3	EXAMPLES OF DATA AVAILABLE FROM SELECTED GOVERNMENT AGENCIES
Government Agency	**Some of the Data Available**
Bureau of the Census	Population data and their distribution, data on number of households and their distribution, data on household income and their distribution
Federal Reserve Board	Data on the money supply, installment credit, exchange rates, and discount rates
Office of Management and Budget	Data on revenue, expenditures, and debt of the federal government
Department of Commerce	Data on business activity—value of shipments by industry, level of profits by industry, and data on growing and declining industries

Many companies have created Internet web sites and provide public access to them. Figure 1.3 shows the Internet address for a variety of companies (*Fortune,* August 4, 1997). By accessing these web sites, one can obtain a variety of product and other types of information concerning these companies. A number of companies now specialize in making information available over the Internet. One can obtain access to stock quotes, meal prices at restaurants, and an almost infinite variety of information. As just one example, the avid golfer will find a variety of news and statistics at www.golf.com.

Figure 1.2   U.S. BUREAU OF THE CENSUS HOMEPAGE

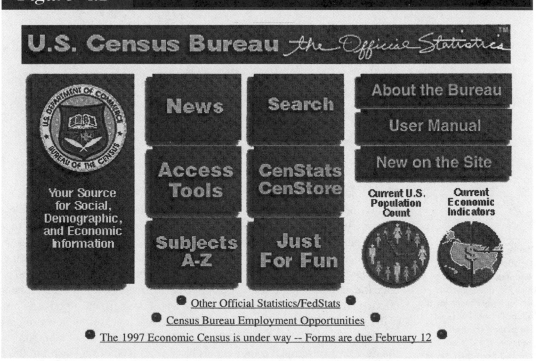

| **Figure 1.3** | **INTERNET ADDRESSES FOR SELECTED COMPANIES** |

Acer Computer International Ltd.
http://www.acer.com.sg

American Airlines, Inc./AAccess via the Web
http://www.americanair.com

Andersen Consulting
http://www.ac.com

American Express
http://www.americanexpress.com

Applied Materials
http://www.appliedmaterials.com

The Baan Company
http://www.baan.com

Black & Veatch
http://www.bv.com

BMW of North America, Inc.
http://www.bmwusa.com

Buick Park Avenue
http://www.parkave.buick.com

Cabletron Systems, Inc.
http://www.cabletron.com

Cadillac Seville
http://www.cadillac.com

Canon U.S.A.
http://www.usa.canon.com

Caterpillar
http://www.caterpillar.com

Charleston Regional Development Alliance
http://www.crda.org

Chevrolet Malibu
http://www.chevrolet.com

Cisco Systems
http://www.cisco.com

Columbia
http://www.Columbia.net

COMSAT World Systems
http://www.COMSAT.com

CONNEXT
http://www.connext.com

Coopers & Lybrand LLP
http://www.colybrand.com

Cushman & Wakefield
http://www.cushwake.com

Dale Carnegie Training
http://www.dale-carnegie.com

Deloitte & Touche
http://www.dttus.com

FEMSA
http://www.femsa.com

First Union National Bank
http://www.firstunion.com

Ford Expedition
http://www.ford.com

France Telecom
http://www.francetelecom.com

Hewlett-Packard
http://www.hp.com

Hitachi
http://www.hitachi.com

Hitachi America, Ltd.
http://www.hitachi.com

In Focus
http://www.infocus.com

Information Builders, Inc.
http://www.ibi.com

International Paper
http://www.ipaper.com

J.P. Morgan
http://www.jpmorgan.com

Jaguar Cars
http://www.jaguarcars.com/us

Johnson Controls, Inc.
http://www.johnsoncontrols.com

Kallback
http://www.kallback.com

Kalthoff International
http://www.kalthoff.com

The Kaufmann Fund
http://www.kaufmann.inter.net

Land Rover North America Inc.
http://www.landrover.com

Levi, Ray & Shoup, Inc.
http://www.lrs.com

Lucent Technologies
http://www.lucent.com

Lufthansa Airlines N.A.
http://www.lufthansa-usa.com

Microsoft
http://www.microsoft.com/internet/go17/

Mitsubishi Motor Sales of America
http://www.mitsucars.com

National Corporate Services, Inc.
http://www.natcorp.com/ir

NCR Corporation
http://www.ncr.com

Novell, Inc.
http://www.novell.com

OLDE Discount Stockbrokers
http://www.OLDE.com

Online Resources & Communications Corporation
http://www.orcc.com

Open Market, Inc.
http://www.openmarket.com

Oracle Corporation
http://www.oracle.com

Panasonic Personal Computer Company
http://www.panasonic.com/ruggedpc

PeopleSoft
http://www.peoplesoft.com

Prudential Securities
http://www.prudential.com

QAD Inc.
http://www.qad.com

QUALCOMM
http://www.qualcomm.com/cdma/

Ralph Lauren
http://www.ralphlaurenfragrance.com

Robertson Stephens & Company
http://www.rsim.com

Royal Insurance
http://www.royal-usa.com

Saab USA
http://www.saabusa.com

SAP America, Inc.
http://www.sap.com

South Carolina Department of Commerce
http://www.state.sc.us/commerce

Sprint
http://www.sprint.com

Sterling Commerce
http://www.stercomm.com

Subaru
http://www.subaru.com

Sybase, Inc.
http://www.sybase.com

T. Rowe Price Blue Chip Growth
http://www.troweprice.com

Toyota In America
http://www.toyotausa.com

U.S. Trust
http://www.ustrust.com

United Technologies
http://www.utc.com

UUNET
http://www.uu.net

Xcellenet
http://www.xcellenet.com

Yaskawa Electric
http://www.yaskawa.com

Yellow Freight System
http://www.yellowfreight.com

© 1997 Time Inc. FORTUNE®

Source: Reprinted from the August 4, 1997 issue of *Fortune* by special permission; copyright 1997, Time Inc.

Statistical Studies

Sometimes the data needed for a particular application are not available through existing sources. In such cases, the data can often be obtained by conducting a statistical study. Statistical studies can be classified as either *experimental* or *observational*.

In an experimental study, a variable of interest is first identified. Then one or more other variables are identified and controlled so that data can be obtained about how they influence the variable of interest. For example, a pharmaceutical firm might be interested in conducting an experiment to learn about how a new drug affects blood pressure. Blood pressure is the variable of interest in the study. The dosage level of the new drug is another variable that is known to have a causal effect on blood pressure. To obtain data about the effect of the new drug, a sample of individuals is selected. The dosage level of the new drug is controlled, with different groups of individuals being given different dosage levels. Data on

The largest experimental statistical study ever conducted is believed to be the 1954 Public Health Service experiment for the Salk polio vaccine. Nearly two million children in grades 1, 2, and 3 were selected from throughout the United States.

blood pressure is collected for each group. Statistical analysis of the experimental data can help determine how the new drug affects blood pressure.

In nonexperimental, or observational, statistical studies, no attempt is made to control the variables of interest. A survey is perhaps the most common type of observational study. For instance, in a personal interview survey, research questions are first identified. Then a questionnaire is designed and administered to a sample of individuals. Some restaurants use observational studies to obtain data about their customers' opinions of the quality of food, service, atmosphere, and so on. A questionnaire used by the Lobster Pot Restaurant in Redington Shores, Florida, is shown in Figure 1.4. Note that the customers completing the questionnaire are asked to provide ratings for five variables: food, friendliness of service, promptness of service, cleanliness, and management. The response categories of excellent, good, satisfactory, and unsatisfactory provide data that enable Lobster Pot's managers to assess the quality of the restaurant's operation.

Managers wanting to use data and statistical analyses as an aid to decision making must be aware of the time and cost required to obtain the data. The use of existing data sources is desirable when data must be obtained in a relatively short period of time. If important data are not readily available from an existing source, the additional time and cost involved in obtaining the data must be taken into account. In all cases, the decision maker should

Studies of smokers and nonsmokers are observational studies because researchers do not determine or control who will smoke and who will not smoke.

Figure 1.4   **CUSTOMER OPINION QUESTIONNAIRE USED BY THE LOBSTER POT RESTAURANT, REDINGTON SHORES, FLORIDA (*USED WITH PERMISSION*)**

The
LOBSTER
Pot
RESTAURANT

*W*e are happy you stopped by the Lobster Pot Restaurant and want to make sure you will come back. So, if you have a little time, we will really appreciate it if you will fill out this card. Your comments and suggestions are extremely important to us. Thank you!

Server's Name ___Eugen_____

	Excellent	Good	Satisfactory	Unsatisfactory
Food Quality	❑	❑	❑	❑
Friendly Service	❑	❑	❑	❑
Prompt Service	❑	❑	❑	❑
Cleanliness	❑	❑	❑	❑
Management	❑	❑	❑	❑

Comments _____

_____

What prompted your visit to us? _____

_____

Please drop in suggestion box at entrance. Thank you.

consider the contribution of the statistical analysis to the decision-making process. The cost of data acquisition and the subsequent statistical analysis should not exceed the savings generated by using the information to make a better decision.

Data Acquisition Errors

Managers should always be aware of the possibility of data errors in statistical studies. Using erroneous data can be worse than not using any data at all. An error in data acquisition occurs whenever the data value obtained is not equal to the true or actual value that would have been obtained with a correct procedure. Such errors can occur in a number of ways. For example, an interviewer might make a recording error, such as a transposition in writing the age of a 24-year-old person as 42, or the person answering an interview question might misinterpret the question and provide an incorrect response.

Experienced data analysts take great care in collecting and recording data to ensure that errors are not made. Special procedures can be used to check for internal consistency of the data. For instance, such procedures would indicate that the analyst should review the accuracy of data for a respondent who is shown to be 22 years of age but who reports 20 years of work experience. Data analysts also review data with unusually large and small values, called outliers, which are candidates for possible data errors. In Chapter 3 we present some of the methods statisticians use to identify outliers.

Errors often occur during data acquisition. Blindly using any data that happen to be available or using data that were acquired with little care can lead to poor and misleading information. Thus, taking steps to acquire accurate data can help ensure reliable and valuable decision-making information.

1.4   DESCRIPTIVE STATISTICS

Most of the statistical information in newspapers, magazines, reports, and other publications consists of data that are summarized and presented in a form that is easy for the reader to understand. Such summaries of data, which may be tabular, graphical, or numerical, are referred to as *descriptive statistics*.

Refer again to the data set in Table 1.1 where financial information on 25 companies is listed. Methods of descriptive statistics can be used to provide summaries of the information in this data set. For example, a tabular summary of the data for the exchange variable is shown in Table 1.4. A graphical summary of the same data is shown in Figure 1.5. The purpose of tabular and graphical summaries such as these is to make the data easier to interpret. Referring to Table 1.4 and Figure 1.5, we can see easily that the majority of the

Table 1.4	FREQUENCIES AND PERCENTAGES FOR THE EXCHANGE OF 25 COMPANY STOCKS	
Exchange	**Frequency**	**Percent**
New York Stock Exchange	5	20
American Stock Exchange	3	12
Over the counter	17	68
Total	25	100

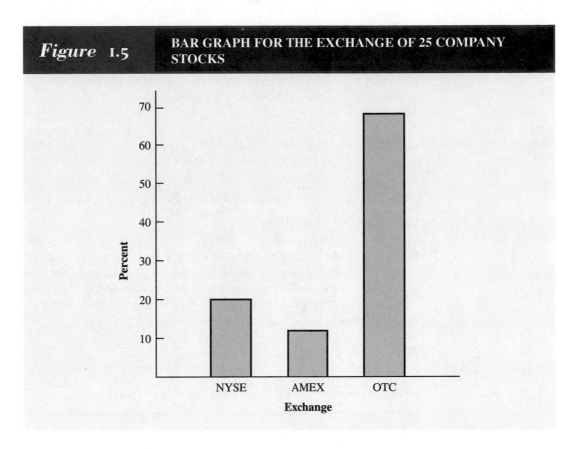

Figure 1.5   BAR GRAPH FOR THE EXCHANGE OF 25 COMPANY STOCKS

stocks in the data set are traded over the counter. On a percentage basis, 68% are traded over the counter, 12% are traded on the American Stock Exchange, and 20% are traded on the New York Stock Exchange.

A graphical summary of the data on price/earnings ratio for the stocks in Table 1.1 is provided by the histogram in Figure 1.6. From the histogram, it is easy to see that the price/earnings ratios range from 0 to 35, with the highest concentrations between 10 and 20.

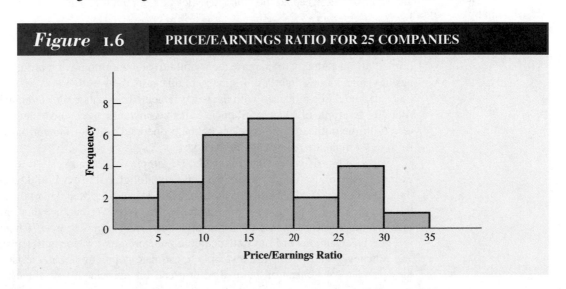

Figure 1.6   PRICE/EARNINGS RATIO FOR 25 COMPANIES

In addition to tabular and graphical displays, numerical descriptive statistics are used to summarize data. The most common numerical descriptive statistic is the *average* or *mean.* Using the data on annual sales in Table 1.1, we can compute the average annual sales by adding the annual sales for all 25 companies and dividing the sum by 25. Doing so tells us that the average annual sales is $68.8 million. This average is taken as a measure of the central value, or central location, of the data.

Methods of descriptive statistics are covered in detail in Chapters 2 and 3.

In recent years interest has grown in statistical methods that can be used for developing and presenting descriptive statistics. Chapters 2 and 3 are devoted to the tabular, graphical, and numerical methods of descriptive statistics.

1.5   STATISTICAL INFERENCE

In many situations, data are sought for a large group of elements (individuals, companies, voters, households, products, customers, and so on). Because of time, cost, and other considerations, data are collected from only a small portion of the group. The larger group of elements in a particular study is called the *population,* and the smaller group is called the *sample.* Formally, we use the following definitions.

Population

A *population* is the set of all elements of interest in a particular study.

Sample

A *sample* is a subset of the population.

A major contribution of statistics is that data from a sample can be used to make estimates and test hypotheses about the characteristics of a population. This process is referred to as *statistical inference.*

As an example of statistical inference, let us consider the study conducted by Norris Electronics. Norris manufactures a high-intensity lightbulb used in a variety of electrical products. In an attempt to increase the useful life of the lightbulb, the product design group has developed a new lightbulb filament. In this case, the population is defined as all lightbulbs that could be produced with the new filament. To evaluate the advantages of the new filament, a sample of 200 new-filament bulbs was manufactured and tested. Data were collected on the number of hours each lighbulb operated before filament burnout. The data from the sample are reported in Table 1.5.

Suppose Norris is interested in using the sample data to make an inference about the average hours of useful life for the population of all lightbulbs that could be produced with the new filament. Adding the 200 values in Table 1.5 and dividing the total by 200 provides the sample average lifetime for the lightbulbs: 76 hours. We can use this sample result to estimate that the average lifetime for the lightbulbs in the population is 76 hours. Figure 1.7 is a graphical summary of the statistical inference process for Norris Electronics.

Whenever statisticians use a sample to estimate population characteristics of interest, they provide a statement of the quality, or precision, associated with the estimate. For the

Table 1.5   HOURS UNTIL BURNOUT FOR A SAMPLE OF 200 LIGHTBULBS FOR NORRIS ELECTRONICS

Norris

107	73	68	97	76	79	94	59	98	57
54	65	71	70	84	88	62	61	79	98
66	62	79	86	68	74	61	82	65	98
62	116	65	88	64	79	78	79	77	86
74	85	73	80	68	78	89	72	58	69
92	78	88	77	103	88	63	68	88	81
75	90	62	89	71	71	74	70	74	70
65	81	75	62	94	71	85	84	83	63
81	62	79	83	93	61	65	62	92	65
83	70	70	81	77	72	84	67	59	58
78	66	66	94	77	63	66	75	68	76
90	78	71	101	78	43	59	67	61	71
96	75	64	76	72	77	74	65	82	86
66	86	96	89	81	71	85	99	59	92
68	72	77	60	87	84	75	77	51	45
85	67	87	80	84	93	69	76	89	75
83	68	72	67	92	89	82	96	77	102
74	91	76	83	66	68	61	73	72	76
73	77	79	94	63	59	62	71	81	65
73	63	63	89	82	64	85	92	64	73

Figure 1.7   THE PROCESS OF STATISTICAL INFERENCE FOR THE NORRIS ELECTRONICS EXAMPLE

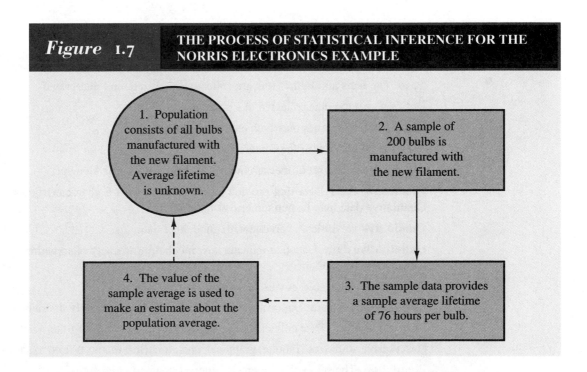

1. Population consists of all bulbs manufactured with the new filament. Average lifetime is unknown.

2. A sample of 200 bulbs is manufactured with the new filament.

3. The sample data provides a sample average lifetime of 76 hours per bulb.

4. The value of the sample average is used to make an estimate about the population average.

Norris example, the statistician might state that the estimate of the average lifetime for the population of new lightbulbs is 76 hours with a precision of ± 4 hours. Thus, an interval estimate of the average lifetime for all lightbulbs produced with the new filament is 72 hours to 80 hours. The statistician can also state how confident he or she is that the interval from 72 hours to 80 hours contains the population average.

SUMMARY

Statistics is the art and science of collecting, analyzing, presenting, and interpreting data. Nearly every college student majoring in business or economics is required to take a course in statistics. We began the chapter by describing typical statistical applications for business and economics.

Data are the facts and figures that are collected, analyzed, presented, and interpreted. For purposes of statistical analysis, data are classified as either qualitative or quantitative. Qualitative data consist of labels or names used to identify an attribute of an element. Qualitative data may be numeric or nonnumeric. Quantitative data are always numeric and indicate how much or how many for the variable of interest. Ordinary arithmetic operations are meaningful only if the data are *quantitative*. Therefore, statistical computations used for quantitative data are not always appropriate for qualitative data.

In Sections 1.4 and 1.5 we introduced the topics of descriptive statistics and statistical inference. Descriptive statistics are the tabular, graphical, and numerical methods used to summarize data. Statistical inference is the process of using data obtained from a sample to make estimates or test hypotheses about the characteristics of a population.

GLOSSARY

Statistics The art and science of collecting, analyzing, presenting, and interpreting data.

Data The facts and figures that are collected, analyzed, and interpreted.

Data set All the data collected in a particular study.

Elements The entities on which data are collected.

Variable A characteristic of interest for the elements.

Observation The set of measurements obtained for a single element.

Qualitative data Data that provide labels or names for a characteristic of an element. Qualitative data may be nonnumeric or numeric.

Qualitative variable A variable with qualitative data.

Quantitative data Data that indicate how much or how many of something. Quantitative data are always numeric.

Quantitative variable A variable with quantitative data.

Cross-sectional data Data collected at the same or approximately the same point in time.

Time series data Data collected at several successive periods of time.

Descriptive statistics Tabular, graphical, and numerical methods used to summarize data.

Population The set of all elements of interest in a particular study.

Sample A subset of the population.

Statistical inference The process of using data obtained from a sample to make estimates or test hypotheses about the characteristics of a population.

EXERCISES

1. Discuss the differences between statistics as numerical facts and statistics as a discipline or field of study.

SELF TEST

2. Table 1.6 shows the chief executive officer (CEO) compensation, industry classification, annual sales, and the CEO compensation versus shareholder return rating data for 10 companies. A CEO compensation versus shareholder return rating of 1 indicates that the company is among the group of companies that have the best ratio of CEO compensation to shareholder return. A rating of 2 indicates that the company is similar to companies that have a very good, but not the best, ratio of CEO compensation to shareholder return. Companies with the worst ratio of CEO compensation to shareholder return have a rating of 5.
   a. How many elements are in this data set?
   b. How many variables are in this data set?
   c. Which variables are qualitative and which variables are quantitative?

SELF TEST

3. Refer to the data in Table 1.6.
   a. Compute the average compensation for the chief executive officers (CEOs).
   b. What percentage of the firms are in the banking industry?
   c. What percentage of the firms have a value of 3 for the CEO compensation versus shareholder return rating?

4. *Fortune* magazine provides data on how the 500 largest U.S. industrial corporations rank in terms of sales and profits. Data for a sample of *Fortune* 500 companies are given in Table 1.7.
   a. How many elements are in this data set?
   b. What is the population?
   c. Compute the average sales for the sample.
   d. Using the results in part (c), what is the estimate of the average sales for the population?

SELF TEST

Table 1.6	EXECUTIVE COMPENSATION FOR A SAMPLE OF 10 COMPANIES			
Company	**CEO Compensation ($1000s)**	**Industry**	**Sales ($ millions)**	**CEO Compensation vs. Shareholder Return Rating**
Bankers Trust	8925	Banking	9565	3
Coca Cola	2437	Beverages	18546	5
General Mills	1410	Food	5567	1
LSI Logic	696	Electronics	1239	2
Motorola	1847	Electronics	27973	4
Readers Digest	1490	Publishing	2968	3
Sears	3414	Retailing	38236	4
Sprint	3344	Telecomm.	14045	4
Walgreen	1490	Retailing	12140	2
Wells Fargo	2861	Banking	8723	3

Source: *Business Week*, April 21, 1997.

Table 1.7   **A SAMPLE OF 10 FORTUNE 500 COMPANIES**

Company	Sales ($ millions)	Profit ($ millions)	Industry Code
Banc One	10272	1427.0	8
CPC Intl.	9844	580.0	19
Tyson Foods	6454	87.0	19
Hewlett-Packard	38420	2586.0	12
Intel	20847	5157.0	15
Northrup	8071	234.0	2
Seagate Tech.	8588	213.3	11
Unisys	6371	49.7	10
Westvaco	3075	212.2	22
Woolworth	8092	168.7	48

Source: *Fortune*, April 28, 1997.

5. Consider the data set for the sample of *Fortune* 500 companies in Table 1.7.
   a. How many variables are in the data set?
   b. Which of the variables are qualitative and which are quantitative?
   c. Compute the average profit for the sample.
   d. What percentage of the companies earned a profit over $100 million?
   e. What percentage of the companies have an industry code of 8?

6. Columbia House provides CDs, tapes, and records to its mail-order club members. A Columbia House Music Survey asked new club members to complete an 11-question survey. Some of the questions asked were:
   a. How many albums (CDs, tapes, or records) have you bought in the last 12 months?
   b. Are you currently a member of a national mail-order book club? (Yes or No)
   c. What is your age?
   d. Including yourself, how many people (adults and children) are in your household?
   e. What kind of music are you interested in buying? (15 categories were listed, including hard rock, soft rock, adult contemporary, heavy metal, rap, and country.)
   Comment on whether each question provides qualitative or quantitative data.

7. A California state agency classifies worker occupations as professional, white collar, or blue collar. The data are recorded with 1 denoting professional, 2 denoting white collar, and 3 denoting blue collar. The variable is worker occupation. Is it a qualitative or quantitative variable?

8. A *Wall Street Journal*/NBC News poll asked 2013 adults, "How satisfied are you with the state of the U.S. economy today?" (*The Wall Street Journal,* December 12, 1997). Response categories were Dissatisfied, Satisfied, and Not Sure.
   a. What was the sample size for this survey?
   b. Are the data qualitative or quantitative?
   c. Would it make more sense to use averages or percentages as a summary of the data for this question?
   d. Of the respondents, 28% said that they were dissatisfied with the state of the U.S. economy. How many individuals provided this response?

9. The Commerce Department reported receiving the following applications for the Malcolm Baldrige National Quality Award: 23 from large manufacturing firms, 18 from large service firms, and 30 from small businesses.
   a. Is type of business a qualitative or quantitative variable?
   b. What percentage of the applications came from small businesses?

10. State whether each of the following variables is qualitative or quantitative.
  a. Age
  b. Gender
  c. Class rank
  d. Make of automobile
  e. Number of people favoring the death penalty

11. State whether each of the following variables is qualitative or quantitative.
  a. Annual sales
  b. Soft-drink size (small, medium, large)
  c. Employee classification (GS1 through GS18)
  d. Earnings per share
  e. Method of payment (cash, check, credit card)

12. The Hawaii Visitors Bureau collects data on visitors to Hawaii. The following questions were among 16 asked in a questionnaire handed out to passengers during incoming airline flights in June 1997.
  • This trip to Hawaii is my: 1st, 2nd, 3rd, 4th, etc.
  • The primary reason for this trip is: (10 categories including vacation, convention, honeymoon)
  • Where I plan to stay: (11 categories including hotel, apartment, relatives, camping)
  • Total days in Hawaii
  a. What is the population being studied?
  b. Is the use of a questionnaire a good way to reach the population of passengers on incoming airline flights?
  c. Comment on each of the four questions in terms of whether it will provide qualitative or quantitative data.

SELF TEST

13. Figure 1.8 is a bar graph providing data on the number of riverboat casinos over the years 1991–1997.
  a. Are the data qualitative or quantitative?
  b. Are the data time series or cross-sectional?
  c. What is the variable of interest?
  d. Comment on the trend over time. Would you expect to see an increase or a decrease in 1998?

Figure **1.8**   **RIVERBOAT CASINOS IN THE UNITED STATES**

Source: Reprinted by permission of *The Wall Street Journal,* ©1997 Dow Jones & Company, Inc. All rights reserved worldwide.

14. The following data set provides a snapshot of the financial performance of Ameritech Corporation (*Barrons,* December 29, 1997).

	1993	1994	1995	1996
Earnings per share	$2.78	$2.13	$3.41	$3.83
Revenues (billions)	$11.87	$12.57	$13.43	$14.92
Net Income (billions)	$1.51	$1.17	$1.89	$2.12
Book Value per share	$14.35	$10.98	$12.67	$13.98

    a. How many variables are there?
    b. Are the data qualitative or quantitative?
    c. Are they cross-sectional or time series data? Why?

15. Refer again to the data in Table 1.7 for *Fortune* 500 companies. Are they cross-sectional or time series data? Why?

16. The marketing group at your company has come up with a new diet soft drink that it claims will capture a large share of the young adult market.
    a. What data would you want to see before deciding to invest substantial funds in introducing the new product into the marketplace?
    b. How would you expect the data mentioned in part (a) to be obtained?

17. A manager of a large corporation has recommended that a $10,000 raise be given to keep a valued subordinate from moving to another company. What internal and external sources of data might be used to decide whether such a salary increase is appropriate?

18. In a recent study of causes of death in men 60 years of age and older, a sample of 120 men indicated that 48 died as a result of some form of heart disease.
    a. Develop a descriptive statistic that can be used as an estimate of the percentage of men 60 years of age or older who die from some form of heart disease.
    b. Are the data on cause of death qualitative or quantitative?
    c. Discuss the role of statistical inference in this type of medical research.

19. The *Business Week* 1996 North American subscriber study collected data from a sample of 2861 subscribers. Fifty-nine percent of the respondents indicated that their annual income was $75,000 or more and 50% reported having an American Express credit card.
    a. What is the population of interest in this study?
    b. Is annual income a qualitative or quantitative variable?
    c. Is ownership of an American Express card a qualitative or quantitative variable?
    d. Does this study involve cross-sectional or time series data?
    e. Describe any statistical inferences *Business Week* might make on the basis of the survey.

20. The Scanner Data User Survey of 50 companies provided the following findings (Mercer Management Consulting, Inc., April 24, 1997):
    • A. C. Nielson earned 56% of the dollar-share of the market.
    • The average amount spent on scanner data per category of consumer goods was $387,325.
    • On a scale of 1 (very dissatisfied) to 5 (very satisfied), the average level of overall satisfaction with scanner data was 3.73.

    a. Cite two descriptive statistics.
    b. Make an inference of the overall satisfaction in the population of all users of scanner data.
    c. Make an inference about the average amount spent per category for scanner data for consumer goods.

21. A seven-year medical research study reported that women whose mothers took the drug DES during pregnancy were *twice* as likely to develop tissue abnormalities that might lead to cancer as women whose mothers did not take the drug.

    a. This study involved the comparison of two populations. What were the populations?

    b. Do you suppose the data were obtained in a survey or an experiment?

    c. For the population of women whose mothers took the drug DES during pregnancy, a sample of 3980 women showed 63 developed tissue abnormalities that might lead to cancer. Provide a descriptive statistic that could be used to estimate the number of women out of 1000 in this population who have tissue abnormalities.

    d. For the population of women whose mothers did not take the drug DES during pregnancy, what is the estimate of the number of women out of 1000 who would be expected to have tissue abnormalities?

    e. Medical studies often use a relatively large sample (in this case, 3980). Why?

22. A firm is interested in testing the advertising effectiveness of a new television commercial. As part of the test, the commercial is shown on a 6:30 P.M. local news program in Denver, Colorado. Two days later, a market research firm conducts a telephone survey to obtain information on recall rates (percentage of viewers who recall seeing the commercial) and impressions of the commercial.

    a. What is the population for this study?

    b. What is the sample for this study?

    c. Why would a sample be used in this situation? Explain.

23. The Nielsen organization conducts weekly surveys of television viewing throughout the United States. The Nielsen statistical ratings indicate the size of the viewing audience for each major network television program. Rankings of the television programs and of the viewing audience market shares for each network are published each week.

    a. What is the Nielsen organization attempting to measure?

    b. What is the population?

    c. Why would a sample be used for this situation?

    d. What kinds of decisions or actions are based on the Nielsen studies?

24. A sample of midterm grades for five students showed the following results: 72, 65, 82, 90, 76. Which of the following statements are correct, and which should be challenged as being too generalized?

    a. The average midterm grade for the sample of five students is 77.

    b. The average midterm grade for all students who took the exam is 77.

    c. An estimate of the average midterm grade for all students who took the exam is 77.

    d. More than half of the students who take this exam will score between 70 and 85.

    e. If five other students are included in the sample, their grades will be between 65 and 90.

2

DESCRIPTIVE STATISTICS I: TABULAR AND GRAPHICAL METHODS

CONTENTS

COLGATE-PALMOLIVE COMPANY*
New York, New York

The Colgate-Palmolive Company started as a small soap and candle shop in New York City in 1806. Today, Colgate-Palmolive is a $8.7 billion company whose products can be found in more than 200 countries and territories around the world. While internationally recognized for its brand names of Colgate, Palmolive, Ajax, and Fab, the company also markets Mennen, Hill's Science Diet, and Hill's Prescription Diet products.

The Colgate-Palmolive Company uses statistics in its quality assurance program for home laundry detergent products. One concern is customer satisfaction with the quantity of detergent in a carton. Every carton in each size category is filled with the same amount of detergent by weight, but the volume of detergent is affected by the density of the detergent powder. For instance, if the powder density is on the heavy side, a smaller volume of detergent is needed to reach the carton's specified weight. As a result, the carton may appear to be underfilled when opened by the consumer.

To control the problem of heavy detergent powder, limits are placed on the acceptable range of powder density. Statistical samples are taken periodically, and the density of each powder sample is measured. Data summaries are then provided for

Statistical summaries help maintain the quality of these Colgate-Palmolive products. © Spencer Grant/PhotoEdit.

operating personnel so that corrective action can be taken if necessary to keep the density within the desired quality specifications.

A frequency distribution for the densities of 150 samples taken over a one-week period and a histogram are shown in the accompanying table and figure. Density levels above .40 are unacceptably high. The frequency distribution and histogram show that the operation is meeting its quality guidelines with all of the densities less than or equal to .40. Managers viewing these statistical summaries would be pleased with the quality of the detergent production process.

In this chapter, you will learn about tabular and graphical methods of descriptive statistics such as frequency distributions, bar graphs, histograms, stem-and-leaf displays, dot plots, crosstabulations, and others. The goal of these methods is to summarize data so that they can be easily understood and interpreted.

Histogram of Density Data

Less than 1% of samples near the undesirable .40 level

*The authors are indebted to William R. Fowle, Manager of Quality Assurance, Colgate-Palmolive Company, for providing this Statistics in Practice.

Frequency Distribution of Density Data

Density	Frequency
.29–.30	30
.31–.32	75
.33–.34	32
.35–.36	9
.37–.38	3
.39–.40	1
Total	150

As indicated in Chapter 1, data can be classified as either *qualitative* or *quantitative*. Qualitative data provide labels or names for categories of like items. Quantitative data indicate how much or how many.

The purpose of this chapter is to introduce tabular and graphical procedures commonly used to summarize both qualitative and quantitative data. Tabular and graphical summaries of data can be found in annual reports, newspaper articles, and research studies. Everyone is exposed to these types of presentations. Hence, it is important to understand how they are prepared and to know how they should be interpreted. We begin with tabular and graphical methods for summarizing data concerning a single variable. The last section introduces methods for summarizing data involving the relationship between two variables.

2.1   SUMMARIZING QUALITATIVE DATA

Frequency Distribution

We begin the discussion of how tabular and graphical methods can be used to summarize qualitative data with the definition of a *frequency distribution*.

Frequency Distribution

A *frequency distribution* is a tabular summary of data showing the frequency (or number) of observations in each of several nonoverlapping classes.

Let us use the following example to demonstrate the construction and interpretation of a frequency distribution for qualitative data. According to *Beverage Digest,* Coke Classic, Diet Coke, Dr. Pepper, Pepsi-Cola, and Sprite are the top five selling soft drinks (*The Wall Street Journal Almanac,* 1998). Assume that the data in Table 2.1 show the soft drink selected for a sample of 50 soft drink purchases. The data are qualitative; each observation in the data set provides the name of the soft drink purchased.

To develop a frequency distribution for these data, we count the number of times each soft drink appears in the data set. Coke Classic appears 19 times, Diet Coke appears 8 times, Dr. Pepper appears 5 times, Pepsi-Cola appears 13 times, and Sprite appears 5 times. These counts are summarized in the frequency distribution in Table 2.2.

The advantage of this frequency distribution is that it provides a data summary showing how the sample of 50 purchases is distributed across the five soft drinks. This summary provides more insight than the original data as shown in Table 2.1. Viewing the frequency distribution, we see that Coke Classic is the leader, Pepsi-Cola is second, Diet Coke is third, and Sprite and Dr. Pepper are tied for fourth and fifth. The frequency distribution has provided information about the relative popularity of the five best-selling soft drinks.

Relative Frequency and Percent Frequency Distributions

A frequency distribution shows the number (frequency) of observations in each of several nonoverlapping classes. However, we are often interested in the proportion, or percentage,

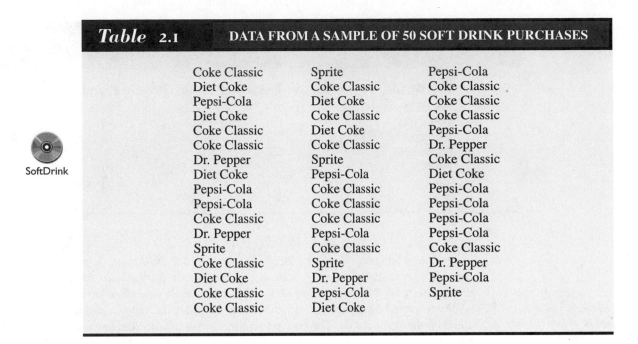

Table 2.1	DATA FROM A SAMPLE OF 50 SOFT DRINK PURCHASES	
Coke Classic	Sprite	Pepsi-Cola
Diet Coke	Coke Classic	Coke Classic
Pepsi-Cola	Diet Coke	Coke Classic
Diet Coke	Coke Classic	Coke Classic
Coke Classic	Diet Coke	Pepsi-Cola
Coke Classic	Coke Classic	Dr. Pepper
Dr. Pepper	Sprite	Coke Classic
Diet Coke	Pepsi-Cola	Diet Coke
Pepsi-Cola	Coke Classic	Pepsi-Cola
Pepsi-Cola	Coke Classic	Pepsi-Cola
Coke Classic	Coke Classic	Pepsi-Cola
Dr. Pepper	Pepsi-Cola	Pepsi-Cola
Sprite	Coke Classic	Coke Classic
Coke Classic	Sprite	Dr. Pepper
Diet Coke	Dr. Pepper	Pepsi-Cola
Coke Classic	Pepsi-Cola	Sprite
Coke Classic	Diet Coke	

SoftDrink

Table 2.2

FREQUENCY DISTRIBUTION OF SOFT DRINK PURCHASES

Soft Drink	Frequency
Coke Classic	19
Diet Coke	8
Dr. Pepper	5
Pepsi-Cola	13
Sprite	5
Total	50

In quality control applications, bar graphs are used to identify the most important causes of problems. When the bars are arranged in descending order of height from left to right with the most frequently occurring cause appearing first, the bar graph is called a *Pareto diagram*. This diagram is named for its founder, Vilfredo Pareto, an Italian economist.

of the observations in each class. The *relative frequency* of a class is the proportion of the observations belonging to the class. For a data set with n observations, the relative frequency of each class is as follows:

Relative Frequency

$$\text{Relative Frequency of a Class} = \frac{\text{Frequency of the Class}}{n} \qquad (2.1)$$

The *percent frequency* of a class is the relative frequency multiplied by 100.

A *relative frequency distribution* is a tabular summary of data showing the relative frequency for each class. A *percent frequency distribution* is a tabular summary of data showing the percent frequency for each class. Using equation (2.1), we can develop a relative frequency distribution for the soft drink data. In Table 2.3 we see that the relative frequency for Coke Classic is 19/50 = .38, the relative frequency for Diet Coke is 8/50 = .16, and so on. Multiplying each of the relative frequencies by 100 provides the percent frequency distribution. From these distributions, we see that on the basis of the sample data, 38% of the purchases were Coke Classic, 16% of the purchases were Diet Coke, and so on. We can also note that 38% + 26% + 16% = 80% of the purchases were of the top three soft drinks.

Bar Graphs and Pie Charts

A *bar graph* is a graphical device for depicting qualitative data that have been summarized in a frequency, relative frequency, or percent frequency distribution. On the horizontal

Table 2.3	RELATIVE AND PERCENT FREQUENCY DISTRIBUTIONS OF SOFT DRINK PURCHASES	
Soft Drink	**Relative Frequency**	**Percent Frequency**
Coke Classic	.38	38
Diet Coke	.16	16
Dr. Pepper	.10	10
Pepsi-Cola	.26	26
Sprite	.10	10
Total	1.00	100

axis of the graph, we specify the labels that are used for the classes. A frequency, relative frequency, or percent frequency scale can be used for the vertical axis of the graph. Then, using a bar of fixed width drawn above each class label, we extend the height of the bar until we reach the frequency, relative frequency, or percent frequency of the class as indicated by the vertical axis. The bars are separated to emphasize the fact that each class is a separate category. Figure 2.1 is a bar graph of the frequency distribution for the 50 soft drink purchases. Note how the graphical presentation shows Coke Classic, Pepsi-Cola, and Diet Coke to be the most preferred brands.

> All bars in a bar graph should be constructed with the same width and the same space between bars. This practice reduces the chances of misleading the user.

The *pie chart* is a commonly used graphical device for presenting relative frequency and percent frequency distributions for qualitative data. To draw a pie chart, we first draw a circle, then use the relative frequencies to subdivide the circle into sectors, or parts, that correspond to the relative frequency for each class. For example, because there are 360 degrees in a circle and because Coke Classic has a relative frequency of .38, the sector of the

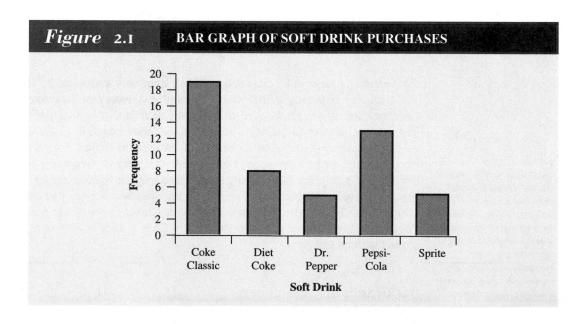

| Figure 2.1 | BAR GRAPH OF SOFT DRINK PURCHASES |

pie chart labeled Coke Classic consists of .38 × 360 = 136.8 degrees. The sector of the pie chart labeled Diet Coke consists of .16 × 360 = 57.6 degrees. Similar calculations for the other classes yield the pie chart in Figure 2.2. The numerical values shown for each sector can be frequencies, relative frequencies, or percentages.

Figure 2.2   PIE CHART OF SOFT DRINK PURCHASES

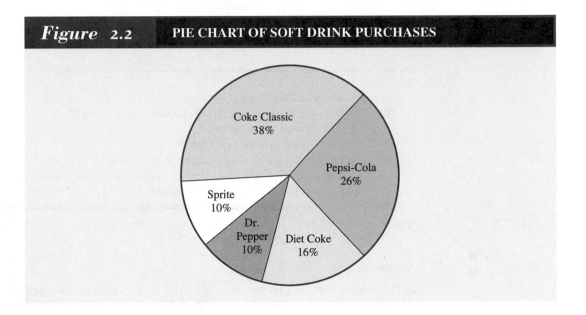

NOTES and Comments

1. Often the number of classes in a frequency distribution is the same as the number of categories found in the data, as is the case for the soft drink purchase data in this section. The data involve only five soft drinks, and a separate frequency distribution class was defined for each one. Data that included all soft drinks would require many categories, most of which would have small numbers of purchases. Most statisticians recommend that classes with smaller frequencies be grouped into an aggregate class called "other."
2. The sum of the frequencies in any frequency distribution always equals the number of observations. The sum of the relative frequencies in any relative frequency distribution always equals 1.00, and the sum of the percentages in a percent frequency distribution always equals 100.

EXERCISES

Methods

1. The response to a question has three alternatives: A, B, and C. A sample of 120 responses provides 60 A, 24 B, and 36 C. Show the frequency and relative frequency distributions.

2. A partial relative frequency distribution is given.

Class	Relative Frequency
A	.22
B	.18
C	.40
D	

a. What is the relative frequency of class D?
b. The total sample size is 200. What is the frequency of class D?
c. Show the frequency distribution.
d. Show the percent frequency distribution.

SELF TEST

3. A questionnaire provides 58 yes, 42 no, and 20 no-opinion answers.
a. In the construction of a pie chart, how many degrees would be in the section of the pie showing the yes answers?
b. How many degrees would be in the section of the pie showing the no answers?
c. Construct a pie chart.
d. Construct a bar graph.

Applications

TVshows

4. According to Nielsen Media Research, the five top TV shows for the week of September 28 to October 4, 1998, were ER, Frasier, Friends, Jesse, and Veronica's Closet. Data for a sample of 50 viewers follow.

Jesse	ER	Veronica	Frasier	Frasier
ER	ER	Frasier	ER	Frasier
Veronica	Friends	Veronica	ER	Frasier
ER	ER	Frasier	Frasier	Friends
ER	ER	Friends	Friends	Frasier
Friends	Frasier	Frasier	ER	ER
Friends	ER	Friends	Frasier	Friends
Veronica	Friends	Veronica	Frasier	ER
Veronica	Veronica	ER	Frasier	Friends
ER	Jesse	Friends	Veronica	ER

a. Are these qualitative or quantitative data?
b. Provide frequency and percent frequency distributions for the data.
c. Construct a bar graph and a pie chart for the data.
d. On the basis of the sample, which show has the largest market share? Which one is second?

5. Freshmen entering the College of Business at Eastern University were asked to indicate their preferred major. The following data were obtained. Summarize the data by constructing:

Major	Number
Management	55
Accounting	51
Finance	28
Marketing	82

     a. Relative and percent frequency distributions.
     b. A bar graph.
     c. A pie chart.

Books

6. The seven best-selling hardcover business books in December 1996 are listed in Table 2.4 (*Business Week,* February 3, 1997). Suppose a sample of book purchases in the St. Louis, Missouri, area provided the following data for these seven books.

Table 2.4

THE SEVEN BEST-SELLING HARDCOVER BUSINESS BOOKS

Only the Paranoid Survive
The Dilbert Principle
Nuts
Forbes Greatest Business Stories
Dogbert's Top Secret Management Handbook
Wall Street Money Machine
Against the Gods

Gods	Wall Street	Paranoid	Forbes	Dogbert	Nuts
Dogbert	Forbes	Dilbert	Paranoid	Dilbert	Gods
Dogbert	Dilbert	Gods	Paranoid	Paranoid	Paranoid
Gods	Dogbert	Dilbert	Forbes	Paranoid	Dilbert
Dogbert	Gods	Dilbert	Paranoid	Dilbert	Forbes
Dilbert	Dilbert	Dilbert	Dogbert	Gods	Nuts
Dilbert	Gods	Forbes	Dogbert	Dogbert	Gods
Forbes	Dilbert	Nuts	Nuts	Forbes	Gods
Dogbert	Forbes	Dogbert	Wall Street	Dilbert	Forbes
Dilbert	Dogbert	Gods	Gods	Dogbert	Dilbert

     a. Construct frequency and percent frequency distributions for the data. Group any books with less than a 10% frequency in an "other" category.
     b. Rank the best-selling books.
     c. What percentages of sales are represented by *The Dilbert Principle* and *Dogbert's Top Secret Management Handbook.*

SELF TEST

7. Leverock's Waterfront Steakhouse in Maderia Beach, Florida, uses a questionnaire to ask customers how they rate the server, food quality, cocktails, prices, and atmosphere at the restaurant. Each characteristic is rated on a scale of outstanding (O), very good (V), good (G), average (A), and poor (P). Use descriptive statistics to summarize the following data collected on food quality. What is your feeling about the food quality ratings at the restaurant?

G	O	V	G	A	O	V	O	V	G	O	V	A
V	O	P	V	O	G	A	O	O	O	G	O	V
V	A	G	O	V	P	V	O	O	G	O	O	V
O	G	A	O	V	O	O	G	V	A	G		

8. Position-by-position data for a sample of 55 members of the Baseball Hall of Fame in Cooperstown, New York, are shown here. Each observation indicates the primary position played by the Hall of Famers: pitcher (P), catcher (H), 1st base (1), 2nd base (2), 3rd base (3), shortstop (S), left field (L), center field (C), and right field (R).

L	P	C	H	2	P	R	1	S	S	1	L	P	R	P
P	P	P	R	C	S	L	R	P	C	C	P	P	R	P
2	3	P	H	L	P	1	C	P	P	P	S	1	L	R
R	1	2	H	S	3	H	2	L	P					

     a. Use frequency and relative frequency distributions to summarize the data.
     b. What position provides the most Hall of Famers?
     c. What position provides the fewest Hall of Famers?
     d. What outfield position (L, C, or R) provides the most Hall of Famers?
     e. Compare infielders (1, 2, 3, and S) to outfielders (L, C, and R).

9. Employees at Electronics Associates are on a flextime system; they can begin their working day at 7:00, 7:30, 8:00, 8:30, or 9:00 A.M. The following data represent a sample of the starting times selected by the employees.

7:00	8:30	9:00	8:00	7:30	7:30	8:30	8:30	7:30	7:00
8:30	8:30	8:00	8:00	7:30	8:30	7:00	9:00	8:30	8:00

Summarize the data by constructing:

a.   A frequency distribution.
b.   A percent frequency distribution.
c.   A bar graph.
d.   A pie chart.
e.   What do the summaries tell you about employee preferences in the flextime system?

10.   Students in the College of Business Administration at the University of Cincinnati are asked to fill out a course evaluation questionnaire upon completion of their courses. It consists of a variety of questions that have a five-category response scale. One of the questions follows.

Compared to other courses you have taken, what is the overall quality of the course you are now completing?

     ____   ____   ____   ____   ____
     Poor   Fair   Good   Very Good   Excellent

A sample of 60 students completing a course in business statistics during the spring quarter of 1998 provided the following responses. To aid in computer processing of the questionnaire results, a numeric scale was used with 1 = poor, 2 = fair, 3 = good, 4 = very good, and 5 = excellent.

```
3   4   4   5   1   5   3   4   5   2   4   5   3   4   4
4   5   5   4   1   4   5   4   2   5   4   2   4   4   4
5   5   3   4   5   5   2   4   3   4   5   4   3   5   4
4   3   5   4   5   4   3   5   3   4   4   3   5   3   3
```

a.   Comment on why these are qualitative data.
b.   Provide a frequency distribution and a relative frequency distribution summary of the data.
c.   Provide a bar graph and a pie chart summary of the data.
d.   On the basis of your summaries, comment on the students' overall evaluation of the course.

2.2   SUMMARIZING QUANTITATIVE DATA

Frequency Distribution

As defined in Section 2.1, a frequency distribution is a tabular summary showing the frequency (or number) of observations in each of several nonoverlapping classes. This definition holds for quantitative as well as qualitative data. However, with quantitative data we have to be more careful in defining the nonoverlapping classes to be used in the frequency distribution.

Table 2.5

YEAR-END AUDIT TIMES (IN DAYS)

12	14	19	18
15	15	18	17
20	27	22	23
22	21	33	28
14	18	16	13

For example, consider the quantitative data in Table 2.5. These data provide the time in days required to complete year-end audits for a sample of 20 clients of Sanderson and Clifford, a small public accounting firm. The three steps necessary to define the classes for a frequency distribution with quantitative data are:

1.   Determine the number of nonoverlapping classes.
2.   Determine the width of each class.
3.   Determine the class limits.

Let us demonstrate these steps by developing a frequency distribution for the audit-time data in Table 2.5.

Number of Classes.   Classes are formed by specifying ranges that will be used to group the observations in the data set. As a general guideline, we recommend using between five and 20 classes. Data sets with a larger number of observations usually require a larger number of classes. Data sets with a smaller number of observations can often be summarized easily with as few as five or six classes. Because the data set in Table 2.5 is relatively small ($n = 20$), we chose to develop a frequency distribution with five classes.

Width of the Classes.   The second step in constructing a frequency distribution for quantitative data is to choose a width for the classes. As a general guideline, we recommend that the width be the same for each class. Thus the choices of the number of classes and the width of classes are not independent decisions. A larger number of classes means a smaller class width and vice versa. To determine an approximate class width, we begin by identifying the largest and smallest data values in the data set. Then, once the desired number of classes has been specified, we can use the following expression to determine the approximate class width.

> Making the classes the same width reduces the chance of inappropriate interpretations by the user.

$$\text{Approximate Class Width} = \frac{\text{Largest Data Value} - \text{Smallest Data Value}}{\text{Number of Classes}} \quad \textbf{(2.2)}$$

The approximate class width given by (2.2) can be rounded to a more convenient value based on the preference of the person developing the frequency distribution. For example, an approximate class width of 9.28 might be rounded to 10 simply because 10 is a more convenient class width to use in constructing a frequency distribution.

For the data set involving the year-end audit times, the largest value is 33 and the smallest value is 12. Because we decided to summarize the data with five classes, using (2.2) provides an approximate class width of $(33 - 12)/5 = 4.2$. We therefore decided to use a class width of five days in the frequency distribution.

In practice, the number of classes and the appropriate class width are determined by trial and error. Once a possible number of classes is chosen, (2.2) is used to find the approximate class width. The process can be repeated for a different number of classes. Ultimately, the analyst uses judgment to determine the combination of number of classes and class width that provides the best means for summarizing the data.

For the audit-time data in Table 2.5, after deciding to use five classes, each with a width of five days, the next task is to specify the class limits for each of the classes.

Class Limits.   Class limits must be chosen so that each observation belongs to one and only one class. The *lower class limit* identifies the smallest possible data value assigned to the class. The *upper class limit* identifies the largest possible data value assigned to the class. In developing frequency distributions for qualitative data, we did not need to specify class limits because each observation naturally fell into a separate class (category). But with quantitative data, such as the audit times in Table 2.5, class limits are necessary to determine where each observation belongs.

> There is no one best frequency distribution for a data set. Different people may construct different, but equally acceptable, frequency distributions. The goal is to reveal the natural grouping and variation in the data.

For the audit-time data in Table 2.5 we defined the class limits as 10–14, 15–19, 20–24, 25–29, and 30–34. The smallest data value, 12, is included in the 10–14 class. The largest data value, 33, is included in the 30–34 class. For the 10–14 class, 10 is the lower class limit and 14 is the upper class limit. The difference between the lower class limits of adjacent classes provides the class width. Using the first two lower class limits of 10 and 15, we see that the class width is $15 - 10 = 5$.

Once the number of classes, class width, and class limits have been determined, a frequency distribution can be obtained by *counting* the number of data values belonging to each class. For example, the data in Table 2.5 show that four values—12, 14, 14, and 13—belong to the 10–14 class. Thus, the frequency for the 10–14 class is 4. Continuing this

Table 2.6

FREQUENCY DISTRIBUTION FOR THE AUDIT-TIME DATA

Audit Time (days)	Frequency
10–14	4
15–19	8
20–24	5
25–29	2
30–34	1
Total	20

counting process for the 15–19, 20–24, 25–29, and 30–34 classes provides the frequency distribution in Table 2.6. Using this frequency distribution, we can observe that:

1. The most frequently occurring audit times are in the class of 15–19 days. Eight of the 20 audit times belong to this class.
2. Only one audit required 30 or more days.

Other conclusions are possible, depending on the interests of the person viewing the frequency distribution. The value of a frequency distribution is that it provides insights about the data that are not easily obtained by viewing the data in their original unorganized form.

Class Midpoint.   In some applications, we want to know the *midpoints* of the classes in a frequency distribution for quantitative data. The class midpoint is the value halfway between the lower and upper class limits. For the audit-time data, the five class midpoints are 12, 17, 22, 27, and 32.

Relative Frequency and Percent Frequency Distributions

We define the relative frequency and percent frequency distributions for quantitative data in the same manner as for qualitative data. First, recall that the relative frequency is simply the proportion of the observations belonging to a class. With n observations,

$$\text{Relative Frequency of Class} = \frac{\text{Frequency of the Class}}{n}$$

The percent frequency of a class is the relative frequency multiplied by 100.

Based on the class frequencies in Table 2.6 and with $n = 20$, Table 2.7 shows the relative frequency distribution and percent frequency distribution for the audit-time data. Note that .40 of the audits, or 40%, required from 15 to 19 days. Only .05 of the audits, or 5%, required 30 or more days. Again, additional interpretations and insights can be obtained by using Table 2.7.

Dot Plot

One of the simplest graphical summaries of data is a *dot plot*. A horizontal axis shows the range of values for the observations. Each observation is represented by a dot placed above the axis. Figure 2.3 is the dot plot for the audit-time data in Table 2.5. The three dots located

Table 2.7   RELATIVE AND PERCENT FREQUENCY DISTRIBUTIONS FOR THE AUDIT-TIME DATA

Audit Time (days)	Relative Frequency	Percent Frequency
10–14	.20	20
15–19	.40	40
20–24	.25	25
25–29	.10	10
30–34	.05	5
Total	1.00	100

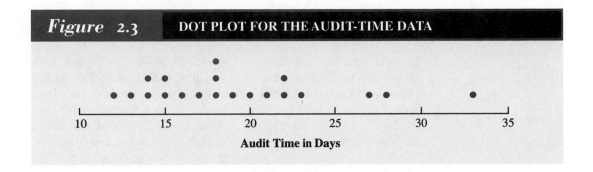

Figure 2.3   DOT PLOT FOR THE AUDIT-TIME DATA

above 18 on the horizontal axis indicate that the data set contains three observations with a value of 18. Dot plots show the details of the data and are useful for comparing two or more data sets.

Histogram

Another common graphical presentation of quantitative data is a *histogram*. This graphical summary can be prepared for data that have been previously summarized in either a frequency, relative frequency, or percent frequency distribution. A histogram is constructed by placing the variable of interest on the horizontal axis and the frequency, relative frequency, or percent frequency on the vertical axis. The frequency, relative frequency, or percent frequency of each class is shown by drawing a rectangle whose base is the class interval on the horizontal axis and whose height is the corresponding frequency, relative frequency, or percent frequency.

Figure 2.4 is a histogram for the audit-time data. Note that the class with the greatest frequency is shown by the rectangle appearing above the class of 15–19 days. The height of the rectangle shows that the frequency of this class is 8. A histogram for the relative or percent frequency distribution of this data would look the same as the histogram in Figure 2.4 with the exception that the vertical axis would be labeled with relative or percent frequency values.

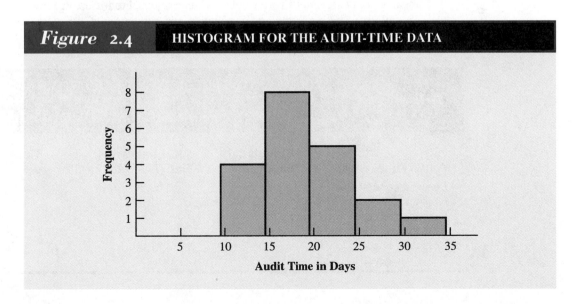

Figure 2.4   HISTOGRAM FOR THE AUDIT-TIME DATA

As Figure 2.4 shows, the adjacent rectangles of a histogram touch one another. Unlike a bar graph, a histogram has no natural separation between the rectangles of adjacent classes. This format is the usual convention for histograms. Because the class limits for the audit-time data are stated as 10–14, 15–19, 20–24, 25–29, and 30–34, there appear to be one-unit intervals of 14 to 15, 19 to 20, 24 to 25, and 29 to 30 between the classes. These spaces are eliminated by drawing the vertical lines of the histogram halfway between the class limits. The vertical lines separating the classes for the histogram in Figure 2.4 are at 9.5, 14.5, 19.5, 24.5, 29.5, and 34.5. This minor adjustment to eliminate the spaces between classes in a histogram helps show that, even though the data are rounded, all values between the lower limit of the first class and the upper limit of the last class are possible.

Cumulative Distributions

A variation of the frequency distribution that provides another tabular summary of quantitative data is the *cumulative frequency distribution*. The cumulative frequency distribution uses the number of classes, class widths, and class limits that were developed for the frequency distribution. However, rather than showing the frequency of each class, the cumulative frequency distribution shows the number of observations with values *less than or equal to the upper class limit* of each class. The first two columns of Table 2.8 provide the cumulative frequency distribution for the audit-time data.

To understand how the cumulative frequencies are determined, consider the class with the description "less than or equal to 24." The cumulative frequency for this class is simply the sum of the frequencies for all classes with observations less than or equal to 24. For the frequency distribution in Table 2.6, the sum of the frequencies for classes 10–14, 15–19, and 20–24 indicates that there are 4 + 8 + 5 = 17 observations with values less than or equal to 24. Hence, the cumulative frequency for this class is 17. In addition, the cumulative frequency distribution in Table 2.8 shows that 4 audits were completed in 14 days or less and 19 audits were completed in 29 days or less.

As a final point, we note that a *cumulative relative frequency distribution* shows the proportion of observations, and a *cumulative percent frequency distribution* shows the percentage of observations with values less than or equal to the upper limit of each class. The cumulative relative frequency distribution can be computed either by summing the relative frequencies in the relative frequency distribution or by dividing the cumulative fre-

Table 2.8	CUMULATIVE FREQUENCY, CUMULATIVE RELATIVE FREQUENCY, AND CUMULATIVE PERCENT FREQUENCY DISTRIBUTIONS FOR THE AUDIT-TIME DATA		
Audit Time (days)	**Cumulative Frequency**	**Cumulative Relative Frequency**	**Cumulative Percent Frequency**
Less than or equal to 14	4	.20	20
Less than or equal to 19	12	.60	60
Less than or equal to 24	17	.85	85
Less than or equal to 29	19	.95	95
Less than or equal to 34	20	1.00	100

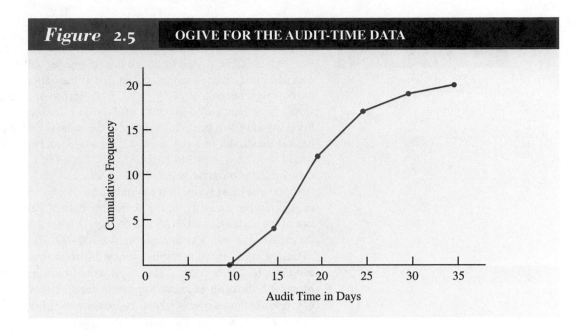

Figure 2.5   OGIVE FOR THE AUDIT-TIME DATA

quencies by the total number of observations. Using the latter approach, we found the cumulative relative frequencies in column 3 of Table 2.8 by dividing the cumulative frequencies in column 2 by the total number of observations ($n = 20$). The cumulative percent frequencies were again computed by multiplying the relative frequencies by 100. The cumulative relative and percent frequency distributions show that .85 of the audits, or 85%, were completed in 24 days or less, .95 of the audits, or 95%, were completed in 29 days or less, and so on.

Ogive

A graph of a cumulative distribution is called an *ogive*. The data values are shown on the horizontal axis and either the cumulative frequencies, the cumulative relative frequencies, or the cumulative percent frequencies are shown on the vertical axis. Figure 2.5 is the ogive for the cumulative frequencies of the audit-time data in Table 2.8.

The ogive is constructed by plotting a point corresponding to the cumulative frequency of each class. Since the class limits for the audit-time data are 10–14, 15–19, 20–24, and so on, there appear to be one-unit intervals for 14 to 15, 19 to 20, and so on. As with the histogram, these spaces are eliminated by plotting points halfway between the class limits. Thus, 14.5 is used for the 10–14 class, 19.5 is used for the 15–19 class, and so on. The "less than or equal to 14" class with a cumulative frequency of 4 is shown on the ogive in Figure 2.5 by the point located at 14.5 on the horizontal axis and 4 on the vertical axis. The "less than or equal to 19" class with a cumulative frequency of 12 is shown by the point located at 19.5 on the horizontal axis and 12 on the vertical axis. Note that one additional point is plotted at the left end of the ogive. This point starts the ogive by showing that there are no data values below the 10–14 class. It is plotted at 9.5 on the horizontal axis and 0 on the vertical axis. The plotted points are connected by straight lines to complete the ogive.

NOTES and Comments

1. The appropriate values for the class limits with quantitative data depend on the level of accuracy of the data. For instance, with the audit-time data of Table 2.5 the limits used were integer values because the data had been rounded to the nearest day. If the data were rounded to the nearest tenth of a day (e.g., 12.3, 14.4, and so on), then the limits would have been stated in tenths of days. For instance, the first class limits would have been 10.0–14.9. If the data were rounded to the nearest hundredth of a day (e.g., 12.34, 14.45, and so on), the limits would have been stated in hundredths of days. For instance, the first class limits would have been 10.00–14.99.

2. An *open-end* class is one that has only a lower class limit or an upper class limit. For example, in the audit-time data of Table 2.5, suppose two of the audits had taken 58 and 65 days. Rather than continue with the classes of width 5 with class intervals 35–39, 40–44, 45–49, and so on, we could simplify the frequency distribution to show an open-end class of "35 or more." This class would have a frequency of 2. Most often the open-end class appears at the upper end of the distribution. Sometimes an open-end class appears at the lower end of the distribution, and occasionally such classes appear at both ends.

3. The last entry in a cumulative frequency distribution is always the total number of observations. The last entry in a cumulative relative frequency distribution is always 1.00 and the last entry in a cumulative percent frequency distribution is always 100.

4. The wide availability of statistical computer software and spreadsheets is a great aid in data analysis. Several software packages are designed especially for statistical analysis. Among the more popular are Minitab, SAS, and SPSS. In Appendix 2.1, we show how dot plots and histograms can be developed using Minitab. Most spreadsheet packages now also provide statistical analysis capability. In Appendix 2.2, we show how to develop a frequency distribution and a histogram using Excel.

EXERCISES

Methods

11. Consider the following data.

14	21	23	21	16
19	22	25	16	16
24	24	25	19	16
19	18	19	21	12
16	17	18	23	25
20	23	16	20	19
24	26	15	22	24
20	22	24	22	20

    a. Develop a frequency distribution using class limits of 12–14, 15–17, 18–20, 21–23, and 24–26.

    b. Develop a relative frequency distribution and a percent frequency distribution using the class limits in part (a).

SELF TEST

12. Consider the following frequency distribution.

Class	Frequency
10–19	10
20–29	14
30–39	17
40–49	7
50–59	2

Construct a cumulative frequency distribution and a cumulative relative frequency distribution.

13. Construct a histogram and an ogive for the data in Exercise 12.

14. Consider the following data.

8.9	10.2	11.5	7.8	10.0	12.2	13.5	14.1	10.0	12.2
6.8	9.5	11.5	11.2	14.9	7.5	10.0	6.0	15.8	11.5

a. Construct a dot plot.
b. Construct a frequency distribution.
c. Construct a percent frequency distribution.

Applications

SELF TEST

15. A doctor's office staff has studied the waiting times for patients who arrive at the office with a request for emergency service. The following data were collected over a one-month period (the waiting times are in minutes).

2   5   10   12   4   4   5   17   11   8   9   8   12   21   6   8   7   13   18   3

Use classes of 0–4, 5–9, and so on.
a. Show the frequency distribution.
b. Show the relative frequency distribution.
c. Show the cumulative frequency distribution.
d. Show the cumulative relative frequency distribution.
e. What proportion of patients needing emergency service have a waiting time of nine minutes or less?

16. A sample of 25 computer hardware companies taken from the *Stock Invester Pro* database is shown in Table 2.9.
a. Develop tabular summaries and a histogram for the stock price data. Comment on typical stock prices and the distribution of stock prices.
b. Develop tabular summaries and a histogram for the earnings per share data. Comment on your results.

17. National Airlines accepts flight reservations by telephone. The following data show the call durations (in minutes) for a sample of 20 telephone reservations. Construct the frequency and relative frequency distributions for the data. Also provide a histogram.

2.1	4.8	5.5	10.4
3.3	3.5	4.8	5.8
5.3	5.5	2.8	3.6
5.9	6.6	7.8	10.5
7.5	6.0	4.5	4.8

Table 2.9	DATA SET FOR 25 COMPUTER HARDWARE COMPANIES			
Company	Stock Price	Institutional Ownership (%)	Price/Book Value	Earnings Per Share (Annual $)
Amdahl	12.31	45.4	2.49	−2.49
Auspex Systems	11.00	66.1	2.22	0.85
Compaq Computer	65.50	83.0	6.84	2.01
Data General	35.94	91.5	4.25	1.15
Digi International	15.00	33.4	2.04	−0.89
Digital Equipment Corp.	43.00	58.8	1.92	−2.93
En Pointe Technologies	14.25	11.8	3.47	0.80
Equitrac	16.25	20.9	2.38	0.76
Franklin Electronic Pbls.	12.88	30.8	1.41	0.82
Gateway 2000	39.13	36.0	6.45	1.74
Hewlett-Packard	61.50	50.2	4.35	2.64
Ingram Micro	28.75	14.4	4.53	1.01
Maxwell Technologies	30.50	26.5	8.07	0.46
MicroAge	27.19	76.6	2.16	1.25
Micron Electronics	16.31	18.8	4.48	1.06
Network Computing Devices	11.88	39.8	3.34	0.15
Pomeroy Computer Resource	33.00	56.9	3.29	1.81
Sequent Computer Systems	28.19	57.0	2.65	0.36
Silicon Graphics	27.44	63.0	3.01	−0.44
Southern Electronics	15.13	41.9	2.46	0.99
Stratus Computer	55.50	77.2	2.48	2.52
Sun Microsystems	48.00	59.3	7.50	1.67
Tandem Computers	34.25	61.3	3.61	1.02
Tech Data	38.94	82.3	3.80	1.50
Unisys	11.31	34.8	16.64	0.08

Source: *Stock Investor Pro,* American Association of Individual Investors, August 31, 1997.

Stocks

Retail

18. The Roth Young Personnel Service reported that annual salaries for department store assistant managers range from $28,000 to $57,000 (*National Business Employment Weekly,* October 16–22, 1994). Assume the following data are a sample of the annual salaries for 40 department store assistant managers (data are in thousands of dollars).

48	35	57	48	52	56	51	44
40	40	50	31	52	37	51	41
47	45	46	42	53	43	44	39
50	50	44	49	45	45	50	42
52	55	46	54	45	41	45	47

a. What are the lowest and highest salaries reported?
b. Use a class width of $5000 and prepare tabular summaries of the annual salary data.
c. What proportion of the annual salaries are $35,000 or less?
d. What percentage of the annual salaries are more than $50,000?
e. Prepare a histogram of the data.

19. The data for the numbers of units produced by a production employee during the most recent 20 days are shown here.

160	170	181	156	176
148	198	179	162	150
162	156	179	178	151
157	154	179	148	156

Summarize the data by constructing:
a. A frequency distribution.
b. A relative frequency distribution.
c. A cumulative frequency distribution.
d. A cumulative relative frequency distribution.
e. An ogive.

20. *Fortune* magazine conducted a survey to learn about its subscribers in the United States and Canada. One survey question asked the value of subscribers' investment portfolios (stocks, bonds, mutual funds, and certificates of deposit). The following percent frequency distribution was prepared from responses to this question (*Fortune* National Subscriber Portrait, 1994).

Value of Investments	Percent Frequency
Under $25,000	17
$25,000–49,999	9
$50,000–99,999	12
$100,000–249,999	20
$250,000–499,999	13
$500,000–999,999	13
$1,000,000 or over	16
Total	100

a. What percentage of subscribers have investments of less than $100,000?
b. What percentage of subscribers have investments in the $100,000–499,999 range?
c. What percentage of subscribers have investments of $500,000 or more?
d. The percent frequency distribution is based on 816 responses. How many of the respondents reported having investments of $100,000 to $249,999?
e. Estimate the number of respondents reporting investments of less than $100,000.

21. The Nielsen Home Technology Report (February 20, 1996) reported on home technology and its usage by persons aged 12 and older. The following data are the hours of personal computer usage during one week for a sample of 50 persons.

Computer

4.1	1.5	10.4	5.9	3.4	5.7	1.6	6.1	3.0	3.7
3.1	4.8	2.0	14.8	5.4	4.2	3.9	4.1	11.1	3.5
4.1	4.1	8.8	5.6	4.3	3.3	7.1	10.3	6.2	7.6
10.8	2.8	9.5	12.9	12.1	0.7	4.0	9.2	4.4	5.7
7.2	6.1	5.7	5.9	4.7	3.9	3.7	3.1	6.1	3.1

Summarize the data by constructing:
a. A frequency distribution (use a class width of three hours).
b. A relative frequency distribution.
c. A histogram.
d. An ogive.
e. Comment on what the data indicate about personal computer usage at home.

2.3 EXPLORATORY DATA ANALYSIS: THE STEM-AND-LEAF DISPLAY

The techniques of *exploratory data analysis* consist of simple arithmetic and easy-to-draw graphs that can be used to summarize data quickly. Many of these techniques were initially developed to provide a simple overview of a data set using pencil and paper; today, extensive use of computers for data analysis has deemphasized many of the techniques of exploratory data analysis. However, one technique—referred to as the *stem-and-leaf display*—is still widely used. A stem-and-leaf display can be used to show both the rank order and shape of a data set simultaneously.

To illustrate the use of a stem-and-leaf display, consider the data set in Table 2.10. These data are the results of a 150-question aptitude test given to 50 individuals who were recently interviewed for a position at Haskens Manufacturing. The data values indicate the number of questions answered correctly.

To develop a stem-and-leaf display, we first arrange the leading digits of each data value to the left of a vertical line. To the right of the vertical line, we record the last digit for each data value as we pass through the observations in the order they were recorded. The last digit for each data value is placed on the line corresponding to its first digit.

```
 6 | 9  8
 7 | 2  3  6  3  6  5
 8 | 6  2  3  1  1  0  4  5
 9 | 7  2  2  6  2  1  5  8  8  5  4
10 | 7  4  8  0  2  6  6  0  6
11 | 2  8  5  9  3  5  9
12 | 6  8  7  4
13 | 2  4
14 | 1
```

ApTest

Table 2.10	NUMBER OF QUESTIONS ANSWERED CORRECTLY ON AN APTITUDE TEST			
112	72	69	97	107
73	92	76	86	73
126	128	118	127	124
82	104	132	134	83
92	108	96	100	92
115	76	91	102	81
95	141	81	80	106
84	119	113	98	75
68	98	115	106	95
100	85	94	106	119

With this organization of the data, sorting the digits on each line into rank order is simple. Doing so leads to the stem-and-leaf display shown here.

```
 6 | 8  9
 7 | 2  3  3  5  6  6
 8 | 0  1  1  2  3  4  5  6
 9 | 1  2  2  2  4  5  5  6  7  8  8
10 | 0  0  2  4  6  6  6  7  8
11 | 2  3  5  5  8  9  9
12 | 4  6  7  8
13 | 2  4
14 | 1
```

Each line in this display is referred to as a *stem,* and each digit on the stem is a *leaf.* For example, consider the first line.

$$6 \mid 8 \quad 9$$

The meaning attached to this line is that two data values have a first digit of six: 68 and 69. Similarly, the second line

$$7 \mid 2 \quad 3 \quad 3 \quad 5 \quad 6 \quad 6$$

indicates that six data values have a first digit of seven: 72, 73, 73, 75, 76, and 76. Thus, we see that the data in this stem-and-leaf display are separated into two parts. The label for each stem is the one or two leading digits of the number (that is, 6, 7, 8, 9, 10, 11, 12, 13, or 14), and the leaf is the single last digit (that is, 0, 1, 2, . . . , 8, 9). The vertical line simply serves to separate the two parts.

To focus on the shape indicated by the stem-and-leaf display, let us use a rectangle to depict the "length" of each stem. Doing so, we obtain the following representation.

```
 6 | 8  9
 7 | 2  3  3  5  6  6
 8 | 0  1  1  2  3  4  5  6
 9 | 1  2  2  2  4  5  5  6  7  8  8
10 | 0  0  2  4  6  6  6  7  8
11 | 2  3  5  5  8  9  9
12 | 4  6  7  8
13 | 2  4
14 | 1
```

Rotating this page counterclockwise onto its side provides a picture of the data that is similar to a histogram with classes of 60–69, 70–79, 80–89, and so on.

Although the stem-and-leaf display may appear to offer the same information as a histogram, it has two primary advantages.

1. The stem-and-leaf display is easier to construct.
2. Within a class interval, the stem-and-leaf display provides more information than the histogram because the stem-and-leaf shows the actual data values.

In a stretched stem-and-leaf display, whenever a stem value is stated twice, the first value corresponds to leaf values of 0–4, and the second value corresponds to leaf values of 5–9.

Just as a frequency distribution or histogram has no absolute number of classes, neither does a stem-and-leaf display have an absolute number of rows or stems. If we believe that our original stem-and-leaf display has condensed the data too much, we can easily stretch the display by using two or more stems for each leading digit(s). For example, to use two lines for each leading digit(s), we would place all data values ending in 0, 1, 2, 3, and 4 on one line and all values ending in 5, 6, 7, 8, and 9 on a second line. The following stretched stem-and-leaf display illustrates this approach.

```
 6 | 8  9
 7 | 2  3  3
 7 | 5  6  6
 8 | 0  1  1  2  3  4
 8 | 5  6
 9 | 1  2  2  2  4
 9 | 5  5  6  7  8  8
10 | 0  0  2  4
10 | 6  6  6  7  8
11 | 2  3
11 | 5  5  8  9  9
12 | 4
12 | 6  7  8
13 | 2  4
13 |
14 | 1
```

Note that data values 72, 73, and 73 have leaves in the 0–4 range and are shown with the first stem value of 7. The data values 75, 76, and 76 have leaves in the 5–9 range and are shown with the second stem value of 7. This stretched stem-and-leaf display is similar to a frequency distribution with intervals of 65–69, 70–74, 75–79, and so on.

The preceding example showed a stem-and-leaf display for data having up to three digits. Stem-and-leaf displays for data with more than three digits are possible. For example, consider the following data on the number of hamburgers sold by a fast-food restaurant for each of 15 weeks.

1565	1852	1644	1766	1888	1912	2044	1812
1790	1679	2008	1852	1967	1954	1733	

A stem-and-leaf display of these data follows.

Leaf Unit = 10

```
15 | 6
16 | 4  7
17 | 3  6  9
18 | 1  5  5  8
19 | 1  5  6
20 | 0  4
```

A single digit is used to define each leaf in a stem-and-leaf display. The leaf unit indicates how to multiply the stem-and-leaf numbers in order to approximate the original data. Leaf units may be 100, 10, 1, 0.1, and so on.

Note that a single digit is used to define each leaf and that only the first three digits of each observation have been used to construct the display. To illustrate how to interpret the values in the display, consider the first stem, 15, and its associated leaf, 6. Combining these, we obtain the number 156. To reconstruct an approximation of the original observation, we must multiply this number by 10, the value of the *leaf unit*. Thus, $156 \times 10 = 1560$ is an approximation of the original observation used to construct the stem-and-leaf display. Although it is not possible to reconstruct the exact data from the stem-and-leaf display, the convention of using a single digit for each leaf enables stem-and-leaf displays to be constructed for data having a large number of digits.

EXERCISES

Methods

22. Construct a stem-and-leaf display for the following data.

| 70 | 72 | 75 | 64 | 58 | 83 | 80 | 82 |
| 76 | 75 | 68 | 65 | 57 | 78 | 85 | 72 |

SELF TEST

23. Construct a stem-and-leaf display for the following data.

| 11.3 | 9.6 | 10.4 | 7.5 | 8.3 | 10.5 | 10.0 |
| 9.3 | 8.1 | 7.7 | 7.5 | 8.4 | 6.3 | 8.8 |

24. Construct a stem-and-leaf display for the following data. Use the first two digits as the stem and the third digit as the leaf.

| 1161 | 1206 | 1478 | 1300 | 1604 | 1725 | 1361 | 1422 |
| 1221 | 1378 | 1623 | 1426 | 1557 | 1730 | 1706 | 1689 |

Applications

SELF TEST

25. A psychologist developed a new test of adult intelligence. The test was administered to 20 individuals, and the following data were obtained.

| 114 | 99 | 131 | 124 | 117 | 102 | 106 | 127 | 119 | 115 |
| 98 | 104 | 144 | 151 | 132 | 106 | 125 | 122 | 118 | 118 |

Construct a stem-and-leaf display for the data.

26. The earnings per share data for a sample of 20 companies from the *Business Week* Corporate Scoreboard follow (*Business Week,* November 17, 1997):

Company	Earnings per Share ($)	Company	Earnings per Share ($)
Barnes & Noble	0.78	Hershey Foods	1.97
Citicorp	7.10	Hewlett-Packard	2.82
Compaq Computer	2.16	Humana	0.89
Dana	3.42	Microsoft	2.66
Dell Computer	2.03	Procter & Gamble	2.53
Digital Equipment	1.28	Quaker State	0.41
General Dynamics	4.82	Sara Lee	2.08
Goodyear	0.94	Snap-On Tools	2.38
Harley-Davidson	1.11	Sunstrand	2.53
Heinz	0.98	Xerox	3.95

Develop a stem-and-leaf display for the data. Use a leaf unit of 0.1. Comment on what you learned about the earnings per share for these companies.

JobSat

27. In a study of job satisfaction, a series of tests was administered to 50 subjects. The following data were obtained; higher scores represent greater dissatisfaction.

87	76	67	58	92	59	41	50	90	75	80	81	70
73	69	61	88	46	85	97	50	47	81	87	75	60
65	92	77	71	70	74	53	43	61	89	84	83	70
46	84	76	78	64	69	76	78	67	74	64		

Construct a stem-and-leaf display for the data.

28. Periodically *Barron's* publishes earnings forecasts for the companies listed in the Dow Jones Industrial Average. The following are the 1998 forecasts of price/earnings (P/E) ratios for these companies implied by *Barron's* earnings forecasts (*Barron's,* December 8, 1997).

PEforcst

Company	1998 P/E Forecast	Company	1998 P/E Forecast
AT&T	20	Hewlett-Packard	18
Alcoa	10	IBM	16
Allied Signal	16	International Paper	17
American Express	18	Johnson & Johnson	23
Boeing	21	McDonald's	18
Caterpillar	11	Merck	24
Chevron	18	Minnesota Mining	21
Coca-Cola	38	J. P. Morgan	15
Disney	27	Philip Morris	13
Dupont	16	Procter & Gamble	27
Eastman Kodak	15	Sears	13
Exxon	20	Travelers	17
General Electric	26	Union Carbide	12
General Motors	8	United Technologies	17
Goodyear	13	Wal-Mart	24

a. Develop a stem-and-leaf display for the data.
b. Use the results of the stem-and-leaf display to develop a frequency distribution and percent frequency distribution for the data.

2.4   CROSSTABULATIONS AND SCATTER DIAGRAMS

Crosstabulations and scatter diagrams are used to summarize data in a way that reveals the relationship between two variables.

Thus far in this chapter, we have focused on tabular and graphical methods that are used to summarize the data for *one variable at a time*. Often a manager or decision maker is interested in tabular and graphical methods that will assist in the understanding of the *relationship between two variables*. Crosstabulation and scatter diagrams are two such methods.

Crosstabulation

Restaurant

Crosstabulation is a method that can be used to summarize the data for two variables simultaneously. Let us illustrate the use of a crosstabulation by considering the following application. Zagat's Restaurant Review is a service that provides data on restaurants located throughout the world. Data on a variety of variables such as the restaurant's quality rating and typical meal price are reported. Quality rating is a qualitative variable with rating categories of good, very good, and excellent. Meal price is a quantitative variable that generally ranges from $10 to $49. The quality rating and the meal price data were collected for a sample of 300 restaurants located in the Los Angeles area.

A crosstabulation of the data for this application is shown in Table 2.11. The left and top margin labels define the classes for the two variables. In the left margin, the row labels (good, very good, and excellent) correspond to the three classes of the quality rating variable. In the top margin, the column labels ($10–19, $20–29, $30–39, and $40–49) correspond to the four classes of the meal price variable. Each restaurant in the sample provides a quality rating and a meal price. Thus, each restaurant in the sample is associated with a cell appearing in one of the rows and one of the columns of the crosstabulation. For example, an Italian restaurant located near Malibu is identified as having a very good quality rating and typical meal price of $32. This restaurant belongs to the cell in row 2 and column 3 of Table 2.11. In constructing a crosstabulation, we simply count the number of restaurants that belong to each of the cells in the crosstabulation table.

In reviewing Table 2.11, we see that the greatest number of restaurants in the sample (64) have a very good rating and a meal price in the $20–29 range. Only two restaurants have an excellent rating and a meal price in the $10–19 range. Similar interpretations of the other frequencies can be made. In addition, note that the right and bottom margins of the crosstabulation provide the frequency distributions for quality rating and

Table 2.11	CROSSTABULATION OF QUALITY RATING AND MEAL PRICE FOR 300 LOS ANGELES RESTAURANTS				

		Meal Price			
Quality Rating	$10–19	$20–29	$30–39	$40–49	Total
Good	42	40	2	0	84
Very Good	34	64	46	6	150
Excellent	2	14	28	22	66
Total	78	118	76	28	300

meal price separately. From the frequency distribution in the right margin, we see that data on quality ratings show 84 good restaurants, 150 very good restaurants, and 66 excellent restaurants. Similarly, the bottom margin shows the frequency distribution for the meal price variable.

The value of a crosstabulation is that it provides insight about the relationship between the variables. From the results in Table 2.11, higher meal prices appear to be associated with the higher quality restaurants and the lower meal prices appear to be associated with the lower quality restaurants.

Converting the entries in the table into row percentages or column percentages can afford additional insight about the relationship between the variables. For example, the results of dividing each frequency in Table 2.11 by its corresponding row total and expressing the values as percentages are shown in Table 2.12. For the lowest quality category (good), we see that the greatest percentages are for the less expensive restaurants (50.0% have \$10–19 meal prices and 47.6% have \$20–29 meal prices). For the highest quality category (excellent), we see that the greatest percentages are for the more expensive restaurants (42.4% have \$30–39 meal prices and 33.4% have \$40–49 meal prices). Thus, we continue to see that the more expensive meals are associated with the higher quality restaurants.

Crosstabulation is widely used for examining the relationship between two variables. In practice, final reports for many statistical surveys include a large number of crosstabulation tables. In the Los Angeles restaurant sample, the crosstabulation is based on one qualitative variable (quality rating) and one quantitative variable (meal price). Crosstabulations can also be developed when both variables are qualitative and when both variables are quantitative.

Scatter Diagram

A *scatter diagram* is a graphical presentation of the relationship between two quantitative variables. As an illustration of a scatter diagram, consider the situation of a stereo and sound equipment store in San Francisco. On 10 occasions during the past three months, the store has used weekend television commercials to promote sales at its stores. The managers want to investigate whether a relationship can be demonstrated between the number of commercials shown and the sales at the store during the following week. Sample data for the 10 weeks with sales in hundreds of dollars are shown in Table 2.13.

Table 2.12   ROW PERCENTAGES FOR EACH QUALITY RATING CATEGORY

	Meal Price				
Quality Rating	\$10–19	\$20–29	\$30–39	\$40–49	Total
Good	50.0	47.6	2.4	0.0	100
Very Good	22.7	42.7	30.6	4.0	100
Excellent	3.0	21.2	42.4	33.4	100

	No. of Commercials	Sales Volume ($100s)
Week	x	y
1	2	50
2	5	57
3	1	41
4	3	54
5	4	54
6	1	38
7	5	63
8	3	48
9	4	59
10	2	46

Table 2.13   SAMPLE DATA FOR THE STEREO AND SOUND EQUIPMENT STORE

Figure 2.6 is the scatter diagram for the data in Table 2.13. The number of commercials (x) is shown on the horizontal axis and the sales (y) are shown on the vertical axis. For week 1, $x = 2$ and $y = 50$. A point with those coordinates is plotted on the scatter diagram. Similar points are plotted for the other nine weeks. The completed scatter diagram in Figure 2.6 indicates a positive relationship between the number of commercials and sales. Higher sales are associated with a higher number of commercials. The relationship is not perfect in that

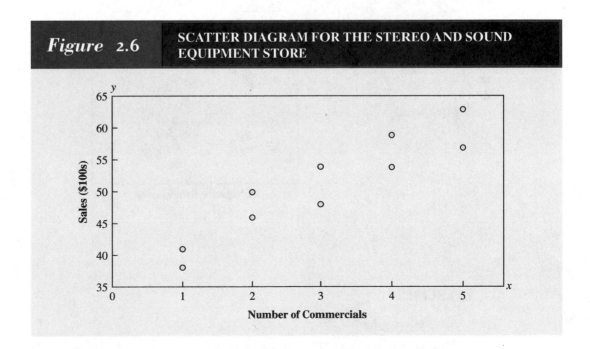

Figure 2.6   SCATTER DIAGRAM FOR THE STEREO AND SOUND EQUIPMENT STORE

all points are not on a straight line. However, the general pattern of the points suggests that the overall relationship is positive.

Some general scatter diagram patterns and the types of relationships they suggest are shown in Figure 2.7. The top left panel depicts a positive relationship similar to the one we saw for the number of commercials and sales example. In the top right panel, the scatter diagram shows no apparent relationship between the variables. The bottom panel depicts a negative relationship where y tends to decrease as x increases.

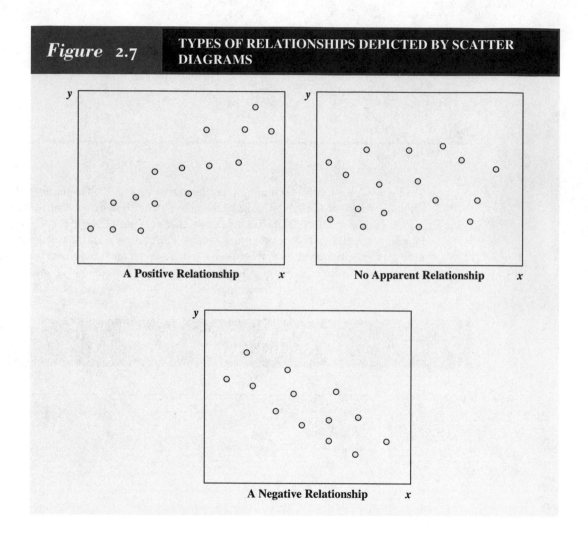

Figure 2.7   TYPES OF RELATIONSHIPS DEPICTED BY SCATTER DIAGRAMS

A Positive Relationship

No Apparent Relationship

A Negative Relationship

EXERCISES

Methods

29. The following data are for 30 observations on two qualitative variables, x and y. The categories for x are A, B, and C; the categories for y are 1 and 2.

SELF TEST

Observation	x	y	Observation	x	y
1	A	1	16	B	2
2	B	1	17	C	1
3	B	1	18	B	1
4	C	2	19	C	1
5	B	1	20	B	1
6	C	2	21	C	2
7	B	1	22	B	1
8	C	2	23	C	2
9	A	1	24	A	1
10	B	1	25	B	1
11	A	1	26	C	2
12	B	1	27	C	2
13	C	2	28	A	1
14	C	2	29	B	1
15	C	2	30	B	2

a. Develop a crosstabulation for the data, using x in the rows and y in the columns.
b. Compute the row percentages.
c. Compute column percentages.
d. What is the relationship, if any, between x and y?

30. The following 20 observations are for two quantitative variables, x and y.

Scatter

Observation	x	y	Observation	x	y
1	−22	22	11	−37	48
2	−33	49	12	34	−29
3	2	8	13	9	−18
4	29	−16	14	−33	31
5	−13	10	15	20	−16
6	21	−28	16	− 3	14
7	−13	27	17	−15	18
8	−23	35	18	12	17
9	14	− 5	19	−20	−11
10	3	− 3	20	− 7	−22

a. Develop a scatter diagram for the relationship between x and y.
b. What is the apparent relationship, if any, between x and y?

Applications

31. Compute column percentages for the restaurant data in Table 2.11. What is the relationship between quality rating and meal price?

SELF TEST

32. Shown in Table 2.14 are financial data for a 30-company sample of the largest U.S. companies whose stock is traded over the counter (*Financial World,* September 1, 1994).
a. Prepare a crosstabulation of the data on earnings (rows) and book value (columns). Use classes 0.00–0.99, 1.00–1.99, and 2.00–2.99 for earnings per share and classes 0.00–4.99, 5.00–9.99, 10.00–14.99, and 15.00–15.99 for book value per share.
b. Compute row percentages and comment on any relationship that you see between the variables.

33. Refer to the data in Table 2.14.
    a. Prepare a crosstabulation of the data on book value and stock price.
    b. Compute column percentages and comment on any relationship that you see between the variables.

34. Refer to the data in Table 2.14.
    a. Prepare a scatter diagram of the data on earnings per share and book value.
    b. Comment on any relationship that you see between the variables.

35. Refer to the data in Table 2.14.
    a. Prepare a scatter diagram of the data on earnings per share and stock price.
    b. Does there appear to be a relationship between the variables? Comment.

Finance

Table 2.14	FINANCIAL DATA FOR A SAMPLE OF 30 COMPANIES		
Company	Earnings per Share ($)	Book Value per Share ($)	Stock Price ($)
Acme	2.59	15.00	25.50
Aldus	1.41	9.22	29.50
American Fed. Bank	1.26	7.75	11.63
Applebees	.49	3.60	14.75
Banta Corp.	2.16	14.89	32.75
Bob Evans	1.15	7.41	21.50
Cintas Corp.	1.12	5.64	31.00
Comm. Clr. Hse.	.72	5.76	19.00
Cracker Barrel	.89	6.09	23.13
Devon Group	2.01	8.86	19.50
Duracraft	1.69	5.41	40.00
First Alert	.79	3.18	25.75
Food Lion	.26	3.71	5.94
Gentex	.83	3.09	21.00
Gould Pumps	1.12	8.80	20.25
Haggar Corp.	2.80	15.26	29.00
Hubco, Inc.	2.27	11.74	21.13
Info. Res.	.74	8.59	13.75
Irwin Financial	2.82	12.08	21.75
Kelly Services	1.35	11.06	28.75
Lone Star	.62	4.44	20.00
Mark Twain	2.40	13.75	27.50
Micro Systems	1.03	4.01	28.50
Novell	.98	3.58	16.13
Pacific Phy.	.55	5.00	11.50
Proffitts Inc.	.50	13.39	18.75
Rival	1.44	6.57	20.38
Sybase	1.07	3.81	37.00
Tyson Foods	1.23	17.06	23.88
Zenith Labs	.85	3.63	15.63

Source: *Financial World,* September 1, 1994.

··/ /··········

SUMMARY

A set of data, even if modest in size, is often difficult to interpret directly in the form in which it is gathered. Tabular and graphical procedures provide means of organizing

| Figure 2.8 | TABULAR AND GRAPHICAL PROCEDURES FOR SUMMARIZING DATA |

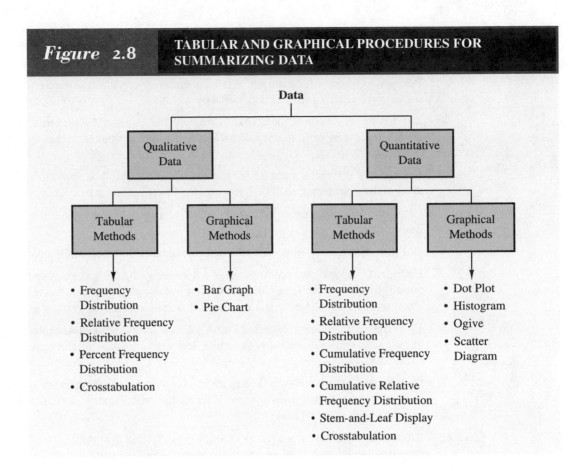

and summarizing data so that patterns are revealed and the data are more easily interpreted. Frequency distributions, relative frequency distributions, percent frequency distributions, bar graphs, and pie charts were presented as tabular and graphical procedures for summarizing qualitative data. Frequency distributions, relative frequency distributions, percent frequency distributions, dot plots, histograms, cumulative frequency distributions, cumulative relative frequency distributions, cumulative percent frequency distributions, and ogives were presented as ways of summarizing quantitative data. A stem-and-leaf display was presented as an exploratory data analysis technique that can be used to summarize quantitative data. Crosstabulation was presented as a tabular method for summarizing data for two variables. The scatter diagram was introduced as a graphical method for showing the relationship between two quantitative variables. Figure 2.8 is a summary of the tabular and graphical methods presented in this chapter.

GLOSSARY

Qualitative data Data that provide labels or names for categories of like items.

Quantitative data Data that indicate how much or how many.

Frequency distribution A tabular summary of data showing the frequency (or number) of observations in each of several nonoverlapping classes.

Relative frequency distribution A tabular summary of data showing the relative frequency—that is, the fraction or proportion—of the observations in each of several nonoverlapping classes.

Percent frequency distribution A tabular summary of data showing the percentage of observations in each of several nonoverlapping classes.

Bar graph A graphical method for depicting the information presented in a frequency distribution, relative frequency distribution, or percent frequency distribution of qualitative data.

Pie chart A graphical method for presenting qualitative data summaries based on subdivision of a circle into sectors that correspond to the relative frequency for each class.

Class midpoint The point in each class that is halfway between the lower and upper class limits.

Dot plot A graphical summary with dots showing the location of the quantitative data.

Histogram A graphical presentation of a frequency distribution, relative frequency distribution, or percent frequency distribution of quantitative data constructed by placing the class intervals on the horizontal axis and the frequencies on the vertical axis.

Cumulative frequency distribution A tabular summary of quantitative data showing the number of observations with values less than or equal to the upper class limit of each class.

Cumulative relative frequency distribution A tabular summary of quantitative data showing the fraction or proportion of observations with values less than or equal to the upper class limit of each class.

Cumulative percent frequency distribution A tabular summary of quantitative data showing the percentage of observations with values less than or equal to the upper class limit of each class.

Ogive A graph of a cumulative distribution.

Exploratory data analysis Methods that use simple arithmetic and easy-to-draw graphs to summarize data quickly.

Stem-and-leaf display An exploratory data analysis technique that simultaneously rank orders quantitative data and provides insight about the shape of the distribution.

Crosstabulation A tabular summary of data for two variables. The classes for one variable are represented by the rows; the classes for the other variable are represented by the columns.

Scatter diagram A graphical means of showing the relationship between two quantitative variables. One variable is shown on the horizontal axis and the other variable is shown on the vertical axis.

KEY FORMULAS

Relative Frequency

$$\frac{\text{Frequency of the Class}}{n} \tag{2.1}$$

Approximate Class Width

$$\frac{\text{Largest Data Value} - \text{Smallest Data Value}}{\text{Number of Classes}} \qquad (2.2)$$

··/ /··············

SUPPLEMENTARY EXERCISES

36. America's five best-selling cars for the first 11 months of the 1997 model year were Honda Accord, Chevy Cavalier, Toyota Camry, Honda Civic, and Ford Taurus (*The Wall Street Journal,* September 30, 1997). Data on 50 car purchases in Cleveland, Ohio, are presented in Table 2.15.
    a. Show a frequency distribution.
    b. Show a relative frequency distribution. What is the best-selling car?
    c. Show a pie chart of the data.

37. Each of the *Fortune* 500 companies is classified as belonging to one of several industries (*Fortune,* April 28, 1997). A sample of 20 companies with their corresponding industry classification follows.

Company	Industry Classification	Company	Industry Classification
IBP	Food	Borden	Food
Intel	Electronics	McDonnell Douglas	Aerospace
Coca-Cola	Beverage	Morton International	Chemicals
Union Carbide	Chemicals	Quaker Oats	Food
General Electric	Electronics	Pepsico	Beverage
Motorola	Electronics	Maytag	Electronics
Kellogg	Food	Textron	Aerospace
Dow Chemical	Chemicals	Sara Lee	Food
Campbell Soup	Food	Harris	Electronics
Ralston Purina	Food	Eaton	Electronics

    a. Provide a frequency distribution showing the number of companies in each industry.
    b. Provide a percent frequency distribution.
    c. Provide a bar graph for the data.

Cars

Table 2.15	A SAMPLE OF 50 CAR PURCHASES

Taurus	Civic	Civic	Taurus	Camry
Taurus	Civic	Cavalier	Cavalier	Taurus
Camry	Civic	Cavalier	Cavalier	Taurus
Camry	Camry	Camry	Civic	Civic
Civic	Accord	Cavalier	Cavalier	Taurus
Cavalier	Taurus	Accord	Civic	Camry
Accord	Camry	Cavalier	Camry	Accord
Accord	Taurus	Accord	Camry	Taurus
Civic	Accord	Camry	Accord	Cavalier
Accord	Taurus	Camry	Camry	Accord

38. The International Organization for Standardization in Geneva, Switzerland, has developed a widely accepted set of quality standards: ISO 9000. Companies all over the world have become ISO 9000 certified. A Grant Thornton survey (*Fifth Annual Grant Thornton Survey of American Manufacturers Report,* 1994) asked U.S. manufacturers about their plans for obtaining certification. Let C = already certified, P = already pursuing certification, W = will pursue certification, N = will not pursue certification, and U = uncertain. The following sample data are consistent with the responses obtained by Grant Thornton.

W	P	N	N	W	P	C	W	W	N
N	W	U	W	P	W	P	C	N	P
P	N	W	W	N	W	N	W	W	N
C	W	P	W	N	N	C	W	P	N
W	W	N	W	N	U	N	W	N	W

a. Prepare a frequency distribution and a percent frequency distribution for the data set.
b. Prepare a pie chart for the data set.
c. Grant Thornton reported that less than 1% of the companies were certified in 1993. Comment on the trend in obtaining ISO certification based on the 1994 sample data.

39. The data in Table 2.16 represent sales in millions of dollars for 20 companies in the health care services industry during third quarter, 1997 (*Business Week,* November 17, 1997).
a. Construct a frequency distribution to summarize the data. Use a class width of 500.
b. Develop a relative frequency distribution for the data.
c. Construct a cumulative frequency distribution for the data.
d. Construct a cumulative relative frequency distribution for the data.
e. Construct a histogram as a graphical representation of the data.

Comstock

40. The closing prices of 40 common stocks follow (*Investor's Daily,* March 25, 1998).

$29\frac{5}{8}$	34	$43\frac{1}{4}$	$8\frac{3}{4}$	$37\frac{7}{8}$	$8\frac{5}{8}$	$7\frac{5}{8}$	$30\frac{3}{8}$	$35\frac{1}{4}$	$19\frac{3}{8}$
$9\frac{1}{4}$	$16\frac{1}{2}$	38	$53\frac{3}{8}$	$16\frac{5}{8}$	$1\frac{1}{4}$	$48\frac{3}{8}$	18	$9\frac{3}{8}$	$9\frac{1}{4}$
10	37	18	8	$28\frac{1}{2}$	$24\frac{1}{4}$	$21\frac{5}{8}$	$18\frac{1}{2}$	$33\frac{5}{8}$	$31\frac{1}{8}$
$32\frac{1}{4}$	$29\frac{5}{8}$	$79\frac{3}{8}$	$11\frac{3}{8}$	$38\frac{7}{8}$	$11\frac{1}{2}$	52	14	9	$33\frac{1}{2}$

a. Construct frequency and relative frequency distributions for the data.
b. Construct cumulative frequency and cumulative relative frequency distributions for the data.
c. Construct a histogram for the data.
d. Using your summaries, make comments and observations about the price of common stock.

41. Ninety-four new shadow stocks were reported by the American Association of Individual Investors (*AAII Journal,* February 1997). The term "shadow" indicates stocks for small to medium-size firms not followed closely by the major brokerage houses. Information on where the stock was traded—New York Stock Exchange (NYSE), American Stock Exchange

Table 2.16	SALES IN HEALTH CARE SERVICES FOR THIRD QUARTER, 1997		
Beverly Ent.	805	Novacare	357
Coventry	307	Phycor	284
Express Scripts	320	Quest Diag.	374
Healthsouth	748	Quorum Health	393
Horizon	445	Sun Healthcare	486
Humana	1968	Tenet Healthcare	2331
Int. Health	472	U. Wisconsin	389
Lab. Corp. Am.	377	Univ. Health	362
Manor Care	274	Vencor	845
Medpartners	1614	Wellpoint	1512

Source: *Business Week,* November 17, 1997.

(AMEX), and over the counter (OTC)—the earnings per share, and the price/earnings ratio was provided for the following sample of 20 shadow stocks.

Shadow

Stock	Exchange	Earnings per Share ($)	Price/Earnings Ratio
Chemi-Trol	OTC	.39	27.30
Candie's	OTC	.07	36.20
TST/Impreso	OTC	.65	12.70
Unimed Pharm.	OTC	.12	59.30
Skyline Chili	AMEX	.34	19.30
Cyanotech	OTC	.22	29.30
Catalina Light.	NYSE	.15	33.20
DDL Elect.	NYSE	.10	10.20
Euphonix	OTC	.09	49.70
Mesa Labs	OTC	.37	14.40
RCM Tech.	OTC	.47	18.60
Anuhco	AMEX	.70	11.40
Hello Direct	OTC	.23	21.10
Hilite Industries	OTC	.61	7.80
Alpha Tech.	OTC	.11	34.60
Wegener Group	OTC	.16	24.50
U.S. Home & Garden	OTC	.24	8.70
Chalone Wine	OTC	.27	44.40
Eng. Support Sys.	OTC	.89	16.70
Int. Remote Imaging	AMEX	.86	4.70

a. Provide frequency and relative frequency distributions for the exchange data. Where are most shadow stocks listed?

b. Provide frequency and relative frequency distributions for the earnings per share and price/earnings ratio data. Use class limits of .00–.19, .20–.39, and so on, for the earnings per share data and class limits of 0.0–9.9, 10.0–19.9, and so on for the price/earnings ratio data. What observations and comments can you make about the shadow stocks?

42. A state-by-state listing of average household incomes for 1995–96 follows.

States

State	Income ($)	State	Income ($)	State	Income ($)
Ala.	28,530	Kent.	31,552	N.D.	30,709
Alaska	51,074	La.	29,518	Ohio	35,022
Ariz.	31,706	Maine	34,777	Okla.	27,263
Ark.	26,850	Md.	43,123	Ore.	36,470
Calif.	38,457	Mass.	39,604	Penn.	35,221
Colo.	41,429	Mich.	38,364	R.I.	36,695
Conn.	41,775	Minn.	40,022	S.C.	32,297
Del.	37,634	Miss.	27,000	S.D.	29,989
D.C.	31,811	Mo.	35,059	Tenn.	30,331
Fla.	30,632	Mont.	28,631	Texas	33,029
Ga.	33,801	Neb.	33,958	Utah	37,298
Hawaii	42,944	Nev.	37,845	Vt.	33,591
Idaho	34,175	N.H.	39,868	Va.	38,252
Ill.	39,375	N.J.	46,345	Wash.	36,647
Ind.	34,759	N.M.	25,922	W.Va.	25,431
Iowa	34,888	N.Y.	34,707	Wis.	41,082
Kan.	31,911	N.C.	34,262	Wyo.	31,707

Source: U.S. Bureau of the Census, March 1997, *Current Population Survey.*

Develop a frequency distribution, a relative frequency distribution, and a histogram for the data.

43. The conclusion from a 40-state poll conducted by the Joint Council on Economic Education is that students do not learn enough economics. The findings were based on test results from 11th- and 12th-grade students who took a 46-question, multiple-choice test on basic economic concepts such as profit and the law of supply and demand. The following table gives sample data on the number of questions answered correctly.

12	10	16	24	12	14	18	23
31	14	15	19	17	9	19	28
24	16	21	13	20	12	22	18
22	18	30	16	26	18	16	14
8	25	22	15	33	24	17	19

Summarize these data using:
a. A stem-and-leaf display.
b. A frequency distribution.
c. A relative frequency distribution.
d. A cumulative frequency distribution.
e. On the basis of these data, do you agree with the claim that students are not learning enough economics? Explain.

44. The daily high and low temperatures for 24 cities follow.

Cities

City	High	Low	City	High	Low
Tampa	78	66	Birmingham	63	51
Kansas City	38	26	Minneapolis	32	17
Boise	28	15	Portland	43	32
Los Angeles	63	46	Memphis	61	45
Philadelphia	41	35	Buffalo	38	32
Milwaukee	37	29	Cincinnati	46	40
Chicago	42	31	Charlotte	48	42
Albany	35	21	Boston	37	29
Houston	63	57	Tulsa	46	35
Salt Lake City	33	16	Washington, D.C.	43	38
Miami	79	70	Las Vegas	48	30
Cheyenne	29	13	Detroit	41	35

Source: *USA Today,* December 22, 1997.

a. Prepare a stem-and-leaf display for the high temperatures.
b. Prepare a stem-and-leaf display for the low temperatures.
c. Compare the stem-and-leaf displays from parts (a) and (b) and make some comments about the differences between daily high and low temperatures.
d. Use the stem-and-leaf display from part (b) to determine the number of cities having a low temperature of freezing (32°F) or below.
e. Provide frequency distributions for both the high and low temperature data.

45. Refer to the data set for high and low temperatures for 24 cities in Exercise 44.
a. Develop a scatter diagram to show the relationship between the two variables, high temperature and low temperature.
b. Comment on the relationship between high and low temperature.

46. Following are financial data for 20 companies in the banking and consumer products industries (*Business Week,* August 15, 1994).

BWdata

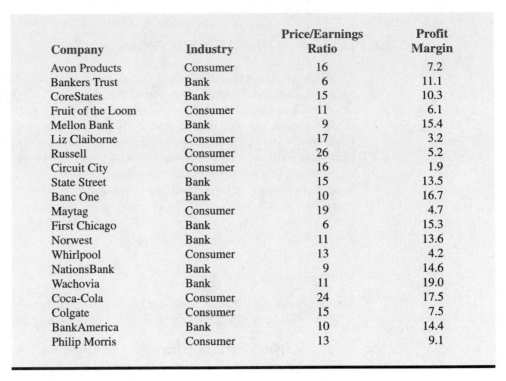

Company	Industry	Price/Earnings Ratio	Profit Margin
Avon Products	Consumer	16	7.2
Bankers Trust	Bank	6	11.1
CoreStates	Bank	15	10.3
Fruit of the Loom	Consumer	11	6.1
Mellon Bank	Bank	9	15.4
Liz Claiborne	Consumer	17	3.2
Russell	Consumer	26	5.2
Circuit City	Consumer	16	1.9
State Street	Bank	15	13.5
Banc One	Bank	10	16.7
Maytag	Consumer	19	4.7
First Chicago	Bank	6	15.3
Norwest	Bank	11	13.6
Whirlpool	Consumer	13	4.2
NationsBank	Bank	9	14.6
Wachovia	Bank	11	19.0
Coca-Cola	Consumer	24	17.5
Colgate	Consumer	15	7.5
BankAmerica	Bank	10	14.4
Philip Morris	Consumer	13	9.1

    a.   Prepare a crosstabulation for the variables industry type and price/earnings ratio. Use industry type as the row labels.

    b.   Compute the row percentages for your crosstabulation in part (a).

    c.   What relationship, if any, do you notice between industry type and price/earnings ratio?

47. Refer to the data set in Exercise 46 containing financial data for 20 companies in the banking and consumer products industries.

    a.   Prepare a scatter diagram to show the relationship between the variables price/earnings ratio and profit margin.

    b.   Comment on any relationship that is apparent between the variables.

48. A survey of commercial buildings served by the Cincinnati Gas & Electric Company was concluded in 1992 (CG&E Commercial Building Characteristics Survey, November 25, 1992). One question asked what main heating fuel was used and another asked the year the commercial building was constructed. A partial crosstabulation of the findings follows.

Year Constructed	Fuel Type				
	Electricity	Natural Gas	Oil	Propane	Other
1973 or before	40	183	12	5	7
1974–1979	24	26	2	2	0
1980–1986	37	38	1	0	6
1987–1991	48	70	2	0	1

    a.   Complete the crosstabulation by showing the row totals and column totals.

    b.   Show the frequency distributions for year constructed and for fuel type.

    c.   Prepare a crosstabulation showing column percentages.

    d.   Prepare a crosstabulation showing row percentages.

    e.   Comment on the relationship between year constructed and fuel type.

..../ /..............

Case Problem   CONSOLIDATED FOODS

Consolidated Foods operates a chain of supermarkets in New Mexico, Arizona, and California. A promotional campaign has advertised the chain's offering of a credit card policy whereby Consolidated Foods' customers have the option of paying for their purchases with credit cards such as Visa and MasterCard in addition to the usual options of cash or personal check. The policy is being implemented on a trial basis with the hope that the credit card option will encourage customers to make larger purchases.

After the first month of operation, a random sample of 100 customers was selected over a one-week period. Data were collected on the method of payment and how much was spent by each of the 100 customers. The sample data are shown in Table 2.17. Prior to the new credit card policy, approximately 50% of Consolidated Foods' customers paid in cash and approximately 50% paid by personal check.

Managerial Report

Use the tabular and graphical methods of descriptive statistics to summarize the sample data in Table 2.17. Your report should contain summaries such as the following.

1. A frequency and relative frequency distribution for the method of payment.
2. A bar graph or pie chart for the method of payment.

Consolid

Table 2.17	PURCHASE AMOUNT AND METHOD OF PAYMENT FOR A SAMPLE OF 100 CONSOLIDATED FOODS CUSTOMERS				
Cash	Personal Check	Credit Card	Cash	Personal Check	Credit Card
$ 7.40	$27.60	$50.30	$ 5.08	$52.87	$69.77
5.15	30.60	33.76	20.48	78.16	48.11
4.75	41.58	25.57	16.28	25.96	
15.10	36.09	46.24	15.57	31.07	
8.81	2.67	46.13	6.93	35.38	
1.85	34.67	14.44	7.17	58.11	
7.41	58.64	43.79	11.54	49.21	
11.77	57.59	19.78	13.09	31.74	
12.07	43.14	52.35	16.69	50.58	
9.00	21.11	52.63	7.02	59.78	
5.98	52.04	57.55	18.09	72.46	
7.88	18.77	27.66	2.44	37.94	
5.91	42.83	44.53	1.09	42.69	
3.65	55.40	26.91	2.96	41.10	
14.28	48.95	55.21	11.17	40.51	
1.27	36.48	54.19	16.38	37.20	
2.87	51.66	22.59	8.85	54.84	
4.34	28.58	53.32	7.22	58.75	
3.31	35.89	26.57		17.87	
15.07	39.55	27.89		69.22	

3. Frequency and relative frequency distributions for the amount spent in each method of payment.
4. Histograms and/or stem-and-leaf plots for the amount spent in each method of payment.

What preliminary insights do you have about the amounts spent and method of payment at Consolidated Foods?

..../ /.............

Appendix 2.1   DOT PLOTS, HISTOGRAMS, AND STEM-AND-LEAF DISPLAYS WITH MINITAB

In this appendix we describe the steps necessary to use Minitab to generate a dot plot, a histogram, and a stem-and-leaf display for the audit-time data in Table 2.5. We first enter the audit-time data into column C1 of a Minitab worksheet. The following steps generate the dot plot of Figure 2.3 using Minitab.

Step 1. Select the **Graph** pull-down menu
Step 2. Select **Dotplot**
Step 3. When the Dotplot dialog box appears:
      Enter C1 in the **Variables** box
      Select **OK**

To obtain the histogram shown in Figure 2.4, the following steps are necessary.

Step 1. Select the **Graph** pull-down menu
Step 2. Select **Histogram**
Step 3. When the Histogram dialog box appears:
      Enter C1 in row 1 of the **Graph variables** box
      Select **Bar** under **Display** and **Graph** under **For each** in the **Data display** box
      Select **Options**
Step 4. When the Histogram Options dialog box appears:
      Select **Frequency** under **Type of Histogram**
      Select **CutPoint** under **Type of Intervals**
      Select **Midpoint/cutpoint positions** under **Definition of Intervals** and enter
          10:35/5 in the box*
      Select **OK**
Step 5. When the Histogram dialog box appears:
      Select **OK**

To obtain the stem-and-leaf display for the audit-time data, the following steps are necessary.

Step 1. Select the **Graph** pull-down menu
Step 2. Select **Stem-and-Leaf**
Step 3. When the Stem-and-Leaf dialog box appears:
      Enter C1 in the **Variables** box
      Select **OK**

_____

*The entry 10:35/5 indicates 10 is the lowest value for the histogram, 35 is the highest-value for the histrogram and 5 is the class width.

Appendix 2.2   FREQUENCY DISTRIBUTIONS AND BAR GRAPHS WITH EXCEL

In this appendix, we show how Excel can be used to construct a frequency distribution and a bar graph for the soft drink purchase data in Table 2.1. Excel provides a worksheet of rows and columns for entering and storing the data. Suppose we enter the heading Brand Purchased and the 50 observations for the soft drink purchases in rows 1 to 51 of column A (see Figure 2.9). We now want to develop a frequency distribution and a bar graph for these data. Excel provides a histogram tool that can be used for this purpose. The histogram tool is designed to work with quantitative data only. So to work with qualitative data we must first develop numeric codes for the data. The soft drink data are coded as follows: 1 for Coke Classic, 2 for Diet Coke, 3 for Dr. Pepper, 4 for Pepsi-Cola, and 5 for Sprite. Note that we have placed the codes for each data item in column B of the spreadsheet in Figure 2.9.

Figure 2.9   SOFT DRINK DATA, CODES, AND BIN VALUES IN AN EXCEL WORKSHEET

	A	B	C
1	**Brand Purchased**	**Code**	
2	Coke Classic	1	**Brand Code**
3	Diet Coke	2	1
4	Pepsi-Cola	4	2
5	Diet Coke	2	3
6	Coke Classic	1	4
7	Coke Classic	1	5
8	Dr. Pepper	3	
9	Diet Coke	2	
10	Pepsi-Cola	4	
11	Pepsi-Cola	4	
12	Coke Classic	1	
13	Dr. Pepper	3	
14	Sprite	5	
15	Coke Classic	1	
16	Diet Coke	2	
17	Coke Classic	1	
18	Coke Classic	1	
19	•	•	
20	•	•	
21	•	•	
49	Dr. Pepper	3	
50	Pepsi-Cola	4	
51	Sprite	5	

Excel now treats the codes as quantitative data. To develop a frequency distribution and bar graph, Excel requires the user to identify what are called *bins* for the data. A bin must be identified for each class (category) and its upper limit must be specified. Five bins, with upper limits of 1, 2, 3, 4, and 5, are needed for the soft drink categories. In constructing the frequency distribution and bar graph, Excel provides a count of the number of observations *less than or equal to* the upper limit of the first bin (1), a count of the number of observations *greater than* the first bin upper limit and *less than or equal to* the second bin upper limit (2), and so on. Thus, the counts provided by Excel are the class frequencies for the frequency distribution.

Prior to implementing the Excel histogram procedure, we must enter the bin upper limits in *ascending order* in a column or row of the worksheet. Let us select column C as a convenient location and enter the label Brand Code in row 2. The bin upper limits are then entered in ascending order in rows 3 through 7 of column C. Figure 2.9 shows the worksheet with the bin upper limits in column C.

The following steps describe how to use Excel to produce a frequency distribution and a bar graph for the data in Figure 2.9.

Step 1. Select the **Tools** pull-down menu
Step 2. Choose the **Data Analysis** option
Step 3. Choose **Histogram** from the list of Analysis Tools
Step 4. When the Histogram dialog box appears:
Enter B1:B51 in the **Input Range** box
Enter C2:C7 in the **Bin Range** box
Select **Labels**
Select **Output Range**
Enter C10 in the **Output Range** box (this identifies the upper left corner of the section of the worksheet where the frequency distribution will appear)
Select **Chart Output** (this requests a histogram)
Select **OK**

Figure 2.10 shows the frequency distribution provided by Excel. The title Brand Code and the upper limits are shown in cells C10 through C15. The frequencies appear in the corresponding cells of column D. Note that Excel includes a last bin labeled More in case the data contains values greater than the upper limit of the last bin specified by the user. When interpreting the output, the user must remember that the bin values are the upper limits of the corresponding classes.

To convert the Excel frequency distribution into an easier-to-read format, the user can replace the upper limits in cells C11 through C15 with the soft drink names: Coke Classic, Diet Coke, Dr. Pepper, Pepsi-Cola, and Sprite. Finally, the title Total and the sum of the frequencies (50) can be entered in cells C16 and D16 to complete the frequency distribution.

Figure 2.11 shows the bar graph generated as a result of the preceding steps. We note that the values shown on the horizontal axis are the brand codes.

The steps necessary to use Excel to construct a frequency distribution and histogram for the audit-time data in Table 2.5 are similar to those described here for the qualitative data describing soft drink purchases. But, since the audit-time data are quantitative, no coding is necessary. We simply enter the data into the spreadsheet, specify the upper limits for the bins, and follow the steps just described.

Figure 2.10 FREQUENCY DISTRIBUTION OF THE SOFT DRINK DATA CONSTRUCTED BY EXCEL

	A	B	C	D
1	**Brand Purchased**	**Code**		
2	Coke Classic	1	**Brand Code**	
3	Diet Coke	2	1	
4	Pepsi-Cola	4	2	
5	Diet Coke	2	3	
6	Coke Classic	1	4	
7	Coke Classic	1	5	
8	Dr. Pepper	3		
9	Diet Coke	2		
10	Pepsi-Cola	4	*Brand Code*	*Frequency*
11	Pepsi-Cola	4	1	19
12	Coke Classic	1	2	8
13	Dr. Pepper	3	3	5
14	Sprite	5	4	13
15	Coke Classic	1	5	5
16	Diet Coke	2	More	0
17	Coke Classic	1		
18	Coke Classic	1		
19	•	•		
20	•	•		
21	•	•		
49	Dr. Pepper	3		
50	Pepsi-Cola	4		
51	Sprite	5		

Figure 2.11 BAR GRAPH OF THE SOFT DRINK DATA CONSTRUCTED BY EXCEL

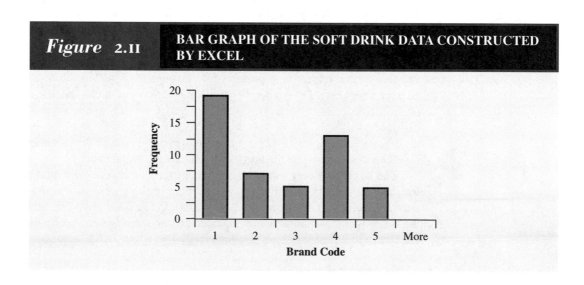

....*/ /*............

Appendix 2.3   CROSSTABULATIONS WITH MINITAB

In Section 2.4 we discussed how to summarize the data for two variables simultaneously using a crosstabulation. Using data from Zagat's restaurant review, we showed a crosstabulation of quality ratings and meal prices for 300 Los Angeles restaurants in Table 2.11. The data used to develop Table 2.11 is on the data disk in the data set named Restaurant. The restaurants are numbered from 1 to 300 in column 1 of the Minitab worksheet; column 2 shows the quality rating (good, very good, or excellent), and column 3 contains the typical meal price for each restaurant.

In this appendix, we describe how Minitab can be used to develop a crosstabulation for these data. First, note that the crosstabulation shown in Table 2.11 has four columns under the heading Meal Price, corresponding to the four categories: $10–19, $20–29, $30–39, and $40–49. Because crosstabulations can only be developed for qualitative (categorical) data, the first step in using Minitab to develop a crosstabulation of quality rating and meal price is to convert the quantitative data for meal price into categories. The following steps will place the categories for meal price in column 4 of the worksheet.

Step 1. Select the **Manip** pull-down menu
Step 2. Select **Code**
Step 3. Select **Numeric to Text . . .**
Step 4. When the Code—Numeric to Text dialog box appears:
Enter C3 in the **Code data from columns** box
Enter C4 in the **Into columns** box
Enter 10:19 in the first **Original values** box and $10–19 in the adjacent **New** box
Enter 20:29 in the second **Original values** box and $20–29 in the adjacent **New** box
Enter 30:39 in the third **Original values** box and $30–39 in the adjacent **New** box
Enter 40:49 in the fourth **Original values** box and $40–49 in the adjacent **New** box
Select **OK**

We can now develop the crosstabulation for quality rating and meal price using the data in columns 2 and 4. The following steps are necessary.

Step 1. Select the **Stat** pull-down menu
Step 2. Select **Tables**
Step 3. Select **Cross Tabulation**
Step 4. When the Cross Tabulation dialog box appears:
Enter C2 and C4 in the **Classification variables** box
Select **Counts**
Select **OK**

The crosstabulation that appears in the session window provides the same information as the crosstabulation shown in Table 2.11.

....*/ /*............

Appendix 2.4   CROSSTABULATIONS WITH EXCEL

In Section 2.4 we discussed how to summarize the data for two variables simultaneously using a crosstabulation. Using data from Zagat's restaurant view, we showed a

Figure 2.12		**WORKSHEET FOR THE FIRST 25 OBSERVATIONS FOR THE RESTAURANT DATA**	

Restaurant

	A	B	C
1	**Restaurant**	**Quality Rating**	**Meal Price ($)**
2	1	Good	18
3	2	Very Good	22
4	3	Good	28
5	4	Excellent	38
6	5	Very Good	33
7	6	Good	28
8	7	Very Good	19
9	8	Very Good	11
10	9	Very Good	23
11	10	Good	13
12	11	Very Good	33
13	12	Very Good	44
14	13	Excellent	42
15	14	Excellent	34
16	15	Good	25
17	16	Good	22
18	17	Good	26
19	18	Excellent	17
20	19	Very Good	30
21	20	Good	19
22	21	Very Good	33
23	22	Very Good	22
24	23	Excellent	32
25	24	Excellent	33
26	25	Very Good	34

crosstabulation of quality ratings and meal prices for 300 Los Angeles restaurants in Table 2.11. The worksheet shown in Figure 2.12 contains the data for the first 25 restaurants that were used to develop Table 2.11. Note that for each of the restaurants in the sample, the original data shows the quality rating (Good, Very Good, or Excellent) and the typical meal price rounded to the nearest dollar.

In this appendix, we describe how Excel's PivotTable Report can be used to develop a crosstabulation of quality rating and meal price. First, note that the crosstabulation shown in Table 2.11 has three rows under the heading Quality Rating, corresponding to the three quality categories: Good, Very Good, and Excellent. Unless we specify differently, the PivotTable report will order the labels alphabetically; in this case, the quality ratings would be listed in the order Excellent, Good, and Very Good. Thus, before using Excel's PivotTable Report to develop a crosstabulation of quality rating and meal price, the following steps must be performed in order to change the sort order Excel uses in developing the PivotTable.

Step 1. Select the **Tools** pull-down menu
Step 2. Choose **Options**
Step 3. When the Options dialog box appears:
Select the **Custom Lists** tab
In the **List entries:** box, type Good and press Enter; type Very Good and press
   Enter; and type Excellent
Select **Add**
Select **OK**

We are now ready to use the PivotTable Report to develop a crosstabulation of quality rating and meal price. The steps necessary to develop a crosstabulation from the spreadsheet in Figure 2.12 follow.

Step 1. Select the **Data** pull-down menu
Step 2. Choose the **PivotTable Report**
Step 3. When the PivotTable Wizard—Step 1 of 4 dialog box appears:
Choose **Microsoft Excel list or database**
Select **Next** >
Step 4. When the PivotTable Wizard—Step 2 of 4 dialog box appears:
Enter A1:C301 in the **Range:** box
Select **Next** >
Step 5. When the PivotTable Wizard—Step 3 of 4 dialog box appears (see Figure 2.13):
Drag the **Quality Rating** field button to the **ROW** section of the diagram
Drag the **Meal Price ($)** field button to the **COLUMN** section of the diagram

Figure 2.13   PIVOTTABLE WIZARD—STEP 3 OF 4 DIALOG BOX

Drag the **Restaurant** field button to the **DATA** section of the diagram

Double click the **Restaurant** field button* in the **DATA** section of the diagram

When the PivotTable Field dialog box appears:

　Choose **Summarize by Count**

　Select **OK**

Step 6. When the PivotTable Wizard—Step 3 of 4 dialog box reappears (see Figure 2.14):

　Select **Next** >

Step 7. When the PivotTable Wizard—Step 4 of 4 dialog box appears:

Choose **New Worksheet**

Select **Finish**

A portion of the output generated by Excel is shown in Figure 2.15. Note that the output that appears in columns E through AK has been hidden so the results can be shown in a reasonably sized figure. The row labels (Good, Very Good, and Excellent) and row totals (84, 150, 66, and 300) that appear in Figure 2.15 are the same as the row labels and row totals shown in Table 2.11. But, in Figure 2.15, there is one column for each possible value of meal price. For example, column B contains the output corresponding to a $10 meal price, column C contains the output corresponding to a meal price of $11, and so on. Thus, to view the output in a form similar to Table 2.11, we must group the columns into four price categories: $10–19, $20–29, $30–39, and $40–49. The steps necessary to group the columns for the spreadsheet shown in Figure 2.15 follow.

Figure 2.14　**PIVOTTABLE WIZARD—STEP 3 OF 4 DIALOG BOX AT THE END OF STEP 5**

---

*Because we are developing a crosstabulation that shows only the number of observations in each cell of the crosstabulation, the Quality Rating or the Meal Price ($) field buttons could be used in this step instead of the Restaurant field button.

Figure 2.15   PIVOTTABLE REPORT OUTPUT (COLUMNS E:AK HAVE BEEN HIDDEN FOR READABILITY)

	A	B	C	D	AL	AM	AN
1	Count of Restaurant	Meal Price ($)					
2	Quality Rating	10	11	12	47	48	Grand Total
3	Good	6	4	3			84
4	Very Good	1	4	3		1	150
5	Excellent				2	2	66
6	Grand Total	7	8	6	2	3	300

Step 1: Select cell B1 in the PivotTable

Step 2: Click the **large right arrow** in the PivotTable toolbar*

Step 3: If necessary, select **Auto** next to the **Starting at** box
If necessary, select **Auto** next to the **Ending at** box
Enter 10 in the **By** box
Select **OK**

The revised PivotTable output is shown in Figure 2.16. Note that the PivotTable provides the same type of information as the crosstabulation shown in Table 2.11.

Figure 2.16   REVISED PIVOTTABLE OUTPUT

	A	B	C	D	E	F
1	Count of Restaurant	Meal Price ($)				
2	Quality Rating	10-19	20-29	30-39	40-49	Grand Total
3	Good	42	40	2		84
4	Very Good	34	64	46	6	150
5	Excellent	2	14	28	22	66
6	Grand Total	78	118	76	28	300

---

*If the PivotTable toolbar is not visible, select the View pull-down menu, choose Toolbars, and select the PivotTable option. Alternatively, right click on any toolbar to display the list of toolbars and select PivotTable.

3

DESCRIPTIVE STATISTICS II: NUMERICAL METHODS

CONTENTS

SMALL FRY DESIGN*
Santa Ana, California

Founded in 1997, Small Fry Design is a toy and accessory company that designs and imports products for infants. The company's product line includes teddy bears, mobiles, musical toys, rattles, and security blankets, and features high-quality soft toy designs with an emphasis on color, texture, and sound. The products are designed in the United States and manufactured in China.

Small Fry Design uses independent representatives to sell the products to infant furnishing retailers, children's accessory and apparel stores, gift shops, upscale department stores, and major catalog companies. Currently, Small Fry Design products are distributed in more than 1000 retail outlets throughout the United States.

Cash flow management is one of the most critical activities in the day-to-day operation of this young company. Ensuring sufficient incoming cash to meet both current and ongoing debt obligations can mean the difference between business success and failure. A critical factor in cash flow management is the analysis and control of accounts receivable. By measuring the average age and dollar value of outstanding invoices, management can predict cash availability and monitor changes in the status of accounts receivable. The company has set the following goals: the average past due time for invoices should not exceed 45 days and the dollar value of invoices more than 60 days old should not exceed 5% of the dollar value of all accounts receivable.

In a recent summary of accounts receivable status, the following descriptive statistics were provided for the age of outstanding invoices:

---

* The authors are indebted to John A. McCarthy, president of Small Fry Design, for providing this Statistics in Practice.

Some of the Small Fry Design products. © Photo courtesy of Small Fry Design.

Mean	40 days
Median	35 days
Mode	31 days

Interpretation of these statistics shows that the mean or average age of an invoice is 40 days. The median shows that half of the invoices have been outstanding 35 days or more. The mode of 31 days is the most frequent invoice age indicating that the most common length of time an invoice has been outstanding is 31 days. The statistical summary also showed that only 3% of the dollar value of all accounts receivable was over 60 days old. Based on the statistical information, management was satisfied that accounts receivable and incoming cash flow were under control.

In this chapter, you will learn how to compute and interpret some of the statistical measures used by Small Fry Design. In addition to the mean, median, and mode, you will learn about other descriptive statistics such as the range, variance, standard deviation, percentiles, and correlation. These numerical measures will assist in the understanding and interpretation of data.

In Chapter 2 we discussed tabular and graphical methods used to summarize data. In this chapter, we present several numerical methods of descriptive statistics that provide additional alternatives for summarizing data.

We start by considering data sets consisting of a single variable. Whenever the data have been obtained from a sample of n elements, the numerical measures are computed by using the n observations. When a data set contains more than one variable, numerical measures can be computed separately for each variable. In the two-variable case, we will also develop measures of the relationship between the variables.

Several numerical measures of location, dispersion, and association are introduced. If the measures are computed for data from a sample, they are called *sample statistics*. If the measures are computed for data from a population, they are called *population parameters*.

3.1 MEASURES OF LOCATION

Mean

Perhaps the most important measure of location is the *mean,* or average value, for a variable. The mean provides a measure of central location. If the data are from a sample, the mean is denoted by $\bar{x}$; if the data are from a population, the mean is denoted by the Greek letter μ.

In statistical formulas, it is customary to denote the value of the first observation by x_1, the value of the second observation by x_2, and so on. In general, the value of the ith observation is denoted by x_i. For a sample with n observations, the formula for the sample mean is as follows.

Sample Mean

$$\bar{x} = \frac{\Sigma x_i}{n} \tag{3.1}$$

In the preceding formula, the numerator is the sum of the values of the n observations. That is,

$$\Sigma x_i = x_1 + x_2 + \cdots + x_n$$

The Greek letter Σ is the summation sign.

To illustrate the computation of a sample mean, let us consider the following class-size data for a sample of five college classes.

$$46 \quad 54 \quad 42 \quad 46 \quad 32$$

We use the notation x_1, x_2, x_3, x_4, x_5 to represent the number of students in each of the five classes.

$$x_1 = 46 \qquad x_2 = 54 \qquad x_3 = 42 \qquad x_4 = 46 \qquad x_5 = 32$$

Hence, to compute the sample mean, we can write

$$\bar{x} = \frac{\Sigma x_i}{n} = \frac{x_1 + x_2 + x_3 + x_4 + x_5}{5} = \frac{46 + 54 + 42 + 46 + 32}{5} = 44$$

The sample mean class size is 44 students.

Another illustration of the computation of a sample mean is given in the following situation. Suppose that a college placement office sent a questionnaire to a sample of business school graduates requesting information on starting salaries. Table 3.1 shows the data that have been collected. The mean monthly starting salary for the sample of 12 business college graduates is computed as

$$\bar{x} = \frac{\Sigma x_i}{n} = \frac{x_1 + x_2 + \cdots + x_{12}}{12}$$

$$= \frac{2350 + 2450 + \cdots + 2380}{12}$$

$$= \frac{29,280}{12} = 2440$$

Equation (3.1) shows how the mean is computed for a sample with n observations. The formula for computing the mean of a population is the same, but we use different notation to indicate that we are working with the entire population. The number of observations in a population is denoted by N and the symbol for a population mean is μ.

Population Mean

$$\mu = \frac{\Sigma x_i}{N} \tag{3.2}$$

Median

The *median* is another measure of central location for a variable. The median is the value in the middle when the data are arranged in ascending order (rank ordered from smallest value to largest value). With an odd number of observations, the median is the middle value. An even number of observations has no single middle value. In this case, we follow the convention of defining the median to be the average of the values for the middle two observations. For convenience the definition of the median is restated as follows.

Table 3.1	MONTHLY STARTING SALARIES FOR A SAMPLE OF 12 BUSINESS SCHOOL GRADUATES		
Graduate	**Monthly Salary ($)**	**Graduate**	**Monthly Salary ($)**
1	2350	7	2390
2	2450	8	2630
3	2550	9	2440
4	2380	10	2825
5	2255	11	2420
6	2210	12	2380

Median

Arrange the data values in ascending order.

(a) For an odd number of observations, the median is the middle value.

(b) For an even number of observations, the median is the average of the middle two values.

Let us apply this definition to compute the median class size for the sample of five college classes. Arranging the five observations in ascending order provides the following list.

$$32 \quad 42 \quad 46 \quad 46 \quad 54$$

Because $n = 5$ is odd, the median is the middle value. Thus the median class size is 46 students. Even though this data set has two data values of 46, each data value is treated separately when we arrange the data in ascending order.

Suppose we also compute the median starting salary for 12 business college graduates. We first arrange the 12 observations in Table 3.1 in ascending order.

$$2210 \quad 2255 \quad 2350 \quad 2380 \quad 2380 \quad \underbrace{2390 \quad 2420}_{\text{Middle Two Values}} \quad 2440 \quad 2450 \quad 2550 \quad 2630 \quad 2825$$

Because $n = 12$ is even, we identify the middle two values: 2390 and 2420. The median is the average of these values.

$$\text{Median} = \frac{2390 + 2420}{2} = 2405$$

The median is the measure of location most often reported for annual income and property value data because a few extremely large incomes or property values can inflate the mean. In such cases, the median is a better measure of central location.

Although the mean is the more commonly used measure of central location, in some situations the median is preferred. The mean is influenced by extremely small and large data values. For instance, suppose that one of the graduates (see Table 3.1) had a starting salary of $10,000 per month (maybe the individual's family owns the company). If we change the highest monthly starting salary in Table 3.1 from $2825 to $10,000 and recompute the mean, the sample mean changes from 2440 to 3038. The median of 2405, however, is unchanged, since 2390 and 2420 are still the middle two values. With the extremely high starting salary included, the median provides a better measure of central location than the mean. We can generalize to say that whenever a data set has extreme data values, the median is often the preferred measure of central location.

Mode

A third measure of location is the *mode*. The mode is defined as follows.

Mode

The mode is the data value that occurs with greatest frequency.

To illustrate the identification of the mode, consider the sample of five class sizes. The only value that occurs more than once is 46. Because this value, occurring with a frequency of 2, has the greatest frequency, it is the mode. As another illustration, consider the sample of starting salaries for the business school graduates. The only monthly starting salary that occurs more than once is 2380. Because this value has the greatest frequency, it is the mode.

Situations can arise for which the greatest frequency occurs at two or more different values. In these instances more than one mode exists. If the data have exactly two modes, we say that the data are *bimodal*. If data have more than two modes, we say that the data are *multimodal*. In multimodal cases the mode is almost never reported because listing three or more modes would not be particularly helpful in describing a location for the data.

The mode is an important measure of location for qualitative data. For example, the qualitative data set in Table 2.2 resulted in the following frequency distribution for soft drink purchases.

Soft Drink	Frequency
Coke Classic	19
Diet Coke	8
Dr. Pepper	5
Pepsi-Cola	13
Sprite	5
Total	50

The mode, or most frequently purchased soft drink, is Coke Classic. For this type of data it obviously makes no sense to speak of the mean or median. The mode provides the information of interest, the most frequently purchased soft drink.

Percentiles

A *percentile* provides information about how the data values are spread over the interval from the smallest value to the largest value. For data that do not have numerous repeated values, the pth percentile divides the data into two parts. Approximately p percent of the observations have values less than the pth percentile; approximately $(100 - p)$ percent of the observations have values greater than the pth percentile. The pth percentile is formally defined as follows.

Percentile

The pth percentile is a value such that *at least* p percent of the observations take this value or less and *at least* $(100 - p)$ percent of the observations take this value or more.

Admission test scores for colleges and universities are frequently reported in terms of percentiles. For instance, suppose an applicant obtains a raw score of 54 on the verbal portion of an admission test. How this student performed in relation to other students taking the same test may not be readily apparent. However, if the raw score of 54 corresponds to the 70th percentile, we know that approximately 70% of the students had scores lower than this individual's and approximately 30% of the students had scores higher than this individual's.

The following procedure can be used to compute the pth percentile.

Calculating the pth Percentile

Following these steps
makes it easy to calculate
percentiles.

Step 1. Arrange the data in ascending order (rank order from smallest value to largest value).

Step 2. Compute an index i

$$i = \left(\frac{p}{100}\right)n$$

where p is the percentile of interest and n is the number of observations.

Step 3. (a) If i *is not an integer, round up*. The next integer *greater* than i denotes the position of the pth percentile.

(b) If i *is an integer*, the pth percentile is the average of the data values in positions i and $i + 1$.

As an illustration of this procedure, let us determine the 85th percentile for the starting salary data in Table 3.1.

Step 1. Arrange the data in ascending order.

2210   2255   2350   2380   2380   2390   2420   2440   2450   2550   2630   2825

Step 2.

$$i = \left(\frac{p}{100}\right)n = \left(\frac{85}{100}\right)12 = 10.2$$

Step 3. Because i is not an integer, *round up*. The position of the 85th percentile is the next integer greater than 10.2, the 11th position.

Returning to the data, we see that the 85th percentile is the data value in the 11th position, or 2630.

As another illustration of this procedure, let us consider the calculation of the 50th percentile for the starting salary data. Applying step 2, we obtain

$$i = \left(\frac{50}{100}\right)12 = 6$$

Because i is an integer, step 3(b) states that the 50th percentile is the average of the sixth and seventh data values; thus the 50th percentile is $(2390 + 2420)/2 = 2405$. Note that the *50th percentile is also the median*.

Quartiles

Quartiles are just specific
percentiles; thus, the steps
for computing percentiles
can be applied directly in
the computation of
quartiles.

It is often desirable to divide data into four parts, with each part containing approximately one-fourth, or 25% of the observations. Figure 3.1 shows a data set divided into four parts. The division points are referred to as the *quartiles* and are defined as

Q_1 = first quartile, or 25th percentile

Q_2 = second quartile, or 50th percentile (also the median)

Q_3 = third quartile, or 75th percentile.

The starting salary data are again arranged in ascending order. Q_2, the second quartile (median), has already been identified as 2405.

2210   2255   2350   2380   2380   2390   2420   2440   2450   2550   2630   2825

The computations of quartiles Q_1 and Q_3 require the use of the rule for finding the 25th and 75th percentiles. These calculations follow.

For Q_1,

$$i = \left(\frac{p}{100}\right)n = \left(\frac{25}{100}\right)12 = 3$$

Because i is an integer, step 3(b) indicates that the first quartile, or 25th percentile, is the average of the third and fourth data values; thus, $Q_1 = (2350 + 2380)/2 = 2365$.

For Q_3,

$$i = \left(\frac{p}{100}\right)n = \left(\frac{75}{100}\right)12 = 9$$

Again, because i is an integer, step 3(b) indicates that the third quartile, or 75th percentile, is the average of the ninth and tenth data values; thus, $Q_3 = (2450 + 2550)/2 = 2500$.

The quartiles have divided the starting salary data into four parts, with each part containing 25% of the observations.

2210   2255   2350 | 2380   2380   2390 | 2420   2440   2450 | 2550   2630   2825

$\qquad\qquad Q_1 = 2365 \qquad\qquad\quad Q_2 = 2405 \qquad\qquad Q_3 = 2500$
$\qquad\qquad\qquad\qquad\qquad\qquad\quad$ (Median)

We have defined the quartiles as the 25th, 50th, and 75th percentiles. Thus, we have computed the quartiles in the same way as percentiles. However, other conventions may be used to compute quartiles. The actual values reported for quartiles may vary slightly depending on the convention used. Nevertheless, the objective of all procedures for computing quartiles is to divide the data into four equal parts.

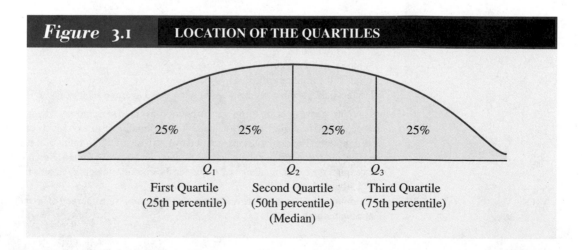

Figure 3.1   **LOCATION OF THE QUARTILES**

25%   25%   25%   25%

Q_1 Q_2 Q_3

First Quartile   Second Quartile   Third Quartile
(25th percentile)   (50th percentile)   (75th percentile)
            (Median)

N O T E S	It is better to use the median than the mean as a measure of central loca-
and Comments	tion when a data set contains extreme values. Another measure, some-

times used when extreme values are present, is the *trimmed mean*. It is
obtained by deleting the smallest and largest observations from a data
set and then computing the mean of the remaining values. For example,
the 5% trimmed mean would be obtained by removing the smallest 5%
and the largest 5% of the data values and then computing the mean of
the remaining values. Using the sample with $n = 12$ starting salaries,
$0.05(12) = 0.6$. Rounding this value to 1 indicates the 5% trimmed mean
would remove the 1 smallest data value and the 1 largest data value. Thus,
the 5% trimmed mean using the 10 remaining observations is 2424.50.

EXERCISES

Methods

1. Consider a sample with data values of 10, 20, 12, 17, and 16. Compute the mean and median.

2. Consider a sample with data values of 10, 20, 21, 17, 16, and 12. Compute the mean and median.

3. Consider a sample with data values of 27, 25, 20, 15, 30, 34, 28, and 25. Compute the 20th, 25th, 65th, and 75th percentiles.

4. Consider a sample with data values of 53, 55, 70, 58, 64, 57, 53, 69, 57, 68, and 53. Compute the mean, median, and mode.

SELF TEST

Applications

5. The 1996–97 average starting salary for new college graduates in accounting was $30,393 (*U.S. News Online, U.S. News and World Report,* December 1997). A sample of starting salaries follows. Data are in thousands of dollars.

AcctSal

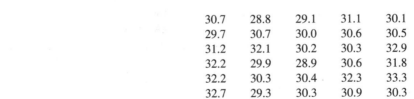

30.7	28.8	29.1	31.1	30.1
29.7	30.7	30.0	30.6	30.5
31.2	32.1	30.2	30.3	32.9
32.2	29.9	28.9	30.6	31.8
32.2	30.3	30.4	32.3	33.3
32.7	29.3	30.3	30.9	30.3

   a. What is the mean starting salary?
   b. What is the median starting salary?
   c. What is the mode?
   d. What is the first quartile?
   e. What is the third quartile?
   f. Do these data seem consistent with the reported average salary of $30,393?

6. More and more investors are turning to discount brokers to save money when buying and selling shares of stock. The American Association of Individual Investors conducts an annual survey of discount brokers. The commissions charged by a sample of 20 discount brokers for two types of trades: 500 shares at $50 per share and 1000 shares at $5 per share are shown in Table 3.2.
   a. Compute the mean, median, and mode for the commission charged on a trade of 500 shares at $50 per share.
   b. Compute the mean, median, and mode for the commission charged on a trade of 1000 shares at $5 per share.

Table 3.2		COMMISSIONS CHARGED BY DISCOUNT BROKERS			
	Commission ($)			**Commission ($)**	
Broker	**500@$50**	**1000@$5**	**Broker**	**500@$50**	**1000@$5**
Peck	73	90	Pacific	25	25
Aufhauser	34	34	People's	131	69
Brown	29	29	Quick & Reilly	120	61
Burke	120	70	Russo	85	110
Schwab	155	90	Seaport	50	70
Downstate	90	65	St. Louis	67	65
Freeman	145	70	T. Rowe	134	80
Kennedy	33	53	Unified	154	90
Max Ule	195	70	White	39	49
Mongerson	95	66	Your	55	70

Source: *AAII Journal,* January 1997.

Discount

   c. Which costs the most: trading 500 shares at $50 per share or trading 1000 shares at $5 per share?

   d. Does the cost of a transaction seem to be related to the amount of the transaction? For example, the amount of the transaction when trading 500 shares at $50 per share is $25,000, while the cost when trading 1000 shares at $5 per share is $5000.

7. The average person spends 45 minutes a day listening to recorded music (*The Des Moines Register,* December 5, 1997). The following data were obtained for the number of minutes spent listening to recorded music for a sample of 30 individuals.

Music

88.3	4.3	4.6	7.0	9.2
0.0	99.2	34.9	81.7	0.0
85.4	0.0	17.5	45.0	53.3
29.1	28.8	0.0	98.9	64.5
4.4	67.9	94.2	7.6	56.6
52.9	145.6	70.4	65.1	63.6

   a. Compute the mean.
   b. Do these data appear to be consistent with the average reported by the newspaper?
   c. Compute the median.
   d. Compute the first and third quartiles.
   e. Compute and interpret the 40th percentile.

8. Millions of Americans get up each morning and go to work in their offices at home. The growing use of personal computers is suggested to be one of the reasons more people can operate at-home businesses. Following is a sample of age data for individuals working at home.

SELF TEST

22	58	24	50	29	52	57	31	30	41
44	40	46	29	31	37	32	44	49	29

   a. Compute the mean and mode.
   b. The median age of the population of all adults is 35.1 years (U.S. Census Bureau, November 1, 1997). Use the median age of the preceding data to comment on whether the at-home workers tend to be younger or older than the population of all adults.
   c. Compute the first and third quartiles.
   d. Compute and interpret the 32nd percentile.

9. The American Association of Advertising Agencies records data on nonprogramming minutes per half hour of prime-time television programming (*U.S. News & World Report,* April 13, 1992). Representative data on nonprogramming minutes follow for a sample of prime-time programs on major networks at 8:30 P.M.

6.0	6.6	5.8	7.0	6.3	6.2	7.2	5.7	6.4	7.0
6.5	6.2	6.0	6.5	7.2	7.3	7.6	6.8	6.0	6.2

   a. Compute the mean and median.
   b. Compute the first and third quartiles.
   c. Using the sample mean, find the percentage of viewing time spent on prime-time advertisements, promotions, and credits. What percentage of viewing time is spent on the programs themselves?

10. The *Los Angeles Times* regularly reports the air quality index for various areas of Southern California. Index ratings of 0–50 are considered good, 51–100 moderate, 101–200 unhealthy, 201–275 very unhealthy, and over 275 hazardous. Recent air quality indexes for Pomona were 28, 42, 58, 48, 45, 55, 60, 49, and 50.
   a. Compute the mean, median, and mode for the data. Should the Pomona air quality index be considered good?
   b. Compute the 25th percentile and 75th percentile for the Pomona air quality data.

11. In automobile mileage and gasoline-consumption testing, 13 automobiles were road tested for 300 miles in both city and country driving conditions. The following data were recorded for miles-per-gallon performance.

City: 16.2 16.7 15.9 14.4 13.2 15.3 16.8 16.0 16.1 15.3 15.2 15.3 16.2
Country: 19.4 20.6 18.3 18.6 19.2 17.4 17.2 18.6 19.0 21.1 19.4 18.5 18.7

Use the mean, median, and mode to make a statement about the difference in performance for city and country driving.

12. Pennsylvania is the nation's fifth largest producer of Christmas trees, with a crop of 1.5 million trees in 1994. Tree prices range from $3.50 to $5.50 per foot (*The Philadelphia Inquirer,* December 3, 1994). Suppose the following data represent the price per foot for 16 trees sold in the Philadelphia area.

3.90	4.20	3.90	5.10
4.20	4.50	4.10	5.10
4.30	4.20	4.00	5.20
4.50	4.20	4.50	5.10

   a. Compute the mean, median, and mode.
   b. Compute the 20th and 90th percentiles.
   c. Compute the quartiles.

3.2 MEASURES OF VARIABILITY

In addition to measures of location, it is often desirable to consider measures of variability, or dispersion. For example, assume that you are a purchasing agent for a large manufacturing firm and that you regularly place orders with two different suppliers. After several months of operation, you find that the mean number of days required to fill orders is 10 days for both of the suppliers. The histograms summarizing the number of working days required to fill orders from the suppliers are shown in Figure 3.2. Although the mean number of days is 10 for both suppliers, do the two suppliers have the same degree of reliability in terms of making deliveries on schedule? Note the disper-

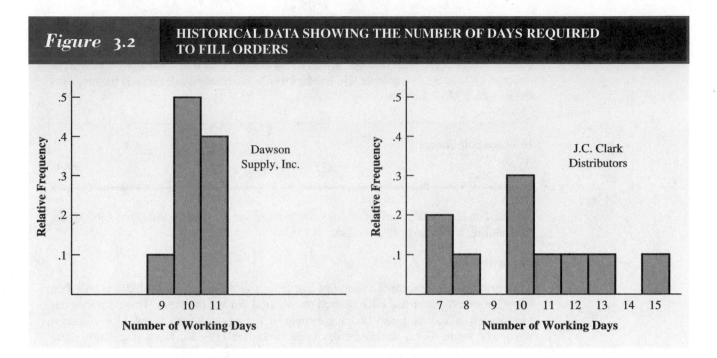

Figure 3.2

HISTORICAL DATA SHOWING THE NUMBER OF DAYS REQUIRED TO FILL ORDERS

sion, or variability, in delivery times indicated by the histograms. Which supplier would you prefer?

For most firms, receiving materials and supplies on schedule is important. The seven- or eight-day deliveries shown for J. C. Clark Distributors might be viewed favorably; however, a few of the slow 13- to 15-day deliveries could be disastrous in terms of keeping a workforce busy and production on schedule. This example illustrates a situation in which the variability in the delivery times may be an overriding consideration in selecting a supplier. For most purchasing agents, the lower variability shown for Dawson Supply, Inc. would make Dawson the more consistent and preferred supplier.

We turn now to a discussion of some commonly used measures of the variability.

Range

Perhaps the simplest measure of variability is the *range*.

Range

$$\text{Range} = \text{Largest Value} - \text{Smallest Value}$$

Let us refer to the data on starting salaries for business school graduates in Table 3.1. The largest starting salary is 2825 and the smallest is 2210. The range is $2825 - 2210 = 615$.

Although the range is the easiest of the measures of variability to compute, it is seldom used as the only measure. The reason is that the range is based on only two of the observations and thus is highly influenced by extreme values. Suppose one of the graduates had a starting salary of $10,000 per month. In this case, the range would be $10,000 - 2210 = 7790$ rather than 615. This large value for the range would not be especially descriptive of the variability in the data, in which 11 of the 12 starting salaries are closely grouped between 2210 and 2630.

The range is easy to compute, but it is sensitive to just two data values: the largest and smallest.

Interquartile Range

A measure of variability that overcomes the dependency on extreme values is the *interquartile range* (IQR). This measure of variability is simply the difference between the third quartile, Q_3, and the first quartile, Q_1. In other words, the interquartile range is the range for the middle 50% of the data.

Interquartile Range

$$IQR = Q_3 - Q_1 \tag{3.3}$$

For the data on monthly starting salaries, the quartiles are $Q_3 = 2500$ and $Q_1 = 2365$. Thus, the interquartile range is $2500 - 2365 = 135$.

Variance

The *variance* is a measure of variability that utilizes all the data. The variance is based on the difference between the value of each observation (x_i) and the mean. The difference between each x_i and the mean ($\bar{x}$ for a sample, μ for a population) is called a *deviation about the mean*. For a sample, a deviation is written ($x_i - \bar{x}$); for a population, it is written ($x_i - \mu$). In the computation of the variance, the deviations about the mean are *squared*.

If the data are for a population, the average of the squared deviations is called the *population variance*. The population variance is denoted by the Greek symbol σ^2. For a population of N observations and with μ denoting the population mean, the definition of the population variance is as follows.

Population Variance

$$\sigma^2 = \frac{\Sigma(x_i - \mu)^2}{N} \tag{3.4}$$

In most statistical applications, the data being analyzed are for a sample. When we compute a sample variance, we are often interested in using it to estimate the population variance σ^2. Although a detailed explanation is beyond the scope of this text, it can be shown that if the sum of the squared deviations about the sample mean is divided by $n - 1$, and not n, the resulting sample variance provides an unbiased estimate of the population variance. For this reason, the *sample variance,* denoted by s^2, is defined as follows.

Sample Variance

$$s^2 = \frac{\Sigma(x_i - \bar{x})^2}{n - 1} \tag{3.5}$$

To illustrate the computation of the variance for a sample, we will use the data on class size for the sample of five college classes as presented in Section 3.1. A summary of the data, including the computation of the deviations about the mean and the squared deviations about the mean, is shown in Table 3.3. The sum of squared deviations about the mean is $\Sigma(x_i - \bar{x})^2 = 256$. Hence, with $n - 1 = 4$, the sample variance is

$$s^2 = \frac{\Sigma(x_i - \bar{x})^2}{n - 1} = \frac{256}{4} = 64$$

Before moving on, let us note that the units associated with the sample variance often cause confusion. Because the values being summed in the variance calculation, $(x_i - \bar{x})^2$, are squared, the units associated with the sample variance are also *squared*. For instance, the sample variance for the class size data is $s^2 = 64$ (students)^2. The squared units associated with variance make it difficult to obtain an intuitive understanding and interpretation of the numerical value of the variance. We recommend that you think of the variance as a measure useful in comparing the amount of variability for two or more variables. In a comparison of the variables, the one with the larger variance has the most variability. Further interpretation of the value of the variance may not be necessary.

The variance is useful in comparing the variability of two variables.

As another illustration of computing a sample variance, consider the starting salaries listed in Table 3.1 for the 12 business school graduates. In Section 3.1, we showed that the sample mean starting salary was 2440. The computation of the sample variance ($s^2 = 27,440.91$) is shown in Table 3.4.

Note that in Tables 3.3 and 3.4 we show both the sum of the deviations about the mean and the sum of the squared deviations about the mean. For any data set, the sum of the deviations about the mean will *always equal zero*. Hence, as shown in Tables 3.3 and 3.4, $\Sigma(x_i - \bar{x}) = 0$. This result is always the case because the positive deviations and negative deviations cancel each other, causing the sum of the deviations about the mean to equal zero.

Standard Deviation

The *standard deviation* is defined to be the positive square root of the variance. Following the notation we adopted for a sample variance and a population variance, we use s to denote the sample standard deviation and σ to denote the population standard deviation. The standard deviation is derived from the variance in the following way.

Table 3.3	COMPUTATION OF DEVIATIONS AND SQUARED DEVIATIONS ABOUT THE MEAN FOR THE CLASS-SIZE DATA

Number of Students in Class (x_i)	Mean Class Size ($\bar{x}$)	Deviation About the Mean ($x_i - \bar{x}$)	Squared Deviation About the Mean ($x_i - \bar{x})^2$
46	44	2	4
54	44	10	100
42	44	-2	4
46	44	2	4
32	44	-12	144
		$\overline{0}$	$\overline{256}$
		$\Sigma(x_i - \bar{x})$	$\Sigma(x_i - \bar{x})^2$

Table 3.4		COMPUTATION OF THE SAMPLE VARIANCE FOR THE STARTING SALARY DATA	
Monthly Salary (x_i)	Sample Mean $(\bar{x})$	Deviation About the Mean $(x_i - \bar{x})$	Squared Deviation About the Mean $(x_i - \bar{x})^2$
2350	2440	−90	8,100
2450	2440	10	100
2550	2440	110	12,100
2380	2440	−60	3,600
2255	2440	−185	34,225
2210	2440	−230	52,900
2390	2440	−50	2,500
2630	2440	190	36,100
2440	2440	0	0
2825	2440	385	148,225
2420	2440	−20	400
2380	2440	−60	3,600
		0	301,850
		$\Sigma(x_i - \bar{x})$	$\Sigma(x_i - \bar{x})^2$

Using (3.5),

$$s^2 = \frac{\Sigma(x_i - \bar{x})^2}{n - 1} = \frac{301,850}{11} = 27,440.91$$

Standard Deviation

$$\text{Sample Standard Deviation} = s = \sqrt{s^2} \tag{3.6}$$

$$\text{Population Standard Deviation} = \sigma = \sqrt{\sigma^2} \tag{3.7}$$

Recall that the sample variance for the sample of class sizes in five college classes is $s^2 = 64$. Thus the sample standard deviation is $s = \sqrt{64} = 8$. For the data on starting salaries, the sample standard deviation is $s = \sqrt{27,440.91} = 165.65$.

The standard deviation is easier to interpret than the variance because the standard deviation is measured in the same units as the data.

What is gained by converting the variance to its corresponding standard deviation? Recall that the units associated with the variance are squared. For example, the sample variance for the starting salary data of business school graduates is $s^2 = 27,440.91$ (dollars)^2. Because the standard deviation is the square root of the variance, the units of the variance, dollars squared, are converted to dollars in the standard deviation. Thus, the standard deviation of the starting salary data is $165.65. In other words, the standard deviation is measured in the same units as the original data. For this reason the standard deviation is more easily compared to the mean and other statistics that are measured in the same units as the original data.

Coefficient of Variation

The coefficient of variation is a relative measure of variability; it measures the standard deviation relative to the mean.

In some situations we may be interested in a descriptive statistic that indicates how large the standard deviation is relative to the mean. This measure is called the *coefficient of variation* and is computed as follows.

Coefficient of Variation

$$\frac{\text{Standard Deviation}}{\text{Mean}} \times 100 \qquad\qquad (3.8)$$

For the class size data, we found a sample mean of 44 and a sample standard deviation of 8. The coefficient of variation is $(8/44) \times 100 = 18.2$. In words, the coefficient of variation tells us that the sample standard deviation is 18.2% of the value of the sample mean. For the starting salary data with a sample mean of 2440 and a sample standard deviation of 165.65, the coefficient of variation, $(165.65/2440) \times 100 = 6.8$, tells us the sample standard deviation is only 6.8% of the value of the sample mean. In general, the coefficient of variation is a useful statistic for comparing the variability of variables that have different standard deviations and different means.

N O T E S
and Comments

1. Statistical software packages and spreadsheets can be used to develop the descriptive statistics presented in this chapter. After the data have been entered into a worksheet, a few simple commands can be used to generate the desired output. In Appendixes 3.1 and 3.2, we show how Minitab and Excel can be used to develop descriptive statistics.

2. The standard deviation is a commonly used measure of the risk associated with investing in stock and stock funds (*Fortune*, December 29, 1997). It provides a measure of how monthly returns fluctuate around the long-run average return.

3. Rounding the value of the sample mean $\bar{x}$ and the values of the squared deviations $(x_i - \bar{x})^2$ may introduce errors when a calculator is used in the computation of the variance and standard deviation. To reduce rounding errors, we recommend carrying at least six significant digits during intermediate calculations. The resulting variance or standard deviation can then be rounded to fewer digits.

4. An alternative formula for the computation of the sample variance is

$$s^2 = \frac{\Sigma x_i^2 - n\bar{x}^2}{n - 1}$$

where $\Sigma x_i^2 = x_1^2 + x_2^2 + \cdots + x_n^2$. Using this formula eases the computational burden slightly and helps reduce rounding errors. Exercise 19 requires use of this alternative formula to compute the sample variance.

EXERCISES

Methods

13. Consider a sample with data values of 10, 20, 12, 17, and 16. Compute the range and interquartile range.

14. Consider a sample with data values of 10, 20, 12, 17, and 16. Compute the variance and standard deviation.

15. Consider the sample with data values of 27, 25, 20, 15, 30, 34, 28, and 25. Compute the range, interquartile range, variance, and standard deviation.

Applications

16. The Hawaii Visitors Bureau collects data on the number of visitors to the islands. The following data are a representative sample of visitors (in thousands) for several days in November 1994 (*The Honolulu Advertiser,* December 28, 1994).

From the mainland, Canada, and Europe:

108.70	112.25	94.01	144.03	162.44	161.61	76.20
102.11	110.87	79.36	129.04	95.16	114.16	121.88

From Asia and the Pacific:

29.89	41.13	40.67	40.41	43.07	24.86
31.61	21.60	27.34	64.57	32.98	41.31

a. Compute the mean and median number of daily visitors from the two sources.
b. Compute the range, the standard deviation, and the coefficient of variation for the two sources of visitors.
c. What comparisons can you make between the numbers of visitors from the two sources?

17. The prices for the population of the 15 basic models of drip coffeemakers follow (*Consumer Reports 1995 Buying Guide*).

Model	Price ($)	Model	Price ($)	Model	Price ($)
Mr. Coffee PR12A	27	Mr. Coffee PR16	25	Braun	60
Krups	50	Mr. Coffee BL110	22	Proctor 42401	35
Proctor 42301	20	Braun	35	Krups	40
Black & Decker 901	22	Bunn	40	Melitta	30
Black & Decker 900	20	West Bend	35	Betty Crocker	19

Compute the range, variance, and standard deviation for this population.

18. The *Los Angeles Times* regularly reports the air quality index for various areas of Southern California. A sample of air quality index values for Pomona provided the following data: 28, 42, 58, 48, 45, 55, 60, 49, and 50.
a. Compute the range and interquartile range.
b. Compute the sample variance and sample standard deviation.
c. A sample of air quality index readings for Anaheim provided a sample mean of 48.5, a sample variance of 136, and a sample standard deviation of 11.66. What comparisons can you make between the air quality in Pomona and that in Anaheim on the basis of these descriptive statistics?

19. The Davis Manufacturing Company has just completed five weeks of operation using a new process that is supposed to increase productivity. The numbers of parts produced each week are 410, 420, 390, 400, and 380. Compute the sample variance and sample standard deviation by using the definition of sample variance (3.5) as well as the alternative formula provided in the Notes and Comments.

20. Assume that the following data are used to construct the histograms of the number of days required to fill orders for Dawson Supply, Inc., and J. C. Clark Distributors (see Figure 3.2).

Dawson Supply Days for Delivery:	11	10	9	10	11	11	10	11	10	10
Clark Distributors Days for Delivery:	8	10	13	7	10	11	10	7	15	12

Use the range and standard deviation to support the previous observation that Dawson Supply provides the more consistent and reliable delivery times.

SELF TEST

Discount

21. A bowler's scores for six games were 182, 168, 184, 190, 170, and 174. Using these data as a sample, compute the following descriptive statistics.
    a. Range.
    b. Variance.
    c. Standard deviation.
    d. Coefficient of variation.

22. The American Association of Individual Investors conducts an annual survey of discount brokers (*AAII Journal*, January 1997). The commissions charged by a sample of 20 discount brokers for two types of trades, 500 shares at $50 per share and 1000 shares at $5 per share, are shown in Table 3.2.
    a. Compute the range and interquartile range for each type of trade.
    b. Compute the variance and standard deviation for each type of trade.
    c. Compute the coefficient of variation for each type of trade.
    d. Compare the variability of cost for the two types of trades.

23. A production department uses a sampling procedure to test the quality of newly produced items. The department employs the following decision rule at an inspection station: If a sample of 14 items has a variance of more than .005, the production line must be shut down for repairs. Suppose the following data have just been collected:

3.43	3.45	3.43	3.48	3.52	3.50	3.39
3.48	3.41	3.38	3.49	3.45	3.51	3.50

Should the production line be shut down? Why or why not?

24. The following times were recorded by the quarter-mile and mile runners of a university track team (times are in minutes).

Quarter-mile Times:	.92	.98	1.04	.90	.99
Mile Times:	4.52	4.35	4.60	4.70	4.50

After viewing this sample of running times, one of the coaches commented that the quarter-milers turned in the more consistent times. Use the standard deviation and the coefficient of variation to summarize the variability in the data. Does the use of the coefficient of variation indicate that the coach's statement should be qualified?

3.3   MEASURES OF RELATIVE LOCATION AND DETECTING OUTLIERS

We have described several measures of location and variability for data. The mean is the most widely used measure of location, whereas the standard deviation and variance are the most widely used measures of variability. Using the mean and the standard deviation, we also can learn about the relative location of observations in a data set.

z-Scores

By using the mean and standard deviation, we can determine the relative location of any observation. Suppose we have a sample of n observations, with the values denoted by x_1, $x_2, \ldots, x_n$. In addition, assume that the sample mean, $\bar{x}$, and the sample standard deviation, s, have been computed. Associated with each value, x_i, is another value called its *z-score*. Equation (3.9) shows how the z-score is computed for each x_i.

z-Score

$$z_i = \frac{x_i - \bar{x}}{s}$$ (3.9)

where

z_i = the z-score for observation i

$\bar{x}$ = the sample mean

s = the sample standard deviation

The z-score is often called the *standardized value*. The z-score, z_i, can be interpreted as the *number of standard deviations x_i is from the mean $\bar{x}$*. For example, $z_1 = 1.2$ would indicate x_1 is 1.2 standard deviations greater than the sample mean. Similarly, $z_2 = -.5$ would indicate x_2 is .5, or 1/2, standard deviation less than the sample mean. As can be seen from (3.9), z-scores greater than zero occur for observations with values greater than the mean, and z-scores less than zero occur for observations with values less than the mean. A z-score of zero indicates that the value of the observation is equal to the mean.

The z-score for any observation can be interpreted as a measure of the relative location of the observation in a data set. Thus, observations in two different data sets with the same z-score can be said to have the same relative location in terms of being the same number of standard deviations from the mean.

The z-scores for the class size data are listed in Table 3.5. Recall that the sample mean, $\bar{x} = 44$, and sample standard deviation, $s = 8$, have been computed previously. The z-score of -1.50 for the fifth observation shows it is farthest from the mean; it is 1.50 standard deviations below the mean.

Chebyshev's Theorem

Chebyshev's theorem enables us to make statements about the percentage of data values that must be within a specified number of standard deviations from the mean.

Table 3.5	z-SCORES FOR THE CLASS SIZE DATA	
Number of Students in Class (x_i)	Deviation About the Mean ($x_i - \bar{x}$)	z-score $\left(\dfrac{x_i - \bar{x}}{s}\right)$
46	2	2/8 = .25
54	10	10/8 = 1.25
42	−2	−2/8 = −.25
46	2	2/8 = .25
32	−12	−12/8 = −1.50

Chebyshev's Theorem

At least $(1 - 1/z^2)$ of the data values must be within z standard deviations of the mean, where z is any value greater than 1.

Some of the implications of this theorem, with $z = 2$, 3, and 4 standard deviations, follow.

- At least .75, or 75%, of the data values must be within $z = 2$ standard deviations of the mean.
- At least .89, or 89%, of the data values must be within $z = 3$ standard deviations of the mean.
- At least .94, or 94%, of the data values must be within $z = 4$ standard deviations of the mean.

For an example using Chebyshev's theorem, assume that the midterm test scores for 100 students in a college business statistics course had a mean of 70 and a standard deviation of 5. How many students had test scores between 60 and 80? How many students had test scores between 58 and 82?

For the test scores between 60 and 80, we note that 60 is two standard deviations below the mean and 80 is two standard deviations above the mean. Using Chebyshev's theorem, we see that at least .75, or at least 75%, of the observations must have values within two standard deviations of the mean. Thus, at least 75% of the students must have scored between 60 and 80.

Chebyshev's theorem requires $z > 1$, but z need not be an integer. Exercise 27 involves noninteger values of z greater than 1.

For the test scores between 58 and 82, we see that $(58 - 70)/5 = -2.4$ indicates 58 is 2.4 standard deviations below the mean and that $(82 - 70)/5 = +2.4$ indicates 82 is 2.4 standard deviations above the mean. Applying Chebyshev's theorem with $z = 2.4$, we have

$$\left(1 - \frac{1}{z^2}\right) = \left[1 - \frac{1}{(2.4)^2}\right] = .826$$

At least 82.6% of the students must have test scores between 58 and 82.

The Empirical Rule

One of the advantages of Chebyshev's theorem is that it applies to any data set regardless of the shape of the distribution of the data. In practical applications, however, it has been found that many data sets have a mound-shaped or bell-shaped distribution like the one shown in Figure 3.3. When the data are believed to approximate this distribution, the *empirical rule* can be used to determine the percentage of data values that must be within a specified number of standard deviations of the mean.

The empirical rule is based on the normal probability distribution, which will be introduced in Chapter 6 and used extensively throughout the text.

Empirical Rule

For data having a bell-shaped distribution:

- Approximately 68% of the data values will be within one standard deviation of the mean.
- Approximately 95% of the data values will be within two standard deviations of the mean.
- Almost all of the data values will be within three standard deviations of the mean.

For example, liquid-detergent cartons are filled automatically on a production line. Filling weights frequently have a bell-shaped distribution. If the mean filling weight is 16 ounces and the standard deviation is .25 ounces, we can use the empirical rule to draw the following conclusions.

- Approximately 68% of the filled cartons will have weights between 15.75 and 16.25 ounces (that is, within one standard deviation of the mean).
- Approximately 95% of the filled cartons will have weights between 15.50 and 16.50 ounces (that is, within two standard deviations of the mean).
- Almost all filled cartons will have weights between 15.25 and 16.75 ounces (that is, within three standard deviations of the mean).

Detecting Outliers

Sometimes a data set will have one or more observations with unusually large or unusually small values. Extreme values such as these are called *outliers*. Experienced statisticians take steps to identify outliers and then review each one carefully. An outlier may be a data value that has been incorrectly recorded. If so, it can be corrected before further analysis. An outlier may also be from an observation that was incorrectly included in the data set; if so, it can be removed. Finally, an outlier may be an unusual data value that has been recorded correctly and belongs in the data set. In such cases it should remain.

It is a good idea to check for outliers before making decisions based on data analysis. Errors are often made in recording data and entering it into the computer. Outliers should not necessarily be deleted, but their accuracy and appropriateness should be verified before further analysis.

Standardized values (z-scores) can be used to identify outliers. Recall that the empirical rule allows us to conclude that for data with a bell-shaped distribution, almost all the data values will be within three standard deviations of the mean. Hence, in using z-scores to identify outliers, we recommend treating any data value with a z-score less than -3 or greater than $+3$ as an outlier. Such data values can then be reviewed for accuracy and to determine whether they belong in the data set.

Refer to the z-scores for the class size data in Table 3.5. The z-score of -1.50 shows the fifth class size is farthest from the mean. However, this standardized value is well within the -3 to $+3$ guideline for outliers. Thus, the z-scores do not indicate that outliers are present in the class size data.

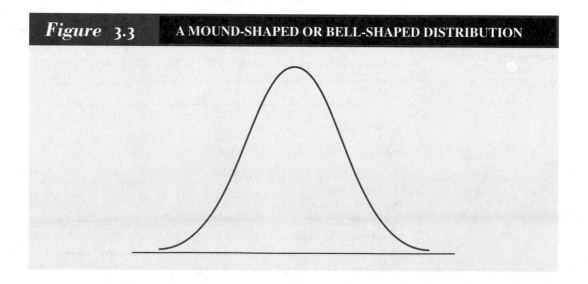

Figure 3.3　　**A MOUND-SHAPED OR BELL-SHAPED DISTRIBUTION**

N O T E S *and Comments*	1. Chebyshev's theorem is applicable for any data set and can be used to state the minimum number of data values that will be within a certain number of standard deviations of the mean. If the data are known to be approximately bell-shaped, more can be said. For instance, the empirical rule allows us to say that *approximately* 95% of the data values will be within two standard deviations of the mean; Chebyshev's theorem allows us to conclude only that at least 75% of the data values will be in that interval.
	2. Before analyzing a data set, statisticians usually make a variety of checks to ensure the validity of data. In a large study it is not uncommon for errors to be made in recording data values or in entering the values into a computer. Identifying outliers is one tool used to check the validity of data.

/ /

EXERCISES

Methods

25. Consider a sample with data values of 10, 20, 12, 17, and 16. Compute the z-score for each of the five observations.

26. Consider a sample with a mean of 500 and a standard deviation of 100. What are the z-scores for 520, 650, 500, 450, and 280?

SELF TEST

27. Consider a sample with a mean of 30 and a standard deviation of 5. Use Chebyshev's theorem to determine the percentage of the data within each of the following ranges.
   a. 20 to 40.
   b. 15 to 45.
   c. 22 to 38.
   d. 18 to 42.
   e. 12 to 48.

28. Data that have a bell-shaped distribution have a mean of 30 and a standard deviation of 5. Use the empirical rule to determine the percentage of data within each of the following ranges.
   a. 20 to 40.
   b. 15 to 45.
   c. 25 to 35.

Applications

29. The average labor cost for color TV repair in Chicago is $90.06 (*The Wall Street Journal*, January 2, 1998). Suppose the standard deviation is $20.00.
   a. What is the z-score for a repair job with a labor cost of $71.00?
   b. What is the z-score for a repair job with a labor cost of $168.00?
   c. Interpret the z-scores in parts (a) and (b). Comment on whether either should be considered an outlier.

SELF TEST

30. A sample of 10 National Basketball Association (NBA) scores provided the following winning teams and the number of points scored (*The Cincinnati Enquirer*, January 5, 1998).

Winner	Score	Winner	Score
Indiana	89	San Antonio	84
Cleveland	95	New York	88
Chicago	105	Minnesota	109
Portland	97	Utah	97
Boston	106	L.A. Clippers	97

a. Compute the mean and standard deviation for the data.
b. In another game, Seattle beat Vancouver 120 to 108. Use the z-score to determine whether the Seattle score should be considered an outlier. Explain.
c. Assume that the distribution of points scored by winning teams is mound-shaped with the mean and standard deviation found in part (a). Estimate the percentage of all NBA games in which the winning team will score 105 or more points. Estimate the percentage of games in which the winning team will score 80 or fewer points.

31. According to the Roth Young Personnel Service, salaries for chain store managers range from $30,000 to $62,000 (*National Business Employment Weekly,* October 16–22, 1994). Assume that the following data are the annual salaries for a sample of chain store managers. Data are in $1000s.

ChainSal

33.7	45.4	44.0	47.5	59.6
45.1	37.7	43.9	48.3	53.0
39.5	42.9	51.0	35.6	41.5
49.5	45.4	58.2	55.4	62.3
32.2	45.9	47.6	56.2	56.8
48.8	31.3	51.2	43.2	54.4

a. Compute the mean and standard deviation.
b. A chain store manager in Memphis, Tennessee, earns $28,500 a year. Compute the z-score for this manager and state whether you believe the manager's salary should be considered an outlier.
c. Compute the z-scores for salaries of $30,000, $45,000, $60,000, and $75,000. Should any of these salaries be considered an outlier?

32. The average American spends 4.4 hours per day watching television (*Statistical Abstract of the United States,* 1996). Suppose the standard deviation is 2.1 hours.
a. Use Chebyshev's theorem to calculate the percentage of individuals watching between 0.2 and 8.6 hours per day.
b. Use Chebyshev's theorem to calculate the percentage of individuals watching between 0.0 and 8.8 hours per day.
c. Use the empirical rule to calculate the percentage of individuals watching between 0.2 and 8.6 hours per day.

33. *Consumer Review* posts reviews and ratings of a variety of products on the Internet. The following is a sample of 20 speaker systems and the ratings posted on January 2, 1998 (see www.audioreview.com). The ratings are on a scale of 1 to 5, with 5 being best.

Speaker	Rating	Speaker	Rating
Infinity Kappa 6.1	4.00	ACI Sapphire III	4.67
Allison One	4.12	Bose 501 Series	2.14
Cambridge Ensemble II	3.82	DCM KX-212	4.09
Dynaudio Contour 1.3	4.00	Eosone RSF1000	4.17
Hsu Rsch. HRSW12V	4.56	Joseph Audio RM7si	4.88
Legacy Audio Focus	4.32	Martin Logan Aerius	4.26
Mission 73li	4.33	Omni Audio SA 12.3	2.32
PSB 400i	4.50	Polk Audio RT12	4.50
Snell Acoustics D IV	4.64	Sunfire True Subwoofer	4.17
Thiel CS1.5	4.20	Yamaha NS-A636	2.17

a. Compute the mean and the median.
b. Compute the first and third quartiles.
c. Compute the standard deviation.
d. What are the z-scores associated with Allison One and Omni Audio?
e. Are there any outliers? Explain.

..../ /.............

3.4   EXPLORATORY DATA ANALYSIS

In Chapter 2 we introduced the stem-and-leaf display as a technique of exploratory data analysis. Recall that exploratory data analysis enables us to use simple arithmetic and easy-to-draw pictures to summarize data. In this section we continue exploratory data analysis by considering five-number summaries and box plots.

Five-Number Summary

In a *five-number summary,* the following five numbers are used to summarize the data.

1. Smallest value
2. First quartile (Q_1)
3. Median (Q_2)
4. Third quartile (Q_3)
5. Largest value

The easiest way to develop a five-number summary is to first place the data in ascending order. Then it is easy to identify the smallest value, the three quartiles, and the largest value. The monthly starting salaries shown in Table 3.1 for a sample of 12 business school graduates are repeated here in ascending order.

2210   2255   2350 | 2380   2380   2390 | 2420   2440   2450 | 2550   2630   2825

$Q_1 = 2365$ $\qquad\qquad$ $Q_2 = 2405$ $\qquad\qquad$ $Q_3 = 2500$

(Median)

The median of 2405 and the quartiles $Q_1 = 2365$ and $Q_3 = 2500$ were computed in Section 3.1. Reviewing the data shows a smallest value of 2210 and a largest value of 2825. Thus the five-number summary for the salary data is 2210, 2365, 2405, 2500, 2825. Approximately one-fourth, or 25%, of the observations are between adjacent numbers in a five-number summary.

Box Plot

The *box plot* is a graphical summary of data that is based on a five-number summary. A key to the development of a box plot is the computation of the median and the quartiles, Q_1 and Q_3. The interquartile range, IQR = $Q_3 - Q_1$, is also used. Figure 3.4 is the box plot for the monthly starting salary data. The steps used to construct the box plot follow.

1. A box is drawn with the ends of the box located at the first and third quartiles. For the salary data, $Q_1 = 2365$ and $Q_3 = 2500$. This box contains the middle 50% of the data.
2. A vertical line is drawn in the box at the location of the median (2405 for the salary data).
3. By using the interquartile range, IQR = $Q_3 - Q_1$, limits are located. The limits for the box plot are 1.5(IQR) below Q_1 and 1.5(IQR) above Q_3. For the salary data, IQR = $Q_3 - Q_1 = 2500 - 2365 = 135$. Thus, the limits are $2365 - 1.5(135) = 2162.5$ and $2500 + 1.5(135) = 2702.5$. Data outside these limits are considered *outliers.*

Box plots provide another way to identify outliers. But they do not necessarily identify the same values as those with a z-score less than -3 or greater than $+3$. Either, or both, procedures may be used.

4. The dashed lines in Figure 3.4 are called *whiskers.* The whiskers are drawn from the ends of the box to the smallest and largest values *inside the limits* computed in step 3. Thus the whiskers end at salary values of 2210 and 2630.
5. Finally, the location of each outlier is shown with the symbol *. In Figure 3.4 we see one outlier, 2825.

In Figure 3.4 we have included lines showing the location of the limits. These lines were drawn to show how the limits are computed and where they are located for the salary data. Although the limits are always computed, generally they are not drawn on the box plots. Figure 3.5 shows the usual appearance of a box plot for the salary data.

Figure **3.4**

BOX PLOT OF THE MONTHLY STARTING SALARIES OF BUSINESS SCHOOL GRADUATES, WITH LINES SHOWING THE LOWER AND UPPER LIMITS

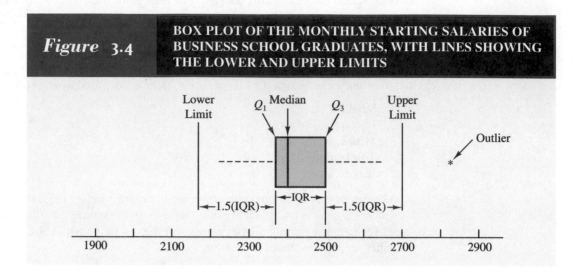

N O T E S
and Comments

1. When using a box plot, we may or may not identify the same outliers as the ones we select when using z-scores less than -3 and greater than $+3$. However, the objective of both approaches is simply to identify extreme data values that should be reviewed to ensure the validity of the data. Outliers identified by either procedure should be reviewed.
2. An advantage of the exploratory data analysis procedures is that they are easy to use; few numerical calculations are necessary. We simply sort the data values into ascending order and identify the five-number summary. The box plot can then easily be constructed. It is not necessary to compute the mean and the standard deviation for the data.

Figure **3.5**

BOX PLOT OF THE MONTHLY STARTING SALARIES OF BUSINESS SCHOOL GRADUATES

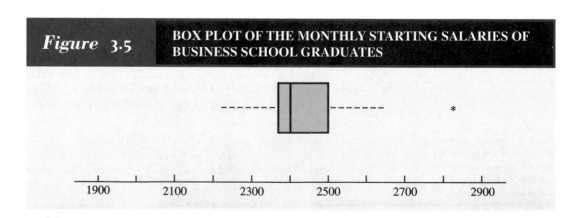

EXERCISES

Methods

34. Consider a sample with data values of 27, 25, 20, 15, 30, 34, 28, and 25. Provide the five-number summary for the data.

35. Show the box plot for the data in Exercise 34.

36. Show the five-number summary and the box plot for the following data: 5, 15, 18, 10, 8, 12, 16, 10, 6.

SELF TEST

37. A data set has a first quartile of 42 and a third quartile of 50. Compute the lower and upper limits. Should a data value of 65 be considered an outlier?

Applications

38. A goal of management is to earn as much as possible relative to the capital invested in their company. One measure of success is return on equity—the ratio of net income to stockholders' equity. Shown here are the most recent return on equity percentages for 25 companies (*Standard & Poor's Stock Reports,* November 1997).

ReEquity

9.0	19.6	22.9	41.6	11.4
15.8	52.7	17.3	12.3	5.1
17.3	31.1	9.6	8.6	11.2
12.8	12.2	14.5	9.2	16.6
5.0	30.3	14.7	19.2	6.2

a. Provide a five-number summary.
b. Compute the lower and upper limits.
c. Do there appear to be outliers? How would this information be helpful to a financial analyst?
d. Show a box plot.

SELF TEST

39. Annual sales, in millions of dollars, for 21 pharmaceutical companies follow (*Business Week,* April 25, 1994).

8408	1374	1872	8879	2459	11413
608	14138	6452	1850	2818	1356
10498	7478	4019	4341	739	2127
3653	5794	8305			

a. Provide a five-number summary.
b. Compute the lower and upper limits.
c. Do there appear to be outliers?
d. Johnson & Johnson's sales are the largest in the list at $14,138 million. Suppose a data entry error had been made and the sales had been entered as $41,138 million. Would the method of detecting outliers in part (c) have identified the problem and allowed correction of the data entry error?
e. Show a box plot.

40. *Consumer Reports* provides performance and quality ratings for numerous consumer products. The overall ratings were provided for a sample of 16 mid-priced VCRs in the *Consumer Reports 1992 Buying Guide*. The manufacturer brands and overall scores are as follows:

Manufacturer	Score
Fisher	77
General Electric	81
Hitachi	89
J. C. Penney	78
JVC	79
Magnavox	80
Montgomery Ward	78
Mitsubishi	90
Panasonic	77
Phillips	73
Quasar	72
Radio Shack	76
RCA	79
Sanyo	75
Sony	86
Toshiba	79

a. Provide the mean and median overall rating.
b. Compute the first and third quartiles.
c. Provide the five-number summary.
d. Similar ratings for camcorders showed a mean of 82.56, a standard deviation of 6.39, and a five-number summary of 75, 77, 82, 86, 93. Compare the *Consumer Reports* ratings data for VCRs and camcorders. Show the box plots for both.
e. Are there any outliers in the VCR data? Explain.

41. The Highway Loss Data Institute's Injury and Collision Loss Experience report rates car models on the basis of the number of insurance claims filed after accidents. Index ratings near 100 are considered average. Lower ratings are better, indicating a safer car model. Shown are ratings for 20 midsize cars and 20 small cars.

Injury

Midsize cars:	81	91	93	127	68	81	60	51	58	75
	100	103	119	82	128	76	68	81	91	82

Small cars:	73	100	127	100	124	103	119	108	109	113
	108	118	103	120	102	122	96	133	80	140

Summarize the data for the midsize and small cars separately.
a. Provide a five-number summary for midsize cars and for small cars.
b. Show the box plots.
c. Make a statement about what your summaries indicate about the safety of midsize cars in comparison to small cars.

42. Birinyi Associates, Inc., conducted a survey of stock markets around the world to assess their performance during 1997. Table 3.6 summarizes the findings for a sample of 30 countries.
a. What are the mean and median percentage changes for these countries?
b. What are the first and third quartiles?
c. Are there any outliers? Show a box plot.
d. What percentile would you report for the United States?

Table 3.6	1997 PERCENT CHANGE IN VALUE FOR WORLD STOCK MARKETS		
Country	Percent Change	Country	Percent Change
Argentina	24.70	Australia	7.91
Bahrain	49.67	Barbados	48.29
Bermuda	51.92	Brazil	44.84
Chile	12.80	Colombia	69.60
Croatia	−1.07	Czech Republic	−3.25
Ecuador	5.37	Estonia	62.34
Finland	32.31	Germany	47.11
Greece	59.19	India	18.60
Israel	27.91	Japan	−21.19
Lithuania	16.82	Mexico	54.92
Namibia	6.52	Nigeria	−7.97
Panama	59.40	Poland	2.27
Russia	125.89	Slovenia	18.71
Sri Lanka	15.49	Taiwan	18.08
Turkey	254.45	United States	22.64

Source: *The Wall Street Journal*, January 2, 1998.

World

3.5   MEASURES OF ASSOCIATION BETWEEN TWO VARIABLES

Thus far we have examined numerical methods used to summarize the data for *one variable at a time*. Often a manager or decision maker is interested in the *relationship between two variables*. In this section we present covariance and correlation as descriptive measures of the relationship between two variables.

We begin by reconsidering the application by a stereo and sound equipment store in San Francisco as presented in Section 2.4. The store's manager is interested in investigating the relationship between the number of weekend television commercials shown and the sales at the store during the following week. Sample data with sales expressed in hundreds of dollars are provided in Table 3.7. The scatter diagram in Figure 3.6 shows a positive relationship, with higher sales (y) associated with a greater number of commercials (x). In fact, the scatter diagram suggests that a straight line could be used as an approximation of the relationship. In the following discussion, we introduce covariance as a descriptive measure of the linear association between two variables.

Covariance

For a sample of size n with the corresponding observations (x_1, y_1), (x_2, y_2), and so on, the *sample covariance* is defined as follows:

Sample Covariance

$$s_{xy} = \frac{\Sigma(x_i - \bar{x})(y_i - \bar{y})}{n - 1} \tag{3.10}$$

Table 3.7	SAMPLE DATA FOR THE STEREO AND SOUND EQUIPMENT STORE	

Week	Number of Commercials x	Sales Volume ($100s) y
1	2	50
2	5	57
3	1	41
4	3	54
5	4	54
6	1	38
7	5	63
8	3	48
9	4	59
10	2	46

In this formula each x_i is paired with a y_i. We then sum the products obtained by multiplying the deviation of each x_i from its sample mean $\bar{x}$ by the deviation of the corresponding y_i from its sample mean $\bar{y}$; this sum is then divided by $n - 1$.

To measure the strength of the linear relationship between the number of commercials x and the sales volume y in the stereo and sound equipment store problem, we use (3.10) to compute the sample covariance. The calculations in Table 3.8 show the computation of $\Sigma(x_i - \bar{x})(y_i - \bar{y})$. Note that $\bar{x} = 30/10 = 3$ and $\bar{y} = 510/10 = 51$. Using (3.10), we obtain a sample covariance of

$$s_{xy} = \frac{\Sigma(x_i - \bar{x})(y_i - \bar{y})}{n - 1} = \frac{99}{9} = 11$$

The formula for computing the covariance of a population of size N is similar to (3.10), but we use different notation to indicate that we are working with the entire population.

Figure 3.6	SCATTER DIAGRAM FOR THE STEREO AND SOUND EQUIPMENT STORE	

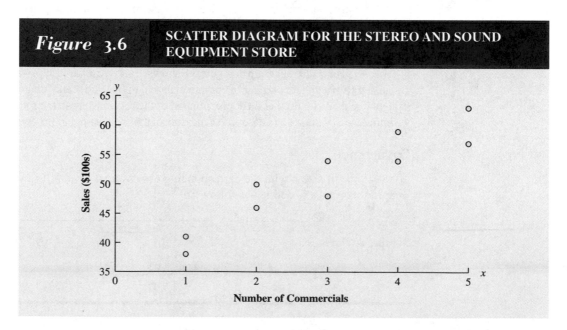

Table 3.8		CALCULATIONS FOR THE SAMPLE COVARIANCE		
x_i	y_i	$x_i - \bar{x}$	$y_i - \bar{y}$	$(x_i - \bar{x})(y_i - \bar{y})$
2	50	−1	−1	1
5	57	2	6	12
1	41	−2	−10	20
3	54	0	3	0
4	54	1	3	3
1	38	−2	−13	26
5	63	2	12	24
3	48	0	−3	0
4	59	1	8	8
2	46	−1	−5	5
Totals 30	510	0	0	99

$$s_{xy} = \frac{\Sigma \, (x_i - \bar{x})(y_i - \bar{y})}{n - 1} = \frac{99}{10 - 1} = 11$$

Population Covariance

$$\sigma_{xy} = \frac{\Sigma(x_i - \mu_x)(y_i - \mu_y)}{N} \qquad (3.11)$$

In (3.11) we use the notation μ_x for the population mean of the variable x and μ_y for the population mean of the variable y. The population covariance σ_{xy} is defined for a population of size N.

Interpretation of the Covariance

To aid in the interpretation of the *sample covariance,* consider Figure 3.7. It is the same as the scatter diagram of Figure 3.6 with a vertical dashed line at $\bar{x} = 3$ and a horizontal dashed line at $\bar{y} = 51$. Four quadrants have been identified on the graph. Points in quadrant I correspond to x_i greater than $\bar{x}$ and y_i greater than $\bar{y}$, points in quadrant II correspond to x_i less than $\bar{x}$ and y_i greater than $\bar{y}$, and so on. Thus, the value of $(x_i - \bar{x})(y_i - \bar{y})$ must be positive for points in quadrant I, negative for points in quadrant II, positive for points in quadrant III, and negative for points in quadrant IV.

> The covariance is a measure of the linear association between two variables.

If the value of s_{xy} is positive, the points that have had the greatest influence on s_{xy} must be in quadrants I and III. Hence, a positive value for s_{xy} is indicative of a positive linear association between x and y; that is, as the value of x increases, the value of y increases. If the value of s_{xy} is negative, however, the points that have had the greatest influence on s_{xy} are in quadrants II and IV. Hence, a negative value for s_{xy} is indicative of a negative linear association between x and y; that is, as the value of x increases, the value of y decreases. Finally, if the points are evenly distributed across all four quadrants, the value of s_{xy} will be close to zero, indicating no linear association between x and y. Figure 3.8 shows the values of s_{xy} that can be expected with three different types of scatter diagrams.

Referring again to Figure 3.7, we see that the scatter diagram for the stereo and sound equipment store follows the pattern in the top panel of Figure 3.8. As we should expect, the value of the sample covariance indicates a positive linear relationship with $s_{xy} = 11$.

Figure 3.7 PARTITIONED SCATTER DIAGRAM FOR THE STEREO AND SOUND EQUIPMENT STORE

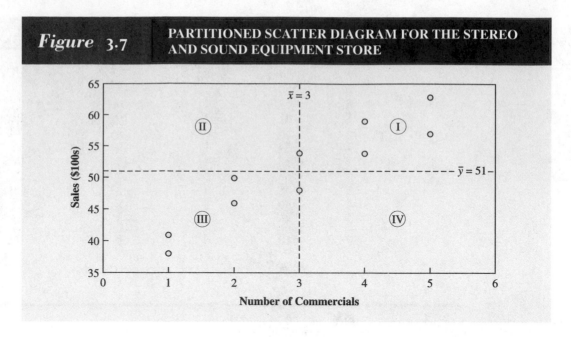

From the preceding discussion, it might appear that a large positive value for the covariance is indicative of a strong positive linear relationship and that a large negative value is indicative of a strong negative linear relationship. However, one problem with using covariance as a measure of the strength of the linear relationship is that the value of the covariance depends on the units of measurement for x and y. For example, suppose we are interested in the relationship between height x and weight y for individuals. Clearly the strength of the relationship should be the same whether we measure height in feet or inches. When height is measured in inches, however, we have much larger numerical values for $(x_i - \bar{x})$ than we have when height is measured in feet. Thus, with height measured in inches, we would obtain a larger value for the numerator $\Sigma(x_i - \bar{x})(y_i - \bar{y})$ in equation (3.10)—and hence a larger covariance—when in fact there is no difference in the relationship. A measure of the relationship between two variables that avoids this difficulty is the *correlation coefficient.*

Correlation Coefficient

For sample data, the Pearson product moment correlation coefficient is defined as follows.

Pearson Product Moment Correlation Coefficient: Sample Data

$$r_{xy} = \frac{s_{xy}}{s_x s_y} \tag{3.12}$$

where

$$r_{xy} = \text{sample correlation coefficient}$$
$$s_{xy} = \text{sample covariance}$$
$$s_x = \text{sample standard deviation of } x$$
$$s_y = \text{sample standard deviation of } y$$

Figure 3.8   INTERPRETATION OF SAMPLE COVARIANCE

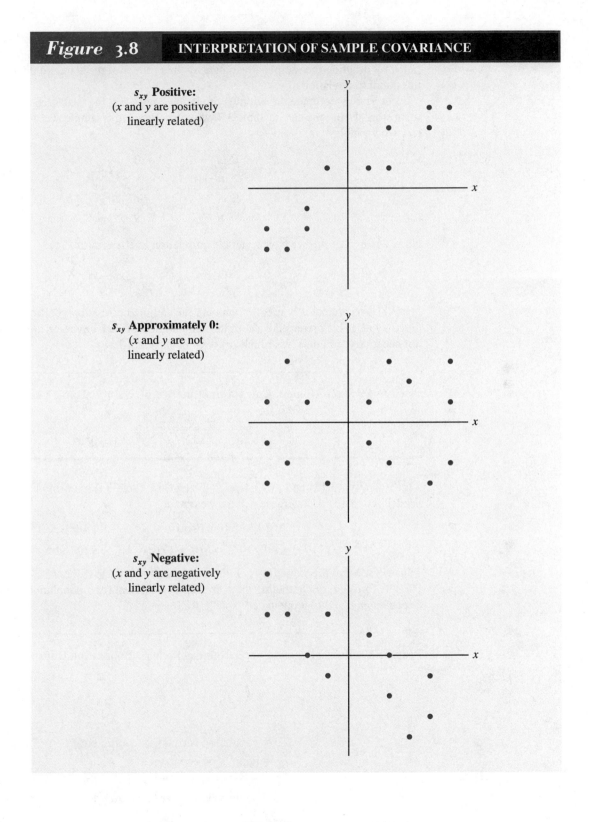

s_{xy} **Positive:**
(x and y are positively linearly related)

s_{xy} **Approximately 0:**
(x and y are not linearly related)

s_{xy} **Negative:**
(x and y are negatively linearly related)

Equation (3.12) shows that the Pearson product moment correlation coefficient for sample data (commonly referred to more simply as the *sample correlation coefficient*) is computed by dividing the sample covariance by the product of the standard deviation of x and the standard deviation of y.

Let us now compute the sample correlation coefficient for the stereo and sound equipment store. Using the data in Table 3.7, we can compute the sample standard deviations for the two variables.

$$s_x = \sqrt{\frac{\Sigma(x_i - \bar{x})^2}{n - 1}} = \sqrt{\frac{20}{9}} = 1.49$$

$$s_y = \sqrt{\frac{\Sigma(y_i - \bar{y})^2}{n - 1}} = \sqrt{\frac{566}{9}} = 7.93$$

Now, when $s_{xy} = 11$, we have a sample correlation coefficient of

$$r_{xy} = \frac{s_{xy}}{s_x s_y} = \frac{11}{(1.49)(7.93)} = +.93$$

When a calculator is used to compute the sample correlation coefficient, the formula given by (3.13) is preferred because the computation of each deviation $x_i - \bar{x}$ and $y_i - \bar{y}$ is not necessary, and thus less round-off error is introduced.

Pearson Product Moment Correlation Coefficient: Sample Data, Alternate Formula

$$r_{xy} = \frac{\Sigma x_i y_i - (\Sigma x_i \Sigma y_i)/n}{\sqrt{\Sigma x_i^2 - (\Sigma x_i)^2/n} \sqrt{\Sigma y_i^2 - (\Sigma y_i)^2/n}} \tag{3.13}$$

Algebraically, (3.12) and (3.13) are equivalent. In Table 3.9 we provide the calculations needed for (3.13). Using these results, we obtain

$$r_{xy} = \frac{1629 - (30)(510)/10}{\sqrt{110 - (30)^2/10} \sqrt{26{,}576 - (510)^2/10}} = \frac{99}{\sqrt{20} \sqrt{566}} = +.93$$

Thus we see that the value for r_{xy} is the same whether we use (3.12) or (3.13).

The formula for computing the correlation coefficient for a population, denoted by the Greek letter ρ_{xy} (rho, pronounced "row"), follows.

Pearson Product Moment Correlation Coefficient: Population Data

$$\rho_{xy} = \frac{\sigma_{xy}}{\sigma_x \sigma_y} \tag{3.14}$$

where

$$\rho_{xy} = \text{population correlation coefficient}$$
$$\sigma_{xy} = \text{population covariance}$$
$$\sigma_x = \text{population standard deviation for } x$$
$$\sigma_y = \text{population standard deviation for } y$$

The sample correlation coefficient r_{xy} is an estimate of the population correlation coefficient ρ_{xy}.

Interpretation of the Correlation Coefficient

First let us consider a simple example that illustrates the concept of a perfect positive linear relationship. The scatter diagram in Figure 3.9 depicts the relationship between x and y based on the following data.

x_i	y_i
5	10
10	30
15	50

The straight line drawn through each of the three points shows a perfect linear relationship between x and y. The calculations needed to compute r_{xy} are shown in Table 3.10. Using (3.13), we obtain

$$r_{xy} = \frac{\Sigma x_i y_i - (\Sigma x_i \Sigma y_i)/n}{\sqrt{\Sigma x_i^2 - (\Sigma x_i)^2/n}\ \sqrt{\Sigma y_i^2 - (\Sigma y_i)^2/n}} = \frac{1100 - 30(90)/3}{\sqrt{350 - (30)^2/3}\ \sqrt{3500 - (90)^2/3}}$$

$$= \frac{200}{\sqrt{50}\ \sqrt{800}} = 1$$

Thus, we see that the value of the sample correlation coefficient is 1.

In general, it can be shown that if all the points in a data set are on a straight line having positive slope, the value of the sample correlation coefficients is $+1$; that is, a sample correlation coefficient of $+1$ corresponds to a perfect positive linear relationship between x and y. Moreover, if the points in the data set are on a straight line having negative slope, the value of the sample correlation coefficient is -1; that is, a sample correlation coefficient of -1 corresponds to a perfect negative linear relationship between x and y.

The correlation coefficient ranges from -1 to $+1$. Values close to -1 or $+1$ indicate a strong linear relationship. The closer the correlation is to zero the weaker the relationship.

Let us now suppose that a certain data set indicates a positive linear relationship between x and y but that the relationship is not perfect. The value of r_{xy} will be less than 1, indicating that the points in the scatter diagram are not all on a straight line. As the points deviate more and more from a perfect positive linear relationship, the value of r_{xy} becomes smaller and smaller. A value of r_{xy} equal to zero indicates no linear relationship between x and y, and values of r_{xy} near zero indicate a weak linear relationship.

| Table 3.9 | COMPUTATIONS FOR USING THE ALTERNATE FORMULA TO COMPUTE r_{xy} | | | |

	x_i	y_i	$x_i y_i$	x_i^2	y_i^2
	2	50	100	4	2500
	5	57	285	25	3249
	1	41	41	1	1681
	3	54	162	9	2916
	4	54	216	16	2916
	1	38	38	1	1444
	5	63	315	25	3969
	3	48	144	9	2304
	4	59	236	16	3481
	2	46	92	4	2116
Totals	30	510	1629	110	26576

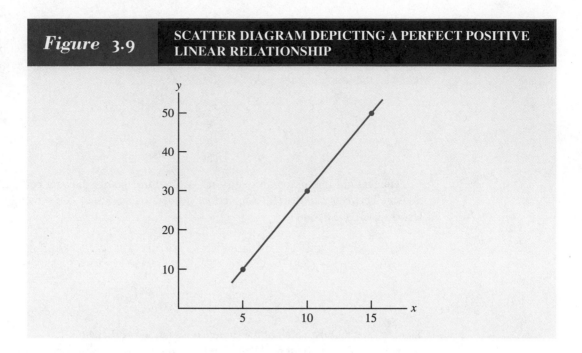

Figure 3.9 SCATTER DIAGRAM DEPICTING A PERFECT POSITIVE LINEAR RELATIONSHIP

Table 3.10 CALCULATIONS FOR COMPUTING r_{xy} FOR THE RELATIONSHIP IN FIGURE 3.9

	x_i	y_i	$x_i y_i$	x_i^2	y_i^2
	5	10	50	25	100
	10	30	300	100	900
	15	50	750	225	2500
Totals	30	90	1100	350	3500

For the data involving the stereo and sound equipment store, recall that $r_{xy} = +.93$. Therefore, we conclude that a strong positive linear relationship occurs between the number of commercials and sales. More specifically, an increase in the number of commercials is associated with an increase in sales.

EXERCISES

Methods

SELF TEST

43. Five observations taken for two variables follow.

x_i	4	6	11	3	16
y_i	50	50	40	60	30

    a. Develop a scatter diagram with x on the horizontal axis.

    b. What does the scatter diagram developed in part (a) indicate about the relationship between the two variables?

    c. Compute and interpret the sample covariance.

    d. Compute and interpret the sample correlation coefficient.

44. Five observations taken for two variables follow.

x_i	6	11	15	21	27
y_i	6	9	6	17	12

    a. Develop a scatter diagram for these data.

    b. What does the scatter diagram indicate about a relationship between x and y?

    c. Compute and interpret the sample covariance.

    d. Compute and interpret the sample correlation coefficient.

Applications

45. A high school guidance counselor collected the following data about the grade point averages (GPA) and the SAT mathematics test scores for six seniors.

GPA	2.7	3.5	3.7	3.3	3.6	3.0
SAT	450	560	700	620	640	570

    a. Develop a scatter diagram for the data with GPA on the horizontal axis.

    b. Does there appear to be any relationship between the GPA and the SAT mathematics test score? Explain.

    c. Compute and interpret the sample covariance.

    d. Compute the sample correlation coefficient. What does this value tell us about the relationship between the two variables?

46. A department of transportation's study on driving speed and mileage for midsize automobiles resulted in the following data.

Driving Speed	30	50	40	55	30	25	60	25	50	55
Mileage	28	25	25	23	30	32	21	35	26	25

Compute and interpret the sample correlation coefficient.

47. The Dow Jones Industrial Average (DJIA) and the Standard & Poor's 500 (S&P 500) index are both used as measures of overall movement in the stock market. The DJIA is based on the price movements of 30 stocks; the S&P 500 is an index composed of 500 stocks. Some say the S&P 500 is a better measure of stock market performance because it is based on more stocks. Table 3.11 shows the closing price for the DJIA and the S&P 500 for 10 weeks in 1997.

    a. Compute the sample correlation coefficient.

    b. What does the sample correlation coefficient tell about the relationship between the DJIA and the S&P 500 indexes?

48. Table 3.12 gives the book value per share and the annual dividend for 15 utility stocks (*Barron's,* January 2, 1995).

    a. Develop a scatter diagram with book value on the horizontal axis.

    b. Compute and interpret the sample correlation coefficient.

DowS&P

Table 3.11	CLOSING PRICES FOR DOW JONES INDUSTRIAL AVERAGE AND S&P 500 INDEXES

Date	Dow Jones	S&P 500
October 24	7715	942
October 31	7442	915
November 7	7581	928
November 14	7572	928
November 21	7881	963
November 28	7823	955
December 5	8149	984
December 12	7838	953
December 19	7756	947
December 26	7679	936

Source: *Barron's* January 5, 1998.

Utility

Table 3.12	BOOK VALUE AND DIVIDENDS PER SHARE FOR 15 UTILITY STOCKS

Company	Book Value ($)	Annual Dividend ($)	Company	Book Value ($)	Annual Dividend ($)
Am Elec	22.44	2.40	Centerior	12.14	.80
Con Ed	20.89	2.98	Cons N Gas	23.31	1.94
Detroit Ed	22.09	2.06	Houston Ind	16.23	3.00
Niag Moh	14.48	1.09	NorAm Enrgy	.56	.28
Pac G&E	20.73	1.96	Panh East	.84	.84
Peco	19.25	1.55	Peoples En	18.05	1.80
Pub Sv Ent	20.37	2.16	SCEcorp	12.45	1.21
UnicomCp	26.43	1.60			

Source: *Barron's,* January 2, 1995.

49. The daily high and low temperatures for 24 cities follow (*USA Today,* December 15, 1997).

Cities

City	High	Low	City	High	Low
Tampa	78	66	Birmingham	63	51
Kansas City	38	26	Minneapolis	32	17
Boise	28	15	Portland	43	32
Los Angeles	63	46	Memphis	61	45
Philadelphia	41	35	Buffalo	38	32
Milwaukee	37	29	Cincinnati	46	40
Chicago	42	31	Charlotte	48	42
Albany	35	21	Boston	37	29
Houston	63	57	Tulsa	46	35
Salt Lake City	33	16	Washington, D.C.	43	38
Miami	79	70	Las Vegas	48	30
Cheyenne	29	13	Detroit	41	35

What is the correlation between the high and low temperatures?

3.6   THE WEIGHTED MEAN AND WORKING WITH GROUPED DATA

In Section 3.1, we presented the mean as one of the most important measures of descriptive statistics. The formula for the mean of a sample with n observations is restated as follows.

$$\bar{x} = \frac{\Sigma x_i}{n} = \frac{x_1 + x_2 + x_3 + \cdots + x_n}{n} \tag{3.15}$$

In this formula, each x_i is given equal importance or weight. Although this practice is most common, in some instances, the mean is computed by giving each observation a weight that reflects its importance. A mean computed in this manner is referred to as a *weighted mean.*

The Weighted Mean

The weighted mean is computed as follows:

The Weighted Mean

$$\bar{x} = \frac{\Sigma w_i x_i}{\Sigma w_i} \tag{3.16}$$

where

$$x_i = \text{value of observation } i$$
$$w_i = \text{weight for observation } i$$

When the data are from a sample, (3.16) provides the weighted sample mean. When the data are from a population, μ replaces $\bar{x}$ and (3.16) provides the weighted population mean.

As an example of the need for a weighted mean, consider the following sample of five purchases of a raw material over the past three months.

Purchase	Cost per Pound ($)	Number of Pounds
1	3.00	1200
2	3.40	500
3	2.80	2750
4	2.90	1000
5	3.25	800

Note that the cost per pound has varied from $2.80 to $3.40 and the quantity purchased has varied from 500 to 2750 pounds. Suppose that a manager has asked for information about the mean cost per pound of the raw material. Because the quantities ordered vary, we must use the formula for a weighted mean. The five cost-per-pound data values are $x_1 = 3.00$, $x_2 = 3.40$, $x_3 = 2.80$, $x_4 = 2.90$, and $x_5 = 3.25$. The weighted mean cost per pound is found by weighting each cost by its corresponding quantity. For this example, the weights are

$w_1 = 1200$, $w_2 = 500$, $w_3 = 2750$, $w_4 = 1000$, and $w_5 = 800$. Using (3.16), the weighted mean is calculated as follows:

$$\bar{x} = \frac{1200(3.00) + 500(3.40) + 2750(2.80) + 1000(2.90) + 800(3.25)}{1200 + 500 + 2750 + 1000 + 800}$$

$$= \frac{18,500}{6250} = 2.96$$

Thus, the weighted mean computation shows that the mean cost per pound for the raw material is $2.96. Note that using (3.15) rather than the weighted mean formula would have provided misleading results. In this case, the mean of the five cost-per-pound values is $(3.00 + 3.40 + 2.80 + 2.90 + 3.25)/5 = 15.35/5 = \$3.07$, which overstates the actual mean cost per pound purchased.

The choice of weights for a particular weighted mean computation depends upon the application. An example that is well known to college students is the computation of a grade point average (GPA). In this computation, the data values generally used are 4 for an A grade, 3 for a B grade, 2 for a C grade, 1 for a D grade, and 0 for an F grade. The weights are the number of credits hours earned for each grade. Exercise 52 at the end of this section provides an example of this weighted mean computation. In other weighted mean computations, quantities such as pounds, dollars, and/or volume are frequently used as weights. In any case, when observations vary in importance, the analyst must choose the weight that best reflects the importance of each observation in the determination of the mean.

Computing a grade point average is a good example of the use of a weighted mean.

Grouped Data

In most cases, measures of location and variability are computed by using the individual data values. Sometimes, however, we have data in only a grouped or frequency distribution form. In the following discussion, we show how the weighted mean formula can be used to obtain approximations of the mean, variance, and standard deviation by using *grouped data*.

In Section 2.2 we provided a frequency distribution of the time in days required to complete year-end audits for the public accounting firm of Sanderson and Clifford. The frequency distribution of audit times based on a sample of 20 clients is shown again in Table 3.13. Based on this frequency distribution, what is the sample mean audit time?

Table 3.13	FREQUENCY DISTRIBUTION OF AUDIT TIMES

Audit Time (days)	Frequency
10–14	4
15–19	8
20–24	5
25–29	2
30–34	1
Total	20

To compute the mean, we treat the midpoint of each class as being representative of the items in the class. Let M_i denote the midpoint for class i and let f_i denote the frequency of class i. The weighted mean formula (3.16) is then used with the data values denoted as M_i and the weights given by the frequencies f_i. In this case, the denominator of (3.16) is the sum of the frequencies, which is the sample size n. That is, $\Sigma f_i = n$. Thus, the equation for the sample mean for grouped data is as follows.

Sample Mean for Grouped Data

$$\bar{x} = \frac{\Sigma f_i M_i}{n} \tag{3.17}$$

where

$$M_i = \text{the midpoint for class } i$$
$$f_i = \text{the frequency for class } i$$
$$n = \text{the sample size}$$

With the class midpoints, M_i, halfway between the class limits, the first class of 10–14 in Table 3.13 has a midpoint at $(10 + 14)/2 = 12$. The five class midpoints and the weighted mean computation for the audit time data are summarized in Table 3.14. As can be seen, the sample mean audit time is 19 days.

To compute the variance for grouped data, we use a slightly altered version of the formula for the variance provided in (3.5). In (3.5), the squared deviations of the data about the sample mean $\bar{x}$ were written $(x_i - \bar{x})^2$. However, with grouped data, the values are not known. In this case, we treat the class midpoint, M_i, as being representative of the x_i values in the corresponding class. Thus the squared deviations about the sample mean, $(x_i - \bar{x})^2$, are replaced by $(M_i - \bar{x})^2$. Then, just as we did with the sample mean calculations for grouped data, we weight each value by the frequency of the class, f_i. The sum of the squared deviations about the mean for all the data is approximated by $\Sigma f_i (M_i - \bar{x})^2$. The term $n - 1$ rather than n appears in the denominator in order to make the sample variance the estimate

Table 3.14	COMPUTATION OF THE SAMPLE MEAN AUDIT TIME FOR GROUPED DATA		
Audit Time (days)	**Class Midpoint (M_i)**	**Frequency (f_i)**	**$f_i M_i$**
10–14	12	4	48
15–19	17	8	136
20–24	22	5	110
25–29	27	2	54
30–34	32	1	32
		20	380

$$\text{Sample mean } \bar{x} = \frac{\Sigma f_i M_i}{n} = \frac{380}{20} = 19 \text{ days}$$

of the population variance. Thus, the following formula is used to obtain the sample variance for grouped data.

Sample Variance for Grouped Data

$$s^2 = \frac{\Sigma f_i(M_i - \bar{x})^2}{n - 1}$$

(3.18)

The calculation of the sample variance for audit times based on the grouped data from Table 3.13 is shown in Table 3.15.

The standard deviation for grouped data is simply the square root of the variance for grouped data. For the audit time data, the sample standard deviation is $s = \sqrt{30} = 5.48$.

Before closing this section on computing measures of location and dispersion for grouped data, we note that the formulas (3.17) and (3.18) are for a sample. Population summary measures are computed similarly. The grouped data formulas for a population mean and variance follow.

Population Mean for Grouped Data

$$\mu = \frac{\Sigma f_i M_i}{N}$$

(3.19)

Population Variance for Grouped Data

$$\sigma^2 = \frac{\Sigma f_i(M_i - \mu)^2}{N}$$

(3.20)

Table 3.15	COMPUTATION OF THE SAMPLE VARIANCE OF AUDIT TIMES FOR GROUPED DATA (SAMPLE MEAN $\bar{x} = 19$)

Audit Time (days)	Class Midpoint (M_i)	Frequency (f_i)	Deviation ($M_i - \bar{x}$)	Squared Deviation ($M_i - \bar{x})^2$	$f_i(M_i - \bar{x})^2$
10–14	12	4	−7	49	196
15–19	17	8	−2	4	32
20–24	22	5	3	9	45
25–29	27	2	8	64	128
30–34	32	1	13	169	169
		20			570
					$\Sigma f_i(M_i - \bar{x})^2$

$$\text{Sample variance } s^2 = \frac{\Sigma f_i(M_i - \bar{x})^2}{n - 1} = \frac{570}{19} = 30$$

N O T E S *and Comments*	1. An alternative formula for the computation of the sample variance for grouped data is

$$s^2 = \frac{\Sigma f_i M_i^2 - n\bar{x}^2}{n - 1}$$

where $\Sigma f_i M_i^2 = f_1 M_1^2 + f_2 M_2^2 + \cdots + f_k M_k^2$ and k is the number of classes used to group the data. Using this formula may ease the computations slightly.

2. In computing descriptive statistics for grouped data, the class midpoints are used to approximate the data values in each class. As a result, the descriptive statistics for grouped data are approximations of the descriptive statistics that would result from using the original data directly. We therefore recommend computing descriptive statistics from the original data rather than from grouped data whenever possible.

EXERCISES

Methods

50.   Consider the following data and corresponding weights.

x_i	Weight (w_i)
3.2	6
2.0	3
2.5	2
5.0	8

    a.   Compute the weighted mean.
    b.   Compute the sample mean of the four data values without weighting. Note the difference in the results provided by the two computations.

SELF TEST

51.   Consider the sample data in the following frequency distribution.

Class	Midpoint	Frequency
3–7	5	4
8–12	10	7
13–17	15	9
18–22	20	5

    a.   Compute the sample mean.
    b.   Compute the sample variance and sample standard deviation.

Applications

SELF TEST

52.   The grade point average for college students is based on a weighted mean computation. For most colleges, the grades are given the following data values: A (4), B (3), C (2), D (1), and F (0). After 60 credit hours of course work, a student at State University has earned 9 credit hours of A, 15 credit hours of B, 33 credit hours of C, and 3 credit hours of D.
    a.   Compute the student's grade point average.
    b.   Students at State University must have a 2.5 grade point average for their first 60 credit hours of course work in order to be admitted to the business college. Will this student be admitted?

53. The dividend yield is the percentage of the value of a share of stock that will be paid as an annual dividend to the stockholder. A sample of eight stocks held by Innis Investments had the following dividend yields (*Barron's,* January 5, 1998). The amount Innis has invested in each stock is also shown. What is the mean dividend yield for the portfolio?

Company	Dividend Yield	Amount Invested ($)
Apple Computer	0.00	37,830
Chevron	2.98	27,667
Eastman Kodak	2.77	31,037
Exxon	2.65	27,336
Merck	1.58	37,553
Franklin Resources	0.57	17,812
Sears	2.00	32,660
Woolworth	0.00	17,775

54. A service station has recorded the following frequency distribution for the number of gallons of gasoline sold per car in a sample of 680 cars.

Gasoline (gallons)	Frequency
0–4	74
5–9	192
10–14	280
15–19	105
20–24	23
25–29	6
Total	680

Compute the mean, variance, and standard deviation for these grouped data. If the service station expects to service about 120 cars on a given day, what is an estimate of the total number of gallons of gasoline that will be sold?

55. In a survey of subscribers to *Fortune* magazine, the following question was asked: "How many of the last four issues have you read or looked through?" The following frequency distribution summarizes 500 responses (*Fortune* National Subscriber Portrait, 1994).

Number Read	Frequency
0	15
1	10
2	40
3	85
4	350
Total	500

a. What is the mean number of issues read by a *Fortune* subscriber?
b. What is the standard deviation of the number of issues read?

..../ /..............

SUMMARY

In this chapter we introduced several descriptive statistics that can be used to summarize the location and variability of data. Unlike the tabular and graphical procedures, the measures introduced in this chapter summarize the data in terms of numerical values. When the numerical values obtained are for a sample, they are called sample statistics. When the numerical values obtained are for a population, they are called population parameters. Some of the notation used for sample statistics and population parameters follow.

	Sample Statistic	Population Parameter
Mean	$\bar{x}$	μ
Variance	s^2	σ^2
Standard deviation	s	σ

As measures of location, we defined the mean, median, and mode. Then the concept of percentiles was used to describe the location of observations in the data set. Next, we presented the range, interquartile range, variance, standard deviation, and coefficient of variation as measures of variability or dispersion. We then described how the mean and standard deviation could be used, applying Chebyshev's theorem and the empirical rule, to provide more information about the distribution of data and to identify outliers.

In Section 3.4 we showed how to develop a five-number summary and a box plot to provide simultaneous information about the location, variability, and shape of the distribution. In Section 3.5 we introduced covariance and the correlation coefficient as measures of association between two variables. In the final section, we showed how to compute a weighted mean.

The descriptive statistics we have discussed can be developed using statistical software packages and spreadsheets. In Appendix 3.1 we show how to develop descriptive statistics using Minitab. In Appendix 3.2, we demonstrate the use of Excel for the same purpose.

..../ /..............

GLOSSARY

Population parameter A numerical value used as a summary measure for a population (e.g., the population mean, μ, the population variance, σ^2, and the population standard deviation, σ).

Sample statistic A numerical value used as a summary measure for a sample (e.g., the sample mean, $\bar{x}$, the sample variance, s^2, and the sample standard deviation, s).

Mean A measure of central location. It is computed by summing the data values and dividing by the number of observations.

Median A measure of central location. It is the value that splits the data into two equal groups, one with values greater than or equal to the median and one with values less than or equal to the median.

Mode A measure of location, defined as the most frequently occurring data value.

Percentile A value such that at least p percent of the observation are less than or equal to this value and at least $(100 - p)$ percent of the observations are greater than or equal to this value. The 50th percentile is the median.

Quartiles The 25th, 50th, and 75th percentiles are referred to as the first quartile, the second quartile (median), and third quartile, respectively. The quartiles can be used to divide a data set into four parts, with each part containing approximately 25% of the data.

Range A measure of variability, defined to be the largest value minus the smallest value.

Interquartile range (IQR) A measure of variability, defined to be the difference between the third and first quartiles.

Variance A measure of variability based on the squared deviations of the data values about the mean.

Standard deviation A measure of variability found by taking the positive square root of the variance.

Coefficient of variation A measure of relative variability found by dividing the standard deviation by the mean and multiplying by 100.

z-score A value found by dividing the deviation about the mean $(x_i - \bar{x})$ by the the standard deviation s. A z-score is referred to as a standardized value and denotes the number of standard deviations x_i is from the mean.

Chebyshev's theorem A theorem that can be used to make statements about the percentage of data values that must be within a specified number of standard deviations of the mean.

Empirical rule A rule that states the percentages of data values that are within one, two, and three standard deviations from the mean for mound-shaped, or bell-shaped, distributions.

Outlier An unusually small or unusually large data value.

Five-number summary An exploratory data analysis technique that uses five numbers to summarize the data: smallest value, first quartile, median, third quartile, and largest value.

Box plot A graphical summary of data. A box, drawn from the first to the third quartiles, shows the location of the middle 50% of the data. Dashed lines, called whiskers, extending from the ends of the box show the location of data values greater than the third quartile and data values less than the first quartile. The locations of outliers are also noted.

Covariance A measure of linear association between two variables. Positive values indicate a positive relationship; negative values indicate a negative relationship.

Correlation coefficient A measure of linear association between two variables that takes values between -1 and $+1$. Values near $+1$ indicate a strong positive linear relationship, values near -1 indicate a strong negative linear relationship, and values near zero indicate the lack of a linear relationship.

Weighted mean The mean obtained by assigning each observation a weight that reflects its importance.

Grouped data Data available in class intervals as summarized by a frequency distribution. Individual values of the original data are not recorded.

KEY FORMULAS

Sample Mean

$$\bar{x} = \frac{\Sigma x_i}{n}$$

(3.1)

Population Mean

$$\mu = \frac{\Sigma x_i}{N} \qquad (3.2)$$

Interquartile Range

$$\text{IQR} = Q_3 - Q_1 \qquad (3.3)$$

Population Variance

$$\sigma^2 = \frac{\Sigma(x_i - \mu)^2}{N} \qquad (3.4)$$

Sample Variance

$$s^2 = \frac{\Sigma(x_i - \bar{x})^2}{n - 1} \qquad (3.5)$$

Standard Deviation

$$\text{Sample Standard Deviation} = s = \sqrt{s^2} \qquad (3.6)$$
$$\text{Population Standard Deviation} = \sigma = \sqrt{\sigma^2} \qquad (3.7)$$

Coefficient of Variation

$$\left(\frac{\text{Standard Deviation}}{\text{Mean}}\right) \times 100 \qquad (3.8)$$

z-score

$$z_i = \frac{x_i - \bar{x}}{s} \qquad (3.9)$$

Sample Covariance

$$s_{xy} = \frac{\Sigma(x_i - \bar{x})(y_i - \bar{y})}{n - 1} \qquad (3.10)$$

Pearson Product Moment Correlation Coefficient: Sample Data

$$r_{xy} = \frac{s_{xy}}{s_x s_y} \qquad (3.12)$$

Pearson Product Moment Correlation Coefficient: Sample Data, Alternate Formula

$$r_{xy} = \frac{\Sigma x_i y_i - (\Sigma x_i \Sigma y_i)/n}{\sqrt{\Sigma x_i^2 - (\Sigma x_i)^2/n} \ \sqrt{\Sigma y_i^2 - (\Sigma y_i)^2/n}} \qquad (3.13)$$

Weighted Mean

$$\bar{x} = \frac{\Sigma w_i x_i}{\Sigma w_i} \qquad (3.16)$$

Sample Mean for Grouped Data

$$\bar{x} = \frac{\Sigma f_i M_i}{n} \qquad (3.17)$$

Sample Variance for Grouped Data

$$s^2 = \frac{\Sigma f_i(M_i - \bar{x})^2}{n - 1}$$

(3.18)

Population Mean for Grouped Data

$$\mu = \frac{\Sigma f_i M_i}{N}$$

(3.19)

Population Variance for Grouped Data

$$\sigma^2 = \frac{\Sigma f_i(M_i - \mu)^2}{N}$$

(3.20)

·· *| |* ···········

SUPPLEMENTARY EXERCISES

Eat

56. The average American spends $65.88 per month dining out (*The Des Moines Register,* December 5, 1997). A sample of young adults provided the following dining out expenditures (in dollars) over the past month.

253	101	245	467	131	0	225
80	113	69	198	95	129	124
11	178	104	161	0	118	151
55	152	134	169			

  a. Compute the mean, median, and mode.
  b. Considering your results in part (a), do these young adults seem to spend about the same as an average American eating out?
  c. Compute the first and third quartiles.
  d. Compute the range and interquartile range.
  e. Compute the variance and standard deviation.
  f. Are there any outliers?

57. Following is a sample of yields for 10 bonds traded on the New York Stock Exchange (*Barron's,* January 5, 1998).

Issuer	Yield (%)	Issuer	Yield (%)
Argosy	12.6	Caterpillar	6.3
Chase Manhattan	6.7	Dow	6.8
IBM	7.0	Lucent	6.7
Mobil	7.3	Pacific Bell	6.7
RJR Nabisco	8.1	Service Mdse.	8.6

Compute the following descriptive statistics.
  a. Mean, median, and mode.
  b. The first and third quartiles.
  c. The range and interquartile range.
  d. The variance and standard deviation.
  e. Coefficient of variation.

58. A survey was conducted concerning the ability of computer manufacturers to handle problems quickly (*PC Computing,* November 1997). The following results were obtained.

Company	Days to Resolve Problems	Company	Days to Resolve Problems
Compaq	13	Gateway	21
Packard Bell	27	Digital	27
Quantex	11	IBM	12
Dell	14	Hewlett-Packard	14
NEC	14	AT&T	20
AST	17	Toshiba	37
Acer	16	Micron	17

   a. What are the mean and median number of days needed to resolve problems?
   b. What is the variance and standard deviation?
   c. Which manufacturer has the best record?
   d. What is the z-score for Packard Bell?
   e. What is the z-score for IBM?
   f. Are there any outliers?

59. A sample of 10 stocks on the New York Stock Exchange (*The Wall Street Journal,* January 26, 1998) has the following price/earnings ratios: 9, 4, 6, 7, 3, 11, 4, 6, 4, 7. Using these data, compute the mean, median, mode, range, variance, and standard deviation.

60. Public transportation and the automobile are two methods an employee can use to get to work each day. Samples of times recorded for each method are shown. Times are in minutes.

   Public Transportation: 28   29   32   37   33   25   29   32   41   34
   Automobile: 29   31   33   32   34   30   31   32   35   33

   a. Compute the sample mean time to get to work for each method.
   b. Compute the sample standard deviation for each method.
   c. On the basis of your results from (a) and (b), which method of transportation should be preferred? Explain.
   d. Develop a box plot for each method. Does a comparison of the box plots support your conclusion in (c)?

61. The median income and the median home price for a sample of six cities follow (*Who's Buying Homes in America,* Chicago Title and Trust Company, 1994). Data are in thousands of dollars.

City	Median Income	Median Home Price
Atlanta, Georgia	$65.2	$120.2
Cleveland, Ohio	49.8	92.7
Denver, Colorado	53.8	111.7
Dallas, Texas	62.7	104.7
Orlando, Florida	50.9	98.5
Minneapolis, Minnesota	53.1	105.8

   a. What is the sample covariance? Does it indicate a positive or negative relationship?
   b. What is the sample correlation coefficient?

62. *Road & Track,* October 1994, provided the following sample of the tire ratings and load-carrying capacity of automobiles tires.

Tire Rating	Load-Carrying Capacity
75	853
82	1047
85	1135
87	1201
88	1235
91	1356
92	1389
93	1433
105	2039

a. Develop a scatter diagram for the data with tire rating on the x-axis.
b. What is the sample correlation coefficient and what does it tell you about the relationship between tire rating and load-carrying capacity?

63. The total returns (dividends plus capital appreciation) for the years 1988 through 1997 for the Dow Jones Industrial Average and the S&P 500 indexes are shown here (*Barron's,* January 5, 1998). Compute the correlation coefficient and comment on how closely the returns on these indexes are related.

Year	Return (%) DJIA	Return (%) S&P 500	Year	Return (%) DJIA	Return (%) S&P 500
1988	16.0	16.6	1993	16.8	10.1
1989	31.7	31.5	1994	4.9	1.3
1990	−0.4	−3.2	1995	36.4	37.6
1991	23.9	30.0	1996	28.6	23.0
1992	7.4	7.6	1997	24.9	33.4

64. A forecasting technique referred to as moving averages uses the average or mean of the most recent n periods to forecast the next value for time series data. With a three-period moving average, the most recent three periods of data are used in the forecast computation. Consider a product with the following demand for the first three months of the current year: January (800 units), February (750 units), and March (900 units).
a. What is the three-month moving average forecast for April?
b. A variation of this forecasting technique is called weighted moving averages. The weighting allows the more recent time series data to receive more weight or more importance in the computation of the forecast. For example, a weighted three-month moving average might give a weight of 3 to data one month old, a weight of 2 to data two months old, and a weight of 1 to data three months old. Use the data above to provide a three-month weighted moving average forecast for April.

65. Automobiles traveling on the New York State Thruway are checked for speed by a state police radar system. Following is a frequency distribution of speeds.

Speed (miles per hour)	Frequency
45–49	10
50–54	40
55–59	150
60–64	175
65–69	75
70–74	15
75–79	10
Total	475

a. What is the mean speed of the automobiles traveling on the New York State Thruway?
b. Compute the variance and the standard deviation.

66. Dinner check amounts at La Maison French Restaurant have the frequency distribution shown as follows. Compute the mean, variance, and standard deviation.

Dinner Check ($)	Frequency
25–34	2
35–44	6
45–54	4
55–64	4
65–74	2
75–84	2
Total	20

··/ /···········

Case Problem 1   CONSOLIDATED FOODS, INC.

Consolidated Foods, Inc., operates a chain of supermarkets in New Mexico, Arizona, and California. Data in Table 3.16 show the dollar amounts and method of payment for a sample of 100 customers. Consolidated's managers requested the sample be taken to learn about payment practices of the store's customers. In particular, managers are interested in learning about how a new credit card payment option is related to the customers' purchase amounts.

Managerial Report

Use the methods of descriptive statistics presented in Chapter 3 to summarize the sample data. Provide summaries of the dollar purchase amounts for cash customers, personal check customers, and credit card customers separately. Your report should contain the following summaries and discussions.

1. A comparison and interpretation of means and medians.
2. A comparison and interpretation of measures of variability such as the range and standard deviation.
3. The identification and interpretation of the five-number summaries for each method of payment.
4. Box plots for each method of payment.

Use the summary section of your report to provide a discussion of what you have learned about the method of payment and the amounts of payments for Consolidated Foods' customers.

Table 3.16		PURCHASE AMOUNT AND METHOD OF PAYMENT FOR A SAMPLE OF 100 CONSOLIDATED FOODS CUSTOMERS				
Cash	Personal Check	Credit Card	Cash	Personal Check	Credit Card
$ 7.40	$27.60	$50.30	$ 5.08	$52.87	$69.77
5.15	30.60	33.76	20.48	78.16	48.11
4.75	41.58	25.57	16.28	25.96	
15.10	36.09	46.24	15.57	31.07	
8.81	2.67	46.13	6.93	35.38	
1.85	34.67	14.44	7.17	58.11	
7.41	58.64	43.79	11.54	49.21	
11.77	57.59	19.78	13.09	31.74	
12.07	43.14	52.35	16.69	50.58	
9.00	21.11	52.63	7.02	59.78	
5.98	52.04	57.55	18.09	72.46	
7.88	18.77	27.66	2.44	37.94	
5.91	42.83	44.53	1.09	42.69	
3.65	55.40	26.91	2.96	41.10	
14.28	48.95	55.21	11.17	40.51	
1.27	36.48	54.19	16.38	37.20	
2.87	51.66	22.59	8.85	54.84	
4.34	28.58	53.32	7.22	58.75	
3.31	35.89	26.57		17.87	
15.07	39.55	27.89		69.22	

Case Problem 2   NATIONAL HEALTH CARE ASSOCIATION

The National Health Care Association is concerned about the shortage of nurses the health care profession is projecting for the future. To learn the current degree of job satisfaction among nurses, the association has sponsored a study of hospital nurses throughout the country. As part of this study, a sample of 50 nurses were asked to indicate their degree of satisfaction in their work, their pay, and their opportunities for promotion. Each of the three aspects of satisfaction was measured on a scale from 0 to 100, with larger values indicating higher degrees of satisfaction. The data in Table 3.17 were collected.

Table 3.17		WORK, PAY, AND PROMOTION JOB SATISFACTION SCORES FOR A SAMPLE OF 50 NURSES			
Work	**Pay**	**Promotion**	**Work**	**Pay**	**Promotion**
71	49	58	72	76	37
84	53	63	71	25	74
84	74	37	69	47	16
87	66	49	90	56	23
72	59	79	84	28	62
72	37	86	86	37	59
72	57	40	70	38	54
63	48	78	86	72	72
84	60	29	87	51	57
90	62	66	77	90	51
73	56	55	71	36	55
94	60	52	75	53	92
84	42	66	74	59	82
85	56	64	76	51	54
88	55	52	95	66	52
74	70	51	89	66	62
71	45	68	85	57	67
88	49	42	65	42	68
90	27	67	82	37	54
85	89	46	82	60	56
79	59	41	89	80	64
72	60	45	74	47	63
88	36	47	82	49	91
77	60	75	90	76	70
64	43	61	78	52	72

Health I

In addition, the sample data in Table 3.17 were broken down by the types of hospitals employing the nurses. The types of hospitals considered were private, Veterans Administration, and University. The data in Table 3.18 are available.

Managerial Report

Use methods of descriptive statistics to summarize the data. Present the summaries that will be beneficial in communicating the results to others. Discuss your findings. Specifically, comment on the following questions.

1. On the basis of the entire data set and the three job satisfaction variables, what aspect of the job is most satisfying for the nurses? What appears to be the least satisfying? In what area(s), if any, do you feel improvements should be made? Discuss.
2. On the basis of descriptive measures of variability, what measure of job satisfaction appears to generate the greatest difference of opinion among the nurses? Explain.

Table 3.18	WORK, PAY, AND PROMOTION JOB SATISFACTION SCORES FOR NURSES IN PRIVATE, VA, AND UNIVERSITY HOSPITALS							
Private Hospitals			**VA Hospitals**			**University Hospitals**		
Work	Pay	Promotion	Work	Pay	Promotion	Work	Pay	Promotion
72	57	40	71	49	58	84	53	63
90	62	66	84	74	37	87	66	49
84	42	66	72	37	86	72	59	79
85	56	64	63	48	78	88	55	52
71	45	68	84	60	29	74	70	51
88	49	42	73	56	55	85	89	46
72	60	45	94	60	52	79	59	41
88	36	47	90	27	67	69	47	16
77	60	75	72	76	37	90	56	23
64	43	61	86	37	59	77	90	51
71	25	74	86	72	72	71	36	55
84	28	62	95	66	52	75	53	92
70	38	54	65	42	68	76	51	54
87	51	57	82	37	54	89	80	64
74	59	82	82	60	56			
89	66	62	90	76	70			
85	57	67	78	52	72			
74	47	63						
82	49	91						

Health2

3. What can be learned about the types of hospitals? Does any particular type of hospital seem to have better levels of job satisfaction than the other types? Do your results suggest any recommendations for learning about and/or improving job satisfaction? Discuss.
4. What additional descriptive statistics and insights can you use to learn about and possibly improve job satisfaction?

Case Problem 3   BUSINESS SCHOOLS OF ASIA-PACIFIC

Asian

The pursuit of a higher education degree in business is now international. A survey shows that more and more Asians are choosing the Master of Business Administration degree route to corporate success (*Asia, Inc.,* September 1997). The number of applicants for MBA courses at Asia-Pacific schools is rising by about 30 percent a year. In 1997, the 74 business schools in the Asia-Pacific region reported a record 170,000 applications for the 11,000 full-time MBA degrees to be awarded in 1999. A main reason for the surge in demand is that an MBA can greatly enhance earning power.

Across the region, thousands of Asians are showing an increasing willingness to temporarily shelve their careers and spend two years in pursuit of a theoretical business qualification. Courses in these schools are notoriously tough and include economics, banking, marketing, behavioral sciences, labor relations, decision making, strategic thinking, business law, and more. *Asia, Inc.* provided the data set in Table 3.19, which shows some of the characteristics of the leading Asia-Pacific business schools.

Table 3.19 DATA FOR 25 ASIA-PACIFIC BUSINESS SCHOOLS

Business School	Full-Time Enrollment	Students per Faculty	Local Tuition	Foreign Tuition	Age	% Foreign	GMAT	English Test	Work Experience	Starting Salary
Melbourne Business School	200	5	$24,420	$29,600	28	47	Yes	No	Yes	$71,400
University of New South Wales (Sydney)	228	4	19,993	32,582	29	28	Yes	No	Yes	65,200
Indian Institute of Management (Ahmedabad)	392	5	4,300	4,300	22	0	No	No	No	7,100
Chinese University of Hong Kong	90	5	11,140	11,140	29	10	Yes	No	No	31,000
International University of Japan (Niigata)	126	4	33,060	33,060	28	60	Yes	Yes	No	87,000
Asian Institute of Management (Manila)	389	5	7,562	9,000	25	50	Yes	No	Yes	22,800
Indian Institute of Management (Bangalore)	380	5	3,935	16,000	23	1	Yes	No	No	7,500
National University of Singapore	147	6	6,146	7,170	29	51	Yes	Yes	Yes	43,300
Indian Institute of Management (Calcutta)	463	8	2,880	16,000	23	0	No	No	No	7,400
Australian National University (Canberra)	42	2	20,300	20,300	30	80	Yes	Yes	Yes	46,600
Nanyang Technological University (Singapore)	50	5	8,500	8,500	32	20	Yes	No	Yes	49,300
University of Queensland (Brisbane)	138	17	16,000	22,800	32	26	No	No	Yes	49,600
Hong Kong University of Science and Technology	60	2	11,513	11,513	26	37	Yes	No	Yes	34,000
Macquarie Graduate School of Management (Sydney)	12	8	17,172	19,778	34	27	No	No	Yes	60,100
Chulalongkorn University (Bangkok)	200	7	17,355	17,355	25	6	Yes	No	Yes	17,600
Monash Mt. Eliza Business School (Melbourne)	350	13	16,200	22,500	30	30	Yes	Yes	Yes	52,500
Asian Institute of Management (Bangkok)	300	10	18,200	18,200	29	90	No	Yes	Yes	25,000
University of Adelaide	20	19	16,426	23,100	30	10	No	No	Yes	66,000
Massey University (Palmerston North, New Zealand)	30	15	13,106	21,625	37	35	No	Yes	Yes	41,400
Royal Melbourne Institute of Technology Business Graduate School	30	7	13,880	17,765	32	30	No	Yes	Yes	48,900
Jammalal Bajaj Institute of Management Studies (Bombay)	240	9	1,000	1,000	24	0	No	No	Yes	7,000
Curtin Institute of Technology (Perth)	98	15	9,475	19,097	29	43	Yes	No	Yes	55,000
Lahore University of Management Sciences	70	14	11,250	26,300	23	2.5	No	No	No	7,500
Universiti Sains Malaysia (Penang)	30	5	2,260	2,260	32	15	No	Yes	Yes	16,000
De La Salle University (Manila)	44	17	3,300	3,600	28	3.5	Yes	No	Yes	13,100

Managerial Report

Use the methods of descriptive statistics to summarize the data in Table 3.19. Discuss your findings.

1. Include a summary for each variable in the data set. Make comments and interpretations based on maximums and minimums, as well as the appropriate means and proportions. What new insights do these descriptive statistics provide concerning Asia-Pacific business schools?
2. Summarize the data to compare the following:
   a. Any difference between local and foreign tuition costs.
   b. Any difference between mean starting salaries for schools requiring and not requiring work experience.
   c. Any difference between starting salaries for schools requiring and not requiring English tests.
3. Present any additional graphical and numerical summaries that will be beneficial in communicating the data in Table 3.19 to others.

Appendix 3.1   DESCRIPTIVE STATISTICS WITH MINITAB

In this appendix, we describe how to use Minitab to develop descriptive statistics. Table 3.1 listed the starting salaries for 12 business school graduates. Panel A of Figure 3.10 shows the descriptive statistics obtained by using Minitab to summarize these data. Definitions of the headings in Panel A follow.

N	number of observations
Mean	mean
Median	median
StDev	standard deviation
Minimum	minimum data value
Maximum	maximum data value
Q1	first quartile
Q3	third quartile

We discussed the measure labeled TrMean in a note and comment at the end of Section 3.1. TrMean is the *trimmed mean,* which indicates the central location of the data after removing the smallest and largest data values. Minitab provides the 5% trimmed mean; the smallest 5% of the data values and the largest 5% of the data values are removed. The 5% trimmed mean is found by computing the mean for the middle 90% of the data. SEMean, which is the *standard error of the mean,* is computed by dividing the standard deviation by the square root of N. The interpretation and use of this measure are discussed in Chapter 7 when we introduce the topics of sampling and sampling distributions.

Although the numerical measures of range, interquartile range, variance, and coefficient of variation do not appear on the Minitab output, these values can be easily computed if desired from the results in Figure 3.10 by the following formulas.

Figure 3.10   **DESCRIPTIVE STATISTICS AND BOX PLOT PROVIDED BY MINITAB**

Panel A
Descriptive Statistics

Variable	N	Mean	Median	TrMean	StDev	SE Mean
Salary	12	2440.0	2405.0	2424.5	165.7	47.8

Variable	Minimum	Maximum	Q1	Q3
Salary	2210.0	2825.0	2357.5	2525.0

Panel B
Box Plot

$$\text{Range} = \text{Maximum} - \text{Minimum}$$
$$\text{IQR} = \text{Q3} - \text{Q1}$$
$$\text{Variance} = (\text{StDev})^2$$
$$\text{Coefficient of Variation} = (\text{StDev/Mean}) \times 100$$

Finally, note that Minitab's quartiles $Q_1 = 2357.5$ and $Q_3 = 2525$ provide values slightly different from the quartiles $Q_1 = 2365$ and $Q_3 = 2500$ that we computed in Section 3.1. The reason is that different conventions* can be used to identify the quartiles. Hence, the values of Q_1 and Q_3 provided by one convention may not be identical to the values of Q_1 and Q_3 provided by another convention. Any differences tend to be negligible,

---

*With the n data values rank ordered from smallest to largest, Minitab uses the positions given by $(n + 1)/4$ and $3(n + 1)/4$ to locate Q_1 and Q_3, respectively. When a position is fractional, Minitab interpolates between the two adjacent rank-ordered data values to determine the corresponding quartile.

however, and the results provided should not mislead the user in making the usual interpretations associated with quartiles.

To generate the descriptive statistics in Figure 3.10, we first entered the starting salary data into column C1 of a Minitab worksheet. Salary is entered as the heading for column C1. The following steps can be used to generate the computer output shown in panel A of Figure 3.10.

Step 1. Select the **Stat** pull-down menu
Step 2. Select the **Basic Statistics** pull-down menu
Step 3. Select the **Display Descriptive Statistics** option
Step 4. When the Display Descriptive Statistics dialog box appears:
  Enter C1 in the **Variables** box
  Select **OK**

Panel B of Figure 3.10 is a box plot provided by Minitab. The box drawn from the first to the third quartiles contains the middle 50% of the data. The line within the box locates the median. The asterisk indicates an outlier at 2825.

The following steps generate the box plot shown in panel B of Figure 3.10.

Step 1. Select the **Graph** pull-down menu
Step 2. Select **Boxplot**
Step 3. When the Boxplot dialog box appears:
  Enter C1 under **Y** in the **Graph variables** box
  Make sure IQ Range Box and Graph appear as Item 1 in the **Data Display** box
  Make sure Outlier Symbol and Graph appear as Item 2 in the **Data Display** box
  Select **OK**

Figure 3.11 shows the covariance and correlation output that Minitab provided for the stereo and sound equipment store data in Table 3.7. The variable Commercial denotes the number of weekend television commercials, and the variable Sales denotes the sales during the following week. The value in column Commercial and row Sales is the sample covariance $s_{xy} = 11$ as computed in Section 3.5. The value in column Commercial and row Commercial is the sample variance for the number of commercials, and the value in column Sales and row Sales is the sample variance for sales. The sample correlation coefficient $r_{xy} = +.93$ is shown at the bottom of the output.

Let us now describe how to obtain the information in Figure 3.11. After entering the data for the number of commercials into column C1 and the data for sales into column C2 of the Minitab worksheet, we named the columns Commercial and Sales, respectively. The steps necessary to generate the covariance output in the first three rows of Figure 3.11 follow.

Figure 3.11	COVARIANCE AND CORRELATION PROVIDED BY MINITAB FOR THE NUMBER OF COMMERCIALS (x) AND SALES (y) DATA

	Commercial	Sales
Commercial	2.22222	
Sales	11.00000	62.88889

Correlation of Commercial and Sales = 0.930

Step 1. Select the **Stat** pull-down menu
Step 2. Select the **Basic Statistics** pull-down menu
Step 3. Select the **Covariance** option
Step 4. When the Covariance dialog box appears:
         Enter C1 C2 in the **Variables** box
         Select **OK**

To obtain the correlation coefficient in the last line of Figure 3.11, only one change is necessary in the steps for obtaining the covariance. In step 3, the **Correlation** option is selected.

Appendix 3.2   DESCRIPTIVE STATISTICS WITH EXCEL

In this appendix, we show how Excel can be used to generate the measures of location and variability for a single variable and to generate the covariance and correlation coefficient as measures of association between two variables.

The starting salary heading, Salary, and the salary data from Table 3.1 have been entered into cells A1 through A13 of the spreadsheet in Figure 3.12. The following steps describe how to use Excel to generate descriptive statistics for these data.

Step 1. Select the **Tools** pull-down menu
Step 2. Choose the **Data Analysis** option
Step 3. Choose **Descriptive Statistics** from the list of Analysis Tools
Step 4. When the Descriptive statistics dialog box appears:
         Enter A1:A13 in the **Input Range** box
         Select **Labels in First Row**
         Select **Output Range**
         Enter C1 in the **Output Range** box (It identifies the upper left corner of the section of the worksheet where the descriptive statistics will appear)
         Select **Summary Statistics**
         Select **OK**

Figure 3.12   MONTHLY STARTING SALARY DATA IN COLUMN A OF A SPREADSHEET

	A	B	C	D
1	**Salary**			
2	2350			
3	2450			
4	2550			
5	2380			
6	2255			
7	2210			
8	2390			
9	2630			
10	2440			
11	2825			
12	2420			
13	2380			

Figure 3.13   **DESCRIPTIVE STATISTICS FOR MONTHLY STARTING SALARIES PROVIDED BY EXCEL**

	A	B	C	D
1	**Salary**		*Salary*	
2	2350			
3	2450		**Mean**	2440
4	2550		Standard Error	47.8199
5	2380		**Median**	2405
6	2255		**Mode**	2380
7	2210		**Standard Deviation**	165.653
8	2390		**Sample Variance**	27440.91
9	2630		Kurtosis	1.718884
10	2440		Skewness	1.091109
11	2825		**Range**	615
12	2420		**Minimum**	2210
13	2380		**Maximum**	2825
14			**Sum**	29280
15			**Count**	12
16				

Figure 3.13 shows the descriptive statistics provided by Excel. The boldfaced entries are the descriptive statistics covered in this chapter. The other descriptive statistics are either covered subsequently in the text or covered in more advanced texts.

We next illustrate the computation of the covariance and correlation coefficient, using the advertising and sales data for the stereo and sound equipment store (see Table 3.7). Figure 3.14 is an Excel spreadsheet with the data on the number of commercials in column A and the data on sales in column B. The steps necessary to generate the covariance for these data follow Figure 3.14.

Figure 3.14   **NUMBER OF COMMERCIALS AND SALES DATA FOR THE STEREO AND SOUND EQUIPMENT STORE**

	A	B	C	D
1	**Commercials**	**Sales**		
2	2	50		
3	5	57		
4	1	41		
5	3	54		
6	4	54		
7	1	38		
8	5	63		
9	3	48		
10	4	59		
11	2	46		

Step 1. Select the **Tools** pull-down menu
Step 2. Choose the **Data Analysis** option
Step 3. Choose **Covariance** from the list of Analysis Tools
Step 4. When the Covariance dialog box appears:
        Enter A1:B11 in the **Input Range** box
        Select **Labels in First Row**
        Select **Output Range**
        Enter D1 in the **Output Range** box
        Select **OK**

Figure 3.15 shows the output of the covariance procedure in columns D, E, and F. The entry in cell E3 is the covariance between the two variables, $s_{xy} = 11$. The entry in cell E2 is the variance for the number of commercials and the entry in cell F3 is the variance for sales.

The steps necessary to compute the correlation coefficient from the spreadsheet in Figure 3.14 follow.

Step 1. Select the **Tools** pull-down menu
Step 2. Choose the **Data Analysis** option
Step 3. Choose **Correlation** from the list of Analysis Tools
Step 4. When the Correlation dialog box appears:
        Enter A1:B11 in the **Input Range** box
        Select **Labels in First Row**
        Select **Output Range**
        Enter D6 in the **Output Range** box
        Select **OK**

The output generated by Excel begins in cell D6 of Figure 3.15. The entry in cell E8 is the correlation coefficient, $r_{xy} = +.93$; note that it is the same value we computed in Section 3.5. The entry in cell E7 is the correlation coefficient of the first variable (number of commercials) with itself, and the entry in cell F8 is the correlation coefficient of the second variable (sales) with itself. Because a variable is always perfectly correlated with itself, these values are always equal to 1.

Figure 3.15   COVARIANCE AND CORRELATION COEFFICIENT FOR COMMERCIALS AND SALES DATA AS PROVIDED BY EXCEL

	A	B	C	D	E	F
1	Commercials	Sales			*Commercials*	*Sales*
2	2	50		**Commercials**	2.222222222	
3	5	57		**Sales**	11	62.88889
4	1	41				
5	3	54				
6	4	54			*Commercials*	*Sales*
7	1	38		**Commercials**	1	
8	5	63		**Sales**	0.930490581	1
9	3	48				
10	4	59				
11	2	46				

4

INTRODUCTION TO PROBABILITY

CONTENTS

MORTON INTERNATIONAL*
Chicago, Illinois

Morton International is a company with businesses in salt, household products, rocket motors, and specialty chemicals. Carstab Corporation, a subsidiary of Morton International, produces specialty chemicals and offers a variety of chemicals designed to meet the unique specifications of its customers. For one particular customer, Carstab produced an expensive catalyst used in chemical processing. Some, but not all, of the lots produced by Carstab met the customer's specifications for the product.

Carstab's customer agreed to test each lot after receiving it and determine whether the catalyst would perform the desired function. Lots that did not pass the customer's test would be returned to Carstab. Over time, Carstab found that the customer was accepting 60% of the lots and returning 40%. In probability terms, each Carstab shipment to the customer had a .60 probability of being accepted and a .40 probability of being returned.

Neither Carstab nor its customer was pleased with these results. In an effort to improve service, Carstab explored the possibility of duplicating the customer's test prior to shipment. However, the high cost of the special testing equipment made that alternative infeasible. Carstab's chemists then proposed a new, relatively low-cost test designed to indicate whether a lot would pass the customer's test. The probability question of interest was: What is the probability that a lot will pass the customer's test if it has passed the new Carstab test?

---

*The authors are indebted to Michael Haskell of Morton International for providing this Statistics in Practice.

Morton Salt: "When It Rains It Pours." © SWCP/Cary Benbow.

A sample of lots was produced and subjected to the new Carstab test. Only lots that passed the new test were sent to the customer. Probability analysis of the data indicated that if a lot passed the Carstab test, it had a .909 probability of passing the customer's test and being accepted. Alternatively, if a lot passed the Carstab test, it had only a .091 probability of being returned. The probability analysis provided key supporting evidence for the adoption and implementation of the new testing procedure at Carstab. The new test resulted in an immediate improvement in customer service and a substantial reduction in shipping and handling costs for returned lots.

The probability of a lot being accepted by the customer after passing the new Carstab test is called a conditional probability. In this chapter, you will learn how to compute this and other probabilities that are helpful in decision making.

Business decisions are often based on an analysis of uncertainties such as the following:

1. What are the chances that sales will decrease if we increase prices?
2. What is the likelihood a new assembly method will increase productivity?
3. How likely is it that the project will be finished on time?
4. What are the odds in favor of a new investment being profitable?

Some of the earliest work on probability originated in a series of letters between Pierre de Fermat and Blaise Pascal in the 1650s.

Probability is a numerical measure of the likelihood that an event will occur. Thus, probabilities could be used as measures of the degree of uncertainty associated with the four events previously listed. If probabilities were available, we could determine the likelihood of each event occurring.

Pierre-Simon de Laplace's book, Theorie Analytique des Probabilities, was published in 1812.

Probability values are always assigned on a scale from 0 to 1. A probability near zero indicates an event is unlikely to occur; a probability near 1 indicates an event is almost certain to occur. Other probabilities between 0 and 1 represent degrees of likelihood that an event will occur. For example, if we consider the event "rain tomorrow," we understand that when the weather report indicates "a near-zero probability of rain," it means almost no chance of rain. However, if a .90 probability of rain is reported, we know that rain is likely to occur. A .50 probability indicates that rain is just as likely to occur as not. Figure 4.1 depicts the view of probability as a numerical measure of the likelihood of an event occurring.

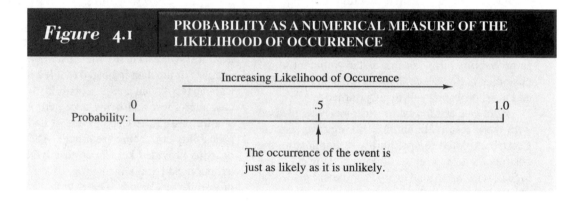

Figure 4.1   PROBABILITY AS A NUMERICAL MEASURE OF THE LIKELIHOOD OF OCCURRENCE

4.1   EXPERIMENTS, COUNTING RULES, AND ASSIGNING PROBABILITIES

In discussing probability, we define an *experiment* to be any process that generates well-defined outcomes. On any single repetition of an experiment, one and only one of the possible experimental outcomes will occur. Several examples of experiments and their associated outcomes follow.

Experiment	Experimental Outcomes
Toss a coin	Head, tail
Select a part for inspection	Defective, nondefective
Conduct a sales call	Purchase, no purchase
Roll a die	1, 2, 3, 4, 5, 6
Play a football game	Win, lose, tie

When we have specified all possible experimental outcomes, we have identified the *sample space* for an experiment.

Sample Space

The sample space for an experiment is the set of all experimental outcomes.

Experimental outcomes are also called sample points.

An experimental outcome is also called a *sample point* to identify it as an element of the sample space.

Consider the first experiment in the preceding table—tossing a coin. The experimental outcomes (sample points) are determined by the upward face of the coin—a head or a tail. If we let S denote the sample space, we can use the following notation to describe the sample space.

$$S = \{\text{Head, Tail}\}$$

The sample space for the second experiment in the table—selecting a part for inspection—has the following sample space and sample points.

$$S = \{\text{Defective, Nondefective}\}$$

Both of the experiments just described have two experimental outcomes (sample points). However, suppose we consider the fourth experiment listed in the table—rolling a die. The possible experimental outcomes defined as the number of dots appearing on the upward face of the die are the six points in the sample space for this experiment.

$$S = \{1, 2, 3, 4, 5, 6\}$$

Counting Rules, Combinations, and Permutations

Being able to identify and count the experimental outcomes is a necessary step in assigning probabilities. We now discuss three counting rules that are useful.

Multiple Step Experiments.   The first counting rule is for multiple-step experiments. Consider the experiment of tossing two coins. Let the experimental outcomes be defined in terms of the pattern of heads and tails appearing on the upward faces of the two coins. How many experimental outcomes are possible for this experiment? It can be thought of as a two-step experiment in which step 1 is the tossing of the first coin and step 2 is the tossing of the second coin. If we use H to denote a head and T to denote a tail, (H, H) indicates the experimental outcome with a head on the first coin and a head on the second coin. Continuing this notation, we can describe the sample space (S) for this coin-tossing experiment as follows:

$$S = \{(H, H), (H, T), (T, H), (T, T)\}$$

Thus, we see that four experimental outcomes are possible. In this case, it is not difficult to list all of the experimental outcomes.

The counting rule for multiple-step experiments makes it possible to determine the number of experimental outcomes without listing them.

A Counting Rule for Multiple-Step Experiments

If an experiment can be described as a sequence of k steps with n_1 possible outcomes on the first step, n_2 possible outcomes on the second step, and so on, then the total number of experimental outcomes is given by $(n_1)(n_2)\cdots(n_k)$.

Viewing the experiment of tossing two coins as a sequence of first tossing one coin ($n_1 = 2$) and then tossing the other coin ($n_2 = 2$), we can see from the counting rule that there are $(2)(2) = 4$ distinct experimental outcomes. As shown, they are $S = \{(H, H), (H, T), (T, H), (T, T)\}$. The number of experimental outcomes in an experiment involving tossing six coins is $(2)(2)(2)(2)(2)(2) = 64$.

A graphical representation that is helpful in visualizing an experiment and enumerating outcomes in a multiple-step experiment is a *tree diagram*. Figure 4.2 shows a tree diagram for the experiment of tossing two coins. The sequence of steps is depicted by moving from left to right through the tree. Step 1 corresponds to tossing the first coin and has two branches corresponding to the two possible outcomes. Step 2 corresponds to tossing the second coin and, for each possible outcome at step 1, has two branches corresponding to the two possible outcomes at step 2. Finally, each of the points on the right end of the tree corresponds to an experimental outcome. Each path through the tree from the leftmost node to one of the nodes at the right side of the tree corresponds to a unique sequence of outcomes.

> Without the tree diagram, one might think there are only three experimental outcomes for two tosses of a coin: 0 heads, 1 head, and 2 heads.

Let us now see how the counting rule for multiple-step experiments can be used in the analysis of a capacity expansion project faced by the Kentucky Power & Light Company (KP&L). KP&L is starting a project designed to increase the generating capacity of one of its plants in northern Kentucky. The project is divided into two sequential stages or steps: stage 1 (design) and stage 2 (construction). While each stage will be scheduled and controlled as closely as possible, management cannot predict beforehand the exact time required to com-

---

Figure 4.2   TREE DIAGRAM FOR THE EXPERIMENT OF TOSSING TWO COINS

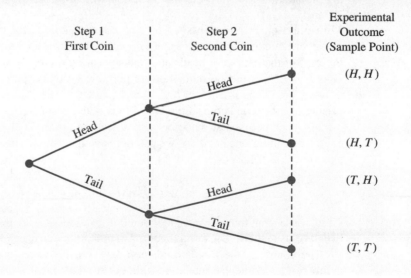

plete each stage of the project. An analysis of similar construction projects has shown completion times for the design stage of 2, 3, or 4 months and completion times for the construction stage of 6, 7, or 8 months. In addition, because of the critical need for additional electrical power, management has set a goal of 10 months for the completion of the entire project.

Because this project has three possible completion times for the design stage (step 1) and three possible completion times for the construction stage (step 2), the counting rule for multiple-step experiments can be applied here to determine a total of (3)(3) = 9 experimental outcomes. To describe the experimental outcomes, we will use a two-number notation; for instance, (2, 6) will indicate that the design stage is completed in 2 months and the construction stage is completed in 6 months. This experimental outcome results in a total of 2 + 6 = 8 months to complete the entire project. Table 4.1 summarizes the nine experimental outcomes for the KP&L problem. The tree diagram in Figure 4.3 shows how the nine outcomes (sample points) occur.

The counting rule and tree diagram have been used to help the project manager identify the experimental outcomes and determine the possible project completion times. From the information in Figure 4.3, we see that the project will be completed in 8 to 12 months, with six of the nine experimental outcomes providing the desired completion time of 10 months or less. While it has been helpful to identify the experimental outcomes, we will need to consider how probability values can be assigned to the experimental outcomes before making an assessment of the probability that the project will be completed within the desired 10 months.

Combinations.   A second counting rule that is often useful allows one to count the number of experimental outcomes when n objects are to be selected from a set of N objects. It is called the counting rule for combinations.

Counting Rule for Combinations

The number of combinations of N objects taken n at a time is

$$C_n^N = \binom{N}{n} = \frac{N!}{n!(N - n)!} \tag{4.1}$$

where

$$N! = N(N - 1)(N - 2) \cdots (2)(1)$$
$$n! = n(n - 1)(n - 2) \cdots (2)(1)$$

and

$$0! = 1$$

The notation ! means *factorial;* for example, 5 factorial is 5! = (5)(4)(3)(2)(1) = 120. By definition, 0! is equal to 1.

As an illustration of the counting rule for combinations, consider a quality control procedure where an inspector randomly selects two of five parts to test for defects. In a group of five parts, how many combinations of two parts can be selected? The counting rule in (4.1) shows that with $N = 5$ and $n = 2$, we have

In sampling from a finite population of size N, the counting rule for combinations is used to find the number of different samples of size n that can be selected.

$$C_2^5 = \binom{5}{2} = \frac{5!}{2!(5 - 2)!} = \frac{(5)(4)(3)(2)(1)}{(2)(1)(3)(2)(1)} = \frac{120}{12} = 10$$

Table 4.1	**LISTING OF EXPERIMENTAL OUTCOMES (SAMPLE POINTS) FOR THE KP&L PROBLEM**		

Completion Time (months)

Stage 1 (Design)	Stage 2 (Construction)	Notation for Experimental Outcome	Total Project Completion Time (months)
2	6	(2, 6)	8
2	7	(2, 7)	9
2	8	(2, 8)	10
3	6	(3, 6)	9
3	7	(3, 7)	10
3	8	(3, 8)	11
4	6	(4, 6)	10
4	7	(4, 7)	11
4	8	(4, 8)	12

Figure 4.3	**TREE DIAGRAM FOR THE KP&L PROJECT**

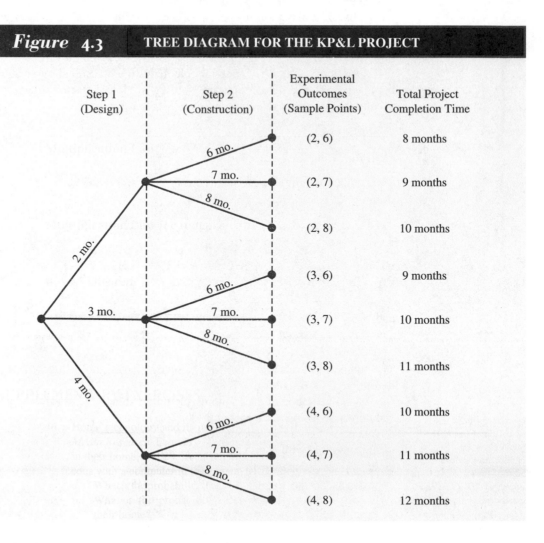

Thus, 10 outcomes are possible for the experiment of randomly selecting two parts from a group of five. If we label the five parts as A, B, C, D, and E, the 10 combinations or experimental outcomes can be identified as AB, AC, AD, AE, BC, BD, BE, CD, CE, and DE.

As another example, consider that the Ohio lottery system uses the random selection of six integers from a group of 47 to determine the weekly lottery winner. The counting rule for combinations, equation (4.1), can be used to determine the number of ways six different integers can be selected from a group of 47.

$$\binom{47}{6} = \frac{47!}{6!(47-6)!} = \frac{47!}{6!41!} = \frac{(47)(46)(45)(44)(43)(42)}{(6)(5)(4)(3)(2)(1)} = 10,737,573$$

The counting rule for combinations shows that the chance of winning the lottery is slim.

The counting rule for combinations tells us that more than 10 million experimental outcomes are possible in the lottery drawing. An individual who buys a lottery ticket has 1 chance in 10,737,573 of winning.

Permutations.   A third counting rule that is sometimes useful is the counting rule for permutations. It allows one to compute the number of experimental outcomes when n objects are to be selected from a set of N objects where the order of selection is important. The same n objects selected in a different order is considered a different experimental outcome.

Counting Rule for Permutations

The number of permutations of N objects taken n at a time is given by

$$P_n^N = n!\binom{N}{n} = \frac{N!}{(N-n)!} \tag{4.2}$$

The counting rule for permutations is closely related to the one for combinations; however, an experiment will have more permutations than combinations for the same number of objects. This is because for every selection of n objects there are $n!$ different ways to order them.

As an example, consider again the quality control process in which an inspector selects two of five parts to inspect for defects. How many permutations may be selected? The counting rule in equation (4.2) shows that with $N = 5$ and $n = 2$, we have

$$P_2^5 = \frac{5!}{(5-2)!} = \frac{5!}{3!} = \frac{(5)(4)(3)(2)(1)}{(3)(2)(1)} = (5)(4) = 20$$

Thus, 20 outcomes are possible for the experiment of randomly selecting two parts from a group of five when the order of selection must be taken into account. If we label the parts A, B, C, D, and E, the 20 permutations are AB, BA, AC, CA, AD, DA, AE, EA, BC, CB, BD, DB, BE, EB, CD, DC, CE, EC, DE, and ED.

Assigning Probabilities

Now let us see how probabilities can be assigned to experimental outcomes. The three approaches most frequently used are the classical, relative frequency, and subjective methods. Regardless of the method used, the probabilities assigned must satisfy two basic requirements.

Basic Requirements for Assigning Probabilities

1. The probability assigned to each experimental outcome must be between 0 and 1, inclusively. If we let E_i denote the ith experimental outcome and $P(E_i)$ be its probability, then this requirement can be written as

$$0 \leq P(E_i) \leq 1 \text{ for all } i \tag{4.3}$$

2. The sum of the probabilities for all the experimental outcomes must equal 1. For n experimental outcomes, this requirement can be written as

$$P(E_1) + P(E_2) + \cdots + P(E_n) = 1 \tag{4.4}$$

The *classical method* of assigning probabilities is appropriate when all the experimental outcomes are equally likely. If n experimental outcomes are possible, a probability of $1/n$ is assigned to each experimental outcome. When using this approach, the two basic requirements for assigning probabilities are automatically satisfied.

For an example, consider the experiment of tossing a fair coin, the two experimental outcomes—head and tail—are equally likely. Because one of the two equally likely outcomes is a head, the probability of observing a head is $\frac{1}{2}$, or .50. Similarly, the probability of observing a tail is also $\frac{1}{2}$, or .50.

As an another example, consider the experiment of rolling a die. It would seem reasonable to conclude that the six possible outcomes are equally likely, and hence each outcome is assigned a probability of $\frac{1}{6}$. If $P(1)$ denotes the probability that one dot appears on the upward face of the die, then $P(1) = \frac{1}{6}$. Similarly, $P(2) = \frac{1}{6}$. $P(3) = \frac{1}{6}$, $P(4) = \frac{1}{6}$, $P(5) = \frac{1}{6}$, and $P(6) = \frac{1}{6}$. Note that requirements (4.3) and (4.4) are both satisfied because each of the probabilities is greater than or equal to zero and they sum to one.

The *relative frequency method* of assigning probabilities is appropriate when data are available to estimate the proportion of the time the experimental outcome will occur if the experiment is repeated a large number of times. As an example consider a study of waiting times in the X-ray department for a local hospital. The number of patients waiting for service at 9:00 A.M. was recorded for 20 successive days. The following results were obtained.

Number Waiting	Number of Days Outcome Occurred
0	2
1	5
2	6
3	4
4	3
Total	20

These data show that on 2 of the 20 days, zero patients were waiting for service; on 5 of the days, one patient was waiting for service; and so on. Using the relative frequency method, we would assign a probability of $2/20 = .10$ to the experimental outcome of zero patients waiting for service, $5/20 = .25$ to the experimental outcome of one patient waiting, $6/20 = .30$ to two patients waiting, $4/20 = .20$ to three patients waiting, and $3/20 = .15$ to four patients waiting.

As with the classical method, the two basic requirements of (4.3) and (4.4) are automatically satisfied when the relative frequency method is used.

The *subjective method* of assigning probabilities is most appropriate when it is unrealistic to assume that the experimental outcomes are equally likely and when little relevant data are available. When the subjective method is used to assign probabilities to the experimental outcomes, we may use any information available, such as our experience or intuition. After considering all available information, a probability value that expresses our *degree of belief* (on a scale from 0 to 1) that the experimental outcome will occur is specified. Because subjective probability expresses a person's degree of belief, it is personal. Using the subjective method, different people can be expected to assign different probabilities to the same experimental outcome.

When using the subjective probability assignment method, extra care must be taken to ensure that requirements (4.3) and (4.4) are satisfied. Regardless of a person's degree of belief, the probability value assigned to each experimental outcome must be between 0 and 1, inclusive, and the sum of all the experimental outcome probabilities must equal one.

Consider the case in which Tom and Judy Elsbernd have just made an offer to purchase a house. Two outcomes are possible:

$$E_1 = \text{their offer is accepted}$$
$$E_2 = \text{their offer is rejected}$$

Judy believes that the probability their offer will be accepted is .8; thus, Judy would set $P(E_1) = .8$ and $P(E_2) = .2$. Tom, however, believes that the probability that their offer will be accepted is .6; hence, Tom would set $P(E_1) = .6$ and $P(E_2) = .4$. Note that Tom's probability estimate for E_1 reflects the fact that he is a bit more pessimistic than Judy about their offer being accepted.

Both Judy and Tom have assigned probabilities that satisfy the two basic requirements. The fact that their probability estimates are different emphasizes the personal nature of the subjective method.

Even in business situations where either the classical or the relative frequency approach can be applied, managers may want to provide subjective probability estimates. In such cases, the best probability estimates often are obtained by combining the estimates from the classical or relative frequency approach with subjective probability estimates.

Bayes' theorem (see Section 4.5) provides a means for combining subjectively determined prior probabilities with probabilities obtained by other means to obtain revised, or posterior, probabilities.

Probabilities for the KP&L Project

To perform further analysis on the KP&L project, we must develop probabilities for each of the nine experimental outcomes listed in Table 4.1. On the basis of experience and judgment, management concluded that the experimental outcomes were not equally likely. Hence, the classical method of assigning probabilities could not be used. Management then decided to conduct a study of the completion times for similar projects undertaken by KP&L over the past three years. The results of a study of 40 similar projects are summarized in Table 4.2.

After reviewing the results of the study, management decided to employ the relative frequency method of assigning probabilities. Management could have provided subjective

Table 4.2   COMPLETION RESULTS FOR 40 KP&L PROJECTS

Completion Time (months)		Sample Point	Number of Past Projects Having These Completion Times
Stage 1	Stage 2		
2	6	(2, 6)	6
2	7	(2, 7)	6
2	8	(2, 8)	2
3	6	(3, 6)	4
3	7	(3, 7)	8
3	8	(3, 8)	2
4	6	(4, 6)	2
4	7	(4, 7)	4
4	8	(4, 8)	6
		Total	40

probability estimates, but felt that the current project was quite similar to the 40 previous projects. Thus, the relative frequency method was judged best.

In using the data in Table 4.2 to compute probabilities, we note that outcome (2, 6)—stage 1 completed in 2 months and stage 2 completed in 6 months—occurred six times in the 40 projects. We can use the relative frequency method to assign a probability of $6/40 = .15$ to this outcome. Similarly, outcome (2, 7) also occurred in six of the 40 projects, providing a $6/40 = .15$ probability. Continuing in this manner, we obtain the probability assignments for the sample points of the KP&L project shown in Table 4.3. Note that $P(2, 6)$ represents the probability of the sample point (2, 6), $P(2, 7)$ represents the probability of the sample point (2, 7), and so on.

Table 4.3   PROBABILITY ASSIGNMENTS FOR THE KP&L PROBLEM BASED ON THE RELATIVE FREQUENCY METHOD

Sample Point	Project Completion Time	Probability of Sample Point
(2, 6)	8 months	$P(2, 6) = 6/40 = .15$
(2, 7)	9 months	$P(2, 7) = 6/40 = .15$
(2, 8)	10 months	$P(2, 8) = 2/40 = .05$
(3, 6)	9 months	$P(3, 6) = 4/40 = .10$
(3, 7)	10 months	$P(3, 7) = 8/40 = .20$
(3, 8)	11 months	$P(3, 8) = 2/40 = .05$
(4, 6)	10 months	$P(4, 6) = 2/40 = .05$
(4, 7)	11 months	$P(4, 7) = 4/40 = .10$
(4, 8)	12 months	$P(4, 8) = 6/40 = .15$
	Total	1.00

N O T E S
and Comments

1. In statistics, the notion of an experiment is somewhat different from the notion of an experiment in the physical sciences. In the physical sciences, an experiment is usually conducted in a laboratory or a controlled environment in order to learn about a scientific occurrence. In statistical experiments, the outcomes are determined by probability. Even though the experiment is repeated in exactly the same way, an entirely different outcome may occur. Because of this influence of probability on the outcome, the experiments of statistics are sometimes called *random experiments*.

2. When drawing a random sample without replacement from a population of size N, the counting rule for combinations is used to find the number of different samples of size n that can be selected.

EXERCISES

Methods

1. An experiment has three steps with three outcomes possible for the first step, two outcomes possible for the second step, and four outcomes possible for the third step. How many experimental outcomes exist for the entire experiment?

2. How many ways can three items be selected from a group of six items? Use the letters A, B, C, D, E, and F to identify the items, and list each of the different combinations of three items.

SELF TEST

3. How many permutations of three items can be selected from a group of six? Use the letters A, B, C, D, E, and F to identify the items, and list each of the permutations when the three items (B, D, F) are selected.

4. Consider the experiment of tossing a coin three times.
   a. Develop a tree diagram for the experiment.
   b. List the experimental outcomes.
   c. What is the probability for each outcome?

5. Suppose an experiment has five equally likely outcomes: E_1, E_2, E_3, E_4, E_5. Assign probabilities to each outcome and show that conditions (4.3) and (4.4) are satisfied. What method did you use?

SELF TEST

6. An experiment with three outcomes has been repeated 50 times, and it was learned that E_1 occurred 20 times. E_2 occurred 13 times, and E_3 occurred 17 times. Assign probabilities to the outcomes. What method did you use?

7. A decision maker has subjectively assigned the following probabilities to the four outcomes of an experiment: $P(E_1) = .10$, $P(E_2) = .15$, $P(E_3) = .40$, and $P(E_4) = .20$. Are these valid probability assignments? Check to see whether (4.3) and (4.4) are satisfied.

Applications

8. In the city of Milford, applications for zoning changes go through a two-step process: a review by the planning commission and a final decision by the city council. At step 1 the planning commission will review the zoning change request and make a positive or negative recommendation concerning the change. At step 2 the city council will review the planning commission's recommendation and then vote to approve or to disapprove the zoning change. An application for a zoning change has just been submitted by the developer of an apartment complex. Consider the application process as an experiment.
   a. How many sample points are there for this experiment? List the sample points.
   b. Construct a tree diagram for the experiment.

9. Simple random sampling uses a sample of size n from a population of size N to obtain data that can be used to make inferences about the characteristics of a population. Suppose we have a population of 50 bank accounts and want to take a random sample of four accounts in order to learn about the population. How many different random samples of four accounts are possible?

10. Many school systems now provide Internet access for their students. As of 1996, Internet access was provided at 21,733 elementary schools, 7286 junior high schools, and 10,682 high schools (*Statistical Abstract of the United States,* 1997). There are a total of 51,745 elementary schools, 14,012 junior high schools, and 17,229 high schools.
    a. If you randomly choose an elementary school to visit, what is the probability it will have Internet access?
    b. If you randomly choose a junior high school to visit, what is the probability it will have Internet access?
    c. If you randomly choose a school to visit, what is the probability it will be an elementary school?
    d. If you randomly choose a school to visit, what is the probability it will have Internet access?

11. Strom Construction has made bids on two contracts. The owner has identified the possible outcomes and subjectively assigned the following probabilities.

Experimental Outcome	Obtain Contract 1	Obtain Contract 2	Probability
1	Yes	Yes	.15
2	Yes	No	.15
3	No	Yes	.30
4	No	No	.25

   a. Are these valid probability assignments? Why or why not?
   b. What would have to be done to make the probability assignments valid?

12. State lotteries have become popular means of fund raising. The Powerball lottery is open to participants across several states. When entering the Powerball lottery, a participant selects five numbers from the digits 1 through 49 and then selects a powerball number from the digits 1 through 42. One week in 1998 the Powerball lottery jackpot reached $150,000,000, in addition to a payoff of $100,000 for anybody selecting the first five numbers correctly.
    a. Compute the number of ways the first five numbers can be selected.
    b. What is the probability of winning the $100,000 prize by selecting the first five numbers correctly?
    c. What is the probability of winning the powerball jackpot?

13. A company that manufactures toothpaste is studying five different package designs. Assuming that one design is just as likely to be selected by a consumer as any other design, what selection probability would you assign to each of the package designs? In an actual experiment, 100 consumers were asked to pick the design they preferred. The following data were obtained. Do the data appear to confirm the belief that one design is just as likely to be selected as another? Explain.

Design	Number of Times Preferred
1	5
2	15
3	30
4	40
5	10

Because this event is given by $C = \{(2, 6), (2, 7), (2, 8), (3, 6), (3, 7), (4, 6)\}$, the probability ($P$) of event C is given by

$$P(C) = P(2, 6) + P(2, 7) + P(2, 8) + P(3, 6) + P(3, 7) + P(4, 6)$$

Refer to the sample point probabilities in Table 4.3; we have

$$P(C) = .15 + .15 + .05 + .10 + .20 + .05 = .70$$

Similarly, because the event that the project is completed in less than 10 months is given by $L = \{(2, 6), (2, 7), (3, 6)\}$, the probability of this event is given by

$$P(L) = P(2, 6) + P(2, 7) + P(3, 6)$$
$$= .15 + .15 + .10 = .40$$

Finally, for the event that the project is completed in more than 10 months, we have $M = \{(3, 8), (4, 7), (4, 8)\}$ and thus

$$P(M) = P(3, 8) + P(4, 7) + P(4, 8)$$
$$= .05 + .10 + .15 = .30$$

Using these probability results, we can now tell KP&L management that there is a .70 probability that the project will be completed in 10 months or less, a .40 probability that the project will be completed in less than 10 months, and a .30 probability that the project will be completed in more than 10 months. This procedure of computing event probabilities can be repeated for any event of interest to the KP&L management.

Any time that we can identify all the sample points of an experiment and assign the corresponding sample point probabilities, we can use the definition to compute the probability of an event. However, in many experiments the number of sample points is large and the identification of the sample points, as well as the determination of their associated probabilities, is extremely cumbersome, if not impossible. In the remaining sections of this chapter, we present some basic probability relationships that can be used to compute the probability of an event without knowledge of all sample point probabilities.

**N O T E S
and Comments**

1. The sample space, S, is an event. Because it contains all the experimental outcomes, it has a probability of 1; that is, $P(S) = 1$.
2. When the classical method is used to assign probabilities, the assumption is that the experimental outcomes are equally likely. In such cases, the probability of an event can be computed by counting the number of experimental outcomes in the event and dividing the result by the total number of experimental outcomes.

EXERCISES

Methods

14. An experiment has four equally likely outcomes: E_1, E_2, E_3, and E_4.
    a. What is the probability that E_2 occurs?
    b. What is the probability that any two of the outcomes occur (e.g., E_1 or E_3)?
    c. What is the probability that any three of the outcomes occur (e.g., E_1 or E_2 or E_4)?

4.2   EVENTS AND THEIR PROBABILITIES

Until now we have used the term "event" much as it would be used in everyday language. We must now introduce the formal definition of an *event* as it relates to probability.

Event

An *event* is a collection of sample points.

For an example, let us return to the KP&L problem and assume that the project manager is interested in the event that the entire project can be completed in 10 months or less. Referring to Table 4.3, we see that six sample points—(2, 6), (2, 7), (2, 8), (3, 6), (3, 7), and (4, 6)—provide a project completion time of 10 months or less. Let C denote the event that the project is completed in 10 months or less; we write

$$C = \{(2, 6), (2, 7), (2, 8), (3, 6), (3, 7), (4, 6)\}$$

Event C is said to occur if *any one* of these six sample points appears as the experimental outcome.

Other events that might be of interest to KP&L management include the following.

L = the event that the project is completed in *less* than 10 months
M = the event that the project is completed in *more* than 10 months

Using the information in Table 4.3, we see that these events consist of the following sample points.

$$L = \{(2, 6), (2, 7), (3, 6)\}$$
$$M = \{(3, 8), (4, 7), (4, 8)\}$$

A variety of additional events can be defined for the KP&L problem, but in each case the event must be identified as a collection of sample points for the experiment.

Given the probabilities of the sample points shown in Table 4.3, we can use the following definition to compute the probability of any event that KP&L management might want to consider.

Probability of an Event

The probability of any event is equal to the sum of the probabilities of the sample points in the event.

Using this definition, we calculate the probability of a particular event by adding the probabilities of the sample points (experimental outcomes) that make up the event. We can now compute the probability that the project will take 10 months or less to complete.

15. Consider the experiment of selecting a card from a deck of 52 cards. Each card corresponds to a sample point with a 1/52 probability.
    a. List the sample points in the event an ace is selected.
    b. List the sample points in the event a club is selected.
    c. List the sample points in the event a face card (jack, queen, or king) is selected.
    d. Find the probabilities associated with each of the events in (a), (b), and (c).

16. Consider the experiment of rolling a pair of dice. Suppose that we are interested in the sum of the face values showing on the dice.
    a. How many sample points are possible? (Hint: Use the counting rule for multiple-step experiments.)
    b. List the sample points.
    c. What is the probability of obtaining a value of 7?
    d. What is the probability of obtaining a value of 9 or greater?
    e. Because each roll has six possible even values (2, 4, 6, 8, 10, and 12) and only five possible odd values (3, 5, 7, 9, and 11), the dice should show even values more often than odd values. Do you agree with this statement? Explain.
    f. What method did you use to assign the probabilities requested above?

Applications

17. Refer to the KP&L sample points and sample point probabilities in Table 4.3.
    a. The design stage (stage 1) will run over budget if it takes 4 months to complete. List the sample points in the event the design stage is over budget.
    b. What is the probability that the design stage is over budget?
    c. The construction stage (stage 2) will run over budget if it takes 8 months to complete. List the sample points in the event the construction stage is over budget.
    d. What is the probability that the construction stage is over budget?
    e. What is the probability that both stages are over budget?

18. Suppose that a manager of a large apartment complex provides the following subjective probability estimates about the number of vacancies that will exist next month.

Vacancies	Probability
0	.05
1	.15
2	.35
3	.25
4	.10
5	.10

List the sample points in each of the following events and provide the probability of the event.
    a. No vacancies.
    b. At least four vacancies.
    c. Two or fewer vacancies.

19. The manager of a furniture store sells from 0 to 4 china hutches each week. On the basis of past experience, the following probabilities are assigned to sales of 0, 1, 2, 3, or 4 hutches: $P(0) = .08$; $P(1) = .18$; $P(2) = .32$; $P(3) = .30$; and $P(4) = .12$.
    a. Are these valid probability assignments? Why or why not?
    b. Let A be the event that 2 or fewer are sold in one week. Find $P(A)$.
    c. Let B be the event that 4 or more are sold in one week. Find $P(B)$.

20. The 1995 *Wall Street Journal* Subscriber Study revealed characteristics of the *Journal's* subscribers, including business responsibilities, investment activities, lifestyle characteristics, and personal affluence. The following data show the total value of stock owned by the 2536 respondents.

Amount	Number
Less than $15,000	347
$15,000–49,999	411
$50,000–99,999	335
$100,000–299,999	619
$300,000 or more	824

Suppose a subscriber is selected at random. What are the probabilities of the following events?
   a. Let A be the event that the total value of stock owned is at least $50,000 but less than $100,000. Find $P(A)$.
   b. Let B be the event that the total value of stock owned is less than $50,000. Find $P(B)$.
   c. Let C be the event that the total value of stock owned is $100,000 or more. Find $P(C)$.

21. A survey of 50 students at Tarpon Springs College about the number of extracurricular activities resulted in the data shown.

Number of Activities	Frequency
0	8
1	20
2	12
3	6
4	3
5	1

   a. Let A be the event that a student participates in at least 1 activity. Find $P(A)$.
   b. Let B be the event that a student participates in 3 or more activities. Find $P(B)$.
   c. What is the probability that a student participates in exactly 2 activities?

4.3   SOME BASIC RELATIONSHIPS OF PROBABILITY

Complement of an Event

Given an event A, the *complement* of A is defined to be the event consisting of all sample points that are *not* in A. The complement of A is denoted by A^c. Figure 4.4 is a diagram, known as a *Venn diagram,* which illustrates the concept of a complement. The rectangular area represents the sample space for the experiment and as such contains all possible sample points. The circle represents event A and contains only the sample points that belong to A. The shaded region of the rectangle contains all sample points not in event A, and is by definition the complement of A.

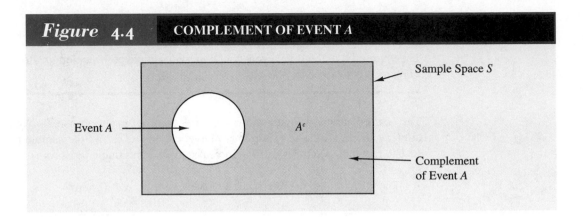

Figure 4.4   COMPLEMENT OF EVENT *A*

Sample Space *S*

Event *A*

A^c

Complement of Event *A*

The union of an event and its complement is the entire sample space.

In any probability application, either event *A* or its complement A^c must occur. Therefore, we have

$$P(A) + P(A^c) = 1$$

Solving for $P(A)$, we obtain the following result.

Computing Probability Using the Complement

$$P(A) = 1 - P(A^c) \tag{4.5}$$

Equation (4.5) shows that the probability of an event *A* can be computed easily if the probability of its complement, $P(A^c)$, is known.

As an example, consider the case of a sales manager who, after reviewing sales reports, states that 80% of new customer contacts result in no sale. By allowing *A* to denote the event of a sale and A^c to denote the event of no sale, the manager is stating that $P(A^c) = .80$. Using (4.5), we see that

$$P(A) = 1 - P(A^c) = 1 - .80 = .20$$

We can conclude that a new customer contact has a .20 probability of resulting in a sale.

In another example, a purchasing agent states that there is a .90 probability that a supplier will send a shipment that is free of defective parts. Using the complement, we can conclude that there is a $1 - .90 = .10$ probability that the shipment will contain defective parts.

Addition Law

The addition law is helpful when we have two events and are interested in knowing the probability that at least one of the events occurs. That is, with events *A* and *B* we are interested in knowing the probability that event *A* or event *B* or both occur.

Before we present the addition law, we need to discuss two concepts related to the combination of events: the *union* of events and the *intersection* of events. Given two events *A* and *B*, the union of *A* and *B* is defined as follows.

Union of Two Events

The *union* of A and B is the event containing *all* sample points belonging to *A or B or both*. The union is denoted by $A \cup B$.

The Venn diagram in Figure 4.5 depicts the union of events A and B. Note that the two circles contain all the sample points in event A as well as all the sample points in event B. The fact that the circles overlap indicates that some sample points are contained in both A and B.

The definition of the intersection of two events A and B follows.

Intersection of Two Events

Given two events A and B, the *intersection* of A and B is the event containing the sample points belonging to *both A and B*. The intersection is denoted by $A \cap B$.

The Venn diagram depicting the intersection of the two events is shown in Figure 4.6. The area where the two circles overlap is the intersection; it contains the sample points that are in both A and B.

Let us now continue with a discussion of the addition law. The *addition law* provides a way to compute the probability of event A or B or both A and B occurring. In other words, the addition law is used to compute the probability of the union of two events, $A \cup B$. The addition law is written as follows.

Addition Law

$$P(A \cup B) = P(A) + P(B) - P(A \cap B) \tag{4.6}$$

To grasp the addition law intuitively, note that the first two terms in the addition law, $P(A) + P(B)$, account for all the sample points in $A \cup B$. However, because the sample points in the intersection $A \cap B$ are in both A and B, when we compute $P(A) + P(B)$, we

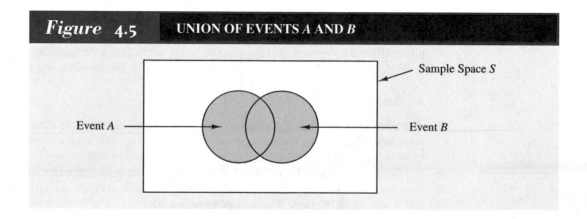

Figure 4.5   UNION OF EVENTS *A* AND *B*

Sample Space *S*

Event *A*   Event *B*

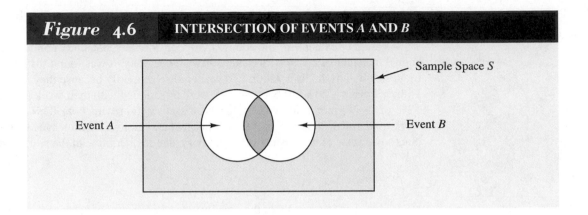

Figure 4.6   **INTERSECTION OF EVENTS *A* AND *B***

Sample Space *S*

Event *A*

Event *B*

are in effect counting each of the sample points in $A \cap B$ twice. We correct for this by subtracting $P(A \cap B)$.

As an example of an application of the addition law, let us consider the case of a small assembly plant with 50 employees. Each worker is expected to complete work assignments on time and in such a way that the assembled product will pass a final inspection. On occasion, some of the workers fail to meet the performance standards by completing work late and/or assembling defective products. At the end of a performance evaluation period, the production manager found that 5 of the 50 workers had completed work late, 6 of the 50 workers had assembled defective products, and 2 of the 50 workers had both completed work late *and* assembled defective products.

Let

$$L = \text{the event that the work is completed late}$$

$$D = \text{the event that the assembled product is defective}$$

The relative frequency information leads to the following probabilities.

$$P(L) = \frac{5}{50} = .10$$

$$P(D) = \frac{6}{50} = .12$$

$$P(L \cap D) = \frac{2}{50} = .04$$

After reviewing the performance data, the production manager decided to assign a poor performance rating to any employee whose work was either late or defective; thus the event of interest is $L \cup D$. What is the probability that the production manager assigned an employee a poor performance rating?

Note that the probability question is about the union of two events. Specifically, we want to know $P(L \cup D)$. Using (4.6), we have

$$P(L \cup D) = P(L) + P(D) - P(L \cap D)$$

Knowing values for the three probabilities on the right side of this expression, we can write

$$P(L \cup D) = .10 + .12 - .04 = .18$$

This calculation tells us that there is a .18 probability that an employee received a poor performance rating.

As another example of the addition law, consider a recent study conducted by the personnel manager of a major computer software company. It was found that 30% of the employees who left the firm within two years did so primarily because they were dissatisfied with their salary, 20% left because they were dissatisfied with their work assignments, and 12% of the former employees indicated dissatisfaction with *both* their salary and their work assignments. What is the probability that an employee who leaves within two years does so because of dissatisfaction with salary, dissatisfaction with the work assignment, or both?

Let

$$S = \text{the event that the employee leaves because of salary}$$
$$W = \text{the event that the employee leaves because of work assignment}$$

We have $P(S) = .30$, $P(W) = .20$, and $P(S \cap W) = .12$. Using (4.6), the addition law, we have

$$P(S \cup W) = P(S) + P(W) - P(S \cap W) = .30 + .20 - .12 = .38.$$

We find that there is a .38 probability that an employee leaves for salary or work assignment reasons.

Before we conclude our discussion of the addition law, let us consider a special case that arises for *mutually exclusive events.*

Mutually Exclusive Events

Two events are said to be *mutually exclusive* if the events have no sample points in common.

Events *A* and *B* are mutually exclusive if, when one event occurs, the other cannot occur. Thus, a requirement for *A* and *B* to be mutually exclusive is that their intersection must contain no sample points. The Venn diagram depicting two mutually exclusive events *A* and *B* is shown in Figure 4.7. In this case $P(A \cap B) = 0$ and the addition law can be written as follows.

Figure 4.7   MUTUALLY EXCLUSIVE EVENTS

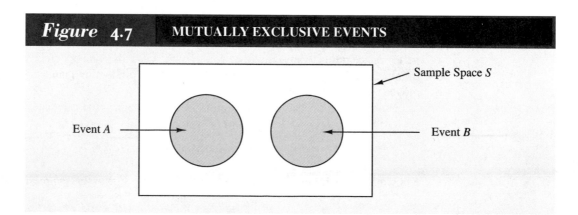

Addition Law for Mutually Exclusive Events

$$P(A \cup B) = P(A) + P(B)$$

..../ /...........

EXERCISES

Methods

22. Suppose that we have a sample space with five equally likely experimental outcomes: E_1, E_2, E_3, E_4, E_5. Let

$$A = \{E_1, E_2\}$$
$$B = \{E_3, E_4\}$$
$$C = \{E_2, E_3, E_5\}$$

a. Find $P(A)$, $P(B)$, and $P(C)$.
b. Find $P(A \cup B)$. Are A and B mutually exclusive?
c. Find A^c, C^c, $P(A^c)$, and $P(C^c)$.
d. Find $A \cup B^c$ and $P(A \cup B^c)$.
e. Find $P(B \cup C)$.

SELF TEST

23. Suppose that we have a sample space $S = \{E_1, E_2, E_3, E_4, E_5, E_6, E_7\}$, where $E_1, E_2, \ldots, E_7$ denote the sample points. The following probability assignments apply: $P(E_1) = .05$, $P(E_2) = .20$, $P(E_3) = .20$, $P(E_4) = .25$, $P(E_5) = .15$, $P(E_6) = .10$, and $P(E_7) = .05$. Let

$$A = \{E_1, E_4, E_6\}$$
$$B = \{E_2, E_4, E_7\}$$
$$C = \{E_2, E_3, E_5, E_7\}$$

a. Find $P(A)$, $P(B)$, and $P(C)$.
b. Find $A \cup B$ and $P(A \cup B)$.
c. Find $A \cap B$ and $P(A \cap B)$.
d. Are events A and C mutually exclusive?
e. Find B^c and $P(B^c)$.

Applications

24. According to a *Business Week/*Harris poll, 14% of adults felt the chance of a big crash in the stock market during 1998 was very likely, and 43% felt the chance of a big crash during 1998 was somewhat likely (*Business Week,* December 29, 1997). If we were to choose an adult at random, what is the probability that she or he would indicate a crash was not likely?

25. A survey of benefits for 254 corporate executives (*Business Week,* October 24, 1994) showed that 155 executives were provided mobile phones, 152 were provided club memberships, and 110 were provided both mobile phones and club memberships as perks associated with their position.
a. Let M be the event of having a mobile phone and C be the event of having a club membership. Find the following probabilities: $P(M)$, $P(C)$, and $P(M \cap C)$.
b. Use the probabilities in part (a) to compute the probability that a corporate executive has at least one of the two perks.
c. What is the probability that a corporate executive does not have either of these perks?

26. A *U.S. News*/UCLA survey of 867 entertainment leaders in Hollywood studied how the entertainment industry views itself in terms of the amount of violence on television and the general quality of television programming (*U.S. News & World Report,* May 9, 1994). Results showed that 624 leaders felt the amount of violent programming had increased in the last 10 years, 390 felt the quality of programming had decreased over the same 10 years, and 234 leaders responded both that the amount of violent programming had increased and that the quality of programming had decreased.

   a. Letting V be the event that the amount of violent programming has increased and Q be the event that the quality of programming has decreased, compute the following probabilities: $P(V)$, $P(Q)$, and $P(V \cap Q)$.

   b. Use the probabilities in part (a) to find the probability that a leader made at least one of the following two comments: the amount of violent programming has increased or the quality of programming has decreased.

   c. What is the probability that a leader did not agree with either of the two comments?

27. *Business Week* surveyed its subscribers concerning whether they consumed or served wine during an average week. The findings were that 57% consumed or served domestic wine, 33% consumed or served imported wine, and 63% consumed or served wine (*Business Week* 1996 Worldwide Subscriber Study). What is the probability that a *Business Week* subscriber consumes or serves both domestic and imported wine in an average week?

SELF TEST

28. A survey of subscribers to *Forbes* showed that 45.8% rented a car during the past 12 months for business reasons, 54% rented a car during the past 12 months for personal reasons, and 30% rented a car during the past 12 months for both business and personal reasons (*Forbes* 1993 Subscriber Study).

   a. What is the probability that a subscriber rented a car during the past 12 months for business or personal reasons?

   b. What is the probability that a subscriber did not rent a car during the past 12 months for either business or personal reasons?

29. According to the Census Bureau, deaths in the United States occur at a rate of 2,425,000 per year. The National Center for Health Statistics reported that the three leading causes of death during 1997 were heart disease (725,790), cancer (537,390), and stroke (159,877). Let H, C, and S represent the events that a person dies of heart disease, cancer, and stroke respectively.

   a. Use the data to estimate $P(H)$, $P(C)$, and $P(S)$.

   b. Are events H and C mutually exclusive? Find $P(H \cap C)$.

   c. What is the probability that a person dies from heart disease or cancer?

   d. What is the probability that a person dies from cancer or a stroke?

   e. Find the probability that someone dies from a cause other than one of these three.

4.4   CONDITIONAL PROBABILITY

Often, the probability of an event is influenced by whether a related event has occurred. Suppose we have an event A with probability $P(A)$. If we obtain new information and learn that a related event, denoted by B, has occurred, we will want to take advantage of this information in calculating a new probability for event A. This new probability of event A is written $P(A \mid B)$. The notation $\mid$ is used to denote the fact that we are considering the probability of event A *given* the condition that event B has occurred. Hence, the notation $P(A \mid B)$ is read "the probability of A given B."

As an illustration of the application of *conditional probability,* consider the situation of the promotion status of male and female officers of a major metropolitan police force in the eastern United States. The police force consists of 1200 officers, 960 men and 240 women.

Table 4.4	PROMOTION STATUS OF POLICE OFFICERS OVER THE PAST TWO YEARS			
		Men	Women	Totals
Promoted		288	36	324
Not Promoted		672	204	876
	Totals	960	240	1200

Over the past two years, 324 officers on the police force have been awarded promotions. The specific breakdown of promotions for male and female officers is shown in Table 4.4.

After reviewing the promotion record, a committee of female officers raised a discrimination case on the basis that 288 male officers had received promotions but only 36 female officers had received promotions. The police administration argued that the relatively low number of promotions for female officers was due not to discrimination, but to the fact that there are relatively few female officers on the police force. Let us show how conditional probability could be used to analyze the discrimination charge.

Let

$$M = \text{event an officer is a man}$$
$$W = \text{event an officer is a woman}$$
$$A = \text{event an officer is promoted}$$
$$A^c = \text{event an officer is not promoted}$$

Dividing the data values in Table 4.4 by the total of 1200 officers enables us to summarize the available information with the following probability values.

$P(M \cap A) = 288/1200 = .24 =$ probability that a randomly selected officer is a man *and* is promoted

$P(M \cap A^c) = 672/1200 = .56 =$ probability that a randomly selected officer is a man *and* is not promoted

$P(W \cap A) = 36/1200 \ \ = .03 =$ probability that a randomly selected officer is a woman *and* is promoted

$P(W \cap A^c) = 204/1200 = .17 =$ probability that a randomly selected officer is a woman *and* is not promoted

Because each of these values gives the probability of the intersection of two events, the probabilities are called *joint probabilities*. Table 4.5, which provides a summary of the probability information for the police officer promotion situation, is referred to as a *joint probability table*.

The values in the margins of the joint probability table provide the probabilities of each event separately. That is, $P(M) = .80$, $P(W) = .20$, $P(A) = .27$, and $P(A^c) = .73$. These probabilities are referred to as *marginal probabilities* because of their location in the margins of the joint probability table. We note that the marginal probabilities are found by summing the joint probabilities in the corresponding row or column of the

Table 4.5		JOINT PROBABILITY TABLE FOR PROMOTIONS	

Joint probabilities appear in the body of the table

	Men (M)	Women (W)	Totals
Promoted (A)	.24	.03	.27
Not Promoted (A^c)	.56	.17	.73
Totals	.80	.20	1.00

Marginal probabilities appear in the margins of the table

joint probability table. For instance, the marginal probability of being promoted is $P(A) = P(M \cap A) + P(W \cap A) = .24 + .03 = .27$. From the marginal probabilities, we see that 80% of the force is male, 20% of the force is female, 27% of all officers received promotions, and 73% were not promoted.

Let us begin the conditional probability analysis by computing the probability that an officer is promoted given that the officer is a man. In conditional probability notation, we are attempting to determine $P(A \mid M)$. To calculate $P(A \mid M)$, we first realize that this notation simply means that we are considering the probability of the event A (promotion) given that the condition designated as event M (the officer is a man) is known to exist. Thus $P(A \mid M)$ tells us that we are now concerned only with the promotion status of the 960 male officers. Because 288 of the 960 male officers received promotions, the probability of being promoted given that the officer is a man is 288/960 = .30. In other words, given that an officer is a man, there has been a 30% chance of receiving a promotion over the past two years.

This procedure was easy to apply because the values in Table 4.4 show the number of officers in each category. We now want to demonstrate how conditional probabilities such as $P(A \mid M)$ can be computed directly from event probabilities rather than the frequency data of Table 4.4.

We have shown that $P(A \mid M) = 288/960 = .30$. Let us now divide both the numerator and denominator of this fraction by 1200, the total number of officers in the study.

$$P(A \mid M) = \frac{288}{960} = \frac{288/1200}{960/1200} = \frac{.24}{.80} = .30$$

We now see that the conditional probability $P(A \mid M)$ can be computed as .24/.80. Refer to the joint probability table (Table 4.5). Note in particular that .24 is the joint probability of A and M; that is, $P(A \cap M) = .24$. Also note that .80 is the marginal probability that a randomly selected officer is a man; that is, $P(M) = .80$. Thus, the conditional probability $P(A \mid M)$ can be computed as the ratio of the joint probability $P(A \cap M)$ to the marginal probability $P(M)$.

$$P(A \mid M) = \frac{P(A \cap M)}{P(M)} = \frac{.24}{.80} = .30$$

The fact that conditional probabilities can be computed as the ratio of a joint probability to a marginal probability provides the following general formula for conditional probability calculations for two events A and B.

Conditional Probability

$$P(A \mid B) = \frac{P(A \cap B)}{P(B)} \tag{4.7}$$

or

$$P(B \mid A) = \frac{P(A \cap B)}{P(A)} \tag{4.8}$$

The Venn diagram in Figure 4.8 is helpful in obtaining an intuitive understanding of conditional probability. The circle on the right shows that event B has occurred; the portion of the circle that overlaps with event A denotes the event $(A \cap B)$. We know that once event B has occurred, the only way that we can also observe event A is for the event $(A \cap B)$ to occur. Thus, the ratio $P(A \cap B)/P(B)$ provides the conditional probability that we will observe event A given event B has already occurred.

Let us return to the issue of discrimination against the female officers. The marginal probability in row 1 of Table 4.5 shows that the probability of promotion of an officer is $P(A) = .27$ (regardless of whether that officer is male or female). However, the critical issue in the discrimination case involves the two conditional probabilities $P(A \mid M)$ and $P(A \mid W)$. That is, what is the probability of a promotion *given* that the officer is a man, and what is the probability of a promotion *given* that the officer is a woman? If these two probabilities are equal, there is no basis for a discrimination argument because the chances of a promotion are the same for male and female officers. However, a difference in the two conditional probabilities will support the position that male and female officers are treated differently in promotion decisions.

We have already determined that $P(A \mid M) = .30$. Let us now use the probability values in Table 4.5 and the basic relationship of conditional probability (4.7) to compute the

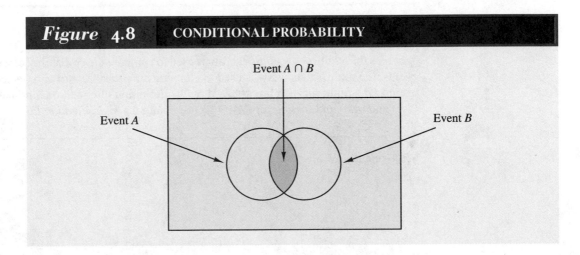

Figure 4.8   CONDITIONAL PROBABILITY

Event $A \cap B$

Event A

Event B

probability that an officer is promoted given that the officer is a woman; that is, $P(A \mid W)$. Using (4.7), we obtain

$$P(A \mid W) = \frac{P(A \cap W)}{P(W)} = \frac{.03}{.20} = .15$$

What conclusions do you draw? The probability of a promotion given that the officer is a man is .30, twice the .15 probability of a promotion given that the officer is a woman. While the use of conditional probability does not in itself prove that discrimination exists in this case, the conditional probability values support the argument presented by the female officers.

Independent Events

In the preceding illustration, $P(A) = .27$, $P(A \mid M) = .30$, and $P(A \mid W) = .15$. We see that the probability of a promotion (event A) is affected or influenced by whether the officer is a man or a woman. Particularly, since $P(A \mid M) \neq P(A)$, we would say that events A and M are *dependent* events. That is, the probability of event A (promotion) is altered or affected by knowing event M (the officer is a man) exists. Similarly, with $P(A \mid W) \neq P(A)$, we would say that events A and W are *dependent* events. However, if the probability of event A is not changed by the existence of event M—that is, $P(A \mid M) = P(A)$—we would say that events A and M are *independent* events. This situation leads to the following definition of the independence of two events.

Independent Events

Two events A and B are independent if

$$P(A \mid B) = P(A) \tag{4.9}$$

Mutually exclusive events with nonzero probabilities cannot be independent.

or

$$P(B \mid A) = P(B). \tag{4.10}$$

Otherwise, the events are dependent.

Multiplication Law

Whereas the addition law of probability is used to compute the probability of a union of two events, the multiplication law is used to compute the probability of an intersection of two events. The multiplication law is based on the definition of conditional probability. Using (4.7) and (4.8) and solving for $P(A \cap B)$, we obtain the *multiplication law*.

Multiplication Law

$$P(A \cap B) = P(B)P(A \mid B) \tag{4.11}$$

or

$$P(A \cap B) = P(A)P(B \mid A) \tag{4.12}$$

To illustrate the use of the multiplication law, consider a newspaper circulation department where it is known that 84% of the households in a particular neighborhood subscribe to the daily edition of the paper. If we let D denote the event that a household subscribes to the daily edition, $P(D) = .84$. In addition, it is known that the probability that a household who already holds a daily subscription also subscribes to the Sunday edition (event S) is .75; that is, $P(S \mid D) = .75$. What is the probability that a household subscribes to both the Sunday and daily editions of the newspaper? Using the multiplication law, we compute the desired $P(S \cap D)$ as

$$P(S \cap D) = P(D)P(S \mid D) = .84(.75) = .63$$

We now know that 63% of the households subscribe to both the Sunday and daily editions.

Before concluding this section, let us consider the special case of the multiplication law when the events involved are independent. Recall that we defined independent events to exist whenever $P(A \mid B) = P(A)$ or $P(B \mid A) = P(B)$. Hence, using (4.11) and (4.12) for the special case of independent events, we obtain the following multiplication law.

Multiplication Law for Independent Events

$$P(A \cap B) = P(A)P(B) \tag{4.13}$$

To compute the probability of the intersection of two independent events, we simply multiply the corresponding probabilities. Note that the multiplication law for independent events provides another way to determine whether A and B are independent. That is, if $P(A \cap B) = P(A)P(B)$, then A and B are independent; if $P(A \cap B) \neq P(A)P(B)$, then A and B are dependent.

As an application of the multiplication law for independent events, consider the situation of a service station manager who knows from past experience that 80% of the customers use a credit card when they purchase gasoline. What is the probability that the next two customers purchasing gasoline will each use a credit card? If we let

A = the event that the first customer uses a credit card

B = the event that the second customer uses a credit card

then the event of interest is $A \cap B$. Given no other information, we can reasonably assume that A and B are independent events. Thus,

$$P(A \cap B) = P(A)P(B) = (.80)(.80) = .64$$

N O T E S
and Comments

Do not confuse the notion of mutually exclusive events with that of independent events. Two events with nonzero probabilities cannot be both mutually exclusive and independent. If one mutually exclusive event is known to occur, the probability of the other occurring is reduced to zero. They are therefore dependent.

..../ /............

EXERCISES

Methods

SELF TEST

30. Suppose that we have two events, A and B, with $P(A) = .50$, $P(B) = .60$, and $P(A \cap B) = .40$.
    a. Find $P(A \mid B)$.
    b. Find $P(B \mid A)$.
    c. Are A and B independent? Why or why not?

31. Assume that we have two events, A and B, that are mutually exclusive. Assume further that we know $P(A) = .30$ and $P(B) = .40$.
    a. What is $P(A \cap B)$?
    b. What is $P(A \mid B)$?
    c. A student in statistics argues that the concepts of mutually exclusive events and independent events are really the same, and that if events are mutually exclusive they must be independent. Do you agree with this statement? Use the probability information in this problem to justify your answer.
    d. What general conclusion would you make about mutually exclusive and independent events given the results of this problem?

Applications

32. A Daytona Beach nightclub has the following data on the age and marital status of 140 customers.

		Marital Status	
		Single	**Married**
Age	**Under 30**	77	14
	30 or Over	28	21

a. Develop a joint probability table for these data.
b. Use the marginal probabilities to comment on the age of customers attending the club.
c. Use the marginal probabilities to comment on the marital status of customers attending the club.
d. What is the probability of finding a customer who is single and under the age of 30?
e. If a customer is under 30, what is the probability that he or she is single?
f. Is marital status independent of age? Explain, using probabilities.

SELF TEST

33. In a survey of MBA students, the following data were obtained on "students' first reason for application to the school in which they matriculated" ("School Selection by Students," *GMAC Occasional Papers,* Stolzenberg and Giarrusso, March 1988).

		Reason for Application			
		School Quality	**School Cost or Convenience**	**Other**	**Totals**
Enrollment	**Full Time**	421	393	76	890
Status	**Part Time**	400	593	46	1039
	Totals	821	986	122	1929

a. Develop a joint probability table for these data.
b. Use the marginal probabilities of school quality, cost/convenience, and other to comment on the most important reason for choosing a school.
c. If a student goes full time, what is the probability that school quality is the first reason for choosing a school?
d. If a student goes part time, what is the probability that school quality is the first reason for choosing a school?
e. Let A be the event that a student is full time and let B be the event that the student lists school quality as the first reason for applying. Are events A and B independent? Justify your answer.

34. The following table shows the distribution of blood types in the general population (Hoxworth Blood Center, Cincinnati, Ohio).

	A	B	AB	O
Rh+	34%	9%	4%	38%
Rh−	6%	2%	1%	6%

a. What is the probability a person will have type O blood?
b. What is the probability a person will be Rh−?
c. What is the probability a married couple will both be Rh−?
d. What is the probability a married couple will both have type AB blood?
e. What is the probability a person will be Rh− given she or he has type O blood?
f. What is the probability a person will have type B blood given he or she is Rh+?

35. "Since 1950, the January Barometer has predicted the annual course of the stock market with amazing accuracy" (*1998 Stock Trader's Almanac*). Over the 48 years from 1950 through 1997, the stock market has been up in January 31 times; it has been up for the year 36 times; and it has been up for the year and up for January 29 times.
a. Estimate the probability the stock market will be up in January.
b. Estimate the probability the stock market will be up for the year.
c. What is the probability the stock market will be up for the year given it is up in January?
d. Do the probabilities suggest that the stock market's January performance and its annual performance are independent events? Explain.

36. The 1995 *Wall Street Journal* Subscriber Study provided the following data on ownership of direct broadcast satellite television. The data are broken down by the four sections of the country in which a separate edition is published.

		Geographic Region			
		East	Midwest	Southwest	West
Satellite Television	**Currently own**	17	8	7	13
	Likely to purchase	107	95	30	93
	Neither	488	403	98	275

a. Construct a joint probability table.
b. What is the probability of a subscriber owning a satellite television?
c. What is the probability one of the subscribers surveyed is from the Southwest?
d. What is the probability of a subscriber from the Southwest owning satellite television?
e. Which region of the country is most likely to own satellite television?
f. Which region of the country is most likely to own satellite television a year from now?

37. A purchasing agent has placed rush orders for a particular raw material with two different suppliers, *A* and *B*. If neither order arrives in four days, the production process must be shut down until at least one of the orders arrives. The probability that supplier *A* can deliver the material in four days is .55. The probability that supplier *B* can deliver the material in four days is .35.
    a. What is the probability that both suppliers will deliver the material in four days? Because two separate suppliers are involved, we are willing to assume independence.
    b. What is the probability that at least one supplier will deliver the material in four days?
    c. What is the probability that the production process will be shut down in four days because of a shortage of raw material (that is, both orders are late)?

38. A survey of 1035 workers by the Institute for the Future and the Gallup Organization found that workers are being inundated by messages (*The Cincinnati Enquirer*, November 2, 1998). The study indicated that each worker gets an average of 190 messages per day. The following table shows the breakdown by type of message.

Source	Daily Messages	Source	Daily Messages
Telephone	52	E-mail	30
Voice mail	22	Interoffice mail	18
U.S. mail	18	Fax	15
Post-it note	11	Phone msg. slip	10
Pager	4	Overnight courier	4
Cellular phone	3	U.S. Express mail	3

    a. For any particular worker, what is the probability the next message will be on the telephone?
    b. For the next two messages, what is the probability the first will be via e-mail and the second will be via fax?
    c. What is the probability the next message received will be via telephone call or interoffice mail?

4.5 BAYES' THEOREM

In the discussion of conditional probability, we indicated that revising probabilities when new information is obtained is an important phase of probability analysis. Often, we begin the analysis with initial or *prior probability* estimates for specific events of interest. Then, from sources such as a sample, a special report, or a product test, we obtain additional information about the events. Given this new information, we update the prior probability values by calculating revised probabilities, referred to as *posterior probabilities*. *Bayes' theorem* provides a means for making these probability calculations. The steps in this probability revision process are shown in Figure 4.9.

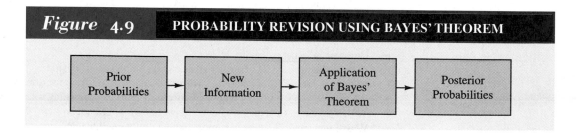

Figure 4.9   PROBABILITY REVISION USING BAYES' THEOREM

Table 4.6	HISTORICAL QUALITY LEVELS OF TWO SUPPLIERS	
	Percentage Good Parts	**Percentage Bad Parts**
Supplier 1	98	2
Supplier 2	95	5

As an application of Bayes' theorem, consider a manufacturing firm that receives shipments of parts from two different suppliers. Let A_1 denote the event that a part is from supplier 1 and A_2 denote the event that a part is from supplier 2. Currently, 65% of the parts purchased by the company are from supplier 1 and the remaining 35% are from supplier 2. Hence, if a part is selected at random, we would assign the prior probabilities $P(A_1) = .65$ and $P(A_2) = .35$.

The quality of the purchased parts varies with the source of supply. Historical data suggest that the quality ratings of the two suppliers are as shown in Table 4.6. If we let G denote the event that a part is good and B denote the event that a part is bad, the information in Table 4.6 provides the following conditional probability values.

$$P(G \mid A_1) = .98 \quad P(B \mid A_1) = .02$$
$$P(G \mid A_2) = .95 \quad P(B \mid A_2) = .05$$

The tree diagram in Figure 4.10 depicts the process of the firm receiving a part from one of the two suppliers and then discovering that the part is good or bad as a two-step experiment. We see that four experimental outcomes are possible; two correspond to the part being good and two correspond to the part being bad.

Each of the experimental outcomes is the intersection of two events, so we can use the multiplication rule to compute the probabilities. For instance,

$$P(A_1, G) = P(A_1 \cap G) = P(A_1)P(G \mid A_1)$$

Figure 4.10	TWO-STEP TREE DIAGRAM

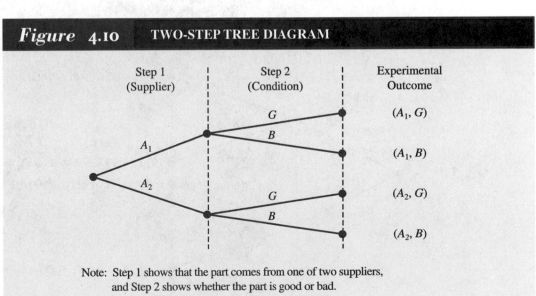

Note: Step 1 shows that the part comes from one of two suppliers,
       and Step 2 shows whether the part is good or bad.

The process of computing these joint probabilities can be depicted in what is called a probability tree (see Figure 4.11). From left to right through the tree, the probabilities for each branch at step 1 are prior probabilities and the probabilities for each branch at step 2 are conditional probabilities. To find the probabilities of each experimental outcome, we simply multiply the probabilities on the branches leading to the outcome. Each of these joint probabilities is shown in Figure 4.11 along with the known probabilities for each branch.

Suppose now that the parts from the two suppliers are used in the firm's manufacturing process and that a machine breaks down because it attempts to process a bad part. Given the information that the part is bad, what is the probability that it came from supplier 1 and what is the probability that it came from supplier 2? With the information in the probability tree (Figure 4.11), Bayes' theorem can be used to answer these questions.

Letting B denote the event that the part is bad, we are looking for the posterior probabilities $P(A_1 \mid B)$ and $P(A_2 \mid B)$. From the law of conditional probability, we know that

$$P(A_1 \mid B) = \frac{P(A_1 \cap B)}{P(B)} \tag{4.14}$$

Referring to the probability tree, we see that

$$P(A_1 \cap B) = P(A_1)P(B \mid A_1) \tag{4.15}$$

To find $P(B)$, we note that event B can occur in only two ways: $(A_1 \cap B)$ and $(A_2 \cap B)$. Therefore, we have

$$P(B) = P(A_1 \cap B) + P(A_2 \cap B)$$
$$= P(A_1)P(B \mid A_1) + P(A_2)P(B \mid A_2) \tag{4.16}$$

Figure 4.11   PROBABILITY TREE FOR TWO-SUPPLIER EXAMPLE

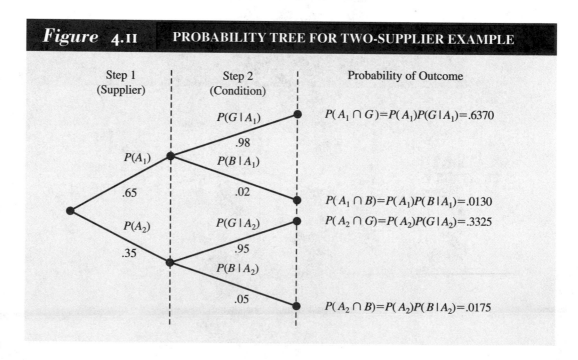

Substituting from (4.15) and (4.16) into (4.14) and writing a similar result for $P(A_2 \mid B)$, we obtain Bayes' theorem for the case of two events.

The Reverend Thomas Bayes (1702–1761), a Presbyterian minister, is credited with the original work leading to the version of Bayes' theorem in use today.

Bayes' Theorem (Two-Event Case)

$$P(A_1 \mid B) = \frac{P(A_1)P(B \mid A_1)}{P(A_1)P(B \mid A_1) + P(A_2)P(B \mid A_2)} \qquad (4.17)$$

$$P(A_2 \mid B) = \frac{P(A_2)P(B \mid A_2)}{P(A_1)P(B \mid A_1) + P(A_2)P(B \mid A_2)} \qquad (4.18)$$

Using (4.17) and the probability values provided in the example, we have

$$P(A_1 \mid B) = \frac{P(A_1)P(B \mid A_1)}{P(A_1)P(B \mid A_1) + P(A_2)P(B \mid A_2)}$$

$$= \frac{(.65)(.02)}{(.65)(.02) + (.35)(.05)} = \frac{.0130}{.0130 + .0175}$$

$$= \frac{.0130}{.0305} = .4262$$

In addition, using (4.18), we find $P(A_2 \mid B)$.

$$P(A_2 \mid B) = \frac{(.35)(.05)}{(.65)(.02) + (.35)(.05)}$$

$$= \frac{.0175}{.0130 + .0175} = \frac{.0175}{.0305} = .5738$$

Note that in this application we started with a probability of .65 that a part selected at random was from supplier 1. However, given information that the part is bad, the probability that the part is from supplier 1 drops to .4262. In fact, if the part is bad, it has better than a 50–50 chance that it came from supplier 2; that is, $P(A_2 \mid B) = .5738$.

Bayes' theorem is applicable when the events for which we want to compute posterior probabilities are mutually exclusive and their union is the entire sample space.* Bayes' theorem can be extended to the case of n mutually exclusive events $A_1, A_2, \ldots, A_n$, whose union is the entire sample space. In such a case, Bayes' theorem for the computation of any posterior probability $P(A_i \mid B)$ has the following form.

Bayes' Theorem

$$P(A_i \mid B) = \frac{P(A_i)P(B \mid A_i)}{P(A_1)P(B \mid A_1) + P(A_2)P(B \mid A_2) + \cdots + P(A_n)P(B \mid A_n)} \qquad (4.19)$$

---

*If the union of events is the entire sample space, the events are said to be *collectively exhaustive*.

With prior probabilities $P(A_1)$, $P(A_2)$, ..., $P(A_n)$ and the appropriate conditional probabilities $P(B \mid A_1)$, $P(B \mid A_2)$, ..., $P(B \mid A_n)$, Equation (4.19) can be used to compute the posterior probability of the events $A_1, A_2, \cdots, A_n$.

The Tabular Approach

A tabular approach is helpful in conducting the Bayes' theorem calculations. Such an approach is shown in Table 4.7 for the parts supplier problem. The computations shown there are done in the following steps.

Step 1. Prepare the following three columns:
Column 1—The mutually exclusive events for which posterior probabilities are desired.
Column 2—The prior probabilities for the events.
Column 3—The conditional probabilities of the new information *given* each event.

Step 2. In column 4, compute the joint probabilities for each event and the new information B by using the multiplication law. These joint probabilities are found by multiplying the prior probabilities in column 2 by the corresponding conditional probabilities in column 3; that is, $P(A_i \cap B) = P(A_i)P(B \mid A_i)$.

Step 3. Sum the joint probabilities in column 4. The sum is the probability of the new information, $P(B)$. Thus we see that in the preceding example there is a .0130 probability of a bad part and supplier 1 and a .0175 probability of a bad part and supplier 2. Because these are the only two ways in which a bad part can be obtained, the sum .0130 + .0175 shows an overall probability of .0305 of finding a bad part from the combined shipments of the two suppliers.

Step 4. In column 5, compute the posterior probabilities using the basic relationship of conditional probability.

$$P(A_i \mid B) = \frac{P(A_i \cap B)}{P(B)}$$

Note that the joint probabilities $P(A_i \cap B)$ are in column 4 and the probability $P(B)$ is the sum of column 4.

Table 4.7	SUMMARY OF BAYES' THEOREM CALCULATIONS FOR THE TWO-SUPPLIER PROBLEM			
(1) Events A_i	(2) Prior Probabilities $P(A_i)$	(3) Conditional Probabilities $P(B \mid A_i)$	(4) Joint Probabilities $P(A_i \cap B)$	(5) Posterior Probabilities $P(A_i \mid B)$
A_1	.65	.02	.0130	.0130/.0305 = .4262
A_2	.35	.05	.0175	.0175/.0305 = .5738
	1.00		$P(B) = .0305$	1.0000

N O T E S	1. Bayes' theorem is used extensively in decision analysis. The prior probabilities are often subjective estimates provided by a decision maker. Sample information is obtained and posterior probabilities are computed for use in developing a decision strategy.
and Comments	2. An event and its complement are mutually exclusive, and their union is the entire sample space. Thus, Bayes' theorem is always applicable for computing posterior probabilities of an event and its complement.

..../ /.............

EXERCISES

Methods

SELF TEST

39. The prior probabilities for events A_1 and A_2 are $P(A_1) = .40$ and $P(A_2) = .60$. It is also known that $P(A_1 \cap A_2) = 0$. Suppose $P(B \mid A_1) = .20$ and $P(B \mid A_2) = .05$.
   a. Are A_1 and A_2 mutually exclusive? Why or why not?
   b. Compute $P(A_1 \cap B)$ and $P(A_2 \cap B)$.
   c. Compute $P(B)$.
   d. Apply Bayes' theorem to compute $P(A_1 \mid B)$ and $P(A_2 \mid B)$.

40. The prior probabilities for events A_1, A_2, and A_3 are $P(A_1) = .20$, $P(A_2) = .50$, and $P(A_3) = .30$. The conditional probabilities of event B given A_1, A_2, and A_3 are $P(B \mid A_1) = .50$, $P(B \mid A_2) = .40$, and $P(B \mid A_3) = .30$.
   a. Compute $P(B \cap A_1)$, $P(B \cap A_2)$, and $P(B \cap A_3)$.
   b. Apply Bayes' theorem, Equation (4.19), to compute the posterior probability $P(A_2 \mid B)$.
   c. Use the tabular approach to applying Bayes' theorem to compute $P(A_1 \mid B)$, $P(A_2 \mid B)$, and $P(A_3 \mid B)$.

Applications

41. A consulting firm has submitted a bid for a large research project. The firm's management initially felt they had a 50–50 chance of getting the project. However, the agency to which the bid was submitted has subsequently requested additional information on the bid. Past experience indicates that on 75% of the successful bids and 40% of the unsuccessful bids the agency requested additional information.
   a. What is the prior probability of the bid being successful (that is, prior to the request for additional information)?
   b. What is the conditional probability of a request for additional information given that the bid will ultimately be successful?
   c. Compute a posterior probability that the bid will be successful given that a request for additional information has been received.

SELF TEST

42. A local bank is reviewing its credit card policy with a view toward recalling some of its credit cards. In the past approximately 5% of cardholders have defaulted and the bank has been unable to collect the outstanding balance. Hence, management has established a prior probability of .05 that any particular cardholder will default. The bank has further found that the probability of missing one or more monthly payments is .20 for customers who do not default. Of course, the probability of missing one or more payments for those who default is 1.
   a. Given that a customer has missed a monthly payment, compute the posterior probability that the customer will default.
   b. The bank would like to recall its card if the probability that a customer will default is greater than .20. Should the bank recall its card if the customer misses a monthly payment? Why or why not?

43. *The Book of Risks* (1994) contains probability information about the chances people take in everyday activities. For example, the probability of a man having a motor vehicle accident during a one-year period is reported to be twice as great as the probability of a woman having a motor vehicle accident during a one-year period. Indicated probabilities are .113 for men and .057 for women. Suppose that 55% of the drivers in Lucas County are men. In filling out a driving history questionnaire, a person from Lucas County indicates involvement in a motor vehicle accident during the past year. What is the probability that the person is a woman?

44. A city has a professional basketball team playing at home and a professional hockey team playing away on the same night. According to probabilities for professional sports published in *Chance* (Fall 1992), a professional basketball team has a .641 probability of winning a home game and a professional hockey team has a .462 probability of winning an away game. Historically, when both teams play on the same night, the chance that the next morning's leading sports story will be about the basketball game is 60% and the chance that it will be about the hockey game is 40%. Suppose that on the morning after these games the newspaper's leading sports story begins with the headline "We Win!!" What is the probability that the story is about the basketball team?

45. *M. D. Computing* (May 1991) describes the use of Bayes' theorem and the use of conditional probability in medical diagnosis. Prior probabilities of diseases are based on the physician's assessment of such things as geographical location, seasonal influence, occurrence of epidemics, and so forth. Assume that a patient is believed to have one of two diseases, denoted D_1 and D_2 with $P(D_1) = .60$ and $P(D_2) = .40$ and that medical research has determined the probability associated with each symptom that may accompany the diseases. Suppose that, given diseases D_1 and D_2, the probabilities that the patient will have symptoms S_1, S_2, or S_3 are as follows.

		Symptoms		
		S_1	S_2	S_3
Disease	D_1	.15	.10	.15
	D_2	.80	.15	.03

$P(S_3 \mid D_1)$

After a certain symptom is found to be present, the medical diagnosis may be aided by finding the revised probabilities of each particular disease. Compute the posterior probabilities of each disease given the following medical findings.
a. The patient has symptom S_1.
b. The patient has symptom S_2.
c. The patient has symptom S_3.
d. For the patient with symptom S_1 in (a), suppose we also find symptom S_2. What are the revised probabilities of D_1 and D_2?

SUMMARY

In this chapter we introduced basic probability concepts and illustrated how probability analysis can be used to provide helpful information for decision making. We described how probability can be interpreted as a numerical measure of the likelihood that an event will occur. In addition, we saw that the probability of an event can be computed either by summing the probabilities of the experimental outcomes (sample points) comprising the event or by using the relationships established by the addition, conditional probability, and multiplication laws of probability. For cases in which additional information is available, we showed how Bayes' theorem can be used to obtain revised or posterior probabilities.

..../ /...............

GLOSSARY

Probability A numerical measure of the likelihood that an event will occur.

Experiment A process that generates well-defined outcomes.

Sample space The set of all experimental outcomes.

Sample point An element of the sample space. A sample point represents an experimental outcome.

Tree diagram A graphical representation helpful in defining sample points of an experiment involving multiple steps.

Basic requirements of probability Two requirements that restrict the manner in which probability assignments can be made:
a. For each experimental outcome E_i we must have $0 \leq P(E_i) \leq 1$.
b. Considering all experimental outcomes, we must have $\Sigma P(E_i) = 1$.

Classical method A method of assigning probabilities that assumes the experimental outcomes are equally likely.

Relative frequency method A method of assigning probabilities on the basis of experimentation or historical data.

Subjective method A method of assigning probabilities on the basis of judgment.

Event A collection of sample points.

Complement of event A The event containing all sample points that are not in A.

Venn diagram A graphical representation for showing symbolically the sample space and operations involving events in which the sample space is represented by a rectangle and events are represented as circles.

Union of events A **and** B The event containing all sample points that are in A, in B, or in both. The union is denoted $A \cup B$.

Intersection of A **and** B The event containing all sample points that are in both A and B. The intersection is denoted $A \cap B$.

Addition law A probability law used to compute the probability of a union, $P(A \cup B)$. It is $P(A \cup B) = P(A) + P(B) - P(A \cap B)$. For mutually exclusive events, because $P(A \cap B) = 0$, it reduces to $P(A \cup B) = P(A) + P(B)$.

Mutually exclusive events Events that have no sample points in common; that is, $A \cap B$ is empty and $P(A \cap B) = 0$.

Conditional probability The probability of an event given that another event has occurred. The conditional probability of A given B is $P(A \mid B) = P(A \cap B)/P(B)$.

Independent events Two events A and B where $P(A \mid B) = P(A)$ or $P(B \mid A) = P(B)$; that is, the events have no influence on each other.

Multiplication law A probability law used to compute the probability of an intersection, $P(A \cap B)$. It is $P(A \cap B) = P(A)P(B \mid A)$ or $P(A \cap B) = P(B)P(A \mid B)$. For independent events it reduces to $P(A \cap B) = P(A)P(B)$.

Prior probabilities Initial estimates of the probabilities of events.

Posterior probabilities Revised probabilities of events based on additional information.

Bayes' theorem A method used to compute posterior probabilities.

···/ /············

KEY FORMULAS

Counting Rule for Combinations

$$C_n^N = \binom{N}{n} = \frac{N!}{n!(N-n)!} \qquad (4.1)$$

Counting Rule for Permutations

$$P_n^N = n!\binom{N}{n} = \frac{N!}{(N-n)!} \qquad (4.2)$$

Computing Probability Using the Complement

$$P(A) = 1 - P(A^c) \qquad (4.5)$$

Addition Law

$$P(A \cup B) = P(A) + P(B) - P(A \cap B) \qquad (4.6)$$

Conditional Probability

$$P(A \mid B) = \frac{P(A \cap B)}{P(B)} \qquad (4.7)$$

$$P(B \mid A) = \frac{P(A \cap B)}{P(A)} \qquad (4.8)$$

Multiplication Law

$$P(A \cap B) = P(B)P(A \mid B) \qquad (4.11)$$
$$P(A \cap B) = P(A)P(B \mid A) \qquad (4.12)$$

Multiplication Law for Independent Events

$$P(A \cap B) = P(A)P(B) \qquad (4.13)$$

Bayes' Theorem

$$P(A_i \mid B) = \frac{P(A_i)P(B \mid A_i)}{P(A_1)P(B \mid A_1) + P(A_2)P(B \mid A_2) + \cdots + P(A_n)P(B \mid A_n)} \qquad (4.19)$$

···/ /············

SUPPLEMENTARY EXERCISES

46. Home technology and its use were the focus of a survey by Nielsen Media Research (*Nielsen Media Research*, February 20, 1996). The survey found that 39.5% of persons have a computer in their home, and 29.3% have both a computer and cable television in their home. Of the persons with a computer in their home 64.1% said they had used it in the past week.
    a. What is the probability that a person has a computer in their home and used it in the past week?
    b. What is the probability a person has cable television given they have a computer in their home?

47. A financial manager has just made two new investments—one in the oil industry and one in municipal bonds. After a one-year period, each of the investments will be classified as either successful or unsuccessful. Consider the making of the two investments as an experiment.
  a. How many sample points exist for this experiment?
  b. Show a tree diagram and list the sample points.
  c. Let O = the event that the oil investment is successful and M = the event that the municipal bond investment is successful. List the sample points in O and in M.
  d. List the sample points in the union of the events $(O \cup M)$.
  e. List the sample points in the intersection of the events $(O \cap M)$.
  f. Are events O and M mutually exclusive? Explain.

48. A survey of American opinion asked: Are you satisfied or dissatisfied with the state of the U.S. economy today? (*The Wall Street Journal,* June 27, 1997). The following table provides the responses for all adults and the distribution by age groups.

	Satisfied (%)	Dissatisfied (%)	Other (%)
All Adults	61	37	2
18–34	64	35	1
35–49	58	41	1
50–64	57	40	3
65+	70	26	4

  a. What is the probability a randomly selected adult is satisfied?
  b. Which age groups report a higher level of satisfaction than the average for all adults?
  c. What is the probability an adult 65 or over did not indicate they were satisfied?

49. A study of 31,000 hospital admissions in New York State was conducted by a Harvard research team led by Paul Weiler (*Business Week,* March 27, 1995). They found that 4% of the admissions led to treatment-caused injuries. One-seventh of these injuries resulted in death, and one-fourth were caused by negligence. Malpractice claims were filed in one out of 7.5 cases involving negligence, and payments were made in one out of every two claims.
  a. What is the probability a person admitted to the hospital will suffer an injury caused by negligence?
  b. What is the probability a person admitted to the hospital will die from a treatment-caused injury?
  c. In the case of a negligent treatment-caused injury, what is the probability a malpractice claim will be paid?

50. A telephone survey was used to determine viewer response to a new television show. The following data were obtained.

Rating	Frequency
Poor	4
Below average	8
Average	11
Above average	14
Excellent	13

  a. What is the probability that a randomly selected viewer rated the new show as average or better?
  b. What is the probability that a randomly selected viewer rated the new show below average or worse?

Table 4.8   NUMBER OF CARS OWNED OR LEASED, AND TOTAL NUMBER OF CARS PER HOUSEHOLD

	Number of Households		
Cars	Own	Lease	Total
0	65	708	19
1	242	168	168
2	401	47	447
3	149	9	186
4 or more	75	0	112
Total	932	932	932

51. *Business Week* surveyed its subscribers concerning the number of cars they owned or leased. Responses were obtained to three questions: How many cars do you own? How many cars do you lease? How many cars do you have (owned or leased)? Table 4.8 contains the results obtained from 932 households (*Business Week* 1996 Worldwide Subscriber Study). In interpreting the table note that the third row shows that 401 households own 2 cars, 47 households lease 2 cars, and 447 households have 2 cars.
    a. What is the probability a household leases 1 car?
    b. What is the probability a household owns 2 or fewer cars?
    c. What is the probability a household has 3 or more cars?
    d. What is the probability a household does not own or lease a car?

52. A GMAC MBA new-matriculants survey provided the following data for 2018 students.

		Applied to More Than One School	
		Yes	No
	23 and under	207	201
	24–26	299	379
Age Group	27–30	185	268
	31–35	66	193
	36 and over	51	169

    a. For a randomly selected MBA student, prepare a joint probability table for the experiment consisting of observing the student's age and whether the student applied to one or more schools.
    b. What is the probability that an applicant was 23 or under?
    c. What is the probability that an applicant was older than 26?
    d. What is the probability that an applicant applied to more than one school?

53. Refer again to the data from the GMAC new-matriculants survey in Exercise 52.
    a. Given that a person applied to more than one school, what is the probability that the person was 24–26 years old?
    b. Given that a person is in the 36-and-over age group, what is the probability that the person applied to more than one school?
    c. What is the probability that a person is 24–26 years old *or* applied to more than one school?
    d. Suppose a person is known to have applied to only one school. What is the probability that the person was 31 or more years old?
    e. Is the number of schools applied to independent of age? Explain.

54. A William M. Mercer Inc. survey provided the following data on salary and bonus compensation for 105 CEOs of technology and financial corporations (*The Wall Street Journal*, April 13, 1994). Total compensation is shown in millions of dollars.

		Total Compensation			
		Under $1M	$1M–$2M	Over $2M	Total
Corporation	Technology	17	21	7	45
	Financial	12	31	17	60
	Total	29	52	24	105

   a. Show the joint probability table for the data.
   b. Use the marginal probabilities to comment on the most probable of the three compensation ranges.
   c. Let T represent technology, F represent financial, and $2M$ represent total compensation over $2 million. Find $P(2M)$. Then compute the conditional probabilities $P(2M \mid T)$ and $P(2M \mid F)$. What conclusion can you draw about the compensation levels for technology and financial CEOs?
   d. Is compensation independent of the type of corporation? Explain.

55. A large consumer goods company has been running a television advertisement for one of its soap products. A survey was conducted. On the basis of this survey, probabilities were assigned to the following events.

$$B = \text{individual purchased the product}$$
$$S = \text{individual recalls seeing the advertisement}$$
$$B \cap S = \text{individual purchased the product and recalls seeing the advertisement}$$

   The probabilities assigned were $P(B) = .20$, $P(S) = .40$, and $P(B \cap S) = .12$.
   a. What is the probability of an individual's purchasing the product given that the individual recalls seeing the advertisement? Does seeing the advertisement increase the probability that the individual will purchase the product? As a decision maker, would you recommend continuing the advertisement (assuming that the cost is reasonable)?
   b. Assume that individuals who do not purchase the company's soap product buy from its competitors. What would be your estimate of the company's market share? Would you expect that continuing the advertisement will increase the company's market share? Why or why not?
   c. The company has also tested another advertisement and assigned it values of $P(S) = .30$ and $P(B \cap S) = .10$. What is $P(B \mid S)$ for this other advertisement? Which advertisement seems to have had the bigger effect on customer purchases?

56. In the evaluation of a sales training program, a firm found that of 50 salespersons making a bonus last year, 20 had attended a special sales training program. The firm has 200 salespersons. Let $B =$ the event that a salesperson makes a bonus and $S =$ the event that a salesperson attends the sales training program.
   a. Find $P(B)$, $P(S \mid B)$, and $P(S \cap B)$.
   b. Assume that 40% of the salespersons have attended the training program. What is the probability that a salesperson makes a bonus given that the salesperson attended the sales training program, $P(B \mid S)$?
   c. If the firm evaluates the training program in terms of its effect on the probability of a salesperson making a bonus, what is your evaluation of the training program? Comment on whether B and S are dependent or independent events.

57. A company has studied the number of lost-time accidents occurring at its Brownsville, Texas, plant. Historical records show that 6% of the employees had lost-time accidents last year. Management believes that a special safety program will reduce such accidents to 5% during the current year. In addition, it estimates that 15% of employees who had lost-time accidents last year will have a lost-time accident during the current year.
   a. What percentage of the employees will have lost-time accidents in both years?
   b. What percentage of the employees will have at least one lost-time accident over the two-year period?

58. The Dallas IRS auditing staff is concerned with identifying potentially fraudulent tax returns. From past experience they believe that the probability of finding a fraudulent return given that the return contains deductions for contributions exceeding the IRS standard is .20. Given that the deductions for contributions do not exceed the IRS standard, the probability of a fraudulent return decreases to .02. If 8% of all returns exceed the IRS standard for deductions due to contributions, what is the best estimate of the percentage of fraudulent returns?

59. An oil company has purchased an option on land in Alaska. Preliminary geologic studies have assigned the following prior probabilities.

$$P(\text{high-quality oil}) = .50$$
$$P(\text{medium-quality oil}) = .20$$
$$P(\text{no oil}) = .30$$

   a. What is the probability of finding oil?
   b. After 200 feet of drilling on the first well, a soil test is taken. The probabilities of finding the particular type of soil identified by the test follow.

$$P(\text{soil} \mid \text{high-quality oil}) = .20$$
$$P(\text{soil} \mid \text{medium-quality oil}) = .80$$
$$P(\text{soil} \mid \text{no oil}) = .20$$

   How should the firm interpret the soil test? What are the revised probabilities, and what is the new probability of finding oil?

60. A Bayesian approach can be used to revise probabilities that a prospect field will produce oil (*Oil & Gas Journal,* January 11, 1988). In one case, geological assessment indicates a 25% chance that the field will produce oil. Further, there is an 80% chance that a particular well will strike oil given that oil is present in the prospect field.
   a. Suppose that one well is drilled on the field and it comes up dry. What is the probability that the prospect field will produce oil?
   b. If two wells come up dry, what is the probability that the field will produce oil?
   c. The oil company would like to keep looking as long as the chances of finding oil are greater than 1%. How many dry wells must be drilled before the field will be abandoned?

Case Problem   HAMILTON COUNTY JUDGES

Hamilton County judges try thousands of cases per year. In an overwhelming majority of the cases disposed, the verdict stands as rendered. However, some cases are appealed, and of those appealed, some of the cases are reversed. Kristen DelGuzzi of *The Cincinnati Enquirer* conducted a study of cases handled by Hamilton County judges over the years 1994 through 1996 (*The Cincinnati Enquirer,* January 11, 1998). Shown in Table 4.9 are the results for 182,908 cases handled (disposed) by 38 judges in Common Pleas Court,

Table 4.9   TOTAL CASES DISPOSED, APPEALED, AND REVERSED IN HAMILTON COUNTY COURTS DURING 1994 THROUGH 1996

Common Pleas Court

Judge	Total Cases Disposed	Appealed Cases	Reversed Cases
Fred Cartolano	3037	137	12
Thomas Crush	3372	119	10
Patrick Dinkelacker	1258	44	8
Timothy Hogan	1954	60	7
Robert Kraft	3138	127	7
William Mathews	2264	91	18
William Morrissey	3032	121	22
Norbert Nadel	2959	131	20
Arthur Ney, Jr.	3219	125	14
Richard Niehaus	3353	137	16
Thomas Nurre	3000	121	6
John O'Connor	2969	129	12
Robert Ruehlman	3205	145	18
J. Howard Sundermann	955	60	10
Ann Marie Tracey	3141	127	13
Ralph Winkler	3089	88	6
Total	43945	1762	199

Domestic Relations Court

Judge	Total Cases Disposed	Appealed Cases	Reversed Cases
Penelope Cunningham	2729	7	1
Patrick Dinkelacker	6001	19	4
Deborah Gaines	8799	48	9
Ronald Panioto	12970	32	3
Total	30499	106	17

Municipal Court

Judge	Total Cases Disposed	Appealed Cases	Reversed Cases
Mike Allen	6149	43	4
Nadine Allen	7812	34	6
Timothy Black	7954	41	6
David Davis	7736	43	5
Leslie Isaiah Gaines	5282	35	13
Karla Grady	5253	6	0
Deidra Hair	2532	5	0
Dennis Helmick	7900	29	5
Timothy Hogan	2308	13	2
James Patrick Kenney	2798	6	1
Joseph Luebbers	4698	25	8
William Mallory	8277	38	9
Melba Marsh	8219	34	7
Beth Mattingly	2971	13	1
Albert Mestemaker	4975	28	9
Mark Painter	2239	7	3
Jack Rosen	7790	41	13
Mark Schweikert	5403	33	6
David Stockdale	5371	22	4
John A. West	2797	4	2
Total	108464	500	104

Judge

Domestic Relations Court, and Municipal Court. Two of the judges (Dinkelacker and Hogan) did not serve in the same court for the entire three-year period.

The purpose of the newspaper's study was to evaluate the performance of the judges. Appeals are often the result of mistakes made by judges, and the newspaper wanted to know which judges were doing a good job and which were making too many mistakes. You have been called in to assist in the data analysis. Use your knowledge of probability and conditional probability to help with the ranking of the judges. You also may be able to analyze the likelihood of cases handled by different courts being appealed and reversed.

Managerial Report

Prepare a report with your rankings of the judges. Also, include an analysis of the likelihood of appeal and case reversal in the three courts. At a minimum, your report should include the following:

1. The probability of cases being appealed and reversed in the three different courts.
2. The probability of a case being appealed for each judge.
3. The probability of a case being reversed for each judge.
4. The probability of reversal given an appeal for each judge.
5. Rank the judges within each court. State the criteria you used and provide a rationale for your choice.

5

DISCRETE PROBABILITY DISTRIBUTIONS

CONTENTS

CITIBANK*
Long Island City, New York

Citibank, a major subsidiary of Citigroup, Inc., provides a wide range of financial services (e.g., checking and savings accounts, loans and mortgages, insurance and investment services) within the framework called Citibanking. Citibanking entails a consistent brand identity, consistent product offerings, and quality customer service all over the world.

Citibanking's state-of-the-art automated teller machines (ATMs) located in Citicard Banking Centers (CBCs), let customers do banking 24 hours a day, 7 days a week. The New York franchise of U.S. Citibanking operates approximately 250 CBCs: 175 are located in Manhattan, the Bronx, Brooklyn, Queens, and Staten Island, with the remaining 75 located in suburban Nassau, Suffolk, Orange, Rockland, and Westchester counties.

Each Citibank CBC operates as a waiting line system with randomly arriving customers seeking service at one of the ATMs. If all ATMs are busy, the arriving customers wait in line. Periodic CBC capacity studies are used to analyze customer waiting times and determine whether additional ATMs are needed.

Data collected by Citibank showed that the random customer arrivals followed a probability distribution known as the Poisson probability distribution. Using the Poisson probability distribution, Citibank can compute probabilities for the number of customers arriving at a CBC during any

© C. Zoltnick; S. Seitz/Woodfin Camp & Associates.

time period and make decisions concerning the number of ATMs needed. For example, let x = the number of customers arriving during a one-minute period, and assume that a particular CBC has a mean arrival rate of 2 customers per minute. The following are the probabilities for the number of customers arriving during a one-minute period.

x	Probability
0	.1353
1	.2707
2	.2707
3	.1804
4	.0902
5 or more	.0527

Discrete probability distributions, such as the one used by Citibank, are the topic of this chapter. In addition to the Poisson probability distribution, you will learn about the binomial and hypergeometric probability distributions and how they can be used to provide helpful probability information.

*The authors are indebted to Ms. Stacey Karter, Citibank, for providing this Statistics in Practice.

In this chapter we continue the study of probability by introducing the concepts of random variables and probability distributions. The focus of this chapter is discrete probability distributions. Three special discrete probability distributions—the binomial, Poisson, and hypergeometric—are covered.

5.1   RANDOM VARIABLES

In Chapter 4 we defined the concept of an experiment and its associated experimental outcomes. A random variable provides a means for describing experimental outcomes by numerical values.

Random variables must assume numerical values.

Random Variable

A *random variable* is a numerical description of the outcome of an experiment.

In effect, a random variable associates a numerical value with each possible experimental outcome. The particular numerical value of the random variable depends on the outcome of the experiment. A random variable can be classified as being either *discrete* or *continuous* depending on the numerical values it assumes.

Discrete Random Variables

A random variable that may assume either a finite number of values or an infinite sequence of values such as 0, 1, 2, . . . is referred to as a *discrete random variable*. For example, consider the experiment of an accountant taking the certified public accountant (CPA) examination. The examination has four parts. We can define the discrete random variable as x = the number of parts of the CPA examination passed. This discrete random variable may assume the finite number of values 0, 1, 2, 3, or 4.

As another example of a discrete random variable, consider the experiment of cars arriving at a tollbooth. The random variable of interest is x = the number of cars arriving during a one-day period. The possible values for x come from the sequence of integers 0, 1, 2, and so on. Hence, x is a discrete random variable assuming one of the values in this infinite sequence.

Although many experiments have outcomes that are naturally described by numerical values, others do not. For example, a survey question might ask an individual to recall the message in a recent television commercial. This experiment would have two possible outcomes: the individual cannot recall the message and the individual can recall the message. We can still describe these experimental outcomes numerically by defining the discrete random variable x as follows: let $x = 0$ if the individual cannot recall the message and $x = 1$ if the individual can recall the message. The numerical values for this random variable are arbitrary (we could have used 5 and 10), but they are acceptable in terms of the definition of a random variable—namely, x is a random variable because it provides a numerical description of the outcome of the experiment.

Table 5.1 provides some additional examples of discrete random variables. Note that in each example the discrete random variable assumes a finite number of values or an infinite

Table 5.1   **EXAMPLES OF DISCRETE RANDOM VARIABLES**

Experiment	Random Variable (x)	Possible Values for the Random Variable
Contact five customers	Number of customers who place an order	0, 1, 2, 3, 4, 5
Inspect a shipment of 50 radios	Number of defective radios	0, 1, 2, $\cdots$, 49, 50
Operate a restaurant for one day	Number of customers	0, 1, 2, 3, $\cdots$
Sell an automobile	Gender of the customer	0 if male; 1 if female

sequence of values such as 0, 1, 2, ... Discrete random variables such as these are discussed in detail in this chapter.

Continuous Random Variables

A random variable that may assume any numerical value in an interval or collection of intervals is called a *continuous random variable*. Experimental outcomes that are based on measurement scales such as time, weight, distance, and temperature can be described by continuous random variables. For example, consider an experiment of monitoring incoming telephone calls to the claims office of a major insurance company. Suppose the random variable of interest is x = the time between consecutive incoming calls in minutes. This random variable may assume any value in the interval $x \geq 0$. Actually, an infinite number of values are possible for x, including values such as 1.26 minutes, 2.751 minutes, 4.3333 minutes, and so on. As another example, consider a 90-mile section of interstate highway I-75 north of Atlanta, Georgia. For an emergency ambulance service located in Atlanta, we might define the random variable as x = the location of the next traffic accident along this section of I-75. In this case, x would be a continuous random variable assuming any value in the interval $0 \leq x \leq 90$. Additional examples of continuous random variables are listed in Table 5.2. Note that each example describes a random variable that may assume any value in an interval of values. Continuous random variables and their probability distributions will be the topic of Chapter 6.

Table 5.2   **EXAMPLES OF CONTINUOUS RANDOM VARIABLES**

Experiment	Random Variable (x)	Possible Values for the Random Variable
Operate a bank	Time between customer arrivals in minutes	$x \geq 0$
Fill a soft drink can (max = 12.1 ounces)	Number of ounces	$0 \leq x \leq 12.1$
Work on a project to construct a new library	Percentage of project complete after six months	$0 \leq x \leq 100$
Test a new chemical process	Temperature when the desired reaction takes place (min 150° F; max 212° F)	$150 \leq x \leq 212$

N O T E S *and Comments*	One way to determine whether a random variable is discrete or continuous is to think of the values of the random variable as points on a line segment. Choose two points representing values of the random variable. If the entire line segment between the two points also represents possible values for the random variable, then the random variable is continuous.

···/ /··············

EXERCISES

Methods

SELF TEST

1. Consider the experiment of tossing a coin twice.
    a. List the experimental outcomes.
    b. Define a random variable that represents the number of heads occurring on the two tosses.
    c. Show what value the random variable would assume for each of the experimental outcomes.
    d. Is this random variable discrete or continuous?

2. Consider the experiment of a worker assembling a product and recording how long it takes.
    a. Define a random variable that represents the time in minutes required to assemble the product.
    b. What values may the random variable assume?
    c. Is the random variable discrete or continuous?

Applications

SELF TEST

3. Three students have interviews scheduled for summer employment at the Brookwood Institute. In each case the result of the interview will be that a position is either offered or not offered. Experimental outcomes are defined in terms of the results of the three interviews.
    a. List the experimental outcomes.
    b. Define a random variable that represents the number of offers made. Is it a discrete or continuous random variable?
    c. Show the value of the random variable for each of the experimental outcomes.

4. Home mortgage rates were listed for 12 Florida lending institutions (*The Tampa Tribune,* February 25, 1995). Assume that the random variable of interest is the number of lending institutions in this group that offer a 30-year fixed rate of 8.5% or less. What values may this random variable assume?

5. To perform a certain type of blood analysis, lab technicians must perform two procedures. The first procedure requires either 1 or 2 separate steps, and the second procedure requires either 1, 2, or 3 steps.
    a. List the experimental outcomes associated with performing an analysis.
    b. If the random variable of interest is the total number of steps required to do the complete analysis, show what value the random variable will assume for each of the experimental outcomes.

6. Listed is a series of experiments and associated random variables. In each case, identify the values that the random variable can assume and state whether the random variable is discrete or continuous.

Experiment	Random Variable (x)
a. Take a 20-question examination	Number of questions answered correctly
b. Observe cars arriving at a tollbooth for one hour	Number of cars arriving at tollbooth
c. Audit 50 tax returns	Number of returns containing errors
d. Observe an employee's work	Number of nonproductive hours in an eight-hour workday
e. Weigh a shipment of goods	Number of pounds

5.2 DISCRETE PROBABILITY DISTRIBUTIONS

The *probability distribution* for a random variable describes how probabilities are distributed over the values of the random variable. For a discrete random variable x, the probability distribution is defined by a *probability function,* denoted by $f(x)$. The probability function provides the probability for each value of the random variable.

As an illustration of a discrete random variable and its probability distribution, consider the sales of automobiles at DiCarlo Motors in Saratoga, New York. Over the past 300 days of operation, sales data show 54 days with no automobiles sold, 117 days with 1 automobile sold, 72 days with 2 automobiles sold, 42 days with 3 automobiles sold, 12 days with 4 automobiles sold, and 3 days with 5 automobiles sold. Suppose we consider the experiment of selecting a day of operation at DiCarlo Motors. We define the random variable of interest as $x =$ the number of automobiles sold during a day. From historical data, we know x is a discrete random variable that can assume the values 0, 1, 2, 3, 4, or 5. In probability function notation, $f(0)$ provides the probability of 0 automobiles sold, $f(1)$ provides the probability of 1 automobile sold, and so on. Because historical data show 54 of 300 days with 0 automobiles sold, we assign the value 54/300 = .18 to $f(0)$, indicating that the probability of 0 automobiles being sold during a day is .18. Similarly, because 117 of 300 days had 1 automobile sold, we assign the value 117/300 = .39 to $f(1)$, indicating that the probability of exactly 1 automobile being sold during a day is .39. Continuing in this way for the other values of the random variable, we compute the values for $f(2)$, $f(3)$, $f(4)$, and $f(5)$ as shown in Table 5.3, the probability distribution for the number of automobiles sold during a day at DiCarlo Motors.

A primary advantage of defining a random variable and its probability distribution is that once the probability distribution is known, it is relatively easy to determine the probability of a variety of events that may be of interest to a decision maker. For example, using the probability distribution for DiCarlo Motors as shown in Table 5.3, we see that the most probable number of automobiles sold during a day is 1 with a probability of $f(1) = .39$. In addition, there is an $f(3) + f(4) + f(5) = .14 + .04 + .01 = .19$ probability of selling 3 or more automobiles during a day. These probabilities, plus others the decision maker may ask about, provide information

Table 5.3 PROBABILITY DISTRIBUTION FOR THE NUMBER OF AUTOMOBILES SOLD DURING A DAY AT DiCARLO MOTORS

x	$f(x)$
0	.18
1	.39
2	.24
3	.14
4	.04
5	.01
Total	1.00

that can help the decision maker understand the process of selling automobiles at DiCarlo Motors.

In the development of a probability function for any discrete random variable, the following two conditions must be satisfied.

These relations are the analogs to the two basic requirements for assigning probabilities to experimental outcomes presented in Chapter 4.

Required Conditions for a Discrete Probability Function

$$f(x) \geq 0 \tag{5.1}$$

$$\Sigma f(x) = 1 \tag{5.2}$$

Table 5.3 shows that the probabilities for the random variable x satisfy condition (5.1); $f(x)$ is greater than or equal to 0 for all values of x. In addition, the probabilities sum to 1 so (5.2) is satisfied. Thus, the DiCarlo Motors probability function is a valid discrete probability function.

We can also present probability distributions graphically. In Figure 5.1 the values of the random variable x for DiCarlo Motors are shown on the horizontal axis and the probability associated with these values is shown on the vertical axis.

In addition to tables and graphs, a formula that gives the probability function, $f(x)$, for every value of x is often used to describe probability distributions. The simplest example of a discrete probability distribution given by a formula is the *discrete uniform probability distribution*. Its probability function is given.

Discrete Uniform Probability Function

$$f(x) = 1/n \tag{5.3}$$

where

$$n = \text{the number of values the random variable may assume}$$

For example, consider the experiment of rolling a die and define the random variable x to be the number coming up. There are $n = 6$ possible values for the random variable; $x = 1, 2, 3, 4, 5, 6$. Thus, the probability function for this random variable is

$$f(x) = 1/6 \qquad x = 1, 2, 3, 4, 5, 6$$

The possible values of the random variable and the associated probabilities are shown.

x	$f(x)$
1	1/6
2	1/6
3	1/6
4	1/6
5	1/6
6	1/6

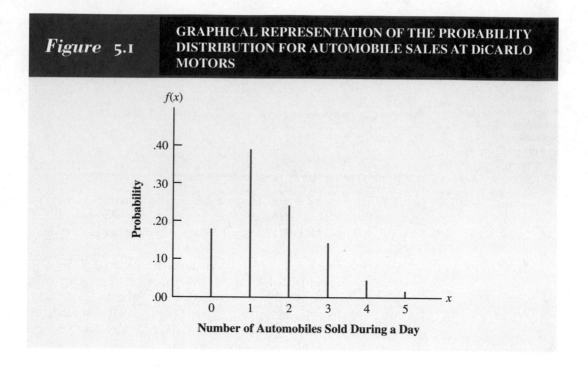

Figure 5.1 GRAPHICAL REPRESENTATION OF THE PROBABILITY DISTRIBUTION FOR AUTOMOBILE SALES AT DiCARLO MOTORS

Note that the values of the random variable are equally likely.

As another example, consider the random variable x with the following discrete probability distribution.

x	$f(x)$
1	1/10
2	2/10
3	3/10
4	4/10

This probability distribution can be defined by the formula

$$f(x) = \frac{x}{10} \qquad \text{for } x = 1, 2, 3, \text{ or } 4$$

Evaluating $f(x)$ for a given value of the random variable will provide the associated probability. For example, using the preceding probability function, we see that $f(2) = 2/10$ provides the probability that the random variable assumes a value of 2.

The more widely used discrete probability distributions generally are specified by formulas. Three important cases are the binomial, Poisson, and hypergeometric probability distributions; they are discussed later in the chapter.

EXERCISES

Methods

SELF TEST

7. The probability distribution of the random variable x is shown as follows.

x	$f(x)$
20	.20
25	.15
30	.25
35	.40
Total	1.00

  a. Is this a proper probability distribution? Check to see that (5.1) and (5.2) are satisfied.
  b. What is the probability that $x = 30$?
  c. What is the probability that x is less than or equal to 25?
  d. What is the probability that x is greater than 30?

Applications

SELF TEST

8. The following data were collected by counting the number of operating rooms in use at Tampa General Hospital over a 20-day period: On 3 of the days only 1 operating room was used, on 5 of the days 2 were used, on 8 of the days 3 were used, and on 4 days all 4 of the hospital's operating rooms were used.
  a. Use the relative frequency approach to construct a probability distribution for the number of operating rooms in use on any given day.
  b. Draw a graph of the probability distribution.
  c. Show that your probability distribution satisfies the required conditions for a valid discrete probability distribution.

9. The following data show the number of employees at each of the five executive levels in the federal government (U.S. Office of Personnel Management, *Pay Structure of the Federal Civil Service,* 1996).

Executive Level	Number of Employees
1	15
2	32
3	84
4	300
5	31
Total	462

Suppose it is of interest to select a sample of executive-level employees for a survey about working conditions. Let x be a random variable indicating the level of an employee selected.
  a. Use the data to develop a probability distribution for x. Specify the values for the random variable and the corresponding values for the probability function $f(x)$.
  b. Draw a graph of the probability distribution.
  c. Show that the probability distribution satisfies (5.1) and (5.2).

10. Shown in Table 5.4 are the percent frequency distributions of job satisfaction scores for a sample of information systems (IS) senior executives and IS middle managers (*Computerworld*, May 26, 1997). The scores range from a low of 1 (very dissatisfied) to a high of 5 (very satisfied).
   a. Develop a probability distribution for the job satisfaction score of a senior executive.
   b. Develop a probability distribution for the job satisfaction score of a middle manager.
   c. What is the probability a senior executive will report a job satisfaction score of 4 or 5?
   d. What is the probability a middle manager is very satisfied?
   e. Compare the overall job satisfaction of senior executives and middle managers.

11. A technician services mailing machines at companies in the Phoenix area. Depending on the type of malfunction, the service call can take 1, 2, 3, or 4 hours. The different types of malfunctions occur at about the same frequency.
   a. Develop a probability distribution for the duration of a service call.
   b. Draw a graph of the probability distribution.
   c. Show that your probability distribution satisfies the conditions required for a discrete probability function.
   d. What is the probability a service call will take 3 hours?
   e. A service call has just come in, but the type of malfunction is unknown. It is 3:00 P.M.; service technicians usually get off at 5:00 P.M. What is the probability the service technician will have to work overtime to fix the machine today?

12. The director of admissions at Lakeville Community College has subjectively assessed a probability distribution for x, the number of entering students, as follows.

x	$f(x)$
1000	.15
1100	.20
1200	.30
1300	.25
1400	.10

   a. Is this a valid probability distribution?
   b. What is the probability there will be 1200 or fewer entering students?

Table 5.4	PERCENT FREQUENCY DISTRIBUTION OF JOB SATISFACTION SCORES FOR INFORMATION SYSTEMS EXECUTIVES AND MIDDLE MANAGERS

Job Satisfaction Score	IS Senior Executives (%)	IS Middle Managers (%)
1	5	4
2	9	10
3	3	12
4	42	46
5	41	28
Total	100	100

13. A psychologist has determined that the number of hours required to obtain the trust of a new patient is either 1, 2, or 3. Let x be a random variable indicating the time in hours required to gain the patient's trust. The following probability function has been proposed.

$$f(x) = \frac{x}{6} \quad \text{for } x = 1, 2, \text{ or } 3$$

   a. Is this a valid probability function? Explain.
   b. What is the probability that it takes exactly 2 hours to gain the patient's trust?
   c. What is the probability that it takes at least 2 hours to gain the patient's trust?

14. The following table is a partial probability distribution for the MRA Company's projected profits (x = profit in $1000s) for the first year of operation (the negative value denotes a loss).

x	$f(x)$
-100	.10
0	.20
50	.30
100	.25
150	.10
200	

   a. What is the proper value for $f(200)$? What is your interpretation of this value?
   b. What is the probability that MRA will be profitable?
   c. What is the probability that MRA will make at least $100,000?

5.3   EXPECTED VALUE AND VARIANCE

Expected Value

The *expected value*, or mean, of a random variable is a measure of the central location for the random variable. The mathematical expression for the expected value of a discrete random variable x follows.

Expected Value of a Discrete Random Variable

$$E(x) = \mu = \Sigma x f(x) \tag{5.4}$$

Both the notations $E(x)$ and μ can be used to denote the expected value of a random variable.

Equation (5.4) shows that to compute the expected value of a discrete random variable, we must multiply each value of the random variable by the corresponding probability $f(x)$ and then add the resulting products. Using the DiCarlo Motors automobile sales example from Section 5.2, we show the calculation of the expected value for the number of automobiles sold during a day in Table 5.5. The sum of the entries in the $xf(x)$ column shows that the expected value is 1.50 automobiles per day. We therefore know that although sales of 0, 1, 2, 3, 4, or 5 automobiles are possible on any one day, over time DiCarlo can anticipate selling an average of 1.50 automobiles per day. Assuming 30 days of operation

The expected value is a weighted average of the values the random variable may assume. The weights are the probabilities.

Table 5.5	CALCULATION OF THE EXPECTED VALUE FOR THE NUMBER OF AUTOMOBILES SOLD DURING A DAY AT DiCARLO MOTORS

x	$f(x)$	$xf(x)$
0	.18	$0(.18) =$ .00
1	.39	$1(.39) =$ .39
2	.24	$2(.24) =$ .48
3	.14	$3(.14) =$ .42
4	.04	$4(.04) =$ .16
5	.01	$5(.01) =$ .05
		1.50

$$E(x) = \mu = \Sigma xf(x)$$

during a month, we can use the expected value of 1.50 to anticipate average monthly sales of $30(1.50) = 45$ automobiles.

Variance

While the expected value provides the mean value for the random variable, we often need a measure of variability, or dispersion. Just as we used the *variance* in Chapter 3 to summarize the variability in a data set, we now use variance to summarize the variability in the values of a random variable. The mathematical expression for the variance of a discrete random variable follows.

Variance of a Discrete Random Variable

$$\text{Var}(x) = \sigma^2 = \Sigma(x - \mu)^2 f(x) \tag{5.5}$$

As (5.5) shows, an essential part of the variance formula is the deviation, $x - \mu$, which measures how far a particular value of the random variable is from the expected value, or mean, μ. In computing the variance of a random variable, the deviations are squared and then weighted by the corresponding value of the probability function. The sum of these weighted squared deviations for all values of the random variable is referred to as the *variance*. The notations $\text{Var}(x)$ and σ^2 are both used to denote the variance of a random variable.

The variance is a weighted average of the squared deviations of a random variable from its mean. The weights are the probabilities.

The calculation of the variance for the probability distribution of the number of automobiles sold during a day at DiCarlo Motors is summarized in Table 5.6. We see that the variance is 1.25. The *standard deviation, σ,* is defined as the positive square root of the variance. Thus, the standard deviation for the number of automobiles sold during a day is

$$\sigma = \sqrt{1.25} = 1.118$$

The standard deviation is measured in the same units as the random variable ($\sigma = 1.118$ automobiles) and therefore is often preferred in describing the variability of a random variable. The variance σ^2 is measured in squared units and is thus more difficult to interpret.

		CALCULATION OF THE VARIANCE FOR THE NUMBER OF		
Table 5.6		AUTOMOBILES SOLD DURING A DAY AT DiCARLO MOTORS		

x	$x - \mu$	$(x - \mu)^2$	$f(x)$	$(x - \mu)^2 f(x)$
0	$0 - 1.50 = -1.50$	2.25	.18	$2.25(.18) = .4050$
1	$1 - 1.50 = -.50$	.25	.39	$.25(.39) = .0975$
2	$2 - 1.50 = .50$	.25	.24	$.25(.24) = .0600$
3	$3 - 1.50 = 1.50$	2.25	.14	$2.25(.14) = .3150$
4	$4 - 1.50 = 2.50$	6.25	.04	$6.25(.04) = .2500$
5	$5 - 1.50 = 3.50$	12.25	.01	$12.25(.01) = .1225$
				1.2500

$$\sigma^2 = \Sigma(x - \mu)^2 f(x)$$

EXERCISES

Methods

15. The following table is a probability distribution for the random variable x.

x	$f(x)$
3	.25
6	.50
9	.25
Total	1.00

    a. Compute $E(x)$, the expected value of x.
    b. Compute σ^2, the variance of x.
    c. Compute σ, the standard deviation of x.

16. The following table is a probability distribution for the random variable y.

SELF TEST

y	$f(y)$
2	.20
4	.30
7	.40
8	.10
Total	1.00

    a. Compute $E(y)$.
    b. Compute $Var(y)$ and σ.

Applications

17. A volunteer ambulance service handles 0 to 5 service calls on any given day. The probability distribution for the number of service calls is as follows.

Number of Service Calls	Probability
0	.10
1	.15
2	.30
3	.20
4	.15
5	.10

    a. What is the expected number of service calls?
    b. What is the variance in the number of service calls? What is the standard deviation?

SELF TEST

18. *The Statistical Abstract of the United States,* 1997, shows that the average number of television sets per household is 2.3. Assume that the probability distribution for the number of television sets per household is as shown in the following table.

x	$f(x)$
0	.01
1	.23
2	.41
3	.20
4	.10
5	.05

    a. Compute the expected value of the number of television sets per household and compare it with the average reported in the *Statistical Abstract.*
    b. What are the variance and standard deviation of the number of television sets per household?

19. The actual shooting records of the 1992 NCAA championship final four teams (*NCAA Final Four Program,* April 1992) showed the probability of making a 2-point basket was .50 and the probability of making a 3-point basket was .39.
    a. What is the expected value of a 2-point shot for these teams?
    b. What is the expected value of a 3-point shot for these teams?
    c. If the probability of making a 2-point basket is greater than the probability of making a 3-point basket, why do coaches allow some players to shoot the 3-point shot if they have the opportunity? Use expected value to explain your answer.

20. The probability distribution for damage claims paid by the Newton Automobile Insurance Company on collision insurance is shown as follows.

Payment ($)	Probability
0	.90
400	.04
1000	.03
2000	.01
4000	.01
6000	.01

a. Use the expected collision payment to determine the collision insurance premium that would enable the company to break even.

b. The insurance company charges an annual rate of $260 for the collision coverage. What is the expected value of the collision policy for a policyholder? (Hint: It is the expected payments from the company minus the cost of coverage.) Why does the policyholder purchase a collision policy with this expected value?

21. Shown are the probability distributions of job satisfaction scores for a sample of information systems (IS) senior executives and IS middle managers (*Computerworld,* May 26, 1997). The scores range from a low of 1 (very dissatisfied) to a high of 5 (very satisfied).

	Probability	
Job Satisfaction Score	IS Senior Executives	IS Middle Managers
1	.05	.04
2	.09	.10
3	.03	.12
4	.42	.46
5	.41	.28
Total	1.00	1.00

a. What is the expected value of the job satisfaction score for senior executives?
b. What is the expected value of the job satisfaction score for middle managers?
c. Compute the variance of job satisfaction scores for executives and middle managers.
d. Compute the standard deviation of job satisfaction scores for both probability distributions.
e. Compare the overall job satisfaction of senior executives and middle managers.

22. The demand for a product of Carolina Industries varies greatly from month to month. The probability distribution in the following table, based on the past two years of data, shows the company's monthly demand.

Unit Demand	Probability
300	.20
400	.30
500	.35
600	.15

a. If the company bases monthly orders on the expected value of the monthly demand, what should Carolina's monthly order quantity be for this product?

b. Assume that each unit demanded generates $70 in revenue and that each unit ordered costs $50. How much will the company gain or lose in a month if it places an order based on your answer to part (a) and the actual demand for the item is 300 units?

23. The *Forbes* 1993 Subscriber Study and the *Fortune* 1994 National Subscriber Portrait reported the following probability distributions for the number of vehicles per subscriber household.

x	*Forbes* $f(x)$	*Fortune* $f(x)$
0	.045	.028
1	.230	.165
2	.449	.489
3	.169	.185
4	.107	.133

a. What is the expected value of the number of vehicles per household for each subscriber group?

b. What is the variance of the number of vehicles per household for each subscriber group?

c. Using your answers to parts (a) and (b), what comparisons can you make about the number of vehicles per household for *Forbes* and *Fortune* subscribers?

24. The J. R. Ryland Computer Company is considering a plant expansion that will enable the company to begin production of a new computer product. The company's president must determine whether to make the expansion a medium- or large-scale project. An uncertainty is the demand for the new product, which for planning purposes may be low demand, medium demand, or high demand. The probability estimates for demand are .20, .50, and .30, respectively. Letting *x* and *y* indicate the annual profits in $1000s, the firm's planners have developed the following profit forecasts for the medium- and large-scale expansion projects.

		Medium-Scale Expansion Profits		Large-Scale Expansion Profits	
		x	$f(x)$	y	$f(y)$
	Low	50	.20	0	.20
Demand	Medium	150	.50	100	.50
	High	200	.30	300	.30

a. Compute the expected value for the profit associated with the two expansion alternatives. Which decision is preferred for the objective of maximizing the expected profit?

b. Compute the variance for the profit associated with the two expansion alternatives. Which decision is preferred for the objective of minimizing the risk or uncertainty?

....*/* */*.............

5.4   BINOMIAL PROBABILITY DISTRIBUTION

The binomial probability distribution is a discrete probability distribution that has many applications. It is associated with a multiple-step experiment that we call the binomial experiment.

A Binomial Experiment

A *binomial experiment* has the following four properties.

Properties of a Binomial Experiment

1. The experiment consists of a sequence of *n* identical trials.
2. Two outcomes are possible on each trial. We refer to one as a *success* and the other as a *failure*.
3. The probability of a success, denoted by *p*, does not change from trial to trial. Consequently, the probability of a failure, denoted by $1 - p$, does not change from trial to trial.
4. The trials are independent.

| **Figure 5.2** | DIAGRAM OF AN EIGHT-TRIAL BINOMIAL EXPERIMENT |

Property 1:   The experiment consists of
$n = 8$ identical trials.

Property 2:   Each trial results in either
success (S) or failure (F).

Trials ⟶	1	2	3	4	5	6	7	8
Outcomes ⟶	S	F	F	S	S	F	S	S

If properties 2, 3, and 4 are present, we say the trials are generated by a Bernoulli process. If, in addition, property 1 is present, we say we have a *binomial experiment.* Figure 5.2 depicts one possible sequence of outcomes of a binomial experiment involving eight trials. This case presents the possibility of 5 successes and 3 failures.

In a binomial experiment, our interest is in the *number of successes occurring in the n trials.* If we let x denote the number of successes occurring in the n trials, we see that x can assume the values of 0, 1, 2, 3, $\cdots$, n. Because the number of values is finite, x is a *discrete* random variable. The probability distribution associated with this random variable is called the *binomial probability distribution.* For example, consider the experiment of tossing a coin five times and on each toss observing whether the coin lands with a head or a tail on its upward face. Suppose we are interested in counting the number of heads appearing over the five tosses. Does this experiment have the properties of a binomial experiment? What is the random variable of interest? Note that:

1. The experiment consists of five identical trials; each trial involves the tossing of one coin.
2. Two outcomes are possible for each trial: a head or a tail. We can designate head a success and tail a failure.
3. The probability of a head and the probability of a tail are the same for each trial, with $p = .5$ and $1 - p = .5$.
4. The trials or tosses are independent because the outcome on any one trial is not affected by what happens on other trials or tosses.

Thus, the properties of a binomial experiment are satisfied. The random variable of interest is $x =$ the number of heads appearing in the five trials. In this case, x can assume the values of 0, 1, 2, 3, 4, or 5.

As another example, consider an insurance salesperson who visits 10 randomly selected families. The outcome associated with each visit is classified as a success if the family purchases an insurance policy and a failure if the family does not. From past experience, the salesperson knows the probability that a randomly selected family will purchase an insurance policy is .10. Checking the properties of a binomial experiment, we observe that:

1. The experiment consists of 10 identical trials; each trial involves contacting one family.
2. Two outcomes are possible on each trial: the family purchases a policy (success) or the family does not purchase a policy (failure).

3. The probabilities of a purchase and a nonpurchase are assumed to be the same for each sales call, with $p = .10$ and $1 - p = .90$.
4. The trials are independent because the families are randomly selected.

Because the four assumptions are satisfied, this example is a binomial experiment. The random variable of interest is the number of sales obtained in contacting the 10 families. In this case, x can assume the values of 0, 1, 2, 3, 4, 5, 6, 7, 8, 9, and 10.

Property 3 of the binomial experiment is called the *stationarity assumption* and is sometimes confused with property 4, independence of trials. To see how they differ, consider again the case of the salesperson calling on families to sell insurance policies. If, as the day wore on, the salesperson got tired and lost enthusiasm, the probability of success (selling a policy) might drop to .05, for example, by the tenth call. In such a case, property 3 (stationarity) would not be satisfied, and we would not have a binomial experiment. Even if property 4 held—that is, the purchase decisions of each family were made independently—it would not be a binomial experiment if property 3 was not satisfied.

In applications involving binomial experiments, a special mathematical formula, called the *binomial probability function,* can be used to compute the probability of x successes in the n trials. Using probability concepts introduced in Chapter 4, we will show in the context of an illustrative problem how the formula can be developed.

Martin Clothing Store Problem

Let us consider the purchase decisions of the next three customers who enter the Martin Clothing Store. On the basis of past experience, the store manager estimates the probability that any one customer will make a purchase is .30. What is the probability that two of the next three customers will make a purchase?

Using a tree diagram (Figure 5.3), we can see that the experiment of observing the three customers each making a purchase decision has eight possible outcomes. Using S to denote success (a purchase) and F to denote failure (no purchase), we are interested in experimental outcomes involving two successes in the three trials (purchase decisions). Next, let us verify that the experiment involving the sequence of three purchase decisions can be viewed as a binomial experiment. Checking the four requirements for a binomial experiment, we note that:

1. The experiment can be described as a sequence of three identical trials, one trial for each of the three customers who will enter the store.
2. Two outcomes—the customer makes a purchase (success) or the customer does not make a purchase (failure)—are possible for each trial.
3. The probability that the customer will make a purchase (.30) or will not make a purchase (.70) is assumed to be the same for all customers.
4. The purchase decision of each customer is independent of the decisions of the other customers.

Hence, the properties of a binomial experiment are present.

The number of experimental outcomes resulting in exactly x successes in n trials can be computed from the following formula.*

---

*This formula is introduced in Chapter 4 to determine the number of combinations of n objects selected x at a time. For the binomial experiment, this combinatorial formula provides the number of experimental outcomes (sequences of n trials) resulting in x successes.

| Figure 5.3 | TREE DIAGRAM FOR THE MARTIN CLOTHING STORE PROBLEM |

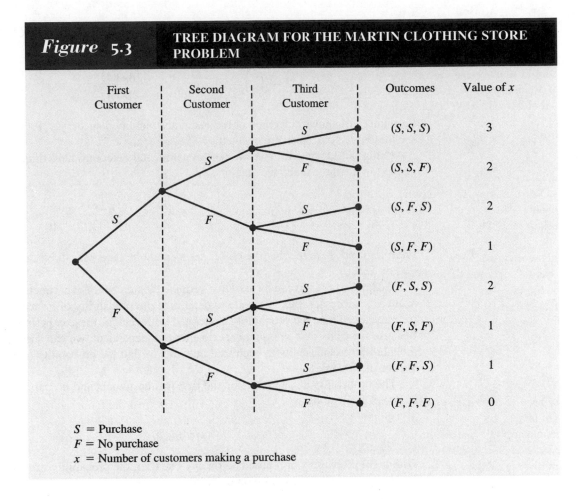

First Customer	Second Customer	Third Customer	Outcomes	Value of x
		S	(S, S, S)	3
	S	F	(S, S, F)	2
S	F	S	(S, F, S)	2
		F	(S, F, F)	1
		S	(F, S, S)	2
	S	F	(F, S, F)	1
F	F	S	(F, F, S)	1
		F	(F, F, F)	0

S = Purchase
F = No purchase
x = Number of customers making a purchase

Number of Experimental Outcomes Providing Exactly x Successes in n Trials

$$\binom{n}{x} = \frac{n!}{x!(n-x)!} \qquad (5.6)$$

where

$$n! = n(n-1)(n-2) \cdots (2)(1)$$

and

$$0! = 1$$

Now let us return to the Martin Clothing Store experiment involving three customer purchase decisions. Equation (5.6) can be used to determine the number of experimental outcomes involving two purchases; that is, the number of ways of obtaining $x = 2$ successes in the $n = 3$ trials. From (5.6) we have

$$\binom{n}{x} = \binom{3}{2} = \frac{3!}{2!(3-2)!} = \frac{(3)(2)(1)}{(2)(1)(1)} = \frac{6}{2} = 3$$

Formula (5.6) shows that three of the outcomes yield two successes. From Figure 5.3 we see these three outcomes are denoted by *SSF*, *SFS*, and *FSS*.

Using (5.6) to determine how many experimental outcomes have three successes (purchases) in the three trials, we obtain

$$\binom{n}{x} = \binom{3}{3} = \frac{3!}{3!(3-3)!} = \frac{3!}{3!0!} = \frac{(3)(2)(1)}{3(2)(1)(1)} = \frac{6}{6} = 1$$

From Figure 5.3 we see that the one experimental outcome with three successes is identified by *SSS*.

We know that (5.6) can be used to determine the number of experimental outcomes that result in x successes. But, if we are to determine the probability of x successes in n trials, we must also know the probability associated with each of these experimental outcomes. Because the trials of a binomial experiment are independent, we can simply multiply the probabilities associated with each trial outcome to find the probability of a particular sequence of outcomes.

The probability of purchases by the first two customers and no purchase by the third customer is given by

$$pp(1-p)$$

With a .30 probability of a purchase on any one trial, the probability of a purchase on the first two trials and no purchase on the third is given by

$$(.30)(.30)(.70) = (.30)^2(.70) = .063$$

Two other sequences of outcomes result in two successes and one failure. The probabilities for all three sequences involving two successes are shown as follows.

1st Customer	2nd Customer	3rd Customer	Success-Failure Notation	Probability of Experimental Outcome
Purchase	Purchase	No purchase	*SSF*	$pp(1-p) = p^2(1-p)$ $= (.30)^2(.70) = .063$
Purchase	No purchase	Purchase	*SFS*	$p(1-p)p = p^2(1-p)$ $= (.30)^2(.70) = .063$
No purchase	Purchase	Purchase	*FSS*	$(1-p)pp = p^2(1-p)$ $= (.30)^2(.70) = .063$

Observe that all three outcomes with two successes have exactly the same probability. This observation holds in general. In any binomial experiment, all sequences of trial outcomes yielding x successes in n trials have the *same probability* of occurrence. The probability of each sequence of trials yielding x successes in n trials follows.

$$\begin{array}{l} \text{Probability of a Particular} \\ \text{Sequence of Trial Outcomes} = p^x(1 - p)^{(n-x)} \\ \text{with } x \text{ Successes in } n \text{ Trials} \end{array} \qquad (5.7)$$

For the Martin Clothing Store, this formula shows that any outcome with two successes has a probability of $p^2(1 - p)^{(3-2)} = p^2(1 - p)^1 = (.30)^2(.70)^1 = .063$, as shown.

Because (5.6) shows the number of outcomes in a binomial experiment with x successes and (5.7) gives the probability for each sequence involving x successes, we combine (5.6) and (5.7) to obtain the following binomial probability function.

Binomial Probability Function

$$f(x) = \binom{n}{x} p^x (1 - p)^{(n-x)} \qquad (5.8)$$

where

$$f(x) = \text{the probability of } x \text{ successes in } n \text{ trials}$$
$$n = \text{the number of trials}$$
$$\binom{n}{x} = \frac{n!}{x!(n - x)!}$$
$$p = \text{the probability of a success on any one trial}$$
$$(1 - p) = \text{the probability of a failure on any one trial}$$

In the Martin Clothing Store example, let us compute the probability that no customer makes a purchase, exactly one customer makes a purchase, exactly two customers make a purchase, and all three customers make a purchase. The calculations are summarized in Table 5.7,

Table 5.7	PROBABILITY DISTRIBUTION FOR THE NUMBER OF CUSTOMERS MAKING A PURCHASE

x	$f(x)$
0	$\dfrac{3!}{0!3!}(.30)^0(.70)^3 = .343$
1	$\dfrac{3!}{1!2!}(.30)^1(.70)^2 = .441$
2	$\dfrac{3!}{2!1!}(.30)^2(.70)^1 = .189$
3	$\dfrac{3!}{3!0!}(.30)^3(.70)^0 = \underline{.027}$
	1.000

which gives the probability distribution of the number of customers purchasing. Figure 5.4 is a graph of this probability distribution.

The binomial probability function can be applied to *any* binomial experiment. If we are satisfied that a situation has the properties of a binomial experiment and if we know the values of n, p, and $(1 - p)$, we can use (5.8) to compute the probability of x successes in the n trials.

If we consider variations of the Martin experiment, such as 10 customers rather than three entering the store, the binomial probability function given by (5.8) is still applicable. For example, the probability of making exactly four sales to 10 potential customers entering the store is

$$f(4) = \frac{10!}{4!6!} (.30)^4(.70)^6 = .2001$$

It is a binomial experiment with $n = 10$, $x = 4$, and $p = .30$.

Using Tables of Binomial Probabilities

Tables have been developed that give the probability of x successes in n trials for a binomial experiment. The tables are generally easy to use and quicker than (5.8). A table of binomial probabilities is provided as Table 5 of Appendix B. A portion of this table is given in Table 5.8. To use this table, we must specify the values of n, p, and x for the binomial experiment of interest. In the example at the top of Table 5.8, we see that the probability of $x = 3$ successes in a binomial experiment with $n = 10$ and $p = .40$ is .2150. You can use (5.8) to verify that you would obtain the same answer if you used the binomial probability function directly.

Now let us use Table 5.8 to verify the probability of four successes in 10 trials for the Martin Clothing Store problem. Note that the value of $f(4) = .2001$ can be read directly from the table of binomial probabilities, with $n = 10$, $x = 4$, and $p = .30$.

Figure 5.4	**GRAPHICAL REPRESENTATION OF THE PROBABILITY DISTRIBUTION FOR THE MARTIN CLOTHING STORE PROBLEM**

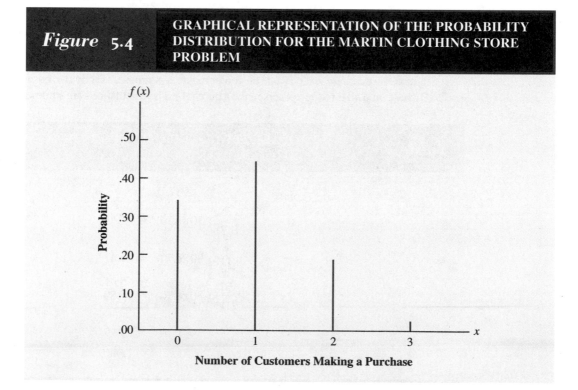

Table 5.8	SELECTED VALUES FROM THE BINOMIAL PROBABILITY TABLE
	EXAMPLE: $n = 10, x = 3, p = .40; f(3) = .2150$

p

n	x	.05	.10	.15	.20	.25	.30	.35	.40	.45	.50
9	0	.6302	.3874	.2316	.1342	.0751	.0404	.0207	.0101	.0046	.0020
	1	.2985	.3874	.3679	.3020	.2253	.1556	.1004	.0605	.0339	.0176
	2	.0629	.1722	.2597	.3020	.3003	.2668	.2162	.1612	.1110	.0703
	3	.0077	.0446	.1069	.1762	.2336	.2668	.2716	.2508	.2119	.1641
	4	.0006	.0074	.0283	.0661	.1168	.1715	.2194	.2508	.2600	.2461
	5	.0000	.0008	.0050	.0165	.0389	.0735	.1181	.1672	.2128	.2461
	6	.0000	.0001	.0006	.0028	.0087	.0210	.0424	.0743	.1160	.1641
	7	.0000	.0000	.0000	.0003	.0012	.0039	.0098	.0212	.0407	.0703
	8	.0000	.0000	.0000	.0000	.0001	.0004	.0013	.0035	.0083	.0176
	9	.0000	.0000	.0000	.0000	.0000	.0000	.0001	.0003	.0008	.0020
10	0	.5987	.3487	.1969	.1074	.0563	.0282	.0135	.0060	.0025	.0010
	1	.3151	.3874	.3474	.2684	.1877	.1211	.0725	.0403	.0207	.0098
	2	.0746	.1937	.2759	.3020	.2816	.2335	.1757	.1209	.0763	.0439
	3	.0105	.0574	.1298	.2013	.2503	.2668	.2522	**.2150**	.1665	.1172
	4	.0010	.0112	.0401	.0881	.1460	.2001	.2377	.2508	.2384	.2051
	5	.0001	.0015	.0085	.0264	.0584	.1029	.1536	.2007	.2340	.2461
	6	.0000	.0001	.0012	.0055	.0162	.0368	.0689	.1115	.1596	.2051
	7	.0000	.0000	.0001	.0008	.0031	.0090	.0212	.0425	.0746	.1172
	8	.0000	.0000	.0000	.0001	.0004	.0014	.0043	.0106	.0229	.0439
	9	.0000	.0000	.0000	.0000	.0000	.0001	.0005	.0016	.0042	.0098
	10	.0000	.0000	.0000	.0000	.0000	.0000	.0000	.0001	.0003	.0010

With modern calculators, these tables are almost unnecessary. It is easy to evaluate (5.8) directly.

While the tables of binomial probabilities are relatively easy to use, it is impossible to have tables that show all possible values of n and p that might be encountered in a binomial experiment. However, with today's calculators, using (5.8) to calculate the desired probability is not difficult, especially if the number of trials is not large. In the exercises, you should practice using (5.8) to compute the binomial probabilities unless the problem specifically requests that you use the binomial probability table.

Statistical software packages such as Minitab and spreadsheet packages such as Excel also provide a capability for computing binomial probabilities. Consider the Martin Clothing Store example with $n = 10$ and $p = .30$. Figure 5.5 shows the binomial probabilities generated by Minitab for all possible values of x. Note that these values are the same as those found in the $p = .30$ column of Table 5.8. The appendixes at the end of this chapter show how Minitab and Excel can be used to generate these probabilities. Appendix 5.1 gives the step-by-step procedure for using Minitab to generate the output in Figure 5.5. Appendix 5.2 describes how Excel can be used to compute binomial probabilities.

Expected Value and Variance for the Binomial Probability Distribution

In Section 5.3 we provided formulas for computing the expected value and variance of a discrete random variable. In the special case where the random variable has a binomial probability distribution with a known number of trials n and a known probability of

Figure 5.5	**MINITAB OUTPUT SHOWING BINOMIAL PROBABILITIES FOR THE MARTIN CLOTHING STORE PROBLEM**	

```
            x          P( X = x)
          0.00           0.0282
          1.00           0.1211
          2.00           0.2335
          3.00           0.2668
          4.00           0.2001
          5.00           0.1029
          6.00           0.0368
          7.00           0.0090
          8.00           0.0014
          9.00           0.0001
         10.00           0.0000
```

success p, the general formulas for the expected value and variance can be simplified. The results follow.

Expected Value and Variance for the Binomial Probability Distribution

$$E(x) = \mu = np \tag{5.9}$$
$$\text{Var}(x) = \sigma^2 = np(1 - p) \tag{5.10}$$

For the Martin Clothing Store problem with three customers, we can use (5.9) to compute the expected number of customers making a purchase.

$$E(x) = np = 3(.30) = .9$$

Suppose that for the next month the Martin Clothing Store forecasts 1000 customers will enter the store. What is the expected number of customers who will make a purchase? The answer is $\mu = np = (1000)(.3) = 300$. Thus, to increase the expected number of sales, Martin's must induce more customers to enter the store and/or somehow increase the probability that any individual customer will make a purchase after entering.

For the Martin Clothing Store problem with three customers, we see that the variance and standard deviation for the number of customers making a purchase are

The *np* chart and lot acceptance sampling as quality control procedures are excellent examples of the binomial distribution. These procedures are discussed in Chapter 13, Statistical Methods for Quality Control.

$$\sigma^2 = np(1 - p) = 3(.3)(.7) = .63$$
$$\sigma = \sqrt{.63} = .79$$

For the next 1000 customers entering the store, the variance and standard deviation for the number of customers making a purchase are

$$\sigma^2 = np(1 - p) = 1000(.3)(.7) = 210$$
$$\sigma = \sqrt{210} = 14.49$$

N O T E S	1. Some binomial tables show values of p only up to and including

N O T E S
and Comments

1. Some binomial tables show values of p only up to and including $p = .50$. It would appear that such tables cannot be used when the probability of success exceeds $p = .50$. However, they can be used by noting that the probability of $n - x$ failures is also the probability of x successes. When the probability of success is greater than $p = .50$, one can compute the probability of $n - x$ failures instead. The probability of failure, $1 - p$, will be less than .50 when $p > .50$.

2. Some sources present binomial tables in a cumulative form. In using such tables, one must subtract to find the probability of x successes in n trials. For example, $f(2) = P(x \le 2) - P(x \le 1)$. Our tables provide these probabilities directly. To compute cumulative probabilities using our tables, one simply sums the individual probabilities. For example, to compute $P(x \le 2)$ using our tables, we sum $f(0) + f(1) + f(2)$.

EXERCISES

Methods

SELF TEST

25. Consider a binomial experiment with two trials and $p = .4$.
    a. Draw a tree diagram showing it as a two-trial experiment (see Figure 5.3).
    b. Compute the probability of one success, $f(1)$.
    c. Compute $f(0)$.
    d. Compute $f(2)$.
    e. Find the probability of at least one success.
    f. Find the expected value, variance, and standard deviation.

26. Consider a binomial experiment with $n = 10$ and $p = .10$. Use the binomial tables (Table 5 of Appendix B) to answer parts (a) through (d).
    a. Find $f(0)$.
    b. Find $f(2)$.
    c. Find $P(x \le 2)$.
    d. Find $P(x \ge 1)$.
    e. Find $E(x)$.
    f. Find Var(x) and σ.

27. Consider a binomial experiment with $n = 20$ and $p = .70$. Use the binomial tables (Table 5 of Appendix B) to answer parts (a) through (d).
    a. Find $f(12)$.
    b. Find $f(16)$.
    c. Find $P(x \ge 16)$.
    d. Find $P(x \le 15)$.
    e. Find $E(x)$.
    f. Find Var(x) and σ.

Applications

28. The greatest number of complaints by owners of two-year-old automobiles pertain to electrical system performance (*Consumer Reports 1995 Buyer's Guide*). Assume that an annual questionnaire sent to owners of more than 300 makes and models of automobiles reveals that 10% of the owners of two-year-old automobiles found trouble spots in the electrical

system that included the starter, alternator, battery, switch controls, instruments, wiring, lights, and radio.

a. What is the probability that a sample of 12 owners of two-year-old automobiles will find exactly two owners with electrical system problems?

b. What is the probability that a sample of 12 owners of two-year-old automobiles will find at least two owners with electrical system problems?

c. What is the probability that a sample of 20 owners of two-year-old automobiles will find at least one owner with an electrical system problem?

29. *The American Almanac of Jobs and Salaries,* 1994–95, reported that 25% of accountants are employed in public accounting. Assume that this percentage applies to a group of 15 college graduates just entering the accounting profession. What is the probability that at least three graduates will be employed in public accounting?

SELF TEST

30. When a new machine is functioning properly, only 3% of the items produced are defective. Assume that we will randomly select two parts produced on the machine and that we are interested in the number of defective parts found.

a. Describe the conditions under which this situation would be a binomial experiment.

b. Draw a tree diagram similar to Figure 5.3 showing this problem as a two-trial experiment.

c. How many experimental outcomes result in exactly one defect being found?

d. Compute the probabilities associated with finding no defects, exactly one defect, and two defects.

31. Five percent of American truck drivers are women (*Statistical Abstract of the United States,* 1997). Suppose 10 truck drivers are selected randomly to be interviewed about quality of work conditions.

a. Is the selection of the 10 drivers a binomial experiment? Explain.

b. What is the probability that two of the drivers will be women?

c. What is the probability that none will be women?

d. What is the probability that at least one will be a woman?

32. Military radar and missile detection systems are designed to warn a country against enemy attacks. A reliability question is whether a detection system will be able to identify an attack and issue a warning. Assume that a particular detection system has a .90 probability of detecting a missile attack. Use the binomial probability distribution to answer the following questions.

a. What is the probability that a single detection system will detect an attack?

b. If two detection systems are installed in the same area and operate independently, what is the probability that at least one of the systems will detect the attack?

c. If three systems are installed, what is the probability that at least one of the systems will detect the attack?

d. Would you recommend that multiple detection systems be used? Explain.

33. Fifty percent of midsize manufacturers planned to have management representatives visit Canada and Mexico to take advantage of opportunities created by the North American Free Trade Agreement (*Grant Thornton Survey of American Manufacturers,* 1995). An export–import group in Toronto, Canada, has invited 20 U.S. midsize manufacturers to participate in a conference to explore trade opportunities.

a. What is the probability that 12 or more companies will send representatives?

b. What is the probability that no more than 5 companies will send representatives?

c. How many companies would you expect to send representatives?

d. What are the variance and standard deviation of the number of companies sending representatives?

34. An American Association of Individual Investors survey found that 23% of AAII members had purchased shares of stock directly through an initial public offering (IPO) (*AAII Journal,* July 1994). In a sample of 12 AAII members,

a. What is the probability exactly three members have purchased IPOs?

b. What is the probability at least one member has purchased IPOs?

c. What is the probability that two or more members have purchased IPOs?

35. A university has found that 20% of its students withdraw without completing the introductory statistics course. Assume that 20 students have registered for the course this quarter.
    a.   What is the probability that two or fewer will withdraw?
    b.   What is the probability that exactly four will withdraw?
    c.   What is the probability that more than three will withdraw?
    d.   What is the expected number of withdrawals?

36. For the special case of a binomial random variable, we stated that the variance measure could be computed from the formula $\sigma^2 = np(1 - p)$. For the Martin Clothing Store problem data in Table 5.7, we found $\sigma^2 = np(1 - p) = .63$. Use the general definition of variance for a discrete random variable, equation (5.5), and the data in Table 5.7 to verify that the variance is in fact .63.

37. Twenty-nine percent of lawyers and judges are women (*Statistical Abstract of the United States, 1997*). In a jurisdiction with 30 lawyers and judges, what is the expected number of women? What are the variance and standard deviation?

5.5   POISSON PROBABILITY DISTRIBUTION

The Poisson probability distribution is often used to model arrival rates in waiting line situations.

In this section we consider a discrete random variable that is often useful in estimating the number of occurrences over a specified interval of time or space. For example, the random variable of interest might be the number of arrivals at a car wash in one hour, the number of repairs needed in 10 miles of highway, or the number of leaks in 100 miles of pipeline. If the following two properties are satisfied, the number of occurrences is a random variable described by the *Poisson probability function*.

Properties of a Poisson Experiment

1. The probability of an occurrence is the same for any two intervals of equal length.
2. The occurrence or nonoccurrence in any interval is independent of the occurrence or nonoccurrence in any other interval.

The Poisson probability function is given by (5.11).

Poisson Probability Function

$$f(x) = \frac{\mu^x e^{-\mu}}{x!}$$

(5.11)

where

$f(x)$ = the probability of x occurrences in an interval

μ = expected value or mean number of occurrences in an interval

e = 2.71828

Before we consider a specific example to see how the Poisson distribution can be applied, note that the number of occurrences, x, has no upper limit. It is a discrete random variable that may assume an infinite sequence of values ($x = 0, 1, 2, \cdots$). The Poisson random variable has no upper limit.

An Example Involving Time Intervals

Suppose that we are interested in the number of arrivals at the drive-in teller window of a bank during a 15-minute period on weekday mornings. If we can assume that the probability of a car arriving is the same for any two time periods of equal length and that the arrival or nonarrival of a car in any time period is independent of the arrival or nonarrival in any other time period, the Poisson probability function is applicable. Suppose these assumptions are satisfied and an analysis of historical data shows that the average number of cars arriving in a 15-minute period of time is 10; then the following probability function applies.

$$f(x) = \frac{10^x e^{-10}}{x!}$$

The random variable here is $x =$ number of cars arriving in any 15-minute period.

If management wanted to know the probability of exactly five arrivals in 15 minutes, we would set $x = 5$ and thus obtain*

$$\text{Probability of Exactly 5 Arrivals in 15 Minutes} = f(5) = \frac{10^5 e^{-10}}{5!} = .0378$$

Although this probability was determined by evaluating the probability function with $\mu = 10$ and $x = 5$, it is often easier to refer to tables for the Poisson probability distribution. These tables provide probabilities for specific values of x and μ. We have included such a table as Table 7 of Appendix B. For convenience, we have reproduced a portion of this table as Table 5.9. Note that to use the table of Poisson probabilities, we need know only the values of x and μ. From Table 5.9 we see that the probability of five arrivals in a 15-minute period is found by locating the value in the row of the table corresponding to $x = 5$ and the column of the table corresponding to $\mu = 10$. Hence, we obtain $f(5) = .0378$.

Our illustration involves computing the probability of five arrivals in a 15-minute period, but other time periods can be used. Suppose we want to compute the probability of one arrival in a three-minute period. Because 10 is the expected number of arrivals in a 15-minute period, we see that $^{10}\!/_{15} = ^{2}\!/_{3}$ is the expected number of arrivals in a one-minute period and that $(2/3)(3 \text{ minutes}) = 2$ is the expected number of arrivals in a three-minute period. Thus, the probability of x arrivals in a three-minute time period with $\mu = 2$ is given by the following Poisson probability function.

$$f(x) = \frac{2^x e^{-2}}{x!}$$

To find the probability of one arrival in a three-minute period, we can either use Table 7 in Appendix B or compute the probability directly.

$$\text{Probability of Exactly 1 Arrival in 3 Minutes} = f(1) = \frac{2^1 e^{-2}}{1!} = .2707$$

*Values of $e^{-\mu}$ can be found in Table 6 of Appendix B. Most calculators also provide these values.

Table 5.9	SELECTED VALUES FROM THE POISSON PROBABILITY TABLES EXAMPLE: $\mu = 10, x = 5; f(5) = .0378$								

	μ									
x	9.1	9.2	9.3	9.4	9.5	9.6	9.7	9.8	9.9	10
0	.0001	.0001	.0001	.0001	.0001	.0001	.0001	.0001	.0001	.0000
1	.0010	.0009	.0009	.0008	.0007	.0007	.0006	.0005	.0005	.0005
2	.0046	.0043	.0040	.0037	.0034	.0031	.0029	.0027	.0025	.0023
3	.0140	.0131	.0123	.0115	.0107	.0100	.0093	.0087	.0081	.0076
4	.0319	.0302	.0285	.0269	.0254	.0240	.0226	.0213	.0201	.0189
5	.0581	.0555	.0530	.0506	.0483	.0460	.0439	.0418	.0398	**.0378**
6	.0881	.0851	.0822	.0793	.0764	.0736	.0709	.0682	.0656	.0631
7	.1145	.1118	.1091	.1064	.1037	.1010	.0982	.0955	.0928	.0901
8	.1302	.1286	.1269	.1251	.1232	.1212	.1191	.1170	.1148	.1126
9	.1317	.1315	.1311	.1306	.1300	.1293	.1284	.1274	.1263	.1251
10	.1198	.1210	.1219	.1228	.1235	.1241	.1245	.1249	.1250	.1251
11	.0991	.1012	.1031	.1049	.1067	.1083	.1098	.1112	.1125	.1137
12	.0752	.0776	.0799	.0822	.0844	.0866	.0888	.0908	.0928	.0948
13	.0526	.0549	.0572	.0594	.0617	.0640	.0662	.0685	.0707	.0729
14	.0342	.0361	.0380	.0399	.0419	.0439	.0459	.0479	.0500	.0521
15	.0208	.0221	.0235	.0250	.0265	.0281	.0297	.0313	.0330	.0347
16	.0118	.0127	.0137	.0147	.0157	.0168	.0180	.0192	.0204	.0217
17	.0063	.0069	.0075	.0081	.0088	.0095	.0103	.0111	.0119	.0128
18	.0032	.0035	.0039	.0042	.0046	.0051	.0055	.0060	.0065	.0071
19	.0015	.0017	.0019	.0021	.0023	.0026	.0028	.0031	.0034	.0037
20	.0007	.0008	.0009	.0010	.0011	.0012	.0014	.0015	.0017	.0019
21	.0003	.0003	.0004	.0004	.0005	.0006	.0006	.0007	.0008	.0009
22	.0001	.0001	.0002	.0002	.0002	.0002	.0003	.0003	.0004	.0004
23	.0000	.0001	.0001	.0001	.0001	.0001	.0001	.0001	.0002	.0002
24	.0000	.0000	.0000	.0000	.0000	.0000	.0000	.0001	.0001	.0001

An Example Involving Length or Distance Intervals

Let us illustrate an application not involving time intervals in which the Poisson probability distribution is useful. Suppose we are concerned with the occurrence of major defects in a highway one month after resurfacing. We will assume that the probability of a defect is the same for any two highway intervals of equal length and that the occurrence or nonoccurrence of a defect in any one interval is independent of the occurrence or nonoccurrence of a defect in any other interval. Hence, the Poisson probability distribution can be applied.

Suppose we learn that major defects one month after resurfacing occur at the average rate of two per mile. Let us find the probability of no major defects in a particular three-mile section of the highway. Because we are interested in an interval with a length of three miles, $\mu = (2 \text{ defects/mile})(3 \text{ miles}) = 6$ represents the expected number of major defects over the three-mile section of highway. By using (5.11) or Table 7 in Appendix B, we see that the probability of no major defects is .0025. Thus, it is unlikely that no major defects will occur in the three-mile section. In fact, this example indicates a $1 - .0025 = .9975$ probability of at least one major defect in the highway section.

Poisson Approximation of the Binomial Probability Distribution

The Poisson probability distribution can be used as an approximation of the binomial probability distribution when p, the probability of success, is small and n, the number of trials, is large. Simply set $\mu = np$ and use the Poisson tables. As a rule of thumb, the approximation will be good whenever $p \leq .05$ and $n \geq 20$.

As an example, suppose we want to compute the binomial probability of $x = 3$ successes in $n = 250$ trials with $p = .01$. To use the Poisson approximation, we set $\mu = np = 250(.01) = 2.5$. Referring to the Poisson probability tables (Table 7 in Appendix B), we find $f(3) = .2138$. So, we would approximate the binomial probability of three successes as $f(3) = .2138$.

The exact binomial probability is .2149; the Poisson approximation is especially good in this case.

EXERCISES

Methods

38. Consider a Poisson probability distribution with $\mu = 3$.
   a. Write the appropriate Poisson probability function.
   b. Find $f(2)$.
   c. Find $f(1)$.
   d. Find $P(x \geq 2)$.

39. Consider a Poisson probability distribution with an average number of occurrences per time period of two.
   a. Write the appropriate Poisson probability function.
   b. What is the average number of occurrences in three time periods?
   c. Write the appropriate Poisson probability function to determine the probability of x occurrences in three time periods.
   d. Find the probability of two occurrences in one time period.
   e. Find the probability of six occurrences in three time periods.
   f. Find the probability of five occurrences in two time periods.

Applications

40. Phone calls arrive at the rate of 48 per hour at the reservation desk for Regional Airways.
   a. Find the probability of receiving three calls in a five-minute interval of time.
   b. Find the probability of receiving exactly 10 calls in 15 minutes.
   c. Suppose no calls are currently on hold. If the agent takes five minutes to complete the current call, how many callers do you expect to be waiting by that time? What is the probability that none will be waiting?
   d. If no calls are currently being processed, what is the probability that the agent can take three minutes for personal time without being interrupted?

41. During the period of time phone-in reservations are being taken at a local university, calls come in at the rate of one every two minutes.
   a. What is the expected number of calls in one hour?
   b. What is the probability of three calls in five minutes?
   c. What is the probability of no calls in a five-minute period?

42. The mean number of times per year that *Barron's* subscribers take domestic flights for personal reasons is four (*Barron's* 1995 Primary Reader Survey).
   a. What is the probability a subscriber takes two domestic flights for personal reasons in a year?
   b. What is the mean number of domestic flights for personal reasons in a 3-month period?
   c. What is the probability a subscriber takes one or more domestic flights for personal reasons in a 6-month period?

43. Airline passengers arrive randomly and independently at the passenger-screening facility at a major international airport. The mean arrival rate is 10 passengers per minute.
    a. What is the probability of no arrivals in a one-minute period?
    b. What is the probability that three or fewer passengers arrive in a one-minute period?
    c. What is the probability of no arrivals in a 15-second period?
    d. What is the probability of at least one arrival in a 15-second period?

44. Investment activities for subscribers to *The Wall Street Journal* show that the average number of security transactions per year is 15 (*The Wall Street Journal* Subscriber Study, 1995). Assume that a particular investor makes transactions at this rate. Furthermore, assume that the probability of a transaction for this investor is the same for any two months and transactions in one month are independent of transactions in any other month. Answer the following questions.
    a. What is the mean number of transactions per month?
    b. What is the probability of no stock transactions during a month?
    c. What is the probability of exactly one stock transaction during a month?
    d. What is the probability of more than one stock transaction during a month?

45. Each year, 450 accidental deaths due to firearms occur in the 15–24 age group (National Safety Council, *Accident Facts,* 1996).
    a. What is the average number of accidental deaths due to firearms per week?
    b. What is the probability of no accidental deaths due to firearms in a typical week?
    c. What is the probability of two or more accidental deaths due to firearms in a typical day?

5.6   HYPERGEOMETRIC PROBABILITY DISTRIBUTION

The hypergeometric probability distribution is closely related to the binomial probability distribution. The key difference between the two probability distributions is that with the hypergeometric distribution, the trials are not independent; and the probability of success changes from trial to trial.

The usual notation in applications of the hypergeometric probability distribution is to let r denote the number of elements in the population of size N that are labeled success and $N - r$ denote the number of elements in the population that are labeled failure. The *hypergeometric probability function* is used to compute the probability that in a random sample of n elements, selected without replacement, we will obtain x elements labeled success and $n - x$ elements labeled failure. For this to occur, we must obtain x successes from the r successes in the population and $n - x$ failures from the $N - r$ failures. The following hypergeometric probability function provides $f(x)$, the probability of obtaining x successes in a sample of size n.

Hypergeometric Probability Function

$$f(x) = \frac{\binom{r}{x}\binom{N - r}{n - x}}{\binom{N}{n}} \qquad \text{for } 0 \le x \le r \qquad (5.12)$$

where

$$f(x) = \text{probability of } x \text{ successes in } n \text{ trials}$$
$$n = \text{number of trials}$$
$$N = \text{number of elements in the population}$$
$$r = \text{number of elements in the population labeled success}$$

Note that $\binom{N}{n}$ represents the number of ways a sample of size n can be selected from a population of size N; $\binom{r}{x}$ represents the number of ways x successes can be selected from a total of r successes in the population; and $\binom{N-r}{n-x}$ represents the number of ways $n-x$ failures can be selected from a total of $N-r$ failures in the population.

To illustrate the computations involved in using (5.12), let us consider the problem of selecting two people from a five-member committee to send to a Las Vegas convention. Assume that the five-member committee consists of three women and two men. To determine the probability of randomly selecting two women, we can use (5.12) with $n=2, N=5, r=3$, and $x=2$.

$$f(2) = \frac{\binom{3}{2}\binom{2}{0}}{\binom{5}{2}} = \frac{\left(\frac{3!}{2!1!}\right)\left(\frac{2!}{2!0!}\right)}{\left(\frac{5!}{2!3!}\right)} = \frac{3}{10} = .30$$

Suppose we learn later that three committee members will be allowed to make the trip. If we use $n=3, N=5, r=3$, and $x=2$, the probability that exactly two of the three members will be women is

$$f(2) = \frac{\binom{3}{2}\binom{2}{1}}{\binom{5}{2}} = \frac{\left(\frac{3!}{2!1!}\right)\left(\frac{2!}{1!1!}\right)}{\left(\frac{5!}{2!3!}\right)} = \frac{6}{10} = .60$$

As another illustration, suppose a population consists of 10 items, four of which are classified as defective and six of which are classified as nondefective. What is the probability that a random sample of size three will contain two defective items? For this problem we can think of obtaining a defective item as a "success." Using (5.12) with $n=3, N=10, r=4$, and $x=2$, we can compute $f(2)$ as follows.

$$f(2) = \frac{\binom{4}{2}\binom{6}{1}}{\binom{10}{3}} = \frac{\left(\frac{4!}{2!2!}\right)\left(\frac{6!}{1!5!}\right)}{\left(\frac{10!}{3!7!}\right)} = \frac{36}{120} = .30$$

EXERCISES

Methods

SELF TEST

46. Suppose $N=10$ and $r=3$. Compute the hypergeometric probabilities for the following values of n and x.
   a. $n=4, x=1$.
   b. $n=2, x=2$.
   c. $n=2, x=0$.
   d. $n=4, x=2$.

47. Suppose $N=15$ and $r=4$. What is the probability of $x=3$ for $n=10$?

Applications

48. According to *Beverage Digest,* Coke Classic and Pepsi rank number one and number two in 1996 sales (*The Wall Street Journal Almanac,* 1998). Assume that in a group of 10 individuals, six prefer Coke Classic and four prefer Pepsi. A random sample of three of these individuals is selected.
    a. What is the probability that exactly two prefer Coke Classic?
    b. What is the probability that the majority (either two or three) prefer Pepsi?

49. Blackjack, or twenty-one as it is frequently called, is a popular gambling game played in Las Vegas casinos. A player is dealt two cards. Face cards (jacks, queens, and kings) and tens have a point value of 10. Aces have a point value of 1 or 11. A 52-card deck has 16 cards with a point value of 10 (jacks, queens, kings, and tens) and four aces.
    a. What is the probability that both cards dealt are from the 20 ace and 10-point cards?
    b. What is the probability that both of the cards are aces?
    c. What is the probability that both of the cards have a point value of 10?
    d. A blackjack is a 10-point card and an ace for a value of 21. Use your answers to parts (a), (b), and (c) to determine the probability that a player is dealt blackjack. (Hint: Part (d) is not a hypergeometric problem. Develop your own logical relationship as to how the hypergeometric probabilities from parts (a), (b), and (c) can be combined to answer this question.)

SELF TEST

50. Axline Computers manufactures personal computers at two plants, one in Texas and the other in Hawaii. The Texas plant has 40 employees; the Hawaii plant has 20. A random sample of 10 employees is to be asked to fill out a benefits questionnaire.
    a. What is the probability that none are at the plant in Hawaii?
    b. What is the probability that one is at the plant in Hawaii?
    c. What is the probability that two or more are at the plant in Hawaii?
    d. What is the probability that nine are at the plant in Texas?

51. Of the 25 students (14 boys and 11 girls) in the sixth-grade class at St. Andrew School, 5 students were absent Thursday.
    a. What is the probability that two of the absent students were girls?
    b. What is the probability that two of the absent students were boys?
    c. What is the probability that all were boys?
    d. What is the probability that none were boys?

52. A shipment of 10 items has two defective and eight nondefective units. In the inspection of the shipment, a sample of units will be selected and tested. If a defective unit is found, the shipment of 10 units will be rejected.
    a. If a sample of three items is selected, what is the probability that the shipment will be rejected?
    b. If a sample of four items is selected, what is the probability that the shipment will be rejected?
    c. If a sample of five items is selected, what is the probability that the shipment will be rejected?
    d. If management would like a .90 probability of rejecting a shipment with two defective and eight nondefective units, how large a sample would you recommend?

SUMMARY

The concept of a random variable was introduced to provide a numerical description of the outcome of an experiment. We saw that the probability distribution for a random variable describes how the probabilities are distributed over the values the random variable can assume. For any discrete random variable x, the probability distribution is defined by a probability function, denoted by $f(x)$, which provides the probability associated with each value of the random variable. Once the probability function has been defined, we can compute the expected value and the variance for the random variable.

The binomial probability distribution can be used to determine the probability of x successes in n trials whenever the experiment has the following properties:

1. The experiment consists of a sequence of n identical trials.
2. Two outcomes are possible on each trial, one called success and the other failure.
3. The probability of a success p does not change from trial to trial. Consequently, the probability of failure, $1 - p$, does not change from trial to trial.
4. The trials are independent.

When the four conditions hold, a binomial probability function, or a table of binomial probabilities, can be used to determine the probability of x successes in n trials. Formulas were also presented for the mean and variance of the binomial probability distribution.

The Poisson probability distribution is used when it is desirable to determine the probability of obtaining x occurrences over an interval of time or space. The following assumptions are necessary for the Poisson distribution to be applicable.

1. The probability of an occurrence of the event is the same for any two intervals of equal length.
2. The occurrence or nonoccurrence of the event in any interval is independent of the occurrence or nonoccurrence of the event in any other interval.

A third discrete probability distribution, the hypergeometric, was introduced in Section 5.6. Like the binomial, it is used to compute the probability of x successes in n trials. But, in contrast to the binomial, the probability of success changes from trial to trial.

GLOSSARY

Random variable A numerical description of the outcome of an experiment.

Discrete random variable A random variable that can assume only a finite or infinite sequence of values.

Continuous random variable A random variable that may assume any value in an interval or collection of intervals.

Probability distribution A description of how the probabilities are distributed over the values the random variable can assume.

Probability function A function, denoted by $f(x)$, that provides the probability that x assumes a particular value for a discrete random variable.

Discrete uniform probability function The function used to define the equal probabilities of the discrete uniform probability distribution.

Expected value A measure of the mean, or central location, of a random variable.

Variance A measure of the variability, or dispersion, of a random variable.

Standard deviation The positive square root of the variance.

Binomial experiment A probability experiment having the four properties stated in Section 5.4.

Binomial probability distribution A probability distribution showing the probability of x successes in n trials of a binomial experiment.

Binomial probability function The function used to compute probabilities in a binomial experiment.

Poisson probability distribution A probability distribution showing the probability of x occurrences of an event over a specified interval of time or space.

Poisson probability function The function used to compute Poisson probabilities.

Hypergeometric probability function The function used to compute the probability of x successes in n trials when the trials are dependent.

KEY FORMULAS

Discrete Uniform Probability Function

$$f(x) = 1/n \tag{5.3}$$

where n = the number of values the random variable may assume

Expected Value of a Discrete Random Variable

$$E(x) = \mu = \Sigma x f(x) \tag{5.4}$$

Variance of a Discrete Random Variable

$$\text{Var}(x) = \sigma^2 = \Sigma(x - \mu)^2 f(x) \tag{5.5}$$

Number of Experimental Outcomes Providing Exactly x Successes in n Trials

$$\binom{n}{x} = \frac{n!}{x!(n-x)!} \tag{5.6}$$

Binomial Probability Function

$$f(x) = \binom{n}{x} p^x (1-p)^{(n-x)} \tag{5.8}$$

Expected Value for the Binomial Probability Distribution

$$E(x) = \mu = np \tag{5.9}$$

Variance for the Binomial Probability Distribution

$$\text{Var}(x) = \sigma^2 = np(1-p) \tag{5.10}$$

Poisson Probability Function

$$f(x) = \frac{\mu^x e^{-\mu}}{x!} \tag{5.11}$$

Hypergeometric Probability Function

$$f(x) = \frac{\binom{r}{x}\binom{N-r}{n-x}}{\binom{N}{n}} \qquad \text{for } 0 \le x \le r \tag{5.12}$$

SUPPLEMENTARY EXERCISES

53. A *Wall Street Journal*/NBC News poll asked 2004 adults how they felt about their opportunities for career advancement (*The Wall Street Journal,* September 19, 1997). Twenty-three percent indicated they were very satisfied; 38% indicated they were somewhat satisfied; 3% indicated they were not sure; 18% indicated they were somewhat dissatisfied; and 18% indicated they were very dissatisfied. Let x be a random variable representing level of satisfaction. We let $x = 5$ for very satisfied, $x = 4$ for somewhat satisfied, $x = 3$ for not sure, $x = 2$ for somewhat dissatisfied, and $x = 1$ for very dissatisfied.
    a. Use the preceding numerical values to develop a probability distribution for level of satisfaction with opportunities for career advancement.
    b. Compute the expected level of satisfaction. Does a higher score indicate more or less satisfaction?
    c. Compute the variance and standard deviation for the satisfaction scores.

54. An opinion survey of 1009 adults was conducted by Louis Harris & Associates, Inc. (*Business Week,* December 29, 1997). Shown in Table 5.10 is the probability distribution of responses to a question concerning the stock market's valuation.
    a. Show that the probability distribution in Table 5.10 satisfies the properties of all probability distributions.
    b. What are the expected value and variance of the probability distribution of opinions?
    c. Comment on whether people think the stock market is overvalued.

55. The budgeting process for a midwestern college resulted in expense forecasts for the coming year (in $millions) of $9, $10, $11, $12, and $13. Because the actual expenses are unknown, the following respective probabilities are assigned: .3, .2, .25, .05, and .2.
    a. Show the probability distribution for the expense forecast.
    b. What is the expected value of the expenses for the coming year?
    c. What is the variance in the expenses for the coming year?
    d. If income projections for the year are estimated at $12 million, comment on the financial position of the college.

56. Kristen DelGuzzi conducted a study of Hamilton County judges and courts over a three-year period (*The Cincinnati Enquirer,* January 11, 1998). One finding was that 4% of the cases decided in Common Pleas Court were appealed.
    a. If 20 cases are heard on a particular day, what is the probability that 3 will be appealed?
    b. If 20 cases are heard on a particular day, what is the probability none will be appealed?
    c. It is not unusual for 1200 cases to be heard in a month. What is the expected number of appeals?
    d. If 1200 cases are heard in a month, what are the variance and standard deviation in the number of appeals?

Table 5.10	PROBABILITY DISTRIBUTION OF OPINIONS CONCERNING STOCK MARKET'S VALUATION	
Market Valuation	**Random Variable (x)**	**Probability $f(x)$**
Very undervalued	1	0.02
Somewhat undervalued	2	0.06
Fairly valued	3	0.28
Somewhat overvalued	4	0.54
Very overvalued	5	0.10

57. A company is planning to host a conference to learn how people are using the Internet. The conference planners want to ensure a good representation across age groups. According to Mediamark Research, 20% of individuals in the 25–34 age group and 8% of individuals in the 55–64 age group use the Internet (*Mediamark Research, Inc.*, New York, Spring 1997).
    a. How many people from the 25–34 age group should be invited to have an expected number of at least 10 attending?
    b. How many people from the 55–64 age group should be invited to have an expected number of at least 10 attending?
    c. If you invite the number suggested in part (a), what is the standard deviation of the number of people 25–34 years old who will attend the conference?
    d. If you invite the number suggested in part (b), what is the standard deviation of the number of people 55–64 years old who will attend the conference?

58. Many companies use a quality control technique called *acceptance sampling* to monitor incoming shipments of parts, raw materials, and so on. In the electronics industry, component parts are commonly shipped from suppliers in large lots. Inspection of a sample of n components can be viewed as the n trials of a binomial experiment. The outcome for each component tested (trial) will be that the component is good or defective. Reynolds Electronics accepts a lot from a particular supplier if the defective components in the lot do not exceed 1%. Suppose a random sample of five items from a recent shipment has been tested.
    a. Assume that 1% of the shipment is defective. Compute the probability that no items in the sample are defective.
    b. Assume that 1% of the shipment is defective. Compute the probability that exactly one item in the sample is defective.
    c. What is the probability of observing one or more defective items in the sample if 1% of the shipment is defective?
    d. Would you feel comfortable accepting the shipment if one item were found to be defective? Why or why not?

59. Cars arrive at a car wash randomly and independently; the probability of an arrival is the same for any two time intervals of equal length. The mean arrival rate is 15 cars per hour. What is the probability that 20 or more cars will arrive during any given hour of operation?

60. A new automated production process has had an average of 1.5 breakdowns per day. Because of the cost associated with a breakdown, management is concerned about the possibility of having three or more breakdowns during a day. Assume that breakdowns occur randomly, that the probability of a breakdown is the same for any two time intervals of equal length, and that breakdowns in one period are independent of breakdowns in other periods. What is the probability of having three or more breakdowns during a day?

61. A regional director responsible for business development in the state of Pennsylvania is concerned about the number of small business failures. If the mean number of small business failures per month is 10, what is the probability that exactly four small businesses will fail during a given month? Assume that the probability of a failure is the same for any two months and that the occurrence or nonoccurrence of a failure in any month is independent of failures in any other month.

62. Customer arrivals at a bank are random and independent; the probability of an arrival in any one-minute period is the same as the probability of an arrival in any other one-minute period. Answer the following questions, assuming a mean arrival rate of three customers per minute.
    a. What is the probability of exactly three arrivals in a one-minute period?
    b. What is the probability of at least three arrivals in a one-minute period?

63. Most people are familiar with the game of five-card draw poker. With 52 cards including four aces, what is the probability that the deal of the five cards provides:
    a. A pair of aces?
    b. Exactly one ace?
    c. No aces?
    d. At least one ace?

64. According to the WTA Tour and ATP Tour, four of the top 10 women tennis players use Wilson rackets (*USA Today,* March 2, 1995). Suppose two of these players have reached the finals of a tournament.
   a. What is the probability that exactly one uses a Wilson racket?
   b. What is the probability that both use Wilson rackets?
   c. What is the probability that neither uses a Wilson racket?

Appendix 5.1   DISCRETE PROBABILITY DISTRIBUTIONS WITH MINITAB

Statistical packages such as Minitab offer a relatively easy and efficient procedure for computing binomial probabilities. In this appendix, we show the step-by-step procedure for determining the binomial probabilities for the Martin Clothing Store problem in Section 5.4. Recall that the desired binomial probability is based on $n = 10$, $x = 4$, and $p = .30$. Before beginning the Minitab routine, the user must enter the desired values of the random variable x into a column of the worksheet. We entered the values 0, 1, 2, . . . , 10 in column 1 (see Figure 5.5) to generate the entire binomial probability distribution. The Minitab steps to obtain the desired binomial probabilities follow.

   Step 1. Select the **Calc** pull-down menu
   Step 2. Select the **Probability Distributions** pull-down menu
   Step 3. Select the **Binomial** option
   Step 4. When the dialog box appears:
      Make sure **Probability** is selected
      Enter 10 in the **Number of trials** box
      Enter .3 in the **Probability of success** box
      Enter C1 in the **Input column** box
      Select **OK** to produce the binomial probabilities

The Minitab output with the binomial probabilities will appear as shown in Figure 5.5.

   Minitab provides Poisson probabilities in a similar manner. The only differences are in step 3, where the Poisson option would be selected, and step 4, where the **Mean** would be entered rather than the number of trials and the probability of success.

Appendix 5.2   DISCRETE PROBABILITY DISTRIBUTIONS WITH EXCEL

Excel has the capability of computing probabilities for several discrete probability distributions including the binomial, Poisson, and hypergeometric. In this appendix, we describe how Excel can be used to compute the probabilities for any binomial probability distribution. The procedures for the Poisson and hypergeometric probability distributions are similar to the one we describe for the binomial probability distribution.

   Let us return to the Martin Clothing Store problem, where the binomial probabilities of interest are based on a binomial experiment with $n = 10$ and $p = .30$. We assume that the user is interested in the probability of $x = 4$ successes in the 10 trials. The following steps describe how to use Excel to produce the desired binomial probability.

   Step 1. Select a cell in the worksheet where you want the binomial probability to appear
   Step 2. Select the **Insert** pull-down menu
   Step 3. Choose the **Function** option

Step 4. When the Paste Function dialog box appears:
Choose **Statistical** from the **Function Category** box
Choose **BINOMDIST** from the **Function Name** box
Select **OK**

Step 5. When the **BINOMDIST** dialog box appears:
Enter 4 in the **Number_s** box (the value of x)
Enter 10 in the **Trials** box (the value of n)
Enter .30 in the **Probability_s** box (the value of p)
Enter false in the **Cumulative** box*
Note: At this point the desired binomial probability of .2001 is automatically computed and appears in the right center of the dialog box.
Select **OK** and the binomial probability will appear in the worksheet cell requested in Step 1

If the user wants other binomial probabilities, that information can be obtained without repeating the steps for each probability desired. Perhaps the easiest alternative is to stay in step 5. After the four entries have been made and the first probability appears, simply return to the **Number_s** box and insert a new value of x. The new probability will appear. Repeated changes can be made in the dialog box, including changes to the trials, probability, and/or cumulative boxes. For each change, the desired probability will appear. When **OK** is selected, only the last binomial probability will be placed in the worksheet.

If the user wants to insert multiple binomial probabilities into the worksheet, the desired values of x should be entered into the worksheet first. Then, in step 5, the user must enter the cell location of one of the values of x in the numbers box. After completing the steps for one binomial probability, individuals experienced with Excel can use Excel's Copy command to copy the binomial function into the cells where the other binomial probabilities are to appear.

The Excel procedure for generating Poisson and hypergeometric probabilities is similar to this procedure we have just described. Step 4 can be used to select either the POISSON or HYPGEOMDIST function name. The dialog box in step 5 will guide the user through the input values required to compute the desired probabilities.

---

*Placing false in the cumulative box provides the probability of exactly four successes. Placing true in this box provides the cumulative probability of four or *fewer* successes.

6

CONTINUOUS PROBABILITY DISTRIBUTIONS

CONTENTS

PROCTER & GAMBLE*
Cincinnati, Ohio

Procter & Gamble (P&G) is in the consumer products business worldwide. P&G produces and markets such products as detergents, disposable diapers, over-the-counter pharmaceuticals, dentifrices, bar soaps, mouthwashes, and paper towels. It has the leading brand in more categories than any other consumer products company.

As a leader in the application of statistical methods to decision making, P&G employs people with diverse academic backgrounds: engineering, statistics, operations research, and business. The major quantitative technologies for which these people provide support are probabilistic decision and risk analysis, advanced simulation, quality improvement, and quantitative methods (e.g., linear programming, regression analysis, probability analysis).

The Industrial Chemicals Division of P&G is a major supplier of fatty alcohols derived from natural substances such as coconut oil and from petroleum-based derivatives. The division wanted to know the economic risks and opportunities of expanding its fatty-alcohol production facilities, and P&G's experts in probabilistic decision and risk analysis were called in to help. After structuring and modeling the problem, they determined that the key to profitability was the cost difference between the petroleum- and coconut-based raw materials. Future costs were unknown, but the analysts were able to represent them with the following continuous random variables.

$$x = \text{the coconut oil price per pound of fatty alcohol}$$

and

$$y = \text{the petroleum raw material price per pound of fatty alcohol}$$

Some of Procter & Gamble's many well-known products. Photo courtesy of Procter & Gamble.

Because the key to profitability was the difference between these two random variables, a third random variable, $d = x - y$, was used in the analysis. Experts were interviewed to determine the probability distribution for x and y. In turn, this information was used to develop a continuous probability distribution for the difference d. The continuous probability distribution showed a .90 probability that the price difference would be $.0655 or less and a .50 probability that the price difference would be $.035 or less. In addition, there was only a .10 probability that the price difference would be $.0045 or less.[†]

The Industrial Chemicals Division thought that being able to quantify the impact of raw material price differences was key to reaching a consensus. The probabilities obtained were used in a sensitivity analysis of the raw material price difference. The analysis yielded sufficient insight to form the basis for a recommendation to management.

The use of continuous random variables and their probability distributions was helpful to P&G in analyzing the economic risks associated with its fatty-alcohol production. In this chapter, you will gain an understanding of continuous random variables and their probability distributions including one of the most important probability distributions in statistics, the normal distribution.

*The authors are indebted to Joel Kahn of Procter & Gamble for providing this Statistics in Practice.

[†]The price differences stated here have been modified to protect proprietary data.

In the preceding chapter we discussed discrete random variables and their probability distributions. In this chapter we turn to the study of continuous random variables. Specifically, we discuss three continuous probability distributions: the uniform, the normal, and the exponential.

A fundamental difference separates discrete and continuous random variables in terms of how probabilities are computed. For a discrete random variable, the probability function $f(x)$ provides the probability that the random variable assumes a particular value. With continuous random variables the counterpart of the probability function is the *probability density function,* also denoted by $f(x)$. The difference is that the probability density function does not directly provide probabilities. However, the area under the graph of $f(x)$ corresponding to a given interval does provide the probability that the continuous random variable x assumes a value in the interval. So when we compute probabilities for continuous random variables we are computing the probability that the random variable assumes any value in an interval.

One of the implications of the definition of probability for continuous random variables is that the probability of any particular value of the random variable is zero, because the area under the graph of $f(x)$ at any particular point is zero. In Section 6.1 we demonstrate these concepts for a continuous random variable that has a uniform probability distribution.

Much of the chapter is devoted to describing and showing applications of the normal probability distribution. The normal probability distribution is of major importance; it is used extensively in statistical inference. The normal distribution can also be used as an approximation to the discrete binomial distribution, as we show in Section 6.3. The chapter closes with a discussion of the exponential probability distribution.

6.1 UNIFORM PROBABILITY DISTRIBUTION

Consider the random variable x that represents the flight time of an airplane traveling from Chicago to New York. Suppose the flight time can be any value in the interval from 120 minutes to 140 minutes. Because the random variable x can assume any value in that interval, x is a continuous rather than a discrete random variable. Let us assume that sufficient actual flight data are available to conclude that the probability of a flight time within any one-minute interval is the same as the probability of a flight time within any other one-minute interval from 120 to 140 minutes. With every one-minute interval being equally likely, the random variable x is said to have a *uniform probability distribution.* The *probability density function,* which defines the uniform probability distribution for the flight time random variable, is

> Whenever the probability is proportional to the length of the interval, the random variable is uniformly distributed.

$$f(x) = \begin{cases} \frac{1}{20} & \text{for } 120 \le x \le 140 \\ 0 & \text{elsewhere} \end{cases}$$

Figure 6.1 is a graph of this probability density function. In general, the uniform probability density function for a random variable x is found by using the following formula.

Uniform Probability Density Function

$$f(x) = \begin{cases} \dfrac{1}{b-a} & \text{for } a \le x \le b \\ 0 & \text{elsewhere} \end{cases} \tag{6.1}$$

In the flight-time example, $a = 120$ and $b = 140$.

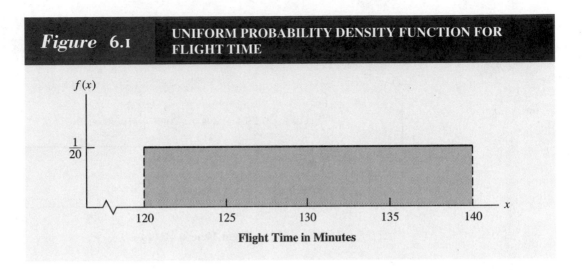

Figure 6.1   UNIFORM PROBABILITY DENSITY FUNCTION FOR FLIGHT TIME

As noted in the introduction, for a continuous random variable, we consider probability only in terms of the likelihood that a random variable has a value within a specified interval. In the flight-time example, an acceptable probability question is: What is the probability that the flight time is between 120 and 130 minutes? That is, what is $P(120 \leq x \leq 130)$? Because the flight time must be between 120 and 140 minutes and because the probability is described as being uniform over this interval, we feel comfortable saying $P(120 \leq x \leq 130) = .50$. In the following subsection we show that this probability can be computed as the area under the graph of $f(x)$ from 120 to 130.

Area as a Measure of Probability

Let us make an observation about the graph in Figure 6.2. Consider the area under the graph of $f(x)$ in the interval from 120 to 130. The region is rectangular, and the area of a rectangle is simply the width multiplied by the height. With the width of the interval equal to $130 - 120 = 10$ and the height equal to the value of the probability density function $f(x) = \frac{1}{20}$, we have area = width × height = $10(\frac{1}{20}) = \frac{10}{20} = .50$.

What observation can you make about the area under the graph of $f(x)$ and probability? They are identical! Indeed, this result is true for all continuous random variables. Once a probability density function $f(x)$ has been identified, the probability that x takes a value between some lower value x_1 and some higher value x_2 can be found by computing the area under the graph of $f(x)$ over the interval x_1 to x_2.

After we have the appropriate probability distribution and accept the interpretation of area as probability, we can answer any number of probability questions. For example, what is the probability of a flight time between 128 and 136 minutes? The width of the interval is $136 - 128 = 8$. With the uniform height of $\frac{1}{20}$, we see that $P(128 \leq x \leq 136) = 8(\frac{1}{20}) = .40$.

Note that $P(120 \leq x \leq 140) = 20(\frac{1}{20}) = 1$. That is, the total area under the graph of $f(x)$ is equal to 1. This property holds for all continuous probability distributions and is the analog of the condition that the sum of the probabilities must equal 1 for a discrete probability function. For a continuous probability density function, we must also require that $f(x) \geq 0$ for all values of x. This requirement is the analog of the requirement that $f(x) \geq 0$ for discrete probability functions.

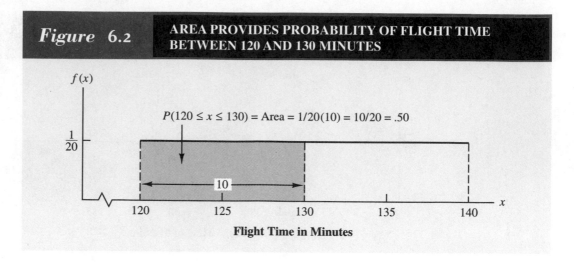

Figure 6.2   **AREA PROVIDES PROBABILITY OF FLIGHT TIME BETWEEN 120 AND 130 MINUTES**

Two major differences stand out between the treatment of continuous random variables and the treatment of their discrete counterparts.

1. We no longer talk about the probability of the random variable assuming a particular value. Instead, we talk about the probability of the random variable assuming a value within some given interval.

2. The probability of the random variable assuming a value within some given interval from x_1 to x_2 is defined to be the area under the graph of the probability density function between x_1 and x_2. It implies that the probability of a continuous random variable assuming any particular value exactly is zero, because the area under the graph of $f(x)$ at a single point is zero.

To see that the probability of any single point is 0, refer to Figure 6.2 and compute the probability of a single point, say, $x = 125$. $P(x = 125) = P(125 \leq x \leq 125) = 0(\frac{1}{20}) = 0$.

The calculation of the expected value and variance for a continuous random variable is analogous to that for a discrete random variable. However, because the computational procedure involves integral calculus, we leave the derivation of the appropriate formulas to more advanced texts.

For the uniform continuous probability distribution introduced in this section, the formulas for the expected value and variance are

$$E(x) = \frac{a + b}{2}$$

$$\text{Var}(x) = \frac{(b - a)^2}{12}$$

In these formulas, a is the smallest value and b is the largest value that the random variable may assume.

Applying these formulas to the uniform probability distribution for flight times from Chicago to New York, we obtain

$$E(x) = \frac{(120 + 140)}{2} = 130$$

$$\text{Var}(x) = \frac{(140 - 120)^2}{12} = 33.33$$

The standard deviation of flight times can be found by taking the square root of the variance. Thus, $\sigma = 5.77$ minutes.

N O T E S
and Comments

1. For a continuous random variable the probability of any particular value is zero, which provides $P(a \leq x \leq b) = P(a < x < b)$. This equation shows that the probability of a random variable assuming a value in any interval is the same whether or not the endpoints are included.

2. To see more clearly why the height of a probability density function is not a probability, think about a random variable with the following uniform probability distribution.

$$f(x) = \begin{cases} 2 & \text{for } 0 \leq x \leq .5 \\ 0 & \text{elsewhere} \end{cases}$$

The height of the probability density function is 2 for values of x between 0 and .5. However, we know probabilities can never be greater than 1.

EXERCISES

Methods

SELF TEST

1. The random variable x is known to be uniformly distributed between 1.0 and 1.5.
   a. Show the graph of the probability density function.
   b. Find $P(x = 1.25)$.
   c. Find $P(1.0 \leq x \leq 1.25)$.
   d. Find $P(1.20 < x < 1.5)$.

2. The random variable x is known to be uniformly distributed between 10 and 20.
   a. Show the graph of the probability density function.
   b. Find $P(x < 15)$.
   c. Find $P(12 \leq x \leq 18)$.
   d. Find $E(x)$.
   e. Find Var(x).

Applications

3. Delta Airlines quotes a flight time of 2 hours, 5 minutes for its flights from Cincinnati to Tampa. Suppose we believe that actual flight times are uniformly distributed between 2 hours and 2 hours, 20 minutes.
   a. Show the graph of the probability density function for flight times.
   b. What is the probability that the flight will be no more than five minutes late?
   c. What is the probability that the flight will be more than 10 minutes late?
   d. What is the expected flight time?

SELF TEST

4. Most computer languages have a function that can be used to generate random numbers. In Excel, the RAND function can be used to generate random numbers between 0 and 1. If we let x denote a random number generated, then x is a continuous random variable with the following probability density function.

$$f(x) = \begin{cases} 1 & \text{for } 0 \leq x \leq 1 \\ 0 & \text{elsewhere} \end{cases}$$

   a. Graph the probability density function.
   b. What is the probability of generating a random number between .25 and .75?
   c. What is the probability of generating a random number with a value less than or equal to .30?
   d. What is the probability of generating a random number with a value greater than .60?

5. The driving distance for the top 60 women golfers on the LPGA tour is between 238.9 and 261.2 yards (*Golfweek,* December 6, 1997). Assume that the driving distance for these women is uniformly distributed over this interval.
   a. Give a mathematical expression for the probability density function of driving distance.
   b. What is the probability the driving distance for one of these women is less than 250 yards?
   c. What is the probability the driving distance for one of these women is at least 255 yards?
   d. What is the probability the driving distance for one of these women is between 245 and 260 yards?
   e. How many of these women drive the ball at least 250 yards?

6. The label on a bottle of liquid detergent shows contents to be 12 ounces per bottle. The production operation fills the bottle uniformly according to the following probability density function.

$$f(x) = \begin{cases} 8 & \text{for } 11.975 \le x \le 12.10 \\ 0 & \text{elsewhere} \end{cases}$$

   a. What is the probability that a bottle will be filled with between 12 and 12.05 ounces?
   b. What is the probability that a bottle will be filled with 12.02 or more ounces?
   c. Quality control accepts production that is within .02 ounces of the number of ounces shown on the container label. What is the probability that a bottle of this liquid detergent will fail to meet the quality control standard?

7. Suppose we are interested in bidding on a piece of land and we know there is one other bidder.* The seller has announced that the highest bid in excess of $10,000 will be accepted. Assume that the competitor's bid x is a random variable that is uniformly distributed between $10,000 and $15,000.
   a. Suppose you bid $12,000. What is the probability that your bid will be accepted?
   b. Suppose you bid $14,000. What is the probability that your bid will be accepted?
   c. What amount should you bid to maximize the probability that you get the property?
   d. Suppose you know someone who is willing to pay you $16,000 for the property. Would you consider bidding less than the amount in part (c)? Why or why not?

..../ /............

6.2   NORMAL PROBABILITY DISTRIBUTION

The most important probability distribution for describing a continuous random variable is the *normal probability distribution.* The normal probability distribution has been used in a wide variety of practical applications in which the random variables are heights and weights of people, IQ scores, scientific measurements, amounts of rainfall, and so on. Use of this probability distribution requires that the random variable be continuous. However, as we shall see in Section 6.3, a continuous normal random variable can be used as an approximation in situations involving discrete random variables.

Normal Curve

The form, or shape, of the normal probability distribution is illustrated by the bell-shaped curve in Figure 6.3. The probability density function that defines the bell-shaped curve of the normal probability distribution follows.

Abraham de Moivre, a French mathematician, published *The Doctrine of Chances* in 1733. He derived the normal probability distribution.

*This exercise is based on a problem suggested to us by Professor Roger Myerson of Northwestern University.

| Figure 6.3 | BELL-SHAPED CURVE FOR THE NORMAL PROBABILITY DISTRIBUTION |

Normal Probability Density Function

$$f(x) = \frac{1}{\sqrt{2\mu}\,\sigma}\, e^{-(x-\mu)^2/2\sigma^2}$$ (6.2)

where

μ = mean
σ = standard deviation
π = 3.14159
e = 2.71828

We make several observations about the characteristics of the normal probability distribution.

The normal curve has two parameters, μ and σ. They determine the location and shape of the distribution.

1. There is an entire family of normal probability distributions. They are differentiated by their mean μ and standard deviation σ.
2. The highest point on the normal curve is at the mean, which is also the median and mode of the distribution.
3. The mean of the distribution can be any numerical value: negative, zero, or positive. Three normal curves with the same standard deviation but three different means (-10, 0, and 20) are shown here.

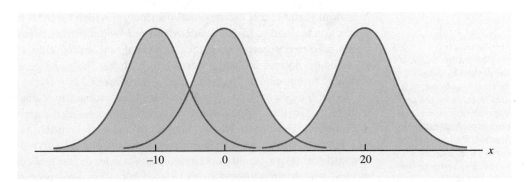

4. The normal probability distribution is symmetric, with the shape of the curve to the left of the mean a mirror image of the shape of the curve to the right of the mean. The tails of the curve extend to infinity in both directions and theoretically never touch the horizontal axis.

5. The standard deviation determines the width of the curve. Larger values of the standard deviation result in wider, flatter curves, showing more variability in the data. Two normal distributions with the same mean but with different standard deviations are shown here.

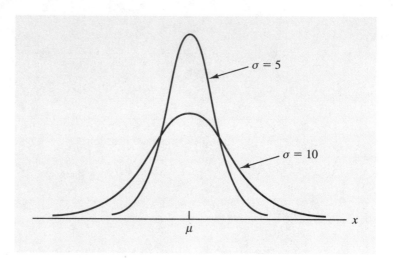

6. The total area under the curve for the normal probability distribution is 1, which is true for all continuous probability distributions.

7. Probabilities for the normal random variable are given by areas under the curve. The percentage of values in some commonly used intervals are:

   a. 68.26% of the values of a normal random variable are within plus or minus one standard deviation of its mean.

   b. 95.44% of the values of a normal random variable are within plus or minus two standard deviations of its mean.

   c. 99.72% of the values of a normal random variable are within plus or minus three standard deviations of its mean.

Figure 6.4 shows properties (a), (b), and (c) graphically.

These percentages are the basis for the empirical rule introduced in Section 3.3.

Standard Normal Probability Distribution

A random variable that has a normal distribution with a mean of zero and a standard deviation of one is said to have a *standard normal probability distribution*. The letter z is commonly used to designate this particular normal random variable. Figure 6.5 is the graph of the standard normal probability distribution. It has the same general appearance as other normal distributions, but with the special properties of $\mu = 0$ and $\sigma = 1$.

As with other continuous random variables, probability calculations with any normal probability distribution are made by computing areas under the graph of the probability density function. Thus, to find the probability that a normal random variable is within any specific interval, we must compute the area under the normal curve over that interval. For the standard normal probability distribution, areas under the normal curve have been computed and are available in tables that can be used in computing probabilities. Table 6.1 is such a table; it is also available as Table 1 of Appendix B and inside the front cover of this text.

For the uniform distribution, the height of the probability density function is constant, so it is easy to compute the area under the curve. For the normal probability density function, the height of the curve varies and calculus is required to compute the areas that represent probability.

Figure 6.4 AREAS UNDER THE CURVE FOR ANY NORMAL PROBABILITY DISTRIBUTION

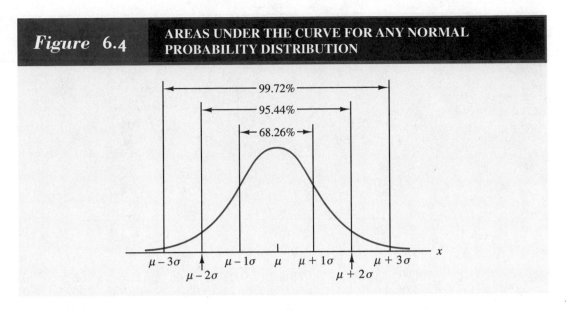

To see how the table of areas under the curve for the standard normal probability distribution (Table 6.1) can be used to find probabilities, let us consider some examples. Later, we will see how this same table can be used to compute probabilities for any normal distribution. To begin, let us see how we can compute the probability that the z value for the standard normal random variable will be between .00 and 1.00; that is, $P(.00 \leq z \leq 1.00)$. The shaded region in the following graph shows this area or probability.

Given a z value, we use the standard normal table to find the appropriate probability (an area under the curve).

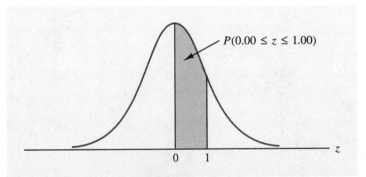

$P(0.00 \leq z \leq 1.00)$

Figure 6.5 THE STANDARD NORMAL PROBABILITY DISTRIBUTION

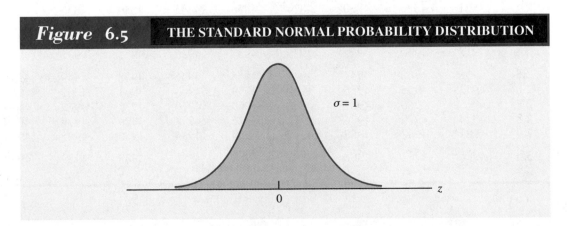

$\sigma = 1$

Table 6.1 **AREAS, OR PROBABILITIES, FOR THE STANDARD NORMAL DISTRIBUTION**

z	.00	.01	.02	.03	.04	.05	.06	.07	.08	.09
.0	.0000	.0040	.0080	.0120	.0160	.0199	.0239	.0279	.0319	.0359
.1	.0398	.0438	.0478	.0517	.0557	.0596	.0636	.0675	.0714	.0753
.2	.0793	.0832	.0871	.0910	.0948	.0987	.1026	.1064	.1103	.1141
.3	.1179	.1217	.1255	.1293	.1331	.1368	.1406	.1443	.1480	.1517
.4	.1554	.1591	.1628	.1664	.1700	.1736	.1772	.1808	.1844	.1879
.5	.1915	.1950	.1985	.2019	.2054	.2088	.2123	.2157	.2190	.2224
.6	.2257	.2291	.2324	.2357	.2389	.2422	.2454	.2486	.2518	.2549
.7	.2580	.2612	.2642	.2673	.2704	.2734	.2764	.2794	.2823	.2852
.8	.2881	.2910	.2939	.2967	.2995	.3023	.3051	.3078	.3106	.3133
.9	.3159	.3186	.3212	.3238	.3264	.3289	.3315	.3340	.3365	.3389
1.0	.3413	.3438	.3461	.3485	.3508	.3531	.3554	.3577	.3599	.3621
1.1	.3643	.3665	.3686	.3708	.3729	.3749	.3770	.3790	.3810	.3830
1.2	.3849	.3869	.3888	.3907	.3925	.3944	.3962	.3980	.3997	.4015
1.3	.4032	.4049	.4066	.4082	.4099	.4115	.4131	.4147	.4162	.4177
1.4	.4192	.4207	.4222	.4236	.4251	.4265	.4279	.4292	.4306	.4319
1.5	.4332	.4345	.4357	.4370	.4382	.4394	.4406	.4418	.4429	.4441
1.6	.4452	.4463	.4474	.4484	.4495	.4505	.4515	.4525	.4535	.4545
1.7	.4554	.4564	.4573	.4582	.4591	.4599	.4608	.4616	.4625	.4633
1.8	.4641	.4649	.4656	.4664	.4671	.4678	.4686	.4693	.4699	.4706
1.9	.4713	.4719	.4726	.4732	.4738	.4744	.4750	.4756	.4761	.4767
2.0	.4772	.4778	.4783	.4788	.4793	.4798	.4803	.4808	.4812	.4817
2.1	.4821	.4826	.4830	.4834	.4838	.4842	.4846	.4850	.4854	.4857
2.2	.4861	.4864	.4868	.4871	.4875	.4878	.4881	.4884	.4887	.4890
2.3	.4893	.4896	.4898	.4901	.4904	.4906	.4909	.4911	.4913	.4916
2.4	.4918	.4920	.4922	.4925	.4927	.4929	.4931	.4932	.4934	.4936
2.5	.4938	.4940	.4941	.4943	.4945	.4946	.4948	.4949	.4951	.4952
2.6	.4953	.4955	.4956	.4957	.4959	.4960	.4961	.4962	.4963	.4964
2.7	.4965	.4966	.4967	.4968	.4969	.4970	.4971	.4972	.4973	.4974
2.8	.4974	.4975	.4976	.4977	.4977	.4978	.4979	.4979	.4980	.4981
2.9	.4981	.4982	.4982	.4983	.4984	.4984	.4985	.4985	.4986	.4986
3.0	.4986	.4987	.4987	.4988	.4988	.4989	.4989	.4989	.4990	.4990

The entries in Table 6.1 give the area under the standard normal curve between the mean, $z = 0$, and a specified positive value of z (see the graph at the top of the table). In this case, we are interested in the area between $z = 0$ and $z = 1.00$. Thus, we must find the entry in the table corresponding to $z = 1.00$. First, we find 1.0 in the left column of the table and then find .00 in the top row of the table. By looking in the body of the table, we find that the 1.0 row and the .00 column intersect at the value of .3413. We have found the desired probability: $P(.00 \leq z \leq 1.00) = .3413$. A portion of Table 6.1 showing these steps follows.

z	.00	.01	.02
.			
.			
.			
.9	.3159	.3186	.3212
1.0	.3413	.3438	.3461
1.1	.3643	.3665	.3686
1.2	.3849	.3869	.3888
.			
.			
.			

$P(.00 \leq z \leq 1.00)$

Using the same approach, we can find $P(.00 \leq z \leq 1.25)$. By first locating the 1.2 row and then moving across to the .05 column, we find $P(.00 \leq z \leq 1.25) = .3944$.

As another example of the use of the table of areas for the standard normal distribution, we compute the probability of obtaining a z value between $z = -1.00$ and $z = 1.00$; that is, $P(-1.00 \leq z \leq 1.00)$.

Note that we have already used Table 6.1 to show that the probability of a z value between $z = .00$ and $z = 1.00$ is .3413, and recall that the normal probability distribution is *symmetric*. Thus, the probability of a z value between $z = .00$ and $z = -1.00$ is the same as the probability of a z value between $z = .00$ and $z = +1.00$. Hence, the probability of a z value between $z = -1.00$ and $z = +1.00$ is

$$P(-1.00 \leq z \leq .00) + P(.00 \leq z \leq 1.00) = .3413 + .3413 = .6826$$

This area is shown graphically in the following figure.

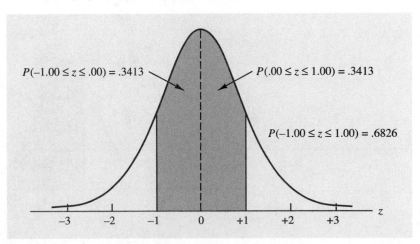

In a similar manner, we can use the values in Table 6.1 to show that the probability of a z value between -2.00 and $+2.00$ is $.4772 + .4772 = .9544$ and that the probability of a z value between -3.00 and $+3.00$ is $.4986 + .4986 = .9972$. Because we know that the total probability or total area under the curve for any continuous random variable must be 1.0000, the probability $.9972$ tells us that the value of z will almost always be between -3.00 and $+3.00$.

Next, we compute the probability of obtaining a z value of at least 1.58; that is, $P(z \geq 1.58)$. First, we use the $z = 1.5$ row and the .08 column of Table 6.1 to find that $P(.00 \leq z \leq 1.58) = .4429$. Now, because the normal probability distribution is symmetric and the total area under the curve equals 1, we know that 50% of the area must be above the mean (i.e., $z = 0$) and 50% of the area must be below the mean. If .4429 is the area between the mean and $z = 1.58$, then the area or probability corresponding to $z \geq 1.58$ must be $.5000 - .4429 = .0571$. This probability is shown in the following figure.

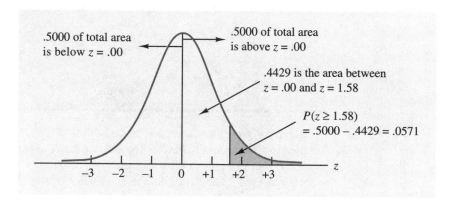

As another illustration, consider the probability that the random variable z assumes a value of $-.50$ or larger; that is, $P(z \geq -.50)$. To make this computation, we note that the probability we are seeking can be written as the sum of two probabilities: $P(z \geq -.50) = P(-.50 \leq z \leq .00) + P(z \geq 0.00)$. We have previously seen that $P(z \geq .00) = .50$. Also, we know that since the normal distribution is symmetric, $P(-.50 \leq z \leq .00) = P(.00 \leq z \leq .50)$. Referring to Table 6.1, we find that $P(.00 \leq z \leq .50) = .1915$. Therefore $P(z \geq -.50) = .1915 + .5000 = .6915$. The following graph shows this area.

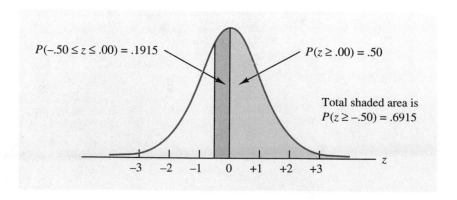

Next, we compute the probability of obtaining a z value between 1.00 and 1.58; that is, $P(1.00 \leq z \leq 1.58)$. From our previous examples, we know that there is a .3413 probability of a z value between $z = 0.00$ and $z = 1.00$ and that there is a .4429 probability of a z value between $z = 0.00$ and $z = 1.58$. Hence, there must be a $.4429 - .3413 = .1016$ probability of a z value between $z = 1.00$ and $z = 1.58$. Thus, $P(1.00 \leq z \leq 1.58) = .1016$. This situation is shown graphically in the following figure.

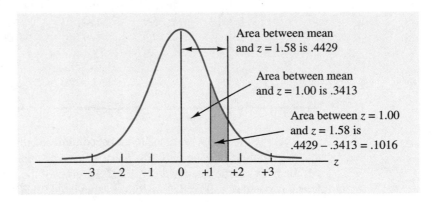

As a final illustration, let us find a z value such that the probability of obtaining a larger z value is only .10. The following figure shows this situation graphically.

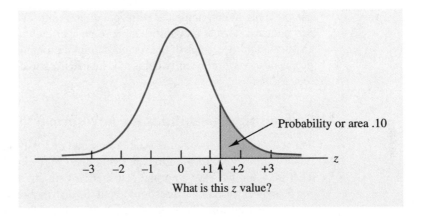

Given a probability, we can use the standard normal table in an inverse fashion to find the corresponding z value.

This problem is the inverse of the preceding examples. Previously, we specified the z value of interest and then found the corresponding probability, or area. In this example, we are given the probability, or area, and asked to find the corresponding z value. To do so, we use the table of areas for the standard normal probability distribution (Table 6.1) somewhat differently.

Recall that the body of Table 6.1 gives the area under the curve between the mean and a particular z value. We have been given the information that the area in the upper tail of the curve is .10. Hence, we must determine how much of the area is between the mean and the z value of interest. Because we know that .5000 of the area is above the mean, $.5000 - .1000 = .4000$ must be the area under the curve between the mean and the desired z value. Scanning the body of the table, we find .3997 as the probability value closest to .4000. The section of the table providing this result follows.

z	.06	.07	.08	.09
.				
.				
.				
1.0	.3554	.3577	.3599	.3621
1.1	.3770	.3790	3810	.3830
1.2	.3962	.3980	.3997	.4015
1.3	.4131	.4147	.4162	.4177
1.4	.4279	.4292	.4306	.4319
.				
.				
.				

Area value in body
of table closest to .4000

Reading the z value from the left most column and the top row of the table, we find that the corresponding z value is 1.28. Thus, an area of approximately .4000 (actually .3997) will be between the mean and $z = 1.28$.* In terms of the question originally asked, there is an approximately .10 probability of a z value larger than 1.28.

The examples illustrate that the table of areas for the standard normal probability distribution can be used to find probabilities associated with values of the standard normal random variable z. Two types of questions can be asked. The first type of question specifies a value, or values, for z and asks us to use the table to determine the corresponding areas, or probabilities. The second type of question provides an area, or probability, and asks us to use the table to determine the corresponding z value. Thus, we need to be flexible in using the standard normal probability table to answer the desired probability question. In most cases, sketching a graph of the standard normal probability distribution and shading the appropriate area or probability helps to visualize the situation and aids in determining the correct answer.

Computing Probabilities for Any Normal Probability Distribution

The reason for discussing the standard normal distribution so extensively is that probabilities for all normal distributions are computed by using the standard normal distribution. That is, when we have a normal distribution with any mean μ and any standard deviation σ, we answer probability questions about the distribution by first converting to the standard normal distribution. Then we can use Table 6.1 and the appropriate z values to find the desired probabilities. The formula used to convert any normal random variable x with mean μ and standard deviation σ to the standard normal distribution follows.

The formula for the standard normal random variable is the same as we introduced in Chapter 3 for computing z scores for a data set.

Converting to the Standard Normal Distribution

$$z = \frac{x - \mu}{\sigma}$$

(6.3)

---

*We could use interpolation in the body of the table to get a better approximation of the z value that corresponds to an area of .4000. Doing so to provide one more decimal place of accuracy would yield a z value of 1.282. However, in most practical situations, sufficient accuracy is obtained by simply using the table value closest to the desired probability.

A value of x equal to its mean μ results in $z = (\mu - \mu)/\sigma = 0$. Thus, we see that a value of x equal to its mean μ corresponds to a value of z at its mean 0. Now suppose that x is one standard deviation above its mean; that is, $x = \mu + \sigma$. Applying (6.3), we see that the corresponding z value is $z = [(\mu + \sigma) - \mu]/\sigma = \sigma/\sigma = 1$. Thus, a value that is one standard deviation above its mean yields $z = 1$. In other words, we can interpret z as the number of standard deviations that the normal random variable x is from its mean μ.

To see how this conversion enables us to compute probabilities for any normal distribution, suppose we have a normal distribution with $\mu = 10$ and $\sigma = 2$. What is the probability that the random variable x is between 10 and 14? Using (6.3) we see that at $x = 10$, $z = (x - \mu)/\sigma = (10 - 10)/2 = 0$ and that at $x = 14$, $z = (14 - 10)/2 = 4/2 = 2$. Thus, the answer to our question about the probability of x being between 10 and 14 is given by the equivalent probability that z is between 0 and 2 for the standard normal distribution. In other words, the probability that we are seeking is the probability that the random variable x is between its mean and two standard deviations above the mean. Using $z = 2.00$ and Table 6.1, we see that the probability is .4772. Hence the probability that x is between 10 and 14 is .4772.

Grear Tire Company Problem

We turn now to an application of the normal probability distribution. Suppose the Grear Tire Company has just developed a new steel-belted radial tire that will be sold through a national chain of discount stores. Because the tire is a new product, Grear's managers believe that the mileage guarantee offered with the tire will be an important factor in the acceptance of the product. Before finalizing the tire mileage guarantee policy, Grear's managers want probability information about the number of miles the tires will last.

From actual road tests with the tires, Grear's engineering group has estimated the mean tire mileage at $\mu = 36,500$ miles and the standard deviation at $\sigma = 5000$. In addition, the data collected indicate that a normal distribution is a reasonable assumption. What percentage of the tires can be expected to last more than 40,000 miles? In other words, what is the probability that the tire mileage will exceed 40,000? This question can be answered by finding the area of the shaded region in Figure 6.6.

At $x = 40,000$, we have

$$z = \frac{x - \mu}{\sigma} = \frac{40,000 - 36,500}{5000} = \frac{3500}{5000} = .70$$

Refer now to the bottom of Figure 6.6. We see that a value of $x = 40,000$ on the Grear Tire normal distribution corresponds to a value of $z = .70$ on the standard normal distribution. Using Table 6.1, we see that the area between the mean and $z = .70$ is .2580. Referring again to Figure 6.6, we see that the area between $x = 36,500$ and $x = 40,000$ on the Grear Tire normal distribution is also .2580. Thus, $.5000 - .2580 = .2420$ is the probability that x will exceed 40,000. We can conclude that about 24.2% of the tires will exceed 40,000 in mileage.

Let us now assume that Grear is considering a guarantee that will provide a discount on replacement tires if the original tires do not exceed the mileage stated in the guarantee. What should the guarantee mileage be if Grear wants no more than 10% of the tires to be eligible for the discount guarantee? This question is interpreted graphically in Figure 6.7.

According to Figure 6.7, 40% of the area must be between the mean and the unknown guarantee mileage. We look up .4000 in the body of Table 6.1 and see that this area is at approximately 1.28 standard deviations below the mean. That is, $z = -1.28$ is the value of

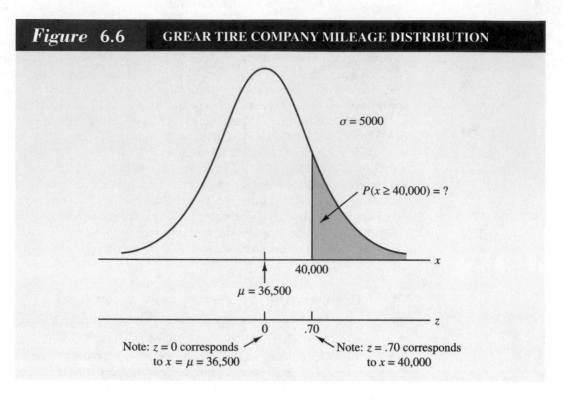

Figure 6.6   GREAR TIRE COMPANY MILEAGE DISTRIBUTION

the standard normal random variable corresponding to the desired mileage guarantee on the Grear Tire normal distribution. To find the mileage x corresponding to $z = -1.28$, we have

$$z = \frac{x - \mu}{\sigma} = -1.28$$

$$x - \mu = -1.28\sigma$$

$$x = \mu - 1.28\sigma$$

Figure 6.7   GREAR'S DISCOUNT GUARANTEE

With $\mu = 36,500$ and $\sigma = 5000$,

$$x = 36,500 - 1.28(5000) = 30,100$$

With the guarantee set at 30,000 miles, the actual percentage eligible for the guarantee will be 9.68%.

Thus, a guarantee of 30,100 miles will meet the requirement that approximately 10% of the tires will be eligible for the guarantee. Perhaps, with this information, the firm will set its tire mileage guarantee at 30,000 miles.

Again, we see the important role that probability distributions play in providing decision-making information. Namely, once a probability distribution is established for a particular application, it can be used quickly and easily to obtain probability information about the problem. Probability does not make a decision recommendation directly, but it provides information that helps the decision maker better understand the risks and uncertainties associated with the problem. Ultimately, this information may assist the decision maker in reaching a good decision.

EXERCISES

Methods

8. Using Figure 6.4 as a guide, sketch a normal curve for a random variable x that has a mean of $\mu = 100$ and a standard deviation of $\sigma = 10$. Label the horizontal axis with values of 70, 80, 90, 100, 110, 120, and 130.

9. A random variable is normally distributed with a mean of $\mu = 50$ and a standard deviation of $\sigma = 5$.
    a. Sketch a normal curve for the probability density function. Label the horizontal axis with values of 35, 40, 45, 50, 55, 60, and 65. Figure 6.4 shows that the normal curve almost touches the horizontal axis at three standard deviations below and at three standard deviations above the mean (in this case at 35 and 65).
    b. What is the probability the random variable will assume a value between 45 and 55?
    c. What is the probability the random variable will assume a value between 40 and 60?

10. Given that z is a standard normal random variable, sketch the standard normal curve. Label the horizontal axis at values of -3, -2, -1, 0, 1, 2, and 3. Then use the table of probabilities for the standard normal distribution to compute the following probabilities.
    a. $P(0 \leq z \leq 1)$
    b. $P(0 \leq z \leq 1.5)$
    c. $P(0 < z < 2)$
    d. $P(0 < z < 2.5)$

11. Given that z is a standard normal random variable, compute the following probabilities.
    a. $P(-1 \leq z \leq 0)$
    b. $P(-1.5 \leq z \leq 0)$
    c. $P(-2 < z < 0)$
    d. $P(-2.5 \leq z \leq 0)$
    e. $P(-3 < z \leq 0)$

12. Given that z is a standard normal random variable, compute the following probabilities.
    a. $P(0 \leq z \leq .83)$
    b. $P(-1.57 \leq z \leq 0)$
    c. $P(z > .44)$
    d. $P(z \geq -.23)$
    e. $P(z < 1.20)$
    f. $P(z \leq -.71)$

SELF TEST

13. Given that z is a standard normal random variable, compute the following probabilities.
    a. $P(-1.98 \leq z \leq .49)$
    b. $P(.52 \leq z \leq 1.22)$
    c. $P(-1.75 \leq z \leq -1.04)$

14. Given that z is a standard normal random variable, find z for each situation.
    a. The area between 0 and z is .4750.
    b. The area between 0 and z is .2291.
    c. The area to the right of z is .1314.
    d. The area to the left of z is .6700.

SELF TEST

15. Given that z is a standard normal random variable, find z for each situation.
    a. The area to the left of z is .2119.
    b. The area between $-z$ and z is .9030.
    c. The area between $-z$ and z is .2052.
    d. The area to the left of z is .9948.
    e. The area to the right of z is .6915.

16. Given that z is a standard normal random variable, find z for each situation.
    a. The area to the right of z is .01.
    b. The area to the right of z is .025.
    c. The area to the right of z is .05.
    d. The area to the right of z is .10.

Applications

17. The average American male adult is 5 feet 9 inches tall (*Astounding Averages,* 1995). Assume the standard deviation is 3 inches in answering the following questions.
    a. What is the probability an adult male is taller than 6 feet?
    b. What is the probability an adult male is shorter than 5 feet?
    c. What is the probability an adult male is between 5 feet 6 inches and 5 feet 10 inches?
    d. What is the probability an adult male is no more than 6 feet tall?

SELF TEST

18. The average time a subscriber spends reading *The Wall Street Journal* is 49 minutes (*The Wall Street Journal* Subscriber Study, 1996). Assume the standard deviation is 16 minutes and that the times are normally distributed.
    a. What is the probability a subscriber will spend at least 1 hour reading the journal?
    b. What is the probability a subscriber will spend no more than 30 minutes reading the journal?
    c. For the 10% who spend the most time reading the journal, how much time do they spend?

19. College presidents receive a housing provision that averages $26,234 annually (*USA Today,* April 18, 1994). Assume that a normal distribution applies and that the standard deviation is $5000.
    a. What percentage of college presidents receive an annual housing provision exceeding $35,000 per year?
    b. What percentage of college presidents receive an annual housing provision less than $20,000 per year?
    c. How large would the provision need to be to put a college president in the top 10%?

20. Trading volume on the New York Stock Exchange has been growing in recent years. For the first two weeks of January 1998, the average daily volume was 646 million shares (*Barron's,* January 1998). The probability distribution of daily volume is approximately normal with a standard deviation of about 100 million shares.
    a. What is the probability trading volume will be less than 400 million shares?
    b. What percentage of the time does the trading volume exceed 800 million shares?
    c. If the exchange wants to issue a press release on the top 5% of trading days, what volume will trigger a release?

21. Mensa is the international high-IQ society. To be a Mensa member, a person must have an IQ of 132 or higher (*USA Today,* February 13, 1992). If IQ scores are normally distributed with a mean of 100 and a standard deviation of 15, what percentage of the population qualifies for membership in Mensa?

22. Drivers who are members of the Teamsters Union earn an average of $17.15 per hour (*U.S. News & World Report,* April 11, 1994). Assume that available data indicate wages are normally distributed with a standard deviation of $2.25.
     a. What is the probability that wages are between $15.00 and $20.00 per hour?
     b. What is the hourly wage of the highest paid 15% of Teamster drivers?
     c. What is the probability that wages are less than $12.00 per hour?

23. The time needed to complete a final examination in a particular college course is normally distributed with a mean of 80 minutes and a standard deviation of 10 minutes. Answer the following questions.
     a. What is the probability of completing the exam in one hour or less?
     b. What is the probability that a student will complete the exam in more than 60 minutes but less than 75 minutes?
     c. Assume that the class has 60 students and that the examination period is 90 minutes in length. How many students do you expect will be unable to complete the exam in the allotted time?

24. The average age for a person getting married for the first time is 26 years (*U.S. News & World Report,* June 6, 1994). Assume the ages for first marriages have a normal distribution with a standard deviation of four years.
     a. What is the probability that a person getting married for the first time is younger than 23 years of age?
     b. What is the probability that a person getting married for the first time is in his or her twenties?
     c. 90% of people getting married for the first time get married before what age?

25. The average ticket price for a major league baseball game was $11.98 in 1998 (*USA Today,* November 11, 1998). Adding the cost of food, parking, and souvenirs, the average cost for a family of four to attend a game was approximately $110.00. Assume the normal distribution applies and that the standard deviation is $20.00.
     a. What is the probability the cost will exceed $100.00?
     b. What is the probability a family will spend $90.00 or less?
     c. What is the probability a family will spend between $80.00 and $130.00?

6.3   NORMAL APPROXIMATION OF BINOMIAL PROBABILITIES

In Section 5.4 we presented the binomial probability distribution. Recall that a binomial experiment consists of a sequence of n identical independent trials with each trial having two possible outcomes, a success or a failure. The probability of a success is the same for all trials and is denoted by p. The binomial random variable is the number of successes in the n trials, and probability questions pertain to the probability of x success in the n trials.

When the number of trials becomes large, evaluating the binomial probability function by hand or with a calculator is difficult. In addition, the binomial tables in Appendix B do not include values of n greater than 20. Hence, when we encounter a binomial probability distribution problem with a large number of trials, we may want to approximate the binomial probability distribution. In cases where the number of trials is greater than 20, $np \geq 5$, and $n(1 - p) \geq 5$, the normal probability distribution provides an easy-to-use approximation of binomial probabilities.

For a given n, the normal approximation will be best when $p = .50$.

When using the normal approximation to the binomial, we set $\mu = np$ and $\sigma = \sqrt{np(1 - p)}$ in the definition of the normal curve. Let us illustrate the normal approximation to the binomial by supposing that a particular company has a history of making errors in 10% of its invoices. A sample of 100 invoices has been taken, and we want to compute the probability that 12 invoices contain errors. That is, we want to find the binomial probability of 12 successes in 100 trials.

In applying the normal approximation to the binomial, we set $\mu = np = (100)(.1) = 10$ and $\sigma = \sqrt{np(1 - p)} = \sqrt{(100)(.1)(.9)} = 3$. A normal distribution with $\mu = 10$ and $\sigma = 3$ is shown in Figure 6.8.

Recall that, with a continuous probability distribution, probabilities are computed as areas under the probability density function. As a result, the probability of any single value for the random variable is zero. To approximate the binomial probability of 12 successes, we must compute the area under the corresponding normal curve between 11.5 and 12.5. The .5 that we add and subtract from 12 is called a *continuity correction factor.* It is introduced because a continuous distribution is being used to approximate a discrete distribution. Thus, $P(x = 12)$ for the *discrete* binomial distribution is approximated by $P(11.5 \leq x \leq 12.5)$ for the *continuous* normal distribution.

Converting to the standard normal distribution to compute $P(11.5 \leq x \leq 12.5)$, we have

$$z = \frac{x - \mu}{\sigma} = \frac{12.5 - 10.0}{3} = .83 \qquad \text{at } x = 12.5$$

and

$$z = \frac{x - \mu}{\sigma} = \frac{11.5 - 10.0}{3} = .50 \qquad \text{at } x = 11.5$$

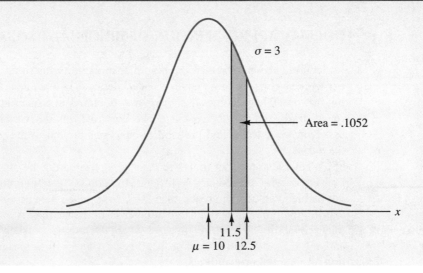

Figure 6.8 **NORMAL APPROXIMATION TO A BINOMIAL PROBABILITY DISTRIBUTION WITH $n = 100$ AND $p = .10$ SHOWING THE PROBABILITY OF 12 ERRORS**

The actual binomial probability is .0988.

From Table 6.1 we find that the area under the curve (in Figure 6.8) between 10 and 12.5 is .2967. Similarly, the area under the curve between 10 and 11.5 is .1915. Therefore, the area between 11.5 and 12.5 is .2967 − .1915 = .1052. The normal approximation to the probability of 12 successes in 100 trials is .1052.

For another illustration, suppose we want to compute the probability of 13 or fewer errors in the sample of 100 invoices. Figure 6.9 shows the area under the normal curve that approximates this probability. Note that the use of the continuity correction factor results in the value of 13.5 being used to compute the desired probability. The z value corresponding to $x = 13.5$ is

$$z = \frac{13.5 - 10.0}{3.0} = 1.17$$

The actual binomial probability is .8761.

Table 6.1 shows that the area under the standard normal curve between 0 and 1.17 is .3790. The area under the normal curve approximating the probability of 13 or fewer errors is given by the heavily shaded portion of the graph in Figure 6.9. The probability is .3790 + .5000 = .8790.

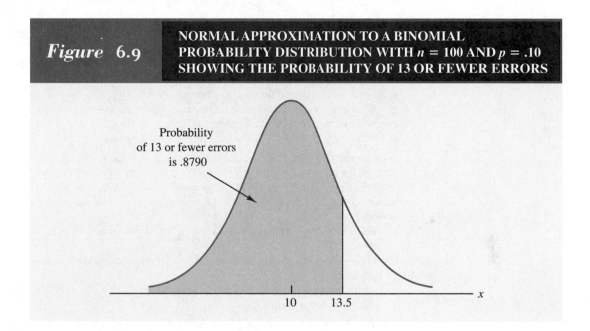

Figure 6.9   NORMAL APPROXIMATION TO A BINOMIAL PROBABILITY DISTRIBUTION WITH $n = 100$ AND $p = .10$ SHOWING THE PROBABILITY OF 13 OR FEWER ERRORS

Probability of 13 or fewer errors is .8790

EXERCISES

Methods

SELF TEST

26. A binomial probability distribution has $p = .20$ and $n = 100$.
    a. What is the mean and standard deviation?
    b. In this situation, can binomial probabilities be approximated by the normal probability distribution? Explain.
    c. What is the probability of exactly 24 successes?
    d. What is the probability of 18 to 22 successes?
    e. What is the probability of 15 or fewer successes?

27. Assume a binomial probability distribution has $p = .60$ and $n = 200$.
   a. What is the mean and standard deviation?
   b. In this situation, can binomial probabilities be approximated by the normal probability distribution? Explain.
   c. What is the probability of 100 to 110 successes?
   d. What is the probability of 130 or more successes?
   e. What is the advantage of using the normal probability distribution to approximate the binomial probabilities? Use part (d) to explain the advantage.

Applications

SELF TEST

28. A *Consumer Reports* survey listed Saturn, Infiniti, and Lexus automobile dealers as the top three in customer service (*Consumer Reports,* April 1994). Saturn ranked number one, with only 4% of the Saturn customers citing some form of dissatisfaction with the dealer. Answer the following questions about a group of 250 Saturn customers.
   a. What is the probability that 12 or fewer customers will have some form of dissatisfaction with the dealer?
   b. What is the probability that five or more customers will have some form of dissatisfaction with the dealer?
   c. What is the probability that eight customers will have some form of dissatisfaction with the dealer?

29. The unemployment rate is 4.6% (*Business Week,* January 5, 1998). Assume that 100 employable people are selected randomly.
   a. What is the expected number who are unemployed?
   b. What is the variance and standard deviation of the number who are unemployed?
   c. What is the probability that exactly six are unemployed?
   d. What is the probability that at least four are unemployed?

30. In December 1997, the U.S. Department of Justice issued an injunction against Microsoft Corporation for bundling its Internet Explorer® Web browser with its Windows 95® operating system (*Fortune,* February 2, 1998). Public opinion was divided on whether Microsoft was a monopoly. In a *Fortune* poll, 41% of respondents agreed with the statement, "Microsoft is a monopoly."
   a. For a sample of 800 people, how many would you expect to agree that Microsoft is a monopoly?
   b. For a sample of 800 people, what is the probability that 300 or fewer agree that Microsoft is a monopoly?
   c. Again for a sample of 800 people, what is the probability that more than 450 do not agree that Microsoft is a monopoly?

31. A Myrtle Beach resort hotel has 120 rooms. In the spring months, hotel room occupancy is approximately 75%. Use the normal approximation to the binomial distribution to answer the following questions.
   a. What is the probability that at least half of the rooms are occupied on a given day?
   b. What is the probability that 100 or more rooms are occupied on a given day?
   c. What is the probability that 80 or fewer rooms are occupied on a given day?

32. It is known that 30% of all holders of a major national credit card pay their bills in full before any interest charges are incurred. Use the normal approximation to the binomial distribution to answer the following questions for a group of 150 credit card holders.
   a. What is the probability that between 40 and 60 customers pay their account balances before any interest charges are incurred? That is, find $P(40 \leq x \leq 60)$.
   b. What is the probability that 30 or fewer customers pay their account balances before any interest charges are incurred?

6.4   EXPONENTIAL PROBABILITY DISTRIBUTION

A continuous probability distribution that is useful in describing the time it takes to complete a task is the *exponential probability distribution*. The exponential random variable can be used to describe such things as the time between arrivals at a car wash, the time required to load a truck, the distance between major defects in a highway, and so on. The exponential probability density function follows.

Exponential Probability Density Function

$$f(x) = \frac{1}{\mu} e^{-x/\mu} \qquad \text{for } x \geq 0, \mu > 0 \qquad\qquad \textbf{(6.4)}$$

As an example of the exponential probability distribution, assume that the time it takes to load a truck at the Schips loading dock follows such a distribution. If the mean, or average, time to load a truck is 15 minutes ($\mu = 15$), the appropriate probability density function is

$$f(x) = \frac{1}{15} e^{-x/15}$$

Figure 6.10 is the graph of this probability density function.

Computing Probabilities for the Exponential Distribution

In waiting line applications, the exponential distribution is often used for service time.

As with any continuous probability distribution, the area under the curve corresponding to an interval provides the probability that the random variable assumes a value in that interval. In the Schips loading dock example, the probability that loading a truck will take 6 minutes or less ($x \leq 6$) is defined to be the area under the curve in Figure 6.10 from $x = 0$

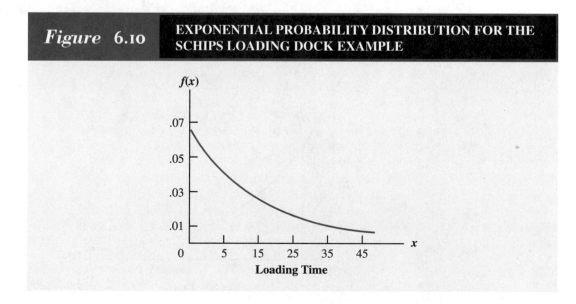

Figure 6.10   **EXPONENTIAL PROBABILITY DISTRIBUTION FOR THE SCHIPS LOADING DOCK EXAMPLE**

to $x = 6$. Similarly, the probability that loading a truck will take 18 minutes or less ($x \leq 18$) is the area under the curve from $x = 0$ to $x = 18$. Note also that the probability that loading a truck will take between 6 minutes and 18 minutes ($6 \leq x \leq 18$) is given by the area under the curve from $x = 6$ to $x = 18$.

To compute exponential probabilities such as those just described, we use the following formula. It provides the probability of obtaining a value for the exponential random variable of less than or equal to some specific value of x, denoted by x_0.

Exponential Distribution Probabilities

$$P(x \leq x_0) = 1 - e^{-x_0/\mu} \tag{6.5}$$

For the Schips loading dock example, (6.5) can be written as

$$P(\text{loading time} \leq x_0) = 1 - e^{-x_0/15}$$

Hence, the probability that loading a truck will take 6 minutes or less ($x \leq 6$) is

$$P(\text{loading time} \leq 6) = 1 - e^{-6/15} = .3297$$

Figure 6.11 shows the area or probability for a loading time of 6 minutes or less. Note also that the probability of loading a truck in 18 minutes or less ($x \leq 18$) is

$$P(\text{loading time} \leq 18) = 1 - e^{-18/15} = .6988$$

Thus, the probability that loading a truck will take between 6 minutes and 18 minutes is equal to $.6988 - .3297 = .3691$. Probabilities for any other interval can be computed similarly.

Figure **6.11**   **PROBABILITY OF A LOADING TIME OF SIX MINUTES OR LESS**

Relationship between the Poisson and Exponential Distributions

In Section 5.5 we introduced the Poisson distribution as a discrete probability distribution that is often useful in examining the number of occurrences of an event over a specified interval of time or space. Recall that the Poisson probability function is

$$f(x) = \frac{\mu^x e^{-\mu}}{x!}$$

where

$$\mu = \text{expected value or mean number of} \\ \text{occurrences in an interval}$$

The continuous exponential probability distribution is related to the discrete Poisson distribution in that, if the Poisson distribution provides an appropriate description of the number of occurrences per interval, the exponential distribution provides a description of the length of the interval between occurrences.

If arrivals follow a Poisson distribution, the time between arrivals must follow an exponential distribution.

To illustrate this relationship, suppose the number of cars that arrive at a car wash during one hour is described by a Poisson probability distribution with a mean of 10 cars per hour. The Poisson probability function that gives the probability of x arrivals per hour is

$$f(x) = \frac{10^x e^{-10}}{x!}$$

Because the average number of arrivals is 10 cars per hour, the average time between cars arriving is

$$\frac{1 \text{ hour}}{10 \text{ cars}} = .1 \text{ hour/car}$$

Thus, the corresponding exponential distribution that describes the time between the arrivals has a mean of $\mu = .1$ hour per car; the appropriate exponential probability density function is

$$f(x) = \frac{1}{.1} e^{-x/.1} = 10e^{-10x}$$

··/ /···········

EXERCISES

Methods

33. Consider the following exponential probability density function.

$$f(x) = \frac{1}{8} e^{-x/8} \qquad \text{for } x \geq 0$$

   a. Find $P(x \leq 6)$.
   b. Find $P(x \leq 4)$.
   c. Find $P(x \geq 6)$.
   d. Find $P(4 \leq x \leq 6)$.

34. Consider the following exponential probability density function.

$$f(x) = \frac{1}{3} e^{-x/3} \qquad \text{for } x \geq 0$$

a. Write the formula for $P(x \leq x_0)$.
b. Find $P(x \leq 2)$.
c. Find $P(x \geq 3)$.
d. Find $P(x \leq 5)$.
e. Find $P(2 \leq x \leq 5)$.

Applications

35. The average life of a television set is 12 years (*Money*, April 1994). Product lifetimes often follow an exponential probability distribution. Assume that this probability distribution applies for the lifetime of a television set.
    a. What is the probability that the lifetime will be 6 years or less?
    b. What is the probability that the lifetime will be 15 years or more?
    c. What is the probability that the lifetime will be between 5 and 10 years?

36. The time between arrivals of vehicles at a particular intersection follows an exponential probability distribution with a mean of 12 seconds.
    a. Sketch this exponential probability distribution.
    b. What is the probability that the arrival time between vehicles is 12 seconds or less?
    c. What is the probability that the arrival time between vehicles is 6 seconds or less?
    d. What is the probability of 30 or more seconds between vehicle arrivals?

37. The lifetime (hours) of an electronic device is a random variable with the following exponential probability density function.

$$f(x) = \frac{1}{50} e^{-x/50} \qquad \text{for } x \geq 0$$

a. What is the mean lifetime of the device?
b. What is the probability that the device will fail in the first 25 hours of operation?
c. What is the probability that the device will operate 100 or more hours before failure?

38. Waiting times are frequently assumed to follow an exponential probability distribution. A study of waiting times at fast-food restaurants conducted by *The Orlando Sentinel* in October 1993 showed that the average waiting time to get food after placing an order at McDonald's, Burger King, and Wendy's was 60 seconds. Assume that an exponential probability distribution applies to the waiting times.
    a. What is the probability that a customer will wait 30 seconds or less?
    b. What is the probability that a customer will wait 45 seconds or less?
    c. What is the probability that a customer will wait more than 2 minutes?

39. How much do people use computers at home? According to a survey, 69.5% of *Barron's* subscribers have a personal computer at home (*Barron's,* 1995 Primary Reader Survey). Of those having a personal computer at home, the average number of hours of weekly usage is 7.4 hours. The number of hours of usage is approximately exponentially distributed.
    a. What is the probability that a subscriber spends 3 hours or less using a personal computer at home?
    b. What is the probability that a subscriber spends more than 10 hours using a personal computer at home?
    c. What is the probability that a subscriber spends between 3 and 10 hours using a personal computer at home?

··/ /··········

SUMMARY

This chapter extended the discussion of probability distributions to the case of continuous random variables. The major conceptual difference between discrete and continuous probability distributions is in the method of computing probabilities. With discrete distributions, the probability function $f(x)$ provides the probability that the random variable x assumes various values. With continuous probability distributions, we associate a probability density function, denoted by $f(x)$. The probability density function does not provide probability values for a continuous random variable directly. Probabilities are given by areas under the curve or graph of the probability density function $f(x)$. Because the area under the curve above a single point is zero, we observe that the probability of any particular value is zero for a continuous random variable.

Three continuous probability distributions—the uniform, normal, and exponential distributions—were treated in detail. The normal probability distribution is used widely in statistical inference and will be used extensively in the remainder of the text.

··/ /··········

GLOSSARY

Uniform probability distribution A continuous probability distribution where the probability that the random variable will assume a value in any interval is the same for each interval of equal length.

Probability density function The function that defines the probability distribution of a continuous random variable.

Normal probability distribution A continuous probability distribution. Its probability density function is bell shaped and determined by the mean μ and standard deviation σ.

Standard normal probability distribution A normal distribution with a mean of zero and a standard deviation of one.

Continuity correction factor A value of .5 that is added and/or subtracted from a value of x when the continuous normal probability distribution is used to approximate the discrete binomial probability distribution.

Exponential probability distribution A continuous probability distribution that is useful in computing probabilities for the time or space between occurrences of an event.

··/ /··········

KEY FORMULAS

Uniform Probability Density Function

$$f(x) = \begin{cases} \dfrac{1}{b-a} & \text{for } a \leq x \leq b \\ 0 & \text{elsewhere} \end{cases} \tag{6.1}$$

Normal Probability Density Function

$$f(x) = \frac{1}{\sqrt{2\pi}\,\sigma}\, e^{-(x-\mu)^2/2\sigma^2} \tag{6.2}$$

Converting to the Standard Normal Distribution

$$z = \frac{x - \mu}{\sigma} \tag{6.3}$$

Exponential Probability Density Function

$$f(x) = \frac{1}{\mu}\, e^{-x/\mu} \qquad \text{for } x \geq 0,\, \mu > 0 \tag{6.4}$$

Exponential Distribution Probabilities

$$P(x \leq x_0) = 1 - e^{-x_0/\mu} \tag{6.5}$$

SUPPLEMENTARY EXERCISES

40. A business executive has been transferred from Chicago to Atlanta and needs to sell her house in Chicago quickly. The executive's employer has offered to buy the house for $210,000, but the offer expires at the end of the week. The executive does not currently have a better offer, but can afford to leave the house on the market for another month. From conversations with her realtor, the executive believes the price she will get by leaving the house on the market for another month is uniformly distributed between $200,000 and $225,000.
  a. If she leaves the house on the market for another month, what is the mathematical expression for the probability density function of the sales price?
  b. If she leaves it on the market for another month, what is the probability she will get at least $215,000 for the house?
  c. If she leaves it on the market for another month, what is the probability she will get less than $210,000?
  d. Should the executive leave the house on the market for another month? Why or why not?

41. Sixty-eight percent of the debt owed by American families is home mortgage or equity credit (*Federal Reserve Bulletin,* January 1997). The median amount of mortgage debt for families with the head of the household under 35 years old is $63,000. Assume the amount of mortgage debt for this group is normally distributed and the standard deviation is $15,000.
  a. What is the mean amount of mortgage debt for this group?
  b. How much mortgage debt do the 10% with the smallest debt have?
  c. What percent of these families have mortgage debt in excess of $80,000?
  d. The upper 5% of mortgage debt is in excess of what amount?

42. Motorola used the normal distribution to determine the probability of defects and the number of defects expected in a production process (*APICS—The Performance Advantage,* July 1991). Assume a production process is designed to produce items with a weight of 10 ounces and that the process mean is 10. Calculate the probability of a defect and the expected number of defects for a 1000-unit production run in the following situations.
  a. The process standard deviation is .15, and the process control is set at plus or minus one standard deviation. Units with weights less than 9.85 or greater than 10.15 ounces will be classified as defects.

b. Through process design improvements, the process standard deviation can be reduced to .05. Assume the process control remains the same, with weights less than 9.85 or greater than 10.15 ounces being classified as defects.

c. What is the advantage of reducing process variation and setting process control limits at a greater number of standard deviations from the mean?

43. The mean hourly operating cost of a USAir 737 airplane is $2071 (*The Tampa Tribune,* February 17, 1995). Assume that the hourly operating cost for the airplane is normally distributed.

a. If 11% of the hourly operating costs are $1800 or less, what is the standard deviation of hourly operating cost?

b. What is the probability that the hourly operating cost of a USAir 737 airplane is between $2000 and $2500?

c. What is the hourly operating cost of the 3% of the airplanes that have the lowest operating cost?

44. The sales of High-Brite Toothpaste are believed to be approximately normally distributed, with a mean of 10,000 tubes per week and a standard deviation of 1500 tubes per week.

a. What is the probability that more than 12,000 tubes will be sold in any given week?

b. To have a .95 probability that the company will have sufficient stock to cover the weekly demand, how many tubes should be produced?

45. Ward Doering Auto Sales is considering offering a special service contract that will cover the total cost of any service work required on leased vehicles. From experience, the company manager estimates that yearly service costs are approximately normally distributed, with a mean of $150 and a standard deviation of $25.

a. If the company offers the service contract to customers for a yearly charge of $200, what is the probability that any one customer's service costs will exceed the contract price of $200?

b. What is Ward's expected profit per service contract?

46. The Asian currency crisis of late 1997 and early 1998 was expected to lead to substantial job losses in the United States as inexpensive imports flooded markets. California was expected to be especially hard hit. The Economic Policy Institute estimated that the mean number of job losses in California would be 126,681 (*St. Petersburg Times,* January 24, 1998). Assume the number of jobs lost is normally distributed with a standard deviation of 30,000.

a. What is the probability the number of lost jobs is between 80,000 and 150,000?

b. What is the probability the number of lost jobs will be less than 50,000?

c. What cutoff value will provide a .95 probability that the number of lost jobs will not exceed the value?

47. Assume that the test scores from a college admissions test are normally distributed, with a mean of 450 and a standard deviation of 100.

a. What percentage of the people taking the test score between 400 and 500?

b. Suppose someone receives a score of 630. What percentage of the people taking the test score better? What percentage score worse?

c. If a particular university will not admit anyone scoring below 480, what percentage of the persons taking the test would be acceptable to the university?

48. The 1996–97 average starting salary for new college graduates in accounting was $30,393 (*U.S. News Online, U.S. News and World Report,* December 1997). Assume salaries are normally distributed with a standard deviation of $3000.

a. What is the probability of a new graduate receiving a starting salary between $28,000 and $32,000?

b. What is the probability of a new graduate getting a starting salary in excess of $35,000?

c. What percent of starting salaries are no more than $25,000?

d. What is the cutoff for the top 1% of the salaries?

49. A machine fills containers with a particular product. The standard deviation of filling weights is known from past data to be .6 ounce. If only 2% of the containers hold less than 18 ounces, what is the mean filling weight for the machine? That is, what must μ equal? Assume the filling weights have a normal distribution.

50. Consider a multiple-choice examination with 50 questions. Each question has four possible answers. Assume that a student who has done the homework and attended lectures has a .75 probability of answering any question correctly.
    a. A student must answer 43 or more questions correctly to obtain a grade of A. What percentage of the students who have done their homework and attended lectures will obtain a grade of A on this multiple-choice examination?
    b. A student who answers 35 to 39 questions correctly will receive a grade of C. What percentage of students who have done their homework and attended lectures will obtain a grade of C on this multiple-choice examination?
    c. A student must answer 30 or more questions correctly to pass the examination. What percentage of the students who have done their homework and attended lectures will pass the examination?
    d. Assume that a student has not attended class and has not done the homework for the course. Furthermore, assume that the student will simply guess at the answer to each question. What is the probability that this student will answer 30 or more questions correctly and pass the examination?

51. A blackjack player at a Las Vegas casino has learned that the house will provide a free room if he plays for four hours at an average bet of $50. His playing strategy provides a probability of .49 of winning on any one hand, and the player knows that about 60 hands per hour are played. Suppose he plays for four hours at a bet of $50 per hand.
    a. What is the player's expected payoff?
    b. What is the probability the player loses $1000 or more?
    c. What is the probability the player actually wins?
    d. Suppose the player has $1500. What is the probability he will go broke?

52. A Labor Department survey asked working women what worries them most. Concern about low wages, job stress, and health benefits were mentioned most often, with 60% of working women concerned about low wages (*Business Week,* October 24, 1994). Consider a random sample of 500 working women from this population.
    a. What is the expected number of women in this group who will express a concern about low wages?
    b. What is the variance and standard deviation of the number who will express a concern about low wages?
    c. What is the probability that 290 to 320 women will express a concern about low wages?
    d. What is the probability that 325 or more women will express a concern about low wages?

53. The time in minutes for which a student uses a computer terminal at the computer center of a major university follows an exponential probability distribution with a mean of 36 minutes. Assume a student arrives at the terminal just as another student is beginning to work on the terminal.
    a. What is the probability that the wait for the second student will be 15 minutes or less?
    b. What is the probability that the wait for the second student will be between 15 and 45 minutes?
    c. What is the probability that the second student will have to wait an hour or more?

54. A new automated production process has been averaging two breakdowns per day, and the number of breakdowns per day follows a Poisson probability distribution.
    a. What is the mean time between breakdowns, assuming eight hours of operation per day?
    b. Show the exponential probability density function that can be used for the time between breakdowns.
    c. What is the probability that the process will run one hour or more before another breakdown?
    d. What is the probability that the process can run a full eight-hour shift without a breakdown?

55. The time (in minutes) a checkout lane is idle between customers at a supermarket follows an exponential probability distribution with a mean of 1.2 minutes.
    a. Show the probability density function for this distribution.
    b. What is the probability that the next customer will arrive between .5 and 1.0 minute after a customer is served?
    c. What is the probability of the checkout lane being idle for more than a minute between customers?

56. The time (in minutes) between telephone calls at an insurance claims office has the following exponential probability distribution.

$$f(x) = .50e^{-.50x} \qquad \text{for } x \geq 0$$

a. What is the mean time between telephone calls?
b. What is the probability of having 30 seconds or less between telephone calls?
c. What is the probability of having 1 minute or less between telephone calls?
d. What is the probability of having 5 or more minutes without a telephone call?

···/ /············

Appendix 6.1   CONTINUOUS PROBABILITY DISTRIBUTIONS WITH MINITAB

Let us demonstrate the Minitab procedure for computing continuous probabilities by referring to the Grear Tire Company problem where tire mileage was described by a normal probability distribution with $\mu = 36{,}500$ and $\sigma = 5000$. One question asked was: What is the probability that the tire mileage will exceed 40,000 miles?

For continuous probability distributions, Minitab gives a cumulative probability; that is, Minitab gives the probability that the random variable will assume a value less than or equal to a specified constant. For the Grear tire mileage question, Minitab can be used to determine the cumulative probability that the tire mileage will be less than or equal to 40,000 miles. (The specified constant in this case is 40,000.) After obtaining the cumulative probability from Minitab, we must subtract it from one to determine the probability that the tire mileage will exceed 40,000 miles.

Prior to using Minitab to compute a probability, one must enter the specified constant into a column of the worksheet. For the Grear tire mileage question we entered the specified constant of 40,000 into column 1 of the Minitab worksheet. The steps in using Minitab to compute the cumulative probability of the normal random variable assuming a value less than or equal to 40,000 follow.

Step 1. Select the **Calc** pull-down menu
Step 2. Select the **Probability Distributions** pull-down menu
Step 3. Select the **Normal** option
Step 4. When the dialog box appears:
  Select **Cumulative probability**
  Enter 36500 in the **Mean** box
  Enter 5000 in the **Standard deviation** box
  Enter C1 in the **Input column** box (the column containing 40,000)
  Select **OK** to produce the cumulative normal probability

After the user selects **OK,** Minitab will print the cumulative probability that the normal random variable assumes a value less than or equal to 40,000. Minitab will show that this probability is .7580. Because we are interested in the probability that the tire mileage will be greater than 40,000, the desired probability is $1 - .7580 = .2420$.

A second question in the Grear Tire Company problem was: What mileage guarantee should Grear set to ensure that no more than 10% of the tires qualify for the guarantee? Here we are given a probability and want to find the corresponding value for the random variable. Minitab uses an inverse calculation routine to find the value of the random variable associated with a given cumulative probability. First, we must enter the cumulative probability into a column of the Minitab worksheet (say C1). In this case, the desired cumulative probability is .10. Then, the first three steps of the Minitab procedure are as already listed. In step 4, we select **Inverse cumulative probability** instead of **Cumulative probability** and complete the remaining step. Minitab then displays the mileage guarantee of 30,100 miles.

Minitab is capable of computing probabilities for other continuous probability distributions, including the exponential probability distribution. To compute exponential probabilities, follow the procedure shown previously for the normal probability distribution and select the **Exponential** option in step 3. Step 4 is as shown, with the exception that entering the standard deviation is not required. Output for cumulative probabilities and inverse cumulative probabilities is identical to that described for the normal probability distribution.

Appendix 6.2   CONTINUOUS PROBABILITY DISTRIBUTIONS WITH EXCEL

Excel has the capability of computing probabilities for several continuous probability distributions, including the normal and exponential probability distributions. In this appendix, we describe how Excel can be used to compute probabilities for any normal probability distribution. The procedures for the exponential and other continuous probability distributions are similar to the one we describe for the normal probability distribution.

Let us return to the Grear Tire Company problem where the tire mileage was described by a normal probability distribution with $\mu = 36,500$ and $\sigma = 5000$. Assume we are interested in the probability that tire mileage will exceed 40,000 miles. The following steps describe how to use Excel to produce the desired normal probability.

Step 1. Select a cell in the worksheet where you want the normal probability to appear
Step 2. Select the **Insert** pull-down menu
Step 3. Choose the **Function** option
Step 4. When the **Paste Function** dialog box appears:
   Choose **Statistical** from the **Function Category** box
   Choose **NORMDIST** from the **Function Name** box
   Select **OK**
Step 5. When the **NORMDIST** dialog box appears:
   Enter 40000 in the **x** box
   Enter 36500 in the **mean** box
   Enter 5000 in the **standard deviation** box
   Enter true in the **cumulative** box
   Select **OK**

At this point, .7580 will appear in the cell selected in step 1, indicating that the probability of tire mileage being less than or equal to 40,000 miles is .7580. Therefore, the probability that tire mileage will exceed 40,000 miles is $1 - .7580 = .2420$.

Excel uses an inverse computation to convert a given cumulative normal probability into a value for the random variable. For example, what mileage guarantee should Grear offer if the company wants no more than 10% of the tires to be eligible for the guarantee? To compute the mileage guarantee by using Excel, follow the procedure just described. However, two changes are necessary: in step 4, choose **NORMINV** from the **Function Name** box; in step 5, enter the cumulative probability of .10 in the **probability** box and then enter the mean and the standard deviation. When **OK** is selected in step 5, the tire mileage guarantee of 30,092 or approximately 30,100 miles appears in the worksheet.

The Excel procedure for generating exponential probabilities is similar to the procedure just described. Step 4 can be used to choose the **EXPONDIST** function name. The dialog box in step 5 will guide the user through the input values required to compute the desired probability. Note that the value entered in the lambda box is $1/\mu$. When **OK** is selected in step 5, the cumulative exponential probability appears in the worksheet.

7

SAMPLING AND SAMPLING DISTRIBUTIONS

CONTENTS

MEAD CORPORATION*
Dayton, Ohio

Mead Corporation, located in Dayton, Ohio, is a diversified paper and forest products company that manufactures paper, pulp, and lumber and converts paperboard into shipping containers and beverage carriers. The company's distribution capability is used to market many of its own products, including paper, school supplies, and stationery. The company's internal consulting group uses sampling for decision analysis to provide a variety of information that enables Mead to obtain significant productivity benefits and remain competitive in its industry.

For example, Mead maintains large woodland holdings, which provide the trees that are the raw material for many of the company's products. Managers need reliable and accurate information about the timberlands and forests to evaluate the company's ability to meet its future raw material needs. What is the present volume in the forests? What is the past growth of the forests? What is the projected future growth of the forests? With answers to these important questions, Mead's managers can develop plans for the future including long-term planting and harvesting schedules for the trees.

How does Mead obtain the information it needs about its vast forest holdings? Data collected from sample plots throughout the forests are the basis for learning about the population of trees owned by the company. To identify the sample plots, the timberland holdings are first divided into three sections based on location and types of trees. Using maps and random numbers, Mead analysts identify random samples of ⅕ to ⅐ acre plots

*The authors are indebted to Dr. Edward P. Winkofsky, Mead Corporation, for providing this Statistics in Practice.

Random sampling of its forest holdings enables Mead Corporation to meet future raw material needs. © Dana White/PhotoEdit.

in each section of the forest. The sample plots are where Mead foresters collect data and learn about the forest population.

Foresters throughout the organization participate in the field data collection process. Periodically, two-person teams gather information on each tree in every sample plot. The sample data are entered into the company's continuous forest inventory (CFI) computer system. Reports from the CFI system include a number of frequency distribution summaries containing statistics on types of trees, present forest volume, past forest growth rates, and projected future forest growth and volume. Sampling and the associated statistical summaries of the sample data provide the reports that are essential for the effective management of Mead's forests and timberlands.

In this chapter you will learn about simple random sampling and the sample selection process. In addition, you will learn how statistics such as the sample mean and sample proportion are used to estimate the population mean and population proportion. The important concept of a sampling distribution is also introduced.

In Chapter 1, we defined a *population* and a *sample* as two important aspects of a statistical study. The definitions are restated here.

1. A *population* is the set of all the elements of interest in a study.
2. A *sample* is a subset of the population.

The purpose of *statistical inference* is to make inferences about a population from information contained in a sample. Let us begin by citing two situations in which sampling is conducted to give a manager or decision maker information about a population.

1. A tire manufacturer developed a new tire designed to provide an increase in mileage over the firm's current line of tires. To estimate the mean number of miles provided by the new tires, the manufacturer selected a sample of 120 new tires for testing. The test results provided a sample mean of 36,500 miles. Hence, an estimate of the mean tire mileage for the population of new tires was 36,500 miles.
2. Members of a political party were considering supporting a particular candidate for election to the U.S. Senate, and party leaders wanted an estimate of the proportion of registered voters favoring the candidate. The time and cost associated with contacting every individual in the population of registered voters were prohibitive. Hence, a sample of 400 registered voters was selected and 160 of the 400 voters indicated a preference for the candidate. An estimate of the proportion of the population of registered voters favoring the candidate was 160/400 = .40.

The preceding examples show how sampling and the sample results can be used to develop estimates of population characteristics. Note that in the tire mileage example, collecting the data on tire life involves wearing out each tire tested. Clearly it is not feasible to test every tire in the population; a sample is the only realistic way to obtain the desired tire mileage data. In the example involving the election, contacting every registered voter in the population is theoretically possible, but the time and cost in doing so are prohibitive; thus, a sample of registered voters is preferred.

The examples illustrate some of the reasons for using samples. However, it is important to realize that sample results provide only *estimates* of the values of the population characteristics. That is, we do not expect the sample mean of 36,500 miles to exactly equal the mean mileage for all tires in the population, nor do we expect exactly 40% of the population of registered voters to favor the candidate. The reason is simply that the sample contains only a portion of the population. With proper sampling methods, the sample results will provide "good" estimates of the population characteristics. But how good can we expect the sample results to be? Fortunately, statistical procedures are available for answering that question.

In this chapter we show how simple random sampling can be used to select a sample from a population. We then show how data obtained from a simple random sample can be used to compute estimates of a population mean, a population standard deviation, and a population proportion. In addition, we introduce the important concept of a sampling distribution. As we show, knowledge of the appropriate sampling distribution is what enables us to make statements about the goodness of the sample results. The last section discusses some alternatives to simple random sampling that are often employed in practice.

A sample mean provides an estimate of a population mean, and a sample proportion provides an estimate of a population proportion. With estimates such as these, some sampling error or ± value can be expected. A key point in this chapter is that statistical methods can be used to make probability statements about the size of the sampling error.

7.1   THE ELECTRONICS ASSOCIATES SAMPLING PROBLEM

The director of personnel for Electronics Associates, Inc. (EAI), has been assigned the task of developing a profile of the company's 2500 managers. The characteristics to be

EAI

identified include the mean annual salary for the managers and the proportion of managers having completed the company's management training program.

Using the 2500 managers as the population for this study, we can find the annual salary and the training program status for each individual by referring to the firm's personnel records. The data file containing this information for all 2500 managers in the population is on the disk at the back of the book.

Using the formulas presented in Chapter 3, we can compute the population mean and the population standard deviation for the annual salary data.

$$\text{Population mean:} \quad \mu = \$51,800$$
$$\text{Population standard deviation:} \quad \sigma = \$4000$$

Furthermore, the data for the training program status show that 1500 of the 2500 managers have completed the training program. Letting p denote the proportion of the population having completed the training program, we see that $p = 1500/2500 = .60$.

A *parameter* is a numerical characteristic of a population. The population mean annual salary ($\mu = \$51,800$), the population standard deviation of annual salary ($\sigma = \$4000$), and the population proportion having completed the training program ($p = .60$) are parameters of the population of EAI managers.

Now, suppose that the necessary information on all the EAI managers was not readily available in the company's database. Employee records for recent hires might not be on the computer. Perhaps only the salary information (and not the training program status) is in the employee's record. Or, maybe the employee records at some locations are on the computer, but records at other locations are not. For whatever reason, it is often the case that it is not possible, or perhaps too costly, to collect and process information on all elements of a population. In such cases, information from a sample can often be used to develop estimates of the population parameters of interest.

The question we now consider is how the firm's director of personnel can obtain estimates of the population parameters of interest by using a sample of managers rather than all 2500 managers in the population. Assume that a sample of 30 managers will be used. Clearly, the time and the cost of developing a profile would be substantially less for 30 managers than for the entire population. If the personnel director could be assured that a sample of 30 managers would provide adequate information about the population of 2500 managers, working with a sample would be preferable to working with the entire population. Let us explore the possibility of using a sample for the EAI study by first considering how we can identify a sample of 30 managers.

Often the cost of collecting information from a sample is substantially less than from a population, especially when personal interviews must be conducted to collect the information.

7.2   SIMPLE RANDOM SAMPLING

Several methods can be used to select a sample from a population; one of the most common is *simple random sampling*. The definition of a simple random sample and the process of selecting a simple random sample depend on whether the population is *finite* or *infinite*. Because the EAI sampling problem involves a finite population of 2500 managers, we first consider sampling from a finite population.

Sampling from a Finite Population

A simple random sample of size *n* from a finite population of size *N* is defined as follows.

Simple Random Sample (Finite Population)

A simple random sample of size *n* from a finite population of size *N* is a sample selected such that each possible sample of size *n* has the same probability of being selected.

One procedure for selecting a simple random sample from a finite population is to choose the elements for the sample one at a time in such a way that each of the elements remaining in the population has the same probability of being selected. Sampling *n* elements in this way will satisfy the definition of a simple random sample from a finite population.

To select a simple random sample from the finite population in the EAI problem, we assume that the 2500 EAI managers have been numbered sequentially (i.e., 1, 2, 3, . . . , 2499, 2500) in the order that their names appear in EAI personnel files. Next, we refer to the table of random numbers* shown in Table 7.1. Referring to the first row of the table, each digit, 6, 3, 2, . . . , is a random digit having an equal chance of occurring. Because the largest number in the population list of EAI managers, 2500, has four digits, we will select random numbers from the table in sets or groups of four digits. Using the first row of Table 7.1, the four-digit random numbers are

> Computer-generated random numbers can also be used to implement the random sample selection process. Excel provides a function for generating random numbers in its worksheets.

$$6327 \quad 1599 \quad 8671 \quad 7445 \quad 1102 \quad 1514 \quad 1807$$

Because the numbers in the table are random, these four-digit numbers are equally probable or equally likely.

We can now use these four-digit random numbers to give each manager in the population an equal chance of being included in the random sample. The first number, 6327, is greater than 2500. It does not correspond to one of the numbered managers in the population, and hence is discarded. The second number, 1599, is between 1 and 2500. Thus the first manager selected for the random sample is number 1599 on the list of EAI managers. Continuing this process, we ignore the numbers 8671 and 7445 before identifying manager numbers 1102, 1514, and 1807 to be included in the random sample. This process continues until the simple random sample of 30 EAI managers has been obtained.

In implementing the simple random sample selection process, it is possible that a random number used previously may appear again in the table before the sample of 30 EAI managers has been selected. Because we do not want to select a manager more than one time, any previously used random numbers are ignored because the corresponding manager is already part of the sample. Selecting a sample in this manner is referred to as *sampling without replacement*. If we had selected the sample such that previously used random numbers were acceptable and specific managers could be included in the sample two or more times, we would be *sampling with replacement*. Sampling with replacement is a valid way of identifying a simple random sample. However, sampling without replacement is the

---

*Tables of random numbers are available in a variety of handbooks such as The Rand Corporation's, *A Million Random Digits with 100,000 Normal Deviates,* The Free Press, 1983.

Table 7.1   RANDOM NUMBERS

63271	59986	71744	51102	15141	80714	58683	93108	13554	79945
88547	09896	95436	79115	08303	01041	20030	63754	08459	28364
55957	57243	83865	09911	19761	66535	40102	26646	60147	15702
46276	87453	44790	67122	45573	84358	21625	16999	13385	22782
55363	07449	34835	15290	76616	67191	12777	21861	68689	03263
69393	92785	49902	58447	42048	30378	87618	26933	40640	16281
13186	29431	88190	04588	38733	81290	89541	70290	40113	08243
17726	28652	56836	78351	47327	18518	92222	55201	27340	10493
36520	64465	05550	30157	82242	29520	69753	72602	23756	54935
81628	36100	39254	56835	37636	02421	98063	89641	64953	99337
84649	48968	75215	75498	49539	74240	03466	49292	36401	45525
63291	11618	12613	75055	43915	26488	41116	64531	56827	30825
70502	53225	03655	05915	37140	57051	48393	91322	25653	06543
06426	24771	59935	49801	11082	66762	94477	02494	88215	27191
20711	55609	29430	70165	45406	78484	31639	52009	18873	96927
41990	70538	77191	25860	55204	73417	83920	69468	74972	38712
72452	36618	76298	26678	89334	33938	95567	29380	75906	91807
37042	40318	57099	10528	09925	89773	41335	96244	29002	46453
53766	52875	15987	46962	67342	77592	57651	95508	80033	69828
90585	58955	53122	16025	84299	53310	67380	84249	25348	04332
32001	96293	37203	64516	51530	37069	40261	61374	05815	06714
62606	64324	46354	72157	67248	20135	49804	09226	64419	29457
10078	28073	85389	50324	14500	15562	64165	06125	71353	77669
91561	46145	24177	15294	10061	98124	75732	00815	83452	97355
13091	98112	53959	79607	52244	63303	10413	63839	74762	50289

sampling procedure used most often. When we refer to simple random sampling, we will assume that the sampling is without replacement.

Random numbers may be selected from anywhere in the random number table. Although we used the first row of the table in the example, we could have started at any other point in the table and continued in any direction. Once the arbitrary starting point is selected, a predetermined systematic procedure, such as reading across rows or down columns, is recommended for picking the subsequent random numbers.

Sampling from an Infinite Population

In practice, a population being studied is usually considered infinite if it involves an ongoing process that makes listing or counting every element in the population impossible.

Many sampling situations in business and economics involve finite populations, but in some situations the population is either infinite or so large that for practical purposes it must be treated as infinite. In sampling from an infinite population, we must use a new definition of a simple random sample. In addition, because the elements in an infinite population cannot be numbered, we must use a different process for selecting elements for the sample.

Suppose we want to estimate the average time between placing an order and receiving food for customers at a fast-food restaurant during the 11:30 A.M. to 1:30 P.M. lunch period. If we consider the population as being all possible customer visits, we see that it would not be feasible to specify a finite limit on the number of possible visits. In fact, if we define the population as being all customer visits that could conceivably occur during the lunch period, we can consider the population as being infinite. Our task is to select a simple random sample of n customers from this population. The definition of a simple random sample from an infinite population follows.

Simple Random Sample (Infinite Population)

A simple random sample from an infinite population is a sample selected such that the following conditions are satisfied.

1. Each element selected comes from the same population.
2. Each element is selected independently.

A random number selection procedure cannot be used for an infinite population because a numbered listing of the population is impossible. In this case, a sample selection procedure must be specially devised to select the items independently and thus avoid a selection bias that gives higher selection probabilities to certain types of elements.

For the problem of selecting a simple random sample of customer visits at a fast-food restaurant, we find that the first condition as defined is satisfied by any customer visit occurring during the 11:30 A.M. to 1:30 P.M. lunch period while the restaurant is operating with its regular staff under "normal" operating conditions. The second condition is satisfied by ensuring that the selection of a particular customer does not influence the selection of any other customer. That is, the customers are selected independently.

A well-known fast-food restaurant has implemented a simple random sampling procedure for just such a situation. The sampling procedure is based on the fact that some customers will present discount coupons for special prices on sandwiches, drinks, french fries, and so on. Whenever a customer presents a discount coupon, the next customer served is selected for the sample. Because the customers present discount coupons randomly and independently, the firm is satisfied that the sampling plan satisfies the two conditions for a simple random sample from an infinite population.

NOTES and Comments

1. Finite populations are often defined by lists such as organization membership rosters, student enrollment records, credit card account lists, inventory product numbers, and so on. Infinite populations are often defined by an ongoing process whereby the elements of the population consist of items generated as though the process would operate indefinitely under the same conditions. In such cases, it is impossible to obtain a list of all elements in the population. For example, populations consisting of all possible parts to be manufactured, all possible customer visits, all possible bank transactions, and so on can be classified as infinite populations.

2. The number of different simple random samples of size n that can be selected from a finite population of size N is

$$\frac{N!}{n!(N-n)!}$$

In this formula, $N!$ and $n!$ are the factorial computations discussed in Chapter 4. For the EAI problem with $N = 2500$ and $n = 30$, this expression can be used to show that there are approximately 2.75×10^{69} different simple random samples of 30 EAI managers.

..../ /...........

EXERCISES

Methods

SELF TEST

1. Consider a finite population with five elements labeled A, B, C, D, and E. Ten possible simple random samples of size two can be selected.
   a. List the 10 samples beginning with AB, AC, and so on.
   b. Using simple random sampling, what is the probability that each sample of size two is selected?
   c. Assume random number 1 corresponds to A, random number 2 corresponds to B, and so on. List the simple random sample of size two that will be selected by using the random digits 8 0 5 7 5 3 2.

2. Assume a finite population has 350 elements. Using the last three digits of each of the following five-digit random numbers, determine the first four elements that will be selected for the simple random sample.

    98601 73022 83448 02147 34229 27553 84147 93289 14209

Applications

SELF TEST

3. *Fortune* publishes data on sales, profits, assets, stockholders' equity, market value, and earnings per share for the 500 largest U.S. industrial corporations (The *Fortune* 500, 1998). Assume that you want to select a simple random sample of 10 corporations from the *Fortune* 500 list. Use the last three digits in column 9 of Table 7.1, beginning with 554. Read down the column and identify the numbers of the 10 corporations that would be selected.

4. The Airport Transport Association of America provided the following list of the ten largest airlines in the world (*The Book of Mosts,* 1997).

1. Aeroflot (Russia)	6. JAL (Japan)
2. Air France (France)	7. Lufthansa (Germany)
3. American Airlines (USA)	8. Northwest Airlines (USA)
4. British Airways (UK)	9. United Airlines (USA)
5. Delta Airlines (USA)	10. USAir (USA)

   a. Assume that a random sample of five of these airlines will be selected for an in-depth study of factors such as the number of aircraft in service, the total annual passenger miles flown, and so on. Beginning with the first random digit in Table 7.1 (6) and reading down the column, use the single-digit random numbers to select a simple random sample of five airlines to be used in the study.
   b. According to the information in Notes and Comments (2) on p. 251, how many different simple random samples of size five can be selected from the list of ten airlines?

5. A student government organization is interested in estimating the proportion of students who favor a mandatory "pass-fail" grading policy for elective courses. A list of names and addresses of the 645 students enrolled during the current quarter is available from the registrar's office. Using three-digit random numbers in row 10 of Table 7.1 and moving across the row from left to right, identify the first 10 students who would be selected using simple random sampling. The three-digit random numbers begin with 816, 283, and 610.

6. The *County and City Data Book,* published by the Bureau of the Census, lists information on 3139 counties throughout the United States. Assume that a national study will collect data from 30 randomly selected counties. Use four-digit random numbers from the last column of Table 7.1 to identify the numbers corresponding to the first five counties selected for the sample. Ignore the first digits and begin with the four-digit random numbers 9945, 8364, 5702, and so on.

7. Assume that we want to identify a simple random sample of 12 of the 372 doctors practicing in a particular city. The doctors' names are available from a local medical organization. Use the eighth column of five-digit random numbers in Table 7.1 to identify the 12 doctors for the sample. Ignore the first two random digits in each five-digit grouping of the random numbers. This process begins with random number 108 and proceeds down the column of random numbers.

8. The following table provides the Men's NCAA Basketball Top 25 Coach's Poll of January 1998 (*USA Today,* January 19, 1998). Use the ninth column of the random numbers in Table 7.1, beginning with 13554, to select a simple random sample of six basketball teams. Begin with team 13 and use the first two digits in each row of the ninth column for your selection process. Which six basketball teams are selected for the simple random sample?

1. Duke	14. Mississippi
2. North Carolina	15. Syracuse
3. Kansas	16. Michigan
4. Utah	17. South Carolina
5. Arizona	18. Xavier
6. Stanford	19. Arkansas
7. Kentucky	20. Florida State
8. Connecticut	21. West Virginia
9. Purdue	22. Rhode Island
10. UCLA	23. Clemson
11. Princeton	24. Hawaii
12. Iowa	25. Cincinnati
13. New Mexico	

9. *Business Week* provided performance data and annual ratings for 895 mutual funds (*Business Week,* February 3, 1997). Assume that a simple random sample of 12 of the 895 mutual funds will be selected for a follow-up study on the performance of mutual funds. Use the fourth column of the random numbers in Table 7.1, beginning with 51102, to select the simple random sample of 12 mutual funds. Begin with mutual fund 511 and use the first three digits in each row of the fourth column for your selection process. What are the numbers of the 12 mutual funds in the simple random sample?

10. Indicate whether the following populations should be considered finite or infinite.
    a. All registered voters in the state of California.
    b. All television sets that could be produced by the Allentown, Pennsylvania, plant of the TV-M Company.
    c. All orders that could be processed by a mail-order firm.
    d. All emergency telephone calls that could come into a local police station.
    e. All components that Fibercon, Inc., produced on the second shift on May 17.

7.3 POINT ESTIMATION

Now that we have described how to select a simple random sample, let us return to the EAI problem. Assume that a simple random sample of 30 managers has been selected and that the corresponding data on annual salary and management training program participation are as shown in Table 7.2. The notation x_1, x_2, and so on is used to denote the annual salary of the first manager in the sample, the annual salary of the second manager in the sample, and

Table 7.2	ANNUAL SALARY AND TRAINING PROGRAM STATUS FOR A SIMPLE RANDOM SAMPLE OF 30 EAI MANAGERS		
Annual Salary ($)	**Management Training Program?**	**Annual Salary ($)**	**Management Training Program?**
$x_1 = 49{,}094.30$	Yes	$x_{16} = 51{,}766.00$	Yes
$x_2 = 53{,}263.90$	Yes	$x_{17} = 52{,}541.30$	No
$x_3 = 49{,}643.50$	Yes	$x_{18} = 44{,}980.00$	Yes
$x_4 = 49{,}894.90$	Yes	$x_{19} = 51{,}932.60$	Yes
$x_5 = 47{,}621.60$	No	$x_{20} = 52{,}973.00$	Yes
$x_6 = 55{,}924.00$	Yes	$x_{21} = 45{,}120.90$	Yes
$x_7 = 49{,}092.30$	Yes	$x_{22} = 51{,}753.00$	Yes
$x_8 = 51{,}404.40$	Yes	$x_{23} = 54{,}391.80$	No
$x_9 = 50{,}957.70$	Yes	$x_{24} = 50{,}164.20$	No
$x_{10} = 55{,}109.70$	Yes	$x_{25} = 52{,}973.60$	No
$x_{11} = 45{,}922.60$	Yes	$x_{26} = 50{,}241.30$	No
$x_{12} = 57{,}268.40$	No	$x_{27} = 52{,}793.90$	No
$x_{13} = 55{,}688.80$	Yes	$x_{28} = 50{,}979.40$	Yes
$x_{14} = 51{,}564.70$	No	$x_{29} = 55{,}860.90$	Yes
$x_{15} = 56{,}188.20$	No	$x_{30} = 57{,}309.10$	No

so on. Participation in the management training program is indicated by Yes in the management training program column.

To estimate the value of a population parameter, we compute a corresponding characteristic of the sample, referred to as a *sample statistic*. For example, to estimate the population mean μ and the population standard deviation σ for the annual salary of EAI managers, we simply use the data in Table 7.2 to calculate the corresponding sample statistics: the sample mean $\bar{x}$ and the sample standard deviation s. Using the formulas for a sample mean and a sample standard deviation presented in Chapter 3, the sample mean is

$$\bar{x} = \frac{\Sigma x_i}{n} = \frac{1{,}554{,}420}{30} = \$51{,}814.00$$

and the sample standard deviation is

$$s = \sqrt{\frac{\Sigma(x_i - \bar{x})^2}{n-1}} = \sqrt{\frac{325{,}009{,}260}{29}} = \$3347.72$$

In addition, by computing the proportion of managers in the sample who responded Yes, we can estimate the proportion of managers in the population who have completed the management training program. Table 7.2 shows that 19 of the 30 managers in the sample have completed the training program. Thus, the sample proportion, denoted by $\bar{p}$, is given by

$$\bar{p} = \frac{19}{30} = .63$$

This value is used as an estimate of the population proportion p.

By making the preceding computations, we have performed the statistical procedure called *point estimation*. In point estimation we use the data from the sample to compute a value of a sample statistic that serves as an estimate of a population parameter. Using the terminology of point estimation, we refer to $\bar{x}$ as the *point estimator* of the population mean μ, s as the *point estimator* of the population standard deviation σ, and $\bar{p}$ as the *point estimator* of the population proportion p. The actual numerical value obtained for $\bar{x}$, s, or $\bar{p}$ in a particular sample is called the *point estimate* of the parameter. Thus, for the sample of 30 EAI managers, \$51,814.00 is the point estimate of μ, \$3,347.72 is the point estimate of σ, and .63 is the point estimate of p. Table 7.3 summarizes the sample results and compares the point estimates to the actual values of the population parameters.

As Table 7.3 shows, none of the point estimates are exactly equal to the corresponding population parameters. This variation is to be expected because only a sample and not a census of the entire population is being used to develop the estimate. The absolute value of the difference between an unbiased point estimate and the corresponding population parameter is called the *sampling error*.* For a sample mean, sample standard deviation, and sample proportion, the sampling errors are $|\bar{x} - \mu|$, $|s - \sigma|$, and $|\bar{p} - p|$, respectively. Thus, for the EAI sample, the sampling errors are $|\$51,814 - \$51,800| = \$14$ for the sample mean, $|\$3,347.72 - \$4000.00| = \$652.28$ for the sample standard deviation, and $|.63 - .60| = .03$ for the sample proportion.

> Sampling error is the result of using a subset of the population (the sample), and not the entire population to develop estimates.

We were able to compute the sampling errors here because the population parameters were known. However, in an actual sampling application we will not be able to calculate the sampling error exactly because the value of the population parameter will not be known. We will show how statisticians analyze the sample data in order to make probability statements about the likely size of the sampling error.

Table 7.3	SUMMARY OF POINT ESTIMATES OBTAINED FROM A SIMPLE RANDOM SAMPLE OF 30 EAI MANAGERS		
Population Parameter	**Parameter Value**	**Point Estimator**	**Point Estimate**
μ = Population mean annual salary	\$51,800.00	$\bar{x}$ = Sample mean annual salary	\$51,814.00
σ = Population standard deviation for annual salary	\$4,000.00	s = Sample standard deviation for annual salary	\$3,347.72
p = Population proportion having completed the management training program	.60	$\bar{p}$ = Sample proportion having completed the management training program	.63

---

*Technically the difference between the point estimate and the population parameter is called sampling error only when the point estimator is unbiased. The point estimators ($\bar{x}$, s, and $\bar{p}$) used here are unbiased.

> N O T E S
> *and Comments*
>
> In our discussion of point estimators, we use $\bar{x}$ to denote a sample mean and $\bar{p}$ to denote a sample proportion. Our use of $\bar{p}$ is based on the fact that the sample proportion is also a *sample mean*. For instance, suppose that in a sample of size n with data values $x_1, x_2, \ldots, x_n$, we let $x_i = 1$ when a characteristic of interest is present for the ith observation and $x_i = 0$ when the characteristic is not present. Then the sample proportion is computed by $\Sigma x_i/n$, which is the formula for a sample mean. We also like the consistency of using the bar over the letter to remind the reader that the sample proportion $\bar{p}$ estimates the population proportion just as the sample mean $\bar{x}$ estimates the population mean. Some texts use $\hat{p}$ instead of $\bar{p}$ to denote the sample proportion.

EXERCISES

Methods

SELF TEST

11. The following data are from a simple random sample.

$$5 \quad 8 \quad 10 \quad 7 \quad 10 \quad 14$$

a. What is the point estimate of the population mean?
b. What is the point estimate of the population standard deviation?

12. A survey question for a sample of 150 individuals yielded 75 Yes responses, 55 No responses, and 20 No Opinions.
a. What is the point estimate of the proportion in the population who respond Yes?
b. What is the point estimate of the proportion in the population who respond No?

Applications

SELF TEST

13. A simple random sample of five months of sales data provided the following information:

Month:	1	2	3	4	5
Units Sold:	94	100	85	94	92

a. What is the point estimate of the population mean number of units sold per month?
b. What is the point estimate of the population standard deviation?

14. A sample of 784 children ages 9 to 14 were asked about cash provided by their parents (*Consumer Reports*, January 1997). The responses were as follows.

Source of Cash	Frequency
Allowance only	149
Handouts & chores plus an allowance	219
Handouts & chores but no allowance	251
Nothing	165
Total	784

a. What proportion of children receive an allowance as their only source of cash?
b. What proportion of children receive cash as handouts and for chores, but nothing in the form of an allowance?
c. Considering all sources, what proportion of children receive at least some cash from their parents?

15. The California Highway Patrol maintains records showing the time between a report of an accident and the arrival of an officer at the accident scene. A simple random sample of 10 records shows the following times in minutes.

    | 12.6 | 3.4 | 4.8 | 5.0 | 6.8 | 2.3 | 3.6 | 8.1 | 2.5 | 10.3 |

    a. What is a point estimate of the population mean time between an accident report and officer arrival?
    b. What is a point estimate of the population standard deviation of the time between an accident report and officer arrival?

16. The U.S. Department of Transportation reports statistics on how frequently major airline flights arrive at or before their scheduled arrival times (*USA Today,* June 26, 1997). Assume that the estimated proportion of flights arriving on time for all airlines is based on a sample of 1400 flights. If 1117 of the flights arrive on time, what is the point estimate of the proportion of all flights that arrive on time?

17. A 1996 Louis Harris poll used a survey of 1005 adults to learn how people are using the Internet (*Business Week,* August 26, 1996). Responses were as follows:

    874 adults were aware of the Internet
    503 adults were users of computers
    191 adults had used the Internet in the past 12 months

    Develop the point estimate of the following population parameters.
    a. The proportion of all adults who are aware of the Internet.
    b. The proportion of all adults who use computers.
    c. The proportion of all adults who have used the Internet in the past 12 months.

7.4 INTRODUCTION TO SAMPLING DISTRIBUTIONS

In the preceding section we used a simple random sample of 30 EAI managers to develop point estimates of the mean and standard deviation of annual salary for the population of all EAI managers as well as the proportion of the managers in the population who have completed the company's management training program. Suppose we select another simple random sample of 30 EAI managers, and an analysis of the data from the second sample provides the following information.

$$\text{Sample Mean } \bar{x} = \$52,669.70$$
$$\text{Sample Standard Deviation } s = \$4,239.07$$
$$\text{Sample Proportion } \bar{p} = .70$$

These results show that different values of $\bar{x}$, s, and $\bar{p}$ have been obtained with the second sample. In general, a second simple random sample will not contain the same elements as the first. Let us imagine carrying out the same process of selecting a new simple random sample of 30 managers over and over again, each time computing values of $\bar{x}$, s, and $\bar{p}$. In this way we could begin to identify the variety of values that these point estimators can have. To illustrate, we repeated the simple random sampling process for the EAI problem until we obtained 500 samples of 30 managers each and the corresponding $\bar{x}$, s, and $\bar{p}$ values. A portion of the results is shown in Table 7.4. Table 7.5 gives the frequency and

Table 7.4	VALUES OF $\bar{x}$, s, and $\bar{p}$ FROM 500 SIMPLE RANDOM SAMPLES OF 30 EAI MANAGERS		
Sample Number	Sample Mean ($\bar{x}$)	Sample Standard Deviation (s)	Sample Proportion ($\bar{p}$)
1	51,814.00	3,347.72	.63
2	52,669.70	4,239.07	.70
3	51,780.30	4,433.43	.67
4	51,587.90	3,985.32	.53
.	.	.	.
.	.	.	.
.	.	.	.
500	51,752.00	3,857.82	.50

relative frequency distributions for the 500 $\bar{x}$ values. Figure 7.1 is the relative frequency histogram for the $\bar{x}$ values.

The concept of a sampling distribution is one of the most important topics in this chapter. The ability to understand the material in subsequent chapters depends heavily on the ability to understand and use the sampling distributions presented in this chapter.

Recall that in Chapter 5 we defined a random variable as a numerical description of the outcome of an experiment. If we consider the process of selecting a simple random sample as an experiment, the sample mean $\bar{x}$ is the numerical description of the outcome of the experiment. Thus, the sample mean $\bar{x}$ is a random variable. As a result, just like other random variables, $\bar{x}$ has a mean or expected value, a variance, and a probability distribution. Because the various possible values of $\bar{x}$ are the result of different simple random samples, the probability distribution of $\bar{x}$ is called the *sampling distribution* of $\bar{x}$. Knowledge of this sampling distribution and its properties will enable us to make probability statements about how close the sample mean $\bar{x}$ is to the population mean μ.

Let us return to Figure 7.1. We would need to enumerate every possible sample of 30 managers and compute each sample mean to completely determine the sampling distribu-

Table 7.5	FREQUENCY DISTRIBUTION OF $\bar{x}$ FROM 500 SIMPLE RANDOM SAMPLES OF 300 EAI MANAGERS	
Mean Annual Salary ($)	Frequency	Relative Frequency
49,500.00–49,999.99	2	.004
50,000.00–50,499.99	16	.032
50,500.00–50,999.99	52	.104
51,000.00–51,499.99	101	.202
51,500.00–51,999.99	133	.266
52,000.00–52,499.99	110	.220
52,500.00–52,999.99	54	.108
53,000.00–53,499.99	26	.052
53,500.00–53,999.99	6	.012
Totals	500	1.000

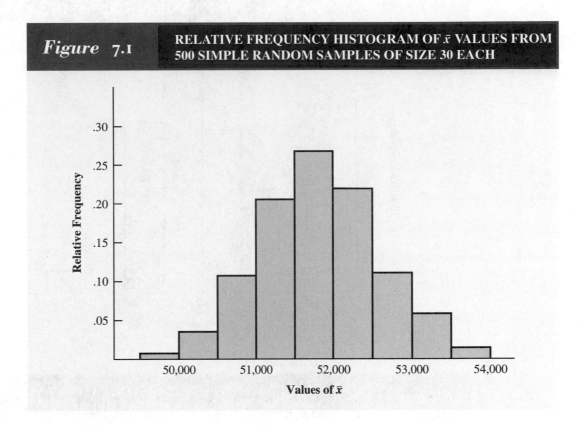

Figure 7.1   RELATIVE FREQUENCY HISTOGRAM OF $\bar{x}$ VALUES FROM 500 SIMPLE RANDOM SAMPLES OF SIZE 30 EACH

tion of $\bar{x}$. However, the histogram of 500 $\bar{x}$ values gives an approximation of this sampling distribution. From the approximation we observe the bell-shaped appearance of the distribution. We note that the estimate of the population mean provided by $\bar{x}$ could be off by more than $2000. But we also note that the largest concentration of the $\bar{x}$ values and the mean of the 500 $\bar{x}$ values is near the population mean $\mu = \$51,800$. We will describe the properties of the sampling distribution of $\bar{x}$ more fully in the next section.

The 500 values of the sample standard deviation s and the 500 values of the sample proportion $\bar{p}$ are summarized by the relative frequency histograms in Figures 7.2 and 7.3. As in the case of $\bar{x}$, both s and $\bar{p}$ are random variables that provide numerical descriptions of the outcome of a simple random sample. If every possible sample of size 30 were selected from the population and if a value of s and a value of $\bar{p}$ were computed for each sample, the resulting probability distributions would be called the sampling distribution of s and the sampling distribution of $\bar{p}$, respectively. The relative frequency histograms of the 500 sample values, Figures 7.2 and 7.3, provide a general idea of the appearance of these two sampling distributions.

In practice, we select only one simple random sample from the population. We repeated the sampling process 500 times in this section simply to illustrate that many different samples are possible and that the different samples generate a variety of values for the sample statistics $\bar{x}$, s, and $\bar{p}$. The probability distribution of any particular sample statistic is called the sampling distribution of the statistic. In Section 7.5 we show the characteristics of the sampling distribution of $\bar{x}$. In Section 7.6 we show the characteristics of the sampling distribution of $\bar{p}$.

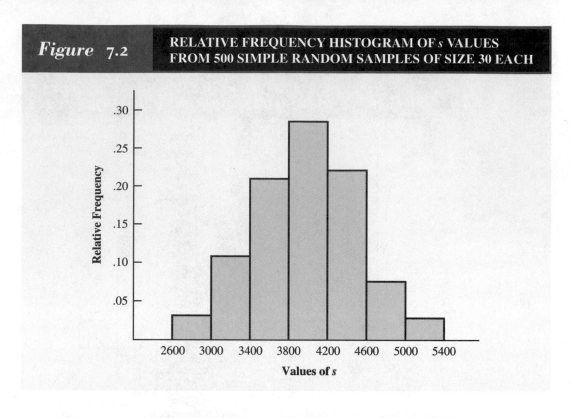

Figure 7.2 RELATIVE FREQUENCY HISTOGRAM OF *s* VALUES FROM 500 SIMPLE RANDOM SAMPLES OF SIZE 30 EACH

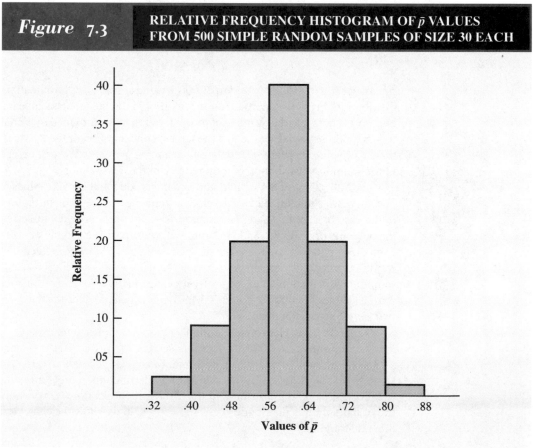

Figure 7.3 RELATIVE FREQUENCY HISTOGRAM OF $\bar{p}$ VALUES FROM 500 SIMPLE RANDOM SAMPLES OF SIZE 30 EACH

7.5   SAMPLING DISTRIBUTION OF $\bar{x}$

One of the most common statistical procedures is the use of a sample mean $\bar{x}$ to make inferences about a population mean μ. This process is shown in Figure 7.4. On each repetition of the process, we can anticipate obtaining a different value for the sample mean $\bar{x}$. The probability distribution for all possible values of the sample mean $\bar{x}$ is called the sampling distribution of the sample mean $\bar{x}$.

Sampling Distribution of $\bar{x}$

The sampling distribution of $\bar{x}$ is the probability distribution of all possible values of the sample mean, $\bar{x}$.

The purpose of this section is to describe the properties of the sampling distribution of $\bar{x}$, including the expected value or mean of $\bar{x}$, the standard deviation of $\bar{x}$, and the shape or form of the sampling distribution itself. As we shall see, knowledge of the sampling distribution of $\bar{x}$ will enable us to make probability statements about the sampling error involved when $\bar{x}$ is used to estimate μ. Let us begin by considering the mean of all possible $\bar{x}$ values, which is referred to as the expected value of $\bar{x}$.

Expected Value of $\bar{x}$

In the EAI sampling problem we saw that different simple random samples result in a variety of values for the sample mean $\bar{x}$. Because many different values of the random variable $\bar{x}$ are possible, we are often interested in the mean of all possible values of $\bar{x}$ that can be generated by the various simple random samples. The mean of the $\bar{x}$ random variable is the expected value of $\bar{x}$. Let $E(\bar{x})$ represent the expected value of $\bar{x}$ and μ represent the mean of the population from which we are sampling. It can be shown that with simple random sampling, $E(\bar{x})$ and μ are equal.

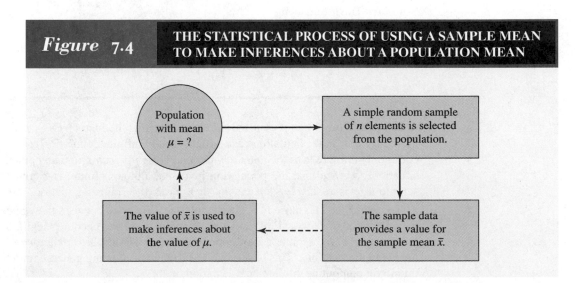

Figure 7.4   THE STATISTICAL PROCESS OF USING A SAMPLE MEAN TO MAKE INFERENCES ABOUT A POPULATION MEAN

Population with mean $\mu = ?$

A simple random sample of n elements is selected from the population.

The value of $\bar{x}$ is used to make inferences about the value of μ.

The sample data provides a value for the sample mean $\bar{x}$.

The expected value of $\bar{x}$ equals the mean of the population from which the sample is drawn.

Expected Value of $\bar{x}$

$$E(\bar{x}) = \mu \tag{7.1}$$

where

$$E(\bar{x}) = \text{the expected value of } \bar{x}$$
$$\mu = \text{the population mean}$$

This result shows that with simple random sampling, the expected value or mean for $\bar{x}$ is equal to the mean of the population from which we are sampling. In Section 7.1 we saw that the mean annual salary for the population of EAI managers is $\mu = \$51,800$. Thus, according to (7.1), the mean of all possible sample means for the EAI study is also $\$51,800$.

Standard Deviation of $\bar{x}$

Let us define the standard deviation of the sampling distribution of $\bar{x}$. We will use the following notation.

$$\sigma_{\bar{x}} = \text{the standard deviation of the sampling distribution of } \bar{x}$$
$$\sigma = \text{the standard deviation of the population}$$
$$n = \text{the sample size}$$
$$N = \text{the population size}$$

It can be shown that with simple random sampling, the standard deviation of $\bar{x}$ depends on whether the population is finite or infinite. The two expressions for the standard deviation of $\bar{x}$ follow.

Standard Deviation of $\bar{x}$

$$\begin{array}{cc} \textit{Finite Population} & \textit{Infinite Population} \\ \sigma_{\bar{x}} = \sqrt{\dfrac{N-n}{N-1}}\left(\dfrac{\sigma}{\sqrt{n}}\right) & \sigma_{\bar{x}} = \dfrac{\sigma}{\sqrt{n}} \end{array} \tag{7.2}$$

In comparing the two expressions in (7.2), we see that the factor $\sqrt{(N-n)/(N-1)}$ is required for the finite population case but not for the infinite population case. This factor is commonly referred to as the *finite population correction factor*. In many practical sampling situations, we find that the population involved, although finite, is "large," whereas the sample size is relatively "small." In such cases the finite population correction factor $\sqrt{(N-n)/(N-1)}$ is close to 1. As a result, the difference between the values of the standard deviation of $\bar{x}$ for the finite and infinite population cases becomes negligible. When this occurs, $\sigma_{\bar{x}} = \sigma/\sqrt{n}$ becomes a good approximation to the standard deviation of $\bar{x}$ even though the population is finite. This observation leads to the following general guideline or rule of thumb for computing the standard deviation of $\bar{x}$.

Use the Following Expression to Calculate the Standard Deviation of $\bar{x}$

$$\sigma_{\bar{x}} = \frac{\sigma}{\sqrt{n}} \qquad (7.3)$$

whenever

1. The population is infinite; or
2. The population is finite *and* the sample size is less than or equal to 5% of the population size; that is, $n/N \leq .05$.

Problem 21 shows that when $n/N \leq .05$, the finite population correction factor has little effect on the value of $\sigma_{\bar{x}}$.

In cases where $n/N > .05$, the finite population version of (7.2) should be used in the computation of $\sigma_{\bar{x}}$. Unless otherwise noted, throughout the text we will assume that the population size is "large," $n/N \leq .05$, and (7.3) can be used to compute $\sigma_{\bar{x}}$.

Now let us return to the EAI study and determine the standard deviation of all possible sample means that can be generated with samples of 30 EAI managers. In Section 7.1 we saw that the population standard deviation for the annual salary data is $\sigma = 4000$. In this case the population is finite, with $N = 2500$. However, with a sample size of 30, we have $n/N = 30/2500 = .012$. Following the rule of thumb given in (7.3), we can ignore the finite population correction factor and use (7.3) to compute the standard deviation of $\bar{x}$.

$$\sigma_{\bar{x}} = \frac{\sigma}{\sqrt{n}} = \frac{4000}{\sqrt{30}} = 730.30$$

Later we will see that the value of $\sigma_{\bar{x}}$ is helpful in determining how far the sample mean may be from the population mean. Because of the role that $\sigma_{\bar{x}}$ plays in computing possible sampling errors, $\sigma_{\bar{x}}$ is referred to as the *standard error of the mean*.

Central Limit Theorem

The final step in identifying the characteristics of the sampling distribution of $\bar{x}$ is to determine the form of the probability distribution of $\bar{x}$. We consider two cases: one in which the population distribution is unknown and one in which the population distribution is known to be normally distributed.

When the population distribution is unknown, we rely on one of the most important theorems in statistics—the *central limit theorem*. A statement of the central limit theorem as it applies to the sampling distribution of $\bar{x}$ follows.

Central Limit Theorem

In selecting simple random samples of size n from a population, the sampling distribution of the sample mean $\bar{x}$ can be approximated by a *normal probability distribution* as the sample size becomes large.

Figure 7.5 shows how the central limit theorem works for three different populations; in each case the population clearly is not normal. However, note what begins to happen to the sampling distribution of $\bar{x}$ as the sample size is increased. When the samples are of size two,

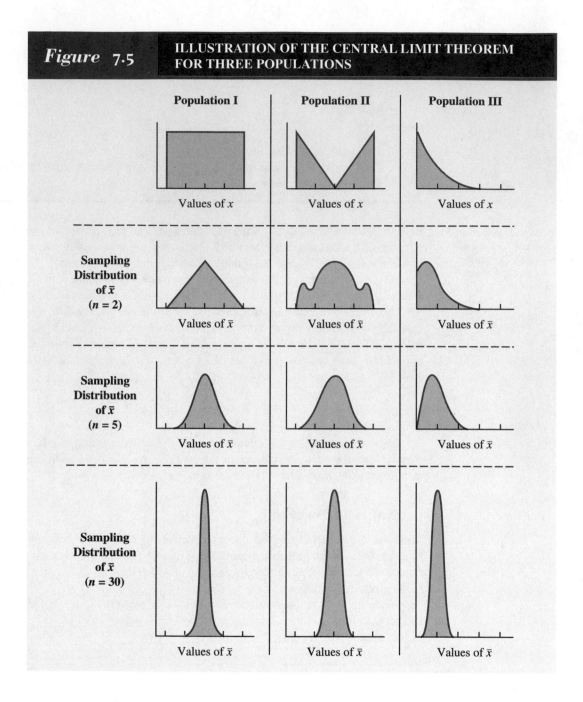

Figure 7·5   ILLUSTRATION OF THE CENTRAL LIMIT THEOREM FOR THREE POPULATIONS

we see that the sampling distribution of $\bar{x}$ begins to take on an appearance different from that of the population distribution. For samples of size five, we see all three sampling distributions beginning to take on a bell-shaped appearance. Finally, the samples of size 30 show all three sampling distributions to be approximately normal. Thus, for sufficiently large samples, the sampling distribution of $\bar{x}$ can be approximated by a normal probability distribution. However, how large must the sample size be before we can assume that the central limit theorem applies? Statistical researchers have investigated this question by studying the sampling distribution of $\bar{x}$ for a variety of populations and a variety of sample sizes. Whenever the population distribution is mound-shaped and symmetrical, sample sizes as small as five to 10 can be enough for the central limit theorem to apply. However, if the population distribution is highly skewed and clearly non-normal, larger sample sizes are needed. General statistical practice is to assume that for most applications, the sampling distribution of $\bar{x}$ can be approximated by a normal probability distribution whenever the sample size is 30 or more. In effect, a sample size of 30 or more is assumed to satisfy the large-sample condition of the central limit theorem. This observation is so important that we restate it.

The sampling distribution of $\bar{x}$ can be approximated by a normal probability distribution whenever the sample size is large. The large-sample condition can be assumed for simple random samples of size 30 or more.

The central limit theorem is the key to identifying the form of the sampling distribution of $\bar{x}$ whenever the population distribution is unknown. However, we may encounter some sampling situations in which the population is assumed or believed to have a normal probability distribution. When this condition occurs, the following result identifies the form of the sampling distribution of $\bar{x}$.

Whenever the population has a normal probability distribution, the sampling distribution of $\bar{x}$ has a normal probability distribution for any sample size.

In summary, if we use a large ($n \geq 30$) simple random sample, the central limit theorem enables us to conclude that the sampling distribution of $\bar{x}$ can be approximated by a normal probability distribution. When the simple random sample is small ($n < 30$), the sampling distribution of $\bar{x}$ can be considered normal only if we assume that the population has a normal probability distribution.

Sampling Distribution of $\bar{x}$ for the EAI Problem

For the EAI study we have shown that $E(\bar{x}) = 51{,}800$ and $\sigma_{\bar{x}} = 730.30$. Because we are using a simple random sample of 30 managers, the central limit theorem enables us to conclude that the sampling distribution of $\bar{x}$ is approximately normal as shown in Figure 7.6.

Practical Value of the Sampling Distribution of $\bar{x}$

Whenever a simple random sample is selected and the value of the sample mean $\bar{x}$ is used to estimate the value of the population mean μ, we cannot expect the sample mean to exactly equal the population mean. As stated earlier, the absolute value of the difference between the value of the sample mean $\bar{x}$ and the value of the population mean μ, $|\bar{x} - \mu|$, is called the *sampling error*. The practical reason we are interested in the sampling distribution of $\bar{x}$ is that it can be used to provide probability information about the size of the sampling error. To demonstrate this use, let us return to the EAI problem.

Suppose the personnel director believes the sample mean will be an acceptable estimate of the population mean if the sample mean is within $500 of the population mean. However, it is not possible to guarantee that the sample mean will be within $500 of the population mean. Indeed, Table 7.5 and Figure 7.1 show that some of the 500 sample means differed by more than $2000 from the population mean. So we must think of the personnel

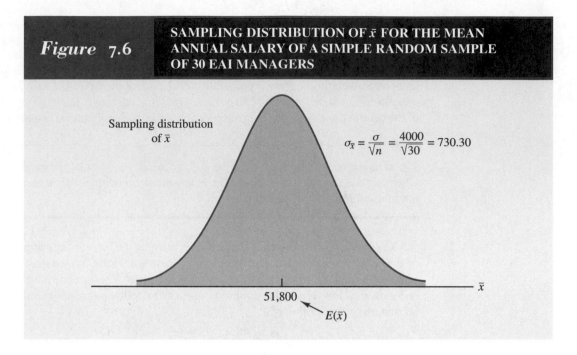

Figure 7.6   SAMPLING DISTRIBUTION OF $\bar{x}$ FOR THE MEAN ANNUAL SALARY OF A SIMPLE RANDOM SAMPLE OF 30 EAI MANAGERS

director's request in probability terms. That is, the personnel director is concerned with the following question: What is the probability that the sample mean from a simple random sample of 30 EAI managers will be within $500 of the population mean?

Since we have identified the properties of the sampling distribution of $\bar{x}$ (see Figure 7.6), we will use this distribution to answer the probability question. Refer to the sampling distribution of $\bar{x}$ shown again in Figure 7.7. The personnel director is asking about the probability that the sample mean is between $51,300 and $52,300. If the value of the sample mean $\bar{x}$ is in this interval, the value of $\bar{x}$ will be within $500 of the population mean. The appropriate probability is given by the shaded area of the sampling distribution shown in Figure 7.7. Because the sampling distribution is normal, with mean 51,800 and standard deviation 730.30, we can use the standard normal probability distribution table to find the area or probability. At $\bar{x} = 51,300$, we have

$$ z = \frac{51,300 - 51,800}{730.30} = -.68 $$

Referring to the standard normal probability distribution table, we find an area between $z = 0$ and $z = -.68$ of .2518. Similar calculations for $\bar{x} = 52,300$ show an area between $z = 0$ and $z = +.68$ of .2518. Thus, the probability of the value of the sample mean being between 51,300 and 52,300 is .2518 + .2518 = .5036.

The preceding computations show that a simple random sample of 30 EAI managers has a .5036 probability of providing a sample mean $\bar{x}$ that is within $500 of the population mean. Thus, there is a $1 - .5036 = .4964$ probability that the sample mean will miss the population mean by more than $500. In other words, a simple random sample of 30 EAI managers has roughly a 50–50 chance of providing a sample mean within the allowable $500. Perhaps a larger sample size should be considered. Let us explore this possibility by considering the relationship between the sample size and the sampling distribution of $\bar{x}$.

The sampling distribution of $\bar{x}$ can be used to provide probability information about how close the sample mean $\bar{x}$ is to the population mean μ.

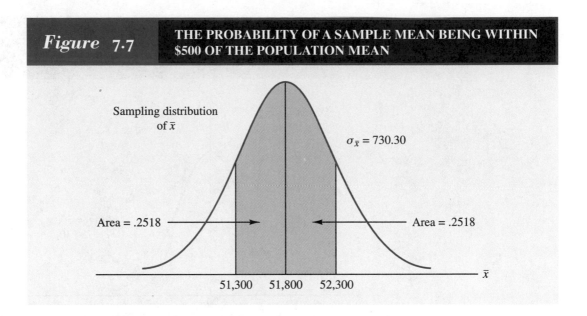

Figure 7.7   THE PROBABILITY OF A SAMPLE MEAN BEING WITHIN $500 OF THE POPULATION MEAN

Relationship between the Sample Size and the Sampling Distribution of $\bar{x}$

Suppose that in the EAI sampling problem we select a simple random sample of 100 EAI managers instead of the 30 originally considered. Intuitively, it would seem that with more data provided by the larger sample size, the sample mean based on $n = 100$ should provide a better estimate of the population mean than the sample mean based on $n = 30$. To see how much better, let us consider the relationship between the sample size and the sampling distribution of $\bar{x}$.

First note that $E(\bar{x}) = \mu$ regardless of the sample size. Thus, the mean of all possible values of $\bar{x}$ is equal to the population mean μ regardless of the sample size n. However, note that the standard error of the mean, $\sigma_{\bar{x}} = \sigma/\sqrt{n}$, is related to the square root of the sample size. Specifically, whenever the sample size is increased, the standard error of the mean $\sigma_{\bar{x}}$ is decreased. With $n = 30$, the standard error of the mean for the EAI problem is 730.30. However, with the increase in the sample size to $n = 100$, the standard error of the mean is decreased to

$$\sigma_{\bar{x}} = \frac{\sigma}{\sqrt{n}} = \frac{4000}{\sqrt{100}} = 400$$

The sampling distributions of $\bar{x}$ with $n = 30$ and $n = 100$ are shown in Figure 7.8. Because the sampling distribution with $n = 100$ has a smaller standard error, the values of $\bar{x}$ have less variation and tend to be closer to the population mean than the values of $\bar{x}$ with $n = 30$.

We can use the sampling distribution of $\bar{x}$ for the case with $n = 100$ to compute the probability that a simple random sample of 100 EAI managers will provide a sample mean that is within $500 of the population mean. Because the sampling distribution is normal, with mean 51,800 and standard deviation 400, we can use the standard normal probability distribution table to find the area or probability. At $\bar{x} = 51,300$ (Figure 7.9), we have

$$z = \frac{51,300 - 51,800}{400} = -1.25$$

Referring to the standard normal probability distribution table, we find an area between $z = 0$ and $z = -1.25$ of .3944. With a similar calculation for $\bar{x} = 52,300$, we see that

Figure 7.8 A COMPARISON OF THE SAMPLING DISTRIBUTIONS OF $\bar{x}$ FOR SIMPLE RANDOM SAMPLES OF $n = 30$ AND $n = 100$ EAI MANAGERS

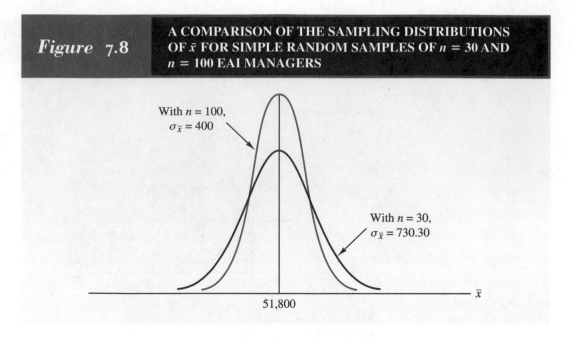

the probability of the value of the sample mean being between 51,300 and 52,300 is .3944 + .3944 = .7888. Thus, by increasing the sample size from 30 to 100 EAI managers, we have increased the probability of obtaining a sample mean within $500 of the population mean from .5036 to .7888.

The important point in this discussion is that as the sample size is increased, the standard error of the mean is decreased. As a result, the larger sample size will provide a higher probability that the sample mean is within a specified distance of the population mean.

Figure 7.9 THE PROBABILITY OF A SAMPLE MEAN BEING WITHIN $500 OF THE POPULATION MEAN WHEN A SIMPLE RANDOM SAMPLE OF 100 EAI MANAGERS IS USED

1. In presenting the sampling distribution of $\bar{x}$ for the EAI problem, we took advantage of the fact that the population mean $\mu = 51{,}800$ and the population standard deviation $\sigma = 4000$ were known. However, in general, the values of the population mean μ and the population standard deviation σ that are needed to determine the sampling distribution of $\bar{x}$ will be unknown. In Chapter 8 we will show how the sample mean $\bar{x}$ and the sample standard deviation s are used when μ and σ are unknown.

2. The theoretical proof of the central limit theorem requires independent observations in the sample. This condition is met for infinite populations and for finite populations where sampling is done with replacement. Although the central limit theorem does not directly address sampling without replacement from finite populations, general statistical practice has been to apply the findings of the central limit theorem in this situation when the population size is large.

EXERCISES

Methods

18. A population has a mean of 200 and a standard deviation of 50. A simple random sample of size 100 will be taken and the sample mean $\bar{x}$ will be used to estimate the population mean.
    a. What is the expected value of $\bar{x}$?
    b. What is the standard deviation of $\bar{x}$?
    c. Show the sampling distribution of $\bar{x}$.
    d. What does the sampling distribution of $\bar{x}$ show?

19. A population has a mean of 200 and a standard deviation of 50. Suppose a simple random sample of size 100 is selected and $\bar{x}$ is used to estimate μ.
    a. What is the probability that the sample mean will be within ± 5 of the population mean?
    b. What is the probability that the sample mean will be within ± 10 of the population mean?

SELF TEST

20. Assume the population standard deviation is $\sigma = 25$. Compute the standard error of the mean, $\sigma_{\bar{x}}$, for sample sizes of 50, 100, 150, and 200. What can you say about the size of the standard error of the mean as the sample size is increased?

21. Suppose a simple random sample of size 50 is selected from a population with $\sigma = 10$. Find the value of the standard error of the mean in each of the following cases (use the finite population correction factor if appropriate).
    a. The population size is infinite.
    b. The population size is $N = 50{,}000$.
    c. The population size is $N = 5000$.
    d. The population size is $N = 500$.

22. A population has a mean of 400 and a standard deviation of 50. The probability distribution of the population is unknown.
    a. A researcher will use simple random samples of either 10, 20, 30, or 40 items to collect data about the population. With which of these sample-size alternatives will we be able to use a normal probability distribution to describe the sampling distribution of $\bar{x}$? Explain.
    b. Show the sampling distribution of $\bar{x}$ for the instances in which the normal probability distribution is appropriate.

23. A population has a mean of 100 and a standard deviation of 16. What is the probability that a sample mean will be within ±2 of the population mean for each of the following sample sizes?
    a. $n = 50$
    b. $n = 100$
    c. $n = 200$
    d. $n = 400$
    e. What is the advantage of a larger sample size?

Applications

24. Refer to the EAI sampling problem. Suppose the simple random sample had contained 60 managers.
    a. Sketch the sampling distribution of $\bar{x}$ when simple random samples of size 60 are used.
    b. What happens to the sampling distribution of $\bar{x}$ if simple random samples of size 120 are used?
    c. What general statement can you make about what happens to the sampling distribution of $\bar{x}$ as the sample size is increased? Does this seem logical? Explain.

SELF TEST

25. In the EAI sampling problem (see Figure 7.7), we showed that for $n = 30$, there was .5036 probability of obtaining a sample mean within ±$500 of the population mean.
    a. What is the probability that $\bar{x}$ is within $500 of the population mean if a sample of size 60 is used?
    b. Answer part (a) for a sample of size 120.

26. The mean price per gallon of regular gasoline sold in the United States is $1.20 (*The Energy Information Administration,* March 3, 1997). Assume the population mean price per gallon is $\mu = 1.20$, and the population standard deviation is $\sigma = .10$. Suppose that a random sample of 50 gasoline stations will be selected, and a sample mean price per gallon will be computed for data collected from the 50 gasoline stations.
    a. Show the sampling distribution of the sample mean $\bar{x}$ where $\bar{x}$ is the sample mean price per gallon for the 50 gasoline stations.
    b. What is the probability that the simple random sample will provide a sample mean within 2 cents, .02, of the population mean?
    c. What is the probability that the simple random sample will provide a sample mean within 1 cent, .01, of the population mean?

27. The College Board American College Testing Program reported a population mean SAT score of $\mu = 960$ (*The New York Times,* 1998 Almanac). Assume that the population standard deviation is $\sigma = 100$.
    a. What is the probability that a random sample of 75 students will provide a sample mean SAT score within 10 of the population mean?
    b. What is the probability a random sample of 75 students will provide a sample mean SAT score within 20 of the population mean?

28. The 1996–97 mean annual starting salary for accounting majors was $30,393 (*U.S. News Online,* December 28, 1997). Assume that for the population of graduates with accounting majors the mean annual starting salary is $\mu = \$30,393$ and the standard deviation is $\sigma = \$2000$.
    a. What is the probability that a simple random sample of accounting graduates will have a sample mean within ±$250 of the population mean for each of the following sample sizes: 30, 50, 100, 200, and 400?
    b. What is the advantage of a larger sample size when attempting to estimate a population mean?

29. In 1993, women took an average of 8.5 weeks of unpaid leave from their jobs after the birth of a child (*U.S. News & World Report,* December 27, 1993). Assume that 8.5 weeks is the population mean and 2.2 weeks is the population standard deviation.
    a. What is the probability that a simple random sample of 50 women provides a sample mean unpaid leave of 7.5 to 9.5 weeks after the birth of a child?
    b. What is the probability that a simple random sample of 50 women provides a sample mean unpaid leave after the birth of a child of between eight and nine weeks?

30. The population mean for the price of a new one-family home is \$166,500 (U.S. Bureau of the Census, *New One-Family Houses Sold,* 1997). Assume that the population standard deviation is \$42,000 and that a sample of 100 new one-family homes will be selected.
    a. Show the sampling distribution of the sample mean price for new homes based on the sample of 100.
    b. What is the probability that the sample mean for the 100 new homes will be within \$10,000 of the population mean?
    c. Repeat part (b) for values of \$5000, \$2500, and \$1000.
    d. To estimate the population mean price to within $\pm$\$2500 or $\pm$\$1000, what would you recommend?

31. *Business Week* reports that its subscribers who plan to purchase a new vehicle within the next 12 months plan to spend a mean of \$27,100 on the new vehicle (*Business Week,* Subscriber Profile, 1996). Assume that the new vehicle price for the population of *Business Week* subscribers has a mean of $\mu = \$27,100$ and a standard deviation of $\sigma = \$5200$.
    a. What is the probability that the sample mean new vehicle price for a sample of 30 subscribers is within \$1000 of the population mean?
    b. What is the probability that the sample mean new vehicle price for a sample of 50 subscribers is within \$1000 of the population mean?
    c. What is the probability that the sample mean new vehicle price for a sample of 100 subscribers is within \$1000 of the population mean?
    d. Would you recommend a sample size of 30, 50, or 100 if it is desired to have at least a .90 probability that the sample mean is within \$1000 of the population mean?

32. To estimate the mean age for a population of 4000 employees, a simple random sample of 40 employees is selected.
    a. Would you use the finite population correction factor in calculating the standard error of the mean? Explain.
    b. If the population standard deviation is $\sigma = 8.2$ years, compute the standard error both with and without using the finite population correction factor. What is the rationale for ignoring the finite population correction factor whenever $n/N \le .05$?
    c. What is the probability that the sample mean age of the employees will be within ± 2 years of the population mean age?

7.6   SAMPLING DISTRIBUTION OF $\bar{p}$

In many situations in business and economics, we use the sample proportion $\bar{p}$ to make statistical inferences about the population proportion p. This process is depicted in Figure 7.10. On each repetition of the process, we can anticipate obtaining a different value for the sample proportion $\bar{p}$. The probability distribution for all possible values of the sample proportion $\bar{p}$ is called the sampling distribution of the sample proportion $\bar{p}$.

Sampling Distribution of $\bar{p}$

The sampling distribution of $\bar{p}$ is the probability distribution of all possible values of the sample proportion $\bar{p}$.

To determine how close the sample proportion $\bar{p}$ is to the population proportion p, we need to understand the properties of the sampling distribution of $\bar{p}$: the expected value of $\bar{p}$, the standard deviation of $\bar{p}$, and the shape of the sampling distribution of $\bar{p}$.

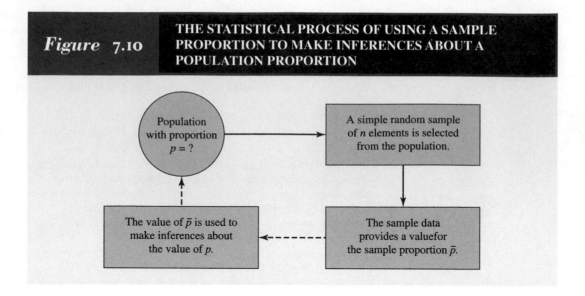

Figure 7.10 — **THE STATISTICAL PROCESS OF USING A SAMPLE PROPORTION TO MAKE INFERENCES ABOUT A POPULATION PROPORTION**

Expected Value of $\bar{p}$

The expected value of $\bar{p}$, the mean of all possible values of $\bar{p}$, can be expressed as follows.

Expected Value of $\bar{p}$

$$E(\bar{p}) = p \tag{7.4}$$

where

$$E(\bar{p}) = \text{the expected value of } \bar{p}$$
$$p = \text{the population proportion}$$

Equation (7.4) shows that the mean of all possible $\bar{p}$ values is equal to the population proportion p. Recall that in Section 7.1 we noted that $p = .60$ for the EAI population, where p is the proportion of the population of managers who had participated in the company's management training program. Thus, the expected value of $\bar{p}$ for the EAI sampling problem is .60.

Standard Deviation of $\bar{p}$

The standard deviation of $\bar{p}$ is referred to as the *standard error of the proportion.* Just as we found for the sample mean $\bar{x}$, the standard deviation of $\bar{p}$ depends on whether the population is finite or infinite. The two expressions for computing the standard deviation of $\bar{p}$ follow.

Standard Deviation of $\bar{p}$

$$\text{\textit{Finite Population}} \qquad\qquad \text{\textit{Infinite Population}}$$

$$\sigma_{\bar{p}} = \sqrt{\frac{N-n}{N-1}}\ \sqrt{\frac{p(1-p)}{n}} \qquad\qquad \sigma_{\bar{p}} = \sqrt{\frac{p(1-p)}{n}} \tag{7.5}$$

Comparing the two expressions in (7.5), we see that the only difference is the use of the finite population correction factor $\sqrt{(N - n)/(N - 1)}$.

As was the case with the sample mean $\bar{x}$, the difference between the expressions for the finite population and the infinite population becomes negligible if the size of the finite population is large in comparison to the sample size. We follow the same rule of thumb that we recommended for the sample mean. That is, if the population is finite with $n/N \le .05$, we will use $\sigma_{\bar{p}} = \sqrt{p(1 - p)/n}$. However, if the population is finite and if $n/N > .05$, the finite population correction factor should be used, as shown in (7.5). Again, unless specifically noted, throughout the text we will assume that the population size is large in relation to the sample size and thus the finite population correction factor is unnecessary.

For the EAI study we know that the population proportion of managers who have participated in the management training program is $p = .60$. With $n/N = 30/2500 = .012$, we can ignore the finite population correction factor when we compute the standard deviation of $\bar{p}$. For the simple random sample of 30 managers, $\sigma_{\bar{p}}$ is

$$\sigma_{\bar{p}} = \sqrt{\frac{p(1 - p)}{n}} = \sqrt{\frac{.60(1 - .60)}{30}} = .0894$$

Form of the Sampling Distribution of $\bar{p}$

Now that we know the mean and standard deviation of $\bar{p}$, we want to consider the form of the sampling distribution of $\bar{p}$. Applying the central limit theorem as it relates to $\bar{p}$ produces the following result.

The sampling distribution of $\bar{p}$ can be approximated by a normal probability distribution whenever the sample size is large.

With $\bar{p}$, the sample size can be considered large whenever the following two conditions are satisfied.

$$np \ge 5$$
$$n(1 - p) \ge 5$$

Recall that for the EAI sampling problem we know that the population proportion of managers who have participated in the training program is $p = .60$. With a simple random sample of size 30, we have $np = 30(.60) = 18$ and $n(1 - p) = 30(.40) = 12$. Thus, the sampling distribution of can be approximated by a normal probability distribution as shown in Figure 7.11.

Practical Value of the Sampling Distribution of $\bar{p}$

Whenever a simple random sample is selected and the value of the sample proportion $\bar{p}$ is used to estimate the value of the population proportion p, we anticipate some sampling error. In this case, the sampling error is the absolute value of the difference between the value of the sample proportion $\bar{p}$ and the value of the population proportion p. The practical value of the sampling distribution of $\bar{p}$ is that it can be used to provide probability information about the sampling error.

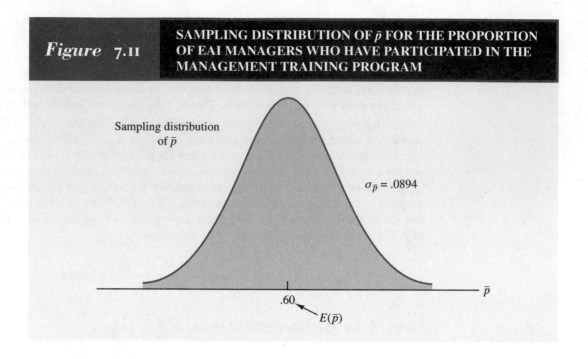

Figure 7.11 SAMPLING DISTRIBUTION OF $\bar{p}$ FOR THE PROPORTION OF EAI MANAGERS WHO HAVE PARTICIPATED IN THE MANAGEMENT TRAINING PROGRAM

Suppose, in the EAI problem, the personnel director wants to know the probability of obtaining a value of $\bar{p}$ that is within .05 of the population proportion of EAI managers who have participated in the training program. That is, what is the probability of obtaining a sample with a sample proportion $\bar{p}$ between .55 and .65? The area in Figure 7.12 shows this probability. Using the fact that the sampling distribution of $\bar{p}$ can be approximated by a normal probability distribution with a mean of .60 and a standard deviation of $\sigma_{\bar{p}} = .0894$,

Figure 7.12 SAMPLING DISTRIBUTION OF $\bar{p}$ FOR THE EAI SAMPLING PROBLEM

we find that the standard normal random variable corresponding to $\bar{p} = .55$ has a value of $z = (.55 - .60)/.0894 = -.56$. Referring to the standard normal probability distribution table, we see that the area between $z = -.56$ and $z = 0$ is .2123. Similarly, at $\bar{p} = .65$ we find an area between $z = 0$ and $z = .56$ of .2123. Thus, the probability of selecting a sample that provides a sample proportion $\bar{p}$ within .05 of the population proportion p is $.2123 + .2123 = .4246$.

If we consider increasing the sample size to $n = 100$, the standard error of the proportion becomes

$$\sigma_{\bar{p}} = \sqrt{\frac{.60(1 - .60)}{100}} = .0490$$

With a sample size of 100 EAI managers, the probability of the sample proportion having a value within .05 of the population proportion can now be computed. Because the sampling distribution is approximately normal, with mean .60 and standard deviation .0490, we can use the standard normal probability distribution table to find the area or probability. At $\bar{p} = .55$, we have $z = (.55 - .60)/.0490 = -1.02$. Referring to the standard normal probability distribution table, we see that the area between $z = -1.02$ and $z = 0$ is .3461. Similarly, at .65 the area between $z = 0$ and $z = 1.02$ is .3461. Thus, if the sample size is increased from 30 to 100, the probability that the sample proportion $\bar{p}$ is within .05 of the population proportion p will increase to $.3461 + .3461 = .6922$.

EXERCISES

Methods

33. A simple random sample of size 100 is selected from a population with $p = .40$.
    a. What is the expected value of $\bar{p}$?
    b. What is the standard deviation of $\bar{p}$?
    c. Show the sampling distribution of $\bar{p}$.
    d. What does the sampling distribution of $\bar{p}$ show?

SELF TEST

34. A population proportion is .40. A simple random sample of size 200 will be taken and the sample proportion $\bar{p}$ will be used to estimate the population proportion.
    a. What is the probability that the sample proportion will be within ±.03 of the population proportion?
    b. What is the probability that the sample proportion will be within ±.05 of the population proportion?

35. Assume that the population proportion is .55. Compute the standard error of the proportion, $\sigma_{\bar{p}}$, for sample sizes of 100, 200, 500, and 1000. What can you say about the size of the standard error of the proportion as the sample size is increased?

36. The population proportion is .30. What is the probability that a sample proportion will be within ±.04 of the population proportion for each of the following sample sizes?
    a. $n = 100$
    b. $n = 200$
    c. $n = 500$
    d. $n = 1000$
    e. What is the advantage of a larger sample size?

Applications

SELF TEST

37. The president of Doerman Distributors, Inc., believes that 30% of the firm's orders come from new or first-time customers. A simple random sample of 100 orders will be used to estimate the proportion of new or first-time customers. The results of the sample will be used to verify the president's claim of $p = .30$.

  a. Assume that the president is correct and $p = .30$. What is the sampling distribution of $\bar{p}$ for this study?

  b. What is the probability that the sample proportion $\bar{p}$ will be between .20 and .40?

  c. What is the probability that the sample proportion will be within $\pm.05$ of the population proportion $p = .30$?

38. The Grocery Manufacturers of America reported that 76% of consumers read the ingredients listed on a product's label (*America by the Numbers,* 1993). Assume the population proportion is $p = .76$ and a sample of 400 consumers is selected from the population.

  a. Show the sampling distribution of the sample proportion $\bar{p}$ where $\bar{p}$ is the proportion of the sampled consumers who read the ingredients listed on a product's label.

  b. What is the probability that the sample proportion will be within $\pm.03$ of the population proportion?

  c. Answer part (b) for a sample of 750 consumers.

39. Louis Harris & Associates conducted a survey of 403 senior executives to learn about how they view the U.S. economy for the coming 12 months (*Business Week,* June 16, 1997). Assume that for the entire population of executives, 80% are optimistic about the U.S. economy. Let $\bar{p}$ be the sample proportion of polled executives who are optimistic about the U.S. economy.

  a. Show the sampling distribution of $\bar{p}$ if the population proportion is $p = .80$.

  b. What is the probability that the Harris poll sample proportion will be within $\pm.02$ of the population proportion?

  c. What is the probability that the Harris poll sample proportion will be within $\pm.03$ of the population proportion?

40. While most people believe breakfast is the most important meal of the day, 25% of adults skip breakfast (*U.S. News & World Report,* November 10, 1997). Assume the population proportion is $p = .25$, and $\bar{p}$ is the sample proportion of adults who skip breakfast based on a sample of 200 adults.

  a. Show the sampling distribution of $\bar{p}$.

  b. What is the probability that the sample proportion will be within $\pm.03$ of the population proportion?

  c. What is the probability that the sample proportion will be within $\pm.05$ of the population proportion?

41. The Institute for Women's Policy Research reported that women now constitute 37% of all union members, an all-time high percentage (*The Wall Street Journal,* July 26, 1994). Suppose the population proportion of women who are union members is $p = .37$, and a simple random sample of 1000 union members is selected.

  a. Show the sampling distribution of $\bar{p}$, the proportion of women in the sample.

  b. What is the probability that the sample proportion will be within $\pm.03$ of the population proportion?

  c. Answer part (b) for a simple random sample of 500.

42. Assume that 15% of the items produced in an assembly line operation are defective, but that the firm's production manager is not aware of this situation. Assume further that 50 parts are tested by the quality assurance department to determine the quality of the assembly operation. Let $\bar{p}$ be the sample proportion found defective by the quality assurance test.

  a. Show the sampling distribution for $\bar{p}$.

  b. What is the probability that the sample proportion will be within $\pm.03$ of the population proportion that is defective?

  c. If the test shows $\bar{p} = .10$ or more, the assembly line operation will be shut down to check for the cause of the defects. What is the probability that the sample of 50 parts will lead to the conclusion that the assembly line should be shut down?

43. The Food Marketing Institute shows that 17% of households spend more than $100 per week on groceries (*USA Today*, June 21, 1994). Assume the population proportion is $p = .17$ and a simple random sample of 800 households will be selected from the population.

    a. Show the sampling distribution of $\bar{p}$, the sample proportion of households spending more than $100 per week on groceries.

    b. What is the probability that the sample proportion will be within ±.02 of the population proportion?

    c. Answer part (b) for a sample of 1600 households.

7.7   OTHER SAMPLING METHODS

This section provides a brief introduction to sampling methods other than simple random sampling.

We have described the simple random sampling procedure and discussed the properties of the sampling distributions of $\bar{x}$ and $\bar{p}$ when simple random sampling is used. However, simple random sampling is not the only sampling method available. Such methods as stratified random sampling, cluster sampling, and systematic sampling are alternatives that in some situations have advantages over simple random sampling. In this section we briefly introduce some of these alternative sampling methods.

Stratified Random Sampling

In *stratified random sampling,* the population is first divided into groups of elements called *strata,* such that each element in the population belongs to one and only one stratum. The basis for forming the strata, such as department, location, age, industry type, and so on, is at the discretion of the designer of the sample. However, the best results are obtained when the elements within each stratum are as much alike as possible. Figure 7.13 is a diagram of a population divided into H strata.

Stratified random sampling works best when the variance among elements in each stratum is relatively small.

After the strata are formed, a simple random sample is taken from each stratum. Formulas are available for combining the results for the individual stratum samples into one estimate of the population parameter of interest. The value of stratified random sampling depends on how homogeneous the elements are within the strata. If elements within strata are alike (homogeneity), the strata will have low variances. Thus relatively small sample sizes can be used to obtain good estimates of the strata characteristics. If strata are homogeneous, the stratified random sampling procedure will provide results just as precise as those of simple random sampling by using a smaller total sample size.

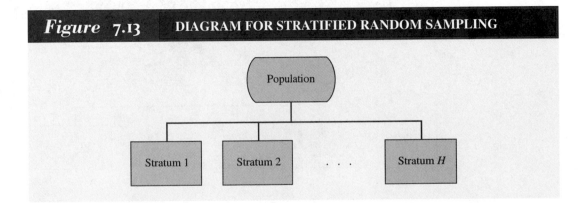

***Figure* 7.13**   **DIAGRAM FOR STRATIFIED RANDOM SAMPLING**

Cluster Sampling

Cluster sampling works best when each cluster provides a small-scale representation of the population.

In *cluster sampling,* the population is first divided into separate groups of elements called *clusters.* Each element of the population belongs to one and only one cluster (see Figure 7.14). A simple random sample of the clusters is then taken. All elements within each sampled cluster form the sample. Cluster sampling tends to provide the best results when the elements within the clusters are heterogeneous (not alike). In the ideal case, each cluster is a representative small-scale version of the entire population. The value of cluster sampling depends on how representative each cluster is of the entire population. If all clusters are alike in this regard, sampling a small number of clusters will provide good estimates of the population parameters.

One of the primary applications of cluster sampling is area sampling, where clusters are city blocks or other well-defined areas. Cluster sampling generally requires a larger total sample size than either simple random sampling or stratified random sampling. However, it can result in cost savings because of the fact that when an interviewer is sent to a sampled cluster (e.g., a city-block location), many sample observations can be obtained in a relatively short time. Hence, a larger sample size may be obtainable with a significantly lower total cost.

Systematic Sampling

In some sampling situations, especially those with large populations, it is time-consuming to select a simple random sample by first finding a random number and then counting or searching through the list of the population until the corresponding element is found. An alternative to simple random sampling is *systematic sampling.* For example, if a sample size of 50 is desired from a population containing 5000 elements, we will sample one element for every 5000/50 = 100 elements in the population. A systematic sample for this case involves selecting randomly one of the first 100 elements from the population list. Other sample elements are identified by starting with the first sampled element and then selecting every 100th element that follows in the population list. In effect, the sample of 50 is identified by moving systematically through the population and identifying every 100th element after the first randomly selected element. The sample of 50 usually will be easier to identify in this way than it would be if simple random sampling were used. Because the first element selected is a random choice, a systematic sample is usually assumed to have the properties of a simple random sample. This

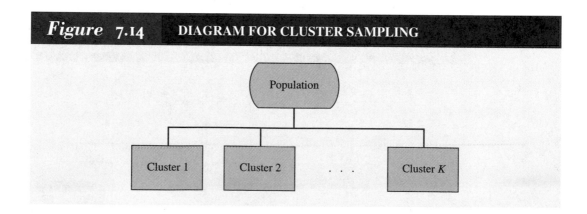

Figure 7.14   **DIAGRAM FOR CLUSTER SAMPLING**

assumption is especially applicable when the list of the population is a random ordering of the elements in the population.

Convenience Sampling

The sampling methods discussed thus far are referred to as *probability sampling* techniques. Elements selected from the population have a known probability of being included in the sample. The advantage of probability sampling is that the sampling distribution of the appropriate sample statistic generally can be identified. Formulas such as the ones for simple random sampling presented in this chapter can be used to determine the properties of the sampling distribution. Then the sampling distribution can be used to make probability statements about the sampling error associated with the results.

Convenience sampling is a *nonprobability sampling* technique. As the name implies, the sample is identified primarily by convenience. Elements are included in the sample without prespecified or known probabilities of being selected. For example, a professor conducting research at a university may use student volunteers to constitute a sample simply because they are readily available and will participate as subjects for little or no cost. Similarly, an inspector may sample a shipment of oranges by selecting oranges haphazardly from among several crates. Labeling each orange and using a probability method of sampling would be impractical. Samples such as wildlife captures and volunteer panels for consumer research are also convenience samples.

Convenience samples have the advantage of relatively easy sample selection and data collection; however, it is impossible to evaluate the "goodness" of the sample in terms of its representativeness of the population. A convenience sample may provide good results or it may not; no statistically justified procedure allows a probability analysis and inference about the quality of the sample results. Sometimes researchers apply statistical methods designed for probability samples to a convenience sample, arguing that the convenience sample can be treated as though it were a probability sample. However, this argument cannot be supported, and we should be cautious in interpreting the results of convenience samples that are used to make inferences about populations.

Judgment Sampling

One additional nonprobability sampling technique is *judgment sampling*. In this approach, the person most knowledgeable on the subject of the study selects elements of the population that he or she feels are most representative of the population. Often this method is a relatively easy way of selecting a sample. For example, a reporter may sample two or three senators, judging that those senators reflect the general opinion of all senators. However, the quality of the sample results depends on the judgment of the person selecting the sample. Again, great caution is warranted in drawing conclusions based on judgment samples used to make inferences about populations.

N O T E S *and Comments*	We recommend using probability sampling methods: simple random sampling, stratified random sampling, cluster sampling, or systematic sampling. For these methods, formulas are available for evaluating the "goodness" of the sample results in terms of the closeness of the results to the population characteristics being estimated. An evaluation of the goodness cannot be made with convenience or judgment sampling. Thus, great care should be used in interpreting the results when nonprobability sampling methods are used.

···/ /············

SUMMARY

In this chapter we presented the concepts of simple random sampling and sampling distributions. We demonstrated how a simple random sample can be selected and how the data collected for the sample can be used to develop point estimates of population parameters. Because different simple random samples provided a variety of different values for the point estimators, point estimators such as $\bar{x}$ and $\bar{p}$ are random variables. The probability distribution of such a random variable is called a sampling distribution. In particular, we described the sampling distributions of the sample mean $\bar{x}$ and the sample proportion $\bar{p}$.

In considering the characteristics of the sampling distributions of $\bar{x}$ and $\bar{p}$, we stated that $E(\bar{x}) = \mu$ and $E(\bar{p}) = p$. After developing the standard deviation or standard error formulas for these estimators, we showed how the central limit theorem provided the basis for using a normal probability distribution to approximate these sampling distributions in the large-sample case. Rules of thumb were given for determining when large-sample conditions were satisfied. Other sampling methods including stratified random sampling, cluster sampling, systematic sampling, convenience sampling, and judgment sampling were discussed.

···/ /············

GLOSSARY

Parameter A numerical characteristic of a population, such as a population mean μ, a population standard deviation σ, a population proportion p, and so on.

Simple random sampling Finite population: a sample selected such that each possible sample of size n has the same probability of being selected. Infinite population: a sample selected such that each element comes from the same population and the elements are selected independently.

Sampling without replacement Once an element has been included in the sample, it is removed from the population and cannot be selected a second time.

Sampling with replacement Once an element has been included in the sample, it is returned to the population. A previously selected element can be selected again and therefore may appear in the sample more than once.

Sample statistic A sample characteristic, such as a sample mean $\bar{x}$, a sample standard deviation s, a sample proportion $\bar{p}$, and so on. The value of the sample statistic is used to estimate the value of the population parameter.

Sampling distribution A probability distribution consisting of all possible values of a sample statistic.

Point estimate A single numerical value used as an estimate of a population parameter.

Point estimator The sample statistic, such as $\bar{x}$, s, or $\bar{p}$, that provides the point estimate of the population parameter.

Sampling error The absolute value of the difference between an unbiased point estimator and the corresponding population parameter. For a sample mean, sample standard deviation, and sample proportion, the sampling errors are $|x^- - \mu|$, $|s - \sigma|$, and $|p^- - p|$, respectively.

Finite population correction factor The term $\sqrt{(N - n)/(N - 1)}$ that is used in the formulas for $\sigma_{\bar{x}}$ and $\sigma_{\bar{p}}$ whenever a finite population, rather than an infinite population, is being sampled. The generally accepted rule of thumb is to ignore the finite population correction factor whenever $n/N \leq .05$.

Standard error The standard deviation of a point estimator.

Central limit theorem A theorem that enables one to use the normal probability distribution to approximate the sampling distribution of $\bar{x}$ and $\bar{p}$ whenever the sample size is large.

Stratified random sampling A probability sampling method in which the population is first divided into strata and a simple random sample is then taken from each stratum.

Cluster sampling A probability sampling method in which the population is first divided into clusters and then a simple random sample of the clusters is taken.

Systematic sampling A probability sampling method in which we randomly select one of the first k elements and then select every kth element thereafter.

Convenience sampling A nonprobability method of sampling whereby elements are selected for the sample on the basis of convenience.

Judgment sampling A nonprobability method of sampling whereby elements are selected for the sample based on the judgment of the person doing the study.

KEY FORMULAS

Expected Value of $\bar{x}$

$$E(\bar{x}) = \mu \tag{7.1}$$

Standard Deviation of $\bar{x}$

Finite Population   *Infinite Population*

$$\sigma_{\bar{x}} = \sqrt{\frac{N-n}{N-1}}\left(\frac{\sigma}{\sqrt{n}}\right) \qquad \sigma_{\bar{x}} = \frac{\sigma}{\sqrt{n}} \tag{7.2}$$

Expected Value of $\bar{p}$

$$E(\bar{p}) = p \tag{7.4}$$

Standard Deviation of $\bar{p}$

Finite Population   *Infinite Population*

$$\sigma_{\bar{p}} = \sqrt{\frac{N-n}{N-1}}\sqrt{\frac{p(1-p)}{n}} \qquad \sigma_{\bar{p}} = \sqrt{\frac{p(1-p)}{n}} \tag{7.5}$$

SUPPLEMENTARY EXERCISES

44. Nationwide Supermarkets has 4800 retail stores in 32 states. At the end of each year, a sample of 35 stores is selected for physical inventories. Results from the inventory samples are used in annual tax reports. Assume that the retail stores are listed sequentially on a computer printout. Begin at the bottom of the second column of random digits in Table 7.1. Ignoring the first digit in each group and using four-digit random numbers beginning with 8112, read *up* the column to identify the first five stores to be included in the simple random sample.

45. A 1993 study conducted by *The Orlando Sentinel* provided data on how much time customers wait for service at Burger King, McDonald's, and Wendy's restaurants. Assume that the population mean waiting time for a drive-through order is four minutes and that the population standard deviation is 1.5 minutes.
    a. Suppose a sample of 60 drive-through customers will be selected and the sample mean waiting time computed. Show the sampling distribution of the sample mean.
    b. What is the probability that the sample mean waiting time will be within ±.25 minutes of the population mean waiting time?

46. The mean travel time to work for individuals in Chicago is 31.5 minutes (*1998 Information Please Almanac*). Assume the population mean is $\mu = 31.5$ minutes and the population standard deviation is $\sigma = 12$ minutes. A sample of 50 Chicago residents is selected.
    a. Show the sampling distribution of $\bar{x}$ where $\bar{x}$ is the sample mean travel time to work for the 50 Chicago residents.
    b. What is the probability that the sample mean will be within ±1 minute of the population mean?
    c. What is the probability that the sample mean will be within ±3 minutes of the population mean?

47. The U.S. Bureau of Labor Statistics reported the mean hourly wage rate for individuals in executive, administrative, and managerial occupations is $24.07 (*The Wall Street Journal Almanac 1998*). Assume the population mean is $\mu = \$24.07$ and the population standard deviation is $\sigma = \$4.80$. A sample of 120 individuals in executive, administrative, and managerial occupations will be selected.
    a. What is the probability that the sample mean will be within ±$0.50 of the population mean?
    b. What is the probability that the sample mean will be within ±$1.00 of the population mean?

48. According to *USA Today* (April 11, 1995), the mean number of days per year that business travelers are on the road for business is 115. The standard deviation is 60 days per year. Assume that these results apply to the population of business travelers and that a sample of 50 business travelers will be selected from the population.
    a. What is the value of the standard error of the mean?
    b. What is the probability that the sample mean will be more than 115 days per year?
    c. What is the probability that the sample mean will be within ±5 days of the population mean?
    d. How would the probability change in part (c) if the sample size were increased to 100?

49. Three firms have inventories that differ in size. Firm A has a population of 2000 items, firm B has a population of 5000 items, and firm C has a population of 10,000 items. The population standard deviation for the cost of the items is $\sigma = 144$. A statistical consultant recommends that each firm take a sample of 50 items from its population to provide statistically valid estimates of the average cost per item. Managers of the small firm state that because it has the smallest population, it should be able to obtain the data from a much smaller sample than that required by the larger firms. However, the consultant states that to obtain the same standard error and thus the same precision in the sample results, all firms should use the same sample size regardless of population size.
    a. Using the finite population correction factor, compute the standard error for each of the three firms given a sample of size 50.
    b. What is the probability that for each firm the sample mean $\bar{x}$ will be within ±25 of the population mean μ?

50. A researcher reports survey results by stating that the standard error of the mean is 20. The population standard deviation is 500.
    a. How large was the sample used in this survey?
    b. What is the probability that the estimate would be within ±25 of the population mean?

51. A production process is checked periodically by a quality control inspector. The inspector selects simple random samples of 30 finished products and computes the sample mean product weights $\bar{x}$. If test results over a long period of time show that 5% of the $\bar{x}$ values are over 2.1 pounds and 5% are under 1.9 pounds, what are the mean and the standard deviation for the population of products produced with this process?

52. What is the most important factor for business travelers when they are staying in a hotel? According to *USA Today,* 74% of business travelers state that having a smoke-free room is the most important factor (*USA Today,* April 11, 1995). Assume that the population proportion is $p = .74$ and that a sample of 200 business travelers will be selected.

   a. Show the sampling distribution of $\bar{p}$, the sample proportion of business travelers stating that a smoke-free room is the most important factor when staying in a hotel.

   b. What is the probability that the sample proportion will be within $\pm.04$ of the population proportion?

   c. What is the probability that the sample proportion will be within $\pm.02$ of the population proportion?

53. A market research firm conducts telephone surveys with a 40% historical response rate. What is the probability that in a new sample of 400 telephone numbers, at least 150 individuals will cooperate and respond to the questions? In other words, what is the probability that the sample proportion will be at least $150/400 = .375$?

54. A production run is not acceptable for shipment to customers if a sample of 100 items contains 5% or more defective items. If a production run has a population proportion defective of $p = .10$, what is the probability that $\bar{p}$ will be at least .05?

55. The proportion of individuals insured by the All-Driver Automobile Insurance Company who have received at least one traffic ticket during a five-year period is .15.

   a. Show the sampling distribution of $\bar{p}$ if a random sample of 150 insured individuals is used to estimate the proportion having received at least one ticket.

   b. What is the probability that the sample proportion will be within $\pm.03$ of the population proportion?

56. Lori Jeffrey is a successful sales representative for a major publisher of college textbooks. Historically, Lori obtains a book adoption on 25% of her sales calls. Viewing her sales calls for one month as a sample of all possible sales calls, assume that a statistical analysis of the data yields a standard error of the proportion of .0625.

   a. How large was the sample used in this analysis? That is, how many sales calls did Lori make during the month?

   b. Let $\bar{p}$ indicate the sample proportion of book adoptions obtained during the month. Show the sampling distribution $\bar{p}$.

   c. Using the sampling distribution of $\bar{p}$, compute the probability that Lori will obtain book adoptions on 30% or more of her sales calls during a one-month period.

8

INTERVAL ESTIMATION

CONTENTS

DOLLAR GENERAL CORPORATION*
Goodlettsville, Tennessee

Dollar General Corporation was founded in 1939 as a dry goods wholesale company. After World War II, the company began opening retail locations in rural south-central Kentucky. Today Dollar General Corporation operates more than 3200 stores in 24 states. Serving predominantly low- and middle-income customers, Dollar General markets health and beauty aids, cleaning supplies, housewares, stationery, apparel, shoes, and domestic items at low everyday prices.

Being in an inventory-intense business with approximately 17,000 products, Dollar General made the decision to adopt the LIFO (last-in-first-out) method of inventory valuation. This method matches current costs against current revenues, which minimizes the effect of radical price changes on profit and loss results. In addition, the LIFO method reduces net income and thereby income taxes during periods of inflation. LIFO also brings disposable cash generated from sales in line with income and allows for the replacement of inventory at current costs.

Accounting practices require that a LIFO index be established for inventory under the LIFO method of valuation. For example, a LIFO index of 1.028 indicates that the company's inventory value at current costs reflects a 2.8% increase due to inflation over the most recent one-year period.

The establishment of a LIFO index requires that the year-end inventory count for each product be valued at the current year-end cost and at the preceding year-end cost. To avoid counting the inventory of every product in more than 3200 retail locations, a random sample of 800 products is selected from 100 retail locations and three ware-

This store in Bedford, Indiana, is one of more than 3200 Dollar General Stores.

houses. Physical inventories for the sampled products are taken at the end of the year. Accounting personnel then provide the current-year and preceding-year costs needed to construct the LIFO index.

For a recent year, the LIFO index was 1.030. However, because this index is a sample estimate of the population's LIFO index, a statement about the precision of the estimate was required. On the basis of the sample results and a 95% confidence level, the margin of error was computed to be .006. Thus, the interval from 1.024 to 1.036 provides the 95% confidence interval estimate of the population LIFO index. This precision was judged to be very good.

In this chapter you will learn how to compute the margin of error associated with a sample mean and a sample proportion. Then, you will learn how to use this information to construct and interpret confidence interval estimates of a population mean and a population proportion. You will also learn how to determine the sample size needed to ensure that the margin of error will be within acceptable limits.

*The authors are indebted to Robert S. Knaul, Controller, Dollar General Corporation, for providing this Statistics in Practice.

In Chapter 7 we showed that the values of the sample mean $\bar{x}$ and the sample proportion $\bar{p}$ provide point estimates of the population mean μ and the population proportion p, respectively. Because a point estimate is based on a sample, it cannot be expected to equal the value of the corresponding population parameter. In this chapter we will show how interval estimates of the population mean and the population proportion can be developed to provide information about the precision of an estimate. As we will show, the sampling distributions of $\bar{x}$ and $\bar{p}$ presented in Chapter 7 play an important role in the development of interval estimates of μ and p.

8.1   INTERVAL ESTIMATION OF A POPULATION MEAN: LARGE-SAMPLE CASE

In this section we show how the sampling distribution of $\bar{x}$ can be used to develop an interval estimate of a population mean μ. We begin with the large-sample case ($n \geq 30$) in which the population standard deviation σ is known. Once we show how to develop an interval estimate of μ for this case, we will show how to do so for the large-sample case in which σ is unknown.

Let us begin by considering a sampling study conducted by CJW, Inc., a mail-order firm that specializes in sporting equipment and accessories. The company works hard to provide the best possible customer service. To monitor the quality of its service, CJW selects a simple random sample of mail-order customers each month; each customer sampled is contacted and asked a series of questions pertaining to the level of customer service. The answers to the questions are used to compute a satisfaction score for each customer sampled; these scores range from 0 (worst possible rating) to 100 (best possible rating). A sample mean satisfaction score is then computed and used as a point estimate of the mean satisfaction score for the population of all CJW customers.

Previous monthly surveys have shown that although the sample mean satisfaction score changes from month to month, the standard deviation of satisfaction scores has tended to stabilize at a value of 20. Hence, we will assume that the population standard deviation is $\sigma = 20$. The most recent CJW customer satisfaction survey provided data on the satisfaction scores of 100 customers ($n = 100$); the sample mean satisfaction score was $\bar{x} = 82$. In the discussion that follows, we will use the sample results to develop an interval estimate of the population mean satisfaction score μ.

Sampling Error

Any time a sample mean is used to provide a point estimate of a population mean, someone may ask: How good is the estimate? The "how good" question is a way of asking about the error involved when the value of $\bar{x}$ is used as the point estimate of μ. In general, the absolute value of the difference between an unbiased point estimator and the population parameter it estimates is called the *sampling error*. For the case of a sample mean estimating a population mean, the sampling error is

Knowledge of the sampling distribution of $\bar{x}$ enables us to make probability statements about the sampling error $|\bar{x} - \mu|$ even though the population mean μ is never known.

$$\text{Sampling Error} = |\bar{x} - \mu| \tag{8.1}$$

In practice, the value of the sampling error cannot be determined because the population mean μ is unknown. However, the sampling distribution of $\bar{x}$ can be used to make probability statements about the size of the sampling error. We will illustrate how it is done for the CJW sampling study.

With a sample size $n = 100$ and a population standard deviation $\sigma = 20$, the central limit theorem, introduced in Chapter 7, enables us to conclude that the sampling distribution of $\bar{x}$ can be approximated by a normal probability distribution with a mean μ and a standard deviation $\sigma_{\bar{x}} = \sigma/\sqrt{n} = 20/\sqrt{100} = 2$. This sampling distribution is shown in Figure 8.1. Since the sampling distribution of $\bar{x}$ shows how values of $\bar{x}$ are distributed around μ, it provides information about the possible differences between $\bar{x}$ and μ. We can use this information to develop probability statements about the sampling error.

Probability Statements about the Sampling Error

Using the table of areas for the standard normal probability distribution, we find that 95% of the values of any normally distributed random variable are within ± 1.96 standard deviations of the mean. Hence, for the sampling distribution in Figure 8.1, 95% of all $\bar{x}$ values must be within ± 1.96 standard deviations of μ. Since $1.96\sigma_{\bar{x}} = 1.96(2) = 3.92$, 95% of the sample means must be within ± 3.92 of the population mean.

> Using terminology introduced in Chapter 7, $\sigma_{\bar{x}} = \sigma/\sqrt{n}$ is called the standard error of the mean. Thus, we can say that 95% of the sample means must be within ± 1.96 standard errors of the population mean.

The location of the sample means that provide a sampling error of 3.92 or less is shown in Figure 8.2. Note that if a sample mean is in the region denoted "95% of all $\bar{x}$ values," it provides a sampling error of 3.92 or less. However, if a sample mean is in either the lower tail or the upper tail of the distribution, the sampling error will be greater than 3.92. We therefore can make the following probability statement about the sampling error for the CJW problem.

> There is a .95 probability that the sample mean will provide a sampling error of 3.92 or less.

This probability statement about the sampling error is a *precision statement* telling CJW about the error that can be expected if a simple random sample of 100 customers is used to estimate the population mean. Although a .95 probability is frequently used in making precision statements, other probability values such as .90 and .99 can be used. For instance, Figure 8.3 shows the location of 99% of the sample means for the CJW problem. Using the standard normal probability distribution table, we find that 99% of the $\bar{x}$ values are within ± 2.576 standard deviations of μ. Because $2.576\sigma_{\bar{x}} = 2.576(2) = 5.15$, there is a .99

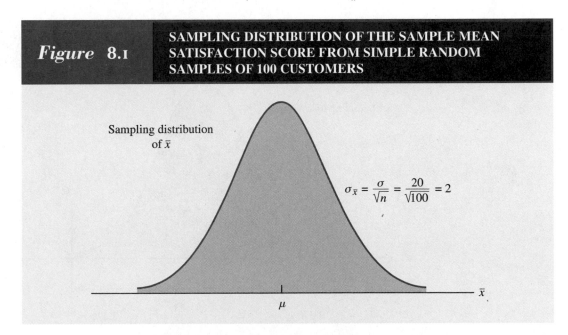

Figure **8.**1   **SAMPLING DISTRIBUTION OF THE SAMPLE MEAN SATISFACTION SCORE FROM SIMPLE RANDOM SAMPLES OF 100 CUSTOMERS**

Sampling distribution of $\bar{x}$

$$\sigma_{\bar{x}} = \frac{\sigma}{\sqrt{n}} = \frac{20}{\sqrt{100}} = 2$$

μ

$\bar{x}$

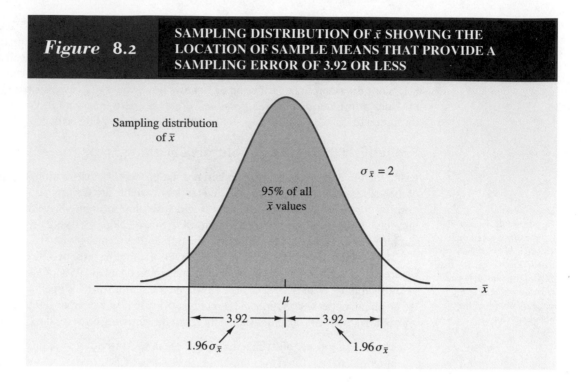

Figure 8.2 SAMPLING DISTRIBUTION OF $\bar{x}$ SHOWING THE LOCATION OF SAMPLE MEANS THAT PROVIDE A SAMPLING ERROR OF 3.92 OR LESS

probability that the sample mean will provide a sampling error of 5.15 or less. Similarly, because 90% of the $\bar{x}$ values are within 1.645 standard deviation of μ, there is a .90 probability that the sample mean will provide a sampling error of $1.645\sigma_{\bar{x}} = 1.645(2) = 3.29$ or less.

Let us generalize the procedure we use to make precision statements about the sampling error whenever the value of a sample mean is used to estimate a population mean. We will use the Greek letter α to indicate the probability that the sampling error is *larger* than the

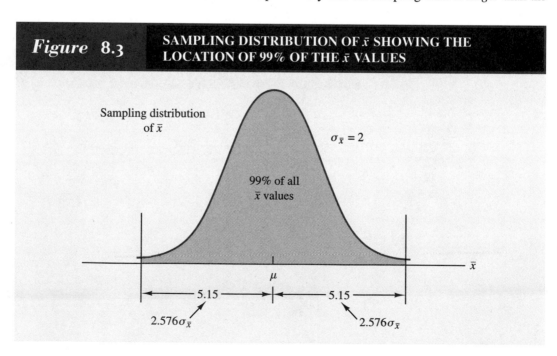

Figure 8.3 SAMPLING DISTRIBUTION OF $\bar{x}$ SHOWING THE LOCATION OF 99% OF THE $\bar{x}$ VALUES

sampling error in the precision statement. In Figure 8.4, $\alpha/2$ denotes the area, or probability, in each tail of the sampling distribution and $1 - \alpha$ denotes the area, or probability, that a sample mean will provide a sampling error less than or equal to the sampling error in the precision statement. For example, the statement that there is a .95 probability that the value of a sample mean will provide a sampling error of 3.92 or less is based on $\alpha = .05$ and $1 - \alpha = .95$. The area in each tail of the sampling distribution is $\alpha/2 = .025$.

Using z to denote the standard normal random variable, we place a subscript on z to denote the area in the upper tail of the distribution. In general, $z_{\alpha/2}$ is the value of the standard normal random variable corresponding to an area of $\alpha/2$ in the upper tail of the distribution. With this notation, the following precision statement defines the size of the sampling error whenever $\bar{x}$ is used to estimate μ.

Precision Statement

There is a $1 - \alpha$ probability that the value of a sample mean will provide a sampling error of $z_{\alpha/2}\sigma_{\bar{x}}$ or less.

Calculating an Interval Estimate: Large-Sample Case with σ Known

In the CJW example, we stated that there is a .95 probability that the value of the sample mean will provide a sampling error of 3.92 or less. We can construct an interval estimate of μ by subtracting 3.92 from $\bar{x}$ and adding 3.92 to $\bar{x}$; that is, $\bar{x} \pm 3.92$. To interpret the interval estimate of μ, let us consider possible values of $\bar{x}$ that could be obtained from three different simple random samples, each consisting of 100 customers.

Suppose the first sample mean turns out to have the value shown in Figure 8.5 as $\bar{x}_1$. In this case, Figure 8.5 shows that the interval formed by subtracting 3.92 from $\bar{x}_1$ and adding 3.92 to $\bar{x}_1$ includes the population mean μ. Now consider what happens if the sample mean turns out to have the value shown in Figure 8.5 as $\bar{x}_2$. Although this sample mean is different from the first sample mean, we see that the interval based on $\bar{x}_2$ also includes the

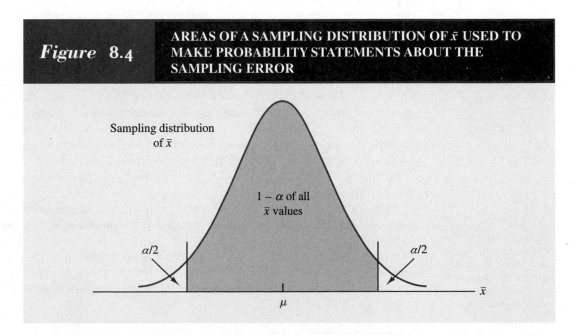

Figure 8.4 — AREAS OF A SAMPLING DISTRIBUTION OF $\bar{x}$ USED TO MAKE PROBABILITY STATEMENTS ABOUT THE SAMPLING ERROR

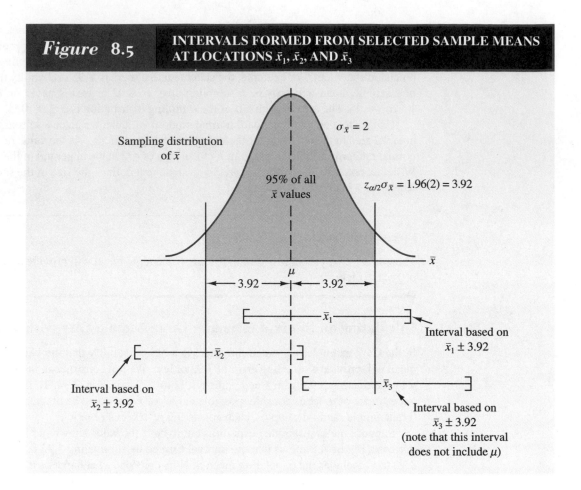

Figure 8.5   INTERVALS FORMED FROM SELECTED SAMPLE MEANS AT LOCATIONS $\bar{x}_1$, $\bar{x}_2$, AND $\bar{x}_3$

population mean μ. However, the interval based on the third sample mean, denoted by $\bar{x}_3$, does not include the population mean; the reason is that $\bar{x}_3$ is in a tail of the distribution at a distance farther than 3.92 from μ. Hence, subtracting and adding 3.92 to $\bar{x}_3$ forms an interval that does not include μ.

Any sample mean $\bar{x}$ that is within the shaded region of Figure 8.5 will provide an interval that contains the population mean μ. Because 95% of the sample means are within this region, 95% of all intervals formed by subtracting 3.92 from $\bar{x}$ and adding 3.92 to $\bar{x}$ will include μ. Thus we are 95% confident that an interval constructed from $\bar{x} - 3.92$ to $\bar{x} + 3.92$ will include the population mean. Using common statistical terminology, we refer to the interval as a *confidence interval*. Because 95% of the sample means will result in a confidence interval that includes the population mean μ, we say that the confidence interval is established at the 95% *confidence level*. The value .95 is referred to as the *confidence coefficient*.

A confidence interval estimate consists of two parts: a point estimate and a $\pm$ value that describes the precision of the estimate. We call the $\pm$ value the *margin of error*. Thus, the CJW sample mean satisfaction score of $\bar{x} = 82$ has a margin of error of 3.92. Using the interval $\bar{x} \pm 3.92$, we find that the 95% confidence interval estimate of the population mean satisfaction score is 82 ± 3.92, or 78.08 to 85.92. Hence, at the 95% confidence level, CJW can conclude that the mean satisfaction score for the population of all mail-order customers is between 78.08 and 85.92.

The margin of error is the $\pm$ value that determines the precision of a point estimate. When estimating a population mean, the margin of error is $z_{\alpha/2}\sigma_{\bar{x}}$.

Let us now state the general procedure for computing an interval estimate of a population mean for the large-sample case with σ known. As previously noted, there is a $1 - \alpha$ probability that the value of the sample mean will provide a margin of error of $z_{\alpha/2}\sigma_{\bar{x}}$. Using the fact that $\sigma_{\bar{x}} = \sigma/\sqrt{n}$, we can write the procedure for calculating the *interval estimate* of a population mean as follows.

Interval Estimate of a Population Mean: Large-Sample Case ($n \geq 30$) with σ Known

$$\bar{x} \pm z_{\alpha/2} \frac{\sigma}{\sqrt{n}} \qquad (8.2)$$

where $1 - \alpha$ is the confidence coefficient and $z_{\alpha/2}$ is the z value providing an area of $\alpha/2$ in the upper tail of the standard normal probability distribution.

The values of $z_{\alpha/2}$ for the most commonly used confidence levels are given in Table 8.1.

Calculating an Interval Estimate: Large-Sample Case with σ Unknown

A difficulty in using (8.2) is that in most applications the value of the population standard deviation σ is unknown. In the large-sample case ($n \geq 30$), we simply use the value of the sample standard deviation, s, as the point estimate of the population standard deviation σ to obtain the following interval estimate.

Interval Estimate of a Population Mean: Large-Sample Case ($n \geq 30$) with σ Unknown

$$\bar{x} \pm z_{\alpha/2} \frac{s}{\sqrt{n}} \qquad (8.3)$$

where s is the sample standard deviation, $1 - \alpha$ is the confidence coefficient, and $z_{\alpha/2}$ is the z value providing an area of $\alpha/2$ in the upper tail of the standard normal probability distribution.

As an illustration of this interval estimation procedure, let us consider a sampling study conducted by the Statewide Insurance Company. Suppose that as part of an annual review of life insurance policies, Statewide selects a simple random sample of 36 Statewide life insurance policyholders. The corresponding life insurance policies are reviewed in terms of the amount of coverage, the cash value of the policy, disability options, and so on. For the

Table **8.1**	VALUES OF $z_{\alpha/2}$ FOR THE MOST COMMONLY USED CONFIDENCE LEVELS			
	Confidence Level	α	$\alpha/2$	$z_{\alpha/2}$
	90%	.10	.05	1.645
	95%	.05	.025	1.96
	99%	.01	.005	2.576

Table 8.2		AGES OF LIFE INSURANCE POLICYHOLDERS FROM A SIMPLE RANDOM SAMPLE OF 36 STATEWIDE POLICYHOLDERS			
Policyholder	Age	Policyholder	Age	Policyholder	Age
1	32	13	39	25	23
2	50	14	46	26	36
3	40	15	45	27	42
4	24	16	39	28	34
5	33	17	38	29	39
6	44	18	45	30	34
7	45	19	27	31	35
8	48	20	43	32	42
9	44	21	54	33	53
10	47	22	36	34	28
11	31	23	34	35	49
12	36	24	48	36	39

Lifelns

current study, a manager has asked for a 90% confidence interval estimate of the mean age for the population of life insurance policyholders.

Table 8.2 reports the age data collected from a simple random sample of 36 policyholders. The sample mean age of $\bar{x} = 39.5$ years is the point estimate of the population mean age. In addition, the sample standard deviation for the data in Table 8.2 is $s = 7.77$. At 90% confidence, $z_{.05} = 1.645$. Using (8.3), we obtain

$$39.5 \pm 1.645 \frac{7.77}{\sqrt{36}}$$

$$39.5 \pm 2.13$$

Hence, the margin of error is 2.13 and the 90% confidence interval estimate of the population mean is 37.37 to 41.63. The manager therefore can be 90% confident that the mean age for the population of Statewide life insurance policyholders is between 37.37 years and 41.63 years.

Minitab can be used to provide a confidence interval estimate of a population mean. The computer output for the Statewide Insurance problem is shown in Figure 8.6. The sample standard deviation, $s = 7.77$, is the assumed value for the population standard deviation σ. The sample of 36 policyholders provides a sample mean of 39.50 years, a standard error of the mean of 1.30 years and a 90% confidence interval from 37.37 to 41.63 years.

In Chapter 7, we pointed out that $\sigma_{\bar{x}} = \sigma/\sqrt{n}$ is the standard error of the mean. Minitab provides an estimate of the standard error of the mean by using s to estimate σ.

Figure 8.6	THE MINITAB CONFIDENCE INTERVAL FOR THE STATEWIDE INSURANCE COMPANY PROBLEM

The assumed sigma = 7.77

Variable	N	Mean	StDev	SE Mean	90.0 % CI
Age	36	39.50	7.77	1.30	(37.37, 41.63)

N O T E S and Comments	1. In developing an interval estimate of the population mean, we specify the desired confidence coefficient $(1 - \alpha)$ before selecting the sample. Thus, prior to selecting the sample, we conclude that there is a $1 - \alpha$ probability that the confidence interval we eventually compute will contain the population mean μ. However, once the sample is taken, the sample mean $\bar{x}$ is computed, and the particular interval estimate is determined, the resulting interval may or may not contain μ. If $1 - \alpha$ is reasonably large, we can be confident that the resulting interval will contain μ because we know that if we use this procedure repeatedly, $100(1 - \alpha)$ percent of all possible intervals developed in this way will contain μ.

2. Note that the sample size n appears in the denominator of the interval estimation expressions (8.2) and (8.3). Thus, if a particular sample size provides too wide an interval to be of any practical use, we may want to consider increasing the sample size. With n in the denominator, a larger sample size will provide a smaller margin of error, a narrower interval, and a greater precision. The procedure for determining the size of a simple random sample necessary to obtain a desired precision is discussed in Section 8.3.

EXERCISES

Methods

1. A simple random sample of 40 items resulted in a sample mean of 25. The population standard deviation is $\sigma = 5$.
   a. What is the standard error of the mean, $\sigma_{\bar{x}}$?
   b. At a 95% probability, what is the margin of error?

SELF TEST

2. A simple random sample of 50 items resulted in a sample mean of 32 and a sample standard deviation of 6.
   a. Provide a 90% confidence interval for the population mean.
   b. Provide a 95% confidence interval for the population mean.
   c. Provide a 99% confidence interval for the population mean.

3. A sample of 60 items resulted in a sample mean of 80 and a sample standard deviation of 15.
   a. Compute the 95% confidence interval for the population mean.
   b. Assume that the same sample mean and sample standard deviation were obtained from a sample of 120 items. Provide a 95% confidence interval for the population mean.
   c. What is the effect of a larger sample size on the interval estimate of a population mean?

4. A 95% confidence interval for a population mean is reported to be 122 to 130. If the sample mean is 126 and the sample standard deviation is 16.07, what sample size was used in this study?

Applications

SELF TEST

5. In an effort to estimate the mean amount spent per customer for dinner at a major Atlanta restaurant, data were collected for a sample of 49 customers over a three-week period.
   a. Assume a population standard deviation of $2.50. What is the standard error of the mean?
   b. At the 95% confidence, what is the margin of error?
   c. If the sample mean is $22.60, what is the 95% confidence interval for the population mean?

6. Mean weekly earnings of individuals working in various industries were reported in *The New York Times 1998 Almanac*. The mean weekly earnings for individuals in the service industry were $369. Assume that this result was based on a sample of 250 service individuals and that the sample standard deviation was $50. Compute the 95% confidence interval for the population mean weekly earnings for individuals working in the service industry.

7. A sample of 532 *Business Week* subscribers showed that the mean time a subscriber spends using the Internet and online services is 6.7 hours per week (*Business Week* 1996 World Wide Subscriber Study). If the sample standard deviation is 5.8 hours, what is the 95% confidence interval for the mean time that the *Business Week* subscriber population spends on the Internet and online services?

8. In a study of student loan subsidies, the Department of Education reported that four-year Stafford Loan borrowers will owe an average of $12,168 upon graduation (*USA Today*, April 5, 1995). Assume that this average or mean amount owed is based on a sample of 480 student loans and that the population standard deviation for the amount owed upon graduation is $2200.
    a. Develop a 90% confidence interval estimate of the population mean amount owed.
    b. Develop a 95% confidence interval estimate of the population mean amount owed.
    c. Develop a 99% confidence interval estimate of the population mean amount owed.
    d. Discuss what happens to the width of the confidence interval as the confidence level is increased. Does this seem reasonable? Explain.

Workers

9. A summary of the mean hourly pay for production workers was reported in *The Wall Street Journal*, November 25, 1997. A sample of 60 hourly pay rates for production workers is contained in the data set Workers.
    a. Use Workers to develop a point estimate of the hourly pay rate for the population of production workers.
    b. What is the sample standard deviation?
    c. What is the 95% confidence interval for the mean hourly pay rate for the population of production workers?

10. The profitability of used car sales was determined in a study conducted by the National Automobile Dealers Association (*USA Today*, April 12, 1995). Assume that a sample of 200 used car sales provided a sample mean profit of $300 and a sample standard deviation of $150. Use this information to develop a 95% confidence interval estimate of the mean profit for the population of used car sales.

11. J. D. Power & Associates' annual quality survey for automobiles found that the industry average number of defects per new car is 1.07 (*The Wall Street Journal*, January 27, 1994). Suppose a sample of 30 new automobiles taken by a particular manufacturer provides the following data on number of defects per car.

    | 0 | 1 | 1 | 2 | 1 | 0 | 2 | 3 | 2 | 1 | 0 | 4 | 3 | 1 | 1 |
    | 0 | 2 | 0 | 0 | 2 | 3 | 0 | 2 | 0 | 2 | 0 | 3 | 1 | 0 | 2 |

    a. Using these data, what is the sample mean number of defects per car?
    b. What is the sample standard deviation?
    c. Provide a 95% confidence interval estimate of the mean number of defects per car for the population of cars produced by this manufacturer.
    d. After viewing the confidence interval estimate in part (c), a statistical analyst suggested that the manufacturer test a larger number of new cars before drawing a conclusion about how the quality of its cars compares to the J. D. Powers & Associates industry average of 1.07 defects per car. Do you support this idea? Why or why not?

12. The International Air Transport Association surveys business travelers to develop quality ratings for transatlantic gateway airports. The maximum possible rating is 10. The highest rated airport is Amsterdam with an average rating of 7.93, followed by Toronto with a rating of 7.17 (*Newsweek*, June 13, 1994). Suppose a simple random sample of 50 business travelers is

selected and each traveler is asked to provide a rating for the Miami International Airport. The ratings obtained from the sample of 50 follow.

Miami

6	4	6	8	7	7	6	3	3	8	10	4	8
7	8	7	5	9	5	8	4	3	8	5	5	4
4	4	8	4	5	6	2	5	9	9	8	4	8
9	9	5	9	7	8	3	10	8	9	6		

Develop a 95% confidence interval estimate of the population mean rating for Miami.

8.2   INTERVAL ESTIMATION OF A POPULATION MEAN: SMALL-SAMPLE CASE

In the small-sample case ($n < 30$), the sampling distribution of $\bar{x}$ depends on the probability distribution of the population. If the population has a normal probability distribution, the methodology presented in this section can be used to develop a confidence interval for a population mean. However, if the assumption of a normal probability distribution for the population is not appropriate, the only alternative is to increase the sample size to $n \geq 30$ and rely on the large-sample interval-estimation procedures given by (8.2) and (8.3).

If the population has a normal probability distribution, the sampling distribution of $\bar{x}$ will be normal regardless of the sample size. In this case, if the population standard deviation σ is known, (8.2) can be used to compute an interval estimate of a population mean even with a small sample. However, if the population standard deviation σ is unknown and the sample standard deviation s is used to estimate σ, the appropriate confidence interval is based on a probability distribution known as the *t distribution*.

William Sealy Gosset, writing under the name "Student," is the founder of the *t* distribution. Gosset, an Oxford graduate in mathematics, worked for the Guinness Brewery in Dublin, Ireland. He developed a new small-sample theory of statistics while working on small-scale materials and temperature experiments in the brewery.

The *t* distribution is a family of similar probability distributions, with a specific *t* distribution depending on a parameter known as the *degrees of freedom*. The *t* distribution with one degree of freedom is unique, as is the *t* distribution with two degrees of freedom, with three degrees of freedom, and so on. As the number of degrees of freedom increases, the difference between the *t* distribution and the standard normal probability distribution becomes smaller and smaller. Figure 8.7 shows *t* distributions with 10 and 20 degrees of freedom and their relationship to the standard normal probability distribution. Note that a *t* distribution with more degrees of freedom has less variability and more closely resembles the standard normal probability distribution. Note also that the mean of the *t* distribution is zero.

We will place a subscript on *t* to indicate the area in the upper tail of the *t* distribution. For example, just as we used $z_{.025}$ to indicate the *z* value providing a .025 area in the upper tail of a standard normal probability distribution, we will use $t_{.025}$ to indicate a .025 area in the upper tail of a *t* distribution. In general, we will use the notation $t_{\alpha/2}$ to represent a *t* value with an area of $\alpha/2$ in the upper tail of the *t* distribution. See Figure 8.8.

As the degrees of freedom increase, the *t* distribution approaches the normal distribution. In fact, normal distribution z values can be found in the infinite degrees of freedom row of the *t* distribution table.

Table 8.3 is a table for the *t* distribution. This table is also shown inside the front cover of the text. Note, for example, that for a *t* distribution with 10 degrees of freedom, $t_{.025} = 2.228$. Similarly, for a *t* distribution with 20 degrees of freedom, $t_{.025} = 2.086$. As the degrees of freedom continue to increase, $t_{.025}$ approaches $z_{.025} = 1.96$.

Now that we have an idea of what the *t* distribution is, let us see how it is used to develop an interval estimate of a population mean. Assume that the population has a normal probability distribution and that the sample standard deviation s is used to estimate the population standard deviation σ. The interval-estimation procedure given by (8.4) is applicable.

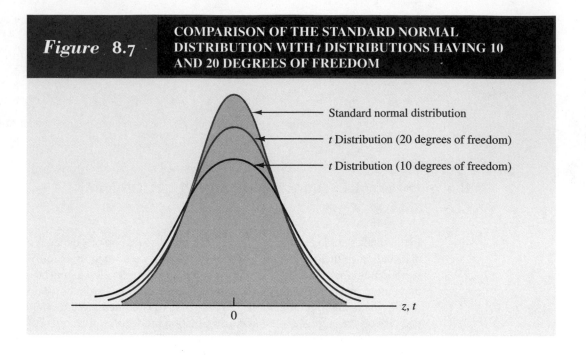

Figure 8.7 COMPARISON OF THE STANDARD NORMAL DISTRIBUTION WITH *t* DISTRIBUTIONS HAVING 10 AND 20 DEGREES OF FREEDOM

Interval Estimate of a Population Mean: Small-Sample Case ($n < 30$) with σ Unknown

$$\bar{x} \pm t_{\alpha/2} \frac{s}{\sqrt{n}} \tag{8.4}$$

where $1 - \alpha$ is the confidence coefficient, $t_{\alpha/2}$ is the *t* value providing an area of $\alpha/2$ in the upper tail of a *t* distribution with $n - 1$ degrees of freedom, and s is the sample standard deviation. The population is assumed to have a normal probability distribution.

Figure 8.8 *t* DISTRIBUTION WITH $\alpha/2$ AREA OR PROBABILITY IN THE UPPER TAIL

| *Table* 8.3 | *t* DISTRIBUTION TABLE FOR AREAS IN THE UPPER TAIL. EXAMPLE: WITH 10 DEGREES OF FREEDOM, $t_{.025} = 2.228$ |

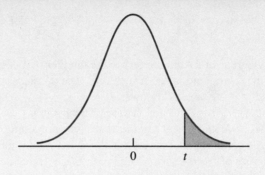

Degrees of Freedom	**Upper-Tail Area (Shaded)**				
	.10	**.05**	**.025**	**.01**	**.005**
1	3.078	6.314	12.706	31.821	63.657
2	1.886	2.920	4.303	6.965	9.925
3	1.638	2.353	3.182	4.541	5.841
4	1.533	2.132	2.776	3.747	4.604
5	1.476	2.015	2.571	3.365	4.032
6	1.440	1.943	2.447	3.143	3.707
7	1.415	1.895	2.365	2.998	3.499
8	1.397	1.860	2.306	2.896	3.355
9	1.383	1.833	2.262	2.821	3.250
10	1.372	1.812	2.228	2.764	3.169
11	1.363	1.796	2.201	2.718	3.106
12	1.356	1.782	2.179	2.681	3.055
13	1.350	1.771	2.160	2.650	3.012
14	1.345	1.761	2.145	2.624	2.977
15	1.341	1.753	2.131	2.602	2.947
16	1.337	1.746	2.120	2.583	2.921
17	1.333	1.740	2.110	2.567	2.898
18	1.330	1.734	2.101	2.552	2.878
19	1.328	1.729	2.093	2.539	2.861
20	1.325	1.725	2.086	2.528	2.845
21	1.323	1.721	2.080	2.518	2.831
22	1.321	1.717	2.074	2.508	2.819
23	1.319	1.714	2.069	2.500	2.807
24	1.318	1.711	2.064	2.492	2.797
25	1.316	1.708	2.060	2.485	2.787
26	1.315	1.706	2.056	2.479	2.779
27	1.314	1.703	2.052	2.473	2.771
28	1.313	1.701	2.048	2.467	2.763
29	1.311	1.699	2.045	2.462	2.756
30	1.310	1.697	2.042	2.457	2.750
40	1.303	1.684	2.021	2.423	2.704
60	1.296	1.671	2.000	2.390	2.660
120	1.289	1.658	1.980	2.358	2.617
∞	1.282	1.645	1.960	2.326	2.576

The reason the number of degrees of freedom associated with the t value in (8.4) is $n - 1$ has to do with the use of s as an estimate of the population standard deviation σ. The expression for the sample standard deviation is

$$s = \sqrt{\frac{\Sigma(x_i - \bar{x})^2}{n - 1}}$$

Degrees of freedom refers to the number of independent pieces of information that go into the computation of $\Sigma(x_i - \bar{x})^2$. The n pieces of information involved in computing $\Sigma(x_i - \bar{x})^2$ are as follows: $x_1 - \bar{x}, x_2 - \bar{x}, \ldots, x_n - \bar{x}$. In Section 3.2 we indicated that $\Sigma(x_i - \bar{x}) = 0$ for any data set. Thus, only $n - 1$ of the $x_i - \bar{x}$ values are independent; that is, if we know $n - 1$ of the values, the remaining value can be determined exactly by using the condition that the sum of the $x_i - \bar{x}$ values must be 0. Thus, $n - 1$ is the number of degrees of freedom associated with $\Sigma(x_i - \bar{x})^2$ and hence the t distribution used in (8.4).

Let us demonstrate the small-sample interval-estimation procedure by considering the training program evaluation conducted by Scheer Industries. Scheer's director of manufacturing is interested in a computer-assisted program that can be used to train the firm's maintenance employees for machine-repair operations. The expectation is that the computer-assisted method will reduce the time needed to train employees. To evaluate the training method, the director of manufacturing has requested an estimate of the mean training time required for the computer-assisted program.

Suppose management has agreed to train 15 employees with the new approach. The data on training days required for each employee in the sample are listed in Table 8.4. The sample mean and sample standard deviation for these data follow.

$$\bar{x} = \frac{\Sigma x_i}{n} = \frac{808}{15} = 53.87 \text{ days}$$

$$s = \sqrt{\frac{\Sigma(x_i - \bar{x})^2}{n - 1}} = \sqrt{\frac{651.73}{14}} = 6.82 \text{ days}$$

The point estimate of the mean training time for the population of employees is 53.87 days. We can obtain information about the precision of this estimate by developing an interval estimate of the population mean. Because the population standard deviation is unknown, we will use the sample standard deviation $s = 6.82$ days. With the small sample size, $n = 15$, we will use (8.4) to develop an interval estimate of the population mean at 95% confidence. If we assume that the population of training times has a normal probability distribution, the t distribution with $n - 1 = 14$ degrees of freedom is the appropriate

Table 8.4	TRAINING TIME IN DAYS FOR THE COMPUTER-ASSISTED TRAINING PROGRAM AT SCHEER INDUSTRIES

Employee	Time	Employee	Time	Employee	Time
1	52	6	59	11	54
2	44	7	50	12	58
3	55	8	54	13	60
4	44	9	62	14	62
5	45	10	46	15	63

The t distribution is based on the assumption that the population has a normal probability distribution. However, confidence intervals based on the t distribution can be used as long as the population distribution does not differ extensively from a normal probability distribution.

probability distribution for the interval-estimation procedure. We see from Table 8.3 that with 14 degrees of freedom, $t_{\alpha/2} = t_{.025} = 2.145$. Using (8.4), we have

$$\bar{x} \pm t_{.025} \frac{s}{\sqrt{n}}$$

$$53.87 \pm 2.145 \left(\frac{6.82}{\sqrt{15}}\right)$$

$$53.87 \pm 3.78$$

Thus, the 95% confidence interval estimate of the population mean training time is 50.09 days to 57.65 days.

Minitab can be used to provide the confidence interval for the population mean in the Scheer Industries example. The output is shown in Figure 8.9. The sample of 15 employees provides a sample mean of 53.87 days, a sample standard deviation of 6.82 days, a standard error of the mean of 1.76 days, and a 95% confidence interval from 50.09 to 57.65 days.

Figure 8.9   **THE MINITAB CONFIDENCE INTERVAL FOR THE SCHEER INDUSTRIES PROBLEM**

Variable	N	Mean	StDev	SE Mean	95.0 % CI
Time	15	53.87	6.82	1.76	(50.09, 57.65)

N O T E S   and Comments

The t distribution is not restricted to the small-sample situation. Actually, the t distribution is applicable whenever the population is normal or near normal and whenever the sample standard deviation is used to estimate the population standard deviation. If these conditions are met, the t distribution can be used for any sample size. However, (8.3) shows that with a large sample ($n \geq 30$), interval estimation of a population mean can be based on the standard normal probability distribution and the value $z_{\alpha/2}$. Thus, with (8.3) available for the large-sample case, we generally do not consider the use of the t distribution until we encounter a small-sample case.

EXERCISES

Methods

13. For a t distribution with 12 degrees of freedom, find the area, or probability, that is in each region.
   a. To the left of 1.782.
   b. To the right of -1.356.
   c. To the right of 2.681.
   d. To the left of -1.782.
   e. Between -2.179 and $+2.179$.
   f. Between -1.356 and $+1.782$.

14. Find the *t* value(s) for each of the following examples.
   a. Upper tail area of .05 with 18 degrees of freedom.
   b. Lower tail area of .10 with 22 degrees of freedom.
   c. Upper tail area of .01 with 5 degrees of freedom.
   d. 90% of the area is between these two *t* values with 14 degrees of freedom.
   e. 95% of the area is between these two *t* values with 28 degrees of freedom.

SELF TEST

15. The following data have been collected for a sample from a normal population: 10, 8, 12, 15, 13, 11, 6, 5.
   a. What is the point estimate of the population mean?
   b. What is the point estimate of the population standard deviation?
   c. What is the 95% confidence interval for the population mean?

16. A simple random sample of 20 observations from a normal population resulted in a sample mean of 17.25 and a sample standard deviation of 3.3.
   a. Develop a 90% confidence interval for the population mean.
   b. Develop a 95% confidence interval for the population mean.
   c. Develop a 99% confidence interval for the population mean.

Applications

SELF TEST

17. In the testing of a new production method, 18 employees were selected randomly and asked to try the new method. The sample mean production rate for the 18 employees was 80 parts per hour and the sample standard deviation was 10 parts per hour. Provide 90% and 95% confidence intervals for the population mean production rate for the new method, assuming the population has a normal probability distribution.

18. The Money & Investing section of the *The Wall Street Journal* contains a summary of daily investment performance for stock exchanges, overseas markets, options, commodities, futures, and so on. In the New York Stock Exchange section, information is provided on each stock's 52-week high price per share, 52-week low price per share, dividend rate, yield, P/E ratio, daily volume, daily high price per share, daily low price per share, closing price per share, and daily net change. The P/E (price/earnings) ratio for each stock is determined by dividing the price of a share of stock by the earnings per share reported by the company for the most recent four quarters. A sample of 10 stocks taken from *The Wall Street Journal* (March 19, 1998) provided the following data on P/E ratios: 5, 7, 9, 10, 14, 23, 20, 15, 3, 26.
   a. What is the point estimate of the mean P/E ratio for the population of all stocks listed on the New York Stock Exchange?
   b. What is the point estimate of the standard deviation of the P/E ratios for the population of all stocks listed on the New York Stock Exchange?
   c. At 95% confidence, what is the interval estimate of the mean P/E ratio for the population of all stocks listed on the New York Stock Exchange? Assume that the population has a normal distribution.
   d. Comment on the precision of the results.

19. The American Association of Advertising Agencies records data on nonprogram minutes on half-hour, prime-time television shows. Representative data in minutes for a sample of 20 prime-time shows on major networks at 8:30 P.M. follows.

TVtime

6.0	6.6	5.8
7.0	6.3	6.2
7.2	5.7	6.4
7.0	6.5	6.2
6.0	6.5	7.2
7.3	7.6	6.8
6.0	6.2	

Provide a point estimate and a 95% confidence interval for the mean number of nonprogram minutes on half-hour, prime-time television shows at 8:30 P.M.

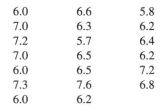

20. Sales personnel for Skillings Distributors are required to submit weekly reports listing the customer contacts made during the week. A sample of 61 weekly contact reports showed a mean of 22.4 customer contacts per week for the sales personnel. The sample standard deviation was 5 contacts.

   a. Use the large-sample case (8.3) to develop a 95% confidence interval for the mean number of weekly customer contacts for the population of sales personnel.
   b. Assume that the population of weekly contact data has a normal distribution. Use the *t* distribution with 60 degrees of freedom to develop a 95% confidence interval for the mean number of weekly customer contacts.
   c. Compare your answers for parts (a) and (b). Comment on why in the large-sample case it is permissible to base interval estimates on the procedure used in part (a) even though the *t* distribution may also be applicable.

21. The U.S. Department of Transportation reported the number of miles that residents of metropolitan areas travel per day in a car (*1994 Information Please Environmental Almanac*). Suppose a simple random sample of 15 residents of Cleveland provided the following data on car miles per day.

20	20	28	16	11	17	23	16	22	18	10	22	29	19	32

   a. Compute a 95% confidence interval estimate of the population mean number of miles residents of Cleveland travel per day in a car.
   b. What assumption about the population was necessary to obtain an answer to part (a)?
   c. Suppose it is desirable to estimate the population mean number of miles with a margin of error of ±2 miles at 95% confidence. Do the data provide this desired level of precision? What action, if any, would you recommend be taken?

22. The number of hours Americans sleep each night varies considerably with 12% of the population sleeping less than six hours to 3% sleeping more than eight hours (*The Macmillan Visual Almanac*, 1996). A following sample of 25 individuals reports the hours of sleep per night.

Sleep

6.9	7.6	6.5	6.2	5.3
7.8	7.0	5.5	7.6	6.7
7.3	6.6	7.1	6.9	6.0
6.8	6.5	7.2	5.8	8.6
7.6	7.1	6.0	7.2	7.7

   a. What is the point estimate of the population mean number of hours of sleep each night?
   b. Assuming that the population has a normal distribution, develop a 95% confidence interval for the population mean number of hours of sleep each night?

8.3   DETERMINING THE SAMPLE SIZE

In the large-sample case with σ known we made the following statement about the sampling error whenever a sample mean was used to provide a point estimate of a population mean:

> There is a $1 - \alpha$ probability that the value of the sample mean will provide a sampling error of $z_{\alpha/2}\sigma_{\bar{x}}$ or less.

Since $\sigma_{\bar{x}} = \sigma/\sqrt{n}$, we can rewrite this statement to read:

> There is a $1 - \alpha$ probability that the value of the sample mean will provide a sampling error of $z_{\alpha/2}(\sigma/\sqrt{n})$ or less.

The quantity $z_{\alpha/2}(\sigma/\sqrt{n})$ is the margin of error. From this statement we see that the values of $z_{\alpha/2}$, σ, and the sample size n combine to determine the margin of error. Once we select a confidence coefficient or probability of $1 - \alpha$, $z_{\alpha/2}$ can be determined. Given values for $z_{\alpha/2}$ and σ, we can determine the sample size n needed to provide any desired margin of error. Development of the formula used to compute the required sample size n follows.

Let E = the desired margin of error

$$E = z_{\alpha/2} \frac{\sigma}{\sqrt{n}}$$

Solving for $\sqrt{n}$, we have

$$\sqrt{n} = \frac{z_{\alpha/2}\sigma}{E}$$

If a desired margin of error E is selected prior to sampling, the procedures in this section can be used to determine the sample size necessary to satisfy the margin of error requirement.

Squaring both sides of this equation, we obtain the following expression for the sample size.

Sample Size for an Interval Estimate of a Population Mean

$$n = \frac{(z_{\alpha/2})^2 \sigma^2}{E^2} \tag{8.5}$$

This sample size will provide the desired margin of error at the chosen confidence level.

In (8.5) the value E is the margin of error that the user is willing to accept at the given confidence level, and the value of $z_{\alpha/2}$ follows directly from the confidence level to be used in developing the interval estimate. Although user preference must be considered, 95% confidence is the most frequently chosen value ($z_{.025} = 1.96$).

Finally, use of (8.5) requires a value for the population standard deviation σ. In most cases, σ will be unknown. However, we can still use (8.5) if we have a preliminary or *planning value* for σ. In practice, one of the following procedures can be chosen.

A planning value for the population standard deviation σ must be known before the sample size can be determined. Three methods of obtaining a planning value for σ are discussed here.

1. Use the sample standard deviation from a previous sample of the same or similar units.
2. Use a pilot study to select a preliminary sample. The sample standard deviation from the preliminary sample can be used as the planning value for σ.
3. Use judgment or a "best guess" for the value of σ. For example, we might begin by estimating the largest and smallest data values in the population. The difference between the largest and smallest values provides an estimate of the range for the data. Finally, the range divided by four is often suggested as a rough approximation of the standard deviation and thus an acceptable planning value for σ.

Let us demonstrate the use of (8.5) to determine the sample size by considering the following example. A previous study that investigated the cost of renting automobiles in the United States found that the cost of renting an intermediate-size automobile ranged from $36 per day in Oakland, California, to $73.50 per day in Hartford, Connecticut (*USA Today,* October 16, 1998). Assume that the organization that conducted this study would like to conduct a new study in order to estimate the current population mean daily rental cost for an intermediate-size automobile in the United States. In designing the new study, the project director has specified that the population mean daily rental cost should be estimated with a margin of error of $2 and a 95% level of confidence.

Using (8.5), we see that the project director has specified a margin of error $E = 2$. The 95% level of confidence indicates $z_{.025} = 1.96$. Thus, we only need a planning value for the population standard deviation σ in order to compute the required sample size. At this point, an analyst reviewed the sample data from the previous study and found that the sample standard deviation for the daily rental cost was $9.65. Using this value as the planning value for σ, we have

Equation (8.5) provides the minimum *sample size needed to satisfy the margin of error requirement. If the computed sample size has a fraction, rounding up to the next integer value will determine the recommended sample size.*

$$n = \frac{(z_{\alpha/2})^2\sigma^2}{E^2} = \frac{(1.96)^2(9.65)^2}{2^2} = 89.43$$

Thus, the sample size for the new study needs to be at least 89.43 intermediate-size automobile rentals in order to satisfy project director's $2 margin-of-error requirement. In cases where the computed n is a fraction, we round up to the next integer value; hence, the recommended sample size is 90 intermediate-size automobile rentals.

EXERCISES

Methods

23. How large a sample should be selected to provide a 95% confidence interval with a margin of error of 5? Assume that the population standard deviation is 25.

24. The range for a set of data is estimated to be 36.
    a. What is the planning value for the population standard deviation?
    b. Using 95% confidence, how large a sample should be used to provide a margin of error of 3?
    c. Using 95% confidence, how large a sample should be used to provide a margin of error of 2?

SELF TEST

Applications

25. Refer to the Scheer Industries example in this section. Use $\sigma = 6.82$ as a planning value for the population standard deviation.
    a. Assuming 95% confidence, what sample size would be required to obtain a margin of error of 1.5 minutes?
    b. If the precision statement was made with 90% confidence, what sample size would be required to obtain a margin of error of 2 minutes?

SELF TEST

26. In Section 8.1 the Statewide Insurance Company used a simple random sample of 36 policyholders to estimate the mean age of the population of policyholders. At 95% confidence, the margin of error was 2.35 years. This result was based on a sample standard deviation of 7.2 years.
    a. How large a simple random sample would have been necessary to reduce the margin of error to 2 years? To 1.5 years? To 1 year?
    b. Would you recommend that Statewide attempt to estimate the population mean age of the policyholders with a margin of error of 1 year? Explain.

27. Annual starting salaries for college graduates with business administration degrees are believed to have a standard deviation of approximately $2000. Assume that a 95% confidence interval estimate of the mean annual starting salary is desired. How large a sample should be taken if the margin of error is
    a. $500?
    b. $200?
    c. $100?

28. The U.S. Department of Housing and Urban Development publishes data on the fair market monthly rent for existing one-bedroom housing by metropolitan area (*The Federal Register,* April 30, 1997). The standard deviation for the monthly rent is approximately $80. Assume that a sample of metropolitan areas will be selected in order to estimate the population mean of the monthly rent for existing one-bedroom housing. Use 95% confidence.
    a. How large should the sample be if the desired margin of error is $25?
    b. How large should the sample be if the desired margin of error is $15?

29. The travel-to-work time for residents of the 15 largest cities in the United States is reported in the *1998 Information Please Almanac.* Suppose that a preliminary simple random sample of residents of San Francisco is used to develop a planning value of 6.25 minutes for the population standard deviation.
    a. If we want to estimate the population mean travel-to-work time for San Francisco residents with a margin of error of 2 minutes, what sample size should be used? Assume a 95% confidence.
    b. If we want to estimate the population mean travel-to-work time for San Francisco residents with a margin of error of 1 minute, what sample size should be used? Assume 95% confidence.

30. From Exercise 18, the sample standard deviation of P/E ratios for stocks listed on the New York Stock Exchange is $s = 7.8$ (*The Wall Street Journal,* March 19, 1998). Assume that we are interested in estimating the population mean P/E ratio for all stocks listed on the New York Stock Exchange. How many stocks should be included in the sample if we want a margin of error of 2? Use 95% confidence.

8.4 INTERVAL ESTIMATION OF A POPULATION PROPORTION

In Chapter 7 we showed that a sample proportion $\bar{p}$ is an unbiased estimator of a population proportion p and that for large samples the sampling probability distribution of $\bar{p}$ can be approximated by a normal probability distribution, as shown in Figure 8.10. Recall that

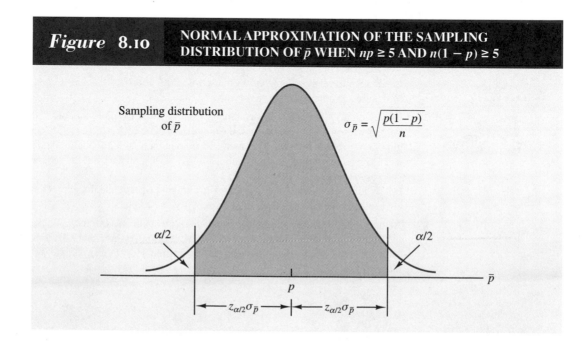

Figure 8.10 NORMAL APPROXIMATION OF THE SAMPLING DISTRIBUTION OF $\bar{p}$ WHEN $np \geq 5$ AND $n(1-p) \geq 5$

Sampling distribution of $\bar{p}$

$$\sigma_{\bar{p}} = \sqrt{\frac{p(1-p)}{n}}$$

$\alpha/2$

$\alpha/2$

p

$\bar{p}$

$z_{\alpha/2}\sigma_{\bar{p}}$ $z_{\alpha/2}\sigma_{\bar{p}}$

the use of the normal distribution as an approximation of the sampling distribution of $\bar{p}$ is based on the condition that both np and $n(1 - p)$ are 5 or more. We will be using the sampling distribution of $\bar{p}$ to make probability statements about the sampling error whenever a sample proportion $\bar{p}$ is used to estimate a population proportion p. In this case, the sampling error is defined as the absolute value of the difference between $\bar{p}$ and p, written $|\bar{p} - p|$.

The probability statements that can be made about the sampling error for the proportion take the following form.

> There is a $1 - \alpha$ probability that the value of the sample proportion will provide a sampling error of $z_{\alpha/2}\sigma_{\bar{p}}$ or less.

Hence, for a proportion, the quantity $z_{\alpha/2}\sigma_{\bar{p}}$ is the margin of error.

The rationale for the preceding statement is the same one we gave when the value of a sample mean was used as an estimate of a population mean. Namely, because we know that the sampling distribution of $\bar{p}$ can be approximated by a normal probability distribution, we can use the value of $z_{\alpha/2}$ and the value of the standard error of the proportion, $\sigma_{\bar{p}}$, to determine the margin of error.

Once we know the margin of error, $z_{\alpha/2}\sigma_{\bar{p}}$, we can subtract and add this value to $\bar{p}$ to obtain an interval estimate of the population proportion. Such an interval estimate is given by

$$\bar{p} \pm z_{\alpha/2}\sigma_{\bar{p}} \tag{8.6}$$

where $1 - \alpha$ is the confidence coefficient. Because $\sigma_{\bar{p}} = \sqrt{p(1 - p)/n}$, we can rewrite (8.6) as

$$\bar{p} \pm z_{\alpha/2}\sqrt{\frac{p(1 - p)}{n}} \tag{8.7}$$

> When developing confidence intervals for proportions, $\sigma_{\bar{p}}$ is referred to as the standard error of the proportion and the quantity $z_{\alpha/2}\sqrt{\bar{p}(1 - \bar{p})/n}$ provides the margin of error.

To use (8.7) to develop an interval estimate of a population proportion p, the value of p would have to be known. Because the value of p is what we are trying to estimate, we simply substitute the sample proportion $\bar{p}$ for p. The resulting general expression for a confidence interval estimate of a population proportion follows.*

Interval Estimate of a Population Proportion

$$\bar{p} \pm z_{\alpha/2}\sqrt{\frac{\bar{p}(1 - \bar{p})}{n}} \tag{8.8}$$

where $1 - \alpha$ is the confidence coefficient and $z_{\alpha/2}$ is the z value providing an area of $\alpha/2$ in the upper tail of the standard normal probability distribution.

Let us use the following example to illustrate the computation of the margin of error and interval estimate for a population proportion. In 1997, Ferrell Calvillo Communications conducted a national survey of 902 women golfers to learn how women golfers view themselves as being treated at golf courses in the United States (*USA Today,* June 3, 1997). The survey

---

*An unbiased estimate of $\sigma_{\bar{p}}^2$ is $\bar{p}(1 - \bar{p})/(n - 1)$, which suggests that $\sqrt{\bar{p}(1 - \bar{p})/(n - 1)}$ should be used in place of $\sqrt{\bar{p}(1 - \bar{p})/n}$ in (8.8). However, the bias introduced by using n in the denominator does not cause any difficulty because large samples are generally used in making estimates about population proportions. In such cases the numerical difference between the results obtained by using n and those obtained by using $n - 1$ is negligible.

found that 397 women golfers were satisfied with the availability of tee times. Thus, the point estimate of the proportion of the population of women golfers who are satisfied with the availability of tee times is 397/902 = .44. Using (8.8) and a 95% confidence level, we have

$$\bar{p} \pm z_{\alpha/2} \sqrt{\frac{\bar{p}(1 - \bar{p})}{n}}$$

$$.44 \pm 1.96 \sqrt{\frac{.44(1 - .44)}{902}}$$

$$.44 \pm .0324$$

Thus, at 95% confidence, the margin of error is .0324 and the interval estimate of the population proportion is .4076 to .4724. Using percentages, the survey results enable us to state that with 95% confidence between 40.76% and 47.24% of all women golfers are satisfied with the availability of tee times.

Determining the Sample Size

Let us consider the question of how large the sample size should be to obtain an estimate of a population proportion at a specified level of precision. The rationale for the sample size determination in developing interval estimates of p is similar to the rationale used in Section 8.3 to determine the sample size for estimating a population mean.

Previously in this section we pointed out that the margin of error associated with an estimate of a population proportion is $z_{\alpha/2}\sigma_{\bar{p}}$. With $\sigma_{\bar{p}} = \sqrt{p(1 - p)/n}$, the margin of error is based on the values of $z_{\alpha/2}$, the population proportion p, and the sample size n. For a given confidence coefficient $1 - \alpha$, $z_{\alpha/2}$ can be determined. Then, for a specified value of the population proportion p, the margin of error is determined by the sample size n. Larger sample sizes provide a smaller margin of error and better precision.

Let E = the desired margin of error

$$E = z_{\alpha/2} \sqrt{\frac{p(1 - p)}{n}}$$

Solving this equation for n provides the following formula for the sample size.

Sample Size for an Interval Estimate of a Population Proportion

$$n = \frac{(z_{\alpha/2})^2 p(1 - p)}{E^2} \qquad (8.9)$$

Because the population proportion p is what we are attempting to estimate from the sample, a planning value for p must be available in order to use (8.9). Four ways to obtain this planning value are listed here.

In (8.9), the margin of error E must be specified by the user; in most cases, E is .10 or less. User preference also specifies the confidence level and thus the corresponding value of $z_{\alpha/2}$. Finally, use of (8.9) requires a planning value for the population proportion p. In practice, this planning value can be chosen by one of the following procedures.

1. Use the sample proportion from a previous sample of the same or similar units.
2. Use a pilot study to select a preliminary sample. The sample proportion from this sample can be used as the planning value for p.
3. Use judgment or a "best guess" for the value of p.
4. If none of the preceding alternatives apply, use a planning value of p = .50.

Let us return to the Ferrell Calvillo Communications survey of women golfers and assume that the company is interested in conducting a new survey to estimate the current proportion of the population of women golfers who are satisfied with the availability of tee times. How large should the sample be if the survey director wants the new study to be able to estimate the population proportion with a margin of error of .025 at a 95% confidence? With $E = .025$ and $z_{\alpha/2} = 1.96$, we need a planning value of p to answer the sample size question. Using the 1997 survey result of $\bar{p} = .44$ as the planning value for p, (8.9) shows that

$$n = \frac{(z_{\alpha/2})^2 p(1-p)}{E^2} = \frac{(1.96)^2(.44)(1-.44)}{(.025)^2} = 1514.51$$

Thus, the sample size must be at least 1514.51 women golfers to satisfy the margin of error requirement. Rounding up to the next integer value indicates that a sample of 1515 women golfers is recommended.

The fourth alternative suggested for selecting a planning value for p is to use $p = .50$. This value of p is frequently used when no other information is available. To understand why, note that the numerator of (8.9) shows that the sample size is proportional to the quantity $p(1-p)$. A larger value for the quantity $p(1-p)$ will result in a larger sample size. Table 8.5 gives some possible values of $p(1-p)$. Note that the largest value of $p(1-p)$ occurs when $p = .50$. Thus, if there is uncertainty about an appropriate planning value for p, we know that $p = .50$ will provide the largest sample size recommendation. In effect, we are being on the safe or conservative side in recommending the largest possible sample size. If the proportion turns out to be different from the .50 planning value, the precision statement will be better than anticipated. Thus, in using $p = .50$, we are guaranteeing that the sample size will be sufficient to obtain the desired margin of error.

Surveys that ask many questions about proportions are often designed by using a planning value $p = .50$ for the sample size computation. Using this planning value gives a sample size that guarantees that all estimates of proportions will meet their margin of error requirements.

In the survey of women golfers example, a planning value of $p = .50$ would have provided the sample size

$$n = \frac{(z_{\alpha/2})^2 p(1-p)}{E^2} = \frac{(1.96)^2(.50)(1-.50)}{(.025)^2} = 1536.64$$

Thus a slightly larger sample size of 1537 women golfers is recommended.

Table 8.5   SOME POSSIBLE VALUES FOR $p(1-p)$

p	$p(1-p)$	
.10	(.10)(.90) = .09	
.30	(.30)(.70) = .21	
.40	(.40)(.60) = .24	
.50	(.50)(.50) = .25 ◄——— Largest value for $p(1-p)$	
.60	(.60)(.40) = .24	
.70	(.70)(.30) = .21	
.90	(.90)(.10) = .09	

N O T E S
and Comments

The margin of error for estimating a population proportion is almost always .10 or less. In national public opinion polls conducted by organizations such as Gallup and Harris, a .03 or .04 margin of error is generally reported. The use of these margins of error [E in equation (8.9)] will generally provide a sample size that is large enough to satisfy the central limit theorem requirements of $np \geq 5$ and $n(1 - p) \geq 5$.

EXERCISES

Methods

SELF TEST

31. A simple random sample of 400 items provides 100 Yes responses.
    a. What is the point estimate of the proportion of the population who would provide Yes responses?
    b. What is the standard error of the proportion, $\sigma_{\bar{p}}$?
    c. Compute the 95% confidence interval for the population proportion.

32. A simple random sample of 800 units generates a sample proportion $\bar{p} = .70$.
    a. Provide a 90% confidence interval for the population proportion.
    b. Provide a 95% confidence interval for the population proportion.

33. In a survey, the planning value for the population proportion p is .35. How large a sample should be taken to provide a 95% confidence interval with a margin of error of .05?

34. Using 95% confidence, how large a sample should be taken to obtain a margin of error for the estimation of a population proportion of .03? Assume that past data are not available for developing a planning value for p.

Applications

SELF TEST

35. A *Time*/CNN poll asked 814 adults to respond to a series of questions about their feelings toward the state of affairs within the United States. A total of 562 adults responded Yes to the question: Do you feel things are going well in the United States these days? (*Time*, August 11, 1997).
    a. What is the point estimate of the proportion of the adult population who feel things are going well in the United States?
    b. At 90% confidence, what is the margin of error?
    c. What is the 90% confidence interval for the proportion of the adult population who feel things are going well in the United States?

36. The Bureau of National Affairs, Inc., selected a sample of 617 companies and found that 56 companies required their employees to surrender airline frequent-flier mileage awards for business-related travel (*The Wall Street Journal*, March 28, 1994).
    a. What is the point estimate of the proportion of all companies that require their employees to surrender airline frequent-flier mileage awards?
    b. Develop a 95% confidence interval estimate of the population proportion.

37. A survey by Wirthlin Worldwide collected data on attitudes toward the quality of customer service in retail stores. The survey found that 28% of Americans feel customer service is better today than it was two years ago (*USA Today*, January 20, 1998). If 650 adults were included in the sample, develop a 95% confidence interval for the proportion of the population of adults who feel customer service is better today than it was two years ago.

38. Audience profile data collected at the ESPN SportsZone web site showed that 26% of the users were women (*USA Today,* January 21, 1998). Assume that this percentage was based on a sample of 400 users.
    a. Using 95% confidence, what is the margin of error associated with the estimated proportion of users who are women?
    b. What is the 95% confidence interval for the population proportion of ESPN Sportszone web site users who are women?
    c. How large a sample should be taken if the desired margin of error is 3%?

SELF TEST

39. The Tourism Institute for the State of Florida plans to sample visitors at major beaches throughout the state to estimate the proportion of beach visitors who are not Florida residents. Preliminary estimates are that 55% of the beach visitors are not Florida residents.
    a. How large a sample should be taken to estimate the proportion of out-of-state visitors with a margin of error of 3%? Use a 95% confidence level.
    b. How large a sample should be taken if the margin of error is increased to 6%?

40. An Associated Press poll of 1018 adults found 255 adults planned to spend less money on gifts during the 1998 holiday season compared to the previous year (ICR Media survey, November 13–17, 1998).
    a. What is the point estimate of the proportion of all adults who planned to spend less money on gifts during the 1998 holiday season?
    b. Using 95% confidence, what is the margin of error associated with this estimate?

41. A *Wall Street Journal*/NBC News survey was used to collect data on how Americans feel about the quality of newspaper and television news coverage (*The Wall Street Journal,* June 27, 1997). One question asked whether the respondent believes that news coverage of the U.S. economy is balanced, too negative, or too positive. Preliminary estimates are that approximately 50% of the population will feel that the news coverage is balanced.
    a. What sample size is recommended if the desired margin of error is 3.3%? Use 95% confidence.
    b. What sample size is recommended if the desired margin of error is 2.5%? Use 95% confidence.

42. A survey of female executives conducted by Louis Harris & Associates showed that 33% of those surveyed rated their own company as an excellent place for women executives to work (*Working Woman,* November 1994). Suppose *Working Woman* wants to conduct an annual survey to monitor this proportion. With $p = .33$ as a planning value for the population proportion, how many female executives should be sampled for each of the following margins of error? Assume that all interval estimates are conducted at the 95% confidence level.
    a. 10%
    b. 5%
    c. 2%
    d. 1%
    e. In general, what happens to the sample size as the margin of error decreases?

43. The League of American Theatres and Producers uses an ongoing audience tracking survey that provides up-to-date information about Broadway theater audiences (*Playbill,* Winter 1997). Every week, the League distributes a one-page survey on random theater seats at a rotation roster of Broadway shows. The survey questionnaire takes only five minutes to complete and enables audiences to communicate their views about the theater industry.
    a. How large a sample should be taken if the desired margin of error on any population proportion is .04? Use 95% confidence and a planning value of $p = .50$.
    b. Assume that the sample size recommended in part (a) is implemented and that during one week 445 theatergoers indicated that they do not live in New York City. What is the point estimate of the proportion of Broadway audiences that do not live in New York City?
    c. Using the data in part (b), what is the 95% confidence interval for the population proportion of Broadway audiences that do not live in New York City?

SUMMARY

In this chapter we presented methods for developing a confidence interval for a population mean μ and a population proportion p. The purpose of developing a confidence interval is to give the user a better understanding of the margin of error that may be present. A wide confidence interval indicates poor precision; in such cases, the sample size can be increased to reduce the width of the confidence interval and improve the precision of the estimate.

Figure 8.11 summarizes the interval-estimation procedures for a population mean and provides a practical guide for computing the interval estimate. The figure shows that the

---

Figure 8.11   SUMMARY OF INTERVAL ESTIMATION PROCEDURES FOR A POPULATION MEAN

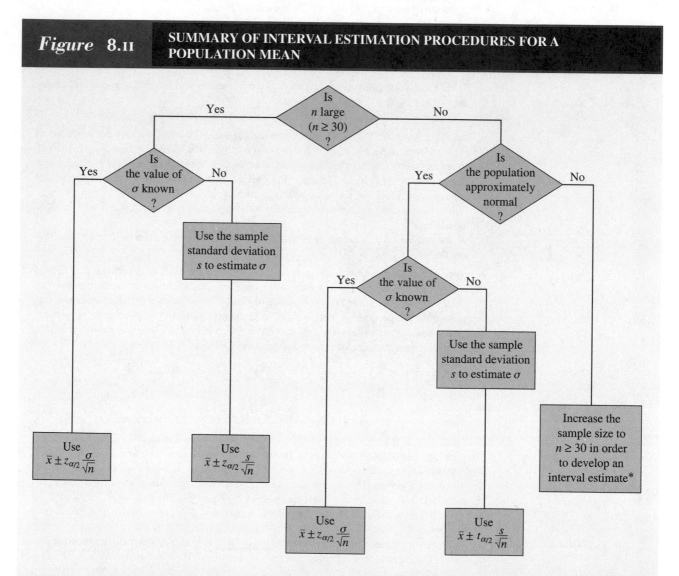

*Sometimes methods from nonparametric statistics can be used in the small-sample case to develop confidence intervals for location parameters of a population.

expression used to compute an interval estimate depends on whether the sample size is large ($n \geq 30$) or small ($n < 30$), whether the population standard deviation is known, and in some cases whether the population has a normal or approximately normal probability distribution. If the sample size is large, no assumption is required about the distribution of the population, and $z_{\alpha/2}$ is used in the computation of the interval estimate. If the sample size is small, the population must have a normal or approximately normal probability distribution in order to develop an interval estimate of μ. For this normal probability distribution, $z_{\alpha/2}$ is used in the computation of the interval estimate when σ is known, whereas $t_{\alpha/2}$ is used when σ is estimated by the sample standard deviation s. Finally, if the sample size is small and the assumption of a normally distributed population is inappropriate, we recommend increasing the sample size to $n \geq 30$ to develop a large-sample interval estimate of the population mean.

In addition, we showed how to determine the sample size so that interval estimates of μ and p would have a specified margin of error. In practice, the sample sizes required for interval estimates of a population proportion are generally large. Hence, we provided the large-sample interval-estimation formulas for a population proportion where both $np \geq 5$ and $n(1 - p) \geq 5$.

GLOSSARY

Interval estimate An estimate of a population parameter that provides an interval believed to contain the value of the parameter.

Sampling error The absolute value of the difference between the value of an unbiased point estimator, such as the sample mean $\bar{x}$, and the value of the population parameter it estimates, such as the population mean μ. In the case of a population mean, the sampling error is $|\bar{x} - \mu|$. In the case of a population proportion, the sampling error is $|\bar{p} - p|$.

Precision A probability statement about the sampling error.

Confidence level The confidence associated with an interval estimate. For example, if an interval-estimation procedure provides intervals such that 95% of the intervals formed using the procedure will include the population parameter, the interval estimate is said to be constructed at the 95% confidence level; note that .95 is referred to as the confidence coefficient.

Margin of error The $\pm$ value added to and subtracted from a point estimate in order to develop a confidence interval.

***t* Distribution** A family of probability distributions that can be used to develop interval estimates of a population mean whenever the population standard deviation is unknown and the population has a normal or near-normal probability distribution.

Degrees of freedom A parameter of the t distribution. When the t distribution is used in the computation of an interval estimate of a population mean, the appropriate t distribution has $n - 1$ degrees of freedom, where n is the size of the simple random sample.

KEY FORMULAS

Sampling Error When Estimating μ

$$|\bar{x} - \mu| \tag{8.1}$$

Interval Estimate of a Population Mean: Large-Sample Case with σ Known

$$\bar{x} \pm z_{\alpha/2} \frac{\sigma}{\sqrt{n}} \tag{8.2}$$

Interval Estimate of a Population Mean: Large-Sample Case with σ Unknown

$$\bar{x} \pm z_{\alpha/2} \frac{s}{\sqrt{n}} \tag{8.3}$$

Interval Estimate of a Population Mean: Small-Sample Case with σ Unknown

$$\bar{x} \pm t_{\alpha/2} \frac{s}{\sqrt{n}} \tag{8.4}$$

Sample Size for an Interval Estimate of a Population Mean

$$n = \frac{(z_{\alpha/2})^2 \sigma^2}{E^2} \tag{8.5}$$

Interval Estimate of a Population Proportion

$$\bar{p} \pm z_{\alpha/2} \sqrt{\frac{\bar{p}(1 - \bar{p})}{n}} \tag{8.8}$$

Sample Size for an Interval Estimate of a Population Proportion

$$n = \frac{(z_{\alpha/2})^2 p(1 - p)}{E^2} \tag{8.9}$$

SUPPLEMENTARY EXERCISES

44. A survey by Day-Timers found that U.S. men work a mean of 52 hours per week (*The Cincinnati Enquirer,* October 23, 1995). Assume the survey used a sample of 650 men and that the sample standard deviation was 8.2 hours. What is the 95% confidence interval for the mean number of hours worked per week for the population of U.S. men?

45. A survey conducted by the American Automobile Association showed that a family of four spends an average of $215.60 per day while on vacation. Suppose a sample of 64 families of four vacationing at Niagara Falls resulted in a sample mean of $252.45 per day and a sample standard deviation of $74.50.

    a. Develop a 95% confidence interval estimate of the mean amount spent per day by a family of four visiting Niagara Falls.

    b. Using the confidence interval from part (a), does it appear that the population mean amount spent per day by families visiting Niagara Falls is different from the mean reported by the American Automobile Association? Explain.

ActTemps

46. A survey by Accountemps asked a sample of 200 executives to provide data on the number of minutes per day office workers waste trying to locate mislabeled, misfiled, or misplaced items (*Astounding Averages,* by D. D. Dauphinais and K. Droste, 1995). Data consistent with this survey are contained in the data set ActTemps.

    a. Use ActTemps to develop a point estimate of the number of minutes per day office workers waste trying to locate mislabeled, misfiled, or misplaced items.

    b. What is the sample standard deviation?

    c. What is the 95% confidence interval for the mean number of minutes wasted per day?

Mail

47. Arthur D. Little, Inc., estimates that approximately 70% of mail received by a household is advertisements (*Time,* July 14, 1997). A sample of 20 households shows the following data for the number of advertisements received and the total number of pieces of mail received during one week.

Household	Advertisements	Total Mail	Household	Advertisements	Total Mail
1	24	35	11	13	19
2	9	14	12	16	28
3	18	30	13	20	27
4	9	12	14	17	22
5	15	28	15	21	24
6	23	33	16	21	33
7	13	20	17	15	25
8	17	20	18	15	24
9	20	23	19	18	24
10	20	25	20	12	16

a. What is the point estimate of the mean number of advertisements received per week? What is the 95% confidence interval for the population mean?

b. What is the point estimate of the mean number of pieces of mail received per week? What is the 95% confidence interval for the population mean?

c. Use the point estimates in parts (a) and (b). Are these estimates in agreement with the statement that approximately 70% of mailings are advertisements?

48. Sample assembly times for a particular manufactured part were 8, 10, 10, 12, 15, and 17 minutes. If the mean of the sample is used to estimate the mean of the population of assembly times, provide a point estimate and a 90% confidence interval for the population mean. Assume that the population has a normal distribution.

49. Many Americans who work in large offices also work at home or in the office on weekends (*USA Today,* June 18, 1997). How large a sample should be taken to estimate the population mean amount of time worked on weekends with a margin of error of 10 minutes. Use 95% confidence and assume that the planning value for the population standard deviation is 45 minutes.

50. Mileage tests are conducted for a particular model of automobile. If the desired precision is a 98% confidence interval with a margin of error of one mile per gallon, how many automobiles should be used in the test? Assume that preliminary mileage tests indicate the standard deviation to be 2.6 miles per gallon.

51. In developing patient appointment schedules, a medical center wants an estimate of the mean time that a staff member spends with each patient. How large a sample should be taken if the margin of error is to be 2 minutes at a 95% level of confidence? How large a sample should be taken for a 99% level of confidence? Use a planning value for the population standard deviation of 8 minutes.

52. Annual salary plus bonus data for chief executive officers are presented in the *Business Week* 47th Annual Pay Survey (*Business Week,* April 21, 1997). A preliminary sample showed that the standard deviation is $675 with data provided in thousands of dollars. How many chief executive officers should be in a sample if we want to estimate the population mean annual salary plus bonus with a margin of error of $100,000. (Note: The margin of error would be $E = 100$ since the data are in thousands of dollars.) Use a 95% confidence interval.

53. The National Center for Education Statistics reported that 47% of college students work to pay for tuition and living expenses (*The Tampa Tribune,* January 22, 1997). Assume that a sample of 450 college students was used in the study.

    a.   Provide a 95% confidence interval for the population proportion of college students who work to pay for tuition and living expenses.

    b.   Provide a 99% confidence interval for the population proportion of college students who work to pay for tuition and living expenses.

    c.   What happens to the margin of error as the confidence is increased from 95% to 99%?

54.   A *USA Today*/CNN Gallup survey of 369 working parents found 200 who said they spend too little time with their children because of work commitments (*USA Today*, April 10, 1995).

    a.   What is the point estimate of the proportion of the population of working parents who feel they spend too little time with their children because of work commitments?

    b.   At 95% confidence, what is the margin of error?

    c.   What is the 95% confidence interval estimate of the population proportion of working parents who feel they spend too little time with their children because of work commitments?

55.   A *Time*/CNN poll of 1400 American adults asked, "Where would you rather go in your spare time?" The top response by 504 adults was a shopping mall.

    a.   What is the point estimate of the proportion of adults who would prefer going to a shopping mall in their spare time?

    b.   At 95% confidence, what is the margin of error associated with this estimate?

56.   A well-known bank credit card firm is interested in estimating the proportion of credit card holders who carry a nonzero balance at the end of the month and incur an interest charge. Assume that the desired margin of error is .03 at 98% confidence.

    a.   How large a sample should be selected if it is anticipated that roughly 70% of the firm's cardholders carry a nonzero balance at the end of the month?

    b.   How large a sample should be selected if no planning value for the population proportion could be specified?

57.   In a survey, 200 people were asked to identify their major source of news information; 110 stated that their major source was television news.

    a.   Construct a 95% confidence interval for the proportion of people in the population who consider television their major source of news information.

    b.   How large a sample would be necessary to estimate the population proportion with a margin of error of .05 at 95% confidence?

58.   A survey of 502 female executives conducted by Louis Harris & Associates showed that 166 of the executives surveyed rated their own company as an excellent place for women executives to work (*Working Woman*, November 1994). Develop a 95% confidence interval of the proportion of all female executives who rate their own company as an excellent place for women executives to work.

59.   The *1997 Statistical Abstract of the United States* reports the percentage of people 18 years of age and older who smoke. Assume that a study is being designed to collect new data on smokers and nonsmokers. The best preliminary estimate of the population proportion who smoke is 30%.

    a.   How large a sample should be taken to estimate the proportion of smokers in the population with a margin of error of .02? Use 95% confidence.

    b.   Assume that the study uses your sample size recommendation in part (a) and finds 520 smokers. What is the point estimate of the proportion of smokers in the population?

    c.   What is the 95% confidence interval for the proportion of smokers in the population?

60.   Although airline schedules and cost are important factors for business travelers when choosing an airline carrier, a *USA Today* survey found that business travelers list an airline's frequent flyer program as the most important factor (*USA Today*, April 11, 1995). From a sample of $n = 1993$ business travelers who responded to the survey, 618 listed a frequent flyer program as the most important factor.

    a.   What is the point estimate of the proportion of the population of business travelers who believe a frequent-flyer program is the most important factor when choosing an airline carrier?

    b.   Develop a 95% confidence interval estimate of the population proportion.

    c.   How large a sample would be required to report the margin of error of .01 at 95% confidence? Would you recommend that *USA Today* attempt to provide this degree of precision? Why or why not?

···/ /·············

Case Problem 1   BOCK INVESTMENT SERVICES

Lisa Rae Bock started Bock Investment Services (BIS) in 1994 with the goal of making BIS the leading money market advisory service in South Carolina. To provide better service for her present clients and to attract new clients, she has developed a weekly newsletter. Lisa has been considering adding a new feature to the newsletter that will report the results of a weekly telephone survey of fund managers. To investigate the feasibility of offering this service, and to determine what type of information to include in the newsletter, Lisa selected a simple random sample of 45 money market funds. A portion of the data obtained is shown in Table 8.6, which reports fund assets and yields for the past seven and 30 days. Before calling the money market fund managers to obtain additional data, Lisa decided to do some preliminary analysis of the data already collected.

Managerial Report

1. Use appropriate descriptive statistics to summarize the data on assets and yields for the money market funds.
2. Develop a 95% confidence interval estimate of the mean assets, mean 7-day yield, and mean 30-day yield for the population of money market funds. Provide a managerial interpretation of each interval estimate.
3. Discuss the implication of your findings in terms of how Lisa could use this type of information in preparing her weekly newsletter.
4. What other information would you recommend that Lisa gather to provide the most useful information to her clients?

···/ /·············

Case Problem 2   METROPOLITAN RESEARCH, INC.

Metropolitan Research, Inc., is a consumer research organization that takes surveys designed to evaluate a wide variety of products and services available to consumers. In one particular study, Metropolitan was interested in learning about consumer satisfaction with the performance of automobiles produced by a major Detroit manufacturer. A questionnaire sent to owners of one of the manufacturer's full-sized cars revealed several complaints about early transmission problems. To learn more about the transmission failures, Metropolitan used a sample of actual transmission repairs provided by a transmission repair firm in the Detroit area. The following data show the actual number of miles that 50 vehicles had been driven at the time of transmission failure.

Auto

85,092	32,609	59,465	77,437	32,534	64,090	32,464	59,902
39,323	89,641	94,219	116,803	92,857	63,436	65,605	85,861
64,342	61,978	67,998	59,817	101,769	95,774	121,352	69,568
74,276	66,998	40,001	72,069	25,066	77,098	69,922	35,662
74,425	67,202	118,444	53,500	79,294	64,544	86,813	116,269
37,831	89,341	73,341	85,288	138,114	53,402	85,586	82,256
77,539	88,798						

Managerial Report

1. Use appropriate descriptive statistics to summarize the transmission failure data.
2. Develop a 95% confidence interval for the mean number of miles driven until transmission failure for the population of automobiles that have had transmission failure. Provide a managerial interpretation of the interval estimate.

Table 8.6	DATA FOR BOCK INVESTMENT SERVICES CASE PROBLEM

Bock

Money Market Fund	Assets (millions $)	7-day Yield (%)	30-day Yield (%)
Amcore	103.9	4.10	4.08
Alger	156.7	4.79	4.73
Arch MM/Trust	496.5	4.17	4.13
BT Instit Treas	197.8	4.37	4.32
Benchmark Div	2755.4	4.54	4.47
Bradford	707.6	3.88	3.83
Capital Cash	1.7	4.29	4.22
Cash Mgt Trust	2707.8	4.14	4.04
Composite	122.8	4.03	3.91
Cowen Standby	694.7	4.25	4.19
Cortland	217.3	3.57	3.51
Declaration	38.4	2.67	2.61
Dreyfus	4832.8	4.01	3.89
Elfun	81.7	4.51	4.41
FFB Cash	506.2	4.17	4.11
Federated Master	738.7	4.41	4.34
Fidelity Cash	13272.8	4.51	4.42
Flex-fund	172.8	4.60	4.48
Fortis	105.6	3.87	3.85
Franklin Money	996.8	3.97	3.92
Freedom Cash	1079.0	4.07	4.01
Galaxy Money	801.4	4.11	3.96
Government Cash	409.4	3.83	3.82
Hanover Cash	794.3	4.32	4.23
Heritage Cash	1008.3	4.08	4.00
Infinity/Alpha	53.6	3.99	3.91
John Hancock	226.4	3.93	3.87
Landmark Funds	481.3	4.28	4.26
Liquid Cash	388.9	4.61	4.64
MarketWatch	10.6	4.13	4.05
Merrill Lynch Money	27005.6	4.24	4.18
NCC Funds	113.4	4.22	4.20
Nationwide	517.3	4.22	4.14
Overland	291.5	4.26	4.17
Pierpont Money	1991.7	4.50	4.40
Portico Money	161.6	4.28	4.20
Prudential MoneyMart	6835.1	4.20	4.16
Reserve Primary	1408.8	3.91	3.86
Schwab Money	10531.0	4.16	4.07
Smith Barney Cash	2947.6	4.16	4.12
Stagecoach	1502.2	4.18	4.13
Strong Money	470.2	4.37	4.29
Transamerica Cash	175.5	4.20	4.19
United Cash	323.7	3.96	3.89
Woodward Money	1330.0	4.24	4.21

Source: *Barron's,* October 3, 1994.

3. Discuss the implication of your statistical finding in terms of the belief that some owners of the automobiles have experienced early transmission failures.
4. How many repair records should be sampled if the research firm wants the population mean number of miles driven until transmission failure to be estimated with a margin of error of 5000 miles. Use 95% confidence.
5. What other information would you like to gather to evaluate the transmission failure problem more fully?

Appendix 8.1   CONFIDENCE INTERVAL ESTIMATION WITH MINITAB

Large-Sample Case

In Section 8.1 we showed the Minitab confidence interval for the population mean in the Statewide Insurance Company study. We will use the data set LifeIns, which contains the data in Table 8.2. With the sample standard deviation, $s = 7.77$, as an estimate of the population standard deviation σ, the following steps can be used to produce the 90% confidence interval output shown in Figure 8.6 (assume the age data have been entered in column C1 of the Minitab worksheet).

Step 1. Select the **Stat** pull-down menu
Step 2. Select the **Basic Statistics** pull-down menu
Step 3. Select the **1-Sample Z** option
Step 4. When the 1-Sample Z dialog box appears:
 Enter C1 in the **Variables** box
 Enter 90 in the **Confidence interval Level** box
 Enter 7.77 in the **Sigma** box
 Select **OK**

Small-Sample Case

In Section 8.2 we showed the Minitab confidence interval for the population mean in the Scheer Industries problem. With the data from Table 8.4 entered in column C1, the following steps can be used to produce the 95% confidence interval shown in Figure 8.9.

Step 1. Select the **Stat** pull-down menu
Step 2. Select the **Basic Statistics** pull-down menu
Step 3. Select the **1-Sample t** option
Step 4. When the 1-Sample t dialog box appears:
 Enter C1 in the **Variables** box
 Enter 95 in the **Confidence interval Level** box
 Select **OK**

Appendix 8.2   CONFIDENCE INTERVAL ESTIMATION WITH EXCEL

Large-Sample Case

We will show how Excel can be used to develop confidence intervals for a population mean in the large-sample case by describing how to develop a 90% confidence interval for the population mean age in the Statewide Insurance Company study introduced in Section 8.1.

We will use the data set LifeIns, which contains the data in Table 8.2. The variable label Age appears in cell A1 and the 36 ages appear in cells A2 to A37.

Step 1. Select the **Tools** pull-down menu
Step 2. Select the **Data Analysis** option
Step 3. When the Data Analysis dialog box appears:
    Choose **Descriptive Statistics**
    Select **OK**
Step 4. When the Descriptive Statistics dialog box appears:
    Enter A1:A37 in the **Input Range** box
    Select **Labels in First Row**
    Select **Summary statistics**
    Select **Output Range** and enter B1 in the box
    Select **OK**
    The value of the standard error appears in cell C4
Step 5. Select cell D3
    Enter the cell formula $= 1.645*C4$

The sample mean, 39.5, appears in cell C3, and the margin of error, 2.13, appears in cell D3. With the sample mean of 39.5, the 90% confidence interval is obtained by subtracting 2.13 from 39.5 and adding 2.13 to 39.5. The confidence interval is 37.37 to 41.63. Note that 1.645 was used in the cell formula in step 5 because a 90% confidence interval was requested. In general, the user must enter the value of z corresponding to the desired confidence level.

Small-Sample Case

To illustrate how to develop a confidence interval for the small-sample case, we will compute a 95% confidence interval for the Scheer Industries study introduced in Section 8.2. We assume that the user has entered the label Time in cell A1 and the training time data from Table 8.4 into worksheet rows 2 to 16 of column A. The following steps can be used to produce the confidence interval.

Step 1. Select the **Tools** pull-down menu
Step 2. Choose the **Data Analysis** option
Step 3. When the Data Analysis dialog box appears:
    Choose **Descriptive Statistics**
    Select **OK**
Step 4. When the Descriptive Statistics dialog box appears:
    Enter A1:A16 in the **Input Range** box
    Select **Labels in First Row**
    Select **Summary statistics**
    Select **Confidence Level for Mean** and enter 95 in the box
    Select **Output Range** and enter B1 in the box
    Select **OK**

The sample mean, 53.87, appears in cell C3 and the margin of error, 3.78, appears in cell C16; note that the Excel label for the margin of error is Confidence Level (95.0%). With the sample mean of 53.87, the 95% confidence interval is obtained by subtracting 3.78 from 53.87 and adding 3.78 to 53.87. This confidence interval is 50.09 to 57.65.

9

HYPOTHESIS TESTING

CONTENTS

HARRIS CORPORATION*
Melbourne, Florida

Harris Corporation's RF Communications Division, in Melbourne, Florida, is a major manufacturer of point-to-point radio communications equipment. It is a horizontally integrated manufacturing company with a multiplant facility. Most of the Harris products require medium- to high-volume production operations, including printed circuit assembly, final product assembly, and testing.

Maintaining quality of components is a high priority at Harris Corporation. © Photo Disc, Inc.

One of the company's high-volume products has an assembly called an RF deck. Each RF deck consists of 16 electronic components soldered to a machined casting that forms the plated surface of the deck. During a manufacturing run, a problem developed in the soldering process; the flow of solder onto the deck did not meet the quality criteria established for the product. After considering a variety of factors that might affect the soldering process, an engineer made the preliminary determination that the soldering problem was most likely due to defective platings.

The engineer wondered whether the proportion of defective platings in the Harris inventory exceeded that set by the supplier's design specifications. With p indicating the proportion of defective platings in the Harris inventory and p_0 indicating the proportion of defective platings set by the supplier's design specifications, the following hypotheses were formulated.

$$H_0: p \leq p_0$$
$$H_a: p > p_0$$

H_0 indicates that the Harris inventory has a defective plating proportion less than or equal to that set by the design specifications. Such a proportion

would be judged acceptable, and the engineer would need to look for other causes of the soldering problem. However, H_a indicates that the Harris inventory has a defective plating proportion greater than that set by the design specifications. In that case, excessive defective platings may well be the cause of the soldering problem and action should be taken to determine why the defective proportion in inventory is so high.

Tests made on a sample of platings from the Harris inventory resulted in the rejection of H_0. The conclusion was that H_a was true and that the proportion of defective platings in inventory exceeded that set by the supplier's design specifications. Further investigation of the inventory area led to the conclusion that the underlying problem was shelf contamination during storage. By altering the storage environment, the engineer was able to solve the problem.

In this chapter you will learn how to formulate hypotheses about a population mean and a population proportion. Through the analysis of sample data, you will be able to determine whether a hypothesis should be rejected. Appropriate conclusions and actions will be demonstrated for testing research hypotheses, testing the validity of assumptions, and decision making.

*The authors are indebted to Richard A. Marshall of the Harris Corporation for providing this Statistics in Practice.

In Chapters 7 and 8 we showed how a sample could be used to develop point and interval estimates of population parameters. In this chapter we continue the discussion of statistical inference by showing how *hypothesis testing* can be used to determine whether a statement about the value of a population parameter should be rejected.

In hypothesis testing we begin by making a tentative assumption about a population parameter. This tentative assumption is called the *null hypothesis* and is denoted by H_0. We then define another hypothesis, called the *alternative hypothesis,* which is the opposite of what is stated in the null hypothesis. The alternative hypothesis is denoted by H_a. The hypothesis-testing procedure involves using data from a sample to test the two competing statements indicated by H_0 and H_a.

The purpose of this chapter is to show how hypothesis tests can be conducted about a population mean and a population proportion. We begin by providing examples that illustrate approaches to developing null and alternative hypotheses.

9.1   DEVELOPING NULL AND ALTERNATIVE HYPOTHESES

In some applications it may not be obvious how the null and alternative hypotheses should be formulated. Care must be taken to be sure the hypotheses are structured appropriately and that the hypothesis-testing conclusion provides the information the researcher or decision maker wants. Guidelines for establishing the null and alternative hypotheses will be given for three types of situations in which hypothesis-testing procedures are commonly employed.

Learning to formulate hypotheses correctly will take practice. Expect some initial confusion over the proper choice of hypotheses H_0 and H_a. The examples in this section show a variety of forms for H_0 and H_a, depending upon the application.

Testing Research Hypotheses

Consider a particular automobile model that currently attains an average fuel efficiency of 24 miles per gallon. A product-research group has developed a new engine specifically designed to increase the miles-per-gallon rating. To evaluate the new engine, several will be manufactured, installed in automobiles, and subjected to research-controlled driving tests. Note that the product-research group is looking for evidence to conclude that the new engine *increases* the mean miles-per-gallon rating. In this case, the research hypothesis is that the new engine will provide a mean miles-per-gallon rating exceeding 24; that is, $\mu > 24$. As a general guideline, a research hypothesis such as this should be formulated as the *alternative hypothesis*. Hence, the appropriate null and alternative hypotheses for the study are:

$$H_0: \mu \leq 24$$
$$H_a: \mu > 24$$

Hypothesis testing is proof by contradiction. Thus, the research hypothesis is the alternative hypothesis. The conclusion that the research hypothesis is true can be made if the sample data indicate that the null hypothesis is rejected.

If the sample results indicate that H_0 cannot be rejected, researchers cannot conclude that the new engine is better. Perhaps more research and subsequent testing should be conducted. However, if the sample results indicate that H_0 can be rejected, researchers can make the inference that $H_a: \mu > 24$ is true. With this conclusion, the researchers have the statistical support necessary to state that the new engine increases the mean number of miles per gallon. Action to begin production with the new engine may be undertaken.

In research studies such as these, the null and alternative hypotheses should be formulated so that the rejection of H_0 supports the conclusion and action being sought. In such cases, the research hypothesis should be expressed as the alternative hypothesis.

Testing the Validity of a Claim

As an illustration of testing the validity of a claim, consider the situation of a manufacturer of soft drinks who states that two-liter containers of its products have an average of at least 67.6 fluid ounces. A sample of two-liter containers will be selected, and the contents will be measured to test the manufacturer's claim. In this type of hypothesis-testing situation, we generally begin by assuming that the manufacturer's claim is true. Using this approach for the soft-drink example, we would state the null and alternative hypotheses as follows.

$$H_0: \mu \geq 67.6$$
$$H_a: \mu < 67.6$$

If the sample results indicate H_0 cannot be rejected, the manufacturer's claim cannot be challenged. However, if the sample results indicate H_0 can be rejected, the inference will be made that $H_a: \mu < 67.6$ is true. With the conclusion, statistical evidence indicates that the manufacturer's claim is incorrect and that the soft-drink containers are being filled with a mean less than the claimed 67.6 ounces. Appropriate action against the manufacturer may be considered.

A manufacturer's claim is usually given the benefit of the doubt and stated as the null hypothesis. The conclusion that the claim is false can be made if the sample data indicate that the null hypothesis is rejected.

In any situation that involves testing the validity of a product claim, the null hypothesis is generally based on the assumption that the claim is true. The alternative hypothesis is then formulated so that rejection of H_0 will provide statistical evidence that the stated assumption is incorrect. Action to correct the claim should be considered whenever H_0 is rejected.

Testing in Decision-Making Situations

In testing research hypotheses or testing the validity of a claim, action is taken if H_0 is rejected. In many instances, however, action must be taken both when H_0 cannot be rejected and when H_0 can be rejected. In general, this type of situation occurs when a decision maker must choose between two courses of action, one associated with the null hypothesis and another associated with the alternative hypothesis. For example, on the basis of a sample of parts from a shipment that has just been received, a quality-control inspector must decide whether to accept the entire shipment or to return the shipment to the supplier because it does not meet specifications. Assume that specifications for a particular part state that a mean length of two inches is desired. If the mean is greater or less than two inches, the parts will cause quality problems in the assembly operation. In this case, the null and alternative hypotheses would be formulated as follows.

$$H_0: \mu = 2$$
$$H_a: \mu \neq 2$$

If the sample results indicate H_0 cannot be rejected, the quality-control inspector will have no reason to doubt that the shipment meets specifications, and the shipment will be accepted. However, if the sample results indicate H_0 should be rejected, the conclusion will be that the parts do not meet specifications. In this case, the quality-control inspector will have sufficient evidence to return the shipment to the supplier. Thus, we see that for these types of situations, action is taken both when H_0 cannot be rejected and when H_0 can be rejected.

Summary of Forms for Null and Alternative Hypotheses

Let μ_0 denote the specific numerical value being considered in the null and alternative hypotheses. In general, a hypothesis test about the values of a population mean μ must take one of the following three forms.

The three possible forms of hypotheses H_0 and H_a are shown here. Note that the equality *always* appears in the null hypothesis H_0. Focusing on what you want to prove and placing it in the alternative hypothesis H_a will help select the proper form of the hypotheses for a particular application.

$$H_0: \mu \geq \mu_0 \qquad H_0: \mu \leq \mu_0 \qquad H_0: \mu = \mu_0$$
$$H_a: \mu < \mu_0 \qquad H_a: \mu > \mu_0 \qquad H_a: \mu \neq \mu_0$$

In many situations, the choice of H_0 and H_a is not obvious and judgment is necessary to select the proper form. However, as the preceding forms show, the equality part of the expression (either $\geq$, $\leq$, or $=$) *always* appears in the null hypothesis. In selecting the proper form of H_0 and H_a, keep in mind that the alternative hypothesis is what the test is attempting to establish. Hence, asking whether the user is looking for evidence to support $\mu < \mu_0$, $\mu > \mu_0$, or $\mu \neq \mu_0$ will help determine H_a. The following exercises are designed to provide practice in choosing the proper form for a hypothesis test.

EXERCISES

1. The manager of the Danvers-Hilton Resort Hotel has stated that the mean amount spent by guests for a weekend is $400 or less. A member of the hotel's accounting staff has noticed that the total charges for weekend guests have been increasing in recent months. The accountant will use a sample of weekend guest bills to test the manager's claim.
   a. Which form of the hypotheses should be used to test the manager's claim? Explain.

   $$H_0: \mu \geq 400 \qquad H_0: \mu \leq 400 \qquad H_0: \mu = 400$$
   $$H_a: \mu < 400 \qquad H_a: \mu > 400 \qquad H_a: \mu \neq 400$$

   b. What conclusion is appropriate when H_0 cannot be rejected?
   c. What conclusion is appropriate when H_0 can be rejected?

SELF TEST

2. The manager of an automobile dealership is considering a new bonus plan designed to increase sales volume. Currently, the mean sales volume is 14 automobiles per month. The manager wants to conduct a research study to see whether the new bonus plan increases sales volume. To collect data on the plan, a sample of sales personnel will be allowed to sell under the new bonus plan for a one-month period.
   a. Develop the null and alternative hypotheses that are most appropriate for this research situation.
   b. Comment on the conclusion when H_0 cannot be rejected.
   c. Comment on the conclusion when H_0 can be rejected.

3. A production-line operation is designed to put 32 ounces of laundry detergent in each carton. A sample of cartons is periodically selected and weighed to determine whether underfilling or overfilling is occurring. If the sample data lead to a conclusion of underfilling or overfilling, the production line will be shut down and adjusted to obtain proper filling.
   a. Formulate the null and alternative hypotheses that will help in deciding whether to shut down and adjust the production line.
   b. Comment on the conclusion and the decision when H_0 cannot be rejected.
   c. Comment on the conclusion and the decision when H_0 can be rejected.

4. Because of high production changeover time and costs, a director of manufacturing must convince management that a proposed manufacturing method reduces costs before the new method can be implemented. The current production method operates with a mean cost of $220 per hour. A research study is to be conducted in which the cost of the new method will be measured over a sample production period.
   a. Develop the null and alternative hypotheses that are most appropriate for this study.
   b. Comment on the conclusion when H_0 cannot be rejected.
   c. Comment on the conclusion when H_0 can be rejected.

..../ /...........

9.2   TYPE I AND TYPE II ERRORS

The null and alternative hypotheses are competing statements about a population parameter. Either the null hypothesis H_0 is true or the alternative hypothesis H_a is true, but not both. Ideally the hypothesis testing procedure should lead to the acceptance of H_0 when H_0 is true and the rejection of H_0 when H_a is true. Unfortunately, this ideal result is not always possible. Because hypothesis tests are based on sample information, we must allow for the possibility of errors. Table 9.1 illustrates the two kinds of errors that can be made in hypothesis testing.

The first row of Table 9.1 shows what can happen when the conclusion is to accept H_0. Because either H_0 is true or H_a is true, if H_0 is true and the conclusion is to accept H_0, this conclusion is correct. However if H_a is true and the conclusion is to accept H_0, we have made a *Type II error;* that is, we have accepted H_0 when it is false. The second row of Table 9.1 shows what can happen when the conclusion is to reject H_0. In this case, if H_0 is true, we have made a *Type I error;* that is, we have rejected H_0 when it is true. However, if H_a is true, and the conclusion is to reject H_0, this conclusion is correct.

Although we cannot eliminate the possibility of errors in hypothesis testing, we can consider the probability of their occurrence. Using common statistical notation, we denote the probabilities of making the two errors as follows.

$$\alpha = \text{the probability of making a Type I error}$$
$$\beta = \text{the probability of making a Type II error}$$

Recall the hypothesis-testing illustration discussed in Section 9.1 in which an automobile product-research group had developed a new engine designed to increase the miles-per-gallon rating of a particular automobile. With the current engine obtaining an average of 24 miles per gallon, the hypothesis test was formulated as follows.

$$H_0: \mu \leq 24$$
$$H_a: \mu > 24$$

The alternative hypothesis, $H_a: \mu > 24$, indicates that the researchers are looking for sample evidence that will support the conclusion that the mean miles per gallon is greater than 24.

Table 9.1	ERRORS AND CORRECT CONCLUSIONS IN HYPOTHESIS TESTING	

| | | **Population Condition** | |
		H_0 **True**	H_a **True**
Conclusion	**Accept H_0**	Correct Conclusion	Type II Error
	Reject H_0	Type I Error	Correct Conclusion

In this application, the Type I error of rejecting H_0 when it is true corresponds to the researchers claiming that the new engine improves the miles per gallon rating ($\mu > 24$) when in fact the new engine is not any better than the current engine. In contrast, the Type II error of accepting H_0 when it is false corresponds to the researchers concluding that the new engine is not any better than the current engine ($\mu \leq 24$) when in fact the new engine improves miles-per-gallon performance.

In practice, the person conducting the hypothesis test specifies the maximum allowable probability of making a Type I error, called the *level of significance* for the test. Common choices for the level of significance are .05 and .01. Referring to the second row of Table 9.1, note that the conclusion to *reject H_0* indicates that either a Type I error or a correct conclusion has been made. Thus, if the probability of making a type I error is controlled for by selecting a small value for the level of significance, we have a high degree of confidence that the conclusion to reject H_0 is correct. In such cases, we have statistical support for concluding that H_0 is false and H_a is true. Any action suggested by the alternative hypothesis H_a is appropriate.

Although most applications of hypothesis testing control for the probability of making a Type I error, they do not always control for the probability of making a Type II error. Hence, if we decide to accept H_0, we cannot determine how confident we can be with that decision. Because of the uncertainty associated with making a Type II error, statisticians often recommend that we use the statement "do not reject H_0" instead of "accept H_0." Using the statement "do not reject H_0" carries the recommendation to withhold both judgment and action. In effect, by never directly accepting H_0, the statistician avoids the risk of making a Type II error. Whenever the probability of making a Type II error has not been determined and controlled, we will not make the conclusion to accept H_0. In such cases, only two conclusions are possible: *do not reject H_0* or *reject H_0*.

> If the sample data are consistent with the null hypothesis H_0, we will follow the practice of concluding "*do not reject H_0.*" This conclusion is preferred over "*accept H_0*" because the conclusion to accept H_0 puts us at risk of making a Type II error.

N O T E S *and Comments*	Many applications of hypothesis testing have a decision-making goal. The conclusion *reject H_0* provides the statistical support to conclude that H_a is true and take whatever action is appropriate. The statement "do not reject H_0," although inconclusive, often forces managers to behave as though H_0 is true. In this case, managers need to be aware of the fact that such behavior may result in a Type II error.

· / / · · · · · · · · · · · ·

EXERCISES

SELF TEST

5. Americans spend an average of 8.6 minutes per day reading newspapers (*USA Today,* April 10, 1995). A researcher believes that individuals in management positions spend more than the national average time per day reading newspapers. A sample of individuals in management positions will be selected by the researcher. Data on newspaper-reading times will be used to test the following null and alternative hypotheses.

$$H_0: \mu \leq 8.6$$
$$H_a: \mu > 8.6$$

    a. What is the Type I error in this situation? What are the consequences of making this error?
    b. What is the Type II error in this situation? What are the consequences of making this error?

6. The label on a three-quart container of orange juice indicates that the orange juice contains an average of one gram of fat or less. Answer the following questions for a hypothesis test that could be used to test the claim on the label.
   a. Develop the appropriate null and alternative hypotheses.
   b. What is the Type I error in this situation? What are the consequences of making this error?
   c. What is the Type II error in this situation? What are the consequences of making this error?

7. Carpetland salespersons have had sales averaging $8000 per week. Steve Contois, the firm's vice president, has proposed a compensation plan with new selling incentives. Steve hopes that the results of a trial selling period will enable him to conclude that the compensation plan increases the mean sales per salesperson.
   a. Develop the appropriate null and alternative hypotheses.
   b. What is the Type I error in this situation? What are the consequences of making this error?
   c. What is the Type II error in this situation? What are the consequences of making this error?

8. Suppose a new production method will be implemented if a hypothesis test supports the conclusion that the new method reduces the mean operating cost per hour.
   a. State the appropriate null and alternative hypotheses if the mean cost for the current production method is $220 per hour.
   b. What is the Type I error in this situation? What are the consequences of making this error?
   c. What is the Type II error in this situation? What are the consequences of making this error?

9.3 ONE-TAILED TESTS ABOUT A POPULATION MEAN: LARGE-SAMPLE CASE

The Federal Trade Commission (FTC) periodically conducts studies designed to test the claims manufacturers make about their products. For example, the label on a large can of Hilltop Coffee states that the can contains at least three pounds of coffee. Suppose we want to check this claim by using hypothesis testing.

The first step is to develop the null and alternative hypotheses. We begin by tentatively assuming that the manufacturer's claim is correct. If the population of coffee cans has a mean weight of three or more pounds per can, Hilltop's claim about its product is correct. However, if the population of coffee cans has a mean weight less than three pounds per can, Hilltop's claim is incorrect.

With μ denoting the mean weight of cans for the population, the null and the alternative hypotheses are as follows.

$$H_0: \mu \geq 3$$
$$H_a: \mu < 3$$

If the sample data indicate that H_0 cannot be rejected, the statistical evidence does not support the conclusion that a label violation has occurred. Hence, no action would be taken against Hilltop. However, if sample data indicate that H_0 can be rejected, we will conclude that the alternative hypothesis, $H_a: \mu < 3$, is true. In that case, a conclusion of underfilling and a charge of a label violation would be appropriate.

Suppose a random sample of 36 cans of coffee is selected. Note that if the mean filling weight for the sample of 36 cans is less than three pounds, the sample results will begin to cast doubt on the null hypothesis $H_0: \mu \geq 3$. But how much less than three pounds must $\bar{x}$ be before we would be willing to risk making a Type I error and falsely accuse the company of a label violation?

To answer this question, let us tentatively assume that the null hypothesis is true with $\mu = 3$. From the study of sampling distributions in Chapter 7, we know that whenever the sample size is large ($n \geq 30$), the sampling distribution of $\bar{x}$ can be approximated by a normal probability distribution. Figure 9.1 shows the sampling distribution of $\bar{x}$ when the null hypothesis is true at $\mu = 3$.

The value of $z = (\bar{x} - 3)/\sigma_{\bar{x}}$ is the number of standard deviations $\bar{x}$ is from $\mu = 3$. For hypothesis tests about a population mean, we will use z as a *test statistic* to determine whether $\bar{x}$ deviates enough from $\mu = 3$ to justify rejecting the null hypothesis. Note that a value of $z = -1$ means that $\bar{x}$ is 1 standard deviation below $\mu = 3$, a value of $z = -2$ means that $\bar{x}$ is 2 standard deviations below $\mu = 3$, and so on. Obtaining a value of $z < -3$ is unlikely if the null hypothesis is true. The key question is: How small must the test statistic z be before we have enough evidence to reject the null hypothesis?

Figure 9.2 shows that the probability of observing a value for $\bar{x}$ of more than 1.645 standard deviations below the mean of $\mu = 3$ is .05. Hence, if we were to reject the null hypothesis whenever the value of the test statistic $z = (\bar{x} - 3)/\sigma_{\bar{x}}$ is less than -1.645, the probability of making a Type I error would be .05. If the FTC considered .05 to be an acceptable probability of making a Type I error, we would reject the null hypothesis whenever the test statistic indicates that the sample mean is more than 1.645 standard deviations below $\mu = 3$. Thus, we would reject H_0 if $z < -1.645$.

The methodology of hypothesis testing requires that we specify the maximum allowable probability of a Type I error. As noted in the preceding section, this maximum probability is called the level of significance for the test; it is denoted by α, and it represents the probability of making a Type I error when the null hypothesis is true as an equality. The manager must specify the level of significance. If the cost of making a Type I error is high, a small value should be chosen for the level of significance. If the cost is not high, a larger value may be appropriate.

In the Hilltop Coffee study, the director of the FTC's testing program has made the following statement: "If the company is meeting its weight specifications exactly ($\mu = 3$), I would like a 99% chance of not taking any action against the company. While I do not want

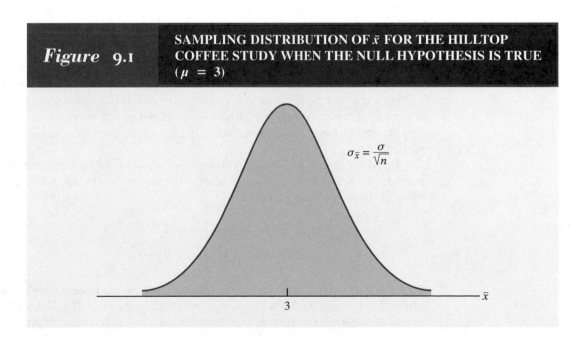

Figure 9.1   SAMPLING DISTRIBUTION OF $\bar{x}$ FOR THE HILLTOP COFFEE STUDY WHEN THE NULL HYPOTHESIS IS TRUE ($\mu = 3$)

$$\sigma_{\bar{x}} = \frac{\sigma}{\sqrt{n}}$$

3

$\bar{x}$

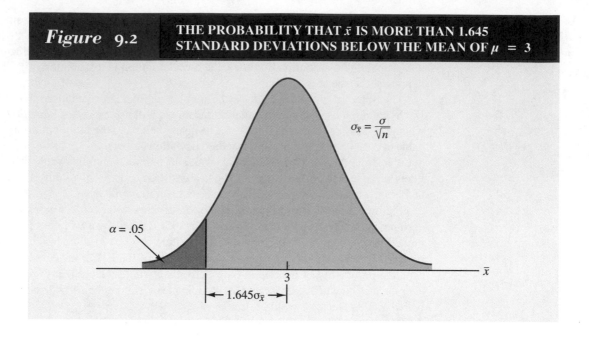

Figure **9.2**   **THE PROBABILITY THAT $\bar{x}$ IS MORE THAN 1.645 STANDARD DEVIATIONS BELOW THE MEAN OF $\mu = 3$**

to accuse the company wrongly of underfilling its product, I am willing to risk a 1% chance of making this error."

From the director's statement, the maximum probability of a Type I error is .01. Hence, the level of significance for the hypothesis test is $\alpha = .01$. Figure 9.3 shows the sampling distributions of both $\bar{x}$ and $z = (\bar{x} - \mu)/\sigma_{\bar{x}}$ for the Hilltop Coffee example. Note that when the null hypothesis is true at $\mu = 3$, the probability is .01 that $\bar{x}$ is more than 2.33 standard deviations below the mean of 3. Therefore, we establish the following rejection rule.

$$\text{Reject } H_0 \text{ if } z = \frac{\bar{x} - \mu}{\sigma_{\bar{x}}} < -2.33$$

If the value of $\bar{x}$ is such that the test statistic z is in the rejection region, we reject H_0 and conclude that H_a is true. If the value of $\bar{x}$ is such that the test statistic z is not in the rejection region, we cannot reject H_0. Note that the rejection region in Figure 9.3 is in only one tail of the sampling distribution. In such cases, we say the test is a *one-tailed* hypothesis test.

Suppose a sample of 36 cans provides a mean of $\bar{x} = 2.92$ pounds and we know from previous studies that the population standard deviation is $\sigma = .18$. With $\sigma_{\bar{x}} = \sigma/\sqrt{n}$, the value of the test statistic is given by

$$z = \frac{\bar{x} - 3}{\sigma/\sqrt{n}} = \frac{2.92 - 3}{.18/\sqrt{36}} = -2.67$$

Figure 9.4 shows that the value of the test statistic is in the rejection region. We are now justified in concluding that $\mu < 3$ at a .01 level of significance. The director has statistical justification for taking action against Hilltop Coffee for underfilling its product.

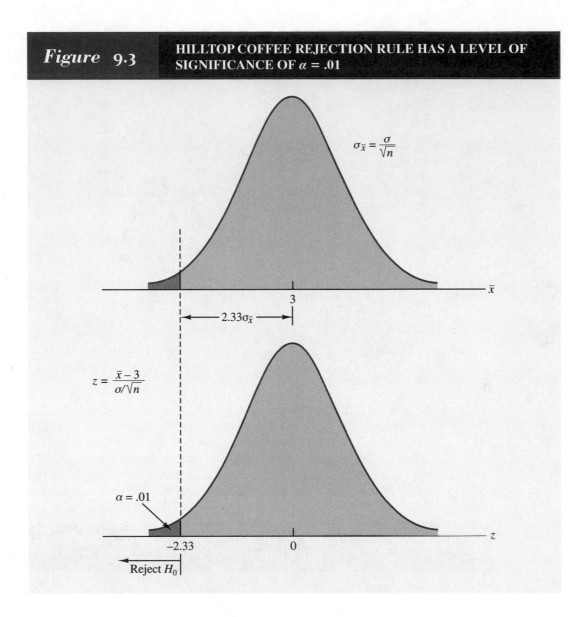

Figure 9.3   HILLTOP COFFEE REJECTION RULE HAS A LEVEL OF SIGNIFICANCE OF $\alpha = .01$

Suppose the sample of 36 cans had provided a sample mean of $\bar{x} = 2.97$. In this case, the value of the test statistic would be

$$z = \frac{\bar{x} - 3}{\sigma/\sqrt{n}} = \frac{2.97 - 3}{.18/\sqrt{36}} = -1.00$$

Because $z = -1.00$ is greater than -2.33, the value of the test statistic is not in the rejection region (see Figure 9.5). Hence we cannot reject the null hypothesis. Thus, with a sample mean of $\bar{x} = 2.97$, no statistical justification is provided for taking action against Hilltop Coffee.

The value $z = -2.33$ establishes the boundary of the rejection region and is called the *critical value*. In establishing the critical value, we tentatively assume the null hypothesis

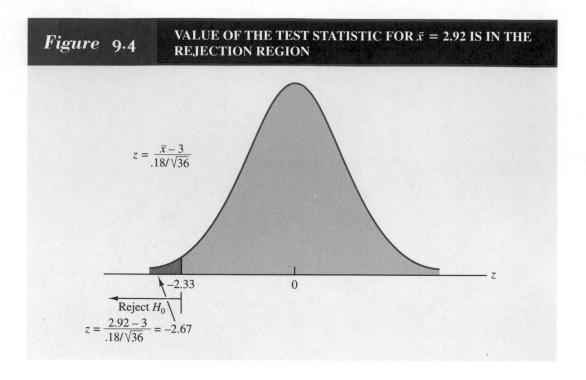

Figure 9.4   VALUE OF THE TEST STATISTIC FOR $\bar{x} = 2.92$ IS IN THE REJECTION REGION

$$z = \frac{\bar{x} - 3}{.18/\sqrt{36}}$$

-2.33 0 z

Reject H_0

$$z = \frac{2.92 - 3}{.18/\sqrt{36}} = -2.67$$

is true. For Hilltop Coffee, the null hypothesis is true whenever $\mu \geq 3$; however, we considered only the case when $\mu = 3$. What about the case when $\mu > 3$? If $\mu > 3$, the probability of making a Type I error will be less than it is when $\mu = 3$; that is, we are even less likely to find a value of the test statistic that is in the rejection region. Because the objective of the hypothesis-testing procedure is to control for the maximum probability of making a Type I error, the critical value for the test is established by assuming $\mu = 3$.

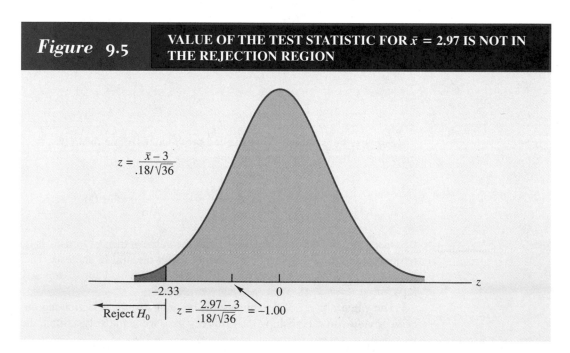

Figure 9.5   VALUE OF THE TEST STATISTIC FOR $\bar{x} = 2.97$ IS NOT IN THE REJECTION REGION

$$z = \frac{\bar{x} - 3}{.18/\sqrt{36}}$$

-2.33 0 z

Reject H_0

$$z = \frac{2.97 - 3}{.18/\sqrt{36}} = -1.00$$

Summary: One-Tailed Tests about a Population Mean

Let us generalize the hypothesis-testing procedure for one-tailed tests about a population mean. We consider the large-sample case ($n \geq 30$) in which the central limit theorem enables us to assume that the sampling distribution $\bar{x}$ can be approximated by a normal probability distribution. In the large-sample case with σ unknown, we simply substitute the sample standard deviation s for σ in computing the test statistic. The general form of a lower-tail test, where μ_0 is a stated value for the population mean, follows.

Large-Sample ($n \geq 30$) Hypothesis Test about a Population Mean for a One-Tailed Test of the Form

$$H_0: \mu \geq \mu_0$$
$$H_a: \mu < \mu_0$$

Test Statistic: σ Known

In most applications the sample standard deviation s is used in the computation of the test statistic because the population standard deviation σ is unknown.

$$z = \frac{\bar{x} - \mu_0}{\sigma/\sqrt{n}} \qquad (9.1)$$

Test Statistic: σ Unknown

$$z = \frac{\bar{x} - \mu_0}{s/\sqrt{n}}$$

Rejection Rule at a Level of Significance of α

$$\text{Reject } H_0 \text{ if } z < -z_\alpha$$

A second form of the one-tailed test rejects the null hypothesis when the test statistic is in the upper tail of the sampling distribution. This one-tailed test and rejection rule are summarized next (see Figure 9.6). Again, we are considering the large-sample case; when σ is unknown, s can be substituted for σ in the computation of the test statistic z.

Large-Sample ($n \geq 30$) Hypothesis Test about a Population Mean for a One-Tailed Test of the Form

$$H_0: \mu \leq \mu_0$$
$$H_a: \mu > \mu_0$$

Test Statistic: σ Known

$$z = \frac{\bar{x} - \mu_0}{\sigma/\sqrt{n}} \qquad (9.2)$$

Test Statistic: σ Unknown

$$z = \frac{\bar{x} - \mu_0}{s/\sqrt{n}}$$

Rejection Rule at a Level of Significance of α

$$\text{Reject } H_0 \text{ if } z > z_\alpha$$

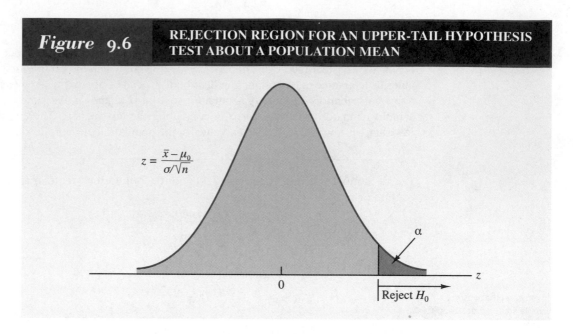

Figure 9.6   REJECTION REGION FOR AN UPPER-TAIL HYPOTHESIS TEST ABOUT A POPULATION MEAN

$$z = \frac{\bar{x} - \mu_0}{\sigma/\sqrt{n}}$$

Use of p-Values

Another approach that can be used to decide whether to reject H_0 is based on a probability called a *p-value*. If we assume that the null hypothesis is true, the p-value is the probability of obtaining a sample result that is at least as unlikely as what is observed. In the Hilltop Coffee example, the rejection region is in the lower tail; therefore the p-value is the probability of observing a sample mean less than or equal to what is observed. The p-value is often called the observed level of significance.

Let us compute the p-value associated with the sample mean $\bar{x} = 2.92$ in the Hilltop Coffee example. The p-value in this case is the probability of obtaining a value for the sample mean that is less than or equal to the observed value of $\bar{x} = 2.92$, given the hypothesized value for the population mean of $\mu = 3$. Previously we showed that the test statistic $z = -2.67$ corresponded to $\bar{x} = 2.92$. Thus, as shown in Figure 9.7, the p-value is the area in the tail of the standard normal probability distribution for $z = -2.67$. Using the standard normal probability distribution table, we find that the area between the mean and $z = -2.67$ is .4962. Hence, there is a $.5000 - .4962 = .0038$ probability of obtaining a sample mean that is less than or equal to the observed $\bar{x} = 2.92$. The p-value is therefore .0038. This p-value shows a small probability of obtaining a sample mean as small as $\bar{x} = 2.92$ when sampling from a population with $\mu = 3$.

The p-value can be used to make the decision in a hypothesis test by noting that if the p-value is *less than the level of significance* α, the value of the test statistic is in the rejection region. Similarly, if the p-value is *greater than or equal to* α, the value of the test statistic is not in the rejection region. For the Hilltop Coffee example, the fact that the p-value of .0038 is less than the level of significance, $\alpha = .01$, indicates that the null hypothesis should be rejected. Given the level of significance α, the decision of whether to reject H_0 can be made as follows.

The p-value for a one-tailed test is always the area from the test statistic toward the rejection tail of the distribution. With a lower one-tailed test and a test statistic value of z greater than zero, the p-value or area toward the lower-tail rejection region will be greater than .50, an indication H_0 cannot be rejected.

---

p-Value Criterion for Hypothesis Testing

$$\text{Reject } H_0 \text{ if } p\text{-value} < \alpha$$

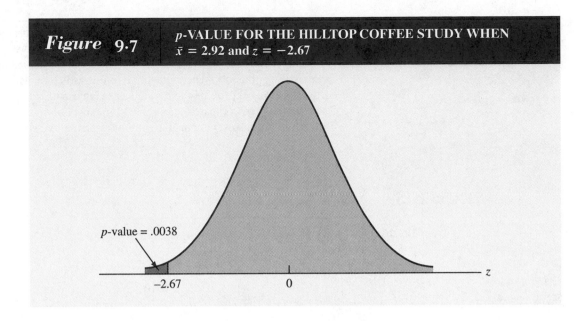

Figure 9.7   *p*-VALUE FOR THE HILLTOP COFFEE STUDY WHEN $\bar{x} = 2.92$ and $z = -2.67$

p-value = .0038

-2.67 0   *z*

The *p*-value and the corresponding test statistic will always provide the same hypothesis-testing conclusion. When the rejection region is in the lower tail of the sampling distribution, the *p*-value is the area under the curve less than or equal to the test statistic. When the rejection region is in the upper tail of the sampling distribution, the *p*-value is the area under the curve greater than or equal to the test statistic. A small *p*-value indicates a sample result that is unusual given the assumption that H_0 is true. Small *p*-values lead to rejection of H_0, whereas large *p*-values indicate that the null hypothesis cannot be rejected.

Steps of Hypothesis Testing

In conducting the Hilltop Coffee hypothesis test, we carried out the steps that are required for any hypothesis-testing procedure. A summary of the steps that can be applied to any hypothesis test follows.

Steps of Hypothesis Testing

1. Determine the null and alternative hypotheses that are appropriate for the application.
2. Select the test statistic that will be used to decide whether to reject the null hypothesis.
3. Specify the level of significance α for the test.
4. Use the level of significance to develop the rejection rule that indicates the values of the test statistic that will lead to the rejection of H_0.
5. Collect the sample data and compute the value of the test statistic.
6. a. Compare the value of the test statistic to the critical value(s) specified in the rejection rule to determine whether H_0 should be rejected.

   or

   b. Compute the *p*-value based on the test statistic in step 5. Use the *p*-value to determine whether H_0 should be rejected.

N O T E S *and Comments*	The *p*-value, the observed level of significance, is a measure of the like- lihood of the sample results when the null hypothesis is assumed to be true. The smaller the *p*-value, the less likely it is that the sample results came from a population where the null hypothesis is true. Most statistical software packages provide the *p*-value associated with a hypothesis test. The user can then compare the *p*-value to the level of significance α and draw a hypothesis test conclusion without referring to a statistical table.

EXERCISES

Methods

9. Consider the following hypothesis test.

$$H_0: \mu \geq 10$$
$$H_a: \mu < 10$$

A sample with $n = 50$ provides a sample mean of 9.46 and sample standard deviation of 2.
   a. At $\alpha = .05$, what is the critical value for z? What is the rejection rule?
   b. Compute the value of the test statistic z. What is your conclusion?

SELF TEST

10. Consider the following hypothesis test.

$$H_0: \mu \leq 15$$
$$H_a: \mu > 15$$

A sample of 40 provides a sample mean of 16.5 and sample standard deviation of 7.
   a. At $\alpha = .02$, what is the critical value for z, and what is the rejection rule?
   b. Compute the value of the test statistic z.
   c. What is the p-value?
   d. What is your conclusion?

11. Consider the following hypothesis test.

$$H_0: \mu \geq 25$$
$$H_a: \mu < 25$$

A sample of 100 is used, and the population standard deviation is 12. Provide the value of the test statistic z and your conclusion for each of the following sample results. Use $\alpha = .05$.
   a. $\bar{x} = 22.0$
   b. $\bar{x} = 24.0$
   c. $\bar{x} = 23.5$
   d. $\bar{x} = 22.8$

12. Consider the following hypothesis test.

$$H_0: \mu \leq 5$$
$$H_a: \mu > 5$$

Assume the following test statistics. Compute the corresponding p-values and make the appro- priate conclusions based on $\alpha = .05$.

a. $z = 1.82$
b. $z = .45$
c. $z = 1.50$
d. $z = 3.30$
e. $z = -1.00$

Applications

SELF TEST

13. Individuals filing 1994 federal income tax returns prior to March 31, 1995, had an average refund of $1056 (*USA Today,* April 5, 1995). Consider the population of "last-minute" filers who mail their returns during the last five days of the income tax period (typically April 10 to April 15).
    a. A researcher suggests that one of the reasons individuals wait until the last five days to file their returns is that on average those individuals have a lower refund than early filers. Develop appropriate hypotheses such that rejection of H_0 will support the researcher's contention.
    b. For a sample of 400 individuals who filed a return between April 10 and April 15, the sample mean refund was $910 and the sample standard deviation was $1600. At $\alpha = .05$, what is your conclusion?
    c. What is the p-value for the test?

14. A Nielsen survey provided the estimate that the mean number of hours of television viewing per household is 7.25 hours per day (*New York Daily News,* November 2, 1997). Assume that the Nielsen survey involved 200 households and that the sample standard deviation was 2.5 hours per day. Ten years ago the population mean number of hours of television viewing per household was reported to be 6.70 hours. Letting μ = the population mean number of hours of television viewing per household in 1997, test the hypotheses $H_0: \mu \leq 6.70$ and $H_a: \mu > 6.70$. Use $\alpha = .01$. What is you conclusion about any change in television viewing time?

15. According to the National Automobile Dealers Association, the mean price for used cars is $10,192 (*USA Today,* April 12, 1995). A manager of a Kansas City used car dealership reviewed a sample of 100 recent used car sales at the dealership. The sample mean price was $9300 and the sample standard deviation was $4500. Letting μ denote the population mean price for used cars at the Kansas City dealership, test $H_0: \mu \geq 10,192$ and $H_a: \mu < 10,192$ at a .05 level of significance.
    a. What is the hypothesis-testing conclusion?
    b. What is the p-value?
    c. What information does the hypothesis test result provide for the manager of the Kansas City dealership? What follow-up action might the manager want to consider?

16. New tires manufactured by a company in Findlay, Ohio, are designed to provide a mean of at least 28,000 miles. Tests with 30 randomly selected tires showed a sample mean of 27,500 miles and a sample standard deviation of 1000 miles. Using a .05 level of significance, test whether there is sufficient evidence to reject the claim of a mean of at least 28,000 miles. What is the p-value?

17. A company currently pays its production employees a mean wage of $15.00 per hour. The company is planning to build a new factory and is considering several locations. The availability of labor at a rate less than $15.00 per hour is a major factor in the location decision. For one location, a sample of 40 workers showed a current mean hourly wage of $\bar{x} = \$14.00$ and a sample standard deviation of $s = \$2.40$.
    a. At a .10 level of significance, do the sample data indicate that the location has a mean wage rate significantly below the $15.00 per hour rate?
    b. What is the p-value?

18. A new diet program claims that participants will lose on average at least eight pounds during the first week of the program. A random sample of 40 people participating in the program showed a sample mean weight loss of seven pounds. The sample standard deviation was 3.2 pounds.
    a. What is the rejection rule with $\alpha = .05$?
    b. What is your conclusion about the claim made by the diet program?
    c. What is the p-value?

9.4   TWO-TAILED TESTS ABOUT A POPULATION MEAN: LARGE-SAMPLE CASE

Two-tailed hypothesis tests differ from one-tailed tests in that the rejection region is placed in both the lower and the upper tails of the sampling distribution. Let us introduce an example to show how and why two-tailed tests are conducted.

The United States Golf Association (USGA) has established rules that manufacturers of golf equipment must meet if their products are to be acceptable for use in USGA events. One of the rules for the manufacture of golf balls states: "A brand of golf ball, when tested on apparatus approved by the USGA on the outdoor range at the USGA Headquarters ... shall not cover an average distance in carry and roll exceeding 280 yards." Suppose Superflight, Inc., has recently developed a high-technology manufacturing method that can produce golf balls having an average distance in carry and roll of 280 yards.

Superflight realizes, however, that if the new manufacturing process goes out of adjustment, the process may produce balls for which the average distance is less than or more than 280 yards. In the former case, sales may decline as a result of marketing an inferior product, and in the latter case the golf balls may be rejected by the USGA. Superflight's managers therefore have instituted a quality-control program to monitor the new manufacturing process.

As part of the quality-control program, an inspector periodically selects a sample of golf balls from the production line and subjects them to tests that are equivalent to those performed by the USGA. Having no reason to doubt that the manufacturing process is functioning correctly, we establish the following null and alternative hypotheses.

$$H_0: \mu = 280$$
$$H_a: \mu \neq 280$$

As usual, we make the tentative assumption that the null hypothesis is true. A rejection region must be established for the test statistic z. We want to reject the claim that $\mu = 280$ when the z value indicates that the population mean is either less than or greater than 280 yards. Thus, H_0 should be rejected for values of the test statistic in either the lower tail or the upper tail of the sampling distribution. As a result, the test is called a *two-tailed* hypothesis test.

Following the hypothesis-testing procedure developed in the previous sections, we specify a level of significance by determining a maximum allowable probability of making a Type I error. Suppose we choose $\alpha = .05$, which means a .05 probability of concluding that the mean distance is not 280 yards when in fact it is. The test statistic is

$$z = \frac{\bar{x} - \mu_0}{\sigma/\sqrt{n}}$$

Figure 9.8 shows the sampling distribution of z with the two-tailed rejection region for $\alpha = .05$. With two-tailed hypothesis tests, we will always determine the rejection region by placing an area or probability of $\alpha/2$ in each tail of the distribution. The values of z that provide an area of .025 in each tail can be found from the standard normal probability distribution table. We see in Figure 9.8 that $-z_{.025} = -1.96$ identifies an area of .025 in the lower

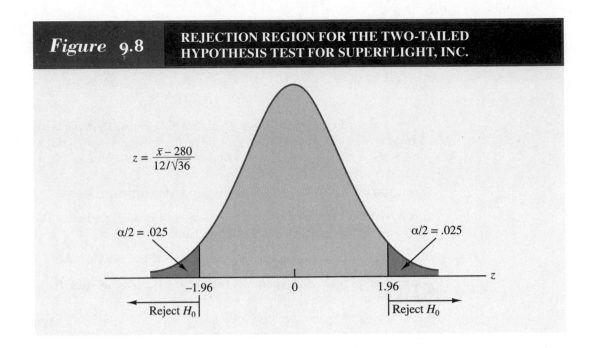

Figure 9.8 REJECTION REGION FOR THE TWO-TAILED HYPOTHESIS TEST FOR SUPERFLIGHT, INC.

$$z = \frac{\bar{x} - 280}{12/\sqrt{36}}$$

$\alpha/2 = .025$

$\alpha/2 = .025$

$-1.96 \qquad 0 \qquad 1.96 \qquad z$

Reject H_0 Reject H_0

tail and $z_{.025} = +1.96$ identifies an area of .025 in the upper tail. Referring to Figure 9.8, we can establish the following rejection rule.

$$\text{Reject } H_0 \text{ if } z < -1.96 \text{ or if } z > 1.96$$

Suppose that a simple random sample of 36 golf balls provided the data in Table 9.2. For these data we obtained a sample mean of $\bar{x} = 278.5$ yards and a sample standard deviation of $s = 12$ yards. Using $\mu_0 = 280$ from the null hypothesis and the sample standard

Table 9.2 DISTANCE DATA FOR A SIMPLE RANDOM SAMPLE OF 36 SUPERFLIGHT GOLF BALLS

Ball	Yards	Ball	Yards	Ball	Yards
1	269	13	296	25	272
2	300	14	265	26	285
3	268	15	271	27	293
4	278	16	279	28	281
5	282	17	284	29	269
6	263	18	260	30	299
7	301	19	275	31	263
8	295	20	282	32	264
9	288	21	260	33	273
10	278	22	266	34	291
11	276	23	270	35	274
12	286	24	293	36	277

Distance

deviation of $s = 12$ as an estimate of the population standard deviation σ, the value of the test statistic is

$$z = \frac{\bar{x} - \mu_0}{\sigma/\sqrt{n}} = \frac{278.5 - 280}{12/\sqrt{36}} = -.75$$

According to the rejection rule, H_0 cannot be rejected. The sample results indicate that the quality-control manager has no reason to doubt the assumption that the manufacturing process is producing golf balls with a population mean distance of 280 yards.

Summary: Two-Tailed Tests about a Population Mean

Let μ_0 represent the value of the population mean in the hypotheses. The general form of the two-tailed hypothesis test about a population mean follows.

Large-Sample ($n \geq 30$) Hypothesis Test about a Population Mean for a Two-Tailed Test of the Form

$$H_0\colon \mu = \mu_0$$
$$H_a\colon \mu \neq \mu_0$$

Test Statistic: σ Known

$$z = \frac{\bar{x} - \mu_0}{\sigma/\sqrt{n}} \qquad\qquad (9.3)$$

Test Statistic: σ Unknown

$$z = \frac{\bar{x} - \mu_0}{s/\sqrt{n}}$$

Rejection Rule at a Level of Significance of α

$$\text{Reject } H_0 \text{ if } z < -z_{\alpha/2} \text{ or if } z > z_{\alpha/2}$$

---

p-Values for Two-Tailed Tests

Let us compute the p-value for the Superflight golf ball example. The sample mean of $\bar{x} = 278.5$ has a corresponding z value of $-.75$. The table for the standard normal probability distribution shows that the area between the mean and $z = -.75$ is .2734. Thus, the area in the lower tail is $.5000 - .2734 = .2266$. Looking at Figure 9.8, we see that the lower-tail portion of the rejection region has an area or probability of $\alpha/2 = .05/2 = .025$. Thus, with $.2266 > .025$, the test statistic is not in the rejection region, and the null hypothesis cannot be rejected.

One question remains: What value should we report as the p-value for the two-tailed test? At first glance, you may be inclined to say the p-value is .2266. If that is your choice, you will have to remember two different rules: one for the one-tailed test, which is to reject H_0 if the p-value $< \alpha$, and another for the two-tailed test, which is to reject H_0 if the p-value $< \alpha/2$. Alternatively, suppose we define the p-value for a two-tailed test as *double*

In a two-tailed test, the *p*-value is found by *doubling* the area in the tail. The doubling of the area is done so that the *p*-value can be compared directly to α and the same rejection rule can be maintained. Without the doubling of the area in the tail, a *p*-value rule based on the tail area of $\alpha/2$ would be needed in two-tailed hypothesis tests.

the area found in the tail of the distribution. Thus, for the Superflight example, we would define the *p*-value to be $2(.2266) = .4532$. The advantage of this definition of the *p*-value for a two-tailed test is that the *p*-value can be compared directly to the level of significance α. Hence, with $.4532 > .05$, we see that the null hypothesis cannot be rejected. By remembering that the *p*-value for a two-tailed test is simply double the area found in the tail of the distribution, the previous rule to reject H_0 if the *p*-value $< \alpha$ can be used for all hypothesis tests.

Minitab can be used to provide hypothesis test information for a population mean. The computer output for the Superflight hypothesis test is shown in Figure 9.9. The sample mean $\bar{x} = 278.5$, the test statistic $z = -.75$ and the *p*-value $= .45$ are computed automatically. The step-by-step procedure used to obtain the Minitab output is described in Appendix 9.1.

Relationship between Interval Estimation and Hypothesis Testing

In Chapter 8 we showed how to develop a confidence interval estimate of a population mean. In the large-sample case, the confidence interval estimate of a population mean corresponding to a $1 - \alpha$ confidence coefficient is given by

$$\bar{x} \pm z_{\alpha/2}\frac{\sigma}{\sqrt{n}} \tag{9.4}$$

when σ is known and

$$\bar{x} \pm z_{\alpha/2}\frac{s}{\sqrt{n}} \tag{9.5}$$

when σ is unknown.

Conducting a hypothesis test requires us first to make an assumption about the value of a population parameter. In the case of the population mean, the two-tailed hypothesis test has the form

$$H_0: \mu = \mu_0$$
$$H_a: \mu \neq \mu_0$$

where μ_0 is the hypothesized value for the population mean. Using the rejection rule provided by (9.3), we see that the region over which we do not reject H_0 includes all values of

Figure 9.9   MINITAB OUTPUT FOR THE SUPERFLIGHT GOLF BALL HYPOTHESIS TEST

```
Test of mu = 280.00 vs mu not = 280.00
The assumed sigma = 12.0


    N      Mean    StDev   SE Mean       Z   P value
   36    278.50    12.00      2.00   -0.75      0.45
```

the sample mean $\bar{x}$ that are within $-z_{\alpha/2}$ and $+z_{\alpha/2}$ standard errors of μ_0. Thus, the do-not-reject region for the sample mean $\bar{x}$ in a two-tailed hypothesis test is given by

$$\mu_0 \pm z_{\alpha/2} \frac{\sigma}{\sqrt{n}} \tag{9.6}$$

when σ is known and

$$\mu_0 \pm z_{\alpha/2} \frac{s}{\sqrt{n}} \tag{9.7}$$

when σ is unknown.

A close look at (9.4) and (9.6) provides insight about the relationship between the estimation and hypothesis-testing approaches to statistical inference. Note in particular that both procedures require the computation of the values $z_{\alpha/2}$ and $\sigma/\sqrt{n}$. Focusing on α, we see that a confidence coefficient of $(1 - \alpha)$ for interval estimation corresponds to a level of significance of α in hypothesis testing. For example, a 95% confidence interval corresponds to a .05 level of significance for hypothesis testing. Furthermore, (9.4) and (9.6) show that because $z_{\alpha/2}(\sigma/\sqrt{n})$ is the plus or minus value for both expressions, if $\bar{x}$ is in the do-not-reject region defined by (9.6), the hypothesized value μ_0 will be in the confidence interval defined by (9.4). Conversely, if the hypothesized value μ_0 is in the confidence interval defined by (9.4), the sample mean $\bar{x}$ will be in the do-not-reject region for the hypothesis H_0: $\mu = \mu_0$ as defined by (9.6). These observations lead to the following procedure for using confidence interval results to draw hypothesis-testing conclusions.

A Confidence Interval Approach to Hypothesis Testing

Form of Hypothesis:

$$H_0: \mu = \mu_0$$
$$H_a: \mu \neq \mu_0$$

1. Select a simple random sample from the population and use the value of the sample mean $\bar{x}$ to develop the confidence interval for the population mean μ. If σ is known, compute the interval estimate by using

$$\bar{x} \pm z_{\alpha/2} \frac{\sigma}{\sqrt{n}}$$

If σ is unknown, compute the interval estimate by using

$$\bar{x} \pm z_{\alpha/2} \frac{s}{\sqrt{n}}$$

2. If the confidence interval contains the hypothesized value μ_0, do not reject H_0. Otherwise, reject H_0.

For a two-tailed hypothesis test, the null hypothesis can be rejected if the confidence interval for the population mean does not include μ_0.

Let us return to the Superflight golf ball study and the following two-tailed test.

$$H_0: \mu = 280$$
$$H_a: \mu \neq 280$$

To test this hypothesis with a level of significance of $\alpha = .05$, we sampled 36 golf balls and found a sample mean of $\bar{x} = 278.5$ yards and a sample standard deviation of $s = 12$ yards. Using these results with $z_{.025} = 1.96$, we find that the 95% confidence interval estimate of the population mean becomes

$$\bar{x} \pm z_{.025} \frac{s}{\sqrt{n}}$$

$$278.5 \pm 1.96 \frac{12}{\sqrt{36}}$$

$$278.5 \pm 3.92$$

or

$$274.58 \text{ to } 282.42$$

This finding enables the quality-control manager to conclude with 95% confidence that the mean distance for the population of golf balls is between 274.58 and 282.42 yards. Because the hypothesized value for the population mean, $\mu_0 = 280$, is in this interval, the hypothesis-testing conclusion is that the null hypothesis, $H_0: \mu = 280$, cannot be rejected.

Note that this discussion and example pertain to two-tailed hypothesis tests about a population mean. However, the same confidence interval and hypothesis-testing relationship exists for other population parameters. In addition, the relationship can be extended to make one-tailed tests about population parameters. Doing so, however, requires the development of one-sided confidence intervals.

N O T E S and Comments

1. The p-value depends only on the sample outcome. However, it is necessary to know whether the hypothesis test being investigated is one-tailed or two-tailed. Given the value of $\bar{x}$ in a sample, the p-value for a two-tailed test will always be *twice* the area in the tail of the sampling distribution.
2. The interval-estimation approach to hypothesis testing helps to highlight the role of the sample size. From (9.4) we can see that larger sample sizes lead to narrower confidence intervals. Thus, for a given level of significance α, a larger sample is less likely to lead to an interval containing μ_0 when the null hypothesis is false. That is, the larger sample size will provide a higher probability of rejecting H_0 when H_0 is false.

EXERCISES

Methods

19. Consider the following hypothesis test.

$$H_0: \mu = 10$$
$$H_a: \mu \neq 10$$

A sample of 36 provides a sample mean of 11 and sample standard deviation of 2.5.
a. At $\alpha = .05$, what is the rejection rule?
b. Compute the value of the test statistic z. What is your conclusion?

20. Consider the following hypothesis test.

$$H_0: \mu = 15$$
$$H_a: \mu \neq 15$$

A sample of 50 gives a sample mean of 14.2 and sample standard deviation of 5.
a.   At $\alpha = .02$, what is the rejection rule?
b.   Compute the value of the test statistic z.
c.   What is the p-value?
d.   What is your conclusion?

21. Consider the following hypothesis test.

$$H_0: \mu = 25$$
$$H_a: \mu \neq 25$$

A sample of 80 is used and the population standard deviation is 10. Use $\alpha = .05$. Compute the value of the test statistic z and specify your conclusion for each of the following sample results.
a. $\bar{x} = 22.0$
b. $\bar{x} = 27.0$
c. $\bar{x} = 23.5$
d. $\bar{x} = 28.0$

22. Consider the following hypothesis test.

$$H_0: \mu = 5$$
$$H_a: \mu \neq 5$$

Assume the following test statistics. Compute the corresponding p-values and specify your conclusions based on $\alpha = .05$.
a. $z = 1.80$
b. $z = -.45$
c. $z = 2.05$
d. $z = -3.50$
e. $z = -1.00$

Applications

23. The Bureau of Economic Analysis in the U.S. Department of Commerce reported that the mean annual income for a resident of North Carolina is $18,688 (*USA Today*, August 24, 1995). A researcher for the state of South Carolina wants to test $H_0: \mu = 18,688$ and $H_a: \mu \neq 18,688$, where μ is the mean annual income for a resident of South Carolina.
a.   What is the appropriate conclusion if a sample of 400 residents of South Carolina shows a sample mean annual income of $16,860 and a sample standard deviation of $14,624? Use a .05 level of significance.
b.   What is the p-value for this test?

24. CNN and ActMedia provided a television channel that showed news, features, and ads, and was targeted to individuals waiting in grocery checkout lines. The television programs were designed with an eight-minute cycle on the assumption that the population mean time a shopper stands in line at a grocery store checkout is eight minutes. (*Astounding Averages*, 1995). A sample of 120 shoppers at a major grocery store showed a sample mean waiting time of 7.5 minutes with a sample standard deviation of 3.2 minutes.
a.   Test $H_0: \mu = 8$ and $H_a: \mu \neq 8$. Use a .05 level of significance. Does the population mean waiting time at the grocery store differ from the 8 minute waiting time assumption?
b.   What is the p-value for the test?

25. A production line operates with a filling mean weight of 16 ounces per container. Overfilling or underfilling is a serious problem, and the production line should be shut down if either occurs. From past data, σ is known to be .8 ounces. A quality-control inspector samples 30 items every two hours and at that time makes the decision of whether to shut the line down for adjustment.
    a. With a .05 level of significance, what is the rejection rule?
    b. If a sample mean of $\bar{x} = 16.32$ ounces were found, what action would you recommend?
    c. If $\bar{x} = 15.82$ ounces, what action would you recommend?
    d. What is the p-value for parts (b) and (c)?

26. An automobile assembly-line operation has a scheduled mean completion time of 2.2 minutes. Because of the effect of completion time on both preceding and subsequent assembly operations, it is important to maintain the 2.2-minute mean completion time. A random sample of 45 assemblies shows a sample mean completion time of 2.39 minutes, with a sample standard deviation of .20 minutes. Use a .02 level of significance and test whether the operation is meeting its 2.2-minute mean completion time.

27. Historically, evening long-distance phone calls from a particular city have averaged 15.2 minutes per call. In a random sample of 35 calls, the sample mean time was 14.3 minutes per call, with a sample standard deviation of five minutes. Use this sample information to test for any change in the mean duration of long-distance phone calls. Use a .05 level of significance. What is the p-value?

28. The mean salary for full professors in the United States is $61,650 (*The American Almanac of Jobs and Salaries*, 1994–1995 Edition). A sample of 36 full professors at business colleges showed $\bar{x} = \$72,800$ and $s = \$5,000$.
    a. Develop a 95% confidence interval for the population mean salary of business college professors.
    b. Use the confidence interval to conduct the hypothesis test: H_0: $\mu = 61,650$ and H_a: $\mu \neq 61,650$. What is your conclusion?

9.5   TESTS ABOUT A POPULATION MEAN: SMALL-SAMPLE CASE

Assume that the sample size is small ($n < 30$) and that the sample standard deviation s is used to estimate the population standard deviation σ. If it is also reasonable to assume that the population has a normal probability distribution, the t distribution can be used to make inferences about the value of the population mean.* In this case, the test statistic is

$$t = \frac{\bar{x} - \mu_0}{s/\sqrt{n}} \qquad (9.8)$$

This test statistic has a t distribution with $n - 1$ degrees of freedom.

Let us consider an example of a one-tailed hypothesis test about a population mean for the small-sample case. The International Air Transport Association surveys business travelers to develop ratings of transatlantic gateway airports. The maximum possible score is 10. A magazine devoted to business travel has decided to classify airports according to the rating they receive. Airports that have a population mean rating of 7 or more will be designated as providing superior service. Suppose a simple random sample of 12 business travelers have been asked to rate London's Heathrow airport, and that the 12 ratings obtained are 7, 8, 10, 8, 6, 9, 6, 7, 7, 8, 9, and 8. The sample mean is $\bar{x} = 7.75$ and the sample standard

---

*If the sample size is small ($n < 30$), if the population standard deviation σ is known, and if the population has a normal probability distribution, $z = (\bar{x} - \mu_0)(\sigma/\sqrt{n})$ can be used as the test statistic for the small-sample hypothesis test.

deviation is $s = 1.215$. Assuming that the population of ratings can be approximated by a normal probability distribution, should Heathrow be designated as providing superior service?

Using a .05 level of significance, we need a test to determine whether the population mean rating for the Heathrow airport is greater than 7. The null and alternative hypotheses follow.

$$H_0: \mu \le 7$$
$$H_a: \mu > 7$$

The Heathrow airport will be designated as providing superior service if H_0 can be rejected indicating that the population mean rating is greater than 7.

The rejection region is in the upper tail of the sampling distribution. With $n - 1 = 12 - 1 = 11$ degrees of freedom, Table 2 of Appendix B shows that $t_{.05} = 1.796$. Thus, the rejection rule is

$$\text{Reject } H_0 \text{ if } t > 1.796$$

Using (9.8) with $\bar{x} = 7.75$ and $s = 1.215$, we have the following value for the test statistic.

$$t = \frac{\bar{x} - \mu_0}{s/\sqrt{n}} = \frac{7.75 - 7}{1.215/\sqrt{12}} = 2.14$$

Because 2.14 is greater than 1.796, the null hypothesis is rejected. At the .05 level of significance, we can conclude that the population mean rating for the Heathrow airport is greater than 7. Thus, Heathrow can be designated as providing superior service. Figure 9.10 shows that the value of the test statistic is in the rejection region.

Figure 9.10   VALUE OF THE TEST STATISTIC ($t = 2.14$) FOR THE HEATHROW AIRPORT HYPOTHESIS TEST

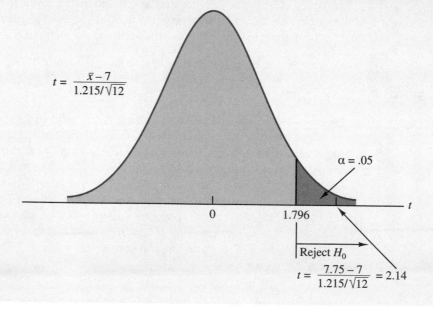

p-Values and the *t* Distribution

Let us consider the *p*-value for the Heathrow airport hypothesis test. The usual rule applies: If the *p*-value is less than the level of significance α, the null hypothesis can be rejected. Unfortunately, the format of the *t* distribution table provided in most statistics textbooks does not have sufficient detail to determine the exact *p*-value for the test. However, we can still use the *t* distribution table to identify a range for the *p*-value. For example, the *t* distribution used in the Heathrow airport hypothesis test has 11 degrees of freedom. Referring to Table 2 of Appendix B, we see that row 11 provides the following information about a *t* distribution with 11 degrees of freedom.

The p-values are difficult to obtain directly from a table of the t distribution. Generally, the best that can be done with the table is to specify a range for the p-value such as between .05 and .025. Computer packages are helpful in that most provide the p-value automatically (see Figure 9.11).

Area in Upper Tail	.10	.05	.025	.01	.005
t Value	1.363	1.796	2.201	2.718	3.106

The computed *t* value for the hypothesis test was $t = 2.14$. The *p*-value is the area in the tail corresponding to $t = 2.14$. From the information above, we see 2.14 is between 1.796 and 2.201. Thus, although we cannot determine the exact *p*-value associated with $t = 2.14$, we do know that the *p*-value must be between .05 and .025. With a level of significance of $\alpha = .05$, we know that the *p*-value must be less than .05; thus, the null hypothesis is rejected.

Minitab can be used to provide small-sample hypothesis test information for a population mean. The computer output for the Heathrow Airport hypothesis test is shown in Figure 9.11. The sample mean $\bar{x} = 7.75$, the test statistic $t = 2.14$, and the *p*-value $= .028$ are computed automatically. The step-by-step procedure used to obtain the Minitab output is described in Appendix 9.1.

A Two-Tailed Test

As an example of a two-tailed hypothesis test about a population mean using a small sample, consider the following production problem. A production process is designed to fill containers with a mean filling weight of $\mu = 16$ ounces. If the process underfills containers, the consumer will not receive the amount of product indicated on the container label. If the process overfills containers, the firm loses money because more product is placed in a container than is required. To monitor the process, quality-assurance personnel periodically select a simple random sample of eight containers and test the following two-tailed hypotheses.

$$H_0: \mu = 16$$
$$H_a: \mu \neq 16$$

Figure 9.11   MINITAB OUTPUT FOR THE HEATHROW AIRPORT RATING HYPOTHESIS TEST

```
Test of mu = 7.000 vs mu > 7.000

     N    Mean   StDev   SE Mean     T   P value
    12   7.750   1.215     0.351   2.14    0.028
```

If H_0 is rejected, the production process will be stopped and the mechanism for regulating filling weights will be readjusted to ensure a mean filling weight of 16 ounces. If the sample yields data values of 16.02, 16.22, 15.82, 15.92, 16.22, 16.32, 16.12, and 15.92 ounces, and the level of significance is .05, what action should be taken? Assume that the population of filling weights is normally distributed.

Because the data have not been summarized, we must first compute the sample mean and sample standard deviation. Doing so provides the following results.

$$\bar{x} = \frac{\Sigma x_i}{n} = \frac{128.56}{8} = 16.07 \text{ ounces}$$

and

$$s = \sqrt{\frac{\Sigma(x_i - \bar{x})^2}{n - 1}} = \sqrt{\frac{.22}{7}} = .18 \text{ ounces}$$

With a two-tailed test and a level of significance of $\alpha = .05$, the value of $-t_{.025}$ and the value of $t_{.025}$ are needed to determine the rejection region for the test. Using the table for the t distribution, we find that with $n - 1 = 8 - 1 = 7$ degrees of freedom, $-t_{.025} = -2.365$ and $t_{.025} = +2.365$. Thus, the rejection rule is written

$$\text{Reject } H_0 \text{ if } t < -2.365 \text{ or if } t > 2.365$$

Using $\bar{x} = 16.07$ and $s = .18$, we have

$$t = \frac{\bar{x} - \mu_0}{s\sqrt{n}} = \frac{16.07 - 16}{.18/\sqrt{8}} = 1.10$$

Because $t = 1.10$ is not in the rejection region, the null hypothesis cannot be rejected. The test did not provide enough evidence to stop the production process.

Using Table 2 of Appendix B and the row for seven degrees of freedom, we see that the computed t value of 1.10 has an upper tail area of *more than* .10. Although the format of the t distribution table prevents us from being more specific, we can at least conclude that the two-tailed p-value is greater than 2(.10) = .20. Because this value is greater than the .05 level of significance, we see that the p-value leads to the same conclusion; that is, do not reject H_0. The computer solution for this problem shows $t = 1.10$ and the exact p-value = .31.

..../ /............

EXERCISES

Methods

29. Consider the following hypothesis test.

$$H_0: \mu \leq 10$$
$$H_a: \mu > 10$$

A sample of 16 provides a sample mean of 11 and sample standard deviation of 3.
a. With $\alpha = .05$, what is the rejection rule?
b. Compute the value of the test statistic t. What is your conclusion?

30. Consider the following hypothesis test.

$$H_0: \mu = 20$$
$$H_a: \mu \neq 20$$

Data from a sample of six items are: 18, 20, 16, 19, 17, 18.
   a. Compute the sample mean.
   b. Compute the sample standard deviation.
   c. With $\alpha = .05$, what is the rejection rule?
   d. Compute the value of the test statistic t.
   e. What is your conclusions?

31. Consider the following hypothesis test.

$$H_0: \mu \geq 15$$
$$H_a: \mu < 15$$

A sample of 22 is used, and the sample standard deviation is 8. Use $\alpha = .05$. Provide the value of the test statistic t and your conclusion for each of the following sample results.
   a. $\bar{x} = 13.0$
   b. $\bar{x} = 11.5$
   c. $\bar{x} = 15.0$
   d. $\bar{x} = 19.0$

32. Consider the following hypothesis test.

$$H_0: \mu \leq 50$$
$$H_a: \mu > 50$$

Assume a sample of 16 items provides the following test statistics. What can you say about the p-values in each case? What are your conclusions based on $\alpha = .05$?
   a. $t = 2.602$
   b. $t = 1.341$
   c. $t = 1.960$
   d. $t = 1.055$
   e. $t = 3.261$

Applications

33. In February 1995, the mean cost for an airline round trip with a discount fare was $258 (*USA Today,* March 30, 1995). A random sample of 15 round-trip discount fares during the month of March provided the following data.

310   260   265   255   300   310   230   250   265   280   290   240   285   250   260

   a. What is the sample mean round trip discount fare in March?
   b. What is the sample standard deviation?
   c. Using $\alpha = .05$, test to see whether the mean round-trip discount fare has *increased* in March. What is your conclusion?
   d. What is the p-value?

34. The average U.S. household spends $90 per day (*American Demographics,* August 1997). Assume a sample of 25 households in Corning, New York, showed a sample mean daily expenditure of $84.50 with a sample standard deviation of $14.50.
   a. Test $H_0: \mu = 90$ and $H_a: \mu \neq 90$ to see whether the population mean in Corning, New York, differs from U.S. mean. Use a .05 level of significance. What is your conclusion?
   b. What is the p-value?

35. On the average, a housewife with a husband and two children is estimated to work 55 hours or less per week on household-related activities. The hours worked during a week for a sample of eight housewives are: 58, 52, 64, 63, 59, 62, 62, and 55.

   a. Use $\alpha = .05$ to test $H_0: \mu \leq 55$, $H_a: \mu > 55$. What is your conclusion about the mean number of hours worked per week?

   b. What can you say about the p-value?

36. A study of a drug designed to reduce blood pressure used a sample of 25 men between the ages of 45 and 55. With μ indicating the mean change in blood pressure for the population of men receiving the drug, the hypotheses in the study were written: $H_0: \mu \geq 0$ and $H_a: \mu < 0$. Rejection of H_0 shows that the mean change is negative, indicating that the drug is effective in lowering blood pressure.

   a. At a .05 level of significance, what conclusion should be drawn if $\bar{x} = -10$ and $s = 15$?

   b. What can you say about the p-value?

37. Last year the number of lunches served at an elementary-school cafeteria was normally distributed with a mean of 300 lunches per day. At the beginning of the current year, the price of a lunch was raised by 25¢. A sample of six days during the months of September, October, and November provided the following numbers of children being served lunches: 290, 275, 310, 260, 270, and 275. Do these data indicate that the mean number of lunches per day has dropped since last year? Test $H_0: \mu \geq 300$ against the alternative $H_a: \mu < 300$ at a .05 level of significance.

38. Joan's Nursery specializes in custom-designed landscaping for residential areas. The estimated labor cost associated with a particular landscaping proposal is based on the number of plantings of trees, shrubs, and so on to be used for the project. For cost-estimating purposes, managers use two hours of labor time for the planting of a medium-size tree. Actual times from a sample of 10 plantings during the past month follow (times in hours).

   1.9   1.7   2.8   2.4   2.6   2.5   2.8   3.2   1.6   2.5

Using a .05 level of significance, test whether the mean tree-planting time exceeds two hours. What is your conclusion, and what recommendations would you consider making to the managers?

9.6 TESTS ABOUT A POPULATION PROPORTION

With p denoting the population proportion and p_0 denoting a particular hypothesized value for the population proportion, the three forms for a hypothesis test about a population proportion are as follows.

$$H_0: p \geq p_0 \qquad H_0: p \leq p_0 \qquad H_0: p = p_0$$
$$H_a: p < p_0 \qquad H_a: p > p_0 \qquad H_a: p \neq p_0$$

The first two forms are one-tailed tests, whereas the third form is a two-tailed test. The specific form used depends on the application.

   Hypothesis tests about a population proportion are based on the difference between the sample proportion $\bar{p}$ and the hypothesized population proportion p_0. The methods used to conduct the tests are similar to the procedures used for hypothesis tests about a population mean. The only difference is that we use the sample proportion $\bar{p}$ and its standard deviation $\sigma_{\bar{p}}$ in developing the test statistic. We begin by formulating null and alternative hypotheses about the value of the population proportion. Then, using the value of the sample proportion $\bar{p}$ and its standard deviation $\sigma_{\bar{p}}$, we compute a value for the test statistic z. Comparing the value of the test statistic to the critical value enables us to determine whether the null hypothesis should be rejected.

Let us illustrate hypothesis testing for a population proportion by considering the situation faced by Pine Creek golf course. Over the past few months, 20% of the players at Pine Creek have been women. In an effort to increase the proportion of women playing, Pine Creek used a special promotion to attract women golfers. After one week, a random sample of 400 players showed 300 men and 100 women. Course managers would like to determine whether the data support the conclusion that the proportion of women playing at Pine Creek has increased.

To determine whether the effect of the promotion has been to increase the proportion of women golfers, we state the following null and alternative hypotheses.

$$H_0: p \leq .20$$
$$H_a: p > .20$$

As usual, we begin the hypothesis-testing procedure by assuming that H_0 is true with $p = .20$. Using the sample proportion $\bar{p}$ to estimate p, we next consider the sampling distribution of $\bar{p}$. Because $\bar{p}$ is an unbiased estimator of p, we know that if $p = .20$, the mean of the sampling distribution of $\bar{p}$ is .20. In addition, we know from Chapter 7 that the standard deviation of $\bar{p}$ is given by

$$\sigma_{\bar{p}} = \sqrt{\frac{p(1 - p)}{n}}$$

With the assumed value of $p = .20$ and a sample size of $n = 400$, the standard deviation of $\bar{p}$ is

$$\sigma_{\bar{p}} = \sqrt{\frac{.20(1 - .20)}{400}} = .02$$

In Chapter 7 we saw that the sampling distribution of $\bar{p}$ can be approximated by a normal probability distribution if both np and $n(1 - p)$ are greater than or equal to 5. In the Pine Creek case, $np = 400(.20) = 80$ and $n(1 - p) = 400(.80) = 320$; thus, the normal probability distribution approximation is appropriate. The sampling distribution of $\bar{p}$ is shown in Figure 9.12.

Because the sampling distribution of $\bar{p}$ is approximately normal, the following test statistic can be used.

Test Statistic for Tests about a Population Proportion

$$z = \frac{\bar{p} - p_0}{\sigma_p} \tag{9.9}$$

where

In hypothesis testing, a value of the population proportion, p_0, is assumed in H_0. Therefore, when H_0 is true, $\sigma_{\bar{p}}$ can be computed by using p_0 as shown in (9.10). The sample proportion, $\bar{p}$, is not used in the computation of $\sigma_{\bar{p}}$.

$$\sigma_{\bar{p}} = \sqrt{\frac{p_0(1 - p_0)}{n}} \tag{9.10}$$

Let us assume that $\alpha = .05$ has been selected as the level of significance for the test. With $z_{.05} = 1.645$, the upper-tail rejection region for the hypothesis test (see Figure 9.13) provides the following rejection rule.

Reject H_0 if $z > 1.645$

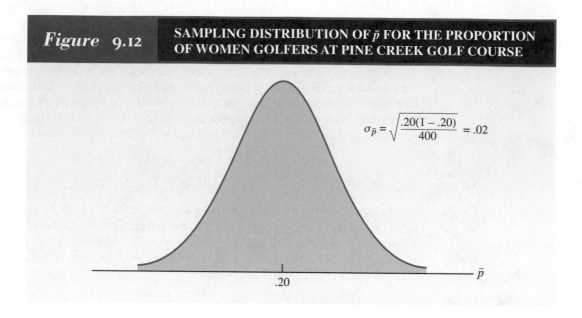

Figure 9.12   SAMPLING DISTRIBUTION OF $\bar{p}$ FOR THE PROPORTION OF WOMEN GOLFERS AT PINE CREEK GOLF COURSE

$$\sigma_{\bar{p}} = \sqrt{\frac{.20(1-.20)}{400}} = .02$$

.20

$\bar{p}$

Because 100 of the 400 players during the promotion were women, we obtain $\bar{p} = 100/400 = .25$. With $\sigma_{\bar{p}} = .02$, the value of the test statistic is

$$z = \frac{\bar{p} - p_0}{\sigma_{\bar{p}}} = \frac{.25 - .20}{.02} = 2.5$$

Thus, since $z = 2.5 > 1.645$, we can reject H_0. The Pine Creek managers can conclude that the proportion of women players has increased.

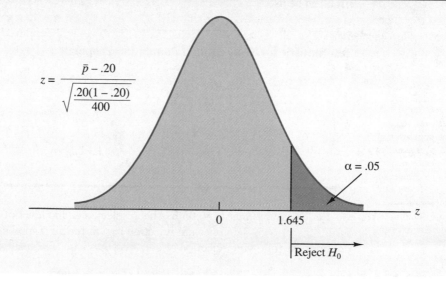

Figure 9.13   REJECTION REGION FOR THE PINE CREEK GOLF COURSE HYPOTHESIS TEST

$$z = \frac{\bar{p} - .20}{\sqrt{\dfrac{.20(1-.20)}{400}}}$$

$\alpha = .05$

0   1.645 z

Reject H_0

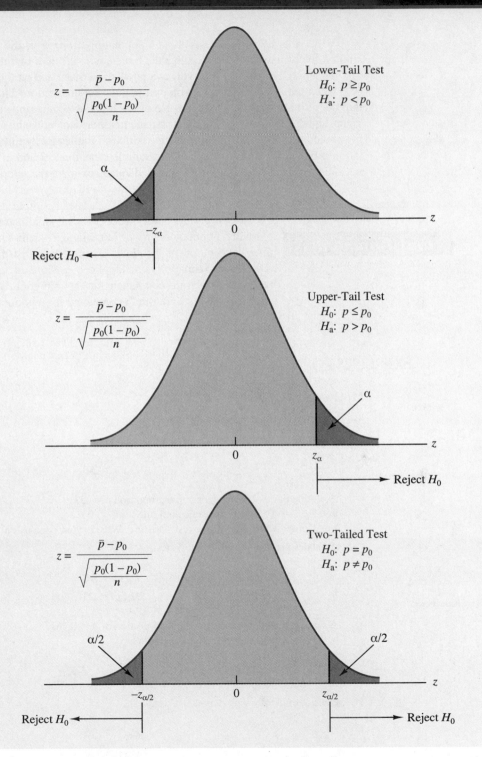

SUMMARY OF REJECTION RULES FOR HYPOTHESIS TESTS ABOUT A POPULATION PROPORTION

Figure 9.14

$$z = \frac{\bar{p} - p_0}{\sqrt{\dfrac{p_0(1 - p_0)}{n}}}$$

Lower-Tail Test
H_0: $p \geq p_0$
H_a: $p < p_0$

α

$-z_\alpha$ 0 z

Reject H_0

$$z = \frac{\bar{p} - p_0}{\sqrt{\dfrac{p_0(1 - p_0)}{n}}}$$

Upper-Tail Test
H_0: $p \leq p_0$
H_a: $p > p_0$

α

0   z_α z

Reject H_0

$$z = \frac{\bar{p} - p_0}{\sqrt{\dfrac{p_0(1 - p_0)}{n}}}$$

Two-Tailed Test
H_0: $p = p_0$
H_a: $p \neq p_0$

$\alpha/2$ $\alpha/2$

$-z_{\alpha/2}$ 0 $z_{\alpha/2}$ z

Reject H_0 Reject H_0

Using the table of areas for the standard normal probability distribution, we find that the p-value for the test can also be computed. For example, with $z = 2.50$, the table of areas shows a .4938 area or probability between the mean and $z = 2.50$. Thus, the p-value for the test is $.5000 - .4938 = .0062$. Because the p-value is less than α, the null hypothesis can be rejected.

We see that hypothesis tests about a population proportion and a population mean are similar; the primary difference is that the test statistic is based on the sampling distribution of $\bar{x}$ when the hypothesis test involves a population mean and on the sampling distribution of $\bar{p}$ when the hypothesis test involves a population proportion. The tentative assumption that the null hypothesis is true, the use of the level of significance to establish the critical value, and the comparison of the test statistic to the critical value are identical in the two testing procedures. Figure 9.14 summarizes the decision rules for hypothesis tests about a population proportion. We assume the large-sample case, $np \geq 5$ and $n(1 - p) \geq 5$, where the normal probability distribution can be used to approximate the sampling distribution of $\bar{p}$.

N O T E S
and Comments

We have not shown the procedure for small-sample hypothesis tests involving population proportions. In the small-sample case, the sampling distribution of $\bar{p}$ follows the binomial distribution and hence the normal approximation is not applicable. More advanced texts show how hypothesis tests are conducted for this situation. However, in practice small-sample tests are rarely conducted for a population proportion.

EXERCISES

Methods

39. Consider the following hypothesis test.

$$H_0: p \leq .50$$
$$H_a: p > .50$$

A sample of 200 provided a sample proportion $\bar{p} = .57$.
a. At $\alpha = .05$, what is the rejection rule?
b. Compute the value of the test statistic z. What is your conclusion?

SELF TEST

40. Consider the following hypothesis test.

$$H_0: p = .20$$
$$H_a: p \neq .20$$

A sample of 400 provided a sample proportion of $\bar{p} = .175$.
a. At $\alpha = .05$, what is the rejection rule?
b. Compute the value of the test statistic z.
c. What is the p-value?
d. What is your conclusion?

41. Consider the following hypothesis test.

$$H_0: p \geq .75$$
$$H_a: p < .75$$

A sample of 300 is selected. Use $\alpha = .05$. Provide the value of the test statistic z, the p-value, and your conclusion for each of the following sample results.

a. $\bar{p} = .68$
b. $\bar{p} = .72$
c. $\bar{p} = .70$
d. $\bar{p} = .77$

Applications

42. The Honolulu Board of Water Supply suggested the water-by-request rule be adopted at restaurants on the island of Oahu to conserve water. A restaurant manager stated that 30% of the patrons do not drink water. Hence, the conservation of water would come not only from the unused water in each glass, but also the water saved in washing the glasses. Test H_0: $p = .30$ versus H_a: $p \neq .30$. Assume a sample of 480 patrons showed that 128 patrons did not drink water. Test the manager's claim at a .05 level of significance. What is the p-value and what is your conclusion?

SELF TEST

43. A study by *Consumer Reports* showed that 64% of supermarket shoppers believed supermarket brands to be as good as national name brands in terms of product quality. To investigate whether this result applies to its own product, the manufacturer of a national name-brand ketchup product asked 100 supermarket shoppers whether they believed the supermarket brand of ketchup was as good as the national name-brand ketchup. Use the fact that 52 of the shoppers in the sample indicated that the supermarket brand was as good as the national name brand to test H_0: $p \geq .64$ and H_a: $p < .64$. Use a .05 level of significance. What is your conclusion?

44. Burger King sponsored what it believed to be the biggest product giveaway in fast-food history when it initiated "FreeFryDay" on Friday, January 2, 1998. Anyone who stopped at one of Burger King's 7400 restaurants received a small order of the new Burger King fries free of charge. A national taste test comparing the new Burger King fries to McDonald's fries was the basis for the launch of the Burger King promotion. Of the 500 customers who participated in the taste test, 285 expressed a taste preference for the Burger King fries (*USA Today*, December 10, 1997). Let p = the population proportion that favors the Burger King fries. Consider the hypothesis following test:

$$H_0: p \leq .50$$
$$H_a: p > .50$$

a. What is the point estimate of the population proportion that favors the Burger King fries?
b. What is your conclusion? Use a .01 level of significance.
c. Do you believe that the national taste test statistics helped Burger King's management decide to implement the "FreeFryDay" campaign? Discuss.

45. A magazine claims that 25% of its readers are college students. A random sample of 200 readers showed 42 were college students. Use a .10 level of significance to test H_0: $p = .25$ and H_a: $p \neq .25$. What is the p-value?

46. A new television series must prove that it has more than 25% of the viewing audience after its initial 13-week run if it is to be judged successful. Assume that in a sample of 400 households, 112 were watching the new series.
a. At a .10 level of significance, can the series be judged successful on the basis of the sample information?
b. What is the p-value? What is your hypothesis-testing conclusion?

47. An accountant believes that a company's cash-flow problems are a direct result of the slow collection of accounts receivable. The accountant claims that at least 70% of the current accounts receivable are more than two months old. A sample of 120 accounts receivable showed that 78 are more than two months old. Test the accountant's claim at the .05 level of significance.

48. In a study of the contamination of fish in the nation's rivers and lakes, the Environmental Protection Agency found that 91% of water quality test sites showed the presence of PCB, a cancer-causing agent (*America by the Numbers,* 1993). Suppose a follow-up study of 200 rivers and lakes in 1998 showed the presence of PCB in 160 cases. Does the statistical evidence support the conclusion that as of 1998 water clean-up programs have reduced the proportion of locations with PCB? Use a .05 level of significance.

49. At least 20% of all workers are believed to be willing to work fewer hours for less pay to obtain more time for personal and leisure activities. A *USA Today*/CNN/Gallup poll with a sample of 596 respondents found 83 willing to work fewer hours for less pay to obtain more personal and leisure time (*USA Today,* April 10, 1995). Test H_0: $p \geq .20$ and H_a: $p < .20$ using a .05 level of significance. What is your conclusion?

SUMMARY

Hypothesis testing is a statistical procedure that uses sample data to determine whether a statement about the value of a population parameter should be rejected. The hypotheses, which come from a variety of sources, are two competing statements about a population parameter: a null hypothesis H_0 and an alternative hypothesis H_a. In some applications it is not obvious how the null and alternative hypotheses should be formulated. We suggested guidelines for developing hypotheses in three types of situations.

1. Testing research hypotheses: The research hypothesis should be formulated as the alternative hypothesis. The null hypothesis is based on an established theory or the statement that the research treatment will have no effect. Whenever the sample data contradict the null hypothesis, the null hypothesis is rejected. In this case, the alternative or research hypothesis is concluded to be true.
2. Testing the validity of a claim: Generally, the claim made is chosen as the null hypothesis; the challenge to the claim is chosen as the alternative hypothesis. Action against the claim will be taken whenever the sample data contradict the null hypothesis. When that occurs, the challenge implied by the alternative hypothesis is concluded to be true.
3. Testing in decision-making situations: Often a decision maker must choose between two courses of action, one associated with the null hypothesis and one associated with the alternative hypothesis.

Figure 9.15 summarizes the test statistics used in hypothesis tests about a population mean and provides a practical guide for selecting the hypothesis-testing procedure. The figure shows that the test statistic depends on whether the sample size is large, whether the population standard deviation is known, and in some cases whether the population has a normal or approximately normal probability distribution. If the sample size is large, $(n \geq 30)$, the z test statistic is used to conduct the hypothesis test. If the sample size is small, $(n < 30)$, the population must have a normal or approximately normal probability distribution to conduct a hypothesis test about the value of μ. If that is the case, the z test statistic is used if σ is known, whereas the t test statistic is used if σ is estimated by the sample standard deviation s. Finally, note that if the sample size is small and the assumption of a normal probability distribution for the population is inappropriate, we recommend increasing the sample size to $n \geq 30$ to test the hypothesis about a population mean.

Figure 9.15   SUMMARY OF THE TEST STATISTICS TO BE USED IN A HYPOTHESIS TEST ABOUT A POPULATION MEAN

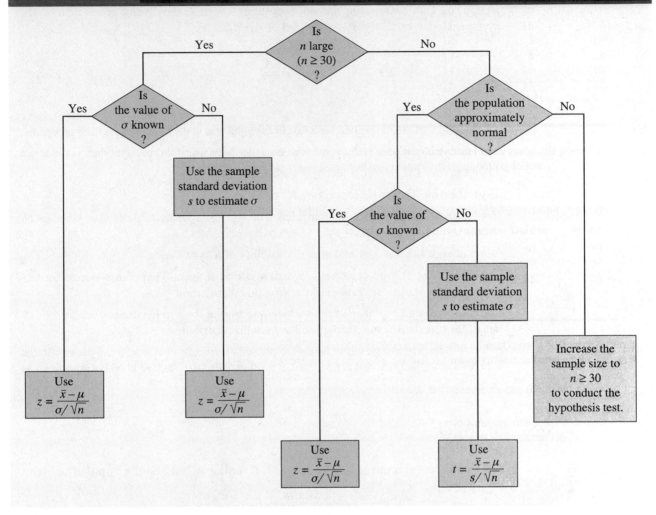

Hypothesis tests about a population proportion were developed for the large-sample case, $np \geq 5$ and $n(1 - p) \geq 5$. The test statistic used is

$$ z = \frac{\bar{p} - p_0}{\sqrt{\dfrac{p_0(1 - p_0)}{n}}} $$

The rejection rule for all the hypothesis-testing procedures involves comparing the value of the test statistic with a critical value. For lower-tail tests, the null hypothesis is rejected if the value of the test statistic is less than the critical value. For upper-tail tests, the null hypothesis is rejected if the test statistic is greater than the critical value. For two-tailed tests, the null hypothesis is rejected for values of the test statistic in either tail of the sampling distribution.

We also saw that p-values could be used for hypothesis testing. The p-value yields the probability, when the null hypothesis is true, of obtaining a sample result that is at least as unlikely as what is observed. When p-values are used to conduct a hypothesis test, the rejection rule calls for rejecting the null hypothesis whenever the p-value is less than α. The p-value is often called the observed level of significance.

GLOSSARY

Null hypothesis The hypothesis tentatively assumed true in the hypothesis-testing procedure.

Alternative hypothesis The hypothesis concluded to be true if the null hypothesis is rejected.

Type I error The error of rejecting H_0 when it is true.

Type II error The error of accepting H_0 when it is false.

Critical value A value that is compared with the test statistic to determine whether H_0 should be rejected.

Level of significance The maximum probability of a Type I error.

One-tailed test A hypothesis test in which rejection of the null hypothesis occurs for values of the test statistic in one tail of the sampling distribution.

Two-tailed test A hypothesis test in which rejection of the null hypothesis occurs for values of the test statistic in either tail of the sampling distribution.

p-Value The probability, when the null hypothesis is true, of obtaining a sample result that is at least as unlikely as what is observed. It is often called the observed level of significance.

KEY FORMULAS

Test Statistics for a Large-Sample ($n \geq 30$) Hypothesis Test about a Population Mean

$$\sigma \text{ Known} \qquad \sigma \text{ Unknown}$$

$$z = \frac{\bar{x} - \mu_0}{\sigma/\sqrt{n}} \qquad z = \frac{\bar{x} - \mu_0}{s/\sqrt{n}} \tag{9.1}$$

Test Statistic for a Small-Sample ($n < 30$) Hypothesis Test about a Population Mean

$$t = \frac{\bar{x} - \mu_0}{s/\sqrt{n}} \tag{9.8}$$

Test Statistic for Hypothesis Tests about a Population Proportion

$$z = \frac{\bar{p} - p_0}{\sigma_{\bar{p}}} \tag{9.9}$$

where

$$\sigma_{\bar{p}} = \sqrt{\frac{p_0(1 - p_0)}{n}} \tag{9.10}$$

SUPPLEMENTARY EXERCISES

50. The Ford Taurus is listed as having a highway fuel efficiency average of 30 miles per gallon (1995 *Motor Trend* New Car Buyer's Guide). A consumer interest group conducts automobile mileage tests seeking statistical evidence to show that automobile manufacturers overstate the miles per gallon ratings for particular models. In the case of the Ford Taurus, hypotheses for the test would be stated $H_0: \mu \geq 30$ and $H_a: \mu < 30$. In a sample of 50 mileage tests with Ford Taurus, the consumer interest group finds a sample mean highway mileage rating of 29.5 miles per gallon and a sample standard deviation of 1.8 miles per gallon. What conclusion should be drawn from the sample results? Use a .01 level of significance.

51. The manager of the Keeton Department Store has assumed that the mean annual income of the store's customers is at least $28,000 per year. A sample of 58 customers shows a sample mean of $27,200 and a sample standard deviation of $3000. At the .05 level of significance, should this assumption be rejected? What is the p-value?

52. The monthly rent for a two-bedroom apartment in a particular city is reported to average $550. Suppose we want to test $H_0: \mu = 550$ versus $H_a: \mu \neq 550$. A sample of 36 two-bedroom apartments is selected. The sample mean is $\bar{x} = \$562$ and the sample standard deviation is $s = \$40$.
    a. Conduct this hypothesis test with a .05 level of significance.
    b. Compute the p-value.
    c. Use the sample results to construct a 95% confidence interval for the population mean. What hypothesis-testing conclusion would you draw from the confidence interval result?

53. In making bids on building projects, Sonneborn Builders, Inc., assumes construction workers are idle no more than 15% of the time. Hence, for a normal eight-hour shift, the mean idle time per worker should be 72 minutes or less per day. A sample of 30 construction workers had a mean idle time of 80 minutes per day. The sample standard deviation was 20 minutes. Suppose a hypothesis test is to be designed to test the validity of the company's assumption.
    a. What is the p-value associated with the sample result?
    b. Using a .05 level of significance and the p-value, test $H_0: \mu \leq 72$. What is your conclusion?

54. The Immigration and Naturalization service reported that 79% of foreign travelers visiting the United States stated that the primary purpose of their visit was to enjoy a vacation (*America by the Numbers,* 1993). As a follow-up study conducted in 1998, suppose a sample of 500 foreign visitors is selected and that 360 say that their primary reason for visiting the United States is to enjoy a vacation. Is the proportion of foreign travelers vacationing in the United States in 1998 less than the proportion reported in 1992? Support your conclusion with a statistical test using a .05 level of significance.

55. In a comprehensive study of workplace communications conducted by Pitney Bowes, 72% of the workers surveyed said they regularly work with coworkers who were not in the office, which made face-to-face meetings or voice-to-voice phone conversations more difficult to schedule and conduct (*ORMS Today,* August 1998). In a related study of 400 workers at Trident Manufacturing, 304 of the individuals surveyed said that they regularly work with coworkers not in the office. Conduct a statistical test to determine whether the proportion of workers who regularly work with coworkers not in the office is greater at Trident Manufacturing than the percentage reported by Pitney Bowes. Use a .05 level of significance.

56. The Gallup Organization conducted a survey of 1350 people for the National Occupational Information Coordinating Committee, a panel Congress created to improve the use of job information (*The Arizona Republic,* January 12, 1990). A research question related to the study was: Do individuals hold jobs that they planned to hold or do they hold jobs for such reasons as chance or lack of choice? Let p indicate the population proportion of individuals who hold jobs that they planned to hold.
    a. If the hypotheses are stated $H_0: p \geq .50$ and $H_a: p < .50$, discuss the research hypothesis H_a in terms of what the researcher is investigating.
    b. The Gallup poll found that 41% of the respondents hold jobs they planned to hold. What is your conclusion at a .01 level of significance? Discuss.

57. A well-known doctor hypothesized that 75% of women wear shoes that are too small. A study of 356 women by the American Orthopedic Foot and Ankle Society found 313 women who wore shoes that were at least one size too small. Test H_0: $p = .75$ and H_a: $p \neq .75$ at $\alpha = .01$. What is your conclusion?

Case Problem 1   UNEMPLOYMENT STUDY

Each month the U.S. Bureau of Labor Statistics publishes a variety of unemployment statistics, including the number of individuals who are unemployed and the mean length of time the individuals have been unemployed. For November 1998, the Bureau of Labor Statistics reported that the national mean length of time of unemployment was 14.6 weeks.

The mayor of Philadelphia has requested a study on the status of unemployment in the Philadelphia area. A sample of 50 unemployed residents of Philadelphia included data on the age and the number of weeks without a job. A portion of the data collected in November 1998 is shown as follows. The complete data set is available in the data file BLS.

BLS

Age	Weeks	Age	Weeks
56	22	25	5
35	19	40	20
22	7	25	12
57	37	25	1
40	18	59	33
22	11	49	26
48	6	33	13
48	22		

Managerial Report

1. Use descriptive statistics to summarize the data.
2. Develop a 95% confidence interval estimate of the mean age of unemployed individuals in Philadelphia.
3. Conduct a hypothesis test to determine whether the mean duration of unemployment in Philadelphia is greater than the national mean duration of 14.6 weeks. Use a .01 level of significance. What is your conclusion?
4. Is there a relationship between the age of an unemployed individual and the number of weeks of unemployment? Explain.

Case Problem 2   QUALITY ASSOCIATES, INC.

Quality Associates, Inc., is a consulting firm that advises its clients about sampling and statistical procedures that can be used to control manufacturing processes. In one particular application, a client provided Quality Associates with a sample of 800 observations that were taken during a time in which the client's process was operating satisfactorily. The sample standard deviation for these data was .21; hence, the population standard deviation was assumed to be .21. Quality Associates then suggested that random samples of size 30 be taken periodically to monitor the process on an ongoing basis. By analyzing the new samples, the client could quickly learn whether the process was operating satisfactorily. When the process was not operating satisfactorily, corrective action could be taken to eliminate the problem. The design specification indicated the mean for the process should be 12. The hypotheses test suggested by Quality Associates follows.

$$H_0: \mu = 12$$
$$H_a: \mu \neq 12$$

Corrective action will be taken any time H_0 is rejected.

The following four samples were collected during the first day of operation of the new statistical process-control procedure. These data are available in the Quality data set.

Quality

Sample 1	Sample 2	Sample 3	Sample 4
11.55	11.62	11.91	12.02
11.62	11.69	11.36	12.02
11.52	11.59	11.75	12.05
11.75	11.82	11.95	12.18
11.90	11.97	12.14	12.11
11.64	11.71	11.72	12.07
11.80	11.87	11.61	12.05
12.03	12.10	11.85	11.64
11.94	12.01	12.16	12.39
11.92	11.99	11.91	11.65
12.13	12.20	12.12	12.11
12.09	12.16	11.61	11.90
11.93	12.00	12.21	12.22
12.21	12.28	11.56	11.88
12.32	12.39	11.95	12.03
11.93	12.00	12.01	12.35
11.85	11.92	12.06	12.09
11.76	11.83	11.76	11.77
12.16	12.23	11.82	12.20
11.77	11.84	12.12	11.79
12.00	12.07	11.60	12.30
12.04	12.11	11.95	12.27
11.98	12.05	11.96	12.29
12.30	12.37	12.22	12.47
12.18	12.25	11.75	12.03
11.97	12.04	11.96	12.17
12.17	12.24	11.95	11.94
11.85	11.92	11.89	11.97
12.30	12.37	11.88	12.23
12.15	12.22	11.93	12.25

Managerial Report

1. Conduct the hypothesis test for each sample at the .01 level of significance and determine what action, if any, should be taken. Provide the test statistic and p-value for each test.
2. Consider the standard deviation for each of the four samples. Does the assumption of .21 for the population standard deviation appear reasonable?
3. Compute limits for the sample mean $\bar{x}$ around $\mu = 12$ such that, as long as a new sample mean is within those limits, the process will be considered to be operating satisfactorily. If $\bar{x}$ exceeds the upper limit or if $\bar{x}$ is below the lower limit, corrective action will be taken. These limits are referred to as upper and lower control limits for quality-control purposes.
4. Discuss the implications of changing the level of significance to a larger value. What mistake or error could increase if the level of significance were changed?

Appendix 9.1   HYPOTHESIS TESTING WITH MINITAB

Large-Sample Case

In Section 9.4 we showed the results obtained using Minitab to perform a hypothesis test for the Superflight golf ball study. Assume that the user has entered the distance data for the 36 golf balls from Table 9.2 into column 1 of a Minitab worksheet. With the sample standard deviation $s = 12$ as an estimate of the population standard deviation σ, the following steps can be used to produce the computer output in Figure 9.9.

Step 1. Select the **Stat** pull-down menu
Step 2. Select the **Basic Statistics** pull-down menu
Step 3. Select the **1-Sample Z** option
Step 4. When the dialog box appears,
   Enter C1 in the **Variables** box
   Select the **Test mean** option and enter 280 in the box
   Select **not equal** in the **Alternative** box
   Enter 12 in the **Sigma** box
   Select **OK**

Although the Superflight golf ball study involved a two-tailed hypothesis test, the procedure described can be easily modified for one-tailed hypothesis tests. In Step 4 we can conduct a one-tailed test by simply selecting the less than or the greater than option in the **Alternative** box.

Small-Sample Case

In Section 9.5 we showed the results obtained using Minitab to perform a hypothesis test for the Heathrow airport rating study. Assume that the user has entered the ratings for the 12 business travelers into column 1 of a Minitab worksheet. The following steps can be used to produce the computer output in Figure 9.11.

Step 1. Select the **Stat** pull-down menu
Step 2. Select the **Basic Statistics** pull-down menu
Step 3. Select the **1-Sample t** option

Step 4. When the dialog box appears,
          Enter C1 in the **Variables** box
          Select the **Test mean** option and enter 7 in the box
          Select the **greater than** option in the **Alternative** box
          Select **OK**

Appendix 9.2   HYPOTHESIS TESTING WITH EXCEL

Large-Sample Case

We will show how Excel can be used to conduct a hypothesis test about a population mean
by using the Superflight example introduced in Section 9.4. The data are available in the
data set Distance. The label Yards appears in cell A1 and the 36 distance values are shown
in cells A2 to A37.

Step 1. Select the **Tools** pull-down menu
Step 2. Select the **Data Analysis** option
Stcp 3. When the Data Analysis dialog box appears:
          Choose **Descriptive Statistics**
          Select **OK**
Step 4. When the Descriptive Statistics dialog box appears:
          Enter A1:A37 in the **Input Range** box
          Select **Labels in First Row**
          Select **Summary statistics**
          Select **Output Range** and enter B1 in the box
          Select **OK**
          (The value of the sample mean appears in cell C3, and the value of the standard
          error appears in cell C4.)
Step 5. Select cell D3
          Enter the cell formula = (C3-280)/C4

The cell formula in step 5 is the formula for the test statistic z. The value 280 is entered because the Superflight null hypothesis is $H_0: \mu = 280$. The cell D3 value of $z = -.75$ indicates that the null hypothesis $H_0: \mu = 280$ cannot be rejected.

Small-Sample Case

Excel can be used to conduct a hypothesis test for a small-sample case by following the
same step-by-step instructions shown for the large-sample case. Using the hypothesized
value for the population mean in the cell formula (step 5), the value of the test statistic t will
appear in cell D3. The hypothesis testing conclusion can be made based on the value of t.

10

COMPARISONS INVOLVING MEANS

CONTENTS

FISONS CORPORATION*
Rochester, New York

Fisons Corporation, Rochester, New York, is a unit of Fisons Plc., UK. Fisons opened its U.S. operations in 1966.

Fisons' Pharmaceutical Division uses extensive statistical procedures to test and develop new drugs. The testing process in the pharmaceutical industry usually consists of three stages: (1) preclinical testing, (2) testing for long-term usage and safety, and (3) clinical efficacy testing. At each successive stage, the chance that a drug will pass the rigorous tests decreases; however, the cost of further testing increases dramatically. Industry surveys indicate that on average the research and development for one new drug costs $250 million and takes 12 years. Hence, it is important to eliminate unsuccessful new drugs in the early stages of the testing process, as well as identify promising ones for further testing.

Statistics plays a major role in pharmaceutical research, where government regulations are stringent and rigorously enforced. In preclinical testing, a two- or three-population statistical study typically is used to determine whether a new drug should continue to be studied in the long-term usage and safety program. The populations may consist of the new drug, a control, and a standard drug. The preclinical testing process begins when a new drug is sent to the pharmacology group for evaluation of efficacy—the capacity of the drug to produce the desired effects. As part of the process, a statistician is asked to design an experiment that can be used to test the new drug. The design must specify the sample size and the statistical methods of analysis. In a two-population study, one sample is used to obtain data on the efficacy of the new drug (population 1) and a second sample is used to obtain data on the efficacy of a standard drug (population 2). Depending on the intended use, the new and standard drugs are tested in such disciplines as neurology, cardiology, and immunology. In most studies, the statistical method involves hypothesis testing for the

Statistical methods are used to test and develop new drugs. © SCI-VU-Genetech/Visuals Unlimited.

difference between the means of the new drug population and the standard drug population. If a new drug lacks efficacy or produces undesirable effects in comparison with the standard drug, the new drug is withdrawn from further testing. Only new drugs that show promising comparisons with the standard drugs are forwarded to the long-term usage and safety testing program.

Further data collection and multipopulation studies are conducted in the long-term usage and safety testing program and in the clinical testing programs. The Food and Drug Administration (FDA) requires that statistical methods be defined prior to such testing to avoid data-related biases. In addition, to avoid human biases, some of the clinical trials are double or triple blind. That is, neither the subject nor the investigator knows what drug is administered to whom. If the new drug meets all requirements in relation to the standard drug, a new drug application is filed with the FDA. The application is rigorously scrutinized by statisticians and scientists at the agency.

In this chapter you will learn how to construct interval estimates and make hypothesis tests about means and proportions with two populations. Techniques will be presented for analyzing independent random samples as well as matched samples.

*The authors are indebted to Dr. M. C. Trivedi for providing this Statistics in Practice.

In Chapters 8 and 9 we showed how to develop interval estimates and conduct hypothesis tests for situations involving one population mean. In this chapter we continue our discussion of statistical inference by showing how interval estimates and hypothesis tests can be developed for situations involving two or more populations. For example, we may want to develop an interval estimate of the difference between the mean starting salary for a population of men and the mean starting salary for a population of women or test a hypothesis that the mean number of hours between breakdowns is the same for four machines. We will begin our discussion by showing how an interval estimate of the difference between the means of two populations can be developed for a sampling study conducted by Greystone Department Stores, Inc.

10.1 ESTIMATION OF THE DIFFERENCE BETWEEN THE MEANS OF TWO POPULATIONS: INDEPENDENT SAMPLES

Greystone Department Stores, Inc., operates two stores in Buffalo, New York; one is in the inner city and the other is in a suburban shopping center. The regional manager has noticed that products that sell well in one store do not always sell well in the other. The manager believes this situation may be attributable to differences in customer demographics at the two locations. Customers may differ in age, education, income, and so on. Suppose the manager has asked us to investigate the difference between the mean ages of the customers who shop at the two stores.

Let us define population 1 as all customers who shop at the inner-city store and population 2 as all customers who shop at the suburban store.

μ_1 = mean of population 1 (i.e., the mean age of all customers who shop at the inner-city store)

μ_2 = mean of population 2 (i.e., the mean age of all customers who shop at the suburban store)

The difference between the two population means is $\mu_1 - \mu_2$.

To estimate $\mu_1 - \mu_2$, we will select a simple random sample of n_1 customers from population 1 and a simple random sample of n_2 customers from population 2. Because the simple random sample of n_1 customers is selected independently of the simple random sample of n_2 customers, we have the case of *independent simple random samples*.

$\bar{x}_1$ = sample mean age for the simple random sample of n_1 inner-city customers

$\bar{x}_2$ = sample mean age for the simple random sample of n_2 suburban customers

Because $\bar{x}_1$ is a point estimator of μ_1 and $\bar{x}_2$ is a point estimator of μ_2, the point estimator of the difference between the two population means is expressed as follows.

Point Estimator of the Difference between the Means of Two Populations

$$\bar{x}_1 - \bar{x}_2 \tag{10.1}$$

Thus, we see that the point estimator of the difference between the two population means is the difference between the sample means of the two independent simple random samples. Figure 10.1 provides an overview of the process used to estimate the difference between two population means based on two independent simple random samples.

Assume the customer age data collected from the two independent simple random samples of Greystone customers provide the following results.

Store	Number of Customers Sampled	Sample Mean Age	Sample Standard Deviation
Inner City	$n_1 = 36$	$\bar{x}_1 = 40$ years	$s_1 = 9$ years
Suburban	$n_2 = 49$	$\bar{x}_2 = 35$ years	$s_2 = 10$ years

Using (10.1), we find that a point estimate of the difference between the mean ages of the two populations is $\bar{x}_1 - \bar{x}_2 = 40 - 35 = 5$ years. Thus, we are led to believe that the customers at the inner-city store have a mean age five years greater than the mean age of the suburban store customers. However, as with all point estimates, we know that five years is only one of many possible estimates of the difference between the mean ages of the two populations. If Greystone selected another simple random sample of 36 inner-city customers and another simple random sample of 49 suburban customers, the difference between the two new sample means would probably not equal five years. The sampling distribution of $\bar{x}_1 - \bar{x}_2$ is the probability distribution of the difference in sample means for all possible sets of two samples.

Sampling Distribution of $\bar{x}_1 - \bar{x}_2$

We can use the sampling distribution of $\bar{x}_1 - \bar{x}_2$ to develop an interval estimate of the difference between the two population means in much the same way as we used the sampling

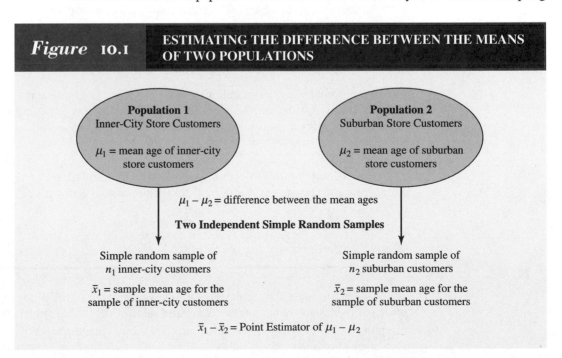

Figure 10.1   ESTIMATING THE DIFFERENCE BETWEEN THE MEANS OF TWO POPULATIONS

distribution of $\bar{x}$ for interval estimation with a single population mean. The sampling distribution of $\bar{x}_1 - \bar{x}_2$ has the following properties.

Sampling Distribution of $\bar{x}_1 - \bar{x}_2$

$$\text{Expected Value:} \quad E(\bar{x}_1 - \bar{x}_2) = \mu_1 - \mu_2 \tag{10.2}$$

$$\text{Standard Deviation:} \quad \sigma_{\bar{x}_1 - \bar{x}_2} = \sqrt{\frac{\sigma_1^2}{n_1} + \frac{\sigma_2^2}{n_2}} \tag{10.3}$$

where

σ_1 = standard deviation of population 1

σ_2 = standard deviation of population 2

n_1 = sample size for the simple random sample from population 1

n_2 = sample size for the simple random sample from population 2

Distribution form: If the sample sizes are both *large* ($n_1 \geq 30$ and $n_2 \geq 30$), the sampling distribution of $\bar{x}_1 - \bar{x}_2$ can be approximated by a normal probability distribution.

Figure 10.2 shows the sampling distribution of $\bar{x}_1 - \bar{x}_2$ and its relationship to the individual sampling distributions of $\bar{x}_1$ and $\bar{x}_2$.

Let us now develop an interval estimate of the difference between the means of two populations. We consider two cases, one in which the sample sizes are large ($n_1 \geq 30$ and $n_2 \geq 30$) and another in which one or both sample sizes are small ($n_1 < 30$ and/or $n_2 < 30$). We consider the large-sample case first.

Interval Estimate of $\mu_1 - \mu_2$: Large-Sample Case

In the large-sample case, the sampling distribution of $\bar{x}_1 - \bar{x}_2$ can be approximated by a normal probability distribution. With this approximation we can use the following expression to develop an interval estimate of the difference between the means of the two populations.

Interval Estimate of the Difference between the Means of Two Populations: Large-Sample Case ($n_1 \geq 30$ and $n_2 \geq 30$) with σ_1 and σ_2 Known

$$\bar{x}_1 - \bar{x}_2 \pm z_{\alpha/2}\sigma_{\bar{x}_1 - \bar{x}_2} \tag{10.4}$$

where $1 - \alpha$ is the confidence coefficient.

Note that to use (10.4) to develop an interval estimate of the difference between the means of two populations, we must know the value of $\sigma_{\bar{x}_1 - \bar{x}_2}$ the standard deviation of the sampling distribution of $\bar{x}_1 - \bar{x}_2$. However, (10.3) shows that the value of $\sigma_{\bar{x}_1 - \bar{x}_2}$ depends on the values of σ_1 and σ_2, the standard deviations of each of the populations. When the pop-

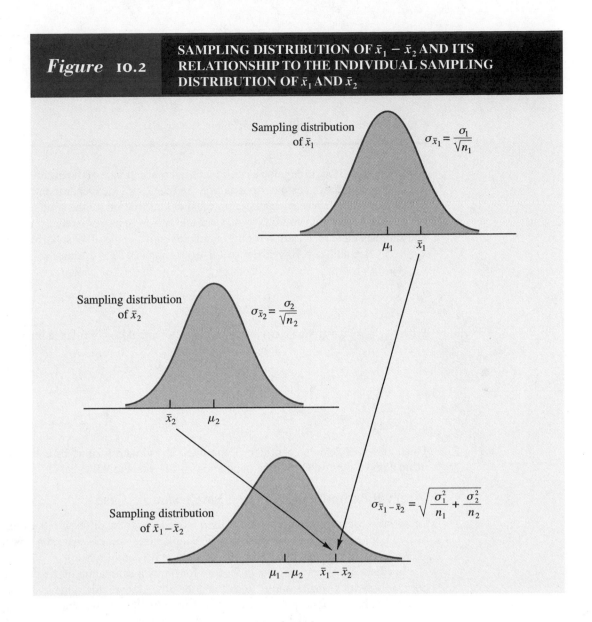

Figure 10.2

SAMPLING DISTRIBUTION OF $\bar{x}_1 - \bar{x}_2$ AND ITS
RELATIONSHIP TO THE INDIVIDUAL SAMPLING
DISTRIBUTION OF $\bar{x}_1$ AND $\bar{x}_2$

ulation standard deviations are unknown, we can use the sample standard deviations as estimates of the population standard deviations and estimate $\sigma_{\bar{x}_1 - \bar{x}_2}$ as follows.

Point Estimator of $\sigma_{\bar{x}_1 - \bar{x}_2}$

$$s_{\bar{x}_1 - \bar{x}_2} = \sqrt{\frac{s_1^2}{n_1} + \frac{s_2^2}{n_2}}$$ (10.5)

In the large-sample case, we can use this point estimator of $\sigma_{\bar{x}_1 - \bar{x}_2}$ to develop the following confidence interval estimate of the difference between the two population means.

Interval Estimate of the Difference between the Means of Two Populations: Large-Sample Case ($n_1 \geq 30$ and $n_2 \geq 30$) with σ_1 and σ_2 Unknown

$$\bar{x}_1 - \bar{x}_2 \pm z_{\alpha/2} s_{\bar{x}_1 - \bar{x}_2} \tag{10.6}$$

where $1 - \alpha$ is the confidence coefficient.

Let us use (10.6) to develop a confidence interval estimate of the difference between the mean ages of the two customer populations in the Greystone Department Store study. Recall that the sample mean age and sample standard deviation for the simple random sample of 36 inner-city customers are $\bar{x}_1 = 40$ years and $s_1 = 9$ years, respectively; the sample mean and sample standard deviation for the simple random sample of 49 suburban customers are $\bar{x}_2 = 35$ years and $s_2 = 10$ years, respectively. Using (10.5) to estimate $\sigma_{\bar{x}_1 - \bar{x}_2}$, we have

$$s_{\bar{x}_1 - \bar{x}_2} = \sqrt{\frac{(9)^2}{36} + \frac{(10)^2}{49}} = 2.07$$

With $z_{\alpha/2} = z_{.025} = 1.96$, (10.6) provides the following 95% confidence interval.

$$5 \pm (1.96)(2.07)$$

or

$$5 \pm 4.06$$

Thus, at a 95% level of confidence, the interval estimate for the difference between the mean ages of the two Greystone populations is .94 years to 9.06 years.

Interval Estimate of $\mu_1 - \mu_2$: Small-Sample Case

Let us now consider the interval-estimation procedure for the difference between the means of two populations whenever one or both sample sizes are less than 30—that is, $n_1 < 30$ and/or $n_2 < 30$, which will be referred to as the small-sample case.

In Chapter 8 we presented a procedure for interval estimation of the mean for a single population with a small sample. Recall that the procedure required the assumption that the population had a normal probability distribution. With the sample standard deviation s used as an estimate of the population standard deviation σ, the t distribution was used to develop an interval estimate of the population mean.

To develop interval estimates for the two-population small-sample case, we will make two assumptions about the two populations and the samples selected from the two populations.

1. Both populations have normal probability distributions.
2. The variances of the populations are equal ($\sigma_1^2 = \sigma_2^2 = \sigma^2$).

If the sample sizes are equal, the procedure in this section provides acceptable results even if the population variances are not equal. Thus, whenever possible, a researcher should use equal sample sizes.

Given these assumptions, the sampling distribution of $\bar{x}_1 - \bar{x}_2$ is normally distributed regardless of the sample sizes. The expected value of $\bar{x}_1 - \bar{x}_2$ is $\mu_1 - \mu_2$. Because of the equal variances assumption, (10.3) can be written

$$\sigma_{\bar{x}_1 - \bar{x}_2} = \sqrt{\frac{\sigma^2}{n_1} + \frac{\sigma^2}{n_2}} = \sqrt{\sigma^2 \left(\frac{1}{n_1} + \frac{1}{n_2} \right)} \tag{10.7}$$

The sampling distribution of $\bar{x}_1 - \bar{x}_2$ is shown in Figure 10.3.

Figure 10.3 SAMPLING DISTRIBUTION OF $\bar{x}_1 - \bar{x}_2$ WHEN THE POPULATIONS HAVE NORMAL DISTRIBUTIONS WITH EQUAL VARIANCES

Sampling distribution of $\bar{x}_1 - \bar{x}_2$

$$\sigma_{\bar{x}_1 - \bar{x}_2} = \sqrt{\sigma^2\left(\frac{1}{n_1} + \frac{1}{n_2}\right)}$$

$\mu_1 - \mu_2$

$\bar{x}_1 - \bar{x}_2$

If the variance σ^2 of the populations is known, (10.4) can be used to develop the interval estimate of the difference between the two population means. However, in most cases, σ^2 is unknown; thus, the two sample variances s_1^2 and s_2^2 must be used to develop the estimate of σ^2. Because (10.7) is based on the assumption that $\sigma_1^2 = \sigma_2^2 = \sigma^2$, we do not need separate estimates of σ_1^2 and σ_2^2. In fact, we can combine the data from the two samples to provide the best single estimate of σ^2. The process of combining the results of two independent simple random samples to provide one estimate of σ^2 is referred to as *pooling*. The *pooled estimator* of σ^2, denoted by s^2, is a weighted average of the two sample variances s_1^2 and s_2^2. The formula for the pooled estimator of σ^2 follows.

A pooled variance estimator of σ^2 is a weighted average of the two sample variances and will always be a value between s_1^2 and s_2^2.

Pooled Estimator of σ^2

$$s^2 = \frac{(n_1 - 1)s_1^2 + (n_2 - 1)s_2^2}{n_1 + n_2 - 2} \tag{10.8}$$

With s^2 as the pooled estimator of σ^2, we can substitute s^2 into (10.7) to obtain the following estimator of $\sigma_{\bar{x}_1 - \bar{x}_2}$.

Point Estimator of $\sigma_{\bar{x}_1 - \bar{x}_2}$ When $\sigma_1^2 = \sigma_2^2 = \sigma^2$

$$s_{\bar{x}_1 - \bar{x}_2} = \sqrt{s^2\left(\frac{1}{n_1} + \frac{1}{n_2}\right)} \tag{10.9}$$

The t distribution can now be used to compute an interval estimate of the difference between the means of the two populations. Because $n_1 - 1$ degrees of freedom are associated with the sample from population 1 and $n_2 - 1$ degrees of freedom are associated with the sample from population 2, the t distribution will have $n_1 + n_2 - 2$ degrees of freedom. The interval-estimation procedure follows.

Interval Estimate of the Difference between the Means of Two Populations: Small-Sample Case ($n_1 < 30$ and/or $n_2 < 30$)

$$\bar{x}_1 - \bar{x}_2 \pm t_{\alpha/2} s_{\bar{x}_1 - \bar{x}_2} \qquad (10.10)$$

where the t value is based on a t distribution with $n_1 + n_2 - 2$ degrees of freedom and where $1 - \alpha$ is the confidence coefficient.

Let us demonstrate the interval-estimation procedure for a sampling study conducted by the Clearview National Bank. Independent random samples of checking account balances for customers at two Clearview branch banks yielded the following results.

Branch Bank	Number of Accounts Sampled	Sample Mean Balance	Sample Standard Deviation
Cherry Grove	$n_1 = 12$	$\bar{x}_1 = \$1000$	$s_1 = \$150$
Beechmont	$n_2 = 10$	$\bar{x}_2 = \$\,920$	$s_2 = \$120$

Let us use these data to develop a 90% confidence interval for the difference between the mean checking account balances at the two branch banks. Suppose that checking account balances are normally distributed at both branches and that the variances of checking account balances at the branches are equal. Using (10.8), the pooled estimate of the population variance becomes

$$s^2 = \frac{(n_1 - 1)s_1^2 + (n_2 - 1)s_2^2}{n_1 + n_2 - 2} = \frac{(11)(150)^2 + (9)(120)^2}{12 + 10 - 2} = 18,855$$

Using (10.9), the corresponding estimate of $\sigma_{\bar{x}_1 - \bar{x}_2}$ is

$$s_{\bar{x}_1 - \bar{x}_2} = \sqrt{s^2\left(\frac{1}{n_1} + \frac{1}{n_2}\right)} = \sqrt{18,855\left(\frac{1}{12} + \frac{1}{10}\right)} = 58.79$$

The appropriate t distribution for the interval-estimation procedure has $n_1 + n_2 - 2 = 12 + 10 - 2 = 20$ degrees of freedom. With $\alpha = .10$, $t_{\alpha/2} = t_{.05} = 1.725$. Thus, using (10.10), we see that the interval estimate becomes

$$\bar{x}_1 - \bar{x}_2 \pm t_{.05} s_{\bar{x}_1 - \bar{x}_2}$$
$$1000 - 920 \pm (1.725)(58.79)$$
$$80 \pm 101.41$$

At a 90% confidence level, the interval estimate of the difference between the mean account balances at the two branch banks is $-\$21.41$ to $\$181.41$. The fact that the interval includes a negative range of values indicates that the actual difference between the two means, $\mu_1 - \mu_2$, may be negative. Thus, μ_2 could actually be larger than μ_1, indicating that the population mean balance could be greater for the Beechmont branch even though the results show a greater sample mean balance at the Cherry Grove branch. The fact that the confidence interval contains the value 0 can be interpreted as indicating that we do not have sufficient evidence to conclude that the population mean account balances differ between the two branches.

N O T E S _and Comments_	1. The use of the t distribution in the small-sample procedure presented in this section is based on the assumptions that both populations have a normal probability distribution and that $\sigma_1^2 = \sigma_2^2$. Fortunately, this procedure is a *robust* statistical procedure, meaning that it is relatively insensitive to these assumptions. For instance, if $\sigma_1^2 \neq \sigma_2^2$ the procedure provides acceptable results if n_1 and n_2 are approximately equal.
	2. The t distribution is not restricted to the small-sample situation; it is applicable whenever both populations are normally distributed and the variances of the populations are equal. However, (10.4) and (10.6) show how to determine an interval estimate of the difference between the means of two populations when the sample sizes are large. Thus, in the large-sample case, use of the t distribution and its corresponding assumptions are not required. We therefore do not need to refer to the t distribution until we have a small-sample case.

EXERCISES

Methods

SELF TEST

1. Consider the following results for two independent random samples taken from two populations.

	Sample 1	**Sample 2**
	$n_1 = 50$	$n_2 = 35$
	$\bar{x}_1 = 13.6$	$\bar{x}_2 = 11.6$
	$s_1 = 2.2$	$s_2 = 3.0$

   a. What is the point estimate of the difference between the two population means?
   b. Provide a 90% confidence interval for the difference between the two population means.
   c. Provide a 95% confidence interval for the difference between the two population means.

2. Consider the following results for two independent random samples taken from two populations.

	Sample 1	**Sample 2**
	$n_1 = 10$	$n_2 = 8$
	$\bar{x}_1 = 22.5$	$\bar{x}_2 = 20.1$
	$s_1 = 2.5$	$s_2 = 2.0$

   a. What is the point estimate of the difference between the two population means?
   b. What is the pooled estimate of the population variance?
   c. Develop a 95% confidence interval for the difference between the two population means.

3. Consider the following data for two independent random samples taken from two populations.

Sample 1		Sample 2	
10	7	8	7
12	7	8	4
7	9	6	9

   a. Compute the two sample means.
   b. Compute the two sample standard deviations.
   c. What is the point estimate of the difference between the two population means?
   d. What is the pooled estimate of the population variance?
   e. Develop a 95% confidence interval for the difference between the two population means.

Applications

4. Data gathered by the U.S. Department of Transportation (*1994 Information Please Environmental Almanac*) show the number of miles that residents of the 75 largest metropolitan areas travel per day in a car. Suppose that for a simple random sample of 50 Buffalo residents the mean is 22.5 miles a day and the standard deviation is 8.4 miles a day, and for an independent simple random sample of 100 Boston residents the mean is 18.6 miles a day and the standard deviation is 7.4 miles a day.
   a. What is the point estimate of the difference between the mean number of miles that Buffalo residents travel per day and the mean number of miles that Boston residents travel per day?
   b. What is the 95% confidence interval for the difference between the two population means?

5. The International Air Transport Association surveyed business travelers to determine ratings of various international airports. The maximum possible score was 10; the highest-rated airport was Amsterdam with an average rating of 7.93, followed by Toronto with a rating of 7.17 (*Newsweek,* June 13, 1994). Suppose a simple random sample of 50 business travelers was asked to rate the Miami airport, and an independent simple random sample of 50 business travelers was asked to rate the Los Angeles airport. The rating scores follow.

Miami

6	4	6	8	7	7	6	3	3	8	10	4	8
7	8	7	5	9	5	8	4	3	8	5	5	4
4	4	8	4	5	6	2	5	9	9	8	4	8
9	9	5	9	7	8	3	10	8	9	6		

Airport

Los Angeles

10	9	6	7	8	7	9	8	10	7	6	5	7
3	5	6	8	7	10	8	4	7	8	6	9	9
5	3	1	8	9	6	8	5	4	6	10	9	8
3	2	7	9	5	3	10	3	5	10	8		

Develop a 95% confidence interval estimate of the difference between the mean ratings of the Miami and Los Angeles airports.

6. The Butler County Bank and Trust Company wants to estimate the difference between the mean credit card balances at two of its branch banks. Independent random samples of credit card customers generated the following results.

Branch 1	Branch 2
$n_1 = 32$	$n_2 = 36$
$\bar{x}_1 = \$500$	$\bar{x}_2 = \$375$
$s_1 = \$150$	$s_2 = \$130$

a. Develop a point estimate of the difference between the mean balances at the two branches.
b. Develop a 99% confidence interval for the difference between the mean balances.

SELF TEST

7. An urban planning group is interested in estimating the difference between the mean household incomes for two neighborhoods in a large metropolitan area. Independent random samples of households in the neighborhoods provided the following results.

Neighborhood 1	Neighborhood 2
$n_1 = 8$	$n_2 = 12$
$\bar{x}_1 = \$15,700$	$\bar{x}_2 = \$14,500$
$s_1 = \$700$	$s_2 = \$850$

a. Develop a point estimate of the difference between the mean incomes in the two neighborhoods.
b. Develop a 95% confidence interval for the difference between the mean incomes in the two neighborhoods.
c. What assumptions were made to compute the interval estimates in part (b)?

8. The National Association of Home Builders provided data on the cost of the most popular home remodeling projects (*USA Today,* June 17, 1997). Sample data on cost in thousands of dollars for two types of remodeling projects are as follows.

Kitchen	Master Bedroom
25.2	18.0
17.4	22.9
22.8	26.4
21.9	24.8
19.7	26.9
23.0	17.8
19.7	24.6
16.9	21.0
21.8	
23.6	

a. Develop a point estimate of the difference between the population mean remodeling costs for the two types of projects.
b. Develop a 90% confidence interval for the difference between the two population means.

9. Women who are union members earn $2.50 per hour more than women who are not union members (*The Wall Street Journal*, July 26, 1994). Suppose independent random samples of 15 unionized women and 20 nonunionized women in manufacturing have been selected and the following hourly wage rates are found.

Union Workers

22.40	18.90	16.70	14.05	16.20	20.00	16.10	16.30	19.10
16.50	18.50	19.80	17.00	14.30	17.20			

Nonunion Workers

17.60	14.40	16.60	15.00	17.65	15.00	17.55	13.30	11.20
15.90	19.20	11.85	16.65	15.20	15.30	17.00	15.10	14.30
13.90	14.50							

Union

a. Suppose we want to develop an interval estimate of the difference in the mean wage rates between unionized and nonunionized women working in manufacturing. What assumptions must be made about the two populations?

b. What is the pooled estimate of the population variance?

c. Develop a 95% confidence interval estimate of the difference between the two population means.

d. Does there appear to be any difference in the mean wage rate between these two groups? Explain.

··/ /············

10.2 HYPOTHESIS TESTS ABOUT THE DIFFERENCE BETWEEN THE MEANS OF TWO POPULATIONS: INDEPENDENT SAMPLES

In this section we present procedures that can be used to test hypotheses about the difference between the means of two populations. The methodology is again divided into large-sample ($n_1 \geq 30$, $n_2 \geq 30$) and small-sample ($n_1 < 30$ and/or $n_2 < 30$) cases.

Large-Sample Case

As part of a study to evaluate differences in educational quality between two training centers, a standardized examination is given to individuals who are trained at the two centers. The examination scores are a major factor in assessing any quality differences between the centers. The means for the two centers are as follows.

μ_1 = the mean examination score for the population of individuals trained at center A

μ_2 = the mean examination score for the population of individuals trained at center B

We begin with the tentative assumption of no difference in the training quality provided at the two centers. Hence, in terms of the mean examination scores, the null hypothesis is that $\mu_1 - \mu_2 = 0$. If sample evidence leads to the rejection of this hypothesis, we will conclude that the mean examination scores differ for the two populations. This conclusion indicates a quality differential between the two centers and that a follow-up study investigating the reasons for the differential may be warranted. The null and alternative hypotheses are written as follows.

$$H_0: \mu_1 - \mu_2 = 0$$
$$H_a: \mu_1 - \mu_2 \neq 0$$

Following the hypothesis testing procedure from Chapter 9, we make the tentative assumption that H_0 is true. Using the difference between the sample means as the point estimator of the difference between the population means, we consider the sampling distribution of $\bar{x}_1 - \bar{x}_2$ when H_0 is true. For the large-sample case, this distribution is as shown in Figure 10.4. Because the sampling distribution of $\bar{x}_1 - \bar{x}_2$ can be approximated by a normal probability distribution, the following test statistic is used.

$$z = \frac{(\bar{x}_1 - \bar{x}_2) - (\mu_1 - \mu_2)}{\sqrt{\sigma_1^2/n_1 + \sigma_2^2/n_2}} \tag{10.11}$$

Whenever $n_1 \geq 30$, $n_2 \geq 30$, and σ_1^2 and σ_2^2 are unknown, we will use s_1^2 and s_2^2 as estimates of σ_1^2 and σ_2^2 to compute the test statistic.

The value of z given by (10.11) can be interpreted as the number of standard deviations $\bar{x}_1 - \bar{x}_2$ is from the value of $\mu_1 - \mu_2$ specified in H_0. For $\alpha = .05$ and thus $z_{\alpha/2} = z_{.025} = 1.96$, the rejection region for the two-tailed hypothesis test is shown in Figure 10.5. The rejection rule is

$$\text{Reject } H_0 \text{ if } z < -1.96 \text{ or if } z > +1.96$$

Let us assume that independent random samples of individuals trained at the two centers provide the examination scores in Table 10.1; summary statistics are given in Table 10.2. Using s_1^2 and s_2^2 to estimate σ_1^2 and σ_2^2, we find that the test statistic z given by (10.11) for the null hypothesis $H_0: \mu_1 - \mu_2 = 0$ becomes

$$z = \frac{(82.5 - 78) - 0}{\sqrt{(8)^2/30 + (10)^2/40}} = 2.09$$

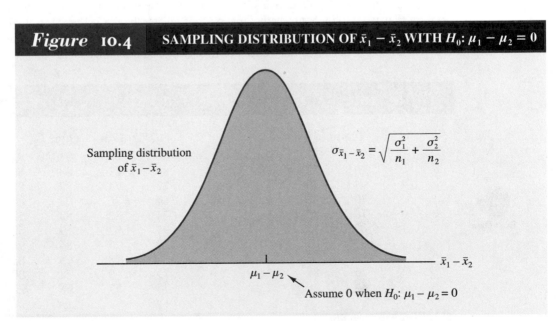

Figure 10.4   SAMPLING DISTRIBUTION OF $\bar{x}_1 - \bar{x}_2$ WITH $H_0: \mu_1 - \mu_2 = 0$

Sampling distribution of $\bar{x}_1 - \bar{x}_2$

$$\sigma_{\bar{x}_1 - \bar{x}_2} = \sqrt{\frac{\sigma_1^2}{n_1} + \frac{\sigma_2^2}{n_2}}$$

$\mu_1 - \mu_2$

$\bar{x}_1 - \bar{x}_2$

Assume 0 when $H_0: \mu_1 - \mu_2 = 0$

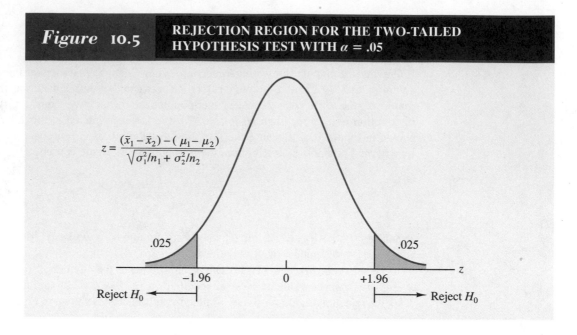

Figure 10.5   REJECTION REGION FOR THE TWO-TAILED HYPOTHESIS TEST WITH $\alpha = .05$

$$z = \frac{(\bar{x}_1 - \bar{x}_2) - (\mu_1 - \mu_2)}{\sqrt{\sigma_1^2/n_1 + \sigma_2^2/n_2}}$$

.025   .025

−1.96   0   +1.96 z

Reject H_0 Reject H_0

Because $z = 2.09 > 1.96$, the conclusion is to reject H_0. Thus, we can conclude that μ_1 and μ_2 are not equal and that the two centers differ in terms of educational quality.

With $z = 2.09$, the standard normal probability distribution table can be used to compute the p-value for this two-tailed test. With an area of .4817 between the mean and $z = 2.09$, the p-value is $2(.5000 - .4817) = .0366$; because the p-value is less than $\alpha = .05$, the p-value approach also results in the rejection of H_0.

In this hypothesis test, we were interested in determining whether the means of the two populations differ. If we have no prior belief that one mean might be greater than or less than the other, then the hypotheses $H_0: \mu_1 - \mu_2 = 0$ and $H_a: \mu_1 - \mu_2 \neq 0$ are appropriate. In other hypothesis tests about the difference between the means of two populations, we may want to find out whether one mean is greater than or perhaps less than the other mean. In these cases, a one-tailed hypothesis test would be appropriate. The two forms of a one-tailed test about the difference between two population means follow.

ExamData

Table 10.1   EXAMINATION SCORE DATA

Training Center A			Training Center B			
97	83	91	64	66	91	84
90	84	87	85	83	78	85
94	76	73	72	74	87	85
79	82	92	64	70	93	84
78	85	64	74	82	89	59
87	85	74	93	82	79	62
83	91	88	70	75	84	91
89	72	88	79	78	65	83
76	86	74	79	99	78	80
84	70	73	75	57	66	76

Table 10.2	EXAMINATION SCORE RESULTS	
	Training Center A	**Training Center B**
	$n_1 = 30$	$n_2 = 40$
	$\bar{x}_1 = 82.5$	$\bar{x}_2 = 78$
	$s_1 = 8$	$s_2 = 10$

$$H_0: \mu_1 - \mu_2 \leq 0 \qquad H_0: \mu_1 - \mu_2 \geq 0$$
$$H_a: \mu_1 - \mu_2 > 0 \qquad H_a: \mu_1 - \mu_2 < 0$$

These hypotheses are tested by using the test statistic z given by (10.11). The rejection region is determined in the same way as in the one-tailed procedure presented in Chapter 9.

Small-Sample Case

For the small-sample case, the use of the t distribution is based on the assumption that both populations have normal distributions.

Let us now consider hypothesis tests about the difference between the means of two populations for the small-sample case; that is, where $n_1 < 30$ and/or $n_2 < 30$. The procedure we will use is based on the t distribution with $n_1 + n_2 - 2$ degrees of freedom. As discussed in Section 10.1, assumptions are made that both populations have normal probability distributions and that the variances of the populations are equal.

The problem situation that we will use to illustrate the small-sample case involves a new computer software package that has been developed to help systems analysts reduce the time required to design, develop, and implement an information system. To evaluate the benefits of the new software package, a random sample of 24 systems analysts is selected. Each analyst is given specifications for a hypothetical information system, and 12 of the analysts are instructed to produce the information system by using current technology. The other 12 analysts are first trained in the use of the new software package and then instructed to use it to produce the information system.

In this study, one population consists of systems analysts using the current technology and the other consists of systems analysts using the new software package. In terms of the time required to complete the information system design project, the population means are as follow.

μ_1 = the mean project completion time for systems analysts using the current technology

μ_2 = the mean project completion time for systems analysts using the new software package

The researcher in charge of the new software evaluation project hopes to show that the new software package will provide a shorter mean project completion time. Thus, the researcher is looking for evidence to conclude that μ_2 is less than μ_1; in this case, the difference between the two population means, $\mu_1 - \mu_2$, will be greater than zero. The research hypothesis $\mu_1 - \mu_2 > 0$ is stated as the alternative hypothesis.

$$H_0: \mu_1 - \mu_2 \leq 0$$
$$H_a: \mu_1 - \mu_2 > 0$$

In tentatively assuming H_0 is true, we are taking the position that using the new software package takes as much time or perhaps even more than the current technology. The researcher is looking for evidence to reject H_0 and conclude that the new software package provides a smaller mean completion time.

Suppose that the 24 analysts complete the study with the results shown in Table 10.3. Under the assumption that the variances of the populations are equal, (10.8) is used to compute the pooled estimate of σ^2.

$$s^2 = \frac{(n_1 - 1)s_1^2 + (n_2 - 1)s_2^2}{n_1 + n_2 - 2} = \frac{11(40)^2 + 11(44)^2}{12 + 12 - 2} = 1768$$

The test statistic for the small-sample case is

$$t = \frac{(\bar{x}_1 - \bar{x}_2) - (\mu_1 - \mu_2)}{\sqrt{s^2\left(\dfrac{1}{n_1} + \dfrac{1}{n_2}\right)}} \qquad (10.12)$$

In the case of two independent random samples of sizes n_1 and n_2, the t distribution will have $n_1 + n_2 - 2$ degrees of freedom. For $\alpha = .05$, the t distribution table shows that with $12 + 12 - 2 = 22$ degrees of freedom, $t_{.05} = 1.717$. Thus, the rejection region for the one-tailed test is

$$\text{Reject } H_0 \text{ if } t > 1.717$$

The sample data and (10.12) provide the following value for the test statistic.

$$t = \frac{(325 - 288) - 0}{\sqrt{1768\left(\dfrac{1}{12} + \dfrac{1}{12}\right)}} = 2.16$$

Software

Table 10.3	COMPLETION TIME DATA AND SUMMARY STATISTICS FOR THE SOFTWARE TESTING STUDY	
	Current Technology	**New Software**
	300	276
	280	222
	344	310
	385	338
	372	200
	360	302
	288	317
	321	260
	376	320
	290	312
	301	334
	283	265
Summary Statistics		
Sample size	$n_1 = 12$	$n_2 = 12$
Sample mean	$\bar{x}_1 = 325$	$\bar{x}_2 = 288$
Sample standard deviation	$s_1 = 40$	$s_2 = 44$

Checking the rejection region, we see that $t = 2.16 > 1.717$ allows the rejection of H_0 at the .05 level of significance. Thus, the sample results enable the researcher to conclude that $\mu_1 - \mu_2 > 0$ and that the new software package provides a smaller mean completion time.

    Minitab can be used for testing hypotheses about the difference between the means of two populations. The output comparing the current and new software technology is shown in Figure 10.6. The next to last line of the output shows $t = 2.16$ and a p-value $= .021$. With $\alpha = .05$, the null hypothesis can be rejected. Thus, the mean completion time for the new software is less than the mean completion time with the current technology. However, note that the Minitab 95% confidence interval information in Figure 10.6 shows that the difference between the two population means may be as little as one hour or as much as 73 hours. This wide confidence interval suggests that further study with larger sample sizes is desirable in order to obtain a more precise estimate of how much time can be saved with the new software package.

Figure 10.6 MINITAB OUTPUT FOR THE HYPOTHESIS TEST ABOUT THE CURRENT AND NEW SOFTWARE TECHNOLOGY

```
Two sample T for Current vs New
              N       Mean      StDev    SE Mean
Current      12       325.0     40.0        12
New          12       288.0     44.0        13
95% CI for mu Current - mu New: (  1,   73)
T-Test mu Current = mu New (vs >): T = 2.16   P=0.021   DF = 22
Both use Pooled StDev = 42.0
```

NOTES and Comments

In hypothesis tests about the difference between the means of two populations, the null hypothesis almost always contains the assumption of no difference between the means. Hence, the following null hypotheses are possible choices.

$$H_0: \mu_1 - \mu_2 = 0 \qquad H_0: \mu_1 - \mu_2 \leq 0 \qquad H_0: \mu_1 - \mu_2 \geq 0$$

In some instances, we may want to determine whether there is a nonzero difference D_0 between the population means. The specific value chosen for D_0 depends on the application under study. However, in this case, the null hypothesis may be one of the following forms.

$$H_0: \mu_1 - \mu_2 = D_0 \qquad H_0: \mu_1 - \mu_2 \leq D_0 \qquad H_0: \mu_1 - \mu_2 \geq D_0$$

The hypothesis testing computations remain the same with the exception that D_0 is used for the value of $\mu_1 - \mu_2$ in (10.11) and (10.12).

EXERCISES

Methods

10. Consider the following hypothesis test.

$$H_0: \mu_1 - \mu_2 \leq 0$$
$$H_a: \mu_1 - \mu_2 > 0$$

SELF TEST

The following results are for two independent samples taken from the two populations.

Sample 1	Sample 2
$n_1 = 40$	$n_2 = 50$
$\bar{x}_1 = 25.2$	$\bar{x}_2 = 22.8$
$s_1 = 5.2$	$s_2 = 6.0$

    a.   With $\alpha = .05$, what is your hypothesis testing conclusion?
    b.   What is the p-value?

11.   Consider the following hypothesis test.

$$H_0: \mu_1 - \mu_2 = 0$$
$$H_a: \mu_1 - \mu_2 \neq 0$$

The following results are for two independent samples taken from the two populations.

Sample 1	Sample 2
$n_1 = 80$	$n_2 = 70$
$\bar{x}_1 = 104$	$\bar{x}_2 = 106$
$s_1 = 8.4$	$s_2 = 7.6$

    a.   With $\alpha = .05$, what is your hypothesis testing conclusion?
    b.   What is the p-value?

12.   Consider the following hypothesis test.

$$H_0: \mu_1 - \mu_2 = 0$$
$$H_a: \mu_1 - \mu_2 \neq 0$$

The following results are for two independent samples taken from the two populations. With $\alpha = .05$, what is your hypothesis testing conclusion?

Sample 1	Sample 2
$n_1 = 8$	$n_2 = 7$
$\bar{x}_1 = 1.4$	$\bar{x}_2 = 1.0$
$s_1 = 0.4$	$s_2 = 0.6$

Applications

13.   Refer to Exercise 5, in which two independent random samples of business travelers rated the Miami and Los Angeles airports. Summary statistics follow.

Airport	Sample Size	Sample Mean	Sample Standard Deviation
Miami	50	6.34	2.163
Los Angeles	50	6.72	2.374

Is the population mean rating for the Los Angeles airport greater than the population mean rating for the Miami airport? Support your conclusion with a statistical test using a .05 level of significance.

SELF TEST

14. The Greystone Department Store study in Section 10.1 supplied the following data on customer ages from independent random samples taken at two store locations.

	Inner-City Store	Suburban Store
	$n_1 = 36$	$n_2 = 49$
	$\bar{x}_1 = 40$ years	$\bar{x}_2 = 35$ years
	$s_1 = 9$ years	$s_2 = 10$ years

For $\alpha = .05$, test $H_0: \mu_1 - \mu_2 = 0$ against the alternative $H_a: \mu_1 - \mu_2 \neq 0$. What is your conclusion about the mean ages of the populations of customers at the two stores?

15. A firm is studying the delivery times of two raw material suppliers. The firm is basically satisfied with supplier A and is prepared to stay with that supplier if the mean delivery time is the same as or less than that of supplier B. However, if the firm finds that the mean delivery time of supplier B is less than that of supplier A, it will begin making raw material purchases from supplier B.
    a. What are the null and alternative hypotheses for this situation?
    b. Assume that independent samples show the following delivery time characteristics for the two suppliers.

	Supplier A	Supplier B
	$n_1 = 50$	$n_2 = 30$
	$\bar{x}_1 = 14$ days	$\bar{x}_2 = 12.5$ days
	$s_1 = 3$ days	$s_2 = 2$ days

With $\alpha = .05$, what is your conclusion for the hypotheses from part (a)? What action do you recommend in terms of supplier selection?

16. In a wage discrimination case involving male and female employees, independent samples of male and female employees with five years' experience or more provided the following hourly wage results. The null hypothesis is that male employees have a mean hourly wage less than or equal to that of the female employees. Rejection of H_0 leads to the conclusion that male employees have a mean hourly wage exceeding that of the female employees. Test the hypothesis with $\alpha = .01$. Does wage discrimination appear to be present in this case?

	Male Employees	Female Employees
	$n_1 = 44$	$n_2 = 32$
	$\bar{x}_1 = \$9.25$	$\bar{x}_2 = \$8.70$
	$s_1 = \$1.00$	$s_2 = \$.80$

17. Starting annual salaries for individuals entering the public accounting and financial planning professions were presented in *Fortune,* June 26, 1995. The starting salaries for a sample of 12 public accountants and a sample of 14 financial planners follow, with data in thousands of dollars.

Public Accountant	Financial Planner
30.6	31.6
31.2	26.6
28.9	25.5
35.2	25.0
25.1	25.9
33.2	32.9
31.3	26.9
35.3	25.8
31.0	27.5
30.1	29.6
29.9	23.9
24.4	26.9
	24.4
	25.5

Starting

a. Using $\alpha = .05$, test for any difference between the population mean starting annual salaries for the two professions. What is your conclusion?

b. What is the point estimate of the difference between the two population means? Which profession has the higher mean annual starting salary?

··/ /············

10.3 INFERENCES ABOUT THE DIFFERENCE BETWEEN THE MEANS OF TWO POPULATIONS: MATCHED SAMPLES

Suppose a manufacturing company has two methods by which employees can perform a production task. To maximize production output, the company wants to identify the method with the shortest mean completion time. Let μ_1 denote the mean completion time for production method 1 and μ_2 denote the mean completion time for production method 2. With no preliminary indication of the preferred production method, we begin by tentatively assuming that the two production methods have the same mean completion time. Thus, the null hypothesis is $H_0: \mu_1 - \mu_2 = 0$. If this hypothesis is rejected, we can conclude that the mean completion times differ. In this case, the method providing the shorter mean completion time would be recommended. The null and alternative hypotheses are written as follows.

$$H_0:\ \mu_1 - \mu_2 = 0$$
$$H_a:\ \mu_1 - \mu_2 \neq 0$$

In choosing the sampling procedure that will be used to collect production time data and test the hypotheses, we consider two alternative designs. One is based on *independent samples,* and the other is based on *matched samples.*

1. *Independent sample design:* A simple random sample of workers is selected and each worker in the sample uses method 1. A second independent simple random sample of workers is selected and each worker in this sample uses method 2. The test of the difference between means is based on the procedures in Section 10.2.

2. *Matched sample design:* One simple random sample of workers is selected. Each worker first uses one method and then uses the other method. The order of the two

methods is assigned randomly to the workers, with some workers performing method 1 first and others performing method 2 first. Each worker provides a pair of data values, one value for method 1 and another value for method 2.

In the matched sample design the two production methods are tested under similar conditions (i.e., with the same workers); hence this design often leads to a smaller sampling error than the independent sample design. The primary reason is that in a matched sample design, variation between workers is eliminated as a source of sampling error.

Let us demonstrate the analysis of a matched sample design by using it to test the difference between the two production methods. A random sample of six workers is used. The data on completion times for the six workers are given in Table 10.4. Note that each worker provides a pair of data values, one for each production method. Also note that the last column contains the difference in completion times d_i for each worker in the sample.

The key to the analysis of the matched sample design is to realize that we consider only the column of differences. We therefore have six data values (.6, −.2, .5, .3, .0, and .6) that will be used to analyze the difference between the means of the two production methods.

Let μ_d = the mean of the *difference* values for the population of workers. With this notation, the null and alternative hypotheses are rewritten as follows.

$$H_0:\ \mu_d = 0$$
$$H_a:\ \mu_d \neq 0$$

If H_0 can be rejected, we can conclude that the mean completion times differ.

The formulas for the sample mean and sample standard deviation use the notation d to remind the user that the data show the *difference* between the matched sample data values. Other than the use of the d notation, the formulas for the sample mean and sample standard deviation are the same ones used previously in the text.

The d notation is a reminder that the matched sample provides *difference* data. The sample mean and sample standard deviation for the six difference values in Table 10.4 follow.

$$\bar{d} = \frac{\Sigma d_i}{n} = \frac{1.8}{6} = .30$$

$$s_d = \sqrt{\frac{\Sigma(d_i - \bar{d})^2}{n - 1}} = \sqrt{\frac{.56}{5}} = .335$$

In Chapter 9 we stated that if the population can be assumed to be normally distributed, the t distribution with $n - 1$ degrees of freedom can be used to test the null hypothesis

Table 10.4	TASK COMPLETION TIMES FOR A MATCHED SAMPLE DESIGN		
Worker	Completion Time for Method 1 (minutes)	Completion Time for Method 2 (minutes)	Difference in Completion Times (d_i)
1	6.0	5.4	.6
2	5.0	5.2	−.2
3	7.0	6.5	.5
4	6.2	5.9	.3
5	6.0	6.0	.0
6	6.4	5.8	.6

about a population mean. Assuming difference data are normally distributed, the test statistic becomes

$$t = \frac{\bar{d} - \mu_d}{s_d/\sqrt{n}} \qquad (10.13)$$

With $\alpha = .05$ and $n - 1 = 5$ degrees of freedom ($t_{.025} = 2.571$), the rejection rule for the two-tailed test becomes

$$\text{Reject } H_0 \text{ if } t < -2.571 \text{ or if } t > 2.571$$

With $\bar{d} = .30$, $s_d = .335$, and $n = 6$, the value of the test statistic for the null hypothesis $H_0: \mu_d = 0$ is

$$t = \frac{\bar{d} - \mu_d}{s_d/\sqrt{n}} = \frac{.30 - 0}{.335/\sqrt{6}} = 2.19$$

Because $t = 2.19$ is not in the rejection region, the sample data do not provide sufficient evidence to reject H_0.

Using the sample results, we can obtain an interval estimate of the difference between the two population means by using the single population methodology of Chapter 8. The calculation follows.

Once the difference data have been computed, the t distribution procedure for matched samples is the same as the one-population procedure described in Chapters 8 and 9.

$$\bar{d} \pm t_{\alpha/2} \frac{s_d}{\sqrt{n}}$$

$$0.3 \pm 2.571 \left(\frac{.335}{\sqrt{6}} \right)$$

$$0.3 \pm .35$$

Thus, the 95% confidence interval for the difference between the means of the two production methods is $-.05$ minutes to $.65$ minutes. Note that because the confidence interval includes the value of zero, the sample data do not provide sufficient evidence to reject H_0.

N O T E S and Comments

1. In the example presented in this section, workers performed the production task with first one method and then the other method. This example illustrates a matched sample design in which each sampled item (worker) provides a pair of data values. It is also possible to use different but "similar" items to provide the pair of data values. For example, a worker at one location could be matched with a similar worker at another location (similarity based on age, education, sex, experience, etc.). The pairs of workers would provide the difference data that could be used in the matched sample analysis.

2. Because a matched sample procedure for inferences about two population means generally provides better precision than the independent sample approach, it is the recommended design. However, in some applications the matching cannot be achieved, or perhaps the time and cost associated with matching are excessive. In such cases, the independent sample design should be used.

3. The example presented in this section had a sample size of six workers and thus was a small-sample case. The t distribution was used in both the hypothesis test and interval-estimation computations. If the sample size is large ($n \geq 30$), use of the t distribution is unnecessary; in such cases, statistical inferences can be based on the z values of the standard normal probability distribution.

..../ /.............

EXERCISES

Methods

SELF TEST

18. Consider the following hypothesis test.

$$H_0: \mu_d \leq 0$$
$$H_a: \mu_d > 0$$

The following data are from matched samples taken from two populations.

	Population	
Element	**1**	**2**
1	21	20
2	28	26
3	18	18
4	20	20
5	26	24

a. Compute the difference value for each element.
b. Compute $\bar{d}$.
c. Compute the standard deviation s_d.
d. Test the hypothesis using $\alpha = .05$. What is your conclusion?

19. The following data are from matched samples taken from two populations.

	Population	
Element	**1**	**2**
1	11	8
2	7	8
3	9	6
4	12	7
5	13	10
6	15	15
7	15	14

a. Compute the difference value for each element.
b. Compute $\bar{d}$.
c. Compute the standard deviation s_d.
d. What is the point estimate of the difference between the two population means?
e. Provide a 95% confidence interval for the difference between the two population means.

Applications

SELF TEST

20. A market research firm used a sample of individuals to rate the purchase potential of a particular product before and after the individuals saw a new television commercial about the product. The purchase potential ratings were based on a 0 to 10 scale, with higher values indicating a higher purchase potential. The null hypothesis stated that the mean rating "after" would be less than or equal to the mean rating "before." Rejection of this hypothesis would show that the commercial improved the mean purchase potential rating. Use $\alpha = .05$ and the following data to test the hypothesis and comment on the value of the commercial.

	Purchase Rating			Purchase Rating	
Individual	After	Before	Individual	After	Before
1	6	5	5	3	5
2	6	4	6	9	8
3	7	7	7	7	5
4	4	3	8	6	6

21. To investigate the amount of savings due to purchasing store-brand versus name-brand products, *Consumer Reports* shopped for a list of items at an A&P grocery store. One cart was filled with national brand products and the other cart was filled with the store brands of the same products (*Consumer Reports,* September 1993). Sample results are as follows.

Product, Size	Name-Brand Price ($)	Store-Brand Price ($)
Ketchup, 2 lb.	1.69	0.79
Coffee, 12 oz.	2.79	1.59
Soda, 6-pack	2.79	1.64
Paper towels, 90 sheets	1.39	0.50
Ice cream, 1/2 gal.	3.99	2.39
American cheese, 1 lb.	3.99	2.99
Thin spaghetti, 1 lb.	0.89	0.53
Butter, 1 lb.	2.39	1.69
White rice, 5 lb.	3.99	1.59
Vegetable oil, qt.	2.19	1.69

a. Does the sampling procedure used by *Consumer Reports* represent an independent sample design or a matched sample design? Explain.

b. Develop a 95% confidence interval for the difference in price between name-brand products and store brand products. What assumption was necessary to develop your interval estimate?

22. The cost of transportation from the airport to the downtown area depends on the method of transportation. One-way costs for taxi and shuttle bus transportation for a sample of 10 major cities follow. Provide a 95% confidence interval for the mean cost increase associated with taxi transportation.

City	Taxi ($)	Shuttle Bus ($)	City	Taxi ($)	Shuttle Bus ($)
Atlanta	15.00	7.00	Minneapolis	16.50	7.50
Chicago	22.00	12.50	New Orleans	18.00	7.00
Denver	11.00	5.00	New York (LaGuardia)	16.00	8.50
Houston	15.00	4.50	Philadelphia	20.00	8.00
Los Angeles	26.00	11.00	Washington, D.C.	10.00	5.00

23. A survey was made of Book-of-the-Month-Club members to ascertain whether members spend more time watching television than they do reading. Assume a sample of 15 respondents provided the following data on weekly hours of television watching and weekly hours of reading. Using a .05 level of significance, can you conclude that Book-of-the-Month-Club members spend more hours per week watching television than reading?

TVRead

Respondent	Television	Reading	Respondent	Television	Reading
1	10	6	9	4	7
2	14	16	10	8	8
3	16	8	11	16	5
4	18	10	12	5	10
5	15	10	13	8	3
6	14	8	14	19	10
7	10	14	15	11	6
8	12	14			

24. A manufacturer produces both a deluxe and a standard model of an automatic sander designed for home use. Selling prices obtained from a sample of retail outlets follow.

	Model Price ($)			Model Price ($)	
Retail Outlet	Deluxe	Standard	Retail Outlet	Deluxe	Standard
1	39	27	5	40	30
2	39	28	6	39	34
3	45	35	7	35	29
4	38	30			

    a. The manufacturer's suggested retail prices for the two models show a $10 price differential. Using a .05 level of significance, test that the mean difference between the prices of the two models is $10.

    b. What is the 95% confidence interval for the difference between the mean prices of the two models?

25. The 1997 price/earnings ratios and estimated 1998 price/earnings ratios for a sample of 12 stocks are shown here (*Kiplinger's Personal Finance Magazine,* November 1997).

PERatio

Stock	1997 P/E Ratio	Est. 1998 P/E Ratio
Coca-Cola	40	32
Walt Disney	33	23
Du Pont	24	16
Eastman Kodak	21	13
General Electric	30	23
General Mills	25	19
IBM	19	14
Merck	29	21
McDonald's	20	17
Motorola	35	20
Philip Morris	17	13
Xerox	20	17

    a. Use $\alpha = .05$ and test for any change in the population mean P/E ratios for the two-year period.

    b. Provide a 95% confidence interval for the change in the population mean price/earnings ratios for the two-year period. What is your conclusion?

10.4   INTRODUCTION TO ANALYSIS OF VARIANCE

Sir Ronald Alymer Fisher (1890–1962) invented the branch of statistics known as experimental design. In addition to being accomplished in statistics, he was a noted scientist in the field of genetics.

In Section 10.2 we showed how a hypothesis test can be conducted to determine whether the means of two populations are equal based upon two independent simple random samples. In this section we introduce a statistical technique called *analysis of variance* (ANOVA), which can be used to test the hypothesis that the means of three or more populations are equal. We begin our discussion of analysis of variance by considering a problem facing National Computer Products, Inc.

National Computer Products, Inc. (NCP), manufactures printers and fax machines at plants located in Atlanta, Dallas, and Seattle. To measure how much employees at these plants know about total quality management, a random sample of six employees was selected from each plant and given a quality-awareness examination. The examination scores obtained for these 18 employees are listed in Table 10.5. The sample means, sample variances, and sample standard deviations for each group are also provided. Managers want to use these data to test the hypothesis that the mean examination score is the same for all three plants.

We will define population 1 as all employees at the Atlanta plant, population 2 as all employees at the Dallas plant, and population 3 as all employees at the Seattle plant. Let

$$\mu_1 = \text{mean examination score for population 1}$$
$$\mu_2 = \text{mean examination score for population 2}$$
$$\mu_3 = \text{mean examination score for population 3}$$

If H_0 is rejected, we cannot conclude that all population means are different. Rejecting H_0 means that at least two population means have different values.

Although we will never know the actual values of μ_1, μ_2, and μ_3, we want to use the sample results to test the following hypotheses.

$$H_0: \mu_1 = \mu_2 = \mu_3$$
$$H_a: \text{ Not all population means are equal}$$

Table 10.5	**EXAMINATION SCORES FOR 18 EMPLOYEES**		
Observation	Plant 1 Atlanta	Plant 2 Dallas	Plant 3 Seattle
1	85	71	59
2	75	75	64
3	82	73	62
4	76	74	69
5	71	69	75
6	85	82	67
Sample mean	79	74	66
Sample variance	34	20	32
Sample standard deviation	5.83	4.47	5.66

As we will demonstrate shortly, analysis of variance is a statistical procedure that can be used to determine whether the observed differences in the three sample means are large enough to reject H_0.

Analysis of variance can be used to analyze data obtained from both an observational study and an experimental study. In order to provide a common set of terminology for discussing the use of analysis of variance in both types of studies, we need to introduce the concepts of a response variable, a factor, and a treatment.

The two variables in the NCP example are plant location and score on the quality-awareness examination. Because the objective is to determine whether the mean examination score is the same for plants located in Atlanta, Dallas, and Seattle, examination score is referred to as the dependent or *response variable* and plant location as the independent variable or *factor*. In general, the values of a factor selected for investigation are referred to as levels of the factor or *treatments*. Thus, in the NCP example the three treatments are Atlanta, Dallas, and Seattle. These three treatments define the populations of interest in the NCP example. For each treatment or population, the response variable is the examination score.

Assumptions for Analysis of Variance

Three assumptions are required to use analysis of variance.

If the sample sizes are equal, analysis of variance is not sensitive to departures from the assumption of normally distributed populations.

1. **For each population, the response variable is normally distributed.** Implication: In the NCP example, the examination scores (response variable) must be normally distributed at each plant.
2. **The variance of the response variable, denoted σ^2, is the same for all of the populations.** Implication: In the NCP example, the variance of examination scores must be the same for all three plants.
3. **The observations must be independent.** Implication: In the NCP example, the examination score for each employee must be independent of the examination score for any other employee.

A Conceptual Overview

If the means for the three populations are equal, we would expect the three sample means to be close together. In fact, the closer the three sample means are to one another, the more evidence we have for the conclusion that the population means are equal. Alternatively, the more the sample means differ, the more evidence we have for the conclusion that the population means are not equal. In other words, if the variability among the sample means is "small," it supports H_0; if the variability among the sample means is "large," it supports H_a.

If the null hypothesis, $H_0: \mu_1 = \mu_2 = \mu_3$, is true, we can use the variability among the sample means to develop an estimate of σ^2. To see how, note that if the assumptions for analysis of variance are satisfied, each sample will have come from the same normal probability distribution with mean μ and variance σ^2. Recall from Chapter 7 that the sampling distribution of the sample mean $\bar{x}$ for a simple random sample of size n from a normal population will be normally distributed with mean μ and variance σ^2/n. Figure 10.7 illustrates such a sampling distribution.

Thus, if the null hypothesis is true, we can think of each of the three sample means, $\bar{x}_1 = 79$, $\bar{x}_2 = 74$, and $\bar{x}_3 = 66$, from Table 10.5 as values drawn at random from the

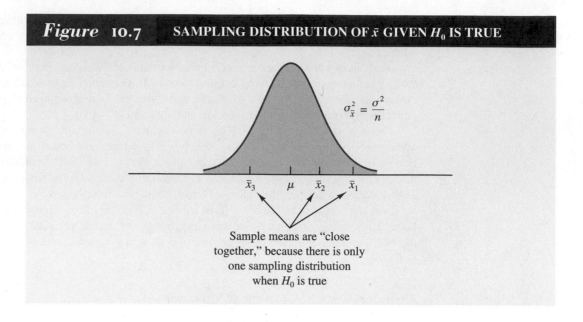

Figure 10.7   SAMPLING DISTRIBUTION OF $\bar{x}$ GIVEN H_0 IS TRUE

$$\sigma^2_{\bar{x}} = \frac{\sigma^2}{n}$$

$\bar{x}_3$ μ $\bar{x}_2$ $\bar{x}_1$

Sample means are "close
together," because there is only
one sampling distribution
when H_0 is true

sampling distribution shown in Figure 10.7. In this case, the mean and variance of the three
$\bar{x}$ values can be used to estimate the mean and variance of the sampling distribution. In the
NCP example, the best estimate of the mean of the sampling distribution of $\bar{x}$ is the mean
or average of the three sample means. That is, $(79 + 74 + 66)/3 = 73$. We refer to this estimate as the *overall sample mean*. An estimate of the variance of the sampling distribution
of $\bar{x}$ is provided by the variance of the three sample means.

$$s^2_{\bar{x}} = \frac{(79 - 73)^2 + (74 - 73)^2 + (66 - 73)^2}{3 - 1} = \frac{86}{2} = 43$$

Because $\sigma^2_{\bar{x}} = \sigma^2/n$, solving for σ^2 gives

$$\sigma^2 = n\sigma^2_{\bar{x}}$$

Hence,

$$\text{Estimate of } \sigma^2 = n \text{ (Estimate of } \sigma^2_{\bar{x}}) = ns^2_{\bar{x}} = 6(43) = 258$$

The result, $ns^2_{\bar{x}} = 258$, is referred to as the *between-treatments* estimate of σ^2.

      The between-treatments estimate of σ^2 is based on the assumption that
the null hypothesis is true. In this case, each sample comes from the same population, and
there is only one sampling distribution of $\bar{x}$. To illustrate what happens when H_0 is false,
suppose the population means *all differ*. Note that because the three samples are from normal populations with different means, there will be three different sampling distributions.
Figure 10.8 shows that in this case, the sample means are not as close together as they were
when H_0 was true. Thus, $s^2_{\bar{x}}$ will be larger, causing the between-treatments estimate of σ^2 to
be larger. In general, when the population means are not equal, the between-treatments estimate will overestimate the population variance σ^2.

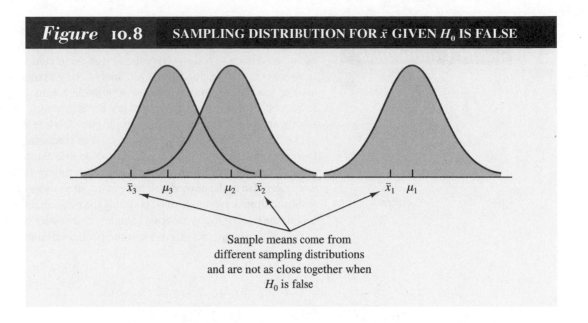

Figure 10.8   SAMPLING DISTRIBUTION FOR $\bar{x}$ GIVEN H_0 IS FALSE

Sample means come from
different sampling distributions
and are not as close together when
H_0 is false

The variation within each of the samples also has an effect on the conclusion we reach in analysis of variance. When a simple random sample is selected from each population, each of the sample variances provides an unbiased estimate of σ^2. Hence, we can combine or pool the individual estimates of σ^2 into one overall estimate. The estimate of σ^2 obtained in this way is called the *pooled* or *within-treatments* estimate of σ^2. Because each sample variance provides an estimate of σ^2 based only on the variation within each sample, the within-treatments estimate of σ^2 is not affected by whether the population means are equal. When the sample sizes are equal, the within-treatments estimate of σ^2 can be obtained by computing the average of the individual sample variances. For the NCP example we obtain

$$\text{Within-Treatments Estimate of } \sigma^2 = \frac{34 + 20 + 32}{3} = \frac{86}{3} = 28.67$$

In the NCP example, the between-treatments estimate of σ^2 (258) is much larger than the within-treatments estimate of σ^2 (28.67). In fact, the ratio of these two estimates is $258/28.67 = 9.00$. Recall, however, that the between-treatments approach provides a good estimate of σ^2 only if the null hypothesis is true; if the null hypothesis is false, the between-treatments approach *overestimates* σ^2. The within-treatments approach provides a good estimate of σ^2 in either case. Thus, if the null hypothesis is true, the two estimates will be similar and their ratio will be close to 1. If the null hypothesis is false, the between-treatments estimate will be larger than the within-treatments estimate, and their ratio will be large. In the next section we will show how large this ratio must be to reject H_0.

In summary, the logic behind ANOVA is based on the development of two independent estimates of the common population variance σ^2. One estimate of σ^2 is based on the variability among the sample means themselves, and the other estimate of σ^2 is based on the variability of the data within each sample. By comparing these two estimates of σ^2, we will be able to determine whether the population means are equal.

<table>
<tr><td>

N O T E S
and Comments

</td><td>

1. In Sections 10.2 and 10.3 we presented statistical methods for testing the hypothesis that the means of two populations are equal. ANOVA can also be used to test the hypothesis that the means of two populations are equal. In practice, however, analysis of variance is usually not used unless there are three or more population means.

2. In Section 10.2 we discussed how to test for the equality of two population means whenever one or both sample sizes are less than 30. As part of that discussion we illustrated the process of combining the results of two independent random samples to provide one estimate of σ^2; that process was referred to as pooling, and the resulting sample variance was referred to as the pooled estimator of σ^2. In analysis of variance, the within-treatments estimate of σ^2 is simply the generalization of that concept to the case of more than two samples; that is why we also referred to the within-treatments estimator as the pooled estimator of σ^2.

</td></tr>
</table>

10.5   ANALYSIS OF VARIANCE: TESTING FOR THE EQUALITY OF k POPULATION MEANS

Analysis of variance can be used to test for the equality of k population means. The general form of the hypotheses tested is

$$H_0: \ \mu_1 = \mu_2 = \cdots = \mu_k$$
$$H_a: \ \text{Not all population means are equal}$$

where

$$\mu_j = \text{mean of the } j\text{th population}$$

We assume that a simple random sample of size n_j has been selected from each of the k populations or treatments. For the resulting sample data, let

$$x_{ij} = \text{value of observation } i \text{ for treatment } j$$
$$n_j = \text{number of observations for treatment } j$$
$$\bar{x}_j = \text{sample mean for treatment } j$$
$$s_j^2 = \text{sample variance for treatment } j$$
$$s_j = \text{sample standard deviation for treatment } j$$

The formulas for the sample mean and sample variance for treatment j are as follow.

$$\bar{x}_j = \frac{\sum_{i=1}^{n_j} x_{ij}}{n_j} \tag{10.14}$$

$$s_j^2 = \frac{\sum_{i=1}^{n_j} (x_{ij} - \bar{x}_j)^2}{n_j - 1} \tag{10.15}$$

The overall sample mean, denoted $\bar{\bar{x}}$, is the sum of all the observations divided by the total number of observations. That is,

$$\bar{\bar{x}} = \frac{\sum\limits_{j=1}^{k} \sum\limits_{i=1}^{n_j} x_{ij}}{n_T} \tag{10.16}$$

where

$$n_T = n_1 + n_2 + \cdots + n_k \tag{10.17}$$

If the size of each sample is n, $n_T = kn$; in this case (10.16) reduces to

$$\bar{\bar{x}} = \frac{\sum\limits_{j=1}^{k} \sum\limits_{i=1}^{n_j} x_{ij}}{nk} = \frac{\sum\limits_{j=1}^{k} \sum\limits_{i=1}^{n_j} x_{ij}/n}{k} = \frac{\sum\limits_{j=1}^{k} \bar{x}_j}{k} \tag{10.18}$$

In other words, whenever the sample sizes are the same, the overall sample mean is just the average of the k sample means.

Because each sample in the NCP example consists of $n = 6$ observations, the overall sample mean can be computed by using (10.18). For the data in Table 10.5 we obtained the following result.

$$\bar{\bar{x}} = \frac{79 + 74 + 66}{3} = 73$$

Thus, if the null hypothesis is true ($\mu_1 = \mu_2 = \mu_3 = \mu$), the overall sample mean of 73 is the best estimate of the population mean μ.

Between-Treatments Estimate of Population Variance

In Section 10.4, we introduced the concept of a between-treatments estimate of σ^2. This estimate of σ^2 is called the *mean square due to treatments* and is denoted MSTR. The formula for computing MSTR is

$$\text{MSTR} = \frac{\sum\limits_{j=1}^{k} n_j(\bar{x}_j - \bar{\bar{x}})^2}{k - 1} \tag{10.19}$$

The numerator in (10.19) is called the *sum of squares due to treatments* and is denoted SSTR. The denominator, $k - 1$, represents the degrees of freedom associated with SSTR. Hence, the mean square due to treatments can be computed by the following formula.

Mean Square Due to Treatments

$$\text{MSTR} = \frac{\text{SSTR}}{k - 1} \tag{10.20}$$

where

$$\text{SSTR} = \sum\limits_{j=1}^{k} n_j(\bar{x}_j - \bar{\bar{x}})^2 \tag{10.21}$$

If H_0 is true, MSTR provides an unbiased estimate of σ^2. However, if the means of the k populations are not equal, MSTR is not an unbiased estimate of σ^2; in fact, in that case, MSTR should overestimate σ^2.

For the NCP data in Table 10.5, we obtain the following results.

$$\text{SSTR} = \sum_{j=1}^{k} n_j(\bar{x}_j - \bar{\bar{x}})^2 = 6(79 - 73)^2 + 6(74 - 73)^2 + 6(66 - 73)^2 = 516$$

$$\text{MSTR} = \frac{\text{SSTR}}{k - 1} = \frac{516}{2} = 258$$

Within-Treatments Estimate of Population Variance

In Section 10.4 we introduced the concept of a within-treatments estimate of σ^2. This estimate of σ^2 is called the *mean square* due to error and is denoted MSE. The formula for computing MSE is

$$\text{MSE} = \frac{\sum_{j=1}^{k}(n_j - 1)s_j^2}{n_T - k} \qquad (10.22)$$

The numerator in (10.22) is called the *sum of squares due to error* and is denoted SSE. The denominator of MSE is referred to as the degrees of freedom associated with SSE. Hence, the formula for MSE can also be stated as follows.

Mean Square Due to Error

$$\text{MSE} = \frac{\text{SSE}}{n_T - k} \qquad (10.23)$$

where

$$\text{SSE} = \sum_{j=1}^{k}(n_j - 1)s_j^2 \qquad (10.24)$$

Note that MSE is based on the variation within each of the treatments; it is not influenced by whether the null hypothesis is true. Thus, MSE always provides an unbiased estimate of σ^2.

For the NCP data in Table 10.5 we obtain the following results.

$$\text{SSE} = \sum_{j=1}^{k}(n_j - 1)s_j^2 = (6 - 1)34 + (6 - 1)20 + (6 - 1)32 = 430$$

$$\text{MSE} = \frac{\text{SSE}}{n_T - k} = \frac{430}{18 - 3} = \frac{430}{15} = 28.67$$

Comparing the Variance Estimates: The *F* Test

Let us assume that the null hypothesis is true. In that case, MSTR and MSE provide two independent, unbiased estimates of σ^2. For normal populations, the sampling distribution of the ratio of two independent estimates of σ^2 follows an F distribution. Hence, if the null hypothesis is true and the ANOVA assumptions are valid, the sampling distribution of MSTR/MSE is an F distribution with numerator degrees of freedom equal to $k - 1$ and denominator degrees of freedom equal to $n_T - k$.

If the means of the k populations are not equal, the value of MSTR/MSE will be inflated because MSTR overestimates σ^2. Hence, we will reject H_0 if the resulting value of MSTR/MSE appears to be too large to have been selected at random from an F distribution with degrees of freedom $k - 1$ in the numerator and $n_T - k$ in the denominator. The value of MSTR/MSE that will cause us to reject H_0 depends on α, the level of significance. Once α is selected, a critical value can be determined. Figure 10.9 shows the sampling distribution of MSTR/MSE and the rejection region associated with a level of significance equal to α where F_α denotes the critical value. A summary of the overall procedure follows.

Test for the Equality of k Population Means

$$H_0:\ \mu_1 = \mu_2 = \cdots = \mu_k$$
$$H_a:\ \text{Not all population means are equal}$$

Test Statistic

$$F = \frac{\text{MSTR}}{\text{MSE}} \qquad\qquad (10.25)$$

Rejection Rule at a Level of Significance α

$$\text{Reject } H_0 \text{ if } F > F_\alpha$$

where the value of F_α is based on an F distribution with $k - 1$ numerator degrees of freedom and $n_T - k$ denominator degrees of freedom.

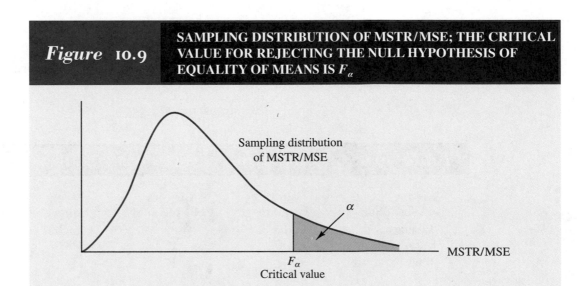

Figure 10.9   SAMPLING DISTRIBUTION OF MSTR/MSE; THE CRITICAL VALUE FOR REJECTING THE NULL HYPOTHESIS OF EQUALITY OF MEANS IS F_α

Suppose the manager responsible for making the decision in the National Computer Products example was willing to accept a probability of a Type I error of $\alpha = .05$. From Table 4 of Appendix B we can determine the critical F value by locating the value corresponding to numerator degrees of freedom equal to $k - 1 = 3 - 1 = 2$ and denominator degrees of freedom equal to $n_T - k = 18 - 3 = 15$. Thus, we obtain the value $F_{.05} = 3.68$, which tells us that if we were to select a value at random from an F distribution with two numerator degrees of freedom and 15 denominator degrees of freedom, only 5% of the time would we observe a value greater than 3.68. Moreover, the theory behind the analysis of variance tells us that if the null hypothesis is true, the ratio of MSTR/MSE would be a value from this F distribution. Hence, the appropriate rejection rule for the NCP example is written

$$\text{Reject } H_0 \text{ if MSTR/MSE} > 3.68$$

Recall that MSTR = 258 and MSE = 28.67. Since MSTR/MSE = 258/28.67 = 9.00 is greater than the critical value, $F_{.05} = 3.68$, we have sufficient evidence to reject the null hypothesis that the means of the three populations are equal. In other words, analysis of variance supports the conclusion that the population mean examination scores at the three NCP plants are not equal.

ANOVA Table

The results of the preceding calculations can be displayed conveniently in a table referred to as the *analysis of variance table*. Table 10.6 is the analysis of variance table for the National Computer Products example. The sum of squares associated with the source of variation referred to as "Total" is called the total sum of squares (SST). Note that the results for the NCP example suggest that SST = SSTR + SSE, and that the degrees of freedom associated with this total sum of squares is the sum of the degrees of freedom associated with the between-treatments estimate of σ^2 and the within-treatments estimate of σ^2.

We point out that SST divided by its degrees of freedom $n_T - 1$ is nothing more than the overall sample variance that would be obtained if we treated the entire set of 18 observations as one data set. With the entire data set as one sample, the formula for computing the total sum of squares, SST, is

$$\text{SST} = \sum_{j=1}^{k} \sum_{i=1}^{n_j} (x_{ij} - \bar{\bar{x}})^2 \tag{10.26}$$

It can be shown that the results we observed for the analysis of variance table for the NCP example also apply to other problems. That is,

$$\text{SST} = \text{SSTR} + \text{SSE} \tag{10.27}$$

Table 10.6   ANALYSIS OF VARIANCE TABLE FOR THE NCP EXAMPLE

Source of Variation	Sum of Squares	Degrees of Freedom	Mean Square	F
Treatments	516	2	258.00	9.00
Error	430	15	28.67	
Total	946	17		

Analysis of variance can be thought of as a statistical procedure for partitioning the total sum of squares into separate components.

In other words, SST can be partitioned into two sums of squares: the sum of squares due to treatments and the sum of squares due to error. The degrees of freedom corresponding to SST, $n_T - 1$, can also be partitioned into the degrees of freedom corresponding to SSTR, $k - 1$, and the degrees of freedom corresponding to SSE, $n_T - k$. The analysis of variance can be viewed as the process of partitioning the total sum of squares and the degrees of freedom into their corresponding sources: treatments and error. Dividing the sum of squares by the appropriate degrees of freedom provides the variance estimates and the F value used to test the hypothesis of equal population means.

Computer Results for Analysis of Variance

Because of the widespread availability of statistical computer packages, analysis of variance computations with large sample sizes and/or a large number of populations can be performed easily. In Figure 10.10 we show output for the NCP example obtained from the Minitab computer package. The first part of the computer output contains the familiar ANOVA table format. Comparing Figure 10.10 with Table 10.6, we see that the same information is available, although some of the headings are slightly different. The heading Source is used for the source of variation column, and Factor identifies the treatments row. The sum of squares and degrees of freedom columns are interchanged, and a p-value is provided for the F test. Given the level of significance α, the decision whether to reject H_0 can be made as follows:

$$\text{Reject } H_0 \text{ if the } p\text{-value} < \alpha.$$

Thus, at the $\alpha = .05$ level of significance, we reject H_0 because the p value $= 0.003 < \alpha = .05$.

Note that following the ANOVA table the computer output contains the respective sample sizes, the sample means, and the standard deviations. In addition, Minitab provides a figure that shows individual 95% confidence interval estimates of each population mean. In developing these confidence interval estimates, Minitab uses MSE as the estimate of σ^2. Thus, the square root of MSE provides the best estimate of the population standard deviation σ. This estimate of σ on the computer output is Pooled StDev; it is equal to 5.354. To

---

Figure 10.10   MINITAB OUTPUT FOR THE NCP ANALYSIS OF VARIANCE

```
Analysis of Variance
Source       DF        SS        MS        F         p
Factor        2     516.0     258.0      9.00     0.003
Error        15     430.0      28.7
Total        17     946.0
                                     Individual 95% CIs For Mean
                                     Based on Pooled StDev
  Level      N      Mean      StDev   ---+---------+---------+---------+---
Atlanta      6    79.000     5.831                           (------*------)
Dallas       6    74.000     4.472                  (------*-----)
Seattle      6    66.000     5.657      (-----*------)
                                     ---+---------+---------+---------+---
Pooled StDev =     5.354              63.0      70.0      77.0      84.0
```

provide an illustration of how the interval estimates in Figure 10.10 are developed, we will compute a 95% confidence interval estimate of the population mean for the Atlanta plant.

From our study of interval estimation in Chapter 8, we know that the general form of an interval estimate of a population mean is

$$\bar{x} \pm t_{\alpha/2} \frac{s}{\sqrt{n}} \tag{10.28}$$

where s is the estimate of the population standard deviation σ. Because in the analysis of variance the best estimate of σ is provided by the square root of MSE or the Pooled StDev, we use a value of 5.354 for s in (10.28). The degrees of freedom for the t value is 15, the degrees of freedom associated with the within-treatments estimate of σ^2. Hence, with $t_{.025} = 2.131$ we obtain

$$79 \pm 2.131 \frac{5.354}{\sqrt{6}} = 79 \pm 4.66$$

Thus, the individual 95% confidence interval for the Atlanta plant goes from $79 - 4.66 = 74.34$ to $79 + 4.6 = 83.66$. Because the sample sizes are equal for the NCP example, the individual confidence intervals for the Dallas and Seattle plants are also constructed by adding and subtracting 4.66 from each sample mean. Thus, in the figure provided by Minitab we see that the widths of the confidence intervals are the same.

N O T E S and Comments

1. The overall sample mean can also be computed as a weighted average of the k sample means.

$$\bar{\bar{x}} = \frac{n_1\bar{x}_1 + n_2\bar{x}_2 + \cdots + n_k\bar{x}_k}{n_T}$$

In problems where the sample means are provided, this formula is simpler than (10.16) for computing the overall mean.

2. If each sample consists of n observations, (10.19) can be written as

$$\text{MSTR} = \frac{n\sum_{j=1}^{k}(\bar{x}_j - \bar{\bar{x}})^2}{k-1} = n\left[\frac{\sum_{j=1}^{k}(\bar{x}_j - \bar{\bar{x}})^2}{k-1}\right] = ns_{\bar{x}}^2$$

Note that this result is the same as presented in Section 10.4 when we introduced the concept of the between-treatments estimate of σ^2. Equation (10.19) is simply a generalization of this result to the unequal sample-size case.

3. If each sample has n observations, $n_T = kn$; thus, $n_T - k = k(n-1)$, and (10.22) can be rewritten as

$$\text{MSE} = \frac{\sum_{j=1}^{k}(n-1)s_j^2}{k(n-1)} = \frac{(n-1)\sum_{j=1}^{k}s_j^2}{k(n-1)} = \frac{\sum_{j=1}^{k}s_j^2}{k}$$

In other words, if the sample sizes are the same, MSE is just the average of the k sample variances. Note that we used this result in Section 10.4 when we introduced the concept of the within-treatments estimate of σ^2.

EXERCISES

Methods

SELF TEST

26. Samples of five observations were selected from each of three populations. The data obtained follow.

Observation	Sample 1	Sample 2	Sample 3
1	32	44	33
2	30	43	36
3	30	44	35
4	26	46	36
5	32	48	40
Sample mean	30	45	36
Sample variance	6.00	4.00	6.50

    a. Compute the between-treatments estimate of σ^2.
    b. Compute the within-treatments estimate of σ^2.
    c. At the $\alpha = .05$ level of significance, can we reject the null hypothesis that the means of the three populations are equal?
    d. Set up the ANOVA table for this problem.

27. Four observations were selected from each of three populations. The data obtained follow.

Observation	Sample 1	Sample 2	Sample 3
1	165	174	169
2	149	164	154
3	156	180	161
4	142	158	148
Sample mean	153	169	158
Sample variance	96.67	97.33	82.00

    a. Compute the between-treatments estimate of σ^2.
    b. Compute the within-treatments estimate of σ^2.
    c. At the $\alpha = .05$ level of significance, can we reject the null hypothesis that the three population means are equal? Explain.
    d. Set up the ANOVA table for this problem.

28. A random sample of 16 observations was selected from each of four populations. A portion of the ANOVA table follows.

Source of Variation	Sum of Squares	Degrees of Freedom	Mean Square	F
Treatments			400	
Error				
Total	1500			

a. Provide the missing entries for the ANOVA table.
b. At the $\alpha = .05$ level of significance, can we reject the null hypothesis that the means of the four populations are equal?

Applications

SELF TEST

29. To test whether the mean time needed to mix a batch of material is the same for machines produced by three manufacturers, the Jacobs Chemical Company obtained the following data on the time (in minutes) needed to mix the material. Use these data to test whether the population mean times for mixing a batch of material differ for the three manufacturers. Use $\alpha = .05$.

	Manufacturer	
1	**2**	**3**
20	28	20
26	26	19
24	31	23
22	27	22

30. Managers at all levels of an organization need adequate information to perform their respective tasks. One study investigated the effect the source has on the dissemination of the information. In this particular study the sources of information were a superior, a peer, and a subordinate. In each case, a measure of dissemination was obtained, with higher values indicating greater dissemination of information. Using $\alpha = .05$ and the following data, test whether the source of information significantly affects dissemination. What is your conclusion, and what does it suggest about the use and dissemination of information?

Superior	Peer	Subordinate
8	6	6
5	6	5
4	7	7
6	5	4
6	3	3
7	4	5
5	7	7
5	6	5

31. A study reported in the *Journal of Small Business Management* concluded that self-employed individuals experience higher job stress than individuals who are not self-employed. In this study job stress was assessed with a 15-item scale designed to measure various aspects of ambiguity and role conflict. Ratings for each of the 15 items were made using a scale with 1–5 response options ranging from strong agreement to strong disagreement. The sum of the ratings for the 15 items for each individual surveyed is between 15 and 75, with higher values indicating a higher degree of job stress (*Journal of Small Business Management,* October 1997). Suppose that a similar approach, using a 20-item scale with 1–5 response options, was used to measure the job stress of individuals for 15 randomly selected real estate agents, 15 architects, and 15 stockbrokers. The results obtained follow.

Stress

Real Estate Agent	Architect	Stockbroker
81	43	65
48	63	48
68	60	57
69	52	91
54	54	70
62	77	67
76	68	83
56	57	75
61	61	53
65	80	71
64	50	54
69	37	72
83	73	65
85	84	58
75	58	58

Using $\alpha = .05$, test for any significant difference in job stress among the three professions.

32. The *Business Week* Global 1000 ranks companies on the basis of their market value (*Business Week*, July 7, 1997). The following table shows the P/E ratios for 29 companies classified as being in the finance economic sector. An industry code of 1 indicates a banking firm, a code of 2 a financial services firm, and a code of 3 an insurance firm. At the .05 level of significance, test whether the mean price/earnings ratio is the same for these three groups of financial firms.

MktValue

Company	Industry Code	P/E	Company	Industry Code	P/E
Citicorp	1	15	MBNA	2	24
NationsBank	1	14	Cincinnati Financial	2	19
Wells Fargo	1	25	Franklin Resources	2	22
First Union	1	13	Fannie Mae	2	17
KeyCorp	1	14	American International	3	21
Chase Manhattan	1	12	Group		
Fifth Third Bancorp	1	23	Allstate	3	14
Bank of New York	1	17	Marsh & McLennan	3	20
First Chicago NBD	1	13	American General	3	16
Mellon Bank	1	16	Cigna	3	12
Fleet Financial	1	15	Lincoln National	3	13
Group			AFLAC	3	21
First Bank System	1	16	Equitable	3	11
American Express	2	19	Chubb	3	20
Travelers	2	15	General Re	3	15
Merrill Lynch	2	12			

SUMMARY

In this chapter we discussed procedures for developing interval estimates and conducting hypothesis tests involving two or more population means. First, we showed how to make inferences about the difference between the means of two populations when independent simple random samples are selected. We considered both the large- and small-sample cases. The z values from the standard normal probability distribution are used for inferences about the difference between two population means when the sample sizes are large. In the small-sample case, if the populations are normally distributed with equal variances, the t distribution is used for inferences.

Inferences about the difference between the means of two populations were then discussed for the matched-sample design. In the matched sample design each element provides a pair of data values, one from each population. The difference between the paired data values is then used in the statistical analysis. The matched sample design is generally preferred to the independent sample design because the matched-sample procedure often reduces the sampling error and improves the precision of the estimate.

Finally, we showed how analysis of variance can be used to test for differences among means of several populations. We showed that the basis for the statistical tests used in analysis of variance is the development of two independent estimates of the population variance, σ^2. By computing the ratio of these two estimates (the F statistic), we developed a rejection rule for determining whether to reject the null hypothesis that the population means are equal.

GLOSSARY

Independent samples Samples selected from two (or more) populations in such a way that the elements making up one sample are chosen independently of the elements making up the other sample(s).

Pooled variance An estimate of the variance of a population based on the combination of two (or more) sample variances. The pooled variance estimate is appropriate whenever the variances of two (or more) populations are assumed equal.

Matched samples Samples in which each data value of one sample is matched with a corresponding data value of the other sample.

Analysis of variance A statistical technique that can be used to test the hypothesis that the means of three or more populations are equal.

ANOVA table A table used to summarize the analysis of variance computations and results.

KEY FORMULAS

Point Estimator of the Difference between the Means of Two Populations

$$\bar{x}_1 - \bar{x}_2 \tag{10.1}$$

Expected Value of $\bar{x}_1 - \bar{x}_2$

$$E(\bar{x}_1 - \bar{x}_2) = \mu_1 - \mu_2 \tag{10.2}$$

Standard Deviation of $\bar{x}_1 - \bar{x}_2$

$$\sigma_{\bar{x}_1-\bar{x}_2} = \sqrt{\frac{\sigma_1^2}{n_1} + \frac{\sigma_2^2}{n_2}} \tag{10.3}$$

Interval Estimate of the Difference between the Means of Two Populations: Large-Sample Case ($n_1 \geq 30$ and $n_2 \geq 30$) with σ_1 and σ_2 Known

$$\bar{x}_1 - \bar{x}_2 \pm z_{\alpha/2}\sigma_{\bar{x}_1-\bar{x}_2} \qquad (10.4)$$

Point Estimator of $\sigma_{\bar{x}_1-\bar{x}_2}$

$$s_{\bar{x}_1-\bar{x}_2} = \sqrt{\frac{s_1^2}{n_1} + \frac{s_2^2}{n_2}} \qquad (10.5)$$

Interval Estimate of the Difference between the Means of Two Populations: Large-Sample Case ($n_1 \geq 30$ and $n_2 \geq 30$) with σ_1 and σ_2 Unknown

$$\bar{x}_1 - \bar{x}_2 \pm z_{\alpha/2}s_{\bar{x}_1-\bar{x}_2} \qquad (10.6)$$

Standard Deviation of $\bar{x}_1 - \bar{x}_2$ When $\sigma_1^2 = \sigma_2^2$

$$\sigma_{\bar{x}_1-\bar{x}_2} = \sqrt{\frac{\sigma^2}{n_1} + \frac{\sigma^2}{n_2}} = \sqrt{\sigma^2\left(\frac{1}{n_1} + \frac{1}{n_2}\right)} \qquad (10.7)$$

Pooled Estimator of σ^2

$$s^2 = \frac{(n_1 - 1)s_1^2 + (n_2 - 1)s_2^2}{n_1 + n_2 - 2} \qquad (10.8)$$

Point Estimator of $\sigma_{\bar{x}_1-\bar{x}_2}$ When $\sigma_1^2 = \sigma_2^2 = \sigma^2$

$$s_{\bar{x}_1-\bar{x}_2} = \sqrt{s^2\left(\frac{1}{n_1} + \frac{1}{n_2}\right)} \qquad (10.9)$$

Interval Estimate of the Difference between the Means of Two Populations: Small-Sample Case ($n_1 < 30$ and/or $n_2 < 30$)

$$\bar{x}_1 - \bar{x}_2 \pm t_{\alpha/2}s_{\bar{x}_1-\bar{x}_2} \qquad (10.10)$$

Test Statistic for Hypothesis Tests about the Difference between the Means of Two Populations (Large-Sample Case)

$$z = \frac{(\bar{x}_1 - \bar{x}_2) - (\mu_1 - \mu_2)}{\sqrt{\sigma_1^2/n_1 + \sigma_2^2/n_2}} \qquad (10.11)$$

Test Statistic for Hypothesis Tests about the Difference between the Means of Two Populations (Small-Sample Case)

$$t = \frac{(\bar{x}_1 - \bar{x}_2) - (\mu_1 - \mu_2)}{\sqrt{s^2\left(\frac{1}{n_1} + \frac{1}{n_2}\right)}} \qquad (10.12)$$

Sample Mean for Matched Samples

$$\bar{d} = \frac{\Sigma d_i}{n}$$

Sample Standard Deviation for Matched Samples

$$s_d = \sqrt{\frac{\Sigma(d_i - \bar{d})^2}{n - 1}}$$

Test Statistic for Matched Samples

$$t = \frac{\bar{d} - \mu_d}{s_d/\sqrt{n}} \tag{10.13}$$

Sample Mean for Treatment j

$$\bar{x}_j = \frac{\displaystyle\sum_{i=1}^{n_j} x_{ij}}{n_j} \tag{10.14}$$

Sample Variance for Treatment j

$$s_j^2 = \frac{\displaystyle\sum_{i=1}^{n_j}(x_{ij} - \bar{x}_j)^2}{n_j - 1} \tag{10.15}$$

Overall Sample Mean

$$\bar{\bar{x}} = \frac{\displaystyle\sum_{j=1}^{k}\sum_{i=1}^{n_j} x_{ij}}{n_T} \tag{10.16}$$

$$n_T = n_1 + n_2 + \cdots + n_k \tag{10.17}$$

Mean Square Due to Treatments

$$\text{MSTR} = \frac{\text{SSTR}}{k - 1} \tag{10.20}$$

Sum of Squares Due to Treatments

$$\text{SSTR} = \sum_{j=1}^{k} n_j(\bar{x}_j - \bar{\bar{x}})^2 \tag{10.21}$$

Mean Square Due to Error

$$\text{MSE} = \frac{\text{SSE}}{n_T - k} \tag{10.23}$$

Sum of Squares Due to Error

$$\text{SSE} = \sum_{j=1}^{k} (n_j - 1)s_j^2 \tag{10.24}$$

Test for the Equality of k Population Means

$$F = \frac{\text{MSTR}}{\text{MSE}} \tag{10.25}$$

Total Sum of Squares

$$SST = \sum_{j=1}^{k} \sum_{i=1}^{n_j} (x_{ij} - \bar{\bar{x}})^2 \qquad\qquad (10.26)$$

Partition of Sum of Squares

$$SST = SSTR + SSE \qquad\qquad (10.27)$$

···/ /············

SUPPLEMENTARY EXERCISES

33. Starting annual salaries for individuals with master's and bachelor's degrees in business were collected in two independent random samples. Use the following data to develop a 90% confidence interval estimate of the increase in starting salary that can be expected upon completion of a master's program.

Master's Degree	Bachelor's Degree
$n_1 = 60$	$n_2 = 80$
$\bar{x}_1 = \$35{,}000$	$\bar{x}_2 = \$30{,}000$
$s_1 = \$2{,}500$	$s_2 = \$2{,}000$

34. Safegate Foods, Inc., is redesigning the checkout lanes in its supermarkets throughout the country. Two designs have been suggested. Tests on customer checkout times have been conducted at two stores where the two new systems have been installed. A summary of the sample data follows.

System A	System B
$n_1 = 120$	$n_2 = 100$
$\bar{x}_1 = 4.1$ minutes	$\bar{x}_2 = 3.3$ minutes
$s_1 = 2.2$ minutes	$s_2 = 1.5$ minutes

Test at the .05 level of significance to determine whether there is a difference between the mean checkout times of the two systems. Which system is preferred?

35. Mutual funds are classified as *load* or *no-load* funds. Load funds require an investor to pay an initial fee based on a percentage of the amount invested in the fund. The no-load funds do not require this initial fee. Some financial advisors argue that the load mutual funds may be worth the extra fee because these funds provide a higher mean rate of return than the no-load mutual funds. A sample of 30 load mutual funds and a sample of 30 no-load mutual funds were selected from *Barron's Lipper Mutual Funds Quarterly,* January 12, 1998. Data were collected on the annual return for the funds over a five-year period. The data are contained in the data set Mutual. The data for the first five load and first five no-load mutual funds are as follows.

Mutual

Mutual Funds—Load	Return	Mutual Funds—No Load	Return
American National Growth	15.51	Amana Income Fund	13.24
Arch Small Cap Equity	14.57	Berger One Hundred	12.13
Bartlett Cap Basic	17.73	Columbia International Stock	12.17
Calvert World International	10.31	Dodge & Cox Balanced	16.06
Colonial Fund A	16.23	Evergreen Fund	17.61

a. Formulate H_0 and H_a such that rejection of H_0 leads to the conclusion that the load mutual funds have a higher mean annual return over the five-year period.

b. Use the 60 mutual funds in the data set Mutual to conduct the hypothesis test. Using $\alpha = .05$, what is your conclusion?

c. What is the p-value?

36. Figure Perfect, Inc., is a women's figure salon that specializes in weight reduction programs. Weights for a sample of clients before and after a six-week introductory program are shown here.

	Weight	
Client	Before	After
1	140	132
2	160	158
3	210	195
4	148	152
5	190	180
6	170	164

Using $\alpha = .05$, test to determine whether the introductory program provides a statistically significant weight loss. What is your conclusion?

37. The Asian economy faltered during the last few months of 1997. Investors anticipated that the downturn in the Asian economy would have a negative effect on the earnings of companies in the United States during the fourth quarter of 1997. The following sample data show the earnings per share for the fourth quarter of 1996 and the fourth quarter of 1997 (*The Wall Street Journal,* January 28, 1998).

Asia

Company	Earnings 1996	Earnings 1997
Atlantic Richfield	1.16	1.17
Balchem Corp.	0.16	0.13
Black & Decker Corp.	0.97	1.02
Dial Corp.	0.18	0.23
DSC Communications	0.15	−0.32
Eastman Chemical	0.77	0.36
Excel Communications	0.28	−0.14
Federal Signal	0.40	0.29
Ford Motor Company	0.97	1.45
GTE Corp	0.81	0.73
ITT Industries	0.59	0.60
Kimberly-Clark	0.61	−0.27
Minnesota Mining & Mfr.	0.91	0.89
Procter & Gamble	0.63	0.71

 a. Formulate H_0 and H_a such that rejection of H_0 leads to the conclusion that the mean earnings per share for the fourth quarter of 1997 are less than for the fourth quarter of 1996.

 b. Use the data in the file Asia to conduct the hypothesis test. Using $\alpha = .05$, what is your conclusion?

38. A simple random sample of the asking prices ($1000s) of four houses currently for sale in each of two residential areas resulted in the following data.

Area 1	Area 2
92	90
89	102
98	96
105	88

 a. Test whether the mean asking price is the same in both areas. Use $\alpha = .05$.

 b. Use the ANOVA procedure to test whether the mean asking price is the same. Compare your analysis with part (a). Use $\alpha = .05$.

39. Suppose that in Exercise 38 data were collected for another residential area. The asking prices for the simple random sample from the third area were $81,000, $86,000, $75,000, and $90,000. Is the mean asking price the same for all three areas? Use $\alpha = .05$.

40. The following data show the age of 12 top executives for major marketers of food, retail, and personal care products (*Advertising Age,* December 1, 1997).

AgeExec

Company	Category	Executive	Age
Campbell Soup Co.	Food	Dale F. Morrison	48
General Mills	Food	Stephen W. Sanger	51
Kellogg Co.	Food	Arnold G. Langbo	59
RJR Nabisco	Food	Stephen F. Goldstone	51
Estee Lauder Cos.	Personal Care	Leonard A. Lauder	64
Gillette Co.	Personal Care	Alfred M. Zeien	67
Procter & Gamble Co.	Personal Care	John E. Pepper	59
Unilever	Personal Care	Morris Tabaksblat	59
Federated Department Stores	Retail	James W. Zimmerman	53
J.C. Penney Co.	Retail	James E. Oesterreicher	55
Sears Roebuck & Co.	Retail	Arthur C. Martinez	57
Kmart Corp.	Retail	Floyd Hall	58

 At the $\alpha = .05$ level of significance, is there a significant difference in the mean age of executives for the three categories of companies?

41. A study reported in the *Journal of Small Business Management* concluded that self-employed individuals do not experience higher job satisfaction than individuals who are not self-employed. In this study, job satisfaction is measured using 18 items, each of which is rated using a Likert-type scale with a 1–5 response scale ranging from strong agreement to strong disagreement. A higher score on this scale indicates a higher degree of job satisfaction. The sum of the ratings for the 18 items, ranging from 18–90, is used as the measure of job satisfaction (*Journal of Small Business Management,* October 1997). Suppose that this approach was used to measure the job satisfaction for lawyers, physical therapists, cabinetmakers, and systems analysts. The results obtained for a sample of 40 individuals follow.

Lawyer	Physical Therapist	Cabinetmaker	Systems Analyst
44	55	54	44
42	78	65	73
74	80	79	71
42	86	69	60
53	60	79	64
50	59	64	66
45	62	59	41
48	52	78	55
64	55	84	76
38	50	60	62

SatisJob

At the $\alpha = .05$ level of significance, is there any difference in the job satisfaction among the four professions?

42. According to the sixth annual survey of ad agency employees conducted by the accounting firm Altschuler, Melvoin & Glasser, ad agency employees can expect another banner year in compensation (*Advertising Age,* December 1, 1997). To investigate whether there is any geographical difference in the annual compensation for art directors, suppose that a sample of ten art directors was selected from each of four regions: West, South, North Central, and Northeast. The base salary ($1000s) for each of the individuals sampled follows.

West	South	North Central	Northeast
60.9	50.8	49.5	65.9
45.9	39.6	42.3	58.6
62.1	44.2	35.5	49.3
66.6	40.0	49.1	52.9
68.0	53.9	56.7	48.5
65.0	45.4	41.4	52.9
49.4	61.1	51.3	52.4
62.3	42.3	49.4	48.1
62.6	38.4	42.1	46.5
57.2	38.3	55.7	45.9

ArtDir

At the $\alpha = .05$ level of significance, test whether the mean base salary for art directors is the same for each of the four regions.

Case Problem 1   PAR, INC.

Par, Inc., is a major manufacturer of golf equipment. Management believes that Par's market share could be increased with the introduction of a cut-resistant, longer-lasting golf ball. Therefore, the research group at Par has been investigating a new golf ball coating designed to resist cuts and provide a more durable ball. The tests with the coating have been very promising.

One of the researchers voiced concern about the effect of the new coating on driving distances. Par would like the new cut-resistant ball to offer driving distances comparable to those of the current-model golf ball. To compare the driving distances for the two balls, 40 balls of each type were subjected to distance tests. The testing was performed with a mechanical hitting machine so that any difference between the mean distances for the two models could be attributed to a difference in the design. The results of the tests, with distances measured to the nearest yard, follow. These data are available on the data disk in the data set Golf.

Golf

Model		Model		Model		Model	
Current	New	Current	New	Current	New	Current	New
264	277	270	272	263	274	281	283
261	269	287	259	264	266	274	250
267	263	289	264	284	262	273	253
272	266	280	280	263	271	263	260
258	262	272	274	260	260	275	270
283	251	275	281	283	281	267	263
258	262	265	276	255	250	279	261
266	289	260	269	272	263	274	255
259	286	278	268	266	278	276	263
270	264	275	262	268	264	262	279

Managerial Report

1. Formulate and present the rationale for a hypothesis test that Par could use to compare the driving distances of the current and new golf balls.
2. Analyze the data to provide the hypothesis testing conclusion. What is the p-value for your test? What is your recommendation for Par, Inc.?
3. Provide descriptive statistical summaries of the data for each model.
4. What is the 95% confidence interval for the population mean of each model, and what is the 95% confidence interval for the difference between the means of the two populations?
5. Do you see a need for larger sample sizes and more testing with the golf balls? Discuss.

Case Problem 2   WENTWORTH MEDICAL CENTER

As part of a long-term study of individuals 65 years of age or older, sociologists and physicians at the Wentworth Medical Center in upstate New York conducted a study to investigate the relationship between geographic location and depression. A sample of 60 individuals, all in reasonably good health, was selected; 20 individuals were residents of Florida, 20 were residents of New York, and 20 were residents of North Carolina. Each of the individuals sampled was given a standardized test to measure depression. The data collected are shown below; higher test scores indicate higher levels of depression. These data are available on the data disk in the file Medical1.

A second part of the study considered the relationship between geographic location and depression for individuals 65 years of age or older who had a chronic health condition such as arthritis, hypertension, and/or heart ailment. A sample of 60 individuals with such conditions was identified. Again, 20 were residents of Florida, 20 were residents of New York, and 20 were residents of North Carolina. The levels of depression recorded for this study follow. These data are available on the data disk in the file Medical2.

Data from Medical1			Data from Medical2		
Florida	New York	North Carolina	Florida	New York	North Carolina
3	8	10	13	14	10
7	11	7	12	9	12
7	9	3	17	15	15
3	7	5	17	12	18
8	8	11	20	16	12
8	7	8	21	24	14
8	8	4	16	18	17
5	4	3	14	14	8
5	13	7	13	15	14
2	10	8	17	17	16
6	6	8	12	20	18
2	8	7	9	11	17
6	12	3	12	23	19
6	8	9	15	19	15
9	6	8	16	17	13
7	8	12	15	14	14
5	5	6	13	9	11
4	7	3	10	14	12
7	7	8	11	13	13
3	8	11	17	11	11

Medical1

Medical2

Managerial Report

1. Use descriptive statistics to summarize the data from the two studies. What are your preliminary observations about the depression scores?
2. Use analysis of variance on both data sets. State the hypotheses being tested in each case. What are your conclusions?
3. Use inferences about individual treatment means where appropriate. What are your conclusions?
4. Discuss extensions of this study or other analyses that you feel might be helpful.

Case Problem 3 COMPENSATION FOR ID PROFESSIONALS

For the last 10 years *Industrial Distribution* has been tracking compensation of industrial distribution (ID) professionals. Results for the 358 respondents in the 1997 Annual Salary Survey showed that 27% of the respondents work for companies with sales over $40 million, with the typical ID professional working for a $12 million firm. Those who work for small to mid-sized companies (between $6 million and $20 million) report higher earnings than those in larger firms. The lowest paid employees work for firms with sales of less than $1 million. The typical outside salesperson made $50,000 in 1996, and the typical inside salesperson earned just $30,000 (*Industrial Distribution,* November 1997). Suppose that a local chapter of ID professionals in the greater San Francisco area conducted a survey of its membership to study the relationship, if any, between years of experience and salary for individuals employed in outside and inside sales positions. In the survey, respondents were asked to specify one of three levels of years of experience: Low (1–10 years); Medium (11–20 years); and High (21 or more years). A portion of the data obtained follow. The complete data set, consisting of 120 observations, is available on the data disk in the file IDSalary.

IDSalary

Observation	Salary $	Position	Experience
1	28938	Inside	Medium
2	27694	Inside	Medium
3	45515	Outside	Low
4	27031	Inside	Medium
5	37283	Outside	Low
6	32718	Inside	Low
7	54081	Outside	High
8	23621	Inside	Low
9	47835	Outside	High
10	29768	Inside	Medium
.	.	.	.
.	.	.	.
115	33080	Inside	High
116	53702	Outside	Medium
117	58131	Outside	Medium
118	32788	Inside	High
119	28070	Inside	Medium
120	35259	Outside	Low

Managerial Report

1. Use descriptive statistics to summarize the data.
2. Develop a 95% confidence interval estimate of the mean annual salary for all salespersons, regardless of years of experience and type of position.
3. Develop a 95% confidence interval estimate of the mean salary for outside salespersons. Compare your results with the national value reported by *Industrial Distribution.*
4. Develop a 95% confidence interval estimate of the mean salary for inside salespersons. Compare your results with the national value reported by *Industrial Distribution.*
5. Ignoring the years of experience, develop a 95% confidence interval estimate of the mean difference between the annual salary for outside salespersons and the mean annual salary for inside salespersons. What is your conclusion?
6. Use analysis of variance to test for any significant differences due to position. Use a .05 level of significance.
7. Use analysis of variance to test for any significant differences due to years of experience. Use a .05 level of significance.

Appendix 10.1 TWO POPULATION MEANS WITH MINITAB

Large-Sample Case

We will show how Minitab can be used to conduct a large-sample hypothesis test about the difference between two population means by using the training center examination scores shown in Table 10.1. The data are available on the data disk in the data set ExamData.

Minitab does not have a two-sample hypothesis procedure based on a z test statistic as described in Section 10.2. However, the Minitab 2-Sample t test procedure can be used to obtain almost identical results. With the ExamData file active, the steps are as follows.

Step 1. Select the **Stat** pull-down menu
Step 2. Select the **Basic Statistics** pull-down menu
Step 3. Select the **2-Sample t** option
Step 4. When the 2-Sample t dialog box appears:
    Select **Samples in different columns**
    Enter C1 in the **First** box
    Enter C2 in the **Second** box
    Select greater than in the **Alternative** box
    Enter 95.0 in the **Confidence Level** box
    Make sure **Assume equal variances** is not selected
    Select **OK**

The value of the test statistic $z = 2.09$ appears as T in the Minitab output. Comparing z to the rejection rule, Reject H_0 if $z < -1.96$ or if $z > 1.96$, leads to the rejection of H_0. The p-value $= .040$ shown with the 2-sample t procedure will always be slightly larger than the p-value based on z. In this example, $z = 2.09$ provides a p-value $= .0366$. Thus, the Minitab 2-Sample t procedure provides useful results in analyzing the difference between population means for the large-sample case.

Small-Sample Case

We will show how Minitab can be used to conduct a small-sample hypothesis test about the difference between two population means with variances assumed equal by using the software completion time data shown in Table 10.3. The data are available on the data disk in the data set Software. With the Software file active, the steps are as follows:

Step 1. Select the **Stat** pull-down menu
Step 2. Select the **Basic Statistics** pull-down menu
Step 3. Select the **2-Sample t** option
Step 4. When the 2-Sample t dialog box appears:
    Select **Samples in different columns**
    Enter C1 in the **First** box
    Enter C2 in the **Second** box
    Select greater than in the **Alternative** box
    Enter 95.0 in the **Confidence Level** box
    Select **Assume equal variances**
    Select **OK**

The output is as shown in Figure 10.6. The value of the test statistic $t = 2.16$ and the p-value $= .021$ indicate H_0 can be rejected. The new software provides a smaller mean completion time.

Appendix 10.2   TWO POPULATION MEANS WITH EXCEL

Large-Sample Case

We will show how Excel can be used to conduct a hypothesis test about the difference between two population means by using the training center examination scores shown in Table 10.1. The data are available on the data disk in the data set ExamData. The label Center A appears in cell A1, and the label Center B appears in cell B1. The examination scores for center A are shown in cells A2:A31, and the examination scores for center B are shown in cells B2:B41.

We will assume that the Excel Data Analysis descriptive statistics routine has been used to compute the two sample standard deviations $s_1 = 8$ and $s_2 = 10$. The Excel procedure for testing the difference between the two population means will require information on the variances of the two populations. Thus, we will use $s_1^2 = (8)^2 = 64$ and $s_2^2 = (10)^2 = 100$. With the ExamData file active, the steps are as follows:

Step 1. Select the **Tools** pull-down menu
Step 2. Select the **Data Analysis** option
Step 3. When the Data Analysis dialog box appears:
  Choose **z-Test: Two Sample for Means**
  Select **OK**
Step 4. When the z-Test: Two Sample for Means dialog box appears:
  Enter A1:A31 in the **Variable 1 Range** box
  Enter B1:B41 in the **Variable 2 Range** box
  Enter 0 in the **Hypothesized Mean Difference** box
  Enter 64 in the **Variable 1 Variance** box
  Enter 100 in the **Variable 2 Variance** box
  Select **Labels**
  Enter .05 in the **Alpha** box
  Select **Output Range** and enter C1 in the box
  Select **OK**

The value of the test statistic $z = 2.09$ appears in cell D8. The two-tailed p-value $= .0366$ appears in cell D11. Because the p-value is less than $\alpha = .05$, H_0 is rejected.

Small-Sample Case

We will show how Excel can be used to conduct a small-sample hypothesis test about the difference between two population means by using the software completion time data shown in Table 10.3. The data are available on the data disk in the data set Software. The label Current appears in cell A1, and the label New Software appears in cell B1. The completion times for the current technology are shown in cells A2:A13, and the completion times for the new software are shown in cells B2:B13. With the Software file active, the steps are as follows:

Step 1. Select **Tools** pull-down menu
Step 2. Select the **Data Analysis** option
Step 3. When the Data Analysis dialog box appears;
Choose **t-Test: Two Sample Assuming Equal Variances**
Select **OK**
Step 4. When the t-Test: Two Sample Assuming Equal Variances dialog box appears:
Enter A1:A13 in the **Variable 1 Range** box
Enter B1:B13 in the **Variable 2 Range** box
Enter 0 in the **Hypothesized Mean Difference** box
Select **Labels**
Enter .05 in the **Alpha** box
Select **Output Range** and enter C1 in the box
Select **OK**

The value of the test statistic $t = 2.16$ appears in cell D10. The one-tailed p-value $= .021$ appears in cell D11. Because the p-value is less than $\alpha = .05$, H_0 is rejected; the new software provides a smaller mean completion time.

Appendix 10.3   ANALYSIS OF VARIANCE WITH MINITAB

To illustrate how Minitab can be used to test for the equality of k population means, we show how to test whether the mean examination score is the same at each plant in the National Computer Products example introduced in Section 10.4. We assume that the user has entered the examination score data into the first three columns of a Minitab worksheet, and that column 1 is labeled Atlanta, column 2 is labeled Dallas, and column 3 is labeled Seattle. The following steps produce the Minitab output in Figure 10.10

Step 1. Select the **Stat** pull-down menu
Step 2. Select the **ANOVA** pull-down menu
Step 3. Choose the **Oneway (Unstacked)** option
Step 4. When the Oneway Analysis of Variance dialog box appears:
Enter C1-C3 in the **Responses (in separate columns)** box
Select **OK**

Appendix 10.4   ANALYSIS OF VARIANCE WITH EXCEL

To illustrate how Excel can be used to test for the equality of k population means, we show how to test whether the mean examination score is the same at each plant in the National Computer Products example introduced in Section 10.4. We assume that the user has entered the examination score data into worksheet rows 2 to 7 of columns A, B, and C as shown in Figure 10.11; note that the cells in row 1 for columns A, B, and C are labeled Atlanta, Dallas, and Seattle. The following steps are used to obtain the output shown in cells A10:G24; the ANOVA portion of this output corresponds to the ANOVA table shown in Table 10.6.

Figure 10.11   EXCEL SOLUTION FOR THE NCP ANALYSIS OF VARIANCE EXAMPLE

	A	B	C	D	E	F	G
1	**Atlanta**	**Dallas**	**Seattle**				
2	85	71	59				
3	75	75	64				
4	82	73	62				
5	76	74	69				
6	71	69	75				
7	85	82	67				
8							
9							
10	Anova: Single Factor						
11							
12	**SUMMARY**						
13	*Groups*	*Count*	*Sum*	*Average*	*Variance*		
14	Atlanta	6	474	79	34		
15	Dallas	6	444	74	20		
16	Seattle	6	396	66	32		
17							
18							
19	ANOVA						
20	*Source of Variation*	*SS*	*df*	*MS*	*F*	*P-value*	*F crit*
21	Between Groups	516	2	258	9	0.002703	3.682317
22	Within Groups	430	15	28.66667			
23							
24	Total	946	17				

Step 1.   Select the **Tools** pull-down menu
Step 2.   Select the **Data Analysis** option
Step 3.   When the Data Analysis dialog box appears:
        Choose the **Anova: Single-Factor** option
Step 4.   When the Anova: Single-Factor dialog box appears:
        Enter A1:C7 in **Input Range** box
        Select **Columns**
        Select **Labels in First Row**
        Select **Output Range** and enter **A10** in the box
        Select **OK**

COMPARISONS INVOLVING PROPORTIONS

CONTENTS

UNITED WAY*
Rochester, New York

United Way of Greater Rochester is a nonprofit organization dedicated to improving the quality of life for all people in the seven counties it serves by meeting the community's most important human care needs.

The annual United Way/Red Cross fund-raising campaign, conducted each spring, funds hundreds of programs offered by more than 200 service providers. These providers meet a wide variety of human needs—physical, mental, and social—and serve people of all ages, backgrounds, and economic means.

Because of enormous volunteer involvement, United Way of Greater Rochester is able to hold its operating costs at just eight cents of every dollar raised.

The United Way of Greater Rochester decided to conduct a survey to learn more about community perceptions of charities. Focus group interviews were held with professional, service, and general worker groups to get preliminary information on perceptions. The information obtained was then used to help develop the questionnaire for the survey. The questionnaire was pretested, modified, and distributed to 440 individuals; 323 completed questionnaires were returned.

A variety of descriptive statistics, including frequency distributions and crosstabulations, were provided from the data collected. An important part of the analysis involved the use of contingency tables and chi-square tests of independence. One use of such statistical tests was to determine whether perceptions of administrative expenses were independent of occupation.

The hypotheses for the test of independence were:

*The authors are indebted to Dr. Philip R. Tyler, Marketing Consultant to the United Way, for providing this Statistics in Practice.

Statistical surveys help United Way adjust its programs to better meet the needs of the people it serves. © Cindy Charles/PhotoEdit.

H_0: Perception of United Way administrative expenses is independent of the occupation of the respondent.

H_a: Perception of United Way administrative expenses is not independent of the occupation of the respondent.

Two questions in the survey provided the data for the statistical test. One question obtained data on perceptions of the percentage of funds going to administrative expenses (up to 10%, 11–20%, and 21% or more). The other question asked for the occupation of the respondent.

The chi-square test at a 5% level of significance led to rejection of the null hypothesis of independence and to the conclusion that perceptions of United Way's administrative expenses did vary by occupation. Actual administrative expenses were less than 9%, but 35% of the respondents perceived that administrative expenses were 21% or more. Hence, many had inaccurate perceptions of administrative costs. In this group, production-line, clerical, sales, and professional-technical employees had more inaccurate perceptions than other groups.

The community perceptions study helped United Way of Rochester to develop adjustments to its program and fund-raising activities. In this chapter, you will learn how a statistical test of independence, such as that described here, is conducted.

In many statistical applications it is of interest to compare population proportions. In Section 11.1 we will describe statistical inferences that can be made concerning differences in the proportions for two populations. Two samples are required, one from each population. The second section is concerned with a hypothesis test comparing the proportions of a single multinomial population with the values stated in a null hypothesis. One sample from the multinomial population is used. In the last section of the chapter, we show how contingency tables are used to test for the independence of two variables. One sample is used for the test of independence, but measures on two variables are required for each sampled element. Both Sections 11.2 and 11.3 rely on the use of a chi-square statistical test.

11.1 INFERENCES ABOUT THE DIFFERENCE BETWEEN THE PROPORTIONS OF TWO POPULATIONS

A tax preparation firm is interested in comparing the quality of work at two of its regional offices. By randomly selecting samples of tax returns prepared at each office and having the sample returns verified for accuracy, the firm will be able to estimate the proportion of erroneous returns prepared at each office. Of particular interest is the difference between these proportions. Let

p_1 = proportion of erroneous returns for population 1 (office 1)

p_2 = proportion of erroneous returns for population 2 (office 2)

$\bar{p}_1$ = sample proportion for a simple random sample from population 1

$\bar{p}_2$ = sample proportion for a simple random sample from population 2

The methods of this section are appropriate for independent random samples from two populations.

The difference between the two population proportions is given by $p_1 - p_2$. The point estimator of $p_1 - p_2$ is the difference between the two sample proportions.

Point Estimator of the Difference between the Proportions of Two Populations

$$\bar{p}_1 - \bar{p}_2 \tag{11.1}$$

Sampling Distribution of $\bar{p}_1 - \bar{p}_2$

In the study of the difference between two population proportions, $\bar{p}_1 - \bar{p}_2$ is the point estimator of interest. As we have seen in several preceding cases, the sampling distribution of a point estimator is a key factor in developing interval estimates and in testing hypotheses about parameters of interest. The properties of the sampling distribution of $\bar{p}_1 - \bar{p}_2$ follow.

Sampling Distribution of $\bar{p}_1 - \bar{p}_2$

Expected value: $E(\bar{p}_1 - \bar{p}_2) = p_1 - p_2$ (11.2)

Standard deviation: $\sigma_{\bar{p}_1 - \bar{p}_2} = \sqrt{\dfrac{p_1(1 - p_1)}{n_1} + \dfrac{p_2(1 - p_2)}{n_2}}$ (11.3)

where

$$n_1 = \text{sample size for the simple random sample from population 1}$$
$$n_2 = \text{sample size for the simple random sample from population 2}$$

Distribution form: If the sample sizes are large—i.e., $n_1 p_1$, $n_1(1 - p_1)$, $n_2 p_2$, and $n_2(1 - p_2)$ are all greater than or equal to 5—the sampling distribution of $\bar{p}_1 - \bar{p}_2$ can be approximated by a normal probability distribution.

Figure 11.1 shows the sampling distribution of $\bar{p}_1 - \bar{p}_2$.

Interval Estimation of $p_1 - p_2$

Suppose that independent simple random samples of tax returns from the two offices provide the following information.

Office 1	Office 2
$n_1 = 250$	$n_2 = 300$
Number of returns with errors $= 35$	Number of returns with errors $= 27$

The sample proportions for the two offices are as follows:

$$\bar{p}_1 = \frac{35}{250} = .14$$

$$\bar{p}_2 = \frac{27}{300} = .09$$

The point estimate of the difference between the proportions of erroneous tax returns for the two populations is $\bar{p}_1 - \bar{p}_2 = .14 - .09 = .05$. Thus, we estimate that office 1 has a .05 greater error rate than office 2.

Figure 11.1   SAMPLING DISTRIBUTION OF $\bar{p}_1 - \bar{p}_2$

Sampling distribution
of $\bar{p}_1 - \bar{p}_2$

$$\sigma_{\bar{p}_1 - \bar{p}_2} = \sqrt{\frac{p_1(1 - p_1)}{n_1} + \frac{p_2(1 - p_2)}{n_2}}$$

$p_1 - p_2$

$\bar{p}_1 - \bar{p}_2$

Before developing a confidence interval for the difference between population proportions, we must estimate $\sigma_{\bar{p}_1-\bar{p}_2}$. Note that (11.3) cannot be used directly because p_1 and p_2 will not be known in practice. The approach taken is to substitute $\bar{p}_1$ as an estimator of p_1 and $\bar{p}_2$ as an estimator of p_2 in (11.3). Doing so provides the point estimator of $\sigma_{\bar{p}_1-\bar{p}_2}$ given by (11.4).

Point Estimator of $\sigma_{\bar{p}_1-\bar{p}_2}$

$$s_{\bar{p}_1-\bar{p}_2} = \sqrt{\frac{\bar{p}_1(1 - \bar{p}_1)}{n_1} + \frac{\bar{p}_2(1 - \bar{p}_2)}{n_2}} \tag{11.4}$$

Using (11.4), the following expression provides an interval estimate of the difference between the proportions of the two populations in the large sample case. The use of $z_{\alpha/2}$ in (11.5) is due to the fact that we can assume a normal sampling distribution for $\bar{p}_1 - \bar{p}_2$ in the large sample case.

Interval Estimate of the Difference between the Proportions of Two Populations: Large-Sample Case with n_1p_1, $n_1(1 - p_1)$, n_2p_2, and $n_2(1 - p_2) \geq 5$

$$\bar{p}_1 - \bar{p}_2 \pm z_{\alpha/2}s_{\bar{p}_1-\bar{p}_2} \tag{11.5}$$

where $1 - \alpha$ is the confidence coefficient

Let us now use (11.5) to develop an interval estimate of the difference between the proportions for the two tax preparation offices in our example. Using (11.4), we find

$$s_{\bar{p}_1-\bar{p}_2} = \sqrt{\frac{.14(.86)}{250} + \frac{.09(.91)}{300}} = .0275$$

With a 90% confidence interval, we have $z_{\alpha/2} = z_{.05} = 1.645$, and a margin of error of $1.645(.0275) = .045$. The interval estimate is

$$(.14 - .09) \pm 1.645(.0275)$$
$$.05 \pm .045$$

Hence, the 90% confidence interval for the difference in error rates at the two offices is .005 to .095.

Hypothesis Tests about $p_1 - p_2$

As an example of a hypothesis test concerning the difference between two population proportions, let us reconsider the example concerning the error rates at two offices of the tax preparation firm. Suppose the firm had simply been interested in whether the two offices experienced a significant difference in error rates. The appropriate null and alternative hypotheses are

$$H_0: p_1 - p_2 = 0$$
$$H_a: p_1 - p_2 \neq 0$$

Figure 11.2 shows the sampling distribution of $\bar{p}_1 - \bar{p}_2$ based on the assumption of no difference between the two population proportions. That is, $p_1 - p_2 = 0$. In the large sample case, the sampling distribution is approximately normal and the test statistic for the difference between two population proportions is

$$z = \frac{(\bar{p}_1 - \bar{p}_2) - (p_1 - p_2)}{\sigma_{\bar{p}_1 - \bar{p}_2}} \tag{11.6}$$

Using $\alpha = .10$ and $z_{\alpha/2} = z_{.05} = 1.645$, the rejection rule is

Reject H_0 if $z < -1.645$ or if $z > 1.645$

The computation of z in (11.6) requires a value for the standard error of the difference between proportions $\sigma_{\bar{p}_1 - \bar{p}_2}$. As in the case of interval estimation, it will be necessary to estimate $\sigma_{\bar{p}_1 - \bar{p}_2}$ because p_1 and p_2 will not be known in practice. But for the special case of a null hypothesis stating that there is no difference in the proportions (H_0: $p_1 = p_2$), we do not use (11.4). This case has only one population proportion; that is, $p_1 = p_2 = p$—and we can combine or *pool* the two sample proportions to provide one estimate of p given by $\bar{p}$.

$$\bar{p} = \frac{n_1 \bar{p}_1 + n_2 \bar{p}_2}{n_1 + n_2} \tag{11.7}$$

With $\bar{p}$ used in place of both $\bar{p}_1$ and $\bar{p}_2$, (11.4) is revised to

$$s_{\bar{p}_1 - \bar{p}_2} = \sqrt{\bar{p}(1 - \bar{p})\left(\frac{1}{n_1} + \frac{1}{n_2}\right)} \tag{11.8}$$

Figure 11.2   SAMPLING DISTRIBUTION OF $\bar{p}_1 - \bar{p}_2$ WITH H_0: $p_1 - p_2 = 0$

Sampling distribution of $\bar{p}_1 - \bar{p}_2$

$\sigma_{\bar{p}_1 - \bar{p}_2} = \sqrt{\dfrac{p_1(1 - p_1)}{n_1} + \dfrac{p_2(1 - p_2)}{n_2}}$

$\bar{p}_1 - \bar{p}_2$

0

Assume 0 when H_0: $p_1 - p_2 = 0$

Using (11.7) and (11.8), we can now proceed with a hypothesis test for the tax preparation firm example.

$$\bar{p} = \frac{250(.14) + 300(.09)}{550} = \frac{62}{550} = .113$$

$$s_{\bar{p}_1 - \bar{p}_2} = \sqrt{(.113)(.887)\left(\frac{1}{250} + \frac{1}{300}\right)} = .0271$$

The value of the test statistic is

$$z = \frac{(\bar{p}_1 - \bar{p}_2) - (p_1 - p_2)}{s_{\bar{p}_1 - \bar{p}_2}} = \frac{(.14 - .09) - 0}{.0271} = 1.85$$

Because $1.85 > 1.645$, at the .10 level of significance the null hypothesis is rejected. The sample evidence indicates a difference between the error proportions at the two offices.

As we saw with the hypothesis tests about differences between two population means (Chapter 10), one-tailed tests can also be developed for the difference between two population proportions. The one-tailed rejection regions are established in a manner similar to the one-tailed hypothesis-testing procedures for a single-population proportion.

EXERCISES

Methods

1. Consider the following results for two independent samples taken from two populations.

Sample 1	Sample 2
$n_1 = 400$	$n_2 = 300$
$\bar{p}_1 = .48$	$\bar{p}_2 = .36$

   a. What is the point estimate of the difference between the two population proportions?
   b. Develop a 90% confidence interval for the difference between the two population proportions.
   c. Develop a 95% confidence interval for the difference between the two population proportions.

SELF TEST

2. Consider the following hypothesis test:

$$H_0: p_1 - p_2 \leq 0$$
$$H_a: p_1 - p_2 > 0$$

The following results are for two independent samples taken from the two populations.

Sample 1	Sample 2
$n_1 = 200$	$n_2 = 300$
$\bar{p}_1 = .22$	$\bar{p}_2 = .16$

    a. Using $\alpha = .05$, what is your hypothesis-testing conclusion?

    b. What is the p-value?

Applications

3. A *Business Week*/Harris survey asked senior executives at large corporations their opinions about the economic outlook for the future (*Business Week,* June 16, 1997). One question was "Do you think that there will be an increase in the number of full-time employees at your company over the next 12 months?" In May 1997, 220 of 400 executives answered yes, while in December 1996, 192 of 400 executives had answered yes. Provide a 95% confidence interval estimate for the difference between the proportions at the two points in time. What is your interpretation of the interval estimate?

4. A 1994 Gallup poll found that 16% of 505 men and 25% of 496 women surveyed favored a law forbidding the sale of all beer, wine, and liquor throughout the nation (*The Gallup Poll Monthly,* June 1994). Develop a 95% confidence interval for the difference between the proportion of women who favor such a ban and the proportion of men who favor such a ban.

5. In December 1993, the women and family issues committee of the American Institute of Certified Public Accountants (AICPA) mailed surveys asking about family-friendly policies and women's upward mobility to 5300 firms of all sizes (excluding sole practitioners). Of the 1710 responses, 57% were from firms with five or fewer AICPA members, 26% were from firms with six to 10 members, 9% were from firms with 11 to 20 members, and 8% were from firms with more than 20 members. For the firms with fewer than five AICPA members, 58% of the hires within the previous three years were women and 42% were men. In contrast, firms with more than 20 AICPA members hired 43% women and 57% men (*Journal of Accountancy,* October 1994). Develop a 95% confidence interval estimate of the difference between the proportion of women hired by firms with fewer than five AICPA members and the proportion of women hired by firms with more than 20 AICPA members.

6. *Fortune* enlisted Yankelovich Partners to poll 600 adults on their ideas about marriage, divorce, and the contribution of the corporate wife to her executive husband (*Fortune,* February 2, 1998). In response to the statement, "In a divorce in a long-term marriage where the husband works outside the home and the wife is not employed for pay, the wife should be entitled to half the assets accumulated during the marriage," 279 of 300 women agreed and 255 of 300 men agreed.

    a. What are the sample proportions for the two populations, women and men?

    b. Test the hypothesis H_0: $p_1 - p_2 = 0$, using $\alpha = .05$. What is your conclusion?

    c. Provide a 95% confidence interval for the difference between the population proportions.

7. A sample of 1545 men and an independent sample of 1691 women were used to compare the amount of housework done by women and men in dual-earner marriages. The study showed that 67.5% of the men felt the division of housework was fair and 60.8% of the women felt the division of housework was fair (*American Journal of Sociology,* September 1994). Is the proportion of men who felt the division of housework was fair greater than the proportion of women who felt the division of housework was fair? Support your conclusion with a statistical test using a .05 level of significance.

8. A survey firm conducts door-to-door surveys on a variety of issues. Some individuals cooperate with the interviewer and complete the interview questionnaire, and others do not. The sample data are shown.

Respondents	Sample Size	Number Cooperating
Men	200	110
Women	300	210

a. Using $\alpha = .05$, test the hypothesis that the response rate is the same for both men and women.

b. Compute a 95% confidence interval for the difference between the proportions of men and women who cooperate with the survey.

9. In a test of the quality of two television commercials, each commercial was shown in a separate test area six times over a one-week period. The following week a telephone survey was conducted to identify individuals who had seen the commercials. The individuals who had seen the commercials were asked to state the primary message in the commercials. The following results were recorded.

Commercial	Number Who Saw Commercial	Number Who Recalled Primary Message
A	150	63
B	200	60

a. Using $\alpha = .05$, test the hypothesis of no difference in the recall proportions for the two commercials.

b. Compute a 95% confidence interval for the difference between the recall proportions for the two populations.

10. In a study designed to test the effectiveness of a new drug for treating rheumatoid arthritis, investigators divided 73 rheumatoid arthritis patients between the ages of 18 and 75 into three groups. Patients in one group were given a high dose of the drug, patients in another group were given a low dose, and patients in the third group were given a placebo. After four weeks, 19 of 24 patients in the high-dosage group indicated that they felt better, whereas 11 of the 25 patients in the low-dosage group and two of the 24 patients in the placebo group felt better (*The Lancet,* October 1994). Is the proportion of patients who felt better in the high-dosage group greater than the proportion of patients who felt better in the low-dosage group? What is your conclusion? Use $\alpha = .05$ for any statistical test.

11.2 HYPOTHESIS TEST FOR PROPORTIONS OF A MULTINOMIAL POPULATION

In this section, we consider hypothesis tests concerning the proportion of elements in a population belonging to each of several classes or categories. In contrast to the preceding section, we will be dealing with a single population: a *multinomial population.* The parameters of the multinomial population are the proportion of elements belonging to each category; the hypothesis tests we describe concern the value of those parameters.

The multinomial probability distribution can be thought of as an extension of the binomial distribution to the case of three or more categories of outcomes. On each trial of a multinomial experiment, such as sampling an item from a multinomial population, one and only one of the outcomes occurs. Each trial of a multinomial experiment is assumed to be independent, and the probabilities must stay the same for each trial.

As an example, consider the market share evaluation being conducted by Scott Marketing Research. Over the past year market shares have stabilized at 30% for company A, 50% for company B, and 20% for company C. Recently company C has developed a "new and improved" product that has replaced its current entry in the market. Scott Marketing Research has been retained by company C to determine whether the new product will alter market shares.

In this example, the population of interest is a multinomial population; each customer is classified as buying from company A, company B, or company C. Thus, we have a multinomial population with three classifications or categories. Let us use the following notation for the proportions.

$$p_A = \text{market share for company A}$$
$$p_B = \text{market share for company B}$$
$$p_C = \text{market share for company C}$$

Scott Marketing Research will conduct a sample survey and compute the proportion preferring each company's product. A hypothesis test will then be conducted to see whether the new product has caused a change in market shares. Assuming that company C's new product will not alter the market shares, the null and alternative hypotheses would be stated as follows.

$$H_0:\ p_A = .30,\ p_B = .50,\ \text{and}\ p_C = .20$$
$$H_a:\ \text{The population proportions are not}$$
$$p_A = .30,\ p_B = .50,\ \text{and}\ p_C = .20$$

If the sample results lead to the rejection of H_0, Scott will have evidence that the introduction of the new product has had an impact on the market shares.

Let us assume that the market research firm has used a consumer panel of 200 customers for the study. Each individual has been asked to specify a purchase preference among the three alternatives: company A's product, company B's product, and company C's new product. The 200 responses are summarized as follows:

The consumer panel of 200 customers in which each individual is asked to select one of three alternatives is equivalent to a multinomial experiment consisting of 200 trials. Choosing a random sample ensures that the independence assumption for the multinomial experiment is satisfied.

Observed Frequency		
Company A's Product	Company B's Product	Company C's New Product
48	98	54

We now can perform a *goodness of fit test* that will determine whether the sample of 200 customer purchase preferences is consistent with the null hypothesis. The goodness of fit test is based on a comparison of the sample of *observed* results, such as those shown, with the *expected* results under the assumption that the null hypothesis is true. Hence, the next step is to compute expected purchase preferences for the 200 customers under the assumption that $p_A = .30$, $p_B = .50$, and $p_C = .20$. Doing so provides the expected results.

Expected Frequency		
Company A's Product	Company B's Product	Company C's New Product
200(.30) = 60	200(.50) = 100	200(.20) = 40

Thus, we see that the expected frequency for each category is found by multiplying the sample size of 200 by the hypothesized proportion for the category.

The goodness of fit test now focuses on the differences between the observed frequencies and the expected frequencies. Large differences between observed and expected frequencies cast doubt on the assumption that the hypothesized proportions or market shares are correct. Whether the differences between the observed and expected frequencies are "large" or "small" is a question answered with the aid of the following test statistic.

Test Statistic for Goodness of Fit

$$\chi^2 = \sum_{i=1}^{k} \frac{(f_i - e_i)^2}{e_i} \tag{11.9}$$

where

f_i = observed frequency for category i

e_i = expected frequency for category i based on the assumption that H_0 is true

k = the number of categories

Note: The test statistic has a chi-square distribution with $k - 1$ degrees of freedom provided that the expected frequencies are 5 *or more* for all categories.

Let us return to the market-share data for the three companies. Because the expected frequencies are all 5 or more, we can proceed with the computation of the chi-square test statistic. The calculations necessary to compute the chi-square test statistic for the Scott Marketing Research market share study are shown in Table 11.1. We see that the value of the test statistic is $\chi^2 = 7.34$.

Suppose we test the null hypothesis that the multinomial population has the proportions of $p_A = .30$, $p_B = .50$, and $p_C = .20$ at the $\alpha = .05$ level of significance. Because we will reject the null hypothesis if the differences between the observed and expected frequencies are *large,* we will place a rejection area of .05 in the upper tail of the chi-square distribution. Checking the chi-square distribution table (Table 3 of Appendix B), we find that with $k - 1 = 3 - 1 = 2$ degrees of freedom, $\chi^2_{.05} = 5.99$. Since $7.34 > 5.99$, we reject H_0. In re-

The test for goodness of fit is always a one-tailed test with the rejection region located in the upper tail of the chi-square distribution.

Table 11.1   COMPUTATION OF THE CHI-SQUARE TEST STATISTIC FOR THE SCOTT MARKETING RESEARCH MARKET SHARE STUDY

Category	Hypothesized Proportion	Observed Frequency (f_i)	Expected Frequency (e_i)	Difference ($f_i - e_i$)	Squared Difference ($f_i - e_i)^2$	Squared Difference Divided by Expected Frequency ($f_i - e_i)^2/e_i$
Company A	.30	48	60	−12	144	2.40
Company B	.50	98	100	−2	4	0.04
Company C	.20	54	40	14	196	4.90
Total		200	200			7.34

jecting H_0 we are concluding that the introduction of the new product by company C will alter the current market share structure.

Computer software packages such as Minitab and Excel can greatly simplify the computations needed to perform a goodness of fit test for a multinomial population. In addition they enable us to conduct the hypothesis testing procedure using the p-value approach. In the appendixes to this chapter we show how to perform the goodness of fit test for a multinomial population using both of these packages. To illustrate how to interpret the results, consider the Excel output shown in Figure 11.3. Note that the p-value for the test is .0255. Given the level of significance α, the decision of whether to reject H_0 can be made as follows:

$$\text{Reject } H_0 \text{ if the } p\text{-value} < \alpha$$

Thus, with $\alpha = 0.05$ and the p-value $= .0255$, we reject H_0.

As we indicated previously, the goodness of fit test enables us to conclude that the introduction of the new product by company C will alter the current market share structure. Although no further conclusions can be made as a result of the test, we can compare the observed and expected frequencies informally to obtain an idea of how the market share structure has changed. Considering company C, we find that the observed frequency of 54 is larger than the expected frequency of 40. Because the expected frequency was based on current market shares, the larger observed frequency suggests that the new product will have a positive effect on company C's market share. Comparisons of the observed and expected frequencies for the other two companies indicate that company C's gain in market share will hurt company A more than company B.

As illustrated in the example, the goodness of fit test uses the chi-square distribution to determine whether a hypothesized multinomial probability distribution for a population provides a good fit. The hypothesis test is based on the differences between the observed frequencies in a sample and the expected frequencies based on the assumed population distribution. Let us outline the general steps that can be used to conduct a goodness of fit test for any hypothesized multinomial population distribution.

Figure 11.3   EXCEL OUTPUT FOR THE SCOTT MARKETING RESEARCH MARKET SHARE STUDY

	A	B	C	D
1	Scott Marketing Research			
2				
3		**Hypothesized**	**Observed**	**Expected**
4	**Category**	**Proportion**	**Frequency**	**Frequency**
5	Company A	0.3	48	60
6	Company B	0.5	98	100
7	Company C	0.2	54	40
8			Total	200	
9			chi-square	**7.34**
10			p-value $=$	**0.0255**

Multinomial Distribution Goodness of Fit Test: A Summary

1. Set up the null and alternative hypotheses.

   H_0: The population follows a multinomial probability distribution with specified probabilities for each of k categories

   H_a: The population does not follow a multinomial probability distribution with the specified probabilities for each of the k categories

2. Select a random sample and record the observed frequencies f_i for each category.
3. Assuming the null hypothesis is true, determine the expected frequency e_i in each category by multiplying the category probability by the sample size.
4. Compute the value of the test statistic.

$$\chi^2 = \sum_{i=1}^{k} \frac{(f_i - e_i)^2}{e_i}$$

5. Rejection rule:

$$\text{Reject } H_0 \text{ if } \chi^2 > \chi_\alpha^2$$

where α is the level of significance for the test and there are $k - 1$ degrees of freedom.

NOTES and Comments

1. For χ^2 goodness of fit tests the rejection region is always in the upper tail. The differences between observed and expected frequencies are squared, and larger differences lead to larger values for χ^2.
2. Many applications of the goodness of fit test involve choosing a sample and observing the category to which each sampled item belongs. In such cases one must take care to choose a random sample. Otherwise, the independence assumption will not be satisfied.

··/ /············

EXERCISES

Methods

SELF TEST

11. Test the following hypotheses using the χ^2 goodness of fit test.

    H_0: $p_A = .40, p_B = .40$, and $p_C = .20$
    H_a: The population proportions are not
    $p_A = .40, p_B = .40$, and $p_C = .20$

    A sample of size 200 yielded 60 in category A, 120 in category B, and 20 in category C. Use $\alpha = .01$.

12. Suppose we have a multinomial population with four categories: A, B, C, and D. The null hypothesis is that the proportion of items is the same in every category. The null hypothesis is

$$H_0: p_A = p_B = p_C = p_D = .25$$

A sample of size 300 yielded the following numbers in each category.

A:85   B:95   C:50   D:70

Use $\alpha = .05$ and the χ^2 goodness of fit test to determine whether H_0 should be rejected.

Applications

SELF TEST

13. During the first 13 weeks of the television season, the Saturday evening 8:00 P.M. to 9:00 P.M. audience proportions were recorded as ABC 29%, CBS 28%, NBC 25%, and independents 18%. A sample of 300 homes two weeks after a Saturday night schedule revision yielded the following viewing audience data: ABC 95 homes, CBS 70 homes, NBC 89 homes, and independents 46 homes. Test with $\alpha = .05$ to determine whether the viewing audience proportions have changed.

14. M&M/MARS, makers of M&M® Chocolate Candies, conducted a national poll in which more than ten million people indicated their preference for a new color. The tally of this poll resulted in the replacement of tan-colored M&Ms with a new blue color. In the brochure "Colors," made available by M&M/MARS Consumer Affairs, the distribution of colors for the plain candies is as follows:

Brown	Yellow	Red	Orange	Green	Blue
30%	20%	20%	10%	10%	10%

In a study reported in *Chance* (no. 4, 1996), samples of one-pound bags were used to determine whether the reported percentages were indeed valid. The following results were obtained for one sample of 506 plain candies.

Brown	Yellow	Red	Orange	Green	Blue
177	135	79	41	36	38

Use $\alpha = .05$ to determine whether these data support the percentages reported by the company.

15. One of the questions on the *Business Week* 1996 Subscriber Study was, "When making investment purchases, do you use full service or discount brokerage firms?" Survey results showed that 264 respondents use full service brokerage firms only, 255 use discount brokerage firms only, and 229 use both full service and discount firms. Use $\alpha = .10$ to determine whether there are any differences in preference among the three service choices.

16. Negative appeals have been recognized as an effective method of persuasion in advertising. A study in *The Journal of Advertising* (Summer 1997) reported the results of a content analysis of guilt advertisements in 24 magazines. The number of ads with guild appeals that appeared in selected magazine types follow.

Magazine Type	Number of Ads with Guilt Appeals
News and opinion	20
General editorial	15
Family-oriented	30
Business/financial	22
Female-oriented	16
African-American	12

Using $\alpha = .10$ test to determine any differences in the proportion of ads with guilt appeals among the six types of magazines.

17. Consumer panel preferences for three proposed store displays follow.

Display A	Display B	Display C
43	53	39

Use $\alpha = .05$ and test to determine any difference in preference among the three display designs.

18. Grade-distribution guidelines for a statistics course at a major university are: 10% A, 30% B, 40% C, 15% D, and 5% F. A sample of 120 statistics grades at the end of a semester showed 18 As, 30 Bs, 40 Cs, 22 Ds, and 10 Fs. Use $\alpha = .05$ and test whether the actual grades deviate significantly from the grade-distribution guidelines.

11.3   TEST OF INDEPENDENCE: CONTINGENCY TABLES

Another important application of the chi-square distribution involves using sample data to test for the independence of two variables. Let us illustrate the test of independence by considering the study conducted by the Alber's Brewery of Tucson, Arizona. Alber's manufactures and distributes three types of beer: light, regular, and dark. In an analysis of the market segments for the three beers, the firm's market research group has raised the question of whether preferences for the three beers differ among male and female beer drinkers. If beer preference is independent of the gender of the beer drinker, one advertising campaign will be initiated for all of Alber's beers. However, if beer preference depends on the gender of the beer drinker, the firm will tailor its promotions to different target markets.

A test of independence addresses the question of whether the beer preference (light, regular, or dark) is independent of the gender of the beer drinker (male, female). The hypotheses for this test of independence are:

H_0: Beer preference is independent of the gender of the beer drinker

H_a: Beer preference is not independent of the gender of the beer drinker

Table 11.2 can be used to describe the situations being studied. After identification of the population as all male and female beer drinkers, a sample can be selected and each individual asked to state his or her preference for the three Alber's beers. Every individual in the sample will be classified in one of the six cells in the table. For example, an individual

| Table 11.2 | CONTINGENCY TABLE FOR BEER PREFERENCE AND GENDER OF BEER DRINKER | | |

		Beer Preference		
		Light	**Regular**	**Dark**
Gender	**Male**	cell(1,1)	cell(1,2)	cell(1,3)
	Female	cell(2,1)	cell(2,2)	cell(2,3)

may be a male preferring regular beer (cell (1,2)), a female preferring light beer (cell (2,1)), a female preferring dark beer (cell (2,3)), and so on. Because we have listed all possible combinations of beer preference and gender or, in other words, listed all possible contingencies, Table 11.2 is called a *contingency table*. The test of independence uses the contingency table format and for that reason is sometimes referred to as a *contingency table test*.

Suppose a simple random sample of 150 beer drinkers has been selected. After tasting each beer, the individuals in the sample are asked to state their preference or first choice. The crosstabulation in Table 11.3 summarizes the responses for the study. As we see, the data for the test of independence are collected in terms of counts or frequencies for each cell or category. Of the 150 individuals in the sample, 20 were men who favored light beer, 40 were men who favored regular beer, 20 were men who favored dark beer, and so on.

To test whether two variables are independent, one sample is selected and crosstabulation is used to summarize the data for the two variables simultaneously.

The data in Table 11.3 are the observed frequencies for the six classes or categories. If we can determine the expected frequencies under the assumption of independence between beer preference and gender of the beer drinker, we can use the chi-square distribution to determine any significant difference between observed and expected frequencies.

Expected frequencies for the cells of the contingency table are based on the following rationale. First we assume that the null hypothesis of independence between beer preference and gender of the beer drinker is true. Then we note that in the entire sample of 150 beer drinkers, a total of 50 prefer light beer, 70 prefer regular beer, and 30 prefer dark beer. In terms of fractions we conclude that $50/150 = 1/3$ of the beer drinkers prefer light beer, $70/150 = 7/15$ prefer regular beer, and $30/150 = 1/5$ prefer dark beer. If the *independence* assumption is valid, we argue that these fractions must be applicable to both male and female beer drinkers. Thus, under the assumption of independence, we would expect the sample of 80 male beer drinkers to show that $(1/3)80 = 26.67$ prefer light beer, $(7/15)80 = 37.33$ prefer regular beer, and $(1/5)80 = 16$ prefer dark beer. Application of the same fractions to the 70 female beer drinkers provides the expected frequencies shown in Table 11.4

| Table 11.3 | SAMPLE RESULTS FOR BEER PREFERENCES OF MALE AND FEMALE BEER DRINKERS (OBSERVED FREQUENCIES) | | | |

		Beer Preference			
		Light	**Regular**	**Dark**	**Total**
Gender	**Male**	20	40	20	80
	Female	30	30	10	70
	Total	50	70	30	150

Table 11.4		EXPECTED FREQUENCIES IF BEER PREFERENCE IS INDEPENDENT OF THE GENDER OF THE BEER DRINKER			
		Beer Preference			
		Light	Regular	Dark	Total
Gender	Male	26.67	37.33	16.00	80
	Female	23.33	32.67	14.00	70
	Total	50.00	70.00	30.00	150

Let e_{ij} denote the expected frequency for the contingency table category in row i and column j. With this notation, let us reconsider the expected frequency calculation for males (row $i = 1$) who prefer regular beer (column $j = 2$); that is, expected frequency e_{12}. Following the preceding argument for the computation of expected frequencies, we can show that

$$e_{12} = (\tfrac{7}{15})80 = 37.33$$

This expression can be written slightly differently as

$$e_{12} = (\tfrac{7}{15})80 = (\tfrac{70}{150})80 = \frac{(80)(70)}{150} = 37.33$$

Note that 80 in the numerator of the expression is the total number of males (row 1 total), 70 is the total number of individuals preferring regular beer (column 2 total), and 150 is the total sample size. Hence, we see that

$$e_{12} = \frac{(\text{Row 1 Total})(\text{Column 2 Total})}{\text{Sample Size}}$$

Generalization of the expression shows that the following formula provides the expected frequencies for a contingency table in the test of independence.

Expected Frequencies for Contingency Tables under the Assumption of Independence

$$e_{ij} = \frac{(\text{Row } i \text{ Total})(\text{Column } j \text{ Total})}{\text{Sample Size}} \qquad (11.10)$$

Using the formula for male beer drinkers who prefer dark beer, we find an expected frequency of $e_{13} = (80)(30)/150 = 16.00$, as shown in Table 11.4. Use (11.10) to verify the other expected frequencies shown in Table 11.4.

The test procedure for comparing the observed frequencies of Table 11.3 with the expected frequencies of Table 11.4 is similar to the goodness of fit calculations made in the preceding section. Specifically, the χ^2 value based on the observed and expected frequencies is computed as follows.

Test Statistic for Independence

$$\chi^2 = \sum_i \sum_j \frac{(f_{ij} - e_{ij})^2}{e_{ij}} \tag{11.11}$$

where

f_{ij} = observed frequency for contingency table category in row i and column j

e_{ij} = expected frequency for contingency table category in row i and column j based on the assumption of independence

Note: With n rows and m columns in the contingency table, the test statistic has a chi-square distribution with $(n - 1)(m - 1)$ degrees of freedom provided that the expected frequencies are 5 *or more* for all categories.

The double summation in (11.11) is used to indicate that the calculation must be made for all the cells in the contingency table.

By reviewing the expected frequencies in Table 11.4, we see that the expected frequencies are 5 or more for each category. We therefore proceed with the computation of the chi-square test statistic. The calculations necessary to compute the chi-square test statistic for determining whether beer preference is independent of the gender of the beer drinker are shown in Table 11.5. We see that the value of the test statistic is $\chi^2 = 6.13$.

The number of degrees of freedom for the appropriate chi-square distribution is computed by multiplying the number of rows minus 1 by the number of columns minus 1. With two rows and three columns, we have $(2 - 1)(3 - 1) = (1)(2) = 2$ degrees of freedom for the test of independence of beer preference and gender of the beer drinker. With $\alpha = .05$ for the level of significance of the test, Table 3 of Appendix B shows an upper-tail χ^2 value of $\chi^2_{.05} = 5.99$. Note that we are again using the upper-tail value because we will reject the

The test for independence is always a one-tailed test with the rejection region located in the upper tail of the chi-square distribution.

Table 11.5	COMPUTATION OF THE CHI-SQUARE TEST STATISTIC FOR DETERMINING WHETHER BEER PREFERENCE IS INDEPENDENT OF THE GENDER OF THE BEER DRINKER

Gender	Beer Preference	Observed Frequency (f_{ij})	Expected Frequency (e_{ij})	Difference $(f_{ij} - e_{ij})$	Squared Difference $(f_{ij} - e_{ij})^2$	Squared Difference Divided by Expected Frequency $(f_{ij} - e_{ij})^2/e_{ij}$
Male	Light	20	26.67	−6.67	44.49	1.67
Male	Regular	40	37.33	2.67	7.13	0.19
Male	Dark	20	16.00	4.00	16.00	1.00
Female	Light	30	23.33	6.67	44.49	1.91
Female	Regular	30	32.67	−2.67	7.13	0.22
Female	Dark	10	14.00	−4.00	16.00	1.14
Total		150	150.00			6.13

null hypothesis only if the differences between observed and expected frequencies provide a large χ^2 value. In our example, $\chi^2 = 6.13$ is greater than the critical value of $\chi^2_{.05} = 5.99$. Thus, we reject the null hypothesis of independence and conclude that beer preference is not independent of the gender of the beer drinker.

Computer software packages such as Minitab and Excel can greatly simplify the computations needed to test for the independence of two variables. In addition they enable us to conduct the hypothesis testing procedure using the p-value approach. In the appendixes to this chapter we show how to perform the test of independence for both of these packages. To illustrate how to interpret the results, consider the Excel output shown in Figure 11.4. The p-value is 0.0467. Given the level of significance α, the decision of whether to reject H_0 can be made as follows:

$$\text{Reject } H_0 \text{ if the } p\text{-value} < \alpha$$

thus, with $\alpha = .05$ and the p-value $= 0.0467$, we reject H_0.

As we indicated previously, the test of independence itself only enables us to conclude that beer preference is not independent of the gender of the beer drinker. Although no further conclusions can be made as a result of the test, we can compare the observed and expected frequencies informally to obtain an idea of how the dependence between beer preference and gender of the beer drinker comes about. Refer to Tables 11.3 and 11.4. We see that male beer drinkers have higher observed than expected frequencies for both regular and dark beers, whereas female beer drinkers have a higher observed than expected frequency only for light beer. These observations give us insight about the beer preference differences between male and female beer drinkers.

Let us summarize the steps in a contingency table test of independence.

Figure 11.4   EXCEL OUTPUT FOR THE ALBER'S BREWERY TEST OF INDEPENDENCE

	A	B	C	D	E
1	Alber's Brewery Test of Independence				
2					
3	Observed Frequencies				
4			Beer Preference		
5	Gender	Light	Regular	Dark	Total
6	Male	20	40	20	80
7	Female	30	30	10	70
8	Total	50	70	30	150
9					
10	Expected Frequencies				
11			Beer Preference		
12	Gender	Light	Regular	Dark	Total
13	Male	26.67	37.33	16	80
14	Female	23.33	32.67	14	70
15	Total	50	70	30	150
16				chi-square	6.13
17				p-value =	0.0467

Test of Independence: A Summary

1. Set up the null and alternative hypotheses.

   H_0: The column variable is independent of the row variable

   H_a: The column variable is not independent of the row variable

2. Select a random sample and record the observed frequencies for each cell of the contingency table.
3. Use (11.10) to compute the expected frequency for each cell.
4. Use (11.11) to compute the value of the χ^2 test statistic.
5. Rejection rule:

$$\text{Reject } H_0 \text{ if } \chi^2 > \chi^2_\alpha$$

   where α is the level of significance; with n rows and m columns there are $(n-1)(m-1)$ degrees of freedom.

**N O T E S
and Comments** | The test statistic for the chi-square tests in this chapter requires an expected frequency of 5 for each category. When a category has fewer than 5, it is often appropriate to combine two adjacent categories to obtain an expected frequency of 5 or more in each category.

EXERCISES

Methods

SELF TEST

19. Shown is a 2 × 3 contingency table with observed frequencies for a sample of 200. Test for independence of the row and column variables by using the χ^2 test with $\alpha = .025$.

		Column Variable		
		A	**B**	**C**
Row Variable	**P**	20	44	50
	Q	30	26	30

20. The following 3 × 3 contingency table has observed frequencies for a sample of 240. Test for independence of the row and column variables by using the χ^2 test with $\alpha = .05$.

		Column Variable		
		A	**B**	**C**
	P	20	30	20
Row Variable	**Q**	30	60	25
	R	10	15	30

Applications

21. One of the questions on the *Business Week* 1996 Subscriber Study was, "In the past 12 months, when traveling for business, what type of airline ticket did you purchase most often?" The data obtained are shown in the following contingency table.

	Type of Flight	
Type of Ticket	**Domestic Flights**	**International Flights**
First class	29	22
Business/executive class	95	121
Full fare economy/coach class	518	135

Using $\alpha = .05$, test for the independence of type of flight and type of ticket. What is your conclusion?

22. The numbers of units sold by three salespersons over a three-month period are shown. Use $\alpha = .05$ and test for the independence of salesperson and type of product. What is your conclusion?

	Product		
Salesperson	**A**	**B**	**C**
Troutman	14	12	4
Kempton	21	16	8
McChristian	15	5	10

23. Starting positions for business and engineering graduates are classified by industry as shown in the following table.

	Industry			
Degree Major	**Oil**	**Chemical**	**Electrical**	**Computer**
Business	30	15	15	40
Engineering	30	30	20	20

Use $\alpha = .01$ and test for independence of degree major and industry type.

24. The results of a study conducted by Marist Institute for Public Opinion showed who men and women say is the most difficult person for them to buy holiday gifts for (*USA Today*, December 15, 1997). Suppose that the following data were obtained in a follow-up study consisting of 100 men and 100 women.

	Gender	
Most Difficult to Buy For	**Men**	**Women**
Spouse	37	25
Parents	28	31
Children	7	19
Siblings	8	3
In-laws	4	10
Other relatives	16	12

Use $\alpha = .05$ and test for independence of gender and the most difficult person to buy for. What is your conclusion?

25. Negative appeals have been recognized as an effective method of persuasion in advertising. A study in *The Journal of Advertising* (Summer 1997) reported the results of a content analysis of guilt and fear advertisements in 24 magazines. The number of ads with guilt and fear appeals that appeared in selected magazine types follows.

	Type of Appeal	
Magazine Type	Number of Ads with Guilt Appeals	Number of Ads with Fear Appeals
News and opinion	20	10
General editorial	15	11
Family-oriented	30	19
Business/financial	22	17
Female-oriented	16	14
African-American	12	15

Use the chi-square test of independence with a .01 level of significance to analyze the data. What is your conclusion?

26. A research study provided data on the primary reason for application to an MBA program by full-time and part-time students. Do the data suggest full-time and part-time students differ in their reasons for applying to MBA programs? Explain. Use $\alpha = .01$.

	Primary Reason for Application		
Student Status	Program Quality	Convenience/Cost	Other
Full-time	421	393	76
Part-time	400	593	46

27. A sport preference poll yielded the following data for men and women:

	Favorite Sport		
Sex	Baseball	Basketball	Football
Men	19	15	24
Women	16	18	16

Use $\alpha = .05$ and test for the same sport preferences by men and women. What is your conclusion?

28. Three suppliers provide the following data on defective parts.

	Part Quality		
Supplier	Good	Minor Defect	Major Defect
A	90	3	7
B	170	18	7
C	135	6	9

Use $\alpha = .05$ and test for independence between supplier and part quality. What does the result of your analysis tell the purchasing department?

29. A study of educational levels of voters and their political party affiliations yielded the following results.

	Party Affiliation		
Educational Level	Democratic	Republican	Independent
Did not complete high school	40	20	10
High school degree	30	35	15
College degree	30	45	25

Use $\alpha = .01$ and determine whether party affiliation is independent of the educational level of the voters.

30. An article in *Chance* (no. 2, 1997) reported the results of ratings of 160 movies by Gene Siskel and Roger Ebert. Each review is categorized as Pro ("thumbs up"), Con ("thumbs down"), or Mixed.

	Ebert Rating		
Siskel Rating	Con	Mixed	Pro
Con	24	8	13
Mixed	8	13	11
Pro	10	9	64

Use the chi-square test of independence with a .01 level of significance to analyze the data. What is your conclusion?

SUMMARY

In this chapter we introduced statistical procedures appropriate for comparisons involving proportions and the contingency table test of independence. In the first section we described how inferences concerning differences between proportions from two different populations could be made. In the second section the focus was on a single multinomial population. There we saw how to conduct hypothesis tests comparing the proportions for the categories of the multinomial population with hypothesized values. The chi-square goodness of fit test was used to make the comparison. The final section was concerned with tests of independence of two variables. Again a chi-square goodness of fit test provided the statistical support for the conclusion.

GLOSSARY

Goodness of fit test A statistical test conducted to determine whether to reject a hypothesized probability distribution for a population.

Contingency table A table used to summarize observed and expected frequencies for a test of independence.

. . . . / | / |. . . . .

KEY FORMULAS

Point Estimator of the Difference between the Proportions of Two Populations

$$\bar{p}_1 - \bar{p}_2 \tag{11.1}$$

Expected Value of $\bar{p}_1 - \bar{p}_2$

$$E(\bar{p}_1 - \bar{p}_2) = p_1 - p_2 \tag{11.2}$$

Standard Deviation of $\bar{p}_1 - \bar{p}_2$

$$\sigma_{\bar{p}_1 - \bar{p}_2} = \sqrt{\frac{p_1(1 - p_1)}{n_1} + \frac{p_2(1 - p_2)}{n_2}} \tag{11.3}$$

Point Estimator of $\sigma_{\bar{p}_1 - \bar{p}_2}$

$$s_{\bar{p}_1 - \bar{p}_2} = \sqrt{\frac{\bar{p}_1(1 - \bar{p}_1)}{n_1} + \frac{\bar{p}_2(1 - \bar{p}_2)}{n_2}} \tag{11.4}$$

Interval Estimate of the Difference between the Proportions of Two Populations: Large-Sample Case with $n_1 p_1, n_1(1 - p_1), n_2 p_2,$ and $n_2(1 - p_2) \geq 5$

$$\bar{p}_1 - \bar{p}_2 \pm z_{\alpha/2} s_{\bar{p}_1 - \bar{p}_2} \tag{11.5}$$

Test Statistic for Hypothesis Tests about the Difference between Proportions of Two Populations

$$z = \frac{(\bar{p}_1 - \bar{p}_2) - (p_1 - p_2)}{\sigma_{\bar{p}_1 - \bar{p}_2}} \tag{11.6}$$

Pooled Estimator of the Population Proportion

$$\bar{p} = \frac{n_1 \bar{p}_1 + n_2 \bar{p}_2}{n_1 + n_2} \tag{11.7}$$

Point Estimator of $\sigma_{\bar{p}_1 - \bar{p}_2}$ when $p_1 = p_2 = p$

$$s_{\bar{p}_1 - \bar{p}_2} = \sqrt{\bar{p}(1 - \bar{p})\left(\frac{1}{n_1} + \frac{1}{n_2}\right)} \tag{11.8}$$

Test Statistic for Goodness of Fit

$$\chi^2 = \sum_{i=1}^{k} \frac{(f_i - e_i)^2}{e_i} \tag{11.9}$$

Expected Frequencies for Contingency Tables under the Assumption of Independence

$$e_{ij} = \frac{(\text{Row } i \text{ Total})(\text{Column } j \text{ Total})}{\text{Sample Size}} \qquad (11.10)$$

Test Statistic for Independence

$$\chi^2 = \sum_i \sum_j \frac{(f_{ij} - e_{ij})^2}{e_{ij}} \qquad (11.11)$$

··/ /············

SUPPLEMENTARY EXERCISES

31. A cable television firm is considering submitting bids for rights to operate in two regions of the state of Florida. Surveys of the two regions provided the following data on customer acceptance of the cable television service.

Region I	Region II
$n_1 = 500$	$n_2 = 800$
Number indicating an intent to purchase = 175	Number indicating an intent to purchase = 360

Develop a 99% confidence interval for the difference between the population proportions of customer acceptance in the two regions.

32. A group of physicians in Denmark conducted a year-long study on the effectiveness of nicotine chewing gum in helping people to stop smoking (*New England Journal of Medicine,* 1988). The 113 people who participated in the study were all smokers. Sixty were given chewing gum with 2 milligrams of nicotine, and 53 were given a placebo chewing gum with no nicotine content. No one in the study knew which type of gum he or she had been given. All were told to use the gum and refrain from smoking.
    a. State the null and alternative hypotheses that would be appropriate if the researchers hoped to show that the group given nicotine chewing gum had a higher proportion of nonsmokers one year after the study began.
    b. Results showed that 23 of the smokers given nicotine chewing gum had remained nonsmokers for the one-year period and 12 of the smokers given the placebo had remained nonsmokers during the same period. Do these results support the conclusion that nicotine chewing gum can help a person to stop smoking? Test using $\alpha = .05$. What is the p-value?

33. A large automobile insurance company selected samples of single and married male policyholders and recorded the number who had made an insurance claim over the preceding three-year period.

Single Policyholders	Married Policyholders
$n_1 = 400$	$n_2 = 900$
Number making claims = 76	Number making claims = 90

    a. Using $\alpha = .05$, test to determine whether the claim rates differ between single and married male policyholders.
    b. Provide a 95% confidence interval for the difference between the proportions for the two populations.

34. Medical tests were conducted to learn about drug-resistant tuberculosis. Of 142 cases tested in New Jersey, nine were found to be drug-resistant. Of 268 cases tested in Texas, five were found to be drug-resistant. Do these data suggest a statistically significant difference between the proportions of drug-resistant cases in the two states? Test $H_0: p_1 - p_2 = 0$ at the .02 level of significance. What is the p-value and what is your conclusion?

35. In setting sales quotas, a marketing manager makes the assumption that order potentials are the same for each of four sales territories. A sample of 200 sales shows the numbers of orders from the territories.

	Sales Territories		
I	II	III	IV
60	45	59	36

Should the manager's assumption be rejected? Use $\alpha = .05$.

36. Seven percent of mutual fund investors rate corporate stocks "very safe," 58% rate them "somewhat safe," 24% rate them "not very safe," 4% rate them "not at all safe," and 7% are "not sure." A *Business Week*/Harris poll asked 529 mutual fund investors how they would rate corporate bonds on safety (*Business Week*, August 15, 1994). The responses are shown.

Safety Rating	Frequency
Very safe	48
Somewhat safe	323
Not very safe	79
Not at all safe	16
Not sure	63
Total	529

Do mutual fund investors' attitudes toward corporate bonds differ from their attitudes toward corporate stock? Support your conclusion with a statistical test using $\alpha = .01$.

37. A community park is to be opened soon. A sample of 140 individuals has been asked to state their preference for when they would most like to visit the park. The sample results follow.

Week Day	Saturday	Sunday	Holiday
20	20	40	60

In developing a staffing plan, should the park manager plan on the same number visiting the park each day? Support your conclusion with a statistical test using $\alpha = .05$.

38. A regional transit authority is concerned about the number of riders on one of its bus routes. In setting up the route, the assumption is that the number of riders is the same on every day from Monday through Friday. Using the data shown, test with $\alpha = .05$ to determine whether the transit authority's assumption is correct.

Day	Number of Riders
Monday	13
Tuesday	16
Wednesday	28
Thursday	17
Friday	16

39. The results of *Computerworld's* Annual Job Satisfaction Survey showed that 28% of Information Systems (IS) managers are very satisfied with their job, 46% are somewhat satisfied, 12% are neither satisfied or dissatisfied, 10% are somewhat dissatisfied, and 4% are very dissatisfied (*Computerworld*, May 26, 1997). Suppose that a sample of 500 computer programmers yielded the following results.

Category	Number of Respondents
Very satisfied	105
Somewhat satisfied	235
Neither	55
Somewhat dissatisfied	90
Very dissatisfied	15

Test using $\alpha = .05$ to determine whether the job satisfaction for computer programmers is different from the job satisfaction for IS managers.

40. A sample of parts provided the following contingency table data on part quality by production shift.

Shift	Number Good	Number Defective
First	368	32
Second	285	15
Third	176	24

Use $\alpha = .05$ and test the hypothesis that part quality is independent of the production shift. What is your conclusion?

41. The 1996 *Wall Street Journal* Subscriber Study showed data on the employment status of subscribers. Sample results corresponding to subscribers of the eastern and western editions are shown here.

	Region	
Employment Status	Eastern Edition	Western Edition
Full-time	1105	574
Part-time	31	15
Self-employed/consultant	229	186
Not employed	485	344

Using $\alpha = .05$, test the hypothesis that employment status is independent of the region. What is your conclusion?

42. A survey of commercial buildings served by the Cincinnati Gas & Electric Company was concluded in 1992 (CG&E Commercial Building Characteristics Survey, November 25, 1992). One question asked the main type of heating fuel used and another asked the year of construction. A crosstabulation of the findings follows.

		Fuel Type					
		Electricity	Natural Gas	Oil	Propane	Other	Total
Year Constructed	1973 or before	40	183	12	5	7	247
	1974–1979	24	26	2	2	0	54
	1980–1986	37	38	1	0	6	82
	1987–1991	48	70	2	0	1	121
	Total	149	317	17	7	14	504

Do fuel type and year constructed appear to be related? Conduct a statistical test with $\alpha = .025$ to support your conclusion.

43. The following is a crosstabulation of industry type and P/E ratio for 20 companies in the consumer products and banking industries (*Business Week,* August 15, 1994).

		P/E Ratio					
		5–9	10–14	15–19	20–24	25–29	Total
Industry	Consumer	0	3	5	1	1	10
	Banking	4	4	2	0	0	10
	Total	4	7	7	1	1	20

Is there a relationship between industry type and P/E ratio? Support your conclusion with a statistical test using $\alpha = .05$.

44. The following data were collected on the number of emergency ambulance calls for an urban county and a rural county in Virginia (*Journal of the Operational Research Society,* November 1986).

		Day of Week							
		Sun	Mon	Tue	Wed	Thur	Fri	Sat	Total
County	Urban	61	48	50	55	63	73	43	393
	Rural	7	9	16	13	9	14	10	78
	Total	68	57	66	68	72	87	53	471

Conduct a test for independence using $\alpha = .05$. What is your conclusion?

45. The 1991 office occupancy rates were reported for four California metropolitan areas. Do the following data suggest that the office vacancies were independent of metropolitan area? Use a .05 level of significance. What is your conclusion?

Occupancy Status	Los Angeles	San Diego	San Francisco	San Jose
Occupied	160	116	192	174
Vacant	40	34	33	26

..../ /............

Case Problem   BIPARTISAN AGENDA FOR CHANGE

In a study conducted by Zogby International for the *Democrat and Chronicle,* more than 700 New Yorkers were polled to determine whether the New York state government works. Respondents surveyed were asked questions involving pay cuts for state legislators, restrictions on lobbyists, term limits for legislators, and whether state citizens should be able to put matters directly on the state ballot for a vote (*Democrat and Chronicle,* December 7, 1997). The results regarding several proposed reforms had broad support, crossing all demographic and political lines.

Suppose that a follow-up survey of 100 individuals who live in the western region of New York was conducted. The party affiliation (Democrat, Independent, Republican) of each individual surveyed was recorded, as well as their responses to the following three questions.

1. Should legislative pay be cut for every day the state budget is late?
   Yes___ No___
2. Should there be more restrictions on lobbyists?
   Yes___ No___
3. Should there be term limits requiring legislators serve a fixed number of years?
   Yes___ No___

NYReform

The responses were coded using 1 for a *yes* response and 2 for a *no* response. The complete data set is available on the data disk in the data set named NYReform.

Managerial Report

1. Use descriptive statistics to summarize the data from this study. What are your preliminary conclusions about the independence of the response (yes or no) and party affiliation for each of the three questions in the survey?
2. With regard to question 1, test for the independence of the response (yes and no) and party affiliation. Use $\alpha = .05$.
3. With regard to question 2, test for the independence of the response (yes and no) and party affiliation. Use $\alpha = .05$.
4. With regard to question 3, test for the independence of the response (yes and no) and party affiliation. Use $\alpha = .05$.
5. Is there broad support for change across all political lines? Explain.

..../ /............

Appendix 11.1   TESTS OF GOODNESS OF FIT AND INDEPENDENCE WITH MINITAB

In this appendix we show how Minitab can be used to conduct a goodness of fit test for the Scott Marketing Research study presented in Section 11.2 and perform a test of independence for the Alber's Brewery example presented in Section 11.3.

Goodness of Fit Test: A Multinomial Population

We begin with a new Minitab worksheet and enter the observed and expected frequency data into columns 1 and 2, respectively. Thus, for the Scott Marketing Research example presented in Section 11.2 we entered the observed frequencies, 48, 98, and 54, in C1 and the expected frequencies, 60, 100, and 40, in C2. The Minitab steps for the goodness of fit test are as follows:

Step 1. Select the **Calc** pull-down menu

Step 2. Choose the **Calculator** option

Step 3. When the Calculator dialog box appears
Enter K1 in the **Store result in variable** box
Enter Sum((C1-C2)**2/C2) in the **Expression** box
Select **OK**

Step 4. Select the **Calc** pull-down menu

Step 5. Select the **Probability Distributions** pull-down menu

Step 6. Choose the **Chisquare** option

Step 7. When the Chisquare Distribution dialog box appears:
Select **Cumulative probability**
Enter 2 in the **Degrees of freedom** box
Select **Input constant**
Enter K1 in the **Input constant** box
Enter K2 in the **Optional storage** box
Select **OK**

Step 8. Select the **Calc** pull-down menu

Step 9. Choose the **Calculator** option

Step 10. When the Calculator dialog box appears
Enter K3 in the **Store result in variable** box
Enter $1 - $ K2 in the **Expression** box
Select **OK**

Step 11. Select the **Window** pull-down menu

Step 12. Choose the **Info** option

The value of constant K1 in the Info window is the test statistic $\chi^2 = 7.34$. The value of constant K3 is the p-value $= .0255$. With $\chi^2_{.05} = 5.99$ and $\alpha = 0.05$, we can reject H_0.

Test of Independence: Contingency Tables

We begin with a new Minitab worksheet and enter the observed frequency data for the Alber's Brewery example into columns 1, 2, and 3, respectively. Thus, we entered the observed frequencies corresponding to a light beer preference (20 and 30) in C1, the observed frequencies corresponding to a regular beer preference (40 and 30) in C2, and the observed frequencies corresponding to a dark beer preference (20 and 10) in C3. The Minitab steps for the test of independence are as follows:

Step 1. Select the **Stat** pull-down menu

Step 2. Select the **Tables** pull-down menu

Step 3. Choose the **Chisquare Test** option

Step 4. When the Chisquare Test dialog box appears:
Enter C1-C3 in the **Columns containing the table** box
Select **OK**

The value of the chisquare test statistic is shown to be $\chi^2 = 6.122$ with a p-value $= 0.047$. With $\chi^2_{.05} = 5.99$ and $\alpha = 0.05$, we reject H_0.

..../ /.............

Appendix 11.2   TESTS OF GOODNESS OF FIT AND INDEPENDENCE WITH EXCEL

In this appendix we show how Excel can be used to conduct a goodness of fit test for the Scott Marketing Research study presented in Section 11.2 and perform a test of independence for the Alber's Brewery example presented in Section 11.3.

Goodness of Fit Test: A Multinomial Population

Figure 11.3 shows the Excel worksheet used to compute the p-value for the test of goodness of fit presented in Section 11.2. Note that the hypothesized proportions for each of the three categories were entered into cells B5:B7, the observed frequencies were entered into cells C5:C7, and the expected frequencies were entered into cells D5:D7; the p-value for the associated test of goodness of fit appears in cell D10. The Excel steps for the goodness of fit test are as follows:

Step 1. Select cell D10 in the worksheet
Step 2. Select the **Insert** pull-down menu
Step 3. Choose the **Function** option
Step 4. When the Paste Function dialog box appears:
      Choose **Statistical** from the **Function category** box
      Choose **CHITEST** from the **Function name** box
      Select **OK**
Step 5. When the CHITEST dialog box appears:
      Enter C5:C7 in the **Actual-range** box
      Enter D5:D7 in the **Expected-range** box
      Select **OK**
Step 6. Select cell D9 in the worksheet
Step 7. Select the **Insert** pull-down menu
Step 8. Choose the **Function** option
Step 9. When the Paste Function dialog box appears:
      Choose **Statistical** from the **Function category** box
      Choose **CHIINV** from the **Function name** box
      Select **OK**
Step 10. When the CHIINV dialog box appears
      Enter D10 in the **Probability** box
      Enter 2 in the **Deg freedom** box
      Select **OK**

The value of the chi-square test statistic, 7.34, is in cell D9, and the p-value, 0.0255, is in cell D10. With $\chi^2_{.05} = 5.99$ and $\alpha = .05$, we can reject H_0.

Test of Independence: Contingency Tables

Figure 11.4 shows the Excel worksheet for the test of independence for the Alber's Brewery example presented in Section 11.3. Note that we entered the observed frequencies into cells B6:D7 and the expected frequencies into cells B13:D14. The Excel steps for the contingency table test of independence are as follows:

Step 1.   Select cell **E17** in the worksheet
Step 2.   Select the **Insert** pull-down menu
Step 3.   Choose the **Function** option
Step 4.   When the Paste Function dialog box appears:
          Choose **Statistical** from the **Function category** box
          Choose **CHITEST** from the **Function name** box
          Select **OK**
Step 5.   When the CHITEST dialog box appears:
          Enter **B6:D7** in the **Actual-range** box
          Enter **B13:D14** in the **Expected-range** box
          Select **OK**
Step 6.   Select cell E16 in the worksheet
Step 7.   Select the **Insert** pull-down menu
Step 8.   Choose the **Function** option
Step 9.   When the Paste Function dialog box appears:
          Choose **Statistical** from the **Function category** box
          Choose **CHIINV** from the **Function name** box
          Select **OK**
Step 10. When the CHIINV dialog box appears
          Enter E17 in the **Probability** box
          Enter 2 in the **Deg freedom** box
          Select **OK**

The value of the chi-square test statistic, 6.13, is in cell E16, and the p-value, .0467, is in cell E17. With $\chi^2_{.05} = 5.99$ and $\alpha = .05$, we can reject H_0.

12

REGRESSION ANALYSIS

CONTENTS

POLAROID CORPORATION*
Cambridge, Massachusetts

Polaroid's consumer photography business began in 1947 when the company's founder, Dr. Edwin Land, announced a one-step dry process for producing a finished photograph within one minute after taking the picture. The first Polaroid Land camera and Polaroid Land film went on sale in 1949. Since then, Polaroid's continuous experimentation and development in chemistry, optics, and electronics have produced photographic systems of ever higher quality, reliability, and convenience.

Polaroid's other major business segment, technical and industrial photography, focuses on making Polaroid's instant photography a key component of the growing number of imaging systems used in today's visual communications environment. To this end, Polaroid markets a wide variety of instant photographic systems, cameras, components, and films for professional, industrial, scientific, and medical uses. Other businesses include magnetics, sunglasses, industrial polarizers, chemicals, custom coating, and holography.

Sensitometry, the measurement of the sensitivity of photographic materials, provides the information on many characteristics of film, such as its useful exposure range. Within Polaroid's central sensitometry laboratory, scientists systematically sample and analyze instant films that have been stored at temperature and humidity levels approximating those to which the films will be subjected after they have been purchased by consumers. To investigate the relationship between film speed and the age of a Polaroid extended range, color professional print film, Polaroid's central sensitometry lab selected film samples ranging in age (time since manufacture) from one to 13 months. The data showed that film speed decreases

Regression analysis enables Polaroid to produce films with the performance levels its customers require. © Polaroid.

with age, and that a straight-line or linear relationship could be used to approximate the relationship between change in film speed and age of the film.

Using regression analysis, Polaroid was able to develop the following equation relating the change in the film speed to the film's age.

$$\hat{y} = -19.8 - 7.6x$$

where

$$\hat{y} = \text{change in film speed}$$
$$x = \text{film age in months}$$

This equation shows that the average decrease in film speed is 7.6 units per month. The information provided by this analysis, when coupled with consumer purchase and use patterns, enables Polaroid to make manufacturing adjustments that help the company produce films with the performance levels its customers require.

In this chapter you will learn how regression analysis can be used to develop an equation relating two variables, such as the change in film speed to the age of the film in the Polaroid example. In the last section of the chapter we will extend this concept to cases involving more than two variables.

*The authors are indebted to Lawrence Friedman, Manager, Photographic Quality, for providing this Statistics in Practice.

Managerial decisions often are based on the relationship between two or more variables. For example, after considering the relationship between advertising expenditures and sales, a marketing manager might attempt to predict sales for a given level of advertising expenditures. In another case, a public utility might use the relationship between the daily high temperature and the demand for electricity to predict electricity usage on the basis of next month's anticipated daily high temperatures. Sometimes a manager will rely on intuition to judge how two variables are related. However, if data can be obtained, a statistical procedure called *regression analysis* can be used to develop an equation showing how the variables are related.

In regression terminology, the variable being predicted is called the *dependent* variable. The variable or variables being used to predict the value of the dependent variable are called the *independent* variables. For example, in analyzing the effect of advertising expenditures on sales, a marketing manager's desire to predict sales would suggest making sales the dependent variable. Advertising expenditure would be the independent variable used to help predict sales. In statistical notation, y denotes the dependent variable and x denotes the independent variable.

The simplest type of regression analysis involving one independent variable and one dependent variable in which the relationship between the variables is approximated by a straight line, which is called *simple linear regression*. Regression analysis involving two or more independent variables is called *multiple regression analysis*.

> The statistical methods used in studying the relationship between two variables were first employed by Sir Francis Galton (1822–1911). Galton was interested in studying the relationship between a father's height and the son's height. Galton's disciple, Karl Pearson (1857–1936), analyzed the relationship between the father's height and the son's height for 1078 pairs of subjects.

12.1 SIMPLE LINEAR REGRESSION MODEL

> In simple linear regression, the analysis of bivariate data involves the measurement of two variables for each element of a sample.

Armand's Pizza Parlors is a chain of Italian-food restaurants located in a five-state area. The most successful locations for Armand's have been near college campuses. The managers believe that quarterly sales for these restaurants (denoted by y) are related positively to the size of the student population (denoted by x); that is, restaurants near campuses with a large student population tend to generate more sales than those located near campuses with a small population. Using regression analysis, we can develop an equation showing how the dependent variable y is related to the independent variable x.

Regression Model and the Regression Equation

In the Armand's Pizza Parlors example, every restaurant has associated with it a value of x (student population) and a corresponding value of y (quarterly sales). The equation that describes how y is related to x and an error term is called the *regression model*. The regression model used in simple linear regression follows.

Simple Linear Regression Model

$$y = \beta_0 + \beta_1 x + \epsilon \tag{12.1}$$

In the simple linear regression model, y is a linear function of x (the $\beta_0 + \beta_1 x$ part) plus ϵ. β_0 and β_1 are referred to as the parameters of the model, and ϵ (the Greek letter epsilon) is a random variable referred to as the error term. The error term accounts for the variability in y that cannot be explained by the linear relationship between x and y.

In Section 12.4 we will discuss the assumptions for the simple linear regression model and ϵ. One of the assumptions is that the mean or expected value of ϵ is zero. A consequence of this assumption is that the mean or expected value of y, denoted $E(y)$, is equal to $\beta_0 + \beta_1 x$; in other words, the mean value of y is a linear function of x. The equation that describes how the mean value of y is related to x is called the *regression equation*. The regression equation for simple linear regression follows.

Simple Linear Regression Equation

$$E(y) = \beta_0 + \beta_1 x \qquad\qquad (12.2)$$

The graph of the simple linear regression equation is a straight line; β_0 is the y intercept of the regression line, β_1 is the slope, and $E(y)$ is the mean or expected value of y for a given value of x. Examples of possible regression lines for simple linear regression are shown in Figure 12.1. The regression line in panel A of the figure shows that the mean value of y is related positively to x, with larger values of $E(y)$ associated with larger values of x. The regression line in panel B shows that the mean value of y is related negatively to x, with smaller values of $E(y)$ associated with larger values of x. The regression line in panel C shows that the mean value of y is not related to x; that is, the mean value of y is the same for every value of x.

Estimated Regression Equation

If the values of the parameters β_0 and β_1 were known, we could use (12.2) to compute the mean value of y for a known value of x. Unfortunately, the parameter values are not known in practice and must be estimated by using sample data. Sample statistics (denoted b_0 and b_1) are computed as estimates of the parameters β_0 and β_1. Substituting the values of the sample statistics b_0 and b_1 for β_0 and β_1 in the regression equation, we obtain the *estimated regression equation*. The estimated regression equation for simple linear regression follows.

Estimated Simple Linear Regression Equation

$$\hat{y} = b_0 + b_1 x \qquad\qquad (12.3)$$

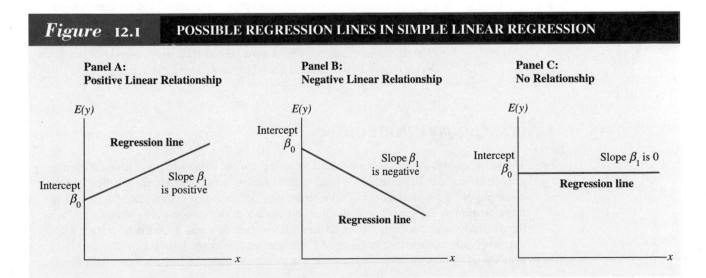

Figure **12.1**   POSSIBLE REGRESSION LINES IN SIMPLE LINEAR REGRESSION

The graph of the estimated simple linear regression equation is called the *estimated regression line;* b_0 is the y intercept, b_1 is the slope, and $\hat{y}$ is the estimated value of y for a given value of x. In the next section, we show how data from a sample can be used to compute the values of b_0 and b_1 in the estimated regression equation. Figure 12.2 is a summary of the estimation process for simple linear regression.

Figure 12.2	THE ESTIMATION PROCESS IN SIMPLE LINEAR REGRESSION

The estimation of β_0 and β_1 is a statistical process much like the estimation of μ discussed in Chapter 7. β_0 and β_1 are the unknown parameters of interest, and b_0 and b_1 are the sample statistics used to estimate the parameters.

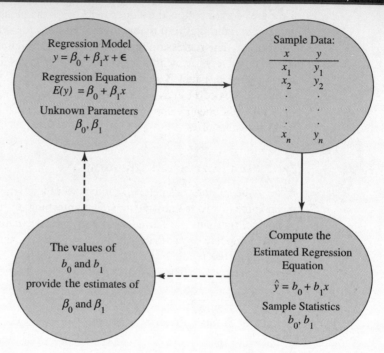

N O T E S *and Comments*	Regression analysis *cannot* be interpreted as a procedure for establishing a *cause-and-effect* relationship between variables. It can only indicate how or to what extent variables are *associated* with each other. Any conclusions about cause and effect must be based on the *judgment* of the individual or individuals most knowledgeable about the application.

12.2   LEAST SQUARES METHOD

The *least squares method* is a procedure for using sample data to compute an estimated regression equation. To illustrate the least squares method, suppose data were collected from a sample of 10 Armand's Pizza Parlor restaurants located near college campuses. For the ith restaurant in the sample, x_i is the size of the student population (in thousands) and y_i is the quarterly sales (in thousands of dollars). The values of x_i and y_i for the 10 restaurants in the sample are summarized in Table 12.1. We see that restaurant 1, with $x_1 = 2$ and $y_1 = 58$, is near a campus with 2000 students and has quarterly sales of $58,000. Restaurant 2, with

Table 12.1	STUDENT POPULATION AND QUARTERLY SALES DATA FOR 10 ARMAND'S PIZZA PARLORS	
Restaurant i	Student Population (1000s) x_i	Quarterly Sales ($1000s) y_i
1	2	58
2	6	105
3	8	88
4	8	118
5	12	117
6	16	137
7	20	157
8	20	169
9	22	149
10	26	202

$x_2 = 6$ and $y_2 = 105$, is near a campus with 6000 students and has quarterly sales of $105,000. The largest sales value is for restaurant 10, which is near a campus with 26,000 students and has quarterly sales of $202,000.

Figure 12.3 is a scatter diagram of the data in Table 12.1. The size of the student population is shown on the horizontal axis and the value of quarterly sales is shown on the vertical axis. Scatter diagrams for regression analysis are constructed with values of the independent variable x on the horizontal axis and values of the dependent variable y on the vertical axis. The scatter diagram enables us to observe the data graphically and to draw preliminary conclusions about the possible relationship between the variables.

What preliminary conclusions can be drawn from Figure 12.3? Quarterly sales appear to be higher at campuses with larger student populations. In addition, for these data the relationship between the size of the student population and quarterly sales appears to be approximated by a straight line; indeed, there seems to be a positive linear relationship between x and y. We therefore choose the simple linear regression model to represent the relationship between quarterly sales and student population. Given that choice, our next task is to use the sample data in Table 12.1 to determine the values of b_0 and b_1 in the estimated simple linear regression equation. For the ith restaurant, the estimated regression equation is

$$\hat{y}_i = b_0 + b_1 x_i \tag{12.4}$$

where

$\hat{y}_i$ = estimated value of quarterly sales ($1000s) for the ith restaurant

b_0 = the y intercept of the estimated regression line

b_1 = the slope of the estimated regression line

x_i = size of the student population (1000s) for the ith restaurant

With y_i denoting the observed (actual) quarterly sales for restaurant i and $\hat{y}_i$ in (12.4) representing the estimated value of quarterly sales for restaurant i, every restaurant in the

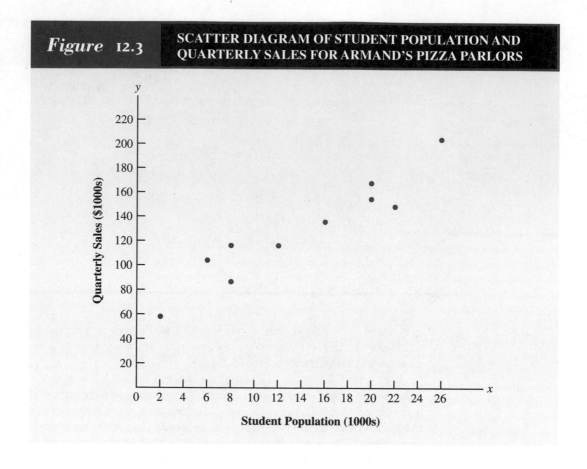

Figure 12.3   SCATTER DIAGRAM OF STUDENT POPULATION AND QUARTERLY SALES FOR ARMAND'S PIZZA PARLORS

sample will have an observed value of quarterly sales y_i and an estimated value of quarterly sales $\hat{y}_i$. For the estimated regression line to provide a good fit to the data, we want the differences between the observed values and the estimated values to be small.

The least squares method uses the sample data to provide the values of b_0 and b_1 that minimize the *sum of the squares of the deviations* between the observed values of the dependent variable y_i and the estimated values of the dependent variable $\hat{y}_i$. The criterion for the least squares method is given by (12.5).

Least Squares Criterion

Carl Friedrich Gauss (1777–1855) proposed the least squares method. Gauss was the first to show that the estimated regression equation minimizes the error sum of squares.

$$\min \Sigma(y_i - \hat{y}_i)^2 \qquad (12.5)$$

where

y_i = observed value of the dependent variable for the ith observation

$\hat{y}_i$ = estimated value of the dependent variable for the ith observation

---

Differential calculus can be used to show that the values of b_0 and b_1 that minimize (12.5) can be found by using (12.6) and (12.7).

Slope and *y*-Intercept for the Estimated Regression Equation

In computing b_1 with a calculator, carry as many significant digits as possible in the intermediate calculations. We recommend carrying at least four significant digits.

$$b_1 = \frac{\Sigma x_i y_i - (\Sigma x_i \Sigma y_i)/n}{\Sigma x_i^2 - (\Sigma x_i)^2/n} \qquad (12.6)$$

$$b_0 = \bar{y} - b_1 \bar{x} \qquad (12.7)$$

where

x_i = value of the independent variable for the *i*th observation

y_i = value of the dependent variable for the *i*th observation

$\bar{x}$ = mean value for the independent variable

$\bar{y}$ = mean value for the dependent variable

n = total number of observations

Some of the calculations necessary to develop the least squares estimated regression equation for Armand's Pizza Parlors are shown in Table 12.2. With the sample of 10 restaurants, we have $n = 10$ observations. Using (12.6), (12.7), and the information in Table 12.2, we can compute the slope and intercept of the estimated regression equation for Armand's Pizza Parlors. The calculation of the slope (b_1) proceeds as follows.

$$b_1 = \frac{\Sigma x_i y_i - (\Sigma x_i \Sigma y_i)/n}{\Sigma x_i^2 - (\Sigma x_i)^2/n}$$

$$= \frac{21{,}040 - (140)(1300)/10}{2528 - (140)^2/10}$$

$$= \frac{2840}{568}$$

$$= 5$$

Table 12.2   CALCULATIONS FOR THE LEAST SQUARES ESTIMATED REGRESSION EQUATION FOR ARMAND'S PIZZA PARLORS

Restaurant i	x_i	y_i	$x_i y_i$	x_i^2
1	2	58	116	4
2	6	105	630	36
3	8	88	704	64
4	8	118	944	64
5	12	117	1,404	144
6	16	137	2,192	256
7	20	157	3,140	400
8	20	169	3,380	400
9	22	149	3,278	484
10	26	202	5,252	676
Totals	140	1300	21,040	2528
	Σx_i	Σy_i	$\Sigma x_i y_i$	Σx_i^2

The calculation of the y intercept (b_0) follows.

$$\bar{x} = \frac{\Sigma x_i}{n} = \frac{140}{10} = 14$$

$$\bar{y} = \frac{\Sigma y_i}{n} = \frac{1300}{10} = 130$$

$$b_0 = \bar{y} - b_1\bar{x}$$
$$= 130 - 5(14)$$
$$= 60$$

Thus, the estimated regression equation is

$$\hat{y} = 60 + 5x$$

Figure 12.4 shows the graph of this equation on the scatter diagram.

The slope of the estimated regression equation ($b_1 = 5$) is positive, implying that as student population increases, quarterly sales increase. In fact, we can conclude (because quarterly sales are measured in $1000s and student population in 1000s) that an increase in the student population of 1000 is associated with an increase of $5000 in expected quarterly sales; that is, quarterly sales are expected to increase by $5.00 per student.

If we believe the least squares estimated regression equation adequately describes the relationship between x and y, it would seem reasonable to use the estimated regression equa-

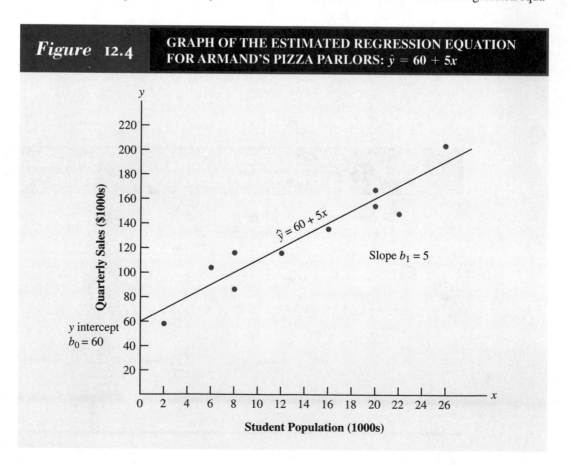

Figure 12.4   **GRAPH OF THE ESTIMATED REGRESSION EQUATION FOR ARMAND'S PIZZA PARLORS: $\hat{y} = 60 + 5x$**

Using the estimated regression equation to make predictions outside the range of the values of the independent variable should be done with caution because outside that range we cannot be sure that the same relationship is valid.

tion to predict the value of y for a given value of x. For example, if we wanted to predict sales for a restaurant to be located near a campus with 16,000 students, we would compute

$$\hat{y} = 60 + 5(16) = 140$$

Hence, we would predict quarterly sales of \$140,000 for this restaurant. In the following sections we will discuss methods for assessing the appropriateness of using the estimated regression equation for prediction.

N O T E S and Comments

The least squares method provides an estimated regression equation that minimizes the sum of squared deviations between the observed values of the dependent variable y_i and the estimated values of the dependent variable $\hat{y}_i$. The least squares criterion chooses the equation that provides the best fit. If some other criterion were used, such as minimizing the sum of the absolute deviations between y_i and $\hat{y}_i$, a different equation would be obtained. In practice, the least squares method is most widely used.

EXERCISES

Methods

SELF TEST

1. Given are five observations for two variables, x and y.

x_i	1	2	3	4	5
y_i	3	7	5	11	14

    a. Develop a scatter diagram for these data.
    b. What does the scatter diagram developed in part (a) indicate about the relationship between the two variables?
    c. Try to approximate the relationship between x and y by drawing a straight line through the data.
    d. Develop the estimated regression equation by computing the values of b_0 and b_1 using (12.6) and (12.7).
    e. Use the estimated regression equation to predict the value of y when $x = 4$.

2. Given are five observations for two variables, x and y.

x_i	2	3	5	1	8
y_i	25	25	20	30	16

    a. Develop a scatter diagram for these data.
    b. What does the scatter diagram developed in part (a) indicate about the relationship between the two variables?
    c. Try to approximate the relationship between x and y by drawing a straight line through the data.
    d. Develop the estimated regression equation by computing the values of b_0 and b_1 using (12.6) and (12.7).
    e. Use the estimated regression equation to predict the value of y when $x = 6$.

3. Given are five observations collected in a regression study with two variables.

x_i	2	4	5	7	8
y_i	2	3	2	6	4

    a. Develop a scatter diagram for these data.
    b. Develop the estimated regression equation for these data.
    c. Use the estimated regression equation to predict the value of y when $x = 4$.

Applications

SELF TEST

4. The following data were collected on the height (inches) and weight (pounds) of women swimmers.

Height	68	64	62	65	66
Weight	132	108	102	115	128

   a. Develop a scatter diagram for these data with height as the independent variable.
   b. What does the scatter diagram developed in part (a) indicate about the relationship between the two variables?
   c. Try to approximate the relationship between height and weight by drawing a straight line through the data.
   d. Develop the estimated regression equation by computing the values of b_0 and b_1 using (12.6) and (12.7).
   e. If a swimmer's height is 63 inches, what would you estimate her weight to be?

5. The following data show the media expenditures (millions of dollars) and the case sales (millions) for seven major brands of soft drinks (*Superbrands '98,* October 20, 1997).

Brand	Media Expenditures ($)	Case Sales
Coca-Cola Classic	131.3	1929.2
Pepsi-Cola	92.4	1384.6
Diet Coke	60.4	811.4
Sprite	55.7	541.5
Dr. Pepper	40.2	536.9
Mountain Dew	29.0	535.6
7-Up	11.6	219.5

   a. Develop a scatter diagram for these data with media expenditures as the independent variable.
   b. What does the scatter diagram developed in part (a) indicate about the relationship between the two variables?
   c. Draw a straight line through the data to approximate a linear relationship between media expenditures and case sales.
   d. Use the least squares method to develop the estimated regression equation.
   e. Provide an interpretation for the slope of the estimated regression equation.
   f. Predict the case sales for a brand with a media expenditure of $70 million.

6. Airline performance data for U.S. airlines were reported in *The Wall Street Journal Almanac 1998.* Data on the percentage of flights arriving on time and the number of complaints per 100,000 passengers follow.

Airline	Percentage on Time	Complaints
Southwest	81.8	0.21
Continental	76.6	0.58
Northwest	76.6	0.85
US Airways	75.7	0.68
United	73.8	0.74
American	72.2	0.93
Delta	71.2	0.72
America West	70.8	1.22
TWA	68.5	1.25

a. Develop a scatter diagram for these data.
b. What does the scatter diagram developed in part (a) indicate about the relationship between the two variables?
c. Develop the estimated regression equation showing how the percentage of flights arriving on time is related to the number of complaints per 100,000 passengers.
d. Provide an interpretation for the slope of the estimated regression equation.
e. What is the estimated number of complaints per 100,000 passengers if the percentage of flights arriving on time is 80%?

7. Major hotels frequently provide special rates for business travelers. The lowest rates are charged when reservations are made 14 days in advance. The following table reports the business rates and the 14-day advance super-saver rates for one night at a sample of six ITT Sheraton Hotels (*Sky Magazine,* January 1995).

Hotel Location	Business Rate ($)	14-Day Advance Rate ($)
Birmingham	89	81
Miami	130	115
Atlanta	98	89
Chicago	149	138
New Orleans	199	149
Nashville	114	94

a. Develop a scatter diagram for these data with business rates as the independent variable.
b. Develop the least squares estimated regression equation.
c. The ITT Sheraton Hotel in Tampa offers a business rate of $135 per night. Estimate the 14-day advance super-saver rate at this hotel.

8. Nielsen Media Research collects data showing which advertisers get the most exposure during prime-time TV on ABC, CBS, NBC, Fox, UPN, and WB networks. Data showing the number of times the ad was aired and the number of household exposures in millions for the week of April 28–May 4, 1997, follow (*USA Today,* May 5, 1997).

Advertised Brand	Times Ad Aired	Household Exposures
Wendy's	28	191.7
Ford Escort	20	174.6
Austin Powers movie	14	161.3
Nissan	16	161.1
Pizza Hut	16	147.7
Saturn	16	146.3
Father's Day movie	11	138.2

a. Develop the estimated regression equation showing how the number of times an ad is aired is related to the number of household exposures.
b. Provide an interpretation for the slope of the estimated regression equation.
c. What is the estimated number of household exposures if an ad is aired 15 times?

9. A sales manager has collected the following data on years of experience and annual sales.

Salesperson	Years of Experience	Annual Sales ($1000s)
1	1	80
2	3	97
3	4	92
4	4	102
5	6	103
6	8	111
7	10	119
8	10	123
9	11	117
10	13	136

a. Develop a scatter diagram for these data with years of experience as the independent variable.
b. Develop an estimated regression equation that can be used to predict annual sales given the years of experience.
c. Use the estimated regression equation to predict annual sales for a salesperson with nine years of experience.

10. The following data show the hotel revenue and the gaming revenue, in millions of dollars, for ten Las Vegas casino hotels (*Cornell Hotel And Restaurant Administration Quarterly*, October 1997).

Casino

Company	Hotel Revenue	Gaming Revenue
Boyd Gaming	$303.5	$548.2
Circus Circus Enterprises	664.8	664.8
Grand Casinos	121.0	270.7
Hilton Corp. Gaming Div.	429.6	511.0
MGM Grand, Inc.	373.1	404.7
Mirage Resorts	670.9	782.8
Primadonna Resorts	66.4	130.7
Rio Hotel & Casino	105.8	105.5
Sahara Gaming	102.4	148.7
Station Casinos	135.8	358.5

a. Develop a scatter diagram for these data with hotel revenue as the independent variable.
b. Is there a linear relationship between the two variables?
c. Develop the estimated regression equation relating the gaming revenue to the hotel revenue.
d. Suppose that the hotel revenue was $500 million. What is an estimate of the gaming revenue?

11. The following table gives the percentage of women working in each company (x) and the percentage of management jobs held by women in that company (y); the data represent companies in retailing and trade (*Louis Rukeyser's Business Almanac*).

Company	x_i	y_i
Federated Department Stores	72	61
Kroger	47	16
Marriott	51	32
McDonald's	57	46
Sears	55	36

a. Develop a scatter diagram for these data.
b. What does the scatter diagram developed in part (a) indicate about the relationship between x and y?
c. Develop the estimated regression equation for these data.
d. Predict the percentage of management jobs held by women in a company that has 60% women employees.
e. Use the estimated regression equation to predict the percentage of management jobs held by women in a company where 55% of the jobs are held by women. How does this predicted value compare to the 36% value observed for Sears, a company in which 55% of the employees are women?

12. To the Internal Revenue Service, the reasonableness of total itemized deductions depends on the taxpayer's adjusted gross income. Large deductions, which include charity and medical deductions, are more reasonable for taxpayers with large adjusted gross incomes. If a taxpayer claims larger than average itemized deductions for a given level of income, the chances of an IRS audit are increased. Data on adjusted gross income and the average or reasonable amount of itemized deductions follow (*Money,* October 1994). The data are in thousands of dollars.

Adjusted Gross Income ($1000s)	Total Itemized Deductions ($1000s)
22	9.6
27	9.6
32	10.1
48	11.1
65	13.5
85	17.7
120	25.5

a. Develop a scatter diagram for these data with adjusted gross income as the independent variable.
b. Use the least squares method to develop the estimated regression equation.
c. Predict a reasonable level of total itemized deductions for a taxpayer with an adjusted gross income of $52,500. If this taxpayer has claimed total itemized deductions of $20,400, would the IRS agent's request for an audit appear justified? Explain.

13. The following data report the occupancy rates (%) and room rates ($) for the largest U.S. hotel markets (*The Wall Street Journal Almanac 1998*).

Hotel

Market	Occupancy Rate (%)	Average Room Rate ($)
Los Angeles–Long Beach	67.9	75.91
Chicago	72.0	92.04
Washington	68.4	94.42
Atlanta	67.7	81.69
Dallas	69.5	74.76
San Diego	68.7	80.86
Anaheim–Santa Ana	69.5	70.04
San Francisco	78.7	106.47
Houston	62.0	66.11
Miami–Hialeah	71.2	85.83
Oahu Island	80.7	107.11
Phoenix	71.4	95.34
Boston	73.5	105.51
Tampa–St. Petersburg	63.4	67.45
Detroit	68.7	64.79
Philadelphia	70.1	83.56
Nashville	67.1	70.12
Seattle	73.4	82.60
Minneapolis–St. Paul	69.8	73.64
New Orleans	70.6	99.00

a. Develop a scatter diagram for these data with average room rate as the independent variable.
b. Develop the estimated regression equation relating the occupancy rate to the average room rate.
c. Predict the occupancy rate for a hotel with an average room rate of $80.

12.3 COEFFICIENT OF DETERMINATION

For the Armand's Pizza Parlors example, we developed the estimated regression equation $\hat{y} = 60 + 5x$ to approximate the linear relationship between the size of the student population x and quarterly sales y. A question now is: How well does the estimated regression equation fit the data? In this section, we show that the *coefficient of determination* provides a measure of the goodness of fit for the estimated regression equation.

For the ith observation, the difference between the observed value of the dependent variable, y_i, and the estimated value of the dependent variable, $\hat{y}_i$, is called the *ith residual*. The ith residual represents the error in using $\hat{y}_i$ to estimate y_i. Thus, for the ith observation, the residual is $y_i - \hat{y}_i$. The sum of squares of these residuals or errors is the quantity that is minimized by the least squares method. This quantity, also known as the *sum of squares due to error,* is denoted by SSE.

Sum of Squares Due to Error

$$\text{SSE} = \Sigma(y_i - \hat{y}_i)^2 \tag{12.8}$$

The value of SSE is a measure of the error in using the estimated regression equation to estimate the values of the dependent variable in the sample.

In Table 12.3 we show the calculations required to compute the sum of squares due to error for the Armand's Pizza Parlors example. For instance, for restaurant 1 the values of the independent and dependent variables are $x_1 = 2$ and $y_1 = 58$. Using the estimated regression equation, we find that the estimated value of quarterly sales for restaurant 1 is $\hat{y}_1 = 60 + 5(2) = 70$. Thus, the error in using $\hat{y}_1$ to estimate y_1 for restaurant 1 is $y_1 - \hat{y}_1 = 58 - 70 = -12$. The squared error, $(-12)^2 = 144$, is shown in the last column of Table 12.3. After computing and squaring the residuals for each restaurant in the sample, we sum them to obtain SSE = 1530. Thus, SSE = 1530 measures the error in using the estimated regression equation $\hat{y} = 60 + 5x$ to predict quarterly sales.

Now suppose we are asked to develop an estimate of quarterly sales without knowledge of the size of the student population. Without knowledge of any related variables, we would use the sample mean as an estimate of quarterly sales at any given restaurant. Table 12.2 shows that $\Sigma y_i = 1300$. Hence, the mean value of quarterly sales for the sample of 10 Armand's restaurants is $\bar{y} = \Sigma y_i/n = 1300/10 = 130$. In Table 12.4 we show the sum of squared deviations obtained by using the sample mean $\bar{y} = 130$ to estimate quarterly sales for each restaurant in the sample. For the ith restaurant in the sample, the difference $y_i - \bar{y}$ provides a measure of the error involved in using $\bar{y}$ to estimate sales. The corresponding sum of squares, called the *total sum of squares,* is denoted SST.

Total Sum of Squares

$$\text{SST} = \Sigma(y_i - \bar{y})^2 \tag{12.9}$$

Table 12.3　　CALCULATION OF SSE FOR ARMAND'S PIZZA PARLORS

Restaurant i	x_i = Student Population (1000s)	y_i = Quarterly Sales ($1000s)	$\hat{y}_i = 60 + 5x_i$	$y_i - \hat{y}_i$	$(y_i - \hat{y}_i)^2$
1	2	58	70	−12	144
2	6	105	90	15	225
3	8	88	100	−12	144
4	8	118	100	18	324
5	12	117	120	−3	9
6	16	137	140	−3	9
7	20	157	160	−3	9
8	20	169	160	9	81
9	22	149	170	−21	441
10	26	202	190	12	144
				SSE =	1530

		COMPUTATION OF THE TOTAL SUM OF SQUARES FOR ARMAND'S PIZZA PARLORS		
Table 12.4				
Restaurant i	x_i = Student Population (1000s)	y_i = Quarterly Sales ($1000s)	$y_i - \bar{y}$	$(y_i - \bar{y})^2$
1	2	58	−72	5,184
2	6	105	−25	625
3	8	88	−42	1,764
4	8	118	−12	144
5	12	117	−13	169
6	16	137	7	49
7	20	157	27	729
8	20	169	39	1,521
9	22	149	19	361
10	26	202	72	5,184
				SST = 15,730

The sum at the bottom of the last column in Table 12.4 is the total sum of squares for Armand's Pizza Parlors; it is SST = 15,730.

In Figure 12.5 we show the estimated regression line $\hat{y} = 60 + 5x$ and the line corresponding to $\bar{y} = 130$. Note that the points cluster more closely around the estimated regression line than they do about the line $\bar{y} = 130$. For example, for the 10th restaurant in the sample we see that the error is much larger when $\bar{y} = 130$ is used as an estimate of y_{10} than when $\hat{y}_{10} = 60 + 5(26) = 190$ is used. We can think of SST as a measure of how well the observations cluster about the $\bar{y}$ line and SSE as a measure of how well the observations cluster about the $\hat{y}$ line.

To measure how much the $\hat{y}$ values on the estimated regression line deviate from $\bar{y}$, another sum of squares is computed. This sum of squares, called the *sum of squares due to regression,* is denoted SSR.

Sum of Squares Due to Regression

$$SSR = \Sigma(\hat{y}_i - \bar{y})^2 \qquad (12.10)$$

From the preceding discussion, we should expect that SST, SSR, and SSE are related. Indeed, the relationship among these three sums of squares provides one of the most important results in statistics.

Relationship Among SST, SSR, and SSE

$$SST = SSR + SSE \qquad (12.11)$$

SSR can be thought of as the explained portion of SST, and SSE can be thought of as the unexplained portion of SST.

where

$$SST = \text{total sum of squares}$$
$$SSR = \text{sum of squares due to regression}$$
$$SSE = \text{sum of squares due to error}$$

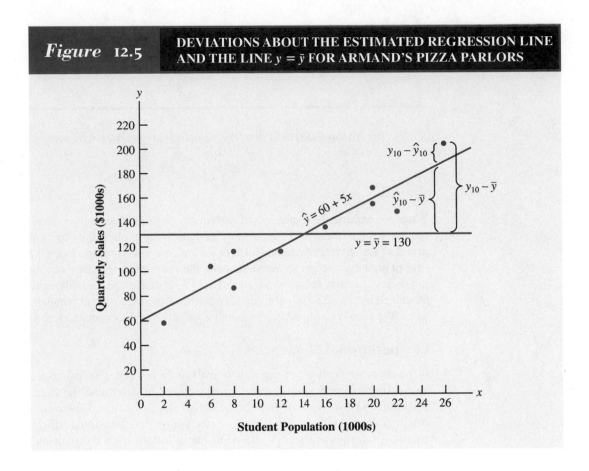

Figure 12.5   DEVIATIONS ABOUT THE ESTIMATED REGRESSION LINE AND THE LINE $y = \bar{y}$ FOR ARMAND'S PIZZA PARLORS

Equation (12.11) shows that the total sum of squares can be partitioned into two components, the regression sum of squares and the sum of squares due to error. Hence, if the values of any two of these sum of squares are known, the third sum of squares can be computed easily. For instance, in the Armand's Pizza Parlors example, we already know that SSE = 1530 and SST = 15,730; therefore, solving for SSR in (12.11), we find that the sum of squares due to regression is

$$SSR = SST - SSE = 15,730 - 1530 = 14,200$$

Now let us see how the three sums of squares, SST, SSR, and SSE, can be used to provide a measure of the goodness of fit for the estimated regression equation. The estimated regression equation would provide a perfect fit if every value of the dependent variable y_i happened to lie on the estimated regression line. In this case, $y_i - \hat{y}_i$ would be zero for each observation, resulting in SSE = 0. Because SST = SSR + SSE, we see that for a perfect fit SSR must equal SST, and the ratio (SSR/SST) must equal one. Poorer fits will result in larger values for SSE. Solving for SSE in (12.11), we see that SSE = SST − SSR. Hence, the largest value for SSE (and hence the poorest fit) occurs when SSR = 0 and SSE = SST.

The ratio SSR/SST, which will be between zero and one, is used to evaluate the goodness of fit for the estimated regression equation. This ratio is called the *coefficient of determination* and is denoted by r^2.

Coefficient of Determination

$$r^2 = \frac{SSR}{SST} \tag{12.12}$$

For the Armand's Pizza Parlors example, the value of the coefficient of determination is

$$r^2 = \frac{SSR}{SST} = \frac{14{,}200}{15{,}730} = .9027$$

When we express the coefficient of determination as a percentage, r^2 can be interpreted as the percentage of the total sum of squares that can be explained by using the estimated regression equation. For Armand's Pizza Parlors, we can conclude that 90.27% of the total sum of squares can be explained by using the estimated regression equation $\hat{y} = 60 + 5x$ to predict quarterly sales. In other words, 90.27% of the variation in quarterly sales can be explained by the linear relationship between the size of the student population and quarterly sales. We should be pleased to find such a good fit for the estimated regression equation.

Computational Efficiencies

In modern applications of regression analysis, a computer software package is almost always used to perform the calculations required to determine the estimated regression equation and the value of the coefficient of determination. However, when solving a small problem with a calculator, we can realize computational efficiencies by using alternative formulas for SST and SSR. We illustrate with the Armand's Pizza Parlors example.

The total sum of squares can be computed by the following alternate formula.

Computational Formula for SST

$$SST = \Sigma y_i^2 - (\Sigma y_i)^2/n \tag{12.13}$$

Using the information in Table 12.5, we obtain $SST = 184{,}730 - (1300)^2/10 = 15{,}730$ (the same value as shown previously). Next, the sum of squares due to regression, SSR, can be calculated directly by the following alternate formula.

Computational Formula for SSR

$$SSR = \frac{[\Sigma x_i y_i - (\Sigma x_i \Sigma y_i)/n]^2}{\Sigma x_i^2 - (\Sigma x_i)^2/n} \tag{12.14}$$

Using the information in Table 12.5, we have

$$SSR = \frac{[21{,}040 - (140)(1300)/10]^2}{2528 - (140)^2/10} = \frac{8{,}065{,}600}{568} = 14{,}200$$

Table 12.5		COMPUTING SST AND SSR FOR ARMAND'S PIZZA PARLORS USING THE COMPUTATIONAL FORMULAS			

Restaurant i	x_i	y_i	$x_i y_i$	x_i^2	y_i^2
1	2	58	116	4	3,364
2	6	105	630	36	11,025
3	8	88	704	64	7,744
4	8	118	944	64	13,924
5	12	117	1,404	144	13,689
6	16	137	2,192	256	18,769
7	20	157	3,140	400	24,649
8	20	169	3,380	400	28,561
9	22	149	3,278	484	22,201
10	26	202	5,252	676	40,804
Totals	140	1300	21,040	2528	184,730
	Σx_i	Σy_i	$\Sigma x_i y_i$	Σx_i^2	Σx_i^2

With SST and SSR known, we can compute the coefficient of determination by using (12.12).

$$r^2 = \frac{\text{SSR}}{\text{SST}} = \frac{14{,}200}{15{,}730} = .9027$$

Finally, if SSE is also desired, we can use the relationship among SST, SSR, and SSE as follows.

$$\text{SSE} = \text{SST} - \text{SSR} = 15{,}730 - 14{,}200 = 1530$$

Correlation Coefficient

In Chapter 3 we introduced the *correlation coefficient* as a descriptive measure of the strength of linear association between two variables, x and y. Values of the correlation coefficient are always between -1 and $+1$. A value of $+1$ indicates that the two variables x and y are perfectly related in a positive linear sense. That is, all data points are on a straight line that has a positive slope. A value of -1 indicates that x and y are perfectly related in a negative linear sense, with all data points on a straight line that has a negative slope. Values of the correlation coefficient close to zero indicate that x and y are not linearly related.

In Section 3.5 we presented the equation for computing sample correlation coefficient. If a regression analysis has already been performed and the coefficient of determination r^2 has been computed, the sample correlation coefficient can be computed as follows.

Sample Correlation Coefficient

$$r_{xy} = (\text{sign of } b_1)\sqrt{\text{Coefficient of Determination}}$$
$$= (\text{sign of } b_1)\sqrt{r^2} \tag{12.15}$$

where

$$b_1 = \text{the slope of the estimated regression equation } \hat{y} = b_0 + b_1 x$$

The sign for the sample correlation coefficient is positive if the estimated regression equation has a positive slope ($b_1 > 0$) and negative if the estimated regression equation has a negative slope ($b_1 < 0$).

For the Armand's Pizza Parlor example, the value of the coefficient of determination corresponding to the estimated regression equation $\hat{y} = 60 + 5x$ is .9027. Because the slope of the estimated regression equation is positive, (12.15) shows that the sample correlation coefficient is $+\sqrt{.9027} = +.9501$. With a sample correlation coefficient of $r_{xy} = +.9501$, we would conclude that there is a strong positive linear association between x and y.

In the case of a linear relationship between two variables, both the coefficient of determination and the sample correlation coefficient provide measures of the strength of the relationship. The coefficient of determination provides a measure between zero and one whereas the sample correlation coefficient provides a measure between -1 and $+1$. Although the sample correlation coefficient is restricted to a linear relationship between two variables, the coefficient of determination can be used for nonlinear relationships and for relationships that have two or more independent variables. In that sense, the coefficient of determination has a wider range of applicability.

N O T E S
and Comments

1. In developing the least squares estimated regression equation and computing the coefficient of determination, we made no probabilistic assumptions and no statistical tests for significance of the relationship between x and y. Larger values of r^2 simply imply that the least squares line provides a better fit to the data; that is, the observations are more closely grouped about the least squares line. But, using only r^2, we can draw no conclusion about whether the relationship between x and y is statistically significant. Such a conclusion must be based on considerations that involve the sample size and the properties of the appropriate sampling distributions of the least squares estimators.

2. As a practical matter, for typical data found in the social sciences, values of r^2 as low as .25 are often considered useful. For data in the physical and life sciences, r^2 values of .60 or greater are often found; in fact, in some cases, r^2 values greater than .90 can be found. In business applications, r^2 values vary greatly, depending on the unique characteristics of each application.

EXERCISES

Methods

SELF TEST

14. The data from Exercise 1 follow.

x_i	1	2	3	4	5
y_i	3	7	5	11	14

The estimated regression equation for these data is $\hat{y} = .20 + 2.60x$.
a. Compute SSE, SST, and SSR using (12.8), (12.9), and (12.10).
b. Compute the coefficient of determination r^2. Comment on the goodness of fit.
c. Recompute SST and SSR using (12.13) and (12.14). Do you get the same results as in part (a)?
d. Compute the sample correlation coefficient.

15. The data from Exercise 2 follow.

x_i	2	3	5	1	8
y_i	25	25	20	30	16

The estimated regression equation for these data is $\hat{y} = 30.33 - 1.88x$.
a. Compute SSE, SST, and SSR.
b. Compute the coefficient of determination r^2. Comment on the goodness of fit.
c. Compute the sample correlation coefficient.

16. The data from Exercise 3 follow.

x_i	2	4	5	7	8
y_i	2	3	2	6	4

The estimated regression equation for these data is $\hat{y} = .75 + .51x$. What percentage of the total sum of squares can be accounted for by the estimated regression equation? What is the value of the sample correlation coefficient?

Applications

SELF TEST

17. The following data are the grade point averages x and the monthly salaries y for students who had obtained a bachelor's degree in business administration with a major in information systems. The estimated regression equation for these data is $\hat{y} = 1290.5 + 581.1x$.

GPA	Monthly Salary ($)
2.6	2800
3.4	3100
3.6	3500
3.2	3000
3.5	3400
2.9	3100

a. Compute SST, SSR, and SSE.
b. Compute the coefficient of determination r^2. Comment on the goodness of fit.
c. What is the value of the sample correlation coefficient?

18. The data from Exercise 7 follow.

Hotel Location	Business Rate ($)	14-Day Advance Rate ($)
Birmingham	89	81
Miami	130	115
Atlanta	98	89
Chicago	149	138
New Orleans	199	149
Nashville	114	94

The estimated regression equation for these data is $\hat{y} = 25.21 + .6608x$. What percentage of the total sum of squares can be accounted for by the estimated regression equation? Comment on the goodness of fit. What is the sample correlation coefficient?

19. A medical laboratory at Duke University estimates the amount of protein in liver samples using regression analysis. A spectrometer emitting light shines through a substance containing the sample, and the amount of light absorbed is used to estimate the amount of protein in the sample. A new estimated regression equation is developed daily because of differing amounts of dye in the solution. On one day, six samples with known protein concentrations gave the following absorbence readings.

Absorbence Reading (x_i)	Milligrams of Protein (y_i)
.509	0
.756	20
1.020	40
1.400	80
1.570	100
1.790	127

   a. Use these data to develop an estimated regression equation relating the light absorbence reading to milligrams of protein present in the sample.
   b. Compute r^2. Would you feel comfortable using this estimated regression equation to estimate the amount of protein in a sample?
   c. In a sample just received, the light absorbence reading was .941. Estimate the amount of protein in the sample.

20. An important application of regression analysis in accounting is in the estimation of cost. By collecting data on volume and cost and using the least squares method to develop an estimated regression equation relating volume and cost, an accountant can estimate the cost associated with a particular manufacturing operation. Consider the following sample of production volumes and total cost data for a manufacturing operation.

Production Volume (units)	Total Cost ($)
400	4000
450	5000
550	5400
600	5900
700	6400
750	7000

   a. Use these data to develop an estimated regression equation that could be used to predict the total cost for a given production volume.
   b. What is the variable, or additional, cost per unit produced?
   c. Compute the coefficient of determination. What percentage of the variation in total cost can be explained by production volume?
   d. The company's production schedule shows 500 units must be produced next month. What is the estimated total cost for this operation?

21. Are company presidents and chief executive officers paid according to the profit performance of the company? The following table lists corporate data on percentage change in return on equity over a two-year period and percentage change in the pay of presidents and chief executive officers immediately after the two-year period (*Business Week*, April 21, 1997).

Company	Two-Year Change in Return on Equity (%)	Change in Executive Compensation (%)
Dow Chemical	201.3	18
Rohm & Haas	146.5	28
Morton International	76.7	10
Union Carbide	158.2	28
Praxair	−34.9	15
Air Products & Chemicals	73.2	−9
Eastman Chemical	−7.9	−20

a. Develop the estimated regression equation with the two-year percentage change in return on equity as the independent variable.

b. Compute r^2. Would you feel comfortable using the percentage change in return on equity over a two-year period to predict the percentage change in the pay of presidents and chief executive officers? Discuss.

c. What is the sample correlation coefficient? Does it reflect a strong or weak relationship between return on equity and executive compensation?

12.4 MODEL ASSUMPTIONS

In simple linear regression analysis, we begin by making an assumption about the appropriate model for the relationship between the dependent variable and the independent variable. In this case, the assumed regression model is

$$y = \beta_0 + \beta_1 x + \epsilon$$

Then, the least squares method is used to develop values for b_0 and b_1, the estimates of the model parameters β_0 and β_1, respectively. The resulting estimated regression equation is

$$\hat{y} = b_0 + b_1 x$$

We saw that the value of the coefficient of determination (r^2) is a measure of the goodness of fit of the estimated regression equation. However, even with a large value of r^2, the estimated regression equation should not be used until further analysis of the appropriateness of the assumed model has been conducted. An important step in determining whether the assumed model is appropriate involves testing for the significance of the relationship. The tests of significance in regression analysis are based on the following assumptions about the error term ϵ.

Assumptions about the Error Term ϵ in the Regression Model

$$y = \beta_0 + \beta_1 x + \epsilon$$

1. The error term ϵ is a random variable with a mean or expected value of zero; that is, $E(\epsilon) = 0$.

   Implication: Because β_0 and β_1 are constants, $E(\beta_0) = \beta_0$ and $E(\beta_1) = \beta_1$; thus, for a given value of x, the expected value of y is

$$E(y) = \beta_0 + \beta_1 x \tag{12.16}$$

As we indicated previously, (12.16) is referred to as the regression equation.

2. The variance of ϵ, denoted by σ^2, is the same for all values of x.
   Implication: The variance of y at a given value of x equals σ^2 and is the same for all values of x.

3. The values of ϵ are independent.
   Implication: The value of ϵ for a particular value of x is not related to the value of ϵ for any other value of x; thus, the value of y for a particular value of x is not related to the value of y for any other value of x.

4. The error term ϵ is a normally distributed random variable.
   Implication: Because y is a linear function of ϵ, y is also a normally distributed random variable.

Figure 12.6 is an illustration of the model assumptions and their implications; note that in this graphical interpretation, the value of $E(y)$ changes according to the specific value of x considered. However, regardless of the x value, the probability distribution of ϵ and hence the probability distributions of y are normally distributed, each with the same variance. The specific value of the error ϵ at any particular point depends on whether the actual value of y is greater than or less than $E(y)$.

At this point, we must keep in mind that we are also making an assumption or hypothesis about the form of the relationship between x and y. That is, we have assumed that a

Figure 12.6   **ASSUMPTIONS FOR THE REGRESSION MODEL**

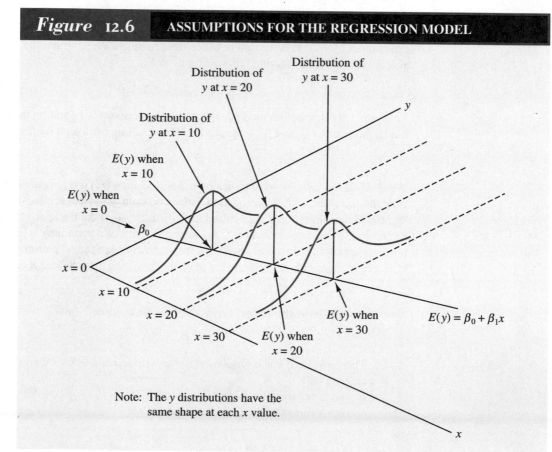

Note: The y distributions have the same shape at each x value.

straight line represented by $\beta_0 + \beta_1 x$ is the basis for the relationship between the variables. We must not lose sight of the fact that some other model, for instance $y = \beta_0 + \beta_1 x^2 + \epsilon$, may turn out to be a better model for the underlying relationship.

..../ /............

12.5   TESTING FOR SIGNIFICANCE

In a simple linear regression equation the mean or expected value of y is a linear function of x: $E(y) = \beta_0 + \beta_1 x$. If the value of β_1 is zero, $E(y) = \beta_0 + (0)x = \beta_0$. In this case, the mean value of y does not depend on the value of x and hence we would conclude that x and y are not linearly related. Alternatively, if the value of β_1 is not equal to zero, we would conclude that the two variables are related. Thus, to test for a significant regression relationship, we must conduct a hypothesis test to determine whether the value of β_1 is zero. Two tests are commonly used. Both require an estimate of σ^2, the variance of ϵ.

An Estimate of σ^2

From the regression model and its assumptions we can conclude that σ^2, the variance of ϵ, also represents the variance of the y values about the regression line. Recall that the deviations of the y values about the estimated regression line are called *residuals*. Thus, SSE, the sum of squared residuals, is a measure of the variability of the y values about the estimated regression line. The mean square error (MSE) provides the estimate of σ^2; it is SSE divided by its degrees of freedom.

With $\hat{y}_i = b_0 + b_1 x_i$, SSE can be written as

$$SSE = \Sigma(y_i - \hat{y}_i)^2 = \Sigma(y_i - b_0 - b_1 x_i)^2$$

Every sum of squares has associated with it a number called its degrees of freedom. Statisticians have shown that SSE has $n - 2$ degrees of freedom because two parameters (β_0 and β_1) must be estimated to compute SSE. Thus, the mean square error is computed by dividing SSE by $n - 2$. Because the value of MSE provides an estimate of σ^2, the notation s^2 is also used.

Mean Square Error (Estimate of σ^2)

$$s^2 = MSE = \frac{SSE}{n - 2} \tag{12.17}$$

In Section 12.3 we showed that for the Armand's Pizza Parlors example, SSE = 1530; hence,

$$s^2 = MSE = \frac{1530}{8} = 191.25$$

provides an estimate of σ^2.

To estimate σ we take the square root of s^2. The resulting value, s, is referred to as the *standard error of the estimate*.

Standard Error of the Estimate

$$s = \sqrt{\text{MSE}} = \sqrt{\frac{\text{SSE}}{n - 2}} \qquad (12.18)$$

For the Armand's Pizza Parlors example, $s = \sqrt{\text{MSE}} = \sqrt{191.25} = 13.829$. In the following discussion, we will use the standard error of the estimate to conduct tests for a significant relationship between x and y.

t Test

The simple linear regression model is $y = \beta_0 + \beta_1 x + \epsilon$. If x and y are linearly related, we must have $\beta_1 \neq 0$. The purpose of the t test is to see whether we can use the sample data to conclude that $\beta_1 \neq 0$. We will test the following hypotheses about β_1.

$$H_0: \beta_1 = 0$$
$$H_a: \beta_1 \neq 0$$

If H_0 is rejected, we will conclude that $\beta_1 \neq 0$ and that the two variables have a statistically significant relationship. However, if H_0 cannot be rejected, we will have insufficient evidence to conclude that a significant relationship exists. The properties of the sampling distribution of b_1, the least squares estimator of β_1, provide the basis for the hypothesis test.

First, let us consider what would have happened if we had used a different random sample for the same regression study. For example, suppose that Armand's Pizza Parlors had used the quarterly sales data for a different sample of 10 restaurants. A regression analysis of this new sample might result in an estimated regression equation similar to our previous estimated regression equation $\hat{y} = 60 + 5x$. However, it is doubtful that we would obtain exactly the same equation (with an intercept of exactly 60 and a slope of exactly 5). Indeed, b_0 and b_1, the least squares estimators, are sample statistics that have their own sampling distributions. The properties of the sampling distribution of b_1 follow.

Sampling Distribution of b_1

Expected Value

$$E(b_1) = \beta_1$$

Standard Deviation

$$\sigma_{b_1} = \frac{\sigma}{\sqrt{\Sigma x_i^2 - (\Sigma x_i)^2/n}} \qquad (12.19)$$

Distribution Form

Normal

Note that the expected value of b_1 is equal to β_1, so b_1 is an unbiased estimator of β_1.

Because we do not know the value of σ, we develop an estimate of σ_{b_1}, denoted s_{b_1}, by estimating σ with s in (12.19). Thus, we obtain the following estimate of σ_{b_1}.

Estimated Standard Deviation of b_1

$$s_{b_1} = \frac{s}{\sqrt{\Sigma x_i^2 - (\Sigma x_i)^2/n}} \tag{12.20}$$

For Armand's Pizza Parlors, $s = 13.829$. Hence, using $\Sigma x_i^2 = 2528$ and $\Sigma x_i = 140$ as shown in Table 12.2, we have

$$s_{b_1} = \frac{13.829}{\sqrt{2528 - (140)^2/10}} = .5803$$

as the estimated standard deviation of b_1.

The t test for a significant relationship is based on the fact that the test statistic

$$\frac{b_1 - \beta_1}{s_{b_1}}$$

follows a t distribution with $n - 2$ degrees of freedom. If the null hypothesis is true, then $\beta_1 = 0$ and $t = b_1/s_{b_1}$. With b_1/s_{b_1} as the test statistic, the steps of the t test for a significant relationship are as follows.

---

t Test for Significance

$$H_0: \beta_1 = 0$$
$$H_a: \beta_1 \neq 0$$

Test Statistic

$$t = \frac{b_1}{s_{b_1}} \tag{12.21}$$

Rejection Rule at a Level of Significance of α

Reject H_0 if $t < -t_{\alpha/2}$ or if $t > t_{\alpha/2}$

where $t_{\alpha/2}$ is based on a t distribution with $n - 2$ degrees of freedom

---

Let us conduct this test of significance for Armand's Pizza Parlors. The test statistic (12.21) is

$$t = \frac{b_1}{s_{b_1}} = \frac{5}{.5803} = 8.62$$

From Table 2 of Appendix B we find that the two-tailed t value corresponding to $\alpha = .01$ and $n - 2 = 10 - 2 = 8$ degrees of freedom is $t_{.005} = 3.355$. With $8.62 > 3.355$, we reject H_0 and conclude at the .01 level of significance that β_1 is not equal to zero. The statistical evidence is sufficient to conclude that we have a significant relationship between student population and sales.

F Test

An F test, based on the F probability distribution, can also be used to test for significance in regression. With only one independent variable, the F test will provide the same conclusion as the t test; that is, if the t test indicates $\beta_1 \neq 0$ and hence a significant relationship, the F test will also indicate a significant relationship. But with more than one independent variable, only the F test can be used to test for an overall significant relationship.

The logic behind the use of the F test for determining whether the regression relationship is statistically significant is based on the development of two independent estimates of σ^2. We have just seen that MSE provides an estimate of σ^2. If the null hypothesis $H_0: \beta_1 = 0$ is true, the sum of squares due to regression, SSR, divided by its degrees of freedom provides another independent estimate of σ^2. This estimate is called the *mean square due to regression,* or simply the *mean square regression,* and is denoted MSR. In general,

$$ \text{MSR} = \frac{\text{SSR}}{\text{regression degrees of freedom}} $$

For the models we consider in this text, the regression degrees of freedom is always equal to the number of independent variables; thus,

$$ \text{MSR} = \frac{\text{SSR}}{\text{number of independent variables}} \tag{12.22} $$

Since there is only one independent variable in the Armand's Pizza Parlors example, we have MSR = SSR/1 = SSR. Hence, for Armand's Pizza Parlors, MSR = SSR = 14,200.

If the null hypothesis ($H_0: \beta_1 = 0$) is true, MSR and MSE are two independent estimates of σ^2 and the sampling distribution of MSR/MSE follows an F distribution with numerator degrees of freedom equal to one and denominator degrees of freedom equal to $n - 2$. Therefore, when $\beta_1 = 0$, the value of MSR/MSE should be close to one. However, if the null hypothesis is false ($\beta_1 \neq 0$), MSR will overestimate σ^2 and the value of MSR/MSE will be inflated; thus, large values of MSR/MSE lead to the rejection of H_0 and the conclusion that the relationship between x and y is statistically significant. A summary of how the F test is used to test for a significant relationship follows.

F Test for Significance

If H_0 is false, MSE still provides an unbiased estimate of σ^2 and MSR overestimates σ^2. If H_0 is true, both MSE and MSR provide unbiased estimates of σ^2; in this case the value of MSR/MSE should be close to 1.

$$ H_0: \beta_1 = 0 $$
$$ H_a: \beta_1 \neq 0 $$

Test Statistic

$$ F = \frac{\text{MSR}}{\text{MSE}} \tag{12.23} $$

Rejection Rule at a Level of Significance of α

$$\text{Reject } H_0 \text{ if } F > F_\alpha$$

where F_α is based on an F distribution with 1 degree of freedom in the numerator and $n - 2$ degrees of freedom in the denominator

---

Let us conduct the F test for the Armand's Pizza Parlors example. The test statistic is

$$F = \frac{\text{MSR}}{\text{MSE}} = \frac{14{,}200}{191.25} = 74.25$$

The *F* test and the *t* test provide identical results for simple linear regression.

From Table 4 of Appendix B we find that the F value corresponding to $\alpha = .01$ with one degree of freedom in the numerator and $n - 2 = 10 - 2 = 8$ degrees of freedom in the denominator is $F_{.01} = 11.26$. With $74.25 > 11.26$, we reject H_0 and conclude at the .01 level of significance that β_1 is not equal to zero. The F test has provided the statistical evidence necessary to conclude that we have a significant relationship between student population and sales.

In Chapter 10 we covered analysis of variance (ANOVA) and showed how an ANOVA table could be used to provide a convenient summary of the computational aspects of analysis of variance. A similar ANOVA table can be used to summarize the results of the F test for significance in regression. Table 12.6 is the general form of the ANOVA table for regression studies involving one independent variable. Table 12.7 is the ANOVA table with the F test computations we have just performed for Armand's Pizza Parlors. Regression, error, and total are listed as the three sources of variation, with SSR, SSE, and SST appearing as the corresponding sum of squares in column two. The degrees of freedom, 1 for regression, $n - 2$ for error, and $n - 1$ for total, are shown in column three. Column 4 contains the values of MSR and MSE, and column 5 contains the value of $F = \text{MSR}/\text{MSE}$. Almost all computer printouts of regression analysis include an ANOVA table summary.

Some Cautions about the Interpretation of Significance Tests

Rejecting the null hypothesis $H_0: \beta_1 = 0$ and concluding that the relationship between x and y is significant does not enable us to conclude that a cause-and-effect relationship is present between x and y. Concluding a cause-and-effect relationship is warranted only if the analyst has some type of theoretical justification that the relationship is in fact causal. In the Armand's Pizza Parlors example, we can conclude that a significant relationship exists

Table 12.6	GENERAL FORM OF THE ANOVA TABLE FOR SIMPLE LINEAR REGRESSION			
Source of Variation	**Sum of Squares**	**Degrees of Freedom**	**Mean Square**	**F**
Regression	SSR	1	$\text{MSR} = \dfrac{\text{SSR}}{1}$	$F = \dfrac{\text{MSR}}{\text{MSE}}$
Error	SSE	$n - 2$	$\text{MSE} = \dfrac{\text{SSE}}{n - 2}$	
Total	SST	$n - 1$		

In every analysis of variance table the total sum of squares is the sum of the regression sum of squares and the error sum of squares; in addition, the total degrees of freedom is the sum of the regression degrees of freedom and the error degrees of freedom.

Table 12.7	ANOVA TABLE FOR THE ARMAND'S PIZZA PARLORS PROBLEM			
Source of Variation	Sum of Squares	Degrees of Freedom	Mean Square	F
Regression	14,200	1	$\dfrac{14,200}{1} = 14,200$	$\dfrac{14,200}{191.25} = 74.25$
Error	1,530	8	$\dfrac{1530}{8} = 191.25$	
Total	15,730	9		

Regression analysis, which can be used to identify how variables are associated with one another, cannot be used as evidence of a cause-and-effect relationship.

between the size of the student population x and quarterly sales y; moreover, the estimated regression equation $\hat{y} = 60 + 5x$ provides the least squares estimate of the relationship. We cannot, however, conclude that changes in student population x *cause* changes in quarterly sales y just because we have identified a statistically significant relationship. The appropriateness of such a cause-and-effect conclusion is left to supporting theoretical justification and to good judgment on the part of the analyst. Armand's managers felt that increases in the student population were a likely cause of increased quarterly sales. Thus, the result of the significance test enabled them to conclude that a cause-and-effect relationship was present.

In addition, just because we are able to reject H_0: $\beta_1 = 0$ and demonstrate statistical significance does not enable us to conclude that the relationship between x and y is linear. We can state only that x and y are related and that a linear relationship explains a significant portion of the variability in y over the range of values for x observed in the sample. Figure 12.7 illustrates this situation. The test for significance has rejected the null hypothesis H_0: $\beta_1 = 0$

Figure 12.7	EXAMPLE OF A LINEAR APPROXIMATION OF A NONLINEAR RELATIONSHIP

and has led to the conclusion that x and y are significantly related, but the figure shows that the actual relationship between x and y is not linear. Although the linear approximation provided by $\hat{y} = b_0 + b_1 x$ is good over the range of x values observed in the sample, it becomes poor for x values outside that range.

Given a significant relationship, we should feel confident in using the estimated regression equation for predictions corresponding to x values within the range of the x values observed in the sample. For Armand's Pizza Parlors, this range corresponds to values of x between 2 and 26. But unless reasons indicate that the model is valid beyond this range, predictions outside the range of the independent variable should be made with caution. For Armand's Pizza Parlors, because the regression relationship has been found significant at the .01 level, we should feel confident using it to predict quarterly sales for restaurants where the associated student population is between 2000 and 26,000.

N O T E S and Comments

1. The assumptions made about the error term (Section 12.4) are what allow the tests of statistical significance in this section. The properties of the sampling distribution of b_1 and the subsequent t and F tests follow directly from these assumptions.
2. Do not confuse statistical significance with practical significance. With very large sample sizes, statistically significant results can be obtained for small values of b_1; in such cases, one must exercise care in concluding that the relationship has practical significance.
3. A test of significance for a linear relationship between x and y can also be performed by using the sample correlation coefficient r_{xy}. With ρ_{xy} denoting the population correlation coefficient, the hypotheses are as follows.

$$H_0: \rho_{xy} = 0$$
$$H_a: \rho_{xy} \neq 0$$

A significant relationship can be conducted if H_0 is rejected. However, the t and F tests presented previously in this section give the same result as the test for significance using the correlation coefficient. Conducting a test for significance using the correlation coefficient therefore is not necessary if a t or F test has already been conducted.

EXERCISES

Methods

22. The data from Exercise 1 follow.

x_i	1	2	3	4	5
y_i	3	7	5	11	14

SELF TEST

a. Compute the mean square error using (12.17).
b. Compute the standard error of the estimate using (12.18).
c. Compute the estimated standard deviation of b_1 using (12.20).
d. Use the t test to test the following hypotheses ($\alpha = .05$):

$$H_0: \beta_1 = 0$$
$$H_a: \beta_1 \neq 0$$

e. Use the F test to test the hypotheses in part (d) at a .05 level of significance. Present the results in the analysis of variance table format (see Table 12.6).

23. The data from Exercise 2 follow.

x_i	2	3	5	1	8
y_i	25	25	20	30	16

     a. Compute the mean square error using (12.17).
     b. Compute the standard error of the estimate using (12.18).
     c. Compute the estimated standard deviation of b_1 using (12.20).
     d. Use the t test to test the following hypotheses ($\alpha = .05$):

$$H_0: \beta_1 = 0$$
$$H_a: \beta_1 \neq 0$$

     e. Use the F test to test the hypotheses in part (d) at a .05 level of significance. Present the results in the analysis of variance table format.

24. The data from Exercise 3 follow.

x_i	2	4	5	7	8
y_i	2	3	2	6	4

     a. What is the value of the standard error of the estimate?
     b. Test for a significant relationship by using the t test. Use $\alpha = .05$.
     c. Use the F test to test for a significant relationship. Use $\alpha = .05$. What is your conclusion?

Applications

SELF TEST

25. In Exercise 17 the following data on grade point average and monthly salary were presented.

GPA	Monthly Salary ($)	GPA	Monthly Salary ($)
2.6	2800	3.2	3000
3.4	3100	3.5	3400
3.6	3500	2.9	3100

     a. Does the t test indicate a significant relationship between grade point average and monthly salary? What is your conclusion? Use $\alpha = .05$.
     b. Test for a significant relationship using the F test. What is your conclusion? Use $\alpha = .05$.
     c. Show the ANOVA table.

26. Refer to Exercise 9, where an estimated regression equation relating years of experience and annual sales was developed. At a .05 level of significance, determine whether years of experience and annual sales are related.

27. Refer to Exercise 19, where an estimated regression equation was developed relating light absorbence readings and milligrams of protein. Test whether the absorbence readings and the amount of protein are related at the .01 level of significance.

28. Refer to Exercise 20, where data on production volume and cost were used to develop an estimated regression equation relating production volume and cost for a particular manufacturing operation. Using $\alpha = .05$, test whether the production volume is significantly related to the total cost. Show the ANOVA table. What is your conclusion?

29. Refer to Exercise 21, where the following data were used to determine whether company presidents and chief executive officers are paid on the basis of company profit performance (*Business Week,* April 21, 1997).

Company	Two-Year Change in Return on Equity (%)	Change in Executive Compensation (%)
Dow Chemical	201.3	18
Rohm & Haas	146.5	28
Morton International	76.7	10
Union Carbide	158.2	28
Praxair	−34.9	15
Air Products & Chemicals	73.2	−9
Eastman Chemical	−7.9	−20

Is a significant relationship evident between the two variables? Conduct the appropriate statistical test and state your conclusion. Use $\alpha = .05$.

12.6 USING THE ESTIMATED REGRESSION EQUATION FOR ESTIMATION AND PREDICTION

The simple linear regression model is an assumption about the relationship between x and y. Using the least squares method, we obtained the estimated simple linear regression equation. If the results show a statistically significant relationship between x and y, and the fit provided by the estimated regression equation appears to be good, the estimated regression equation should be useful for estimation and prediction.

Point Estimation

In the Armand's Pizza Parlors example, the estimated regression equation $\hat{y} = 60 + 5x$ provides an estimate of the relationship between the size of the student population x and quarterly sales y. We can use the estimated regression equation to develop a point estimate of the mean value of y for a particular value of x or to predict an individual value of y corresponding to a given value of x. For instance, suppose Armand's managers want a point estimate of the mean quarterly sales for all restaurants located near college campuses with 10,000 students. Using the estimated regression equation $\hat{y} = 60 + 5x$, we see that for $x = 10$ (or 10,000 students), $\hat{y} = 60 + 5(10) = 110$. Thus, a point estimate of the mean quarterly sales for all restaurants located near campuses with 10,000 students is $110,000.

Now suppose Armand's managers want to predict sales for an individual restaurant located near Talbot College, a school with 10,000 students. In this case we are not interested in the mean value for all restaurants located near campuses with 10,000 students; we are just interested in predicting quarterly sales for one individual restaurant. As it turns out, the point estimate is the same as the point estimate for the mean value of y. Hence, we would predict quarterly sales of $\hat{y} = 60 + 5(10) = 110$ or $110,000 for this one restaurant.

Interval Estimation

Confidence intervals and prediction intervals indicate the precision of the regression results. Narrower intervals indicate a higher degree of precision.

Point estimates do not provide any information on the precision associated with the estimates. For that we must develop interval estimates much like those in Chapters 8, 10, and 11. The first type of interval estimate, a *confidence interval estimate,* is an interval estimate of the *mean value of y* for a given value of x. The second type of interval estimate, a *prediction interval estimate,* is used whenever we want an interval estimate of an *indvidual value of y* corresponding to a given value of *x*. With point estimation we obtain the same value whether we are estimating the mean value of *y* or predicting an individual value of *y*, but with interval estimates we obtain different values.

Confidence Interval Estimate of the Mean Value of *y*

The estimated regression equation provides a point estimate of the mean value of *y* for a given value of *x*. In describing the confidence interval estimation procedure, we will use the following notation.

$$x_p = \text{the particular or given value of the independent variable } x$$

$$E(y_p) = \text{the mean or expected value of the dependent variable } y \\ \text{corresponding to the given } x_p$$

$$\hat{y}_p = b_0 + b_1 x_p = \text{the estimate of } E(y_p) \text{ when } x = x_p$$

Using this notation to estimate the mean quarterly sales for all Armand's restaurants located near a campus with 10,000 students, we have $x_p = 10$, and $E(y_p)$ denotes the unknown mean value of sales for all restaurants where $x_p = 10$. The point estimate of $E(y_p)$ is provided by $\hat{y}_p = 60 + 5(10) = 110$.

In general, we cannot expect $\hat{y}_p$ to equal $E(y_p)$ exactly. If we want to make an inference about how close $\hat{y}_p$ is to the true mean value $E(y_p)$, we will have to estimate the variance of $\hat{y}_p$. The formula for estimating the variance of $\hat{y}_p$ given x_p, denoted by $s_{\hat{y}_p}^2$, is

$$s_{\hat{y}_p}^2 = s^2 \left[\frac{1}{n} + \frac{(x_p - \bar{x})^2}{\Sigma x_i^2 - (\Sigma x_i)^2/n} \right] \tag{12.24}$$

The estimate of the standard deviation of $\hat{y}_p$ is given by the square root of (12.24).

$$s_{\hat{y}_p} = s \sqrt{\frac{1}{n} + \frac{(x_p - \bar{x})^2}{\Sigma x_i^2 - (\Sigma x_i)^2/n}} \tag{12.25}$$

The computational results for Armand's Pizza Parlors in Section 12.5 provided $s = 13.829$. With $\Sigma x_i^2 = 2528$, $\Sigma x_i = 140$, $\bar{x} = \Sigma x_i/n = 140/10 = 14$, and $x_p = 10$, we can use (12.25) to obtain

$$s_{\hat{y}_p} = 13.829 \sqrt{\frac{1}{10} + \frac{(10 - 14)^2}{2528 - (140)^2/10}}$$

$$= 13.829 \sqrt{.1282} = 4.95$$

The general expression for a confidence interval estimate of $E(y_p)$ follows.

Confidence Interval Estimate of $E(y_p)$

$$\hat{y}_p \pm t_{\alpha/2} s_{\hat{y}_p} \tag{12.26}$$

where the confidence coefficient is $1 - \alpha$ and $t_{\alpha/2}$ is based on a t distribution with $n - 2$ degrees of freedom

---

Using (12.26) to develop a 95% confidence interval estimate of the mean quarterly sales for all Armand's restaurants located near campuses with 10,000 students, we need the value of t for $\alpha/2 = .025$ and $n - 2 = 10 - 2 = 8$ degrees of freedom. Using Table 2 of Appendix B, we have $t_{.025} = 2.306$. Thus, with $\hat{y}_p = 110$ and $s_{\hat{y}_p} = 4.95$, we have

$$110 \pm 2.306(4.95)$$
$$110 \pm 11.415$$

In dollars, the 95% confidence interval for the mean quarterly sales of all restaurants near campuses with 10,000 students is $110,000 \pm 11,415. Therefore, the confidence interval estimate for the mean quarterly sales when the student population is 10,000 is $98,585 to $121,415.

Note that the estimated standard deviation of x_p given by (12.25) is smallest when $x_p = \bar{x}$ and the quantity $x_p - \bar{x} = 0$. In this case, the estimated standard deviation of $\hat{y}_p$ becomes

$$s_{\hat{y}_p} = s \sqrt{\frac{1}{n} + \frac{(x_p - \bar{x})^2}{\Sigma x_i^2 - (\Sigma x_i)^2/n}} = s \sqrt{\frac{1}{n}}$$

This result implies that we can make the best or most precise estimate of the mean value of y whenever $x_p = \bar{x}$. In fact, the further x_p is from $\bar{x}$, the larger $x_p - \bar{x}$ becomes. As a result, confidence intervals for the mean value of y will become wider as x_p deviates more from $\bar{x}$. This pattern is shown graphically in Figure 12.8.

Figure 12.8   CONFIDENCE INTERVALS FOR THE MEAN QUARTERLY SALES y AT GIVEN VALUES OF STUDENT POPULATION x

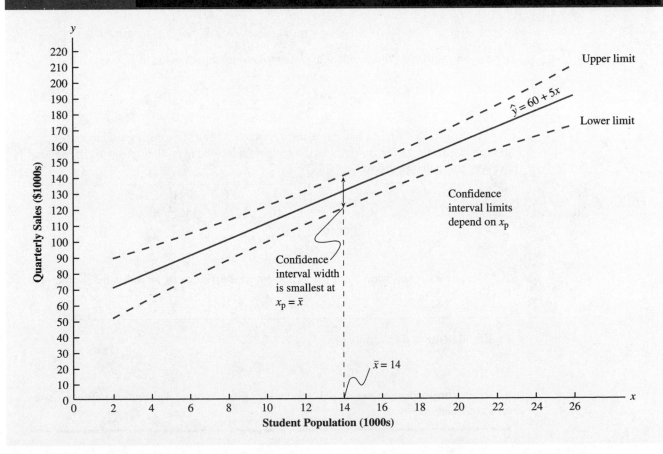

Prediction Interval Estimate of an Individual Value of y

Suppose that instead of estimating the mean value of quarterly sales for all Armand's restaurants located near campuses with 10,000 students, we want to estimate the quarterly sales for an individual restaurant located near Talbot College, a school with 10,000 students. As noted previously, the point estimate of an individual value of y given $x = x_p$ is provided by the estimated regression equation with $\hat{y}_p = b_0 + b_1 x_p$. For the restaurant at Talbot College, we have $x_p = 10$ and a corresponding estimated quarterly sales of $\hat{y}_p = 60 + 5(10) = 110$, or \$110,000. Note that this value is the same as the point estimate of the mean quarterly sales for all restaurants located near campuses with 10,000 students.

To develop a prediction interval estimate, we must first estimate the variance associated with using $\hat{y}_p$ as an estimate of an individual value of y when $x = x_p$. This variance is made up of the sum of the following two components.

1. The variance of individual y values about the mean $E(y_p)$, an estimate of which is given by s^2.
2. The variance associated with using $\hat{y}_p$ to estimate $E(y_p)$, an estimate of which is given by $s_{\hat{y}_p}^2$.

The formula for estimating the variance of an individual value of y_p, denoted by s_{ind}^2, is

$$
\begin{aligned}
s_{\text{ind}}^2 &= s^2 + s_{\hat{y}_p}^2 \\
&= s^2 + s^2 \left[\frac{1}{n} + \frac{(x_p - \bar{x})^2}{\Sigma x_i^2 - (\Sigma x_i)^2/n} \right] \\
&= s^2 \left[1 + \frac{1}{n} + \frac{(x_p - \bar{x})^2}{\Sigma x_i^2 - (\Sigma x_i)^2/n} \right]
\end{aligned}
\tag{12.27}
$$

Hence, an estimate of the standard deviation of an individual value of y_p is given by

$$
s_{\text{ind}} = s \sqrt{1 + \frac{1}{n} + \frac{(x_p - \bar{x})^2}{\Sigma x_i^2 - (\Sigma x_i)^2/n}}
\tag{12.28}
$$

For Armand's Pizza Parlors, the estimated standard deviation corresponding to the prediction of quarterly sales for one specific restaurant located near a campus with 10,000 students is computed as follows.

$$
\begin{aligned}
s_{\text{ind}} &= 13.829 \sqrt{1 + \frac{1}{10} + \frac{(10 - 14)^2}{2528 - (140)^2/10}} \\
&= 13.829 \sqrt{1.1282} \\
&= 14.69
\end{aligned}
$$

The general expression for a prediction interval estimate of an individual value of y follows.

Prediction Interval Estimate of y_p

$$
\hat{y}_p \pm t_{\alpha/2} s_{\text{ind}}
\tag{12.29}
$$

where the confidence coefficient is $1 - \alpha$ and $t_{\alpha/2}$ is based on a t distribution with $n - 2$ degrees of freedom.

The 95% prediction interval for quarterly sales at Armand's Talbot College restaurant can be found by using $t_{.025} = 2.306$ and $s_{ind} = 14.69$. Expression (12.29) provides

$$110 \pm 2.306(14.69)$$
$$110 \pm 33.875$$

In dollars, this prediction interval is \$110,000 $\pm$ \$33,875 or \$76,125 to \$143,875. Note that the prediction interval for an individual restaurant is wider than the confidence interval for the mean sales of all restaurants located near campuses with 10,000 students (\$98,585 to \$121,415). The difference reflects the fact that we are able to estimate the mean value of y more precisely than we can an individual value of y.

Both confidence interval estimates and prediction interval estimates are most precise when the value of the independent variable is $x_p = \bar{x}$. The general shapes of confidence intervals and the wider prediction intervals are shown together in Figure 12.9.

Figure 12.9   **CONFIDENCE AND PREDICTION INTERVALS FOR QUARTERLY SALES y AT GIVEN VALUES OF STUDENT POPULATION x**

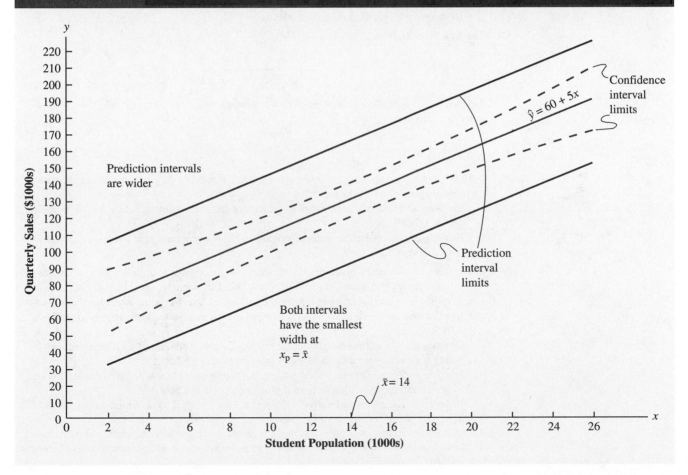

···/ /············

EXERCISES

Methods

30. The data from Exercise 1 follow.

x_i	1	2	3	4	5
y_i	3	7	5	11	14

a. Use (12.25) to estimate the standard deviation of $\hat{y}_p$ when $x = 4$.
b. Use (12.26) to develop a 95% confidence interval estimate of the expected value of y when $x = 4$.
c. Use (12.28) to estimate the standard deviation of an individual value when $x = 4$.
d. Use (12.29) to develop a 95% prediction interval for $x = 4$.

31. The data from Exercise 2 follow.

x_i	2	3	5	1	8
y_i	25	25	20	30	16

a. Estimate the standard deviation of $\hat{y}_p$ when $x = 3$.
b. Develop a 95% confidence interval estimate of the expected value of y when $x = 3$.
c. Estimate the standard deviation of an individual value when $x = 3$.
d. Develop a 95% prediction interval when $x = 3$.

32. The data from Exercise 3 follow.

x_i	2	4	5	7	8
y_i	2	3	2	6	4

Develop the 95% confidence and prediction intervals when $x = 3$. Explain why these two intervals are different.

Applications

33. In Exercise 17, the data on grade point average x and monthly salary y provided the estimated regression equation $\hat{y} = 1290.5 + 581x$.
a. Develop a 95% confidence interval estimate of the mean starting salary for all students with a 3.0 GPA.
b. Develop a 95% prediction interval estimate of the starting salary for Joe Heller, a student with a GPA of 3.0.

34. In Exercise 12, data were given on the adjusted gross income x and the amount of itemized deductions taken by taxpayers (*Money,* October 1994). Data were reported in thousands of dollars. With the estimated regression equation $\hat{y} = 4.68 + .16x$, the point estimate of a reasonable level of total itemized deductions for a taxpayer with an adjusted gross income of $52,500 is $13,080.
a. Develop a 95% confidence interval estimate of the mean amount of total itemized deductions for all taxpayers with an adjusted gross income of $52,500.
b. Develop a 95% prediction interval estimate for the amount of total itemized deductions for a particular taxpayer with an adjusted gross income of $52,500.
c. If the particular taxpayer referred to in part (b) has claimed total itemized deductions of $20,400, would the IRS agent's request for an audit appear to be justified?
d. Using your answer to part (b), give the IRS agent a guideline as to the amount of total itemized deductions a taxpayer with an adjusted gross income of $52,500 should have before an audit is recommended.

35. Refer to Exercise 20, where data on the production volume *x* and total cost *y* for a particular manufacturing operation were used to develop the estimated regression equation $\hat{y} = 1246.67 + 7.6x$.

    a. The company's production schedule shows that 500 units must be produced next month. What is the point estimate of the total cost for the next month?

    b. Develop a 99% production interval estimate of the total cost for next month.

    c. If an accounting cost report at the end of next month shows that the actual production cost during the month was $6000, should managers be concerned about incurring such a high total cost for the month? Discuss.

36. Nielsen Media Research collects data showing the number of households tuned in to shows that carry a particular advertisement. This information is useful to advertisers because it tells them how many consumers they are reaching. The following data show the number of times the ad was aired and the number of household exposures in millions for the week of October 27—November 2, 1997 (*USA Today*, November 17, 1997).

Nielsen I

Advertised Brand	Times Ad Aired	Household Exposures
McDonald's	49	359.6
Burger King	42	296.1
HBO	30	271.6
Red Corner movie	26	251.1
Pizza Hut	31	229.3
Sears	20	186.9
Isuzu Rodeo	21	186.3
MCI	24	172.7
Sprint	15	166.0
J. C. Penney	19	162.1

    a. Use these data to develop an estimated regression equation that could be used to predict the number of household exposures given the number of times the ad is aired.

    b. Did the estimated regression equation provide a good fit? Explain.

    c. Develop a 95% confidence interval estimate for the number of household exposures for all ads that are aired 35 times.

    d. Suppose that Wendy's was considering airing a particular ad 35 times. Develop a 95% prediction interval estimate for the number of household exposures for this particular ad.

12.7   COMPUTER SOLUTION

Performing the regression analysis computations without the help of a computer can be quite time consuming. In this section we discuss how the computational burden can be minimized by using a computer software package such as Minitab.

    We entered Armand's student population and quarterly sales data into a Minitab worksheet. The independent variable was named POP and the dependent variable was named SALES to assist with interpretation of the computer output. Using Minitab, we obtained the printout for Armand's Pizza Parlors shown in Figure 12.10.* The interpretation of this printout follows.

---
*The Minitab steps necessary to generate the output are given in Appendix 12.1.

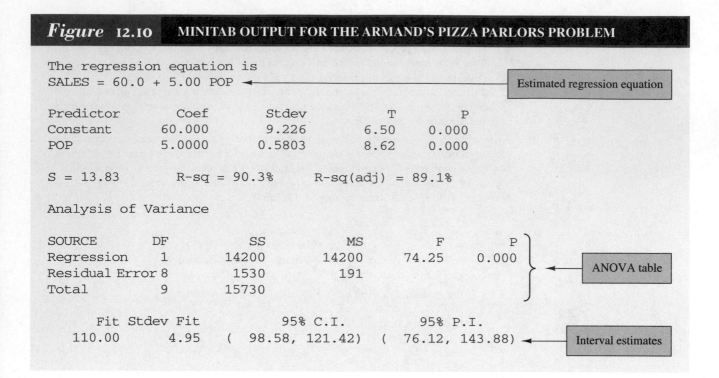

Figure 12.10   MINITAB OUTPUT FOR THE ARMAND'S PIZZA PARLORS PROBLEM

```
The regression equation is
SALES = 60.0 + 5.00 POP  ◄──────────────────  Estimated regression equation

Predictor       Coef       Stdev          T        P
Constant      60.000       9.226       6.50    0.000
POP           5.0000      0.5803       8.62    0.000

S = 13.83       R-sq = 90.3%      R-sq(adj) = 89.1%

Analysis of Variance

SOURCE          DF          SS          MS          F        P
Regression       1       14200       14200      74.25    0.000
Residual Error 8        1530         191                              ANOVA table
Total            9       15730

    Fit  Stdev Fit            95% C.I.            95% P.I.
  110.00        4.95    (  98.58, 121.42)   (  76.12, 143.88)  ◄──  Interval estimates
```

1. Minitab prints the estimated regression equation as SALES = 60.0 + 5.00 POP.
2. A table is printed that shows the values of the coefficients b_0 and b_1, the standard deviation of each coefficient, the t value obtained by dividing each coefficient value by its standard deviation, and the p-value associated with the t test. Thus, to test H_0: $\beta_1 = 0$ versus H_a: $\beta_1 \neq 0$, we could compare 8.62 (located in the T column) to the appropriate critical value. This same procedure was described for the t test in Section 12.5. Alternatively, we could use the p-value provided by Minitab to perform the same test. Recall from Chapter 9 that the p-value is the probability of obtaining a sample result more unlikely than what is observed. Because the p-value in this case is zero (to three decimal places), the sample results indicate that the null hypothesis (H_0: $\beta_1 = 0$) should be rejected. In general, we reject H_0: $\beta_1 = 0$ if the p-value $< \alpha$.
3. Minitab prints the standard error of the estimate, $s = 13.83$, as well as information about the goodness of fit. Note that "R-sq = 90.3%" is the coefficient of determination expressed as a percentage. The output "R-Sq (adj) = 89.1%" is discussed in Section 12.9.
4. The ANOVA table is printed below the heading Analysis of Variance. Note that DF is an abbreviation for degrees of freedom and that MSR is given as 14,200 and MSE as 191. The ratio of these two values provides the F value of 74.25. In Section 12.5, we showed how the F value can be used to test for a significant relationship between SALES and POP. Minitab also prints the p-value associated with this F test. Because the p-value is zero (to three decimal places), the relationship is judged statistically significant. In general, we reject H_0: $\beta_1 = 0$ if the p-value $< \alpha$.
5. The 95% confidence interval estimate of the expected quarterly sales and the 95% prediction interval estimate of quarterly sales for an individual restaurant located near a campus with 10,000 students are printed below the ANOVA table. The confidence interval is (98.58, 121.42) and the prediction interval is (76.12, 143.88).

··· */ /*··············

EXERCISES

Applications

SELF TEST

37. The commercial division of a real estate firm is conducting a regression analysis of the relationship between x, annual gross rents ($1000s), and y, selling price ($1000s) for apartment buildings. Data have been collected on several properties recently sold, and the following output has been obtained in a computer run.

```
The regression equation is
Y = 20.0 + 7.21 X

Predictor       Coef      Stdev        T
Constant      20.000     3.2213      6.21
X           · 7.210     1.3626      5.29

Analysis of Variance

SOURCE            DF         SS
Regression         1     41587.3
Residual Error     7
Total              8     51984.1
```

    a. How many apartment buildings were in the sample?
    b. Write the estimated regression equation.
    c. What is the value of s_{b_1}?
    d. Use the F statistic to test the significance of the relationship at a .05 level of significance.
    e. Estimate the selling price of an apartment building with gross annual rents of $50,000.

38. Following is a portion of the computer output for a regression analysis relating y = maintenance expense (dollars per month) to x = usage (hours per week) of a particular brand of computer terminal.

```
The regression equation is

Y = 6.1092 + .8951 X

Predictor       Coef      Stdev
Constant      6.1092     0.9361
X             0.8951     0.1490

Analysis of Variance

SOURCE            DF          SS         MS

Regression         1      1575.76     1575.76
Residual Error     8       349.14       43.64
Total              9      1924.90
```

    a. Write the estimated regression equation.
    b. Use a t test to determine whether monthly maintenance expense is related to usage at the .05 level of significance.
    c. Use the estimated regression equation to predict monthly maintenance expense for any terminal that is used 25 hours per week.

39. A regression model relating x, number of salespersons at a branch office, to y, annual sales at the office ($1000s), has been developed. The computer output from a regression analysis of the data follows.

```
The regression equation is
Y = 80.0 + 50.00 X

Predictor        Coef        Stdev            T
Constant         80.0       11.333         7.06
X                50.0        5.482         9.12

Analysis of Variance

SOURCE              DF           SS           MS
Regression           1       6828.6       6828.6
Residual Error      28       2298.8         82.1
Total               29       9127.4
```

a. Write the estimated regression equation.
b. How many branch offices were involved in the study?
c. Compute the F statistic and test the significance of the relationship at a .05 level of significance.
d. Predict the annual sales at the Memphis branch office. This branch has 12 salespersons.

40. The National Association of Home Builders ranks the most and least affordable housing markets, based on the proportion of homes that a family earning the median income in that market could afford to buy. Data showing the median income ($1000s) and the median sale price ($1000s) for a sample of 12 housing markets that appeared on the list of most affordable markets follow (*The Wall Street Journal Almanac 1998*).

HomeBldg

Market	Income ($1000s)	Price ($1000s)
Syracuse, NY	41.8	76
Springfield, IL	47.7	91
Lima, OH	40.0	65
Dayton, OH	44.3	88
Beaumont, TX	37.3	70
Lakeland, FL	35.9	73
Baton Rouge, LA	39.3	85
Nashua, NH	56.9	118
Racine, WI	46.7	81
Des Moines, IA	48.3	89
Minneapolis–St. Paul, MN	54.6	110
Wilmington, DE–MD	55.5	110

a. Use these data to develop an estimated regression equation that could be used to predict the median price for a market given the median income for the market.
b. Did the estimated regression equation provide a good fit? Explain.
c. Develop a 95% confidence interval estimate of the median price for all homes sold in a market in which the median income is $40,100.
d. The median income in Binghamton, New York, was reported to be $40,100. Develop a 95% prediction interval estimate of the median sales price for homes sold in the Binghamton market.

41. Cushman & Wakefield, Inc., collects data showing the office building vacancy rates and rental rates for markets in the United States. The following data show the overall vacancy rates (%) and the average rental rates (per square foot) for the central business district for 18 selected markets (*The Wall Street Journal Almanac 1998*).

OffRates

Market	Vacancy Rate (%)	Average Rental Rate ($)
Atlanta	21.9	18.54
Boston	6.0	33.70
Hartford	22.8	19.67
Baltimore	18.1	21.01
Washington	12.7	35.09
Philadelphia	14.5	19.41
Miami	20.0	25.28
Tampa	19.2	17.02
Chicago	16.0	24.04
San Francisco	6.6	31.42
Phoenix	15.9	18.74
San Jose	9.2	26.76
West Palm Beach	19.7	27.72
Detroit	20.0	18.20
Brooklyn	8.3	25.00
Downtown, NY	17.1	29.78
Midtown, NY	10.8	37.03
Midtown South, NY	11.1	28.64

a. Develop a scatter diagram for these data; plot the vacancy rate on the horizontal axis.
b. Does there appear to be any relationship between these two variables?
c. Develop the estimated regression equation that could be used to predict the average rental rate given the overall vacancy rate.
d. Test the significance of the relationship at the .05 level of significance.
e. Did the estimated regression equation provide a good fit? Explain.
f. Predict the expected rental rate for markets with a 25% vacancy rate in the central business district.
g. The overall vacancy rate in the central business district in Ft. Lauderdale is 11.3%. Predict the expected rental rate for Ft. Lauderdale.

12.8   RESIDUAL ANALYSIS: VALIDATING MODEL ASSUMPTIONS

Residual analysis is the primary tool for determining whether the assumed regression model is appropriate.

As we have previously noted, the *residual* for observation i is the difference between the observed value of the dependent variable (y_i) and the estimated value of the dependent variable ($\hat{y}_i$).

Residual for Observation i

$$y_i - \hat{y}_i \tag{12.30}$$

where

$\quad\quad y_i$ is the observed value of the dependent variable

$\quad\quad \hat{y}_i$ is the estimated value of the dependent variable

---

In other words, the ith residual is the error resulting from using the estimated regression equation to predict the value of y_i. The residuals for the Armand's Pizza Parlors example are computed in Table 12.8. The observed values of the dependent variable are in the second column and the estimated values of the dependent variable, obtained using the estimated regression equation $\hat{y} = 60 + 5x$, are in the third column. The corresponding residuals are in the fourth column. An analysis of these residuals will help determine whether the assumptions that have been made about the regression model are appropriate.

Let us now review the regression assumptions for the Armand's Pizza Parlors example. A simple linear regression model was assumed.

$$y = \beta_0 + \beta_1 x + \epsilon \tag{12.31}$$

This model indicates that we assumed sales (y) to be a linear function of the size of the student population (x) plus an error term ϵ. In Section 12.4 we made the following assumptions about the error term ϵ.

1. $E(\epsilon) = 0$.
2. The variance of ϵ, denoted by σ^2, is the same for all values of x.
3. The values of ϵ are independent.
4. The error term ϵ has a normal probability distribution.

These assumptions provide the theoretical basis for the t test and the F test used to determine whether the relationship between x and y is significant, and for the confidence and prediction interval estimates presented in Section 12.6. If the assumptions about the error term ϵ appear questionable, the hypothesis tests about the significance of the regression relationship and the interval estimation results may not be valid.

The residuals provide the best information about ϵ; hence an analysis of the residuals is an important step in determining whether the assumptions for ϵ are appropriate. Much of residual analysis is based on an examination of graphical plots. In this section, we discuss a plot of the residuals against values of the independent variable x.

Residual Plot against x

A residual plot against the independent variable x is a graph in which the values of the independent variable are represented by the horizontal axis and the corresponding residual values are represented by the vertical axis. A point is plotted for each residual. The first coordinate for each point is given by the value of x_i and the second coordinate is given by the corre-

Table 12.8	**RESIDUALS FOR ARMAND'S PIZZA PARLORS**		
Student Population x_i	**Sales** y_i	**Estimated Sales** $\hat{y}_i = 60 + 5x_i$	**Residuals** $y_i - \hat{y}_i$
2	58	70	−12
6	105	90	15
8	88	100	−12
8	118	100	18
12	117	120	−3
16	137	140	−3
20	157	160	−3
20	169	160	9
22	149	170	−21
26	202	190	12

sponding value of the residual $y_i - \hat{y}_i$. For a residual plot against x with the Armand's Pizza Parlors data from Table 12.8, the coordinates of the first point are $(2, -12)$, corresponding to $x_1 = 2$ and $y_1 - \hat{y}_1 = -12$; the coordinates of the second point are $(6, 15)$, corresponding to $x_2 = 6$ and $y_2 - \hat{y}_2 = 15$, and so on. Figure 12.11 is the resulting residual plot.

Before interpreting the results for this residual plot, let us consider some general patterns that might be observed in any residual plot. Three examples are shown in Figure 12.12. If the assumption that the variance of ϵ is the same for all values of x and the assumed regression model is an adequate representation of the relationship between the variables, the residual plot should give an overall impression of a horizontal band of points such as the one in panel A of Figure 12.12. However, if the variance of ϵ is not the same for all values of x—for example, if variability about the regression line is greater for larger values of x—a pattern such as the one in panel B of Figure 12.12 could be observed. In this case, the assumption of a constant variance of ϵ is violated. Another possible residual plot is shown in panel C. In this case, we would conclude that the assumed regression model is not an adequate representation of the relationship between the variables. A curvilinear regression model or multiple regression model should be considered.

Now let us return to the residual plot for Armand's Pizza Parlors shown in Figure 12.11. The residuals appear to approximate the horizontal pattern in panel A of Figure 12.12. Hence, we conclude that the residual plot does not provide evidence that the assumptions made for Armand's regression model should be challenged. At this point, we are confident in the conclusion that Armand's simple linear regression model is valid.

Experience and good judgment are always factors in the effective interpretation of residual plots. Seldom does a residual plot conform precisely to one of the patterns shown in Figure 12.12. Yet analysts who frequently conduct regression studies and frequently

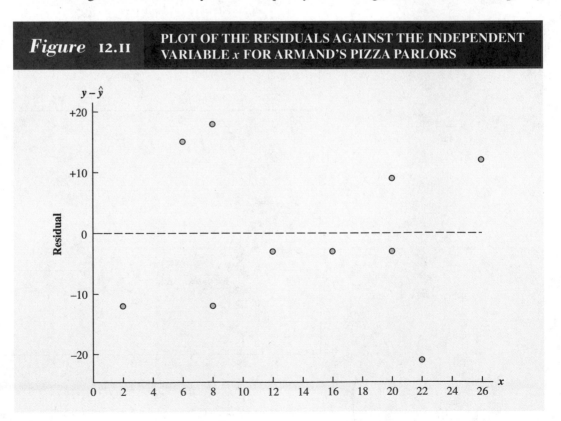

Figure 12.11   PLOT OF THE RESIDUALS AGAINST THE INDEPENDENT VARIABLE x FOR ARMAND'S PIZZA PARLORS

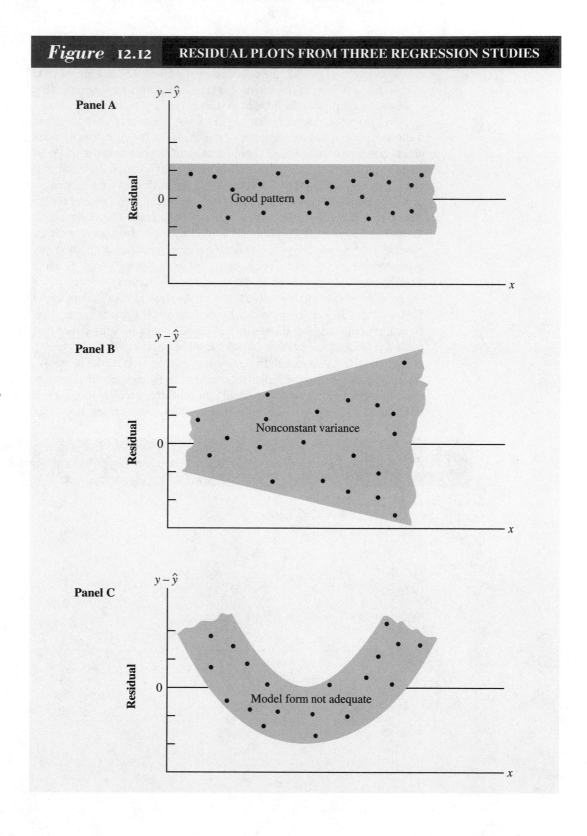

Figure 12.12 **RESIDUAL PLOTS FROM THREE REGRESSION STUDIES**

Panel A

Good pattern

Panel B

Nonconstant variance

Panel C

Model form not adequate

review residual plots become adept at understanding the differences between patterns that are reasonable and patterns that indicate the assumptions of the model should be questioned. A residual plot as shown here is one of the techniques that is used to assess the validity of the assumptions for a regression model.

N O T E S *and Comments*	1. The analysis of residuals is the primary method statisticians use to verify that the assumptions associated with a regression model are valid. Even if no violations are found, it does not necessarily follow that the model will yield good predictions. However, if in addition the statistical tests support the conclusion of significance and the coefficient of determination is large, we should be able to develop good estimates using the estimated regression equation.

2. We use residual plots to validate the assumptions of a regression model. The appropriate corrective action when assumptions are violated must be based on good judgment; recommendations from an experienced statistician can be valuable. If the residual analysis indicates that the one or more assumptions are questionable, but not necessarily invalid, the user should take caution in using and interpreting the regression results.

3. Another residual plot places the predicted value of the dependent variable $\hat{y}$ on the horizontal axis and the residual values on the vertical axis. A point is plotted for each residual; the first coordinate for each point is given by $\hat{y}_i$ and the second coordinate is given by the corresponding value of the ith residual $y_i - \hat{y}_i$. For simple linear regression, both the residual plot against x and the residual plot against $\hat{y}$ provide the same information. In multiple regression analysis, the residual plot against $\hat{y}$ is more widely used.

4. Many of the residual plots provided by computer software packages use a standardized version of the residuals, which are obtained by dividing each residual by its standard deviation. We should expect to see approximately 95% of the standardized residuals between -2 and $+2$ if the normal probability assumption for the error term ϵ is appropriate.

EXERCISES

Methods

42.   Given are data for two variables, x and y.

x_i	6	11	15	18	20
y_i	6	8	12	20	30

SELF TEST

a.   Develop an estimated regression equation for these data.
b.   Compute the residuals.
c.   Develop a plot of the residuals against the independent variable x. Do the assumptions about the error terms seem to be satisfied?

43. The following data were used in a regression study.

Observation	x_i	y_i	Observation	x_i	y_i
1	2	4	6	7	6
2	3	5	7	7	9
3	4	4	8	8	5
4	5	6	9	9	11
5	7	4			

a. Develop an estimated regression equation for these data.
b. Construct a plot of the residuals. Do the assumptions about the error terms seem to be satisfied?

Applications

44. Data on advertising expenditures ($1000s) and revenue ($1000s) for the Four Seasons Restaurant follow.

Advertising Expenditures	Revenue
1	19
2	32
4	44
6	40
10	52
14	53
20	54

a. Let x equal advertising expenditures ($1000s) and y equal revenue ($1000s). Use the method of least squares to develop a straight-line approximation of the relationship between the two variables.
b. Test whether revenue and advertising expenditures are related at a .05 level of significance.
c. Develop a plot of the residuals against the independent variable.
d. What conclusions can you draw from residual analysis? Should this model be used, or should we look for a better one?

45. Refer to Exercise 9, where an estimated regression equation relating years of experience and annual sales was developed.
a. Compute the residuals and construct a residual plot for this problem.
b. Do the assumptions about the error terms seem reasonable in light of the residual plot?

46. The following table lists the number of employees and the yearly revenue for the 10 largest wholesale bakers (*Louis Rukeyser's Business Almanac*).

Bakers

Company	Employees	Revenues ($ millions)
Nabisco Brands USA	9,500	1,734
Continental Baking Co.	22,400	1,600
Campbell Taggart, Inc.	19,000	1,044
Keebler Company	8,943	988
Interstate Bakeries Corp.	11,200	704
Flowers Industries, Inc.	10,200	557
Sunshine Biscuits, Inc.	5,000	490
American Bakeries, Co.	6,600	461
Entenmann's Inc.	3,734	450
Kitchens of Sara Lee	1,550	405

a. Use a computer package to develop an estimated regression equation relating yearly revenues y to the number of employees x.

b. Construct a residual plot of the standardized residuals against the independent variable.

c. Do the assumptions about the error terms and model form seem reasonable in light of the residual plot?

12.9   MULTIPLE REGRESSION

Multiple regression analysis is the study of how a dependent variable y is related to two or more independent variables. In the general case, we will use p to denote the number of independent variables. The concepts of a regression model and a regression equation introduced in Section 12.1 are applicable in the multiple regression case. The equation that describes how the dependent variable y is related to the independent variables $x_1, x_2, \ldots, x_p$ and an error term is called the *regression model*. We begin with the assumption that the multiple regression model has the following form.

Multiple Regression Model

$$y = \beta_0 + \beta_1 x_1 + \beta_2 x_2 + \cdots + \beta_p x_p + \epsilon \qquad \textbf{(12.32)}$$

The assumptions about the error term ϵ in the multiple regression model are the same as the assumptions for ϵ in the simple linear regression model (see Section 12.4). Recall that one of the assumptions is that the mean or expected value of ϵ is zero. A consequence of this assumption is that the mean or expected value of y, denoted $E(y)$, is equal to $\beta_0 + \beta_1 x_1 + \beta_2 x_2 + \ldots + \beta_p x_p$. The equation that describes how the mean value of y is related to $x_1, x_2, \ldots, x_p$ is called the *multiple regression equation*.

Multiple Regression Equation

$$E(y) = \beta_0 + \beta_1 x_1 + \beta_2 x_2 + \cdots + \beta_p x_p \qquad \textbf{(12.33)}$$

If the values of $\beta_0, \beta_1, \beta_2, \ldots, \beta_p$ were known, (12.33) could be used to compute the mean value of y at given values of $x_1, x_2, \ldots, x_p$. Unfortunately, these parameter values will not, in general, be known and must be estimated from sample data. A simple random sample is used to compute sample statistics $b_0, b_1, b_2, \ldots, b_p$ that are used as the point estimators of the parameters $\beta_0, \beta_1, \beta_2, \ldots, \beta_p$. These sample statistics provide the following estimated multiple regression equation.

Estimated Multiple Regression Equation

$$\hat{y} = b_0 + b_1 x_1 + b_2 x_2 + \cdots + b_p x_p \qquad \textbf{(12.34)}$$

where

$$b_0, b_1, b_2, \ldots, b_p \text{ are the estimates of } \beta_0, \beta_1, \beta_2, \ldots, \beta_p$$
$$\hat{y} = \text{estimated value of the dependent variable}$$

The estimation process for multiple regression is shown in Figure 12.13.

Figure **12.13**   **THE ESTIMATION PROCESS FOR MULTIPLE REGRESSION**

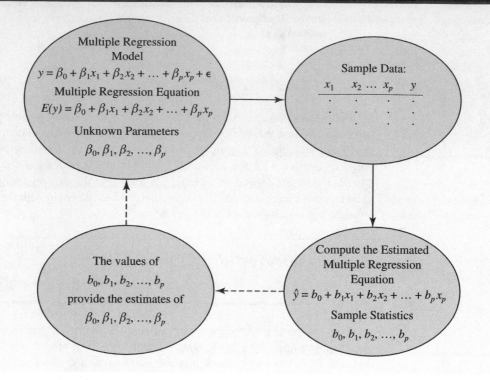

In Section 12.2, we used the least squares method to develop the estimated regression equation for simple linear regression. This same approach is used to develop the estimated multiple regression equation. The least squares criterion is restated as follows.

Least Squares Criterion

$$\min \Sigma(y_i - \hat{y}_i)^2 \tag{12.35}$$

where

y_i = observed value of the dependent variable for the ith observation

$\hat{y}_i$ = estimated value of the dependent variable for the ith observation

The estimated values of the dependent variable are computed using the estimated multiple regression equation,

$$\hat{y} = b_0 + b_1x_1 + b_2x_2 + \cdots + b_px_p$$

As (12.35) shows, the least squares method uses sample data to provide the values of b_0, b_1, b_2, . . . , b_p that make the sum of squared residuals [the deviations between the observed values of the dependent variable (y_i) and the estimated values of the dependent variable ($\hat{y}_i$)] a minimum.

In Section 12.2 we presented formulas for computing the least squares estimators b_0 and b_1 for the estimated simple linear regression equation $\hat{y} = b_0 + b_1 x$. In multiple regression, the presentation of the formulas for the regression coefficients $b_0, b_1, b_2, \ldots, b_p$ involves the use of matrix algebra and is beyond the scope of this text. Therefore, in presenting multiple regression, we will focus on how computer software packages can be used to obtain the estimated regression equation and other information. The emphasis will be on how to interpret the computer output rather than on how to make the multiple regression computations.

An Example: Butler Trucking Company

As an illustration of multiple regression analysis, we will consider a problem faced by the Butler Trucking Company, an independent trucking company in southern California. A major portion of Butler's business involves deliveries throughout its local area. To develop better work schedules, the managers want to estimate the total daily travel time for their drivers.

Initially the managers believed that the total daily travel time would be closely related to the number of miles traveled in making the daily deliveries. A simple random sample of 10 driving assignments provided the data shown in Table 12.9 and the scatter diagram shown in Figure 12.14. After reviewing this scatter diagram, the managers hypothesized that the simple linear regression model $y = \beta_0 + \beta_1 x_1 + \epsilon$ could be used to describe the relationship between the total travel time (y) and the number of miles traveled (x_1). To estimate the parameters β_0 and β_1, the least squares method was used to develop the estimated regression equation,

$$\hat{y} = b_0 + b_1 x_1 \qquad (12.36)$$

In Figure 12.15, we show the Minitab computer output from applying simple linear regression to the data in Table 12.9. The estimated regression equation is

$$\hat{y} = 1.27 + .0678 x_1$$

Table 12.9	PRELIMINARY DATA FOR BUTLER TRUCKING	
Driving Assignment	x_1 = Miles Traveled	y = Travel Time (hours)
1	100	9.3
2	50	4.8
3	100	8.9
4	100	6.5
5	50	4.2
6	80	6.2
7	75	7.4
8	65	6.0
9	90	7.6
10	90	6.1

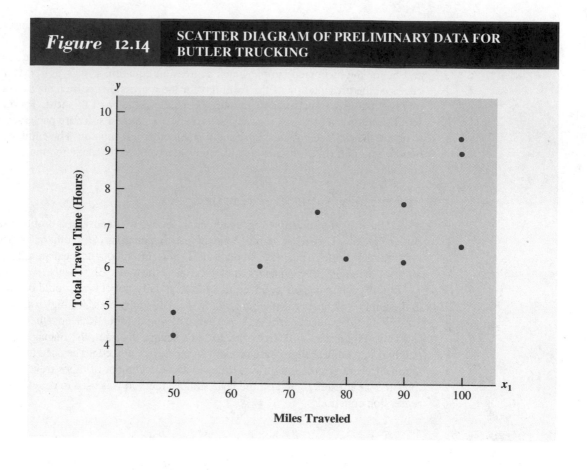

Figure 12.14 SCATTER DIAGRAM OF PRELIMINARY DATA FOR BUTLER TRUCKING

Figure 12.15 MINITAB OUTPUT FOR BUTLER TRUCKING WITH ONE INDEPENDENT VARIABLE

```
The regression equation is
Y = 1.27 + 0.0678 X1

Predictor      Coef        Stdev           T          P
Constant       1.274       1.401          0.91       0.390
X1             0.06783     0.01706        3.98       0.004

S = 1.002      R-sq = 66.4%      R-sq(adj) = 62.2%

Analysis of Variance

SOURCE           DF          SS             MS          F         P
Regression        1        15.871         15.871      15.81     0.004
Residual Error    8         8.029          1.004
Total             9        23.900
```

At the .05 level of significance, the F value of 15.81 and its corresponding p-value of .004 indicate that the relationship is significant; that is, we can reject H_0: $\beta_1 = 0$ when the p-value is less than $\alpha = .05$. Note that the same conclusion is obtained based upon the t value of 3.98 and its associated p-value of .004. Thus, we can conclude that the relationship between the total travel time and the number of miles traveled is significant; longer travel times are associated with more miles traveled. With a coefficient of determination (expressed as a percentage) of R-sq = 66.4%, we see that 66.4% of the variability in travel time can be explained by the linear effect of the number of miles traveled. This finding is fairly good, but the managers might want to consider adding a second independent variable to explain some of the remaining variability in the dependent variable.

In attempting to identify another independent variable, the managers felt that the number of deliveries could also contribute to the total travel time. The Butler Trucking data, with the number of deliveries added, are shown in Table 12.10. The Minitab computer solution with both miles traveled (x_1) and number of deliveries (x_2) as independent variables is shown in Figure 12.16. The estimated regression equation is

$$\hat{y} = -.869 + .0611x_1 + .923x_2 \tag{12.37}$$

A Note on Interpretation of Coefficients

Compare the relationship between the estimated regression equation with only the miles traveled as an independent variable and the equation that includes the number of deliveries as a second independent variable. Note that the value of b_1 is not the same in both cases. In simple linear regression, we interpret b_1 as an estimate of the change in y for a one-unit change in the independent variable. For example, in the Butler Trucking Company problem involving only one independent variable, number of miles traveled, $b_1 = .0678$. Thus, .0678 is an estimate of the expected increase in travel time corresponding to an increase of one mile in the distance traveled. In multiple regression analysis, this interpretation must be modified somewhat. That is, in multiple regression analysis, we interpret each regression coefficient as follows: b_i represents an estimate of the change in y corresponding to a one-unit change in x_i when all other independent variables are held constant. In the Butler Trucking example

Table 12.10	DATA FOR BUTLER TRUCKING WITH MILES TRAVELED (x_1) AND NUMBER OF DELIVERIES (x_2) AS THE INDEPENDENT VARIABLES		
Driving Assignment	x_1 = Miles Traveled	x_2 = Number of Deliveries	y = Travel Time (hours)
1	100	4	9.3
2	50	3	4.8
3	100	4	8.9
4	100	2	6.5
5	50	2	4.2
6	80	2	6.2
7	75	3	7.4
8	65	4	6.0
9	90	3	7.6
10	90	2	6.1

Figure 12.16	MINITAB OUTPUT FOR BUTLER TRUCKING WITH TWO INDEPENDENT VARIABLES

```
The regression equation is
Y = - 0.869 + 0.0611 X1 + 0.923 X2

Predictor       Coef        Stdev          T        P
Constant      -0.8687      0.9515       -0.91     0.392
X1            0.061135     0.009888      6.18     0.000
X2            0.9234       0.2211        4.18     0.004

S = 0.5731        R-sq = 90.4%      R-sq(adj) = 87.6%

Analysis of Variance

SOURCE            DF          SS          MS        F        P
Regression         2        21.601      10.800    32.88    0.000
Residual Error     7         2.299       0.328
Total              9        23.900
```

involving two independent variables, $b_1 = .0611$. Thus, .0611 hours is an estimate of the expected increase in travel time corresponding to an increase of one mile in the distance traveled when the number of deliveries is held constant. Similarly, since $b_2 = .923$, an estimate of the expected increase in travel time corresponding to an increase of one delivery when the number of miles traveled is held constant is .923 hours.

Testing for Significance

The significance tests used in simple linear regression were a t and an F test. In simple linear regression, both tests provided the same conclusion; that is, if the null hypothesis was rejected, we concluded $\beta_1 \neq 0$. In multiple regression, the t and the F test have different purposes.

1. The F test is used to determine whether there is a significant relationship between the dependent variable and the set of all the independent variables; we will refer to the F test as the test for *overall significance*.
2. The t test is used to determine whether each of the individual independent variables is significant. A separate t test is conducted for each of the independent variables; we refer to each of these t tests as a test for *individual significance*.

In the following discussion, we will show how the F test and the t test apply to the Butler Trucking Company multiple regression problem.

With two independent variables, the hypotheses used to determine whether a significant relationship can be found between travel time and the two independent variables, miles traveled and number of deliveries, are written as follows:

$$H_0: \beta_1 = \beta_2 = 0$$
$$H_a: \beta_1 \text{ and/or } \beta_2 \neq 0$$

Recall that in simple linear regression the F test statistic is MSR/MSE. In multiple regression the F test statistic is also MSR/MSE; however, the degrees of freedom associated with MSR and MSE change because of the additional independent variables. In the analysis of variance portion of Figure 12.16, we see that MSR = 10.8, MSE = .328, and the value of the F test statistic is 32.88. With a level of significance $\alpha = .01$, Table 4 of Appendix B shows that with 2 degrees of freedom in the numerator (the degrees of freedom associated with MSR) and 7 degrees of freedom in the denominator (the degrees of freedom associated with MSE), $F_{.01} = 9.55$. Because $32.88 > 9.55$, we reject $H_0: \beta_1 = \beta_2 = 0$ and conclude that a significant relationship exists between travel time y and the two independent variables, miles traveled and number of deliveries. The p-value $= 0.000$ in the last column of the analysis of variance table (Figure 12.16) also indicates that we can reject $H_0: \beta_1 = \beta_2 = 0$ because the p-value $< \alpha$.

If the F test first shows that the multiple regression relationship is significant, a t test can be conducted to determine the significance of each of the individual variables. The t test for individual significance is $t = b_i / s_{b_i}$. In this test statistic, s_{b_i} is the estimate of the standard deviation of b_i. The value of s_{b_i} will be provided by the computer software package. Let us conduct the t test for the Butler Trucking multiple regression problem. The Minitab output shown in Figure 12.16 shows that $b_1 = .061135$, $b_2 = .9234$, $s_{b_1} = .009888$ and $s_{b_2} = .2211$. Thus, the test statistics for the hypotheses involving parameters β_1 and β_2 are as follows:

$$t = .061135/.009888 = 6.18$$
$$t = .9234/.2211 = 4.18$$

Note that both of these t-ratios are provided by the Minitab output of Figure 12.16. Using $\alpha = .01$ and $n - p - 1 = 10 - 2 - 1 = 7$ degrees of freedom, Table 2 of Appendix B can be used to show $t_{.005} = 3.499$. With $6.18 > 3.499$, we reject the hypothesis $H_0: \beta_1 = 0$. Similarly, with $4.18 > 3.499$, we also reject the hypothesis $H_0: \beta_2 = 0$. Note also that the p-values of .000 and .004 on the Minitab output indicate rejection of these hypotheses. Thus, both independent variables tested individually are statistically significant.

Multiple Coefficient of Determination

The multiple coefficient of determination, denoted by R^2, is computed using the same formula as for the coefficient of determination in simple linear regression; that is $R^2 = $ SSR/SST. As was the case for the coefficient of determination in simple linear regression, the multiple coefficient of determination can be interpreted as the proportion of the variability in the dependent variable that can be explained by the estimated multiple regression equation. Thus, when it is multiplied by 100, it can be interpreted as the percentage of variation in y that can be explained by the estimated regression equation. In the Minitab output shown in Figure 12.16 the multiple coefficient of determination is denoted by R-sq = 90.4%. Thus, the estimated multiple regression equation has explained 90.4% of the variability in travel time.

Figure 12.15 shows that the R-sq value for the estimated regression equation with only one independent variable, the number of miles traveled (x_1), is 66.4%. Thus, the percentage of the variability in travel times that is explained by the estimated regression equation increased from 66.4% to 90.4% by adding the number of deliveries as a second independent variable. In general, R^2 always increases as more independent variables are added to the model.

Estimation and Prediction

Estimating the mean value of y and predicting an individual value of y in multiple regression is similar to that for the case of simple linear regression. In multiple regression analysis we substitute the given values of the independent variables into the estimated regression equation and use the corresponding value of $\hat{y}$ as the point estimate. Although the methodology behind the development of confidence interval estimates and prediction interval estimates in multiple regression analysis is beyond the scope of the text, computer software packages such as Minitab can be used to develop the interval estimates.

NOTES and Comments

1. As pointed out earlier, the mean square error is an unbiased estimator of σ^2, the variance of the error term ϵ. Thus, referring to Figure 12.16, we see that the estimate of σ^2 is MSE = .328. The square root of MSE is the estimate of the standard deviation of the error term. As defined in Section 12.5, this standard deviation is called the *standard error of the estimate* and is denoted by s. Thus we have $s = \sqrt{\text{MSE}} = \sqrt{.328} = .5731$. Note that the value of the standard error of the estimate also appears in the Minitab output shown in Figure 12.16.

2. Many analysts prefer adjusting R^2 for the number of independent variables to avoid overestimating the impact of adding an independent variable on the amount of variability explained by the estimated regression equation; the resulting measure is referred to as the *adjusted multiple coefficient of determination*. Although the computation of the adjusted multiple coefficient of determination is beyond the scope of the text, its value is routinely provided by computer packages. On the Minitab output in Figure 12.16 the adjusted multiple coefficient of determination is denoted by R-sq(adj) = 87.6%.

EXERCISES

Methods

47. The estimated regression equation for a model involving two independent variables and 10 observations follows.

$$\hat{y} = 29.1270 + .5906x_1 + .4980x_2$$

  a. Interpret b_1 and b_2 in this estimated regression equation.
  b. Estimate y when $x_1 = 180$ and $x_2 = 310$.

48. Consider the following data for a dependent variable y and two independent variables, x_1 and x_2.

SELF TEST

x_1	x_2	y
30	12	94
47	10	108
25	17	112
51	16	178
40	5	94
51	19	175
74	7	170
36	12	117
59	13	142
76	16	211

a. Using these data, develop an estimated regression equation relating y to x_1. Estimate y if $x_1 = 45$.
b. Using these data, develop an estimated regression equation relating y to x_2. Estimate y if $x_2 = 15$.
c. Using these data, develop an estimated regression equation relating y to x_1 and x_2. Estimate y if $x_1 = 45$ and $x_2 = 15$.

49. In a regression analysis involving 30 observations, the following estimated regression equation was obtained.

$$\hat{y} = 17.6 + 3.8x_1 - 2.3x_2 + 7.6x_3 + 2.7x_4$$

a. Interpret b_1, b_2, b_3, and b_4 in this estimated regression equation.
b. Estimate y when $x_1 = 10$, $x_2 = 5$, $x_3 = 1$, and $x_4 = 2$.

Applications

50. The owner of Showtime Movie Theaters, Inc., would like to estimate weekly gross revenue as a function of advertising expenditures. Historical data for a sample of eight weeks follow.

Weekly Gross Revenue ($1000s)	Television Advertising ($1000s)	Newspaper Advertising ($1000s)
96	5.0	1.5
90	2.0	2.0
95	4.0	1.5
92	2.5	2.5
95	3.0	3.3
94	3.5	2.3
94	2.5	4.2
94	3.0	2.5

a. Develop an estimated regression equation with the amount of television advertising as the independent variable.
b. Develop an estimated regression equation with both television advertising and newspaper advertising as the independent variables.
c. Is the estimated regression equation coefficient for television advertising expenditures the same in parts (a) and (b)? Interpret the coefficient in each case.
d. What is the estimate of the gross revenue for a week when $3500 is spent on television advertising and $1800 is spent on newspaper advertising?

51. The following table reports the horsepower, curb weight, and the speed at ¼ mile for 16 sports and GT cars (*1998 Road & Track Sports & GT Cars*).

Auto1

Sports & GT Car	Curb Weight (lbs.)	Horsepower	Speed at ¼ mile (mph)
Acura Integra Type R	2577	195	90.7
Acura NSX-T	3066	290	108.0
BMW Z3 2.8	2844	189	93.2
Chevrolet Camaro Z28	3439	305	103.2
Chevrolet Corvette Convertible	3246	345	102.1
Dodge Viper RT/10	3319	450	116.2
Ford Mustang GT	3227	225	91.7
Honda Prelude Type SH	3042	195	89.7
Mercedes-Benz CLK320	3240	215	93.0
Mercedes-Benz SLK230	3025	185	92.3
Mitsubishi 3000GT VR-4	3737	320	99.0
Nissan 240SX SE	2862	155	84.6
Pontiac Firebird Trans Am	3455	305	103.2
Porsche Boxster	2822	201	93.2
Toyota Supra Turbo	3505	320	105.0
Volvo C70	3285	236	97.0

a. Use curb weight as the independent variable and the speed at ¼ mile as the dependent variable. What is the estimated regression equation?

b. Use curb weight and horsepower as two independent variables and the speed at ¼ mile as the dependent variable. What is the estimated regression equation?

c. The 1999 Porsche 911 Carrera has been advertised as having a curb weight of 2910 pounds and an engine with 296 horsepower. Use the results of part (b) to predict the speed at ¼ mile for the Porsche 911.

52. Heller Company manufactures lawn mowers and related lawn equipment. The managers believe the quantity of lawn mowers sold depends on the price of the mower and the price of a competitor's mower. Let

$$y = \text{quantity sold (1000s)}$$
$$x_1 = \text{price of competitor's mower (\$)}$$
$$x_2 = \text{price of Heller's mower (\$)}$$

The managers want an estimated regression equation that relates quantity sold to the prices of the Heller mower and the competitor's mower. The following table lists prices in 10 cities.

Mower

Competitor's Price (x_1)	Heller's Price (x_2)	Quantity sold (y)
120	100	102
140	110	100
190	90	120
130	150	77
155	210	46
175	150	93
125	250	26
145	270	69
180	300	65
150	250	85

a. Determine the estimated regression equation that can be used to predict the quantity sold given the competitor's price and Heller's price.
b. Interpret b_1 and b_2.
c. Predict the quantity sold in a city where Heller prices its mower at $160 and the competitor prices its mower at $170.

53. *Auto Rental News* provided the following data, which show the number of cars in service (1000s), the number of locations, and the rental revenue ($ millions) for 15 car rental companies. (*The Wall Street Journal Almanac 1998*).

CarRent

Company	Cars	Locations	Revenue
Alamo	130	171	1180
Avis	190	1130	1500
Budget	126	1052	1500
Dollar	63.5	450	560
Enterprise	315.1	2636	2060
FRCS (Ford)	55.25	1784	312.5
Hertz	250	1200	2400
National	135	935	1200
Payless	15	100	47
PROP (Chrysler)	27	1500	160
Rent-A-Wreck	10.9	460	78
Snappy	15.5	259	85
Thrifty	34	480	340
U-Save	13.5	500	95
Value	18	45	150.1

a. Determine the estimated regression equation that can be used to predict the rental revenue given the number of cars in service.
b. Provide an interpretation for the slope of the estimated regression equation developed in part (a).
c. Determine the estimated regression equation that can be used to predict the rental revenue given the number of cars in service and the number of locations.

SUMMARY

In this chapter we first showed how regression analysis can be used to determine how a dependent variable y is related to an independent variable x. In simple linear regression, the regression model is $y = \beta_0 + \beta_1 x + \epsilon$. The simple linear regression equation $E(y) = \beta_0 + \beta_1 x$ describes how the mean or expected value of y is related to x. We used sample data and the least squares method to develop the estimated regression equation $\hat{y} = b_0 + b_1 x$. In effect, b_0 and b_1 are the sample statistics used to estimate the unknown model parameters β_0 and β_1.

The coefficient of determination was presented as a measure of the goodness of fit for the estimated regression equation; it can be interpreted as the proportion of the variation in the dependent variable y that can be explained by the estimated regression equation. We reviewed correlation as a descriptive measure of the strength of a linear relationship between two variables.

The assumptions about the regression model and its associated error term ϵ were discussed, and t and F tests, based on those assumptions, were presented as a means for determining whether the relationship between two variables is statistically significant. We showed how to use the estimated regression equation to develop confidence interval estimates of the mean value of y and prediction interval estimates of individual values of y. We concluded the discussion of simple linear regression by showing how computer software can ease the computational burden of regression analysis; we then showed how residual analysis can be used to validate the model assumptions.

Multiple regression analysis was introduced as an extension of simple linear regression analysis. Multiple regression analysis enables us to understand how a dependent variable is related to two or more independent variables. Computer printouts were used throughout the discussion of multiple regression analysis to emphasize the fact that statistical software packages are the only realistic means of performing the numerous computations required in multiple regression analysis.

GLOSSARY

Dependent variable The variable that is being predicted or explained. It is denoted by y.

Independent variable The variable that is doing the predicting or explaining. It is denoted by x.

Simple linear regression Regression analysis involving one independent variable and one dependent variable in which the relationship between the variables is approximated by a straight line.

Simple linear regression model The equation that describes how y is related to x and an error term ϵ; $y = \beta_0 + \beta_1 x + \epsilon$.

Simple linear regression equation The equation that describes how the mean or expected value of the dependent variable is related to the independent variable; $E(y) = \beta_0 + \beta_1 x$.

Estimated simple linear regression equation The estimate of the regression equation developed from sample data by using the least squares method; $\hat{y} = b_0 + b_1 x$.

Scatter diagram A graph of bivariate data in which the independent variable is on the horizontal axis and the dependent variable is on the vertical axis.

Least squares method The procedure used to develop the estimated regression equation. The objective is to minimize $\Sigma(y_i - \hat{y}_i)^2$.

Coefficient of determination A measure of the goodness of fit of the estimated regression equation. It can be interpreted as the proportion of the variation in the dependent variable y that is explained by the estimated regression equation.

Residual The difference between the observed value of the dependent variable and the value predicted by using the estimated regression equation; that is, for the ith observation the residual is $y_i - \hat{y}_i$.

Correlation coefficient A measure of the strength of the linear relationship between two variables.

Mean square error The estimate of σ^2, the variance of the error term ϵ. It is denoted by MSE or s^2.

Standard error of the estimate The square root of the mean square error, denoted by s. It is the estimate of σ, the standard deviation of the error term ϵ.

ANOVA table The analysis of variance table used to summarize the computations associated with the F test for significance.

Confidence interval estimate The interval estimate of the mean value of y for a given value of x.

Prediction interval estimate The interval estimate of an individual value of y for a given value of x.

Residual analysis The analysis of the residuals used to determine whether the assumptions made about the regression model appear to be valid.

Residual plots Graphical representations of the residuals that can be used to determine whether the assumptions made about the regression model appear to be valid.

Multiple regression Regression analysis involving two or more independent variables.

Multiple regression model The equation that describes how the dependent variable y is related to the independent variables $x_1, x_2, \ldots, x_p$ and the error term ϵ; $y = \beta_0 + \beta_1 x_1 + \beta_2 x_2 + \cdots + \beta_p x_p + \epsilon$.

Multiple regression equation The equation that describes how the expected value or mean value of the dependent variable is related to the values of the independent variables; $E(y) = \beta_0 + \beta_1 x_1 + \beta_2 x_2 + \cdots + \beta_p x_p$.

Estimated multiple regression equation The estimate of the multiple regression equation based on sample data and the least squares method; $\hat{y} = b_0 + b_1 x_1 + b_2 x_2 + \cdots + b_p x_p$.

Multiple coefficient of determination A measure of the goodness of fit of the estimated multiple regression equation. It can be interpreted as the proportion of the variation in the dependent variable that is explained by the estimated regression equation.

Adjusted multiple coefficient of determination A measure of the goodness of fit of the estimated multiple regression equation that adjusts for the number of independent variables in the model and thus avoids overestimating the impact of adding more independent variables.

KEY FORMULAS

Simple Linear Regression Model

$$y = \beta_0 + \beta_1 x + \epsilon \tag{12.1}$$

Simple Linear Regression Equation

$$E(y) = \beta_0 + \beta_1 x \tag{12.2}$$

Estimated Simple Linear Regression Equation

$$\hat{y} = b_0 + b_1 x \tag{12.3}$$

Least Squares Criterion

$$\text{Min} \, \Sigma (y_i - \hat{y}_i)^2 \tag{12.5}$$

Slope and y-Intercept for the Estimated Regression Equation

$$b_1 = \frac{\Sigma x_i y_i - (\Sigma x_i \Sigma y_i)/n}{\Sigma x_i^2 - (\Sigma x_i)^2/n} \tag{12.6}$$

$$b_0 = \bar{y} - b_1 \bar{x} \tag{12.7}$$

Sum of Squares Due to Error

$$SSE = \Sigma(y_i - \hat{y}_i)^2 \tag{12.8}$$

Total Sum of Squares

$$SST = \Sigma(y_i - \bar{y})^2 \tag{12.9}$$

Sum of Squares Due to Regression

$$SSR = \Sigma(\hat{y}_i - \bar{y})^2 \tag{12.10}$$

Relationship among SST, SSR, and SSE

$$SST = SSR + SSE \tag{12.11}$$

Coefficient of Determination

$$r^2 = \frac{SSR}{SST} \tag{12.12}$$

Computational Formula for SST

$$SST = \Sigma y_i^2 - (\Sigma y_i)^2/n \tag{12.13}$$

Computational Formula for SSR

$$SSR = \frac{[\Sigma x_i y_i - (\Sigma x_i \Sigma y_i)/n]^2}{\Sigma x_i^2 - (\Sigma x_i)^2/n} \tag{12.14}$$

Sample Correlation Coefficient

$$r_{xy} = (\text{sign of } b_1)\sqrt{\text{Coefficient of Determination}} = \pm\sqrt{r^2} \tag{12.15}$$

Mean Square Error (Estimate of σ^2)

$$s^2 = MSE = \frac{SSE}{n-2} \tag{12.17}$$

Standard Error of the Estimate

$$s = \sqrt{MSE} = \sqrt{\frac{SSE}{n-2}} \tag{12.18}$$

Standard Deviation of b_1

$$\sigma_{b_1} = \frac{\sigma}{\sqrt{\Sigma x_i^2 - (\Sigma x_i)^2/n}} \tag{12.19}$$

Estimated Standard Deviation of b_1

$$s_{b_1} = \frac{s}{\sqrt{\Sigma x_i^2 - (\Sigma x_i)^2/n}} \tag{12.20}$$

t **Test Statistic**

$$t = \frac{b_1}{s_{b_1}} \tag{12.21}$$

Mean Square Due to Regression

$$MSR = \frac{SSR}{\text{Number of independent variables}} \tag{12.22}$$

F **Test Statistic**

$$F = \frac{MSR}{MSE} \tag{12.23}$$

Estimated Standard Deviation of $\hat{y}_p$

$$s_{\hat{y}_p} = s \sqrt{\frac{1}{n} + \frac{(x_p - \bar{x})^2}{\Sigma x_i^2 - (\Sigma x_i)^2/n}} \tag{12.25}$$

Confidence Interval Estimate of $E(\hat{y}_p)$

$$\hat{y}_p \pm t_{\alpha/2} s_{\hat{y}_p} \tag{12.26}$$

Estimated Standard Deviation When Predicting an Individual Value

$$s_{ind} = s \sqrt{1 + \frac{1}{n} + \frac{(x_p - \bar{x})^2}{\Sigma x_i^2 - (\Sigma x_i)^2/n}} \tag{12.28}$$

Prediction Interval Estimate of y_p

$$\hat{y}_p \pm t_{\alpha/2} s_{ind} \tag{12.29}$$

Residual for Observation *i*

$$y_i - \hat{y}_i \tag{12.30}$$

Multiple Regression Model

$$y = \beta_0 + \beta_1 x_1 + \beta_2 x_2 + \cdots + \beta_p x_p + \epsilon \tag{12.32}$$

Multiple Regression Equation

$$E(y) = \beta_0 + \beta_1 x_1 + \beta_2 x_2 + \cdots + \beta_p x_p \tag{12.33}$$

Estimated Multiple Regression Equation

$$\hat{y} = b_0 + b_1 x_1 + b_2 x_2 + \cdots + b_p x_p \tag{12.34}$$

··/ /··············

SUPPLEMENTARY EXERCISES

54. The data in the following table show the number of shares selling (millions) and the expected price (average of projected low price and projected high price) for ten selected initial public stock offerings (*USA Today*, November 17, 1997).

IPO

Company	Shares Selling	Expected Price ($)
American Physician	5.0	15
Apex Silver Mines	9.0	14
Dan River	6.7	15
Franchise Mortgage	8.75	17
Gene Logic	3.0	11
International Home Foods	13.6	19
PRT Group	4.6	13
Rayovac	6.7	14
RealNetworks	3.0	10
Software AG Systems	7.7	13

a. Develop an estimated regression equation with the number of shares selling as the independent variable and the expected price as the dependent variable.
b. At the .05 level of significance, is there a significant relationship between the two variables?
c. Did the estimated regression equation provide a good fit? Explain.
d. Use the estimated regression equation to estimate the expected price for a firm considering an initial public offering of 6 million shares.

55. The law in Hamilton County, Ohio, requires the publication of delinquent property tax information. The county publication lists the name of the property owner, the property valuation, and the amount of taxes, assessments, and interest, and penalties due. The property valuation and the amount of taxes due for a sample of 10 delinquent properties are shown as follow (*Delinquent Land Tax, Hamilton County,* November 17, 1994). The property valuation is in thousands of dollars.

Property Valuation ($1000s)	Amount Due ($)
18.8	445
24.4	539
20.4	1212
35.8	2237
14.8	479
40.4	1181
49.0	4187
14.5	409
37.3	1002
54.7	2062

a. Develop the estimated regression equation that could be used to estimate the amount of taxes due given the property valuation.
b. Use the estimated regression equation to estimate the taxes due for a property located on Red Bank Road. The valuation of the property is $42,400.
c. Do you believe the estimated regression equation would provide a good prediction of the amount of tax due? Use r^2 to support your answer.

56. *Value Line* (February 24, 1995) reported that the market beta for Woolworth Corporation is 1.25. Market betas for individual stocks are determined by simple linear regression. For each stock, the dependent variable is its quarterly percentage return (capital appreciation plus dividends) minus the percentage return that could be obtained from a risk-free investment (the Treasury Bill rate is used as the risk-free rate). The independent variable is the quarterly percentage return (capital appreciation plus dividends) for the stock market (S&P500) minus the percentage return from a risk-free investment. An estimated regression equation is developed with quar-

terly data; the market beta for the stock is the slope of the estimated regression equation (b_1). The value of the market beta is often interpreted as a measure of the risk associated with the stock. Market betas greater than 1 indicate that the stock is more volatile than the market average; market betas less than 1 indicate that the stock is less volatile than the market average. The differences between the percentage return and the risk-free return for 10 quarters for the S&P 500 and IBM are shown here.

S&P 500	IBM
1.2	-0.7
-2.5	-2.0
-3.0	-5.5
2.0	4.7
5.0	1.8
1.2	4.1
3.0	2.6
-1.0	2.0
.5	-1.3
2.5	5.5

a. Develop an estimated regression equation that can be used to determine the market beta for IBM. What is IBM's market beta?
b. Test for a significant relationship at the .05 level of significance.
c. Did the estimated regression equation provide a good fit? Explain.
d. Use the market betas of Woolworth and IBM to compare the risk associated with the two stocks.

57. In a manufacturing process the assembly line speed (feet per minute) was thought to affect the number of defective parts found during the inspection process. To test this theory, managers devised a situation in which the same batch of parts was inspected visually at a variety of line speeds. The table following lists the collected data.

Line Speed	Number of Defective Parts Found
20	21
20	19
40	15
30	16
60	14
40	17

a. Develop the estimated regression equation that relates line speed to the number of defective parts found.
b. At a .05 level of significance, determine whether line speed and number of defective parts found are related.
c. Did the estimated regression equation provide a good fit to the data?
d. Develop a 95% confidence interval to predict the mean number of defective parts for a line speed of 50 feet per minute.

58. A sociologist was hired by a large city hospital to investigate the relationship between the number of unauthorized days that employees are absent per year and the distance (miles) between home and work for the employees. A sample of 10 employees was chosen, and the following data were collected.

Distance to Work	Number of Days Absent
1	8
3	5
4	8
6	7
8	6
10	3
12	5
14	2
14	4
18	2

a. Develop a scatter diagram for these data. Does a linear relationship appear reasonable? Explain.
b. Develop the least squares estimated regression equation.
c. Is there a significant relationship between the two variables? Use $\alpha = .05$.
d. Did the estimated regression equation provide a good fit? Explain.
e. Use the estimated regression equation developed in part (b) to develop a 95% confidence interval estimate of the expected number of days absent for employees living five miles from the company.

59. The Transactional Records Access Clearinghouse at Syracuse University reported data showing the odds of an Internal Revenue Service audit. The following table shows the average adjusted gross income reported and the percent of the returns that were audited for 20 selected IRS districts (*The Wall Street Journal Almanac 1998*).

IRSAudit

District	Adjusted Gross Income	Percent Audited
Los Angeles	$36,664	1.3
Sacramento	38,845	1.1
Atlanta	34,886	1.1
Boise	32,512	1.1
Dallas	34,531	1.0
Providence	35,995	1.0
San Jose	37,799	0.9
Cheyenne	33,876	0.9
Fargo	30,513	0.9
New Orleans	30,174	0.9
Oklahoma City	30,060	0.8
Houston	37,153	0.8
Portland	34,918	0.7
Phoenix	33,291	0.7
Augusta	31,504	0.7
Albuquerque	29,199	0.6
Greensboro	33,072	0.6
Columbia	30,859	0.5
Nashville	32,566	0.5
Buffalo	34,296	0.5

a. Develop the estimated regression equation that could be used to predict the percent audited given the average adjusted gross income reported.
b. At the .05 level of significance, determine whether the adjusted gross income and the percent audited are related.

c. Did the estimated regression equation provide a good fit? Explain.
d. Use the estimated regression equation developed in part (a) to calculate a 95% confidence interval estimate of the expected percent audited for districts with an average adjusted gross income of $35,000.

60. The admissions officer for Clearwater College developed the following estimated regression equation relating the final college GPA to the student's SAT mathematics score and high school GPA.

$$\hat{y} = -1.41 + .0235x_1 + .00486x_2$$

where

$$x_1 = \text{high school grade point average}$$
$$x_2 = \text{SAT mathematics score}$$
$$y = \text{final college grade point average}$$

a. Interpret the coefficients in this estimated regression equation.
b. Estimate the final college GPA for a student who has a high school average of 84 and a score of 540 on the SAT mathematics test.

61. The personnel director for Electronics Associates developed the following estimated regression equation relating an employee's score on a job satisfaction test to his or her length of service and wage rate.

$$\hat{y} = 14.4 - 8.69x_1 + 13.5x_2$$

where

$$x_1 = \text{length of service (years)}$$
$$x_2 = \text{wage rate (dollars)}$$
$$y = \text{job satisfaction test score (higher scores indicate more job satisfaction)}$$

a. Interpret the coefficients in this estimated regression equation.
b. Develop an estimate of the job satisfaction test score for an employee who has four years of service and makes $6.50 per hour.

62. A partial computer output from a regression analysis follows.

```
The regression equation is
Y = 8.103 + 7.602 X1 + 3.111 X2

Predictor        Coef           Stdev          T
Constant         _____         2.667          _____
X1               _____         2.105          _____
X2               _____         0.613          _____

S = 3.35      R-sq = 92.3%      R-sq (adj) = _____%

Analysis of Variance

SOURCE           DF             SS             MS        F
Regression       _____          1612           _____    _____
Residual Error   12             _____         _____
Total            _____          _____
```

    a. Compute the appropriate *t*-ratios.
    b. Test for the significance of β_1 and β_2 at $\alpha = .05$.
    c. Compute the entries in the DF, SS, and MS = SS/DF columns.
    d. Compute R_a^2.

63. Recall that in Exercise 60, the admissions officer for Clearwater College developed the following estimated regression equation relating final college GPA to the student's SAT mathematics score and high school GPA.

$$\hat{y} = -1.41 + .0235x_1 + .00486x_2$$

where

$$x_1 = \text{high school grade point average}$$
$$x_2 = \text{SAT mathematics score}$$
$$y = \text{final college grade point average}$$

A portion of the Minitab computer output follows.

```
The regression equation is
Y = -1.41 + .0235 X1 + .00486 X2

Predictor              Coef            Stdev              T
Constant             -1.4053          0.4848          _____
X1                    0.023467        0.008666        _____
X2                    _____         0.001077        _____

S = 0.1298     R-sq = _____     R-sq (adj) = _____

Analysis of Variance

SOURCE              DF              SS            MS         F
Regression        _____          1.76209       _____      _____
Residual Error    _____          _____       _____
Total               9            1.88000
```

    a. Complete the missing entries in this output.
    b. Compute *F* and test at a .05 level of significance to see whether a significant relationship is present.
    c. Did the estimated regression equation provide a good fit to the data? Explain.
    d. Use the *t* test and $\alpha = .05$ to test $H_0: \beta_1 = 0$ and $H_0: \beta_2 = 0$.

64. Recall that in Exercise 61 the personnel director for Electronics Associates developed the following estimated regression equation relating an employee's score on a job satisfaction test to length of service and wage rate.

$$\hat{y} = 14.4 - 8.69x_1 + 13.5x_2$$

where

$$x_1 = \text{length of service (years)}$$
$$x_2 = \text{wage rate (dollars)}$$
$$y = \text{job satisfaction test score (higher}$$
$$\text{scores indicate more job satisfaction)}$$

A portion of the Minitab computer output follows.

```
The regression equation is
Y = 14.4 - 8.69 X1 + 13.52 X2

Predictor              Coef           Stdev              T
Constant             14.448          8.191            1.76
X1                   _____         1.555           _____
X2                   13.517          2.085           _____


S = 3.773      R-sq = _____%  R-sq (adj) = _____%


Analysis of Variance

SOURCE                DF             SS             MS            F
Regression            2           _____        _____       _____
Residual Error     _____        71.17          _____
Total                 7           720.0
```

a. Complete the missing entries in this output.
b. Compute F and test using $\alpha = .05$ to see whether a significant relationship is present.
c. Did the estimated regression equation provide a good fit to the data? Explain.
d. Use the t test and $\alpha = .05$ to test H_0: $B_1 = 0$ and H_0: $\beta_2 = 0$.

65. A sample of 25 computer hardware companies taken from *Stock Investor Pro* provided the following data on the price per share, book value per share, and the return on equity per share for each (*Stock Investor Pro,* American Association of Individual Investors, August 21, 1997).

Computer

Company	Price per Share	Book Value per Share	Return on Equity per Share (%)
Amdahl Corporation	12.31	4.94	−49.7
Apple Computer, Inc.	21.75	9.46	−71.8
Auspex Systems, Inc.	11	4.95	17.2
Capital Associates	3.25	4.33	5.1
Compaq Computer Corp.	65.5	9.58	20.8
Data General Corporation	35.94	8.46	13.3
Dell Computer Corporation	82.06	2.33	74.5
Digi International	15	7.35	−11.9
Digital Equipment Corp.	43	22.4	−12.9
En Pointe Technologies	14.25	4.11	18.8
Equitrac Corporation	16.25	6.83	10.7
Franklin Electronic Pbls.	12.88	9.13	9
Gateway 2000, Inc.	39.13	6.07	28.8
Hewlett-Packard Company	61.5	14.14	18.7
IBM	101.38	20.12	29.9
Ingram Micro, Inc.	28.75	6.35	15.1
Maxwell Technologies, Inc.	30.5	3.78	11.8
MicroAge, Inc.	27.19	12.59	9.8
Micron Electronics, Inc.	16.31	3.64	28.3
Network Computing Devices	11.88	3.56	4
Pomeroy Computer Resources	33	10.03	16.5
Sequent Computer Systems	28.19	10.64	3.3

Company	Price per Share	Book Value per Share	Return on Equity per Share (%)
Silicon Graphics, Inc.	27.44	9.12	−4.3
Southern Electronics Corp.	15.13	6.15	16.1
Stratus Computer, Inc.	55.5	22.38	11.1
Sun Microsystems, Inc.	48	6.4	26.2
Tandem Computers, Inc.	34.24	9.49	8.7
Tech Data Corporation	38.94	10.25	14.3
Unisys Corporation	11.31	0.68	1.6
Vitech America, Inc.	14.63	3.48	24.3

a. Develop an estimated regression equation that can be used to predict the price per share given the book value per share. At the .05 level of significance, test for a significant relationship.

b. Did the estimated regression equation developed in part (a) provide a good fit to the data? Explain.

c. Develop an estimated regression equation that can be used to predict the price per share given the book value per share and the return on equity per share. At the .05 level of significance, test for overall significance.

66. Following are data on price, curb weight, horsepower, time to go from 0 to 60 miles per hour, and the speed at ¼ mile for 16 sports and GT cars (*1998 Road & Track Sports & GT Cars*).

Auto3

Sports & GT Car	Price ($1000s)	Curb Weight (lbs.)	Horse-power	Zero to 60 (seconds)	Speed at ¼ mile (mph)
Acura Integra Type R	25.035	2577	195	7.0	90.7
Acura NSX-T	93.758	3066	290	5.0	108
BMW Z3 2.8	40.900	2844	189	6.6	93.2
Chevrolet Camaro Z28	24.865	3439	305	5.4	103.2
Chevrolet Corvette Convertible	50.144	3246	345	5.2	102.1
Dodge Viper RT/10	69.742	3319	450	4.4	116.2
Ford Mustang GT	23.200	3227	225	6.8	91.7
Honda Prelude Type SH	26.382	3042	195	7.7	89.7
Mercedes-Benz CLK320	44.988	3240	215	7.2	93
Mercedes-Benz SLK230	42.762	3025	185	6.6	92.3
Mitsubishi 3000GT VR-4	47.518	3737	320	5.7	99
Nissan 240SX SE	25.066	2862	155	9.1	84.6
Pontiac Firebird Trans Am	27.770	3455	305	5.4	103.2
Porsche Boxster	45.560	2822	201	6.1	93.2
Toyota Supra Turbo	40.989	3505	320	5.3	105
Volvo C70	41.120	3285	236	6.3	97

a. Develop an estimated regression equation with price, curb weight, horsepower, and time to go from zero to 60 mph as four independent variables to predict the speed at ¼ mile.

b. Use the F test to determine the significance of the regression results. At a .05 level of significance, what is your conclusion?

c. Use the t test to determine the significance of each independent variable. At a .05 level of significance, what is your conclusion?

d. Delete any independent variable that is not significant and provide your recommended estimated regression equation.

Case Problem 1   SPENDING AND STUDENT ACHIEVEMENT

Is the educational achievement level of students related to how much the state in which they reside spends on education? In many communities this important question is being asked by taxpayers who are being asked by their school districts to increase the amount of tax revenue spent on education. In this case, you will be asked to analyze data on spending and achievement scores in order to determine whether any relationship is evident between spending and student achievement in the public schools.

The federal government's National Assessment of Educational Progress (NAEP) program is frequently used to measure the educational achievement of students. Table 12.11 shows the

NAEP

Table 12.11	SPENDING PER PUPIL AND COMPOSITE SCORES FOR STATES PARTICIPATING IN THE NAEP PROGRAM

State	Spending per Pupil ($)	Composite Score
Louisiana	4049	581
Mississippi	3423	582
California	4917	580
Hawaii	5532	580
South Carolina	4304	603
Alabama	3777	604
Georgia	4663	611
Florida	4934	611
New Mexico	4097	614
Arkansas	4060	615
Delaware	6208	615
Tennesse	3800	618
Arizona	4041	618
West Virginia	5247	625
Maryland	6100	625
Kentucky	5020	626
Texas	4520	627
New York	8162	628
North Carolina	4521	629
Rhode Island	6554	638
Washington	5338	639
Missouri	4483	641
Colorado	4772	644
Indiana	5128	649
Utah	3280	650
Wyoming	5515	657
Connecticut	7629	657
Massachusetts	6413	658
Nebraska	5410	660
Minnesota	5477	661
Iowa	5060	665
Montana	4985	667
Wisconsin	6055	667
North Dakota	4374	671
Maine	5561	675

total current spending per pupil per year, and the composite NAEP test score for 35 states that participated in the NAEP program. These data are available on the data disk in the file named NAEP. The composite score is the sum of the math, science, and reading scores on the 1996 (1994 for reading) NAEP test. Pupils tested are in grade 8, except for reading, which is given to fourth-graders only. The maximum possible score is 1300. Table 12.12 shows the spending per pupil for 14 states that did not participate in relevant NAEP surveys. These data were reported in an article on spending and achievement level appearing in *Forbes* (November 3, 1997).

Managerial Report

1. Develop numerical and graphical summaries of the data.
2. Use regression analysis to investigate the relationship between the amount spent per pupil and the composite score on the NAEP test. Discuss your findings.
3. Do you think that the estimated regression equation developed for these data could be used to estimate the composite scores for the states that did not participate in the NAEP program?
4. Suppose that you only considered states that spend at least $4000 per pupil but not more than $6000 per pupil. For these states, does the relationship between the two variables appear to be any different from the complete data set? Discuss the results of your findings and whether you think deleting states spending less than $4000 per year and more than $6000 per pupil is appropriate.
5. Develop estimates of the composite scores for the states that did not participate in the NAEP program.
6. Based upon your analyses, do you think that the educational achievement level of students is related to how much the state spends on education?

Table 12.12 SPENDING PER PUPIL AND FOR STATES NOT PARTICIPATING IN THE NAEP PROGRAM

State	Spending per Pupil ($)
Idaho	3602
South Dakota	4067
Oklahoma	4265
Nevada	4658
Kansas	5164
Illinois	5297
New Hampshire	5387
Ohio	5438
Oregon	5588
Vermont	6269
Michigan	6391
Pennsylvania	6579
Alaska	7890

Case Problem 2   U.S. DEPARTMENT OF TRANSPORTATION

As part of a study on transportation safety, the U.S. Department of Transportation collected data on the number of fatal accidents per 1000 licenses and the percentage of licensed drivers under the age of 21 in a sample of 42 cities. Data collected over a one-year period follow. These data are available on the data disk in the file named Safety.

Safety

Percent Under 21	Fatal Accidents per 1000 Licenses	Percent Under 21	Fatal Accidents per 1000 Licenses
13	2.962	17	4.100
12	0.708	8	2.190
8	0.885	16	3.623
12	1.652	15	2.623
11	2.091	9	0.835
17	2.627	8	0.820
18	3.830	14	2.890
8	0.368	8	1.267
13	1.142	15	3.224
8	0.645	10	1.014
9	1.028	10	0.493
16	2.801	14	1.443
12	1.405	18	3.614
9	1.433	10	1.926
10	0.039	14	1.643
9	0.338	16	2.943
11	1.849	12	1.913
12	2.246	15	2.814
14	2.855	13	2.634
14	2.352	9	0.926
11	1.294	17	3.256

Managerial Report

1. Develop numerical and graphical summaries of the data.
2. Use regression analysis to investigate the relationship between the number of fatal accidents and the percentage of drivers under the age of 21. Discuss your findings.
3. What conclusion and/or recommendations can you derive from your analysis?

Appendix 12.1   REGRESSION ANALYSIS WITH MINITAB

In Section 12.7 we discussed the computer solution of regression problems by showing Minitab's output for the Armand's Pizza Parlors problem. In this appendix, we describe the steps required to generate the Minitab computer solution. First, the data must be entered in a Minitab worksheet. Student population data were entered in column C1 and quarterly sales data were entered in column C2. The variable names POP and SALES were entered as the column headings on the worksheet. In subsequent steps, we could refer to the data by using the variable names POP and SALES or the column indicators C1 and C2. The following steps describe how to use Minitab to produce the regression results.

Step 1. Select the **Stat** pull-down menu
Step 2. Select the **Regression** pull-down menu
Step 3. Choose the **Regresssion** option
Step 4. When the Regression dialog box appears:
Enter SALES in the **Response** box
Enter POP in the **Predictors** box
Select **OK** to obtain the regression analysis

The summary output is shown in Figure 12.10. The Minitab regression dialog box provides additional output information that can be obtained by selecting the desired options. For example, residuals, standardized residuals, high leverage data points, and the correlation matrix can be obtained in that way.

Appendix 12.2   REGRESSION ANALYSIS WITH EXCEL

Let us demonstrate regression analysis with spreadsheets by using Excel to provide the computations for the Armand's Pizza Parlors problem. Figure 12.17 shows that we have entered Armand's data in columns A and B of the spreadsheet. Student population data are in cells 2 to 11 of column A and sales data are in cells 2 to 11 of column B. The following steps describe how to use Excel to produce the regression results.

Step 1. Select the **Tools** pull-down menu
Step 2. Choose the **Data Analysis** option
Step 3. When the Data Analysis dialog box appears:
Choose **Regression**
Select **OK**
Step 4. When the Regression dialog box appears:
Enter B1:B11 in the **Input Y Range** box
Enter A1:A11 in the **Input X Range** box
Select **Labels**
Select **Output Range**
Enter A14 in the **Output Range** box
(Any upper-left corner cell indicating where the output is to begin may be entered here.)
Select **OK** to begin the regression analysis

The summary output begins with row 14 in Figure 12.17. The Multiple R cell gives the sample correlation coefficient of .9501 as before. The coefficient of determination (90.27%) and the standard error of the estimate (13.829) are also shown as before. The analysis of variance table is next. The p-value under the heading Significance F shows that the null hypothesis H_0: $\beta_1 = 0$ can be rejected, indicating that the relationship between student popu-

Figure 12.17   EXCEL SPREADSHEET SOLUTION TO THE ARMAND'S PIZZA PARLORS PROBLEM

	A	B	C	D	E	F	G
1	Population	Sales					
2	2	58					
3	6	105					
4	8	88					
5	8	118					
6	12	117					
7	16	137					
8	20	157					
9	20	169					
10	22	149					
11	26	202					
12							
13							
14	SUMMARY OUTPUT						
15							
16	*Regression Statistics*						
17	Multiple R	0.9501					
18	R Square	0.9027					
19	Adjusted R Square	0.8906					
20	Standard Error	13.829					
21	Observations	10					
22							
23	ANOVA						
24		*df*	*SS*	*MS*	*F*	*Significance F*	
25	Regression	1	14200	14200	74.25	0.000	
26	Residual	8	1530	191.25			
27	Total	9	15730				
28							
29		*Coefficients*	*Standard Error*	*t Stat*	*P-value*	*Lower 95%*	*Upper 95%*
30	Intercept	60	9.226	6.5	0.000	38.72	81.28
31	Population	5	0.5803	8.62	0.000	3.66	6.34

lation and sales is significant. The regression coefficients of 60 for the intercept and 5 for the independent variable population are significant. They show that the estimated regression equation is $\hat{y} = 60 + 5x$. The t statistic and the p-value for the t test show that the relationship is significant. Finally, the Lower 95% and Upper 95% cells provide the 95% confidence interval estimates for the regression model parameters β_0 and β_1. For example, using 95% confidence, β_0 is between 38.72 and 81.28 and β_1 is between 3.66 and 6.34.

13

STATISTICAL METHODS FOR QUALITY CONTROL

DOW CHEMICAL*
Freeport, Texas

Dow Chemical, Texas Operations, began in 1940 when The Dow Chemical Company purchased 800 acres of Texas land on the Gulf Coast to build a magnesium production facility. That original site has expanded to cover more than 5000 acres and is now one of the largest petrochemical complexes in the world. Among the products from Texas Operations are magnesium, styrene, plastics, adhesives, solvent, glycol, and chlorine. Some products are made solely for use in other processes, but many end up as essential ingredients in products such as pharmaceuticals, toothpastes, dog food, water hoses, ice chests, milk cartons, garbage bags, shampoos, and furniture.

Dow's Texas Operations produces more than 30% of the world's magnesium, an extremely lightweight metal used in products ranging from tennis rackets to suitcases to "mag" wheels. The Magnesium Department was the first group in Texas Operations to train its technical people and managers in the use of statistical quality control. Some of the earliest successful applications of statistical quality control were in chemical processing.

In one application involving the operation of a drier, samples of the output were taken at periodic intervals; the average value for each sample was computed and recorded on a chart called an $\bar{x}$ chart. Such a chart enabled Dow analysts to monitor trends in the output that might indicate the process

Statistical quality control has enabled Dow Chemical to improve its processing methods and output. Photo courtesy of Dow Chemical U.S.A.

was not operating correctly. In one instance, analysts began to observe values for the sample mean that were not indicative of a process operating within its design limits. On further examination of the control chart and the operation itself, the analysts found that the variation could be traced to problems involving one operator. The $\bar{x}$ chart recorded after that operator was retrained showed a significant improvement in the process quality.

Dow Chemical has achieved quality improvements everywhere statistical quality control has been used. Documented savings of several hundred thousand dollars per year have been realized, and new applications are continually being discovered.

In this chapter we will show how an $\bar{x}$ chart such as the one used by Dow Chemical can be developed. Such charts are a part of statistical quality control known as statistical process control. We will also discuss methods of quality control for situations in which a decision to accept or reject a group of items is based on a sample.

---

*The authors are indebted to Clifford B. Wilson, Magnesium Technical Manager, The Dow Chemical Company, for providing this Statistics in Practice.

The American Society for Quality Control (ASQC) defines *quality* as "the totality of features and characteristics of a product or service that bears on its ability to satisfy given needs." In other words, quality measures how well a product or service meets customer needs. Organizations recognize that to be competitive in today's global economy, they must strive for high levels of quality. As a result, they have increased the emphasis on methods for monitoring and maintaining quality.

Quality assurance refers to the entire system of policies, procedures, and guidelines established by an organization to achieve and maintain quality. Quality assurance consists of two principal functions: quality engineering and quality control. The objective of *quality engineering* is to include quality in the design of products and processes and to identify potential quality problems prior to production. *Quality control* consists of making a series of inspections and measurements to determine whether quality standards are being met. If quality standards are not being met, corrective and/or preventive action can be taken to achieve and maintain conformance. As we will show in this chapter, statistical techniques are extremely useful in quality control.

Traditional manufacturing approaches to quality control have been found to be less than satisfactory and are being replaced by improved managerial tools and techniques. Ironically, it was two U.S. consultants, Dr. W. Edwards Deming and Dr. Joseph Juran, who helped educate the Japanese in quality management.

Although quality is everybody's job, Deming stressed that quality must be led by managers. He developed a list of 14 points that he believed are the key responsibilities of managers. For instance, Deming stated that managers must cease dependence on mass inspection; must end the practice of awarding business solely on the basis of price; must seek continual improvement in all production processes and services; must foster a team-oriented environment; and must eliminate numerical goals, slogans, and work standards that prescribe numerical quotas. Perhaps most important, managers must create a work environment in which a commitment to quality and productivity is maintained at all times.

In 1987, the U.S. Congress enacted Public Law 107, the Malcolm Baldrige National Quality Improvement Act. The Baldrige Award is given annually to U.S. firms that excel in quality. This award, along with the perspectives of individuals such as Dr. Deming and Dr. Juran, has helped top managers recognize that improving service quality and product quality is the most critical challenge facing their companies. Winners of the Malcolm Baldrige Award include Motorola, IBM, Xerox, and Federal Express. In this chapter we present two statistical methods used in quality control. The first method, *statistical process control,* uses graphical displays known as *control charts* to monitor a production process; the goal is to determine whether the process can be continued or whether it should be adjusted to achieve a desired quality level. The second method, *acceptance sampling,* is used in situations where a decision to accept or reject a group of items must be based on the quality found in a sample.

> After World War II, Dr. W. Edwards Deming became a consultant to Japanese industry; he is credited with being the person who convinced top managers in Japan to use the methods of statistical quality control.

13.1 STATISTICAL PROCESS CONTROL

> Continual improvement is one of the most important concepts of the total quality management movement. The most important use of a control chart is in improving the process.

In this section we consider quality control procedures for a production process whereby goods are manufactured continuously. On the basis of sampling and inspection of production output, a decision will be made to either continue the production process or adjust it to bring the items or goods being produced up to acceptable quality standards.

Despite high standards of quality in manufacturing and production operations, machine tools will invariably wear out, vibrations will throw machine settings out of adjustment, purchased materials will be defective, and human operators will make mistakes. Any or all of these factors can result in poor quality output. Fortunately, procedures are available for monitoring production output so that poor quality can be detected early and the production process can be adjusted or corrected.

If the variation in the quality of the production output is due to *assignable causes* such as tools wearing out, incorrect machine settings, poor quality raw materials, or operator error, the process should be adjusted or corrected as soon as possible. Alternatively, if the variation is due to what are called *common causes*—that is, randomly occurring variations in materials, temperature, humidity, and so on, which the manufacturer cannot possibly control—the process does not need to be adjusted. The main objective of statistical process control is to determine whether variations in output are due to assignable causes or common causes.

Whenever assignable causes are detected, we conclude that the process is *out of control.* In that case, corrective action will be taken to bring the process back to an acceptable level of quality. However, if the variation in the output of a production process is due only to common causes, we conclude that the process is *in statistical control,* or simply *in control;* in such cases, no changes or adjustments are necessary.

The statistical procedures for process control are based on the hypothesis-testing methodology presented in Chapter 9. The null hypothesis H_0 is formulated in terms of the production process being in control. The alternative hypothesis H_a is formulated in terms of the production process being out of control. Table 13.1 shows that correct decisions to continue an in-control process and adjust an out-of-control process are possible. However, as with other hypothesis-testing procedures, both a Type I error (adjusting an in-control process) and a Type II error (allowing an out-of-control process to continue) are also possible.

Control Charts

A *control chart* provides a basis for deciding whether the variation in the output is due to common causes (in control) or assignable causes (out of control). Whenever an out-of-control situation is detected, adjustments and/or other corrective action will be taken to bring the process back into control.

Control charts can be classified by the type of data they contain. An $\bar{x}$ chart is used if the quality of the output is measured in terms of a variable such as length, weight, temperature, and so on. In that case, the decision to continue or to adjust the production process will be based on the mean value found in a sample of the output. To introduce some of the concepts common to all control charts, let us consider some specific features of an $\bar{x}$ chart.

Figure 13.1 shows the general structure of an $\bar{x}$ chart. The center line of the chart corresponds to the mean of the process when the process is in control. The vertical line

Control charts are closely related to hypothesis testing procedure discussed earlier in this text. In essence, control charts provide an ongoing test of the hypothesis that the process is in control.

Control charts that are based on data that can be measured on a continuous scale are called variables control charts. The $\bar{x}$ chart is a variables control chart.

Table 13.1   THE OUTCOMES OF STATISTICAL PROCESS CONTROL

		State of Production Process	
		H_0 True Process in Control	H_0 False Process Out of Control
Decision	**Continue Process**	Correct decision	Type II error (allowing an out-of-control process to continue)
	Adjust Process	Type I error (adjusting an in-control process)	Correct decision

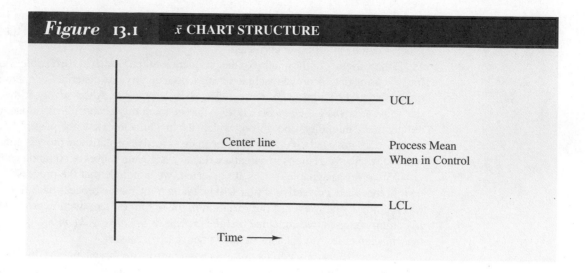

Figure 13.1   x̄ CHART STRUCTURE

identifies the scale of measurement for the variable of interest. Each time a sample is taken from the production process, a value of the sample mean $\bar{x}$ is computed and a data point showing the value of $\bar{x}$ is plotted on the control chart.

The two lines labeled UCL and LCL are important in determining whether the process is in control or out of control. The lines are called the *upper control limit* and the *lower control limit,* respectively. They are chosen so that when the process is in control, there will be a high probability that the value of $\bar{x}$ will be between the two control limits. Values outside the control limits provide strong statistical evidence that the process is out of control and corrective action should be taken.

Over time, more and more data points will be added to the control chart. The order of the data points will be from left to right as the process is sampled. In essence, every time a point is plotted on the control chart, we are carrying out a hypothesis test to determine whether the process is in control.

In addition to the $\bar{x}$ chart, other control charts can be used to monitor the range of the measurements in the sample (*R* chart), the proportion defective in the sample (*p* chart), and the number of defective items in the sample (*np* chart). In each case, the general structure of the control chart follows the format of the $\bar{x}$ chart in Figure 13.1. The major difference among the charts is the measurement scale used; for instance, in a *p* chart the measurement scale denotes the proportion of defective items in the sample instead of the sample mean. In the following discussion, we will illustrate the construction and use of the $\bar{x}$ chart, *R* chart, *p* chart, and *np* chart.

x̄ Chart: Process Mean and Standard Deviation Known

To illustrate the construction of an $\bar{x}$ chart, let us consider the situation at KJW Packaging. This company operates a production line where cartons of cereal are filled. Suppose KJW knows that when the process is operating correctly—and hence the system is in control— the mean filling weight is $\mu = 16.05$ ounces, and the process standard deviation is $\sigma = .10$ ounces. In addition, assume the filling weights are normally distributed. This distribution is shown in Figure 13.2.

The sampling distribution of $\bar{x}$, as presented in Chapter 7, can be used to determine the variation that can be expected in $\bar{x}$ values for a process that is in control. To show how it is done, let us first briefly review the properties of the sampling distribution of $\bar{x}$. First, recall that the expected value or mean of $\bar{x}$ is equal to μ, the mean filling weight when the pro-

Figure 13.2   DISTRIBUTION OF CEREAL-CARTON FILLING WEIGHTS

$\sigma = .10$

16.05

Process mean μ

duction line is in control. For samples of size n, the formula for the standard deviation of $\bar{x}$, called the standard error of the mean, is

$$\sigma_{\bar{x}} = \frac{\sigma}{\sqrt{n}} \qquad\qquad (13.1)$$

In addition, because the filling weights are normally distributed, the sampling distribution of $\bar{x}$ is normal for any sample size. Thus, the sampling distribution of $\bar{x}$ is a normal probability distribution with mean μ and standard deviation $\sigma_{\bar{x}}$. This distribution is shown in Figure 13.3.

The sampling distribution of $\bar{x}$ is used to determine what values of $\bar{x}$ are reasonable if the process is in control. The general practice in quality control is to define as reasonable any value of $\bar{x}$ that is within 3 standard deviations above or below the mean value. Recall from the study of the normal probability distribution that approximately 99.7% of the values of a normally distributed random variable are within ± 3 standard deviations of its mean value. Thus, if a value of $\bar{x}$ is within the interval $\mu - 3\sigma_{\bar{x}}$ to $\mu + 3\sigma_{\bar{x}}$, we will assume that the process is in control. In summary, then, the control limits for an $\bar{x}$ chart are as follows.

Control Limits for an $\bar{x}$ Chart: Process Mean and Standard Deviation Known

$$\text{UCL} = \mu + 3\sigma_{\bar{x}} \qquad\qquad (13.2)$$
$$\text{LCL} = \mu - 3\sigma_{\bar{x}} \qquad\qquad (13.3)$$

Reconsider the KJW Packaging example with the process distribution of filling weights shown in Figure 13.2 and the sampling distribution of $\bar{x}$ shown in Figure 13.3. Assume that a quality control inspector periodically samples six cartons and uses the sample mean filling weight to determine whether the process is in control or out of control. Using (13.1), we find that the standard error of the mean is $\sigma_{\bar{x}} = \sigma/\sqrt{n} = .10/\sqrt{6} = .04$. Thus, with the process mean at 16.05, the control limits are UCL $= 16.05 + 3(.04) = 16.17$ and

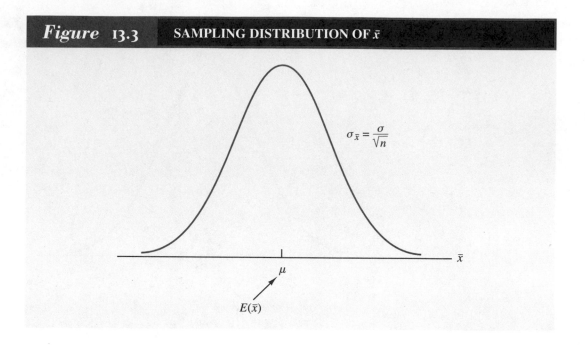

Figure 13.3   SAMPLING DISTRIBUTION OF $\bar{x}$

LCL = 16.05 − 3(.04) = 15.93. Figure 13.4 is the control chart with the results of 10 samples taken over a 10-hour period. For ease of reading, the sample numbers 1 through 10 are listed below the chart.

Note that the mean for the fifth sample in Figure 13.4 shows that the process is out of control. In other words, the fifth sample mean is below the LCL indicating that assignable causes of output variation are present and that underfilling is occurring. As a result, corrective action was taken at this point to bring the process back into control. The fact that the remaining points on the $\bar{x}$ chart are within the upper and lower control limits indicates that the corrective action was successful.

$\bar{x}$ Chart: Process Mean and Standard Deviation Unknown

In the KJW Packaging example, we showed how an $\bar{x}$ chart can be developed when the mean and standard deviation of the process are known. In most situations, those values must be estimated by using samples that are selected from the process when it is known to be operating in control. For instance, KJW might select a random sample of five boxes each morning and five boxes each afternoon for 10 days of in-control operation. For each subgroup, or sample, the mean and standard deviation of the sample are computed. The overall averages of both the sample means and the sample standard deviations are used to construct control charts for both the process mean and the process standard deviation.

It is important to maintain control over both the mean and the variability of a process.

In practice, it is more common to monitor the variability of the process by using the range instead of the standard deviation because the range is easier to compute. In addition to providing good estimates of the process standard deviation, the range can be used to construct upper and lower control limits for the $\bar{x}$ chart with little computational effort. To illustrate, let us consider the problem facing Jensen Computer Supplies, Inc.

Jensen Computer Supplies (JCS) manufactures 3.5-inch-diameter floppy disks that are used in personal computers. For example, random samples of five disks could be taken during the first hour of operation, during the second hour of operation, and so on, until 20 samples have been selected. Table 13.2 lists the data, including the mean $\bar{x}_j$ and range R_j for each of the samples.

Figure 13.4 $\bar{x}$ CHART FOR THE CEREAL-CARTON FILLING PROCESS

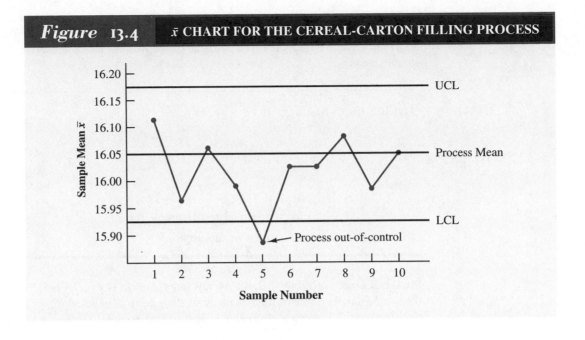

Table 13.2   DATA FOR THE JENSEN COMPUTER SUPPLIES PROBLEM

Jensen

Sample Number	Observations					Sample Mean $\bar{x}_j$	Sample Range R_j
1	3.5056	3.5086	3.5144	3.5009	3.5030	3.5065	.0135
2	3.4882	3.5085	3.4884	3.5250	3.5031	3.5026	.0368
3	3.4897	3.4898	3.4995	3.5130	3.4969	3.4978	.0233
4	3.5153	3.5120	3.4989	3.4900	3.4837	3.5000	.0316
5	3.5059	3.5113	3.5011	3.4773	3.4801	3.4951	.0340
6	3.4977	3.4961	3.5050	3.5014	3.5060	3.5012	.0099
7	3.4910	3.4913	3.4976	3.4831	3.5044	3.4935	.0213
8	3.4991	3.4853	3.4830	3.5083	3.5094	3.4970	.0264
9	3.5099	3.5162	3.5228	3.4958	3.5004	3.5090	.0270
10	3.4880	3.5015	3.5094	3.5102	3.5146	3.5047	.0266
11	3.4881	3.4887	3.5141	3.5175	3.4863	3.4989	.0312
12	3.5043	3.4867	3.4946	3.5018	3.4784	3.4932	.0259
13	3.5043	3.4769	3.4944	3.5014	3.4904	3.4935	.0274
14	3.5004	3.5030	3.5082	3.5045	3.5234	3.5079	.0230
15	3.4846	3.4938	3.5065	3.5089	3.5011	3.4990	.0243
16	3.5145	3.4832	3.5188	3.4935	3.4989	3.5018	.0356
17	3.5004	3.5042	3.4954	3.5020	3.4889	3.4982	.0153
18	3.4959	3.4823	3.4964	3.5082	3.4871	3.4940	.0259
19	3.4878	3.4864	3.4960	3.5070	3.4984	3.4951	.0206
20	3.4969	3.5144	3.5053	3.4985	3.4885	3.5007	.0259

Assume that the diameter of disks produced when the process is in control is a normally distributed random variable with mean μ and standard deviation σ, and that k samples, each of size n, have been selected. The estimate of the process mean μ is given by the overall sample mean.

Overall Sample Mean

$$\bar{\bar{x}} = \frac{\bar{x}_1 + \bar{x}_2 + \cdots + \bar{x}_k}{k} \tag{13.4}$$

where

$$\bar{x}_j = \text{mean of the } j\text{th sample } j = 1, 2, \ldots, k$$
$$k = \text{number of samples}$$

For the JCS data in Table 13.2, the overall sample mean is $\bar{\bar{x}} = 3.4995$. This value will be the center line for the $\bar{x}$ chart. The range of each sample, denoted R_j, is simply the difference between the largest and smallest values in each sample. The average range follows.

Average Range

$$\bar{R} = \frac{R_1 + R_2 + \cdots + R_k}{k} \tag{13.5}$$

where

$$R_j = \text{range of the } j\text{th sample}, j = 1, 2, \ldots, k$$
$$k = \text{number of samples}$$

For the JCS data in Table 13.2, the average range is $\bar{R} = .0253$.

In the preceding section we showed that the upper and lower control limits for the $\bar{x}$ chart are

$$\bar{x} \pm 3\frac{\sigma}{\sqrt{n}} \tag{13.6}$$

Hence, to construct the control limits for the $\bar{x}$ chart, we need to estimate σ, the standard deviation of the process. An estimate of σ can be developed by using the range data.

It can be shown that an estimator of the process standard deviation σ is the average range divided by d_2, a constant that depends on the sample size n. That is,

$$\text{Estimator of } \sigma = \frac{\bar{R}}{d_2} \tag{13.7}$$

The American Society for Testing and Materials Manual on Presentation of Data and Control Chart Analysis provides values for d_2 as shown in Table 9 of Appendix B. For instance, when $n = 5, d_2 = 2.326$, and the estimate of σ is the average range divided by 2.326. If we substitute $\bar{R}/d_2$ for σ in (13.6), we can write the control limits for the $\bar{x}$ chart as

$$\bar{\bar{x}} \pm 3\frac{\bar{R}/d_2}{\sqrt{n}} = \bar{\bar{x}} \pm \frac{3}{d_2\sqrt{n}}\bar{R} = \bar{\bar{x}} \pm A_2\bar{R} \qquad (13.8)$$

Note that $A_2 = 3/(d_2\sqrt{n})$ is a constant that depends only on the sample size. Values for A_2 are provided in Table 9 in Appendix B. For $n = 5, A_2 = .577$; thus, the control limits for the $\bar{x}$ chart are

$$3.4995 \pm (.577)(.0253) = 3.4995 \pm .0146$$

Hence, UCL = 3.514 and LCL = 3.485.

Figure 13.5 shows the $\bar{x}$ chart for the Jensen Computer Supplies problem. We used the data in Table 13.2 and Minitab's control chart routine to construct the chart. The center line is shown at the overall sample mean $\bar{\bar{x}} = 3.499$. The upper control limit (UCL) is 3.514. Minitab uses the notation 3.0SL to indicate the UCL is 3 standard deviations or 3 "sigma limits" (SL) above $\bar{\bar{x}}$. The lower control (LCL) is 3.485, which is -3.0SL or 3 "sigma limits" below $\bar{\bar{x}}$. The $\bar{x}$ chart shows the 20 sample means plotted over time. Because all 20 sample means are within the control limits, the mean of the Jensen manufacturing process shows no indication of being out of control.

R Chart

Let us now consider a range chart (R chart) that can be used to control the variability of a process. To develop the R chart, we need to think of the range of a sample as a random variable with its own mean and standard deviation. The average range $\bar{R}$ provides an estimate of the mean of this random variable. Moreover, it can be shown that an estimate of the standard deviation of the range is

$$\hat{\sigma}_R = d_3\frac{\bar{R}}{d_2} \qquad (13.9)$$

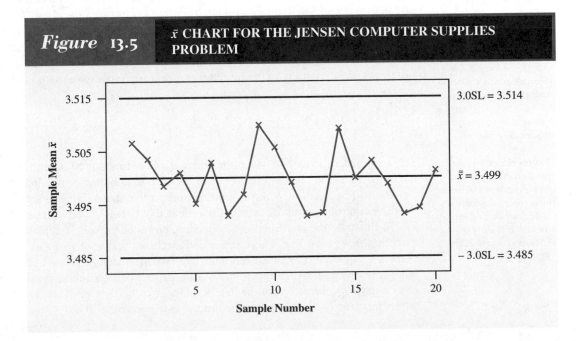

Figure 13.5 $\bar{x}$ CHART FOR THE JENSEN COMPUTER SUPPLIES PROBLEM

where d_2 and d_3 are constants that depend on the sample size; values of d_2 and d_3 are also provided in Table 9 of Appendix B. Thus, the UCL for the R chart is given by

$$\bar{R} + 3\hat{\sigma}_R = \bar{R} + 3d_3\frac{\bar{R}}{d_2} \tag{13.10}$$

and the LCL is

$$\bar{R} - 3\hat{\sigma}_R = \bar{R} - 3d_3\frac{\bar{R}}{d_2} \tag{13.11}$$

If we let

$$D_4 = 1 + 3\frac{d_3}{d_2} \tag{13.12}$$

$$D_3 = 1 - 3\frac{d_3}{d_2} \tag{13.13}$$

we can write the control limits for the R chart as

$$\text{UCL} = \bar{R}D_4 \tag{13.14}$$
$$\text{LCL} = \bar{R}D_3 \tag{13.15}$$

If the R chart indicates that the process is out of control, the $\bar{x}$ chart should not be interpreted until the R chart indicates the process variability is in control.

Values for D_3 and D_4 are also provided in Table 9 of Appendix B. Note that for $n = 5$, $D_3 = 0$, and $D_4 = 2.115$. Thus, with $\bar{R} = .0253$, the control limits are

$$\text{UCL} = .0253(2.115) = .0535$$
$$\text{LCL} = .0253(0) = 0$$

To monitor process variability, a sample standard deviation control chart (s chart) can be constructed instead of an R chart. If the sample size is 10 or less, the R chart and the s chart provide similar results. If the sample size is greater than 10, the s chart is generally preferred.

Figure 13.6 shows the R chart for the Jensen Computer Supplies problem. We used the data in Table 13.2 and Minitab's control chart routine to construct the chart. The center line is shown at the overall mean of the 20 sample ranges, $\bar{R} = .02527$. The UCL is .05344 or 3 sigma limits (3.0SL) above $\bar{R}$. The LCL is 0.0 or 3 sigma limits below $\bar{R}$. The R chart shows the 20 sample ranges plotted over time. Because all 20 sample ranges are within the control limits, the variability in the Jensen manufacturing process shows no indications of being out of control.

p Chart

Control charts that are based on data indicating the presence of a defect or the number of defects are called attributes control charts. A p chart is an attributes control chart.

Let us consider the case in which the output quality is measured in terms of the items being either nondefective or defective. The decision to continue or to adjust the production process will be based on $\bar{p}$, the proportion of defective items found in a sample of the output. The control chart used for proportion-defective data is called a p chart.

To illustrate the construction of a p chart, consider the use of automated mail-sorting machines in a post office. These automated machines scan the zip codes on letters and divert each letter to its proper carrier route. Even when a machine is operating properly, some letters are diverted to incorrect routes. Assume that when a machine is operating correctly, or in a state of control, 3% of the letters are incorrectly diverted. Thus p, the proportion of letters incorrectly diverted when the process is in control, is .03.

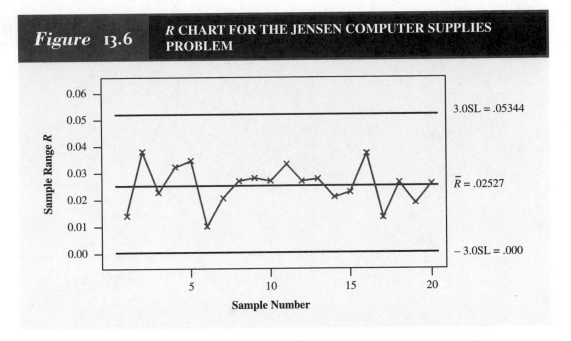

Figure 13.6   R CHART FOR THE JENSEN COMPUTER SUPPLIES PROBLEM

The sampling distribution of $\bar{p}$, as presented in Chapter 7, can be used to determine the variation that can be expected in $\bar{p}$ values for a process that is in control. Recall that the expected value or mean of $\bar{p}$ is p, the proportion defective when the process is in control. With samples of size n, the formula for the standard deviation of $\bar{p}$, called the standard error of the proportion, is

$$\sigma_{\bar{p}} = \sqrt{\frac{p(1-p)}{n}} \qquad (13.16)$$

We also learned in Chapter 7 that the sampling distribution of $\bar{p}$ can be approximated by a normal probability distribution whenever the sample size is large. With $\bar{p}$, the sample size can be considered large whenever the following two conditions are satisfied.

$$np \geq 5$$
$$n(1-p) \geq 5$$

In summary, whenever the sample size is large, the sampling distribution of $\bar{p}$ can be approximated by a normal probability distribution with mean p and standard deviation $\sigma_{\bar{p}}$. This distribution is shown in Figure 13.7.

To establish control limits for a p chart, we follow the same procedure we used to establish control limits for an $\bar{x}$ chart. That is, the limits for the control chart are set at 3 standard deviations, or standard errors, above and below the proportion defective when the process is in control. Thus, we have the following control limits.

Control Limits for a p Chart

$$UCL = p + 3\sigma_{\bar{p}} \qquad (13.17)$$
$$LCL = p - 3\sigma_{\bar{p}} \qquad (13.18)$$

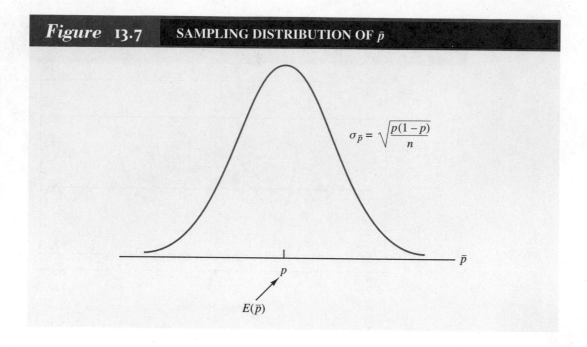

Figure 13.7   SAMPLING DISTRIBUTION OF $\bar{p}$

With $p = .03$ and samples of size $n = 200$, (13.16) shows that the standard error is

$$\sigma_{\bar{p}} = \sqrt{\frac{.03(1 - .03)}{200}} = .0121$$

Hence, the control limits are UCL $= .03 + 3(.0121) = .0663$, and LCL $= .03 - 3(.0121) = -.0063$. Because LCL is negative, LCL is set equal to zero in the control chart.

Figure 13.8 is the control chart for the mail-sorting process. The points plotted show the sample proportion defective found in samples of letters taken from the process. All points are within the control limits, and the sorting process shows no evidence of being out of control. In fact, the p chart indicates that the process should continue to operate.

If the proportion of defective items for a process that is in control is not known, that value is first estimated by using sample data. Suppose, for example, that M different samples, each of size n, are selected from a process that is in control. The fraction or proportion of defective items in each sample is then determined. Treating all the data collected as one large sample, we can determine the average number of defective items for all the data; that value can then be used to provide an estimate of p, the proportion of defective items observed when the process is in control. Note that this estimate of p also enables us to estimate the standard error of the proportion; upper and lower control limits can then be established.

np Chart

An *np* chart is a control chart developed for the number of defective items observed in a sample. With p denoting the probability of observing a defective item when the process is in control, the binomial probability distribution, as presented in Chapter 5, can be used to determine the probability of observing x defective items in a sample size of n. The expected value or mean of a binomial distribution is np and the standard deviation is $\sqrt{np(1 - p)}$.

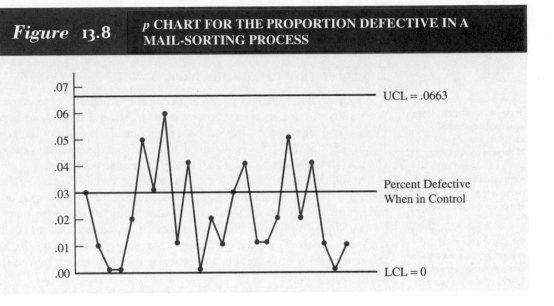

Figure 13.8   *p* CHART FOR THE PROPORTION DEFECTIVE IN A MAIL-SORTING PROCESS

In Chapter 7 we learned that the normal probability distribution can be used to approximate the binomial probability distribution whenever the sample size is large. The sample size can be considered large whenever the following two conditions are satisfied.

$$np \geq 5$$
$$n(1 - p) \geq 5$$

In summary, whenever the sample size is large, the distribution of the number of defective items observed in a sample size n can be approximated by a normal probability distribution with mean np and standard deviation $\sqrt{np(1 - p)}$. Thus, for the mail-sorting example, with $n = 200$ and $p = .03$, the number of defective items observed in a sample of 200 letters can be approximated by a normal probability distribution with a mean of $200(.03) = 6$ and a standard deviation of $\sqrt{200(.03)(.97)} = 2.4125$.

The control limits for an *np* chart are set at 3 standard deviations above and below the expected number of defective items observed when the process is in control. Thus, we have the following control limits.

Control Limits for an *np* Chart

$$\text{UCL} = np + 3\sqrt{np(1 - p)} \tag{13.19}$$
$$\text{LCL} = np - 3\sqrt{np(1 - p)} \tag{13.20}$$

For the mail-sorting process example, with $p = .03$ and $n = 200$, the control limits are UCL = 6 + 3(2.4125) = 13.2375, and LCL = 6 − 3(2.4125) = −1.2375. Because LCL is negative, LCL is set equal to zero in the control chart. Hence, if the number of letters diverted to incorrect routes is greater than 13, the process is concluded to be out of control.

The information provided by an *np* chart is equivalent to the information provided by the *p* chart; the only difference is that the *np* chart is a plot of the number of defective items observed whereas the p chart is a plot of the proportion of defective items observed. Thus, if we were to conclude that a particular process is out of control on the basis of a p chart, the process would also be concluded to be out of control on the basis of an np chart.

Interpretation of Control Charts

Control charts are designed to identify when assignable causes of variation are present. Managers must then authorize action to eliminate the assignable cause and return in-control status to the process.

Even if all points are within the upper and lower control limits, a process may not be in control. Trends in the sample data points or unusually long runs above or below the center line may also indicate out-of-control conditions.

The location and pattern of points in a control chart enable us to determine, with a small probability of error, whether a process is in statistical control. A primary indication that a process may be out of control is a data point outside the control limits, such as point 5 in Figure 13.4. Such a point is statistical evidence that the process is out of control; in such cases, corrective action should be taken as soon as possible.

In addition to points outside the control limits, certain patterns of the points within the control limits can be warning signals of quality control problems. For example, assume that all the data points are within the control limits but that a large number of points are on one side of the center line. This pattern may indicate that an equipment problem, a change in materials, or some other assignable cause of a shift in quality has occurred. Careful investigation of the production process should be undertaken to determine whether quality has changed.

Another pattern to watch for in control charts is a gradual shift, or trend, over time. For example, as tools wear out, the dimensions of machined parts will gradually deviate from their designed levels. Gradual changes in temperature or humidity, general equipment deterioration, dirt buildup, or operator fatigue may also result in a trend pattern in control charts. Six or seven points in a row that indicate either an increasing or decreasing trend should be cause for concern, even if the data points are all within the control limits. When such a pattern occurs, the process should be reviewed for possible changes or shifts in quality. Corrective action to bring the process back into control may be necessary.

NOTES and Comments

1. Because the control limits for the $\bar{x}$ chart depend on the value of the average range, these limits will not have much meaning unless the process variability is in control. In practice, the R chart is usually constructed before the $\bar{x}$ chart; if the R chart indicates that the process variability is in control, then the $\bar{x}$ chart is constructed. Minitab's Xbar-R option provides the $\bar{x}$ chart and the R chart simultaneously. The steps of this procedure are described in the appendix.

2. An np chart is used to monitor a process in terms of the number of defects. The Motorola Six Sigma Quality Level sets a goal of producing no more than 3.4 defects per million operations (*American Production and Inventory Control,* July 1991); this goal implies $p = .0000034$.

EXERCISES

Methods

1. A process that is in control has a mean of $\mu = 12.5$ and a standard deviation of $\sigma = .8$.
   a. Construct an $\bar{x}$ chart if samples of size four are to be used.
   b. Repeat part (a) for samples of size eight and 16.
   c. What happens to the limits of the control chart as the sample size is increased? Discuss why this change is reasonable.

2. Twenty-five samples, each of size five, were selected from a process that was in control. The sum of all the data collected was 677.5 pounds.
   a. What is an estimate of the process mean (in terms of pounds per unit) when the process is in control?
   b. Develop the control chart for this process if samples of size five will be used. Assume that the process standard deviation is .5 when the process is in control, and that the mean of the process is the estimate developed in part (a).

3. Twenty-five samples of 100 items each were inspected when a process was considered to be operating satisfactorily. In the 25 samples, 135 items were found to be defective.
   a. What is an estimate of the proportion defective when the process is in control?
   b. What is the standard error of the proportion if samples of size 100 will be used for statistical process control?
   c. Compute the upper and lower control limits for the control chart.

4. A process sampled 20 times with a sample of size eight resulted in $\bar{\bar{x}} = 28.5$ and $\bar{R} = 1.6$. Compute the upper and lower control limits for the $\bar{x}$ and R charts for this process.

SELF TEST

Applications

5. Temperature is used to measure the output of a production process. When the process is in control, the mean of the process is $\mu = 128.5$ and the standard deviation is $\sigma = .4$.
   a. Construct an $\bar{x}$ chart if samples of size six are to be used.
   b. Is the process in control for a sample providing the following data?

   128.8   128.2   129.1   128.7   128.4   129.2

   c. Is the process in control for a sample providing the following data?

   129.3   128.7   128.6   129.2   129.5   129.0

6. A quality control process monitors the weight per carton of laundry detergent. Control limits are set at UCL = 20.12 ounces and LCL = 19.90 ounces. Samples of size five are used for the sampling and inspection process. What are the process mean and process standard deviation for the manufacturing operation?

7. The Goodman Tire and Rubber Company periodically tests its tires for tread wear under simulated road conditions. To study and control the manufacturing process, 20 samples, each containing three radial tires, were chosen from different shifts over several days of operation, resulting in the following data. Assuming that these data were collected when the manufacturing process was believed to be operating in control, develop the R and $\bar{x}$ charts.

Tires

Sample	Tread Wear*		
1	31	42	28
2	26	18	35
3	25	30	34
4	17	25	21
5	38	29	35
6	41	42	36
7	21	17	29
8	32	26	28
9	41	34	33
10	29	17	30
11	26	31	40

*Hundredths of an inch   **(Additional data on p. 540.)**

Sample		Tread Wear*	
12	23	19	25
13	17	24	32
14	43	35	17
15	18	25	29
16	30	42	31
17	28	36	32
18	40	29	31
19	18	29	28
20	22	34	26

*Hundredths of an inch

8. Over several weeks of normal, or in-control, operation, 20 samples of 150 packages each of synthetic-gut tennis strings were tested for breaking strength. A total of 141 packages of the 3000 tested failed to conform to the manufacturer's specifications.
   a. What is an estimate of the process proportion defective when the system is in control?
   b. Compute the upper and lower control limits for a p chart.
   c. With the results of part (b), what conclusion should be made about the process if tests on a new sample of 150 packages find 12 defective? Do there appear to be assignable causes in this situation?
   d. Compute the upper and lower control limits for an np chart.
   e. Answer part (c) using the results of part (d).
   f. Which control chart would be preferred in this situation? Explain.

9. An automotive industry supplier produces pistons for several models of automobiles. Twenty samples, each consisting of 200 pistons, were selected when the process was known to be operating correctly. The numbers of defective pistons found in the samples follow.

8	10	6	4	5	7	8	12	8	15
14	10	10	7	5	8	6	10	4	8

   a. What is an estimate of the proportion defective for the piston manufacturing process when it is in control?
   b. Construct a p chart for the manufacturing process, assuming each sample has 200 pistons.
   c. With the results of part (b), what conclusion should be made if a sample of 200 has 20 defective pistons?
   d. Compute the upper and lower control limits for an np chart.
   e. Answer part (c) using the results of part (d).

···/ /············

13.2   ACCEPTANCE SAMPLING

In acceptance sampling, the items of interest can be incoming shipments of raw materials or purchased parts as well as finished goods from final assembly. Suppose we want to decide whether to accept or reject a group of items on the basis of specified quality characteristics. In quality control terminology, the group of items is a *lot*, and *acceptance sampling* is a statistical method that enables us to make an accept-reject decision based on the sample of items from the lot.

The general steps of acceptance sampling are shown in Figure 13.9. After a lot is received, a sample is selected for inspection. The results of the inspection are compared to

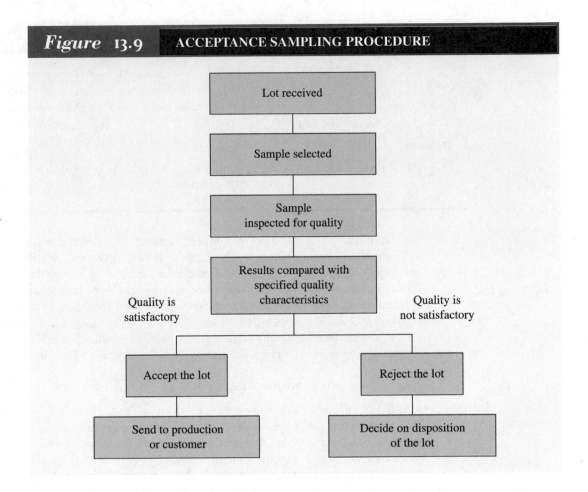

Figure 13.9   ACCEPTANCE SAMPLING PROCEDURE

Lot received

Sample selected

Sample
inspected for quality

Results compared with
specified quality
characteristics

Quality is
satisfactory

Quality is
not satisfactory

Accept the lot

Reject the lot

Send to production
or customer

Decide on disposition
of the lot

Acceptance sampling has
the following advantages
over 100% inspection:
1. Usually less expensive
2. Less product damage
   due to less handling and
   testing
3. Fewer inspectors
   required
4. Provides only approach
   possible if destructive
   testing must be used

specified quality characteristics. If the quality is satisfactory, the lot is accepted and sent to production or shipped to customers. If the quality is not satisfactory, the lot is rejected. Managers must then decide on the disposition of the lot. In some cases, the decision may be to keep the lot and remove the unacceptable or nonconforming items. In other cases, the lot may be returned to the supplier at the supplier's expense; the extra work and cost placed on the supplier can motivate the supplier to provide high-quality lots. Finally, if the rejected lot consists of finished goods, the goods must be scrapped or reworked to meet acceptable quality standards.

The statistical procedure of acceptance sampling is based on the hypothesis-testing methodology presented in Chapter 9. The null and alternative hypotheses are stated as follows.

$$H_0: \text{Good-quality lot}$$

$$H_a: \text{Poor-quality lot}$$

Table 13.3 shows the results of the hypothesis-testing procedure. Note that correct decisions correspond to accepting a good-quality lot and rejecting a poor-quality lot. However, as with other hypothesis-testing procedures, we need to be aware of the possibilities of making a Type I error (rejecting a good-quality lot) or a Type II error (accepting a poor-quality lot).

Table 13.3 THE OUTCOMES OF ACCEPTANCE SAMPLING

		State of the Lot	
		H_0 True Good-Quality Lot	H_0 False Poor-Quality Lot
Decision	Accept the Lot	Correct decision	Type II error (accepting a poor-quality lot)
	Reject the Lot	Type I error (rejecting a good-quality lot)	Correct decision

Because the probability of a Type I error creates a risk for the producer of the lot, it is known as the *producer's risk*. For example, a producer's risk of .05 indicates a 5% chance that a good-quality lot will be erroneously rejected. Because the probability of a Type II error creates a risk for the consumer of the lot, it is known as the *consumer's risk*. For example, a consumer's risk of .10 means that there is a 10% chance that a poor-quality lot will be erroneously accepted and thus used in production or shipped to the customer. Specific values for the producer's risk and the consumer's risk can be controlled by the person designing the acceptance sampling procedure. To illustrate how controlling for risk is done, let us consider the problem faced by KALI, Inc.

KALI, Inc.: An Example of Acceptance Sampling

KALI, Inc., manufactures home appliances that are marketed under a variety of trade names. However, KALI does not manufacture every component used in its products. Several components are purchased directly from suppliers. For example, one of the components that KALI purchases for use in home air conditioners is an overload protector, a device that turns off the compressor if it overheats. Because the compressor can be seriously damaged if the overload protector does not function properly, KALI is concerned about the quality of the overload protectors. One way to ensure quality would be to test every component received; this approach is known as 100% inspection. However, to determine proper functioning of an overload protector, the device must be subjected to time-consuming and expensive tests, and KALI cannot justify testing every overload protector it receives.

Instead, KALI uses an acceptance sampling plan to monitor the quality of the overload protectors. The acceptance sampling plan requires that KALI's quality control inspectors select and test a sample of overload protectors from each shipment. If very few defective units are found in the sample, the lot is probably of good quality and should be accepted. However, if a large number of defective units are found in the sample, the lot is probably of poor quality and should be rejected.

An *acceptance sampling plan* consists of a sample size n and an acceptance criterion c. The *acceptance criterion* is the maximum number of defective items that can be found in the sample and still indicate an acceptable lot. For example, for the KALI problem let us assume that a sample of 15 items will be selected from each incoming shipment or lot. Furthermore, assume that the manager of quality control states that the lot can be accepted only if no defective items are found. In this case, the acceptance sampling plan established by the quality control manager is $n = 15$ and $c = 0$.

This acceptance sampling plan is easy for the quality control inspector to implement. The inspector simply selects a sample of 15 items, performs the tests, and reaches a conclusion based on the following decision rule.

- *Accept the lot* if zero defects are found.
- *Reject the lot* if one or more defects are found.

Before implementing this acceptance sampling plan, the quality control manager wants to evaluate the risks or errors possible under the plan. The plan will be implemented only if both the producer's risk (Type I error) and the consumer's risk (Type II error) are controlled at reasonable levels.

Computing the Probability of Accepting a Lot

The key to analyzing both the producer's risk and the consumer's risk is a "What-if?" type of analysis. That is, we will assume that a lot has some known percentage of defective items and compute the probability of accepting the lot for a given sampling plan. By varying the assumed percentage of defective items, we can examine the effect of the sampling plan on both types of risks.

Let us begin by assuming that a large shipment of overload protectors has been received and that 5% of the overload protectors in the shipment are defective. For a shipment or lot with 5% of the items defective, what is the probability that the $n = 15$, $c = 0$ sampling plan will lead us to accept the lot? Because each overload protector tested will be either defective or nondefective and because the lot size is large, the number of defective items in a sample of 15 has a *binomial probability distribution*. The binomial probability function, which was presented in Chapter 5, follows.

Binomial Probability Function for Acceptance Sampling

$$f(x) = \frac{n!}{x!(n-x)!} p^x (1-p)^{(n-x)} \tag{13.21}$$

where

$$n = \text{the sample size}$$
$$p = \text{the proportion of defective items in the lot}$$
$$x = \text{the number of defects in the sample}$$
$$f(x) = \text{the probability of } x \text{ defects in the sample}$$

For the KALI acceptance sampling plan, $n = 15$; thus, for a lot with 5% defective ($p = .05$), we have

$$f(x) = \frac{15!}{x!(15-x)!} (.05)^x (1-.05)^{(15-x)} \tag{13.22}$$

Using (13.22), $f(0)$ will provide the probability that zero overload protectors will be defective and the lot will be accepted. In using (13.22), recall that $0! = 1$. Thus, the probability computation for $f(0)$ is

$$f(0) = \frac{15!}{0!(15-0)!} (.05)^0 (1-.05)^{(15-0)}$$

$$= \frac{15!}{0!(15)!} (.05)^0 (.95)^{15} = (.95)^{15} = .4633$$

We now know that the $n = 15$, $c = 0$ sampling plan has a .4633 probability of accepting a lot with 5% defective items. Hence, there must be a corresponding $1 - .4633 = .5367$ probability of rejecting a lot with 5% defective items.

In Table 13.4 we show the probability that the $n = 15$, $c = 0$ sampling plan will lead to the acceptance of lots with 1%, 2%, 3%, ... defective items. The probabilities in the table were computed by using $p = .01$, $p = .02$, $p = .03$, ... in the binomial probability function (13.1).

Tables of binomial probabilities (see Table 5, Appendix B) can help reduce the computational effort in determining the probabilities of accepting lots. Selected binomial probabilities for $n = 15$ and $n = 20$ are listed in Table 13.5. Using this table, we can determine that a lot containing 10% defective items has a .2059 probability that the $n = 15$, $c = 0$ sampling plan will indicate an acceptable lot.

With the data in Table 13.4, a graph of the probability of accepting the lot versus the percent defective in the lot can be drawn as shown in Figure 13.10. This graph, or curve, is called the *operating characteristic* (OC) *curve* for the $n = 15$, $c = 0$ acceptance sampling plan.

Perhaps we should consider other sampling plans, ones with different sample sizes n and/or different acceptance criteria c. First consider the case in which the sample size remains $n = 15$ but the acceptance criterion increases from $c = 0$ to $c = 1$. That is, we will now accept the lot if zero or one defective component is found in the sample. For a lot with 5% defective items ($p = .05$), the binomial probability function in (13.21) can be used to compute $f(0)$ and $f(1)$. Summing these two probabilities provides the probability that the $n = 15$, $c = 1$ sampling plan will accept the lot. Alternatively, using Table 13.5, we find that with $n = 15$ and $p = .05$, $f(0) = .4633$ and $f(1) = .3658$. Thus, we find a $.4633 + .3658 = .8291$ probability that the $n = 15$, $c = 1$ plan will lead to the acceptance of a lot with 5% defective items.

Figure 13.11 shows the operating characteristic curves for four alternative acceptance sampling plans for the KALI problem. Samples of size 15 and 20 are considered. Note that regardless of the proportion defective in the lot, the $n = 15$, $c = 1$ sampling plan provides the highest probabilities of accepting the lot. The $n = 20$, $c = 0$ sampling plan provides the lowest probabilities of accepting the lot; however, that plan also provides the highest probabilities of rejecting the lot.

Selecting an Acceptance Sampling Plan

Now that we know how to use the binomial probability distribution to compute the probability of accepting a lot with a given proportion defective, we are ready to select the values of n and c that determine the desired acceptance sampling plan for the application being

Table 13.4	PROBABILITY OF ACCEPTING THE LOT FOR THE KALI PROBLEM WITH $n = 15$ AND $c = 0$
Percent Defective in the Lot	**Probability of Accepting the Lot**
1	.8601
2	.7386
3	.6333
4	.5421
5	.4633
10	.2059
15	.0874
20	.0352
25	.0134

Table 13.5	SELECTED BINOMIAL PROBABILITIES FOR SAMPLES OF SIZES 15 AND 20

						p					
n	x	.05	.10	.15	.20	.25	.30	.35	.40	.45	.50
15	0	.4633	.2059	.0874	.0352	.0134	.0047	.0016	.0005	.0001	.0000
	1	.3658	.3432	.2312	.1319	.0668	.0305	.0126	.0047	.0016	.0005
	2	.1348	.2669	.2856	.2309	.1559	.0916	.0476	.0219	.0090	.0032
	3	.0307	.1285	.2184	.2501	.2252	.1700	.1110	.0634	.0318	.0139
	4	.0049	.0428	.1156	.1876	.2252	.2186	.1792	.1268	.0780	.0417
	5	.0006	.0105	.0449	.1032	.1651	.2061	.2123	.1859	.1404	.0916
	6	.0000	.0019	.0132	.0430	.0917	.1472	.1906	.2066	.1914	.1527
	7	.0000	.0003	.0030	.0138	.0393	.0811	.1319	.1771	.2013	.1964
	8	.0000	.0000	.0005	.0035	.0131	.0348	.0710	.1181	.1647	.1964
	9	.000	.0000	.0001	.0007	.0034	.0116	.0298	.0612	.1048	.1527
	10	.0000	.0000	.0000	.0001	.0007	.0030	.0096	.0245	.0515	.0916
	11	.0000	.0000	.0000	.0000	.0001	.0006	.0024	.0074	.0191	.0417
	12	.0000	.0000	.0000	.0000	.0000	.0001	.0004	.0016	.0052	.0139
	13	.0000	.0000	.0000	.0000	.0000	.0000	.0001	.0003	.0010	.0032
	14	.0000	.0000	.0000	.0000	.0000	.0000	.0000	.0000	.0001	.0005
	15	.0000	.0000	.0000	.0000	.0000	.0000	.0000	.0000	.0000	.0000
20	0	.3585	.1216	.0388	.0115	.0032	.0008	.0002	.0000	.0000	.0000
	1	.3774	.2702	.1368	.0576	.0211	.0068	.0020	.0005	.0001	.0000
	2	.1887	.2852	.2293	.1369	.0669	.0278	.0100	.0031	.0008	.0002
	3	.0596	.1901	.2428	.2054	.1339	.0716	.0323	.0123	.0040	.0011
	4	.0133	.0898	.1821	.2182	.1897	.1304	.0738	.0350	.0139	.0046
	5	.0022	.0319	.1028	.1746	.2023	.1789	.1272	.0746	.0365	.0148
	6	.0003	.0089	.0454	.1091	.1686	.1916	.1712	.1244	.0746	.0370
	7	.0000	.0020	.0160	.0545	.1124	.1643	.1844	.1659	.1221	.0739
	8	.0000	.0004	.0046	.0222	.0609	.1144	.1614	.1797	.1623	.1201
	9	.0000	.0001	.0011	.0074	.0271	.0654	.1158	.1597	.1771	.1602
	10	.0000	.0000	.0002	.0020	.0099	.0308	.0686	.1171	.1593	.1762
	11	.0000	.0000	.0000	.0005	.0030	.0120	.0336	.0710	.1185	.1602
	12	.0000	.0000	.0000	.0001	.0008	.0039	.0136	.0355	.0727	.1201
	13	.0000	.0000	.0000	.0000	.0002	.0010	.0045	.0146	.0366	.0739
	14	.0000	.0000	.0000	.0000	.0000	.0002	.0012	.0049	.0150	.0370
	15	.0000	.0000	.0000	.0000	.0000	.0000	.0003	.0013	.0049	.0148
	16	.0000	.0000	.0000	.0000	.0000	.0000	.0000	.0003	.0013	.0046
	17	.0000	.0000	.0000	.0000	.0000	.0000	.0000	.0000	.0002	.0011
	18	.0000	.0000	.0000	.0000	.0000	.0000	.0000	.0000	.0000	.0002
	19	.0000	.0000	.0000	.0000	.0000	.0000	.0000	.0000	.0000	.0000
	20	.0000	.0000	.0000	.0000	.0000	.0000	.0000	.0000	.0000	.0000

studied. In formulating an acceptance plan, managers must specify two values for the fraction defective in the lot. One value, denoted p_0, will be used to control for the producer's risk, and the other value, denoted p_1, will be used to control for the consumer's risk.

In showing how this can be done, we will use the following notation.

α = the producer's risk; the probability that a lot with p_0 defective will be rejected

β = the consumer's risk; the probability that a lot with p_1 defective will be accepted

Figure 13.10 **OPERATING CHARACTERISTIC CURVE FOR THE $n = 15$, $c = 0$ ACCEPTANCE SAMPLING PLAN**

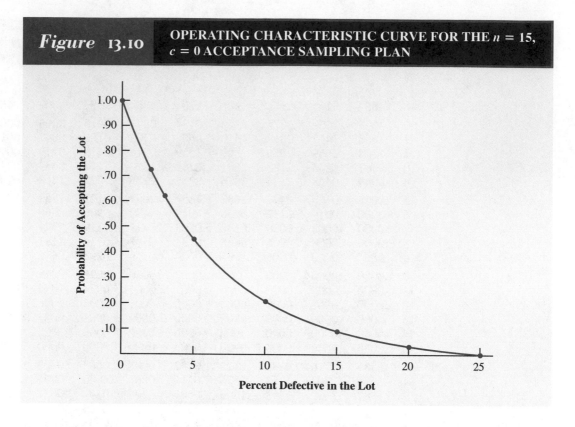

Figure 13.11 **OPERATING CHARACTERISTIC CURVES FOR FOUR ACCEPTANCE SAMPLING PLANS**

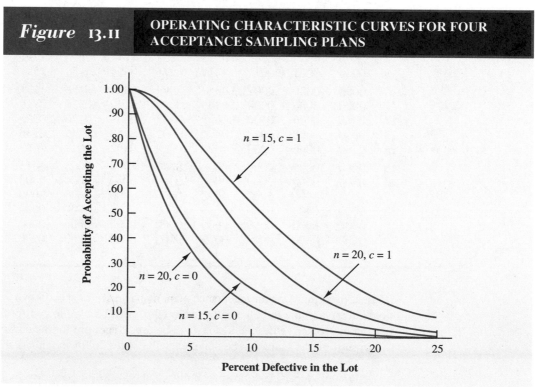

Suppose that for the KALI problem, the managers specify that $p_0 = .03$ and $p_1 = .15$. From the OC curve for $n = 15, c = 0$ in Figure 13.12, we see that $p_0 = .03$ provides a producer's risk of approximately $1 - .63 = .37$, and $p_1 = .15$ provides a consumer's risk of approximately .09. Thus, if the managers are willing to tolerate both a .37 probability of rejecting a lot with 3% defective items (producer's risk) and a .09 probability of accepting a lot with 15% defective items (consumer's risk), the $n = 15, c = 0$ acceptance sampling plan would be acceptable.

Suppose, however, that the managers request a producer's risk of $\alpha = .10$ and a consumer's risk of $\beta = .20$. We see that now the $n = 15, c = 0$ sampling plan has a better-than-desired consumer's risk but an unacceptably large producer's risk. The fact that $\alpha = .37$ indicates that 37% of the lots will be erroneously rejected when only 3% of the items in them are defective. The producer's risk is too high, and a different acceptance sampling plan should be considered.

Using $p_0 = .03$, $\alpha = .10$, $p_1 = .15$, and $\beta = .20$ in Figure 13.11 shows that the acceptance sampling plan with $n = 20$ and $c = 1$ comes closest to meeting both the producer's and the consumer's risk requirements. Exercise 13 at the end of this section will ask you to compute the producer's risk and the consumer's risk for the $n = 20, c = 1$ sampling plan.

As shown in this section, several computations and several operating characteristic curves may need to be considered to determine the sampling plan with the desired producer's and consumer's risk. Fortunately, tables of sampling plans are published. For example, the American Military Standard Table, MIL-STD-105D, provides information helpful in designing acceptance sampling plans. More advanced texts on quality control, such as those listed in the bibliography, describe the use of such tables. The advanced texts also discuss the role of sampling costs in determining the optimal sampling plan.

Figure **13.12** **OPERATING CHARACTERISTIC CURVE FOR $n = 15, c = 0$ WITH $p_0 = .03$ and $p_1 = .15$**

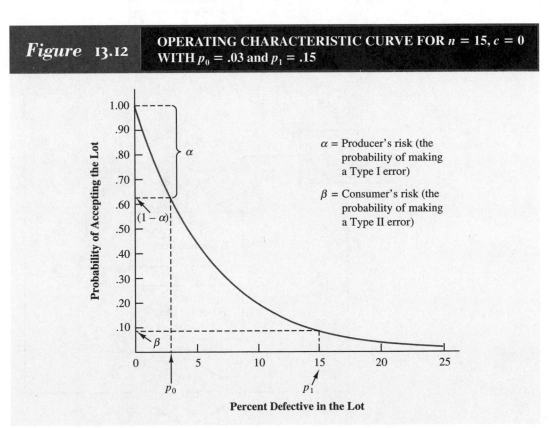

Multiple Sampling Plans

The acceptance sampling procedure that we have presented for the KALI problem is a *single-sample* plan. It is called a single-sample plan because only one sample or sampling stage is used. After the number of defective components in the sample is determined, a decision must be made to accept or reject the lot. An alternative to the single-sample plan is a *multiple sampling plan,* in which two or more stages of sampling are used. At each stage a decision is made among three possibilities: stop sampling and accept the lot, stop sampling and reject the lot, or continue sampling. Although more complex, multiple sampling plans often result in a smaller total sample size than single-sample plans with the same α and β probabilities.

The logic of a two-stage, or double-sample, plan is shown in Figure 13.13. Initially a sample of n_1 items is selected. If the number of defective components x_1 is less than or equal

Figure 13.13   A TWO-STAGE ACCEPTANCE SAMPLING PLAN

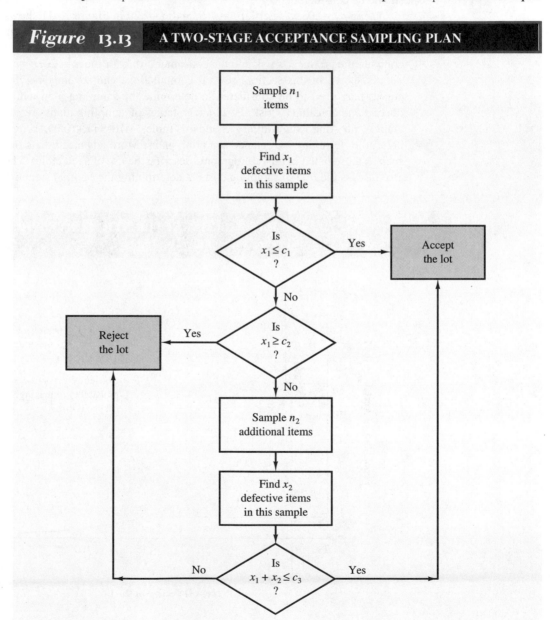

to c_1, accept the lot. If x_1 is greater than or equal to c_2, reject the lot. If x_1 is between c_1 and c_2 $(c_1 < x_1 < c_2)$, select a second sample of n_2 items. Determine the combined, or total number of defects from the first sample (x_1) and the second sample (x_2). If $x_1 + x_2 \leq c_3$, accept the lot; otherwise reject the lot. The development of the double-sample plan is more difficult because the sample sizes n_1 and n_2 and the acceptance numbers c_1, c_2, and c_3 must meet both the producer's and consumer's risks desired.

N O T E S *and Comments*

1. The use of the binomial probability distribution for acceptance sampling is based on the assumption of large lots. If the lot size is small, the hypergeometric probability distribution is the appropriate distribution. Experts in the field of quality control indicate that the Poisson distribution provides a good approximation for acceptance sampling when the sample size is at least 16, the lot size is at least 10 times the sample size, and p is less than .1. For larger sample sizes, the normal approximation to the binomial probability distribution can be used.

2. In the MIL-ST-105D sampling tables, p_0 is called the acceptable quality level (AQL). In some sampling tables, p_1 is called the lot tolerance percent defective (LTPD) or the rejectable quality level (RQL). Many of the published sampling plans also use quality indexes such as the indifference quality level (IQL) and the average outgoing quality limit (AOQL). The more advanced texts listed in the bibliography provide a complete discussion of these other indexes.

3. In this section we provided an introduction to *attributes sampling plans.* In these plans each item sampled is classified as nondefective or defective. In *variables sampling plans,* a sample is taken and a measurement of the quality characteristic is taken. For example, for gold jewelry a measurement of quality may be the amount of gold it contains. A simple statistic such as the average amount of gold in the sample jewelry is computed and compared with an allowable value to determine whether to accept or reject the lot.

EXERCISES

Methods

SELF TEST

10. For an acceptance sampling plan with $n = 25$ and $c = 0$, find the probability of accepting a lot that has a defect rate of 2%. What is the probability of accepting the lot if the defect rate is 6%?

11. Consider an acceptance sampling plan with $n = 20$ and $c = 0$. Compute the producer's risk for each of the following cases.
    a.   The lot has a defect rate of 2%.
    b.   The lot has a defect rate of 6%.

12. Repeat Exercise 11 for the acceptance sampling plan with $n = 20$ and $c = 1$. What happens to the producer's risk as the acceptance number c is increased? Explain.

Applications

13. Refer to the KALI problem presented in this section. The quality-control manager requested a producer's risk of .10 when p_0 was .03 and a consumer's risk of .20 when p_1 was .15. Consider the acceptance sampling plan based on a sample size of 20 and an acceptance number of 1. Answer the following questions.

    a. What is the producer's risk for the $n = 20$, $c = 1$ sampling plan?

    b. What is the consumer's risk for the $n = 20$, $c = 1$ sampling plan?

    c. Does the $n = 20$, $c = 1$ sampling plan satisfy the risks requested by the quality-control manager? Discuss.

14. To inspect incoming shipments of raw materials, a manufacturer is considering samples of sizes 10, 15, and 20. Use the binomial probabilities from Table 5 of Appendix B to select a sampling plan that provides a producer's risk of $\alpha = .03$ when p_0 is .05 and a consumer's risk of $\beta = .12$ when p_1 is .30.

15. A domestic manufacturer of watches purchases quartz crystals from a Swiss firm. The crystals are shipped in lots of 1000. The acceptance sampling procedure uses 20 randomly selected crystals.

    a. Construct operating characteristic curves for acceptance numbers of 0, 1, and 2.

    b. If p_0 is .01 and $p_1 = .08$, what are the producer's and consumer's risks for each sampling plan in part (a)?

··/ /············

SUMMARY

In this chapter we discussed how statistical methods can be used to assist in the control of quality. We first presented the $\bar{x}$, R, p, and np control charts as graphical aids in monitoring process quality. Control limits are established for each chart; samples are selected periodically and the data plotted on the control chart. Data outside the control limits indicate that the process is out of control and that corrective action should be taken. Patterns of data within the control limits can also indicate potential quality control problems and suggest that corrective action may be warranted.

We also considered the technique known as acceptance sampling. With this procedure, a sample is selected and inspected. The number of defective items in the sample provides the basis for accepting or rejecting the lot. The sample size and the acceptance criterion can be adjusted to control both the producer's risk (Type I error) and the consumer's risk (Type II error).

··/ /············

GLOSSARY

Quality control A series of inspections and measurements that determine whether quality standards are being met.

Assignable causes Variations in process outputs that are due to factors such as machine tools wearing out, incorrect machine settings, poor-quality raw materials, operator error, and so on. Corrective action should be taken when assignable causes of output variation are detected.

Common causes Normal or natural variations in process outputs that are due purely to chance. No corrective action is necessary when output variations are due to common causes.

Control chart A graphical tool used to help determine whether a process is in control or out of control.

$\bar{x}$ chart A control chart used when the output of a process is measured in terms of the mean value of a variable such as a length, weight, temperature, and so on.

R chart A control chart used when the output of a process is measured in terms of the range of a variable.

p chart A control chart used when the output of a process is measured in terms of the proportion defective.

np chart A control chart used to monitor the output of a process in terms of the number of defective items.

Lot A group of items such as incoming shipments of raw materials or purchased parts as well as finished goods from final assembly.

Acceptance sampling A statistical procedure in which the number of defective items found in a sample is used to determine whether a lot should be accepted or rejected.

Producer's risk The risk of rejecting a good-quality lot; a Type I error.

Consumer's risk The risk of accepting a poor-quality lot; a Type II error.

Acceptance criterion The maximum number of defective items that can be found in the sample and still allow acceptance of the lot.

Operating characteristic curve A graph showing the probability of accepting the lot as a function of the percentage defective in the lot. This curve can be used to help determine whether a particular acceptance sampling plan meets both the producer's and the consumer's risk requirements.

Multiple sampling plan A form of acceptance sampling in which more than one sample or stage is used. On the basis of the number of defective items found in a sample, a decision will be made to accept the lot, reject the lot, or continue sampling.

KEY FORMULAS

Standard Error of the Mean

$$\sigma_{\bar{x}} = \frac{\sigma}{\sqrt{n}} \tag{13.1}$$

Control Limits for an $\bar{x}$ Chart: Process Mean and Standard Deviation Known

$$\text{UCL} = \mu + 3\sigma_{\bar{x}} \tag{13.2}$$
$$\text{LCL} = \mu - 3\sigma_{\bar{x}} \tag{13.3}$$

Overall Sample Mean

$$\bar{\bar{x}} = \frac{\bar{x}_1 + \bar{x}_2 + \cdots + \bar{x}_k}{k} \tag{13.4}$$

Average Range

$$\bar{R} = \frac{R_1 + R_2 + \cdots + R_k}{k} \tag{13.5}$$

Control Limits for an $\bar{x}$ Chart: Process Mean and Standard Deviation Unknown

$$\bar{\bar{x}} \pm A_2\bar{R} \tag{13.8}$$

Control Limits for an *R* Chart

$$UCL = \bar{R}D_4 \qquad (13.14)$$
$$LCL = \bar{R}D_3 \qquad (13.15)$$

Standard Error of the Proportion

$$\sigma_{\bar{p}} = \sqrt{\frac{p(1-p)}{n}} \qquad (13.16)$$

Control Limits for a *p* Chart

$$UCL = p + 3\sigma_{\bar{p}} \qquad (13.17)$$
$$LCL = p - 3\sigma_{\bar{p}} \qquad (13.18)$$

Control Limits for an *np* Chart

$$UCL = np + 3\sqrt{np(1-p)} \qquad (13.19)$$
$$LCL = np - 3\sqrt{np(1-p)} \qquad (13.20)$$

Binomial Probability Function for Acceptance Sampling

$$f(x) = \frac{n!}{x!(n-x)!} p^x(1-p)^{(n-x)} \qquad (13.21)$$

SUPPLEMENTARY EXERCISES

16. Samples of size five provided the following 20 sample means for a production process that is believed to be in control.

95.72	95.24	95.18
95.44	95.46	95.32
95.40	95.44	95.08
95.50	95.80	95.22
95.56	95.22	95.04
95.72	94.82	95.46
95.60	95.78	

   a. Based on these data, what is an estimate of the mean when the process is in control?
   b. Assuming that the process standard deviation is $\sigma = .50$, develop a control chart for this production process. Assume that the mean of the process is the estimate developed in part (a).
   c. Do any of the 20 sample means indicate that the process is out of control?

17. Product filling weights are normally distributed with a mean of 350 grams and a standard deviation of 15 grams.
   a. Develop the control limits for samples of size 10, 20, and 30.
   b. What happens to the control limits as the sample size is increased?
   c. What happens when a Type I error is made?
   d. What happens when a Type II error is made?
   e. What is the probability of a Type I error for samples of size 10, 20, and 30?
   f. What is the advantage of increasing the sample size for control chart purposes? What error probability is reduced as the sample size is increased?

18. Twenty-five samples of size five resulted in $\bar{\bar{x}} = 5.42$ and $R = 2.0$. Compute control limits for the $\bar{x}$ and R charts, and estimate the standard deviation of the process.

19. The following are quality control data for a manufacturing process at Kensport Chemical Company. The data show the temperature in degrees centigrade at five points in time during a manufacturing cycle. The company is interested in using control charts to monitor the temperature of its manufacturing process. Construct the $\bar{x}$ chart and R chart. What conclusions can be made about the quality of the process?

Sample	$\bar{x}$	R	Sample	$\bar{x}$	R
1	95.72	1.0	11	95.80	.6
2	95.24	.9	12	95.22	.2
3	95.18	.8	13	95.56	1.3
4	95.44	.4	14	95.22	.5
5	95.46	.5	15	95.04	.8
6	95.32	1.1	16	95.72	1.1
7	95.40	.9	17	94.82	.6
8	95.44	.3	18	95.46	.5
9	95.08	.2	19	95.60	.4
10	95.50	.6	20	95.74	.6

20. The following were collected for the Master Blend Coffee production process. The data show the filling weights based on samples of 3-pound cans of coffee. Use these data to construct the $\bar{x}$ and R chart. What conclusions can be made about the quality of the production process?

Coffee

			Observations		
Sample	1	2	3	4	5
1	3.05	3.08	3.07	3.11	3.11
2	3.13	3.07	3.05	3.10	3.10
3	3.06	3.04	3.12	3.11	3.10
4	3.09	3.08	3.09	3.09	3.07
5	3.10	3.06	3.06	3.07	3.08
6	3.08	3.10	3.13	3.03	3.06
7	3.06	3.06	3.08	3.10	3.08
8	3.11	3.08	3.07	3.07	3.07
9	3.09	3.09	3.08	3.07	3.09
10	3.06	3.11	3.07	3.09	3.07

21. Consider the following situations. For each, comment on whether it indicates reason for concern about the quality of the process.
    a. A p chart has LCL = 0 and UCL = .068. When the process is in control, the proportion defective is .033. Plot the following seven sample results: .035, .062, .055, .049, .058, .066, and .055. Discuss.
    b. An $\bar{x}$ chart has LCL = 22.2 and UCL = 24.5. The mean is $\mu = 23.35$ when the process is in control. Plot the following seven sample results: 22.4, 22.6, 22.65, 23.2, 23.4, 23.85, and 24.1. Discuss.

22. Managers of 1200 different retail outlets make twice-a-month restocking orders from a central warehouse. Past experience has shown that 4% of the orders have one or more errors such as wrong item shipped, wrong quantity shipped, and item requested but not shipped. Random samples of 200 orders are selected monthly and checked for accuracy.
    a. Construct a control chart for this situation.
    b. Six months of data show the following numbers of orders with one or more errors: 10, 15, 6, 13, 8, and 17. Plot the data on the control chart. What does your plot indicate about the order process?

23. An $n = 10$, $c = 2$ acceptance sampling plan is being considered; assume that $p_0 = .05$ and $p_1 = .20$.
    a. Compute both the producer's and the consumer's risk for this acceptance sampling plan.
    b. Would the producer, the consumer, or both be unhappy with the proposed sampling plan?
    c. What change in the sampling plan, if any, would you recommend?

24. An acceptance sampling plan with $n = 15$ and $c = 1$ has been designed with a producer's risk of .075.
    a. Was the value of p_0 .01, .02, .03, .04, or .05? What does this value mean?
    b. What is the consumer's risk associated with this plan if p_1 is .25?

25. A manufacturer produces lots of a canned food product. Let p denote the proportion of the lots that do not meet the product quality specifications. An $n = 25$, $c = 0$ acceptance sampling plan will be used.
    a. Compute points on the operating characteristic curve when $p = .01, .03, .10$, and $.20$.
    b. Plot the operating characteristic curve.
    c. What is the probability that the acceptance sampling plan will reject a lot that has .01 defective?

26. Sometimes an acceptance sampling plan will be based on a large sample. In this case, the normal approximation to the binomial probability distribution can be used to compute the producer's and the consumer's risk associated with the plan. Referring to Chapter 6, we know that the normal distribution used to approximate binomial probabilities has a mean of np and a standard deviation of $\sqrt{np(1 - p)}$. Assume that an acceptance sampling plan is $n = 250$, $c = 10$.
    a. What is the producer's risk if p_0 is .02? As discussed in Chapter 6, a continuity correction factor should be used in this case. Thus, the probability of acceptance is based on the normal probability of the random variable being less than or equal to 10.5.
    b. What is the consumer's risk of p_1 is .08?
    c. What is an advantage of a large sample size for acceptance sampling? What is a disadvantage?

Appendix 13.1   CONTROL CHARTS WITH MINITAB

In Section 13.1, we described how to construct and interpret the $\bar{x}$ chart and the R chart for the Jensen Computer Supplies manufacturing process. We showed the corresponding Minitab's control charts in Figures 13.5 and 13.6. In this appendix, we describe the steps required to generate the Minitab computer solution. First, the Jensen sample data shown in Table 13.2 must be entered into a Minitab worksheet. The sample number was entered in column C1. The first observation from each sample was entered into column C2, the second observation was entered into column C3, and so on. The fifth observation was entered into column C6. The following steps describe how to use Minitab to produce both the $\bar{x}$ chart and R chart simultaneously.

Step 1. Select the **Stat** pull-down menu
Step 2. Select the **Control Charts** pull-down menu
Step 3. Choose the **Xbar-R** option

Step 4. When the Xbar-R Chart dialog box appears:
        Select **Subgroups across rows of:**
        Enter C2-C6 in the Subgroups across rows of: box
        Select the **Tests** option

Step 5. When the Tests dialog box appears:
        Select **One point more than 3 sigmas from center line***
        Select **OK**

Step 6. When the Xbar-R Chart dialog box appears
        Select **OK**

The $\bar{x}$ chart and the R chart will be shown together on the Minitab output. The choices available under Step 3 of the preceding Minitab procedure provide access to a variety of control chart options. For example, the $\bar{x}$ and the R charts can be selected separately. Additional options include the p chart, the np chart, and others.

---

*Minitab provides several additional tests for detecting special causes of variation and out-of-control conditions. The user may select several of these tests simultaneously.

General

Bowerman, B. L., and R. T. O'Connell, *Applied Statistics: Improving Business Processes*, Irwin, 1996.

Freedman, D., R. Pisani, and R. Purves, *Statistics*, 3rd ed., W. W. Norton, 1997.

Freund, J. E., *Mathematical Statistics*, 5th ed., Prentice-Hall, 1992.

Hogg, R. V., and A. T. Craig, *Introduction to Mathematical Statistics*, 5th ed., Prentice-Hall, 1995.

McClave, J. T., and P. G. Benson, *Statistics: For Business and Economics*, 6th ed., MacMillan, 1994.

Moore, D. S., and G. P. McCabe, *Introduction to the Practice of Statistics*, 3rd ed., W. H. Freeman & Co., 1998.

Neter, J., W. Wasserman, and G. A. Whitmore, *Applied Statistics*, 4th ed., Allyn & Bacon, 1992.

Roberts, H., *Data Analysis for Managers with Minitab*, Scientific Press, 1991.

Ryan, B. F., and B. L. Joiner, *Minitab Handbook*, 3rd ed., Duxbury Press, 1994.

Tanur, J. M., *Statistics: A Guide to the Unknown*, 3rd ed., Brooks/Cole, 1989.

Tukey, J. W., *Exploratory Data Analysis*, Addison-Wesley, 1977.

Probability

Feller, W., *An Introduction to Probability Theory and Its Application*, Vol. I, 3rd ed., Wiley, 1968.

Hogg, R. V., and E. A. Tanis, *Probability and Statistical Inference*, 5th ed., Prentice-Hall, 1996.

Ross, S. M., *Introduction to Probability Models*, 6th ed., Academic Press, 1997.

Wackerly, D. D., W. Mendenhall, and R. L. Scheaffer, *Mathematical Statistics with Applications*, 5th ed., PWS, 1996.

Regression Analysis

Belsley, D. A., *Conditioning Diagnostics: Collinearity and Weak Data in Regression*, Wiley, 1991.

Chatterjee, S., and B. Price, *Regression Analysis by Example*, 2d ed., Wiley, 1991.

Cook, R. D., and S. Weisberg, *Residuals and Influence in Regression*, Chapman & Hall, 1982.

Draper, N. R., S. Draper, and H. Smith, *Applied Regression Analysis*, 3rd ed., Wiley, 1998.

Graybill, F. A., and H. K. Iyer, *Regression Analysis: Concepts and Applications*, Duxbury Press, 1994.

Kleinbaum, D. G., L. L. Kupper, and K. E. Muller, *Applied Regression Analysis and Other Multivariate Methods*, 3rd ed., Duxbury Press, 1997.

Myers, R. H., *Classical and Modern Regression with Applications*, 2d ed., PWS, 1990.

Neter, J., W. Wasserman, and M. H. Kutner, *Applied Linear Statistical Models: Regression, Analysis of Variance and Experimental Design*, 4th ed., Irwin, 1990.

Wonnacott, T. H., and R. J. Wonnacott, *Regression: A Second Course in Statistics*, Krieger, 1986.

Quality Control

Deming, W. E., *Quality, Productivity, and Competitive Position*, MIT, 1982.

Duncan, A. J., *Quality Control and Industrial Statistics*, 5th ed., Irwin, 1986.

Evans, J. R., and W. M. Lindsay, *The Management and Control of Quality*, 3rd ed., West/Wadsworth, 1995.

Hunt, V. D., and H. S. Gitlow, *Managing for Quality: Integrating Quality and Business Strategy*, Irwin, 1992.

Ishikawa, K., *Introduction to Quality Control*, Quality Resources, 1990.

Juran, J. M., and F. M. Gryna, *Quality Planning and Analysis: From Product Development Through Use*, 3rd ed., McGraw-Hill, 1993.

Montgomery, D. C., *Introduction to Statistical Quality Control*, 3rd ed., Wiley, 1996.

Appendixes

APPENDIX B: TABLES

TABLE I   Standard Normal Distribution

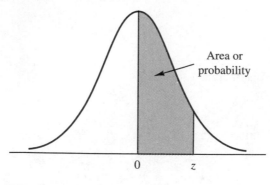

Area or probability

Entries in the table give the area under the curve between the mean and z standard deviations above the mean. For example, for $z = 1.25$ the area under the curve between the mean and z is .3944.

z	.00	.01	.02	.03	.04	.05	.06	.07	.08	.09
.0	.0000	.0040	.0080	.0120	.0160	.0199	.0239	.0279	.0319	.0359
.1	.0398	.0438	.0478	.0517	.0557	.0596	.0636	.0675	.0714	.0753
.2	.0793	.0832	.0871	.0910	.0948	.0987	.1026	.1064	.1103	.1141
.3	.1179	.1217	.1255	.1293	.1331	.1368	.1406	.1443	.1480	.1517
.4	.1554	.1591	.1628	.1664	.1700	.1736	.1772	.1808	.1844	.1879
.5	.1915	.1950	.1985	.2019	.2054	.2088	.2123	.2157	.2190	.2224
.6	.2257	.2291	.2324	.2357	.2389	.2422	.2454	.2486	.2518	.2549
.7	.2580	.2612	.2642	.2673	.2704	.2734	.2764	.2794	.2823	.2852
.8	.2881	.2910	.2939	.2967	.2995	.3023	.3051	.3078	.3106	.3133
.9	.3159	.3186	.3212	.3238	.3264	.3289	.3315	.3340	.3365	.3389
1.0	.3413	.3438	.3461	.3485	.3508	.3531	.3554	.3577	.3599	.3621
1.1	.3643	.3665	.3686	.3708	.3729	.3749	.3770	.3790	.3810	.3830
1.2	.3849	.3869	.3888	.3907	.3925	.3944	.3962	.3980	.3997	.4015
1.3	.4032	.4049	.4066	.4082	.4099	.4115	.4131	.4147	.4162	.4177
1.4	.4192	.4207	.4222	.4236	.4251	.4265	.4279	.4292	.4306	.4319
1.5	.4332	.4345	.4357	.4370	.4382	.4394	.4406	.4418	.4429	.4441
1.6	.4452	.4463	.4474	.4484	.4495	.4505	.4515	.4525	.4535	.4545
1.7	.4554	.4564	.4573	.4582	.4591	.4599	.4608	.4616	.4625	.4633
1.8	.4641	.4649	.4656	.4664	.4671	.4678	.4686	.4693	.4699	.4706
1.9	.4713	.4719	.4726	.4732	.4738	.4744	.4750	.4756	.4761	.4767
2.0	.4772	.4778	.4783	.4788	.4793	.4798	.4803	.4808	.4812	.4817
2.1	.4821	.4826	.4830	.4834	.4838	.4842	.4846	.4850	.4854	.4857
2.2	.4861	.4864	.4868	.4871	.4875	.4878	.4881	.4884	.4887	.4890
2.3	.4893	.4896	.4898	.4901	.4904	.4906	.4909	.4911	.4913	.4916
2.4	.4918	.4920	.4922	.4925	.4927	.4929	.4931	.4932	.4934	.4936
2.5	.4938	.4940	.4941	.4943	.4945	.4946	.4948	.4949	.4951	.4952
2.6	.4953	.4955	.4956	.4957	.4959	.4960	.4961	.4962	.4963	.4964
2.7	.4965	.4966	.4967	.4968	.4969	.4970	.4971	.4972	.4973	.4974
2.8	.4974	.4975	.4976	.4977	.4977	.4978	.4979	.4979	.4980	.4981
2.9	.4981	.4982	.4982	.4983	.4984	.4984	.4985	.4985	.4986	.4986
3.0	.4986	.4987	.4987	.4988	.4988	.4989	.4989	.4989	.4990	.4990

TABLE 2   *t* Distribution

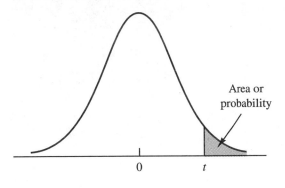

Area or probability

Entries in the table give *t* values for an area or probability in the upper tail of the *t* distribution. For example, with 10 degrees of freedom and a .05 area in the upper tail, $t_{.05} = 1.812$.

Degrees of Freedom	Area in Upper Tail				
	.10	.05	.025	.01	.005
1	3.078	6.314	12.706	31.821	63.657
2	1.886	2.920	4.303	6.965	9.925
3	1.638	2.353	3.182	4.541	5.841
4	1.533	2.132	2.776	3.747	4.604
5	1.476	2.015	2.571	3.365	4.032
6	1.440	1.943	2.447	3.143	3.707
7	1.415	1.895	2.365	2.998	3.499
8	1.397	1.860	2.306	2.896	3.355
9	1.383	1.833	2.262	2.821	3.250
10	1.372	1.812	2.228	2.764	3.169
11	1.363	1.796	2.201	2.718	3.106
12	1.356	1.782	2.179	2.681	3.055
13	1.350	1.771	2.160	2.650	3.012
14	1.345	1.761	2.145	2.624	2.977
15	1.341	1.753	2.131	2.602	2.947
16	1.337	1.746	2.120	2.583	2.921
17	1.333	1.740	2.110	2.567	2.898
18	1.330	1.734	2.101	2.552	2.878
19	1.328	1.729	2.093	2.539	2.861
20	1.325	1.725	2.086	2.528	2.845
21	1.323	1.721	2.080	2.518	2.831
22	1.321	1.717	2.074	2.508	2.819
23	1.319	1.714	2.069	2.500	2.807
24	1.318	1.711	2.064	2.492	2.797
25	1.316	1.708	2.060	2.485	2.787
26	1.315	1.706	2.056	2.479	2.779
27	1.314	1.703	2.052	2.473	2.771
28	1.313	1.701	2.048	2.467	2.763
29	1.311	1.699	2.045	2.462	2.756
30	1.310	1.697	2.042	2.457	2.750
40	1.303	1.684	2.021	2.423	2.704
60	1.296	1.671	2.000	2.390	2.660
120	1.289	1.658	1.980	2.358	2.617
∞	1.282	1.645	1.960	2.326	2.576

This table is reprinted by permission of Oxford University Press on behalf of The Biometrika Trustees from Table 12, Percentage Points of the *t* Distribution, by E. S. Pearson and H. O. Hartley, *Biometrika Tables for Statisticians,* Vol. 1, 3rd ed., 1966.

TABLE 3 Chi-Square Distribution

Entries in the table give χ_α^2 values, where α is the area or probability in the upper tail of the chi-square distribution. For example, with 10 degrees of freedom and a .01 area in the upper tail, $\chi_{.01}^2 = 23.2093$.

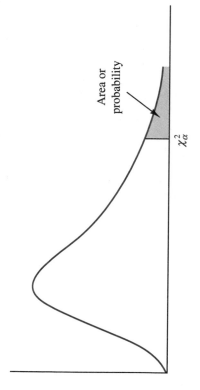

Area or probability

χ_α^2

Degrees of Freedom	Area in Upper Tail									
	.995	.99	.975	.95	.90	.10	.05	.025	.01	.005
1	$392{,}704 \times 10^{-10}$	$157{,}088 \times 10^{-9}$	$982{,}069 \times 10^{-9}$	$393{,}214 \times 10^{-8}$	.0157908	2.70554	3.84146	5.02389	6.63490	7.87944
2	.0100251	.0201007	.0506356	.102587	.210720	4.60517	5.99147	7.37776	9.21034	10.5966
3	.0717212	.114832	.215795	.351846	.584375	6.25139	7.81473	9.34840	11.3449	12.8381
4	.206990	.297110	.484419	.710721	1.063623	7.77944	9.48773	11.1433	13.2767	14.8602
5	.411740	.554300	.831211	1.145476	1.61031	9.23635	11.0705	12.8325	15.0863	16.7496
6	.675727	.872085	1.237347	1.63539	2.20413	10.6446	12.5916	14.4494	16.8119	18.5476
7	.989265	1.239043	1.68987	2.16735	2.83311	12.0170	14.0671	16.0128	18.4753	20.2777
8	1.344419	1.646482	2.17973	2.73264	3.48954	13.3616	15.5073	17.5346	20.0902	21.9550
9	1.734926	2.087912	2.70039	3.32511	4.16816	14.6837	16.9190	19.0228	21.6660	23.5893
10	2.15585	2.55821	3.24697	3.94030	4.86518	15.9871	18.3070	20.4831	23.2093	25.1882
11	2.60321	3.05347	3.81575	4.57481	5.57779	17.2750	19.6751	21.9200	24.7250	26.7569
12	3.07382	3.57056	4.40379	5.22603	6.30380	18.5494	21.0261	23.3367	26.2170	28.2995
13	3.56503	4.10691	5.00874	5.89186	7.04150	19.8119	22.3621	24.7356	27.6883	29.8194
14	4.07468	4.66043	5.62872	6.57063	7.78953	21.0642	23.6848	26.1190	29.1413	31.3193
15	4.60094	5.22935	6.26214	7.26094	8.54675	22.3072	24.9958	27.4884	30.5779	32.8013
16	5.14224	5.81221	6.90766	7.96164	9.31223	23.5418	26.2962	28.8454	31.9999	34.2672
17	5.69724	6.40776	7.56418	8.67176	10.0852	24.7690	27.5871	30.1910	33.4087	35.7185
18	6.26481	7.01491	8.23075	9.39046	10.8649	25.9894	28.8693	31.5264	34.8053	37.1564
19	6.84398	7.63273	8.90655	10.1170	11.6509	27.2036	30.1435	32.8523	36.1908	38.5822

Area in Upper Tail

Degrees of Freedom	.995	.99	.975	.95	.90	.10	.05	.025	.01	.005
20	7.43386	8.26040	9.59083	10.8508	12.4426	28.4120	31.4104	34.1696	37.5662	39.9968
21	8.03366	8.89720	10.28293	11.5913	13.2396	29.6151	32.6705	35.4789	38.9321	41.4010
22	8.64272	9.54249	10.9823	12.3380	14.0415	30.8133	33.9244	36.7807	40.2894	42.7958
23	9.26042	10.19567	11.6885	13.0905	14.8479	32.0069	35.1725	38.0757	41.6384	44.1813
24	9.88623	10.8564	12.4011	13.8484	15.6587	33.1963	36.4151	39.3641	42.9798	45.5585
25	10.5197	11.5240	13.1197	14.6114	16.4734	34.3816	37.6525	40.6465	44.3141	46.9278
26	11.1603	12.1981	13.8439	15.3791	17.2919	35.5631	38.8852	41.9232	45.6417	48.2899
27	11.8076	12.8786	14.5733	16.1513	18.1138	36.7412	40.1133	43.1944	46.9630	49.6449
28	12.4613	13.5648	15.3079	16.9279	18.9392	37.9159	41.3372	44.4607	48.2782	50.9933
29	13.1211	14.2565	16.0471	17.7083	19.7677	39.0875	42.5569	45.7222	49.5879	52.3356
30	13.7867	14.9535	16.7908	18.4926	20.5992	40.2560	43.7729	46.9792	50.8922	53.6720
40	20.7065	22.1643	24.4331	26.5093	29.0505	51.8050	55.7585	59.3417	63.6907	66.7659
50	27.9907	29.7067	32.3574	34.7642	37.6886	63.1671	67.5048	71.4202	76.1539	79.4900
60	35.5346	37.4848	40.4817	43.1879	46.4589	74.3970	79.0819	83.2976	88.3794	91.9517
70	43.2752	45.4418	48.7576	51.7393	55.3290	85.5271	90.5312	95.0231	100.425	104.215
80	51.1720	53.5400	57.1532	60.3915	64.2778	96.5782	101.879	106.629	112.329	116.321
90	59.1963	61.7541	65.6466	69.1260	73.2912	107.565	113.145	118.136	124.116	128.299
100	67.3276	70.0648	74.2219	77.9295	82.3581	118.498	124.342	129.561	135.807	140.169

TABLE 4 ***F* Distribution**

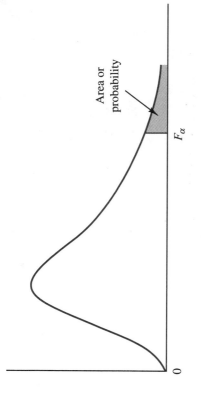

Area or probability

F_α

Entries in the table give F_α values, where α is the area or probability in the upper tail of the F distribution. For example, with 12 numerator degress of freedom, 15 denominator degrees of freedom, and a .05 area in the upper tail, $F_{.05} = 2.48$.

Table of $F_{.05}$ Values

Denominator Degrees of Freedom	Numerator Degrees of Freedom																		
	1	2	3	4	5	6	7	8	9	10	12	15	20	24	30	40	60	120	∞
1	161.4	199.5	215.7	224.6	230.2	234.0	236.8	238.9	240.5	241.9	243.9	245.9	248.0	249.1	250.1	251.1	252.2	253.3	254.3
2	18.51	19.00	19.16	19.25	19.30	19.33	19.35	19.37	19.38	19.40	19.41	19.43	19.45	19.45	19.46	19.47	19.48	19.49	19.50
3	10.13	9.55	9.28	9.12	9.01	8.94	8.89	8.85	8.81	8.79	8.74	8.70	8.66	8.64	8.62	8.59	8.57	8.55	8.53
4	7.71	6.94	6.59	6.39	6.26	6.16	6.09	6.04	6.00	5.96	5.91	5.86	5.80	5.77	5.75	5.72	5.69	5.66	5.63
5	6.61	5.79	5.41	5.19	5.05	4.95	4.88	4.82	4.77	4.74	4.68	4.62	4.56	4.53	4.50	4.46	4.43	4.40	4.36
6	5.99	5.14	4.76	4.53	4.39	4.28	4.21	4.15	4.10	4.06	4.00	3.94	3.87	3.84	3.81	3.77	3.74	3.70	3.67
7	5.59	4.74	4.35	4.12	3.97	3.87	3.79	3.73	3.68	3.64	3.57	3.51	3.44	3.41	3.38	3.34	3.30	3.27	3.23
8	5.32	4.46	4.07	3.84	3.69	3.58	3.50	3.44	3.39	3.35	3.28	3.22	3.15	3.12	3.08	3.04	3.01	2.97	2.93
9	5.12	4.26	3.86	3.63	3.48	3.37	3.29	3.23	3.18	3.14	3.07	3.01	2.94	2.90	2.86	2.83	2.79	2.75	2.71
10	4.96	4.10	3.71	3.48	3.33	3.22	3.14	3.07	3.02	2.98	2.91	2.85	2.77	2.74	2.70	2.66	2.62	2.58	2.54
11	4.84	3.98	3.59	3.36	3.20	3.09	3.01	2.95	2.90	2.85	2.79	2.72	2.65	2.61	2.57	2.53	2.49	2.45	2.40
12	4.75	3.89	3.49	3.26	3.11	3.00	2.91	2.85	2.80	2.75	2.69	2.62	2.54	2.51	2.47	2.43	2.38	2.34	2.30
13	4.67	3.81	3.41	3.18	3.03	2.92	2.83	2.77	2.71	2.67	2.60	2.53	2.46	2.42	2.38	2.34	2.30	2.25	2.21
14	4.60	3.74	3.34	3.11	2.96	2.85	2.76	2.70	2.65	2.60	2.53	2.46	2.39	2.35	2.31	2.27	2.22	2.18	2.13

Table of $F_{.05}$ Values

Denominator Degrees of Freedom	Numerator Degrees of Freedom																		
	1	2	3	4	5	6	7	8	9	10	12	15	20	24	30	40	60	120	∞
15	4.54	3.68	3.29	3.06	2.90	2.79	2.71	2.64	2.59	2.54	2.48	2.40	2.33	2.29	2.25	2.20	2.16	2.11	2.07
16	4.49	3.63	3.24	3.01	2.85	2.74	2.66	2.59	2.54	2.49	2.42	2.35	2.28	2.24	2.19	2.15	2.11	2.06	2.01
17	4.45	3.59	3.20	2.96	2.81	2.70	2.61	2.55	2.49	2.45	2.38	2.31	2.23	2.19	2.15	2.10	2.06	2.01	1.96
18	4.41	3.55	3.16	2.93	2.77	2.66	2.58	2.51	2.46	2.41	2.34	2.27	2.19	2.15	2.11	2.06	2.02	1.97	1.92
19	4.38	3.52	3.13	2.90	2.74	2.63	2.54	2.48	2.42	2.38	2.31	2.23	2.16	2.11	2.07	2.03	1.98	1.93	1.88
20	4.35	3.49	3.10	2.87	2.71	2.60	2.51	2.45	2.39	2.35	2.28	2.20	2.12	2.08	2.04	1.99	1.95	1.90	1.84
21	4.32	3.47	3.07	2.84	2.68	2.57	2.49	2.42	2.37	2.32	2.25	2.18	2.10	2.05	2.01	1.96	1.92	1.87	1.81
22	4.30	3.44	3.05	2.82	2.66	2.55	2.46	2.40	2.34	2.30	2.23	2.15	2.07	2.03	1.98	1.94	1.89	1.84	1.78
23	4.28	3.42	3.03	2.80	2.64	2.53	2.44	2.37	2.32	2.27	2.20	2.13	2.05	2.01	1.96	1.91	1.86	1.81	1.76
24	4.26	3.40	3.01	2.78	2.62	2.51	2.42	2.36	2.30	2.25	2.18	2.11	2.03	1.98	1.94	1.89	1.84	1.79	1.73
25	4.24	3.39	2.99	2.76	2.60	2.49	2.40	2.34	2.28	2.24	2.16	2.09	2.01	1.96	1.92	1.87	1.82	1.77	1.71
26	4.23	3.37	2.98	2.74	2.59	2.47	2.39	2.32	2.27	2.22	2.15	2.07	1.99	1.95	1.90	1.85	1.80	1.75	1.69
27	4.21	3.35	2.96	2.73	2.57	2.46	2.37	2.31	2.25	2.20	2.13	2.06	1.97	1.93	1.88	1.84	1.79	1.73	1.67
28	4.20	3.34	2.95	2.71	2.56	2.45	2.36	2.29	2.24	2.19	2.12	2.04	1.96	1.91	1.87	1.82	1.77	1.71	1.65
29	4.18	3.33	2.93	2.70	2.55	2.43	2.35	2.28	2.22	2.18	2.10	2.03	1.94	1.90	1.85	1.81	1.75	1.70	1.64
30	4.17	3.32	2.92	2.69	2.53	2.42	2.33	2.27	2.21	2.16	2.09	2.01	1.93	1.89	1.84	1.79	1.74	1.68	1.62
40	4.08	3.23	2.84	2.61	2.45	2.34	2.25	2.18	2.12	2.08	2.00	1.92	1.84	1.79	1.74	1.69	1.64	1.58	1.51
60	4.00	3.15	2.76	2.53	2.37	2.25	2.17	2.10	2.04	1.99	1.92	1.84	1.75	1.70	1.65	1.59	1.53	1.47	1.39
120	3.92	3.07	2.68	2.45	2.29	2.17	2.09	2.02	1.96	1.91	1.83	1.75	1.66	1.61	1.55	1.50	1.43	1.35	1.25
∞	3.84	3.00	2.60	2.37	2.21	2.10	2.01	1.94	1.88	1.83	1.75	1.67	1.57	1.52	1.46	1.39	1.32	1.22	1.00

TABLE 4 *F* Distribution *(Continued)*

Table of $F_{.01}$ Values

Denominator Degrees of Freedom	Numerator Degrees of Freedom																		
	1	2	3	4	5	6	7	8	9	10	12	15	20	24	30	40	60	120	∞
1	4,052	4,999.5	5,403	5,625	5,764	5,859	5,928	5,982	6,022	6,056	6,106	6,157	6,209	6,235	6,261	6,287	6,313	6,339	6,366
2	98.50	99.00	99.17	99.25	99.30	99.33	99.36	99.37	99.39	99.40	99.42	99.43	99.45	99.46	99.47	99.47	99.48	99.49	99.50
3	34.12	30.82	29.46	28.71	28.24	27.91	27.67	27.49	27.35	27.23	27.05	26.87	26.69	26.60	26.50	26.41	26.32	26.22	26.13
4	21.20	18.00	16.69	15.98	15.52	15.21	14.98	14.80	14.66	14.55	14.37	14.20	14.02	13.93	13.84	13.75	13.65	13.56	13.46
5	16.26	13.27	12.06	11.39	10.97	10.67	10.46	10.29	10.16	10.05	9.89	9.72	9.55	9.47	9.38	9.29	9.20	9.11	9.06
6	13.75	10.92	9.78	9.15	8.75	8.47	8.26	8.10	7.98	7.87	7.72	7.56	7.40	7.31	7.23	7.14	7.06	6.97	6.88
7	12.25	9.55	8.45	7.85	7.46	7.19	6.99	6.84	6.72	6.62	6.47	6.31	6.16	6.07	5.99	5.91	5.82	5.74	5.65
8	11.26	8.65	7.59	7.01	6.63	6.37	6.18	6.03	5.91	5.81	5.67	5.52	5.36	5.28	5.20	5.12	5.03	4.95	4.86
9	10.56	8.02	6.99	6.42	6.06	5.80	5.61	5.47	5.35	5.26	5.11	4.96	4.81	4.73	4.65	4.57	4.48	4.40	4.31
10	10.04	7.56	6.55	5.99	5.64	5.39	5.20	5.06	4.94	4.85	4.71	4.56	4.41	4.33	4.25	4.17	4.08	4.00	3.91
11	9.65	7.21	6.22	5.67	5.32	5.07	4.89	4.74	4.63	4.54	4.40	4.25	4.10	4.02	3.94	3.86	3.78	3.69	3.60
12	9.33	6.93	5.95	5.41	5.06	4.82	4.64	4.50	4.39	4.30	4.16	4.01	3.86	3.78	3.70	3.62	3.54	3.45	3.36
13	9.07	6.70	5.74	5.21	4.86	4.62	4.44	4.30	4.19	4.10	3.96	3.82	3.66	3.59	3.51	3.43	3.34	3.25	3.17
14	8.86	6.51	5.56	5.04	4.69	4.46	4.28	4.14	4.03	3.94	3.80	3.66	3.51	3.43	3.35	3.27	3.18	3.09	3.00
15	8.68	6.36	5.42	4.89	4.56	4.32	4.14	4.00	3.89	3.80	3.67	3.52	3.37	3.29	3.21	3.13	3.05	2.96	2.87
16	8.53	6.23	5.29	4.77	4.44	4.20	4.03	3.89	3.78	3.69	3.55	3.41	3.26	3.18	3.10	3.02	2.93	2.84	2.75
17	8.40	6.11	5.18	4.67	4.34	4.10	3.93	3.79	3.68	3.59	3.46	3.31	3.16	3.08	3.00	2.92	2.83	2.75	2.65
18	8.29	6.01	5.09	4.58	4.25	4.01	3.84	3.71	3.60	3.51	3.37	3.23	3.08	3.00	2.92	2.84	2.75	2.66	2.57
19	8.18	5.93	5.01	4.50	4.17	3.94	3.77	3.63	3.52	3.43	3.30	3.15	3.00	2.92	2.84	2.76	2.67	2.58	2.49

Table of $F_{.01}$ Values

Numerator Degrees of Freedom

Denominator Degrees of Freedom	1	2	3	4	5	6	7	8	9	10	12	15	20	24	30	40	60	120	∞
20	8.10	5.85	4.94	4.43	4.10	3.87	3.70	3.56	3.46	3.37	3.23	3.09	2.94	2.86	2.78	2.69	2.61	2.52	2.42
21	8.02	5.78	4.87	4.37	4.04	3.81	3.64	3.51	3.40	3.31	3.17	3.03	2.88	2.80	2.72	2.64	2.55	2.46	2.36
22	7.95	5.72	4.82	4.31	3.99	3.76	3.59	3.45	3.35	3.26	3.12	2.98	2.83	2.75	2.67	2.58	2.50	2.40	2.31
23	7.88	5.66	4.76	4.26	3.94	3.71	3.54	3.41	3.30	3.21	3.07	2.93	2.78	2.70	2.62	2.54	2.45	2.35	2.26
24	7.82	5.61	4.72	4.22	3.90	3.67	3.50	3.36	3.26	3.17	3.03	2.89	2.74	2.66	2.58	2.49	2.40	2.31	2.21
25	7.77	5.57	4.68	4.18	3.85	3.63	3.46	3.32	3.22	3.13	2.99	2.85	2.70	2.62	2.54	2.45	2.36	2.27	2.17
26	7.72	5.53	4.64	4.14	3.82	3.59	3.42	3.29	3.18	3.09	2.96	2.81	2.66	2.58	2.50	2.42	2.33	2.23	2.13
27	7.68	5.49	4.60	4.11	3.78	3.56	3.39	3.26	3.15	3.06	2.93	2.78	2.63	2.55	2.47	2.38	2.29	2.20	2.10
28	7.64	5.45	4.57	4.07	3.75	3.53	3.36	3.23	3.12	3.03	2.90	2.75	2.60	2.52	2.44	2.35	2.26	2.17	2.06
29	7.60	5.42	4.54	4.04	3.73	3.50	3.33	3.20	3.09	3.00	2.87	2.73	2.57	2.49	2.41	2.33	2.23	2.14	2.03
30	7.56	5.39	4.51	4.02	3.70	3.47	3.30	3.17	3.07	2.98	2.84	2.70	2.55	2.47	2.39	2.30	2.21	2.11	2.01
40	7.31	5.18	4.31	3.83	3.51	3.29	3.12	2.99	2.89	2.80	2.66	2.52	2.37	2.29	2.20	2.11	2.02	1.92	1.80
60	7.08	4.98	4.13	3.65	3.34	3.12	2.95	2.82	2.72	2.63	2.50	2.35	2.20	2.12	2.03	1.94	1.84	1.73	1.60
120	6.85	4.79	3.95	3.48	3.17	2.96	2.79	2.66	2.56	2.47	2.34	2.19	2.03	1.95	1.86	1.76	1.66	1.53	1.38
∞	6.63	4.61	3.78	3.32	3.02	2.80	2.64	2.51	2.41	2.32	2.18	2.04	1.88	1.79	1.70	1.59	1.47	1.32	1.00

TABLE 4 *F* Distribution (Continued)

Table of $F_{.025}$ Values

Denominator Degrees of Freedom	Numerator Degrees of Freedom																		
	1	2	3	4	5	6	7	8	9	10	12	15	20	24	30	40	60	120	∞
1	647.8	799.5	864.2	899.6	921.8	937.1	948.2	956.7	963.3	968.6	976.7	984.9	993.1	997.2	1,001	1,006	1,010	1,014	1,018
2	38.51	39.00	39.17	39.25	39.30	39.33	39.36	39.37	39.39	39.40	39.41	39.43	39.45	39.46	39.46	39.47	39.48	39.49	39.50
3	17.44	16.04	15.44	15.10	14.88	14.73	14.62	14.54	14.47	14.42	14.34	14.25	14.17	14.12	14.08	14.04	13.99	13.95	13.90
4	12.22	10.65	9.98	9.60	9.36	9.20	9.07	8.98	8.90	8.84	8.75	8.66	8.56	8.51	8.46	8.41	8.36	8.31	8.26
5	10.01	8.43	7.76	7.39	7.15	6.98	6.85	6.76	6.68	6.62	6.52	6.43	6.33	6.28	6.23	6.18	6.12	6.07	6.02
6	8.81	7.26	6.60	6.23	5.99	5.82	5.70	5.60	5.52	5.46	5.37	5.27	5.17	5.12	5.07	5.01	4.96	4.90	4.85
7	8.07	6.54	5.89	5.52	5.29	5.21	4.99	4.90	4.82	4.76	4.67	4.57	4.47	4.42	4.36	4.31	4.25	4.20	4.14
8	7.57	6.06	5.42	5.05	4.82	4.65	4.53	4.43	4.36	4.30	4.20	4.10	4.00	3.95	3.89	3.84	3.78	3.73	3.67
9	7.21	5.71	5.08	4.72	4.48	4.32	4.20	4.10	4.03	3.96	3.87	3.77	3.67	3.61	3.56	3.51	3.45	3.39	3.33
10	6.94	5.46	4.83	4.47	4.24	4.07	3.95	3.85	3.78	3.72	3.62	3.52	3.42	3.37	3.31	3.26	3.20	3.14	3.08
11	6.72	5.26	4.63	4.28	4.04	3.88	3.76	3.66	3.59	3.53	3.43	3.33	3.23	3.17	3.12	3.06	3.00	2.94	2.88
12	6.55	5.10	4.47	4.12	3.89	3.73	3.61	3.51	3.44	3.37	3.28	3.18	3.07	3.02	2.96	2.91	2.85	2.79	2.72
13	6.41	4.97	4.35	4.00	3.77	3.60	3.48	3.39	3.31	3.25	3.15	3.05	2.95	2.89	2.84	2.78	2.72	2.66	2.60
14	6.30	4.86	4.24	3.89	3.66	3.50	3.38	3.29	3.21	3.15	3.05	2.95	2.84	2.79	2.73	2.67	2.61	2.55	2.49
15	6.20	4.77	4.15	3.80	3.58	3.41	3.29	3.20	3.12	3.06	2.96	2.86	2.76	2.70	2.64	2.59	2.52	2.46	2.40
16	6.12	4.69	4.08	3.73	3.50	3.34	3.22	3.12	3.05	2.99	2.89	2.79	2.68	2.63	2.57	2.51	2.45	2.38	2.32
17	6.04	4.62	4.01	3.66	3.44	3.28	3.16	3.06	2.98	2.92	2.82	2.72	2.62	2.56	2.50	2.44	2.38	2.32	2.25
18	5.98	4.56	3.95	3.61	3.38	3.22	3.10	3.01	2.93	2.87	2.77	2.67	2.56	2.50	2.44	2.38	2.32	2.26	2.19
19	5.92	4.51	3.90	3.56	3.33	3.17	3.05	2.96	2.88	2.82	2.72	2.62	2.51	2.45	2.39	2.33	2.27	2.20	2.13

Table of $F_{.025}$ Values

Numerator Degrees of Freedom

Denominator Degrees of Freedom	1	2	3	4	5	6	7	8	9	10	12	15	20	24	30	40	60	120	∞
20	5.87	4.46	3.86	3.51	3.29	3.13	3.01	2.91	2.84	2.77	2.68	2.57	2.46	2.41	2.35	2.29	2.22	2.16	2.09
21	5.83	4.42	3.82	3.48	3.25	3.09	2.97	2.87	2.80	2.73	2.64	2.53	2.42	2.37	2.31	2.25	2.18	2.11	2.04
22	5.79	4.38	3.78	3.44	3.22	3.05	2.93	2.84	2.76	2.70	2.60	2.50	2.39	2.33	2.27	2.21	2.14	2.08	2.00
23	5.75	4.35	3.75	3.41	3.18	3.02	2.90	2.81	2.73	2.67	2.57	2.47	2.36	2.30	2.24	2.18	2.11	2.04	1.97
24	5.72	4.32	3.72	3.38	3.15	2.99	2.87	2.78	2.70	2.64	2.54	2.44	2.33	2.27	2.21	2.15	2.08	2.01	1.94
25	5.69	4.29	3.69	3.35	3.13	2.97	2.85	2.75	2.68	2.61	2.51	2.41	2.30	2.24	2.18	2.12	2.05	1.98	1.91
26	5.66	4.27	3.67	3.33	3.10	2.94	2.82	2.73	2.65	2.59	2.49	2.39	2.28	2.22	2.16	2.09	2.03	1.95	1.88
27	5.63	4.24	3.65	3.31	3.08	2.92	2.80	2.71	2.63	2.57	2.47	2.36	2.25	2.19	2.13	2.07	2.00	1.93	1.85
28	5.61	4.22	3.63	3.29	3.06	2.90	2.78	2.69	2.61	2.55	2.45	2.34	2.23	2.17	2.11	2.05	1.98	1.91	1.83
29	5.59	4.20	3.61	3.27	3.04	2.88	2.76	2.67	2.59	2.53	2.43	2.32	2.21	2.15	2.09	2.03	1.96	1.89	1.81
30	5.57	4.18	3.59	3.25	3.03	2.87	2.75	2.65	2.57	2.51	2.41	2.31	2.20	2.14	2.07	2.01	1.94	1.87	1.79
40	5.42	4.05	3.46	3.13	2.90	2.74	2.62	2.53	2.45	2.39	2.29	2.18	2.07	2.01	1.94	1.88	1.80	1.72	1.64
60	5.29	3.93	3.34	3.01	2.79	2.63	2.51	2.41	2.33	2.27	2.17	2.06	1.94	1.88	1.82	1.74	1.67	1.58	1.48
120	5.15	3.80	3.23	2.89	2.67	2.52	2.39	2.30	2.22	2.16	2.05	1.94	1.82	1.76	1.69	1.61	1.53	1.43	1.31
∞	5.02	3.69	3.12	2.79	2.57	2.41	2.29	2.19	2.11	2.05	1.94	1.83	1.71	1.64	1.57	1.48	1.39	1.27	1.00

This table is reprinted by permission of Oxford University Press on behalf of The Biometrika Trustees from Table 18, Percentage Points of the *F* Distribution, by E. S. Pearson and H. O. Hartley, *Biometrika Tables for Statisticians*, Vol. 1, 3rd ed., 1966.

TABLE 5   Binomial Probabilities

Entries in the table give the probability of x successes in n trials of a binomial experiment, where p is the probability of a success on one trial. For example, with six trials and p = .05, the probability of two successes is .0305.

						p				
n	x	.01	.02	.03	.04	.05	.06	.07	.08	.09
2	0	.9801	.9604	.9409	.9216	.9025	.8836	.8649	.8464	.8281
	1	.0198	.0392	.0582	.0768	.0950	.1128	.1302	.1472	.1638
	2	.0001	.0004	.0009	.0016	.0025	.0036	.0049	.0064	.0081
3	0	.9703	.9412	.9127	.8847	.8574	.8306	.8044	.7787	.7536
	1	.0294	.0576	.0847	.1106	.1354	.1590	.1816	.2031	.2236
	2	.0003	.0012	.0026	.0046	.0071	.0102	.0137	.0177	.0221
	3	.0000	.0000	.0000	.0001	.0001	.0002	.0003	.0005	.0007
4	0	.9606	.9224	.8853	.8493	.8145	.7807	.7481	.7164	.6857
	1	.0388	.0753	.1095	.1416	.1715	.1993	.2252	.2492	.2713
	2	.0006	.0023	.0051	.0088	.0135	.0191	.0254	.0325	.0402
	3	.0000	.0000	.0001	.0002	.0005	.0008	.0013	.0019	.0027
	4	.0000	.0000	.0000	.0000	.0000	.0000	.0000	.0000	.0001
5	0	.9510	.9039	.8587	.8154	.7738	.7339	.6957	.6591	.6240
	1	.0480	.0922	.1328	.1699	.2036	.2342	.2618	.2866	.3086
	2	.0010	.0038	.0082	.0142	.0214	.0299	.0394	.0498	.0610
	3	.0000	.0001	.0003	.0006	.0011	.0019	.0030	.0043	.0060
	4	.0000	.0000	.0000	.0000	.0000	.0001	.0001	.0002	.0003
	5	.0000	.0000	.0000	.0000	.0000	.0000	.0000	.0000	.0000
6	0	.9415	.8858	.8330	.7828	.7351	.6899	.6470	.6064	.5679
	1	.0571	.1085	.1546	.1957	.2321	.2642	.2922	.3164	.3370
	2	.0014	.0055	.0120	.0204	.0305	.0422	.0550	.0688	.0833
	3	.0000	.0002	.0005	.0011	.0021	.0036	.0055	.0080	.0110
	4	.0000	.0000	.0000	.0000	.0001	.0002	.0003	.0005	.0008
	5	.0000	.0000	.0000	.0000	.0000	.0000	.0000	.0000	.0000
	6	.0000	.0000	.0000	.0000	.0000	.0000	.0000	.0000	.0000
7	0	.9321	.8681	.8080	.7514	.6983	.6485	.6017	.5578	.5168
	1	.0659	.1240	.1749	.2192	.2573	.2897	.3170	.3396	.3578
	2	.0020	.0076	.0162	.0274	.0406	.0555	.0716	.0886	.1061
	3	.0000	.0003	.0008	.0019	.0036	.0059	.0090	.0128	.0175
	4	.0000	.0000	.0000	.0001	.0002	.0004	.0007	.0011	.0017
	5	.0000	.0000	.0000	.0000	.0000	.0000	.0000	.0001	.0001
	6	.0000	.0000	.0000	.0000	.0000	.0000	.0000	.0000	.0000
	7	.0000	.0000	.0000	.0000	.0000	.0000	.0000	.0000	.0000
8	0	.9227	.8508	.7837	.7214	.6634	.6096	.5596	.5132	.4703
	1	.0746	.1389	.1939	.2405	.2793	.3113	.3370	.3570	.3721
	2	.0026	.0099	.0210	.0351	.0515	.0695	.0888	.1087	.1288
	3	.0001	.0004	.0013	.0029	.0054	.0089	.0134	.0189	.0255
	4	.0000	.0000	.0001	.0002	.0004	.0007	.0013	.0021	.0031
	5	.0000	.0000	.0000	.0000	.0000	.0000	.0001	.0001	.0002
	6	.0000	.0000	.0000	.0000	.0000	.0000	.0000	.0000	.0000
	7	.0000	.0000	.0000	.0000	.0000	.0000	.0000	.0000	.0000
	8	.0000	.0000	.0000	.0000	.0000	.0000	.0000	.0000	.0000

TABLE 5   Binomial Probabilities (*Continued*)

n	x	.01	.02	.03	.04	.05	.06	.07	.08	.09
9	0	.9135	.8337	.7602	.6925	.6302	.5730	.5204	.4722	.4279
	1	.0830	.1531	.2116	.2597	.2985	.3292	.3525	.3695	.3809
	2	.0034	.0125	.0262	.0433	.0629	.0840	.1061	.1285	.1507
	3	.0001	.0006	.0019	.0042	.0077	.0125	.0186	.0261	.0348
	4	.0000	.0000	.0001	.0003	.0006	.0012	.0021	.0034	.0052
	5	.0000	.0000	.0000	.0000	.0000	.0001	.0002	.0003	.0005
	6	.0000	.0000	.0000	.0000	.0000	.0000	.0000	.0000	.0000
	7	.0000	.0000	.0000	.0000	.0000	.0000	.0000	.0000	.0000
	8	.0000	.0000	.0000	.0000	.0000	.0000	.0000	.0000	.0000
	9	.0000	.0000	.0000	.0000	.0000	.0000	.0000	.0000	.0000
10	0	.9044	.8171	.7374	.6648	.5987	.5386	.4840	.4344	.3894
	1	.0914	.1667	.2281	.2770	.3151	.3438	.3643	.3777	.3851
	2	.0042	.0153	.0317	.0519	.0746	.0988	.1234	.1478	.1714
	3	.0001	.0008	.0026	.0058	.0105	.0168	.0248	.0343	.0452
	4	.0000	.0000	.0001	.0004	.0010	.0019	.0033	.0052	.0078
	5	.0000	.0000	.0000	.0000	.0001	.0001	.0003	.0005	.0009
	6	.0000	.0000	.0000	.0000	.0000	.0000	.0000	.0000	.0001
	7	.0000	.0000	.0000	.0000	.0000	.0000	.0000	.0000	.0000
	8	.0000	.0000	.0000	.0000	.0000	.0000	.0000	.0000	.0001
	9	.0000	.0000	.0000	.0000	.0000	.0000	.0000	.0000	.0001
	10	.0000	.0000	.0000	.0000	.0000	.0000	.0000	.0000	.0001
12	0	.8864	.7847	.6938	.6127	.5404	.4759	.4186	.3677	.3225
	1	.1074	.1922	.2575	.3064	.3413	.3645	.3781	.3837	.3827
	2	.0060	.0216	.0438	.0702	.0988	.1280	.1565	.1835	.2082
	3	.0002	.0015	.0045	.0098	.0173	.0272	.0393	.0532	.0686
	4	.0000	.0001	.0003	.0009	.0021	.0039	.0067	.0104	.0153
	5	.0000	.0000	.0000	.0001	.0002	.0004	.0008	.0014	.0024
	6	.0000	.0000	.0000	.0000	.0000	.0000	.0001	.0001	.0003
	7	.0000	.0000	.0000	.0000	.0000	.0000	.0000	.0000	.0000
	8	.0000	.0000	.0000	.0000	.0000	.0000	.0000	.0000	.0000
	9	.0000	.0000	.0000	.0000	.0000	.0000	.0000	.0000	.0000
	10	.0000	.0000	.0000	.0000	.0000	.0000	.0000	.0000	.0000
	11	.0000	.0000	.0000	.0000	.0000	.0000	.0000	.0000	.0000
	12	.0000	.0000	.0000	.0000	.0000	.0000	.0000	.0000	.0000
15	0	.8601	.7386	.6333	.5421	.4633	.3953	.3367	.2863	.2430
	1	.1303	.2261	.2938	.3388	.3658	.3785	.3801	.3734	.3605
	2	.0092	.0323	.0636	.0988	.1348	.1691	.2003	.2273	.2496
	3	.0004	.0029	.0085	.0178	.0307	.0468	.0653	.0857	.1070
	4	.0000	.0002	.0008	.0022	.0049	.0090	.0148	.0223	.0317
	5	.0000	.0000	.0001	.0002	.0006	.0013	.0024	.0043	.0069
	6	.0000	.0000	.0000	.0000	.0000	.0001	.0003	.0006	.0011
	7	.0000	.0000	.0000	.0000	.0000	.0000	.0000	.0001	.0001
	8	.0000	.0000	.0000	.0000	.0000	.0000	.0000	.0000	.0000
	9	.0000	.0000	.0000	.0000	.0000	.0000	.0000	.0000	.0000
	10	.0000	.0000	.0000	.0000	.0000	.0000	.0000	.0000	.0000
	11	.0000	.0000	.0000	.0000	.0000	.0000	.0000	.0000	.0000
	12	.0000	.0000	.0000	.0000	.0000	.0000	.0000	.0000	.0000
	13	.0000	.0000	.0000	.0000	.0000	.0000	.0000	.0000	.0000
	14	.0000	.0000	.0000	.0000	.0000	.0000	.0000	.0000	.0000
	15	.0000	.0000	.0000	.0000	.0000	.0000	.0000	.0000	.0000

TABLE 5   Binomial Probabilities (*Continued*)

						p				
n	*x*	.01	.02	.03	.04	.05	.06	.07	.08	.09
18	0	.8345	.6951	.5780	.4796	.3972	.3283	.2708	.2229	.1831
	1	.1517	.2554	.3217	.3597	.3763	.3772	.3669	.3489	.3260
	2	.0130	.0443	.0846	.1274	.1683	.2047	.2348	.2579	.2741
	3	.0007	.0048	.0140	.0283	.0473	.0697	.0942	.1196	.1446
	4	.0000	.0004	.0016	.0044	.0093	.0167	.0266	.0390	.0536
	5	.0000	.0000	.0001	.0005	.0014	.0030	.0056	.0095	.0148
	6	.0000	.0000	.0000	.0000	.0002	.0004	.0009	.0018	.0032
	7	.0000	.0000	.0000	.0000	.0000	.0000	.0001	.0003	.0005
	8	.0000	.0000	.0000	.0000	.0000	.0000	.0000	.0000	.0001
	9	.0000	.0000	.0000	.0000	.0000	.0000	.0000	.0000	.0000
	10	.0000	.0000	.0000	.0000	.0000	.0000	.0000	.0000	.0000
	11	.0000	.0000	.0000	.0000	.0000	.0000	.0000	.0000	.0000
	12	.0000	.0000	.0000	.0000	.0000	.0000	.0000	.0000	.0000
	13	.0000	.0000	.0000	.0000	.0000	.0000	.0000	.0000	.0000
	14	.0000	.0000	.0000	.0000	.0000	.0000	.0000	.0000	.0000
	15	.0000	.0000	.0000	.0000	.0000	.0000	.0000	.0000	.0000
	16	.0000	.0000	.0000	.0000	.0000	.0000	.0000	.0000	.0000
	17	.0000	.0000	.0000	.0000	.0000	.0000	.0000	.0000	.0000
	18	.0000	.0000	.0000	.0000	.0000	.0000	.0000	.0000	.0000
20	0	.8179	.6676	.5438	.4420	.3585	.2901	.2342	.1887	.1516
	1	.1652	.2725	.3364	.3683	.3774	.3703	.3526	.3282	.3000
	2	.0159	.0528	.0988	.1458	.1887	.2246	.2521	.2711	.2818
	3	.0010	.0065	.0183	.0364	.0596	.0860	.1139	.1414	.1672
	4	.0000	.0006	.0024	.0065	.0133	.0233	.0364	.0523	.0703
	5	.0000	.0000	.0002	.0009	.0022	.0048	.0088	.0145	.0222
	6	.0000	.0000	.0000	.0001	.0003	.0008	.0017	.0032	.0055
	7	.0000	.0000	.0000	.0000	.0000	.0001	.0002	.0005	.0011
	8	.0000	.0000	.0000	.0000	.0000	.0000	.0000	.0001	.0002
	9	.0000	.0000	.0000	.0000	.0000	.0000	.0000	.0000	.0000
	10	.0000	.0000	.0000	.0000	.0000	.0000	.0000	.0000	.0000
	11	.0000	.0000	.0000	.0000	.0000	.0000	.0000	.0000	.0000
	12	.0000	.0000	.0000	.0000	.0000	.0000	.0000	.0000	.0000
	13	.0000	.0000	.0000	.0000	.0000	.0000	.0000	.0000	.0000
	14	.0000	.0000	.0000	.0000	.0000	.0000	.0000	.0000	.0000
	15	.0000	.0000	.0000	.0000	.0000	.0000	.0000	.0000	.0000
	16	.0000	.0000	.0000	.0000	.0000	.0000	.0000	.0000	.0000
	17	.0000	.0000	.0000	.0000	.0000	.0000	.0000	.0000	.0000
	18	.0000	.0000	.0000	.0000	.0000	.0000	.0000	.0000	.0000
	19	.0000	.0000	.0000	.0000	.0000	.0000	.0000	.0000	.0000
	20	.0000	.0000	.0000	.0000	.0000	.0000	.0000	.0000	.0000

TABLE 5   Binomial Probabilities (*Continued*)

n	x	.10	.15	.20	.25	p .30	.35	.40	.45	.50
2	0	.8100	.7225	.6400	.5625	.4900	.4225	.3600	.3025	.2500
	1	.1800	.2550	.3200	.3750	.4200	.4550	.4800	.4950	.5000
	2	.0100	.0225	.0400	.0625	.0900	.1225	.1600	.2025	.2500
3	0	.7290	.6141	.5120	.4219	.3430	.2746	.2160	.1664	.1250
	1	.2430	.3251	.3840	.4219	.4410	.4436	.4320	.4084	.3750
	2	.0270	.0574	.0960	.1406	.1890	.2389	.2880	.3341	.3750
	3	.0010	.0034	.0080	.0156	.0270	.0429	.0640	.0911	.1250
4	0	.6561	.5220	.4096	.3164	.2401	.1785	.1296	.0915	.0625
	1	.2916	.3685	.4096	.4219	.4116	.3845	.3456	.2995	.2500
	2	.0486	.0975	.1536	.2109	.2646	.3105	.3456	.3675	.3750
	3	.0036	.0115	.0256	.0469	.0756	.1115	.1536	.2005	.2500
	4	.0001	.0005	.0016	.0039	.0081	.0150	.0256	.0410	.0625
5	0	.5905	.4437	.3277	.2373	.1681	.1160	.0778	.0503	.0312
	1	.3280	.3915	.4096	.3955	.3602	.3124	.2592	.2059	.1562
	2	.0729	.1382	.2048	.2637	.3087	.3364	.3456	.3369	.3125
	3	.0081	.0244	.0512	.0879	.1323	.1811	.2304	.2757	.3125
	4	.0004	.0022	.0064	.0146	.0284	.0488	.0768	.1128	.1562
	5	.0000	.0001	.0003	.0010	.0024	.0053	.0102	.0185	.0312
6	0	.5314	.3771	.2621	.1780	.1176	.0754	.0467	.0277	.0156
	1	.3543	.3993	.3932	.3560	.3025	.2437	.1866	.1359	.0938
	2	.0984	.1762	.2458	.2966	.3241	.3280	.3110	.2780	.2344
	3	.0146	.0415	.0819	.1318	.1852	.2355	.2765	.3032	.3125
	4	.0012	.0055	.0154	.0330	.0595	.0951	.1382	.1861	.2344
	5	.0001	.0004	.0015	.0044	.0102	.0205	.0369	.0609	.0938
	6	.0000	.0000	.0001	.0002	.0007	.0018	.0041	.0083	.0156
7	0	.4783	.3206	.2097	.1335	.0824	.0490	.0280	.0152	.0078
	1	.3720	.3960	.3670	.3115	.2471	.1848	.1306	.0872	.0547
	2	.1240	.2097	.2753	.3115	.3177	.2985	.2613	.2140	.1641
	3	.0230	.0617	.1147	.1730	.2269	.2679	.2903	.2918	.2734
	4	.0026	.0109	.0287	.0577	.0972	.1442	.1935	.2388	.2734
	5	.0002	.0012	.0043	.0115	.0250	.0466	.0774	.1172	.1641
	6	.0000	.0001	.0004	.0013	.0036	.0084	.0172	.0320	.0547
	7	.0000	.0000	.0000	.0001	.0002	.0006	.0016	.0037	.0078
8	0	.4305	.2725	.1678	.1001	.0576	.0319	.0168	.0084	.0039
	1	.3826	.3847	.3355	.2670	.1977	.1373	.0896	.0548	.0312
	2	.1488	.2376	.2936	.3115	.2965	.2587	.2090	.1569	.1094
	3	.0331	.0839	.1468	.2076	.2541	.2786	.2787	.2568	.2188
	4	.0046	.0185	.0459	.0865	.1361	.1875	.2322	.2627	.2734
	5	.0004	.0026	.0092	.0231	.0467	.0808	.1239	.1719	.2188
	6	.0000	.0002	.0011	.0038	.0100	.0217	.0413	.0703	.1094
	7	.0000	.0000	.0001	.0004	.0012	.0033	.0079	.0164	.0312
	8	.0000	.0000	.0000	.0000	.0001	.0002	.0007	.0017	.0039

TABLE 5   Binomial Probabilities (*Continued*)

n	x	.10	.15	.20	.25	*p* .30	.35	.40	.45	.50
9	0	.3874	.2316	.1342	.0751	.0404	.0207	.0101	.0046	.0020
	1	.3874	.3679	.3020	.2253	.1556	.1004	.0605	.0339	.0176
	2	.1722	.2597	.3020	.3003	.2668	.2162	.1612	.1110	.0703
	3	.0446	.1069	.1762	.2336	.2668	.2716	.2508	.2119	.1641
	4	.0074	.0283	.0661	.1168	.1715	.2194	.2508	.2600	.2461
	5	.0008	.0050	.0165	.0389	.0735	.1181	.1672	.2128	.2461
	6	.0001	.0006	.0028	.0087	.0210	.0424	.0743	.1160	.1641
	7	.0000	.0000	.0003	.0012	.0039	.0098	.0212	.0407	.0703
	8	.0000	.0000	.0000	.0001	.0004	.0013	.0035	.0083	.0176
	9	.0000	.0000	.0000	.0000	.0000	.0001	.0003	.0008	.0020
10	0	.3487	.1969	.1074	.0563	.0282	.0135	.0060	.0025	.0010
	1	.3874	.3474	.2684	.1877	.1211	.0725	.0403	.0207	.0098
	2	.1937	.2759	.3020	.2816	.2335	.1757	.1209	.0763	.0439
	3	.0574	.1298	.2013	.2503	.2668	.2522	.2150	.1665	.1172
	4	.0112	.0401	.0881	.1460	.2001	.2377	.2508	.2384	.2051
	5	.0015	.0085	.0264	.0584	.1029	.1536	.2007	.2340	.2461
	6	.0001	.0012	.0055	.0162	.0368	.0689	.1115	.1596	.2051
	7	.0000	.0001	.0008	.0031	.0090	.0212	.0425	.0746	.1172
	8	.0000	.0000	.0001	.0004	.0014	.0043	.0106	.0229	.0439
	9	.0000	.0000	.0000	.0000	.0001	.0005	.0016	.0042	.0098
	10	.0000	.0000	.0000	.0000	.0000	.0000	.0001	.0003	.0010
12	0	.2824	.1422	.0687	.0317	.0138	.0057	.0022	.0008	.0002
	1	.3766	.3012	.2062	.1267	.0712	.0368	.0174	.0075	.0029
	2	.2301	.2924	.2835	.2323	.1678	.1088	.0639	.0339	.0161
	3	.0853	.1720	.2362	.2581	.2397	.1954	.1419	.0923	.0537
	4	.0213	.0683	.1329	.1936	.2311	.2367	.2128	.1700	.1208
	5	.0038	.0193	.0532	.1032	.1585	.2039	.2270	.2225	.1934
	6	.0005	.0040	.0155	.0401	.0792	.1281	.1766	.2124	.2256
	7	.0000	.0006	.0033	.0115	.0291	.0591	.1009	.1489	.1934
	8	.0000	.0001	.0005	.0024	.0078	.0199	.0420	.0762	.1208
	9	.0000	.0000	.0001	.0004	.0015	.0048	.0125	.0277	.0537
	10	.0000	.0000	.0000	.0000	.0002	.0008	.0025	.0068	.0161
	11	.0000	.0000	.0000	.0000	.0000	.0001	.0003	.0010	.0029
	12	.0000	.0000	.0000	.0000	.0000	.0000	.0000	.0001	.0002
15	0	.2059	.0874	.0352	.0134	.0047	.0016	.0005	.0001	.0000
	1	.3432	.2312	.1319	.0668	.0305	.0126	.0047	.0016	.0005
	2	.2669	.2856	.2309	.1559	.0916	.0476	.0219	.0090	.0032
	3	.1285	.2184	.2501	.2252	.1700	.1110	.0634	.0318	.0139
	4	.0428	.1156	.1876	.2252	.2186	.1792	.1268	.0780	.0417
	5	.0105	.0449	.1032	.1651	.2061	.2123	.1859	.1404	.0916
	6	.0019	.0132	.0430	.0917	.1472	.1906	.2066	.1914	.1527
	7	.0003	.0030	.0138	.0393	.0811	.1319	.1771	.2013	.1964
	8	.0000	.0005	.0035	.0131	.0348	.0710	.1181	.1647	.1964
	9	.0000	.0001	.0007	.0034	.0016	.0298	.0612	.1048	.1527
	10	.0000	.0000	.0001	.0007	.0030	.0096	.0245	.0515	.0916
	11	.0000	.0000	.0000	.0001	.0006	.0024	.0074	.0191	.0417
	12	.0000	.0000	.0000	.0000	.0001	.0004	.0016	.0052	.0139
	13	.0000	.0000	.0000	.0000	.0000	.0001	.0003	.0010	.0032
	14	.0000	.0000	.0000	.0000	.0000	.0000	.0000	.0001	.0005
	15	.0000	.0000	.0000	.0000	.0000	.0000	.0000	.0000	.0000

TABLE 5   Binomial Probabilities (*Continued*)

n	x	.10	.15	.20	.25	.30	.35	.40	.45	.50
18	0	.1501	.0536	.0180	.0056	.0016	.0004	.0001	.0000	.0000
	1	.3002	.1704	.0811	.0338	.0126	.0042	.0012	.0003	.0001
	2	.2835	.2556	.1723	.0958	.0458	.0190	.0069	.0022	.0006
	3	.1680	.2406	.2297	.1704	.1046	.0547	.0246	.0095	.0031
	4	.0700	.1592	.2153	.2130	.1681	.1104	.0614	.0291	.0117
	5	.0218	.0787	.1507	.1988	.2017	.1664	.1146	.0666	.0327
	6	.0052	.0301	.0816	.1436	.1873	.1941	.1655	.1181	.0708
	7	.0010	.0091	.0350	.0820	.1376	.1792	.1892	.1657	.1214
	8	.0002	.0022	.0120	.0376	.0811	.1327	.1734	.1864	.1669
	9	.0000	.0004	.0033	.0139	.0386	.0794	.1284	.1694	.1855
	10	.0000	.0001	.0008	.0042	.0149	.0385	.0771	.1248	.1669
	11	.0000	.0000	.0001	.0010	.0046	.0151	.0374	.0742	.1214
	12	.0000	.0000	.0000	.0002	.0012	.0047	.0145	.0354	.0708
	13	.0000	.0000	.0000	.0000	.0002	.0012	.0045	.0134	.0327
	14	.0000	.0000	.0000	.0000	.0000	.0002	.0011	.0039	.0117
	15	.0000	.0000	.0000	.0000	.0000	.0000	.0002	.0009	.0031
	16	.0000	.0000	.0000	.0000	.0000	.0000	.0000	.0001	.0006
	17	.0000	.0000	.0000	.0000	.0000	.0000	.0000	.0000	.0001
	18	.0000	.0000	.0000	.0000	.0000	.0000	.0000	.0000	.0000
20	0	.1216	.0388	.0115	.0032	.0008	.0002	.0000	.0000	.0000
	1	.2702	.1368	.0576	.0211	.0068	.0020	.0005	.0001	.0000
	2	.2852	.2293	.1369	.0669	.0278	.0100	.0031	.0008	.0002
	3	.1901	.2428	.2054	.1339	.0716	.0323	.0123	.0040	.0011
	4	.0898	.1821	.2182	.1897	.1304	.0738	.0350	.0139	.0046
	5	.0319	.1028	.1746	.2023	.1789	.1272	.0746	.0365	.0148
	6	.0089	.0454	.1091	.1686	.1916	.1712	.1244	.0746	.0370
	7	.0020	.0160	.0545	.1124	.1643	.1844	.1659	.1221	.0739
	8	.0004	.0046	.0222	.0609	.1144	.1614	.1797	.1623	.1201
	9	.0001	.0011	.0074	.0271	.0654	.1158	.1597	.1771	.1602
	10	.0000	.0002	.0020	.0099	.0308	.0686	.1171	.1593	.1762
	11	.0000	.0000	.0005	.0030	.0120	.0336	.0710	.1185	.1602
	12	.0000	.0000	.0001	.0008	.0039	.0136	.0355	.0727	.1201
	13	.0000	.0000	.0000	.0002	.0010	.0045	.0146	.0366	.0739
	14	.0000	.0000	.0000	.0000	.0002	.0012	.0049	.0150	.0370
	15	.0000	.0000	.0000	.0000	.0000	.0003	.0013	.0049	.0148
	16	.0000	.0000	.0000	.0000	.0000	.0000	.0003	.0013	.0046
	17	.0000	.0000	.0000	.0000	.0000	.0000	.0000	.0002	.0011
	18	.0000	.0000	.0000	.0000	.0000	.0000	.0000	.0000	.0002
	19	.0000	.0000	.0000	.0000	.0000	.0000	.0000	.0000	.0000
	20	.0000	.0000	.0000	.0000	.0000	.0000	.0000	.0000	.0000

TABLE 5   Binomial Probabilities (*Continued*)

						p				
n	*x*	.55	.60	.65	.70	.75	.80	.85	.90	.95
2	0	.2025	.1600	.1225	.0900	.0625	.0400	.0225	.0100	.0025
	1	.4950	.4800	.4550	.4200	.3750	.3200	.2550	.1800	.0950
	2	.3025	.3600	.4225	.4900	.5625	.6400	.7225	.8100	.9025
3	0	.0911	.0640	.0429	.0270	.0156	.0080	.0034	.0010	.0001
	1	.3341	.2880	.2389	.1890	.1406	.0960	.0574	.0270	.0071
	2	.4084	.4320	.4436	.4410	.4219	.3840	.3251	.2430	.1354
	3	.1664	.2160	.2746	.3430	.4219	.5120	.6141	.7290	.8574
4	0	.0410	.0256	.0150	.0081	.0039	.0016	.0005	.0001	.0000
	1	.2005	.1536	.1115	.0756	.0469	.0256	.0115	.0036	.0005
	2	.3675	.3456	.3105	.2646	.2109	.1536	.0975	.0486	.0135
	3	.2995	.3456	.3845	.4116	.4219	.4096	.3685	.2916	.1715
	4	.0915	.1296	.1785	.2401	.3164	.4096	.5220	.6561	.8145
5	0	.0185	.0102	.0053	.0024	.0010	.0003	.0001	.0000	.0000
	1	.1128	.0768	.0488	.0284	.0146	.0064	.0022	.0005	.0000
	2	.2757	.2304	.1811	.1323	.0879	.0512	.0244	.0081	.0011
	3	.3369	.3456	.3364	.3087	.2637	.2048	.1382	.0729	.0214
	4	.2059	.2592	.3124	.3601	.3955	.4096	.3915	.3281	.2036
	5	.0503	.0778	.1160	.1681	.2373	.3277	.4437	.5905	.7738
6	0	.0083	.0041	.0018	.0007	.0002	.0001	.0000	.0000	.0000
	1	.0609	.0369	.0205	.0102	.0044	.0015	.0004	.0001	.0000
	2	.1861	.1382	.0951	.0595	.0330	.0154	.0055	.0012	.0001
	3	.3032	.2765	.2355	.1852	.1318	.0819	.0415	.0146	.0021
	4	.2780	.3110	.3280	.3241	.2966	.2458	.1762	.0984	.0305
	5	.1359	.1866	.2437	.3025	.3560	.3932	.3993	.3543	.2321
	6	.0277	.0467	.0754	.1176	.1780	.2621	.3771	.5314	.7351
7	0	.0037	.0016	.0006	.0002	.0001	.0000	.0000	.0000	.0000
	1	.0320	.0172	.0084	.0036	.0013	.0004	.0001	.0000	.0000
	2	.1172	.0774	.0466	.0250	.0115	.0043	.0012	.0002	.0000
	3	.2388	.1935	.1442	.0972	.0577	.0287	.0109	.0026	.0002
	4	.2918	.2903	.2679	.2269	.1730	.1147	.0617	.0230	.0036
	5	.2140	.2613	.2985	.3177	.3115	.2753	.2097	.1240	.0406
	6	.0872	.1306	.1848	.2471	.3115	.3670	.3960	.3720	.2573
	7	.0152	.0280	.0490	.0824	.1335	.2097	.3206	.4783	.6983
8	0	.0017	.0007	.0002	.0001	.0000	.0000	.0000	.0000	.0000
	1	.0164	.0079	.0033	.0012	.0004	.0001	.0000	.0000	.0000
	2	.0703	.0413	.0217	.0100	.0038	.0011	.0002	.0000	.0000
	3	.1719	.1239	.0808	.0467	.0231	.0092	.0026	.0004	.0000
	4	.2627	.2322	.1875	.1361	.0865	.0459	.0185	.0046	.0004
	5	.2568	.2787	.2786	.2541	.2076	.1468	.0839	.0331	.0054
	6	.1569	.2090	.2587	.2965	.3115	.2936	.2376	.1488	.0515
	7	.0548	.0896	.1373	.1977	.2670	.3355	.3847	.3826	.2793
	8	.0084	.0168	.0319	.0576	.1001	.1678	.2725	.4305	.6634

TABLE 5   Binomial Probabilities (*Continued*)

n	x	.55	.60	.65	.70	.75	.80	.85	.90	.95
9	0	.0008	.0003	.0001	.0000	.0000	.0000	.0000	.0000	.0000
	1	.0083	.0035	.0013	.0004	.0001	.0000	.0000	.0000	.0000
	2	.0407	.0212	.0098	.0039	.0012	.0003	.0000	.0000	.0000
	3	.1160	.0743	.0424	.0210	.0087	.0028	.0006	.0001	.0000
	4	.2128	.1672	.1181	.0735	.0389	.0165	.0050	.0008	.0000
	5	.2600	.2508	.2194	.1715	.1168	.0661	.0283	.0074	.0006
	6	.2119	.2508	.2716	.2668	.2336	.1762	.1069	.0446	.0077
	7	.1110	.1612	.2162	.2668	.3003	.3020	.2597	.1722	.0629
	8	.0339	.0605	.1004	.1556	.2253	.3020	.3679	.3874	.2985
	9	.0046	.0101	.0207	.0404	.0751	.1342	.2316	.3874	.6302
10	0	.0003	.0001	.0000	.0000	.0000	.0000	.0000	.0000	.0000
	1	.0042	.0016	.0005	.0001	.0000	.0000	.0000	.0000	.0000
	2	.0229	.0106	.0043	.0014	.0004	.0001	.0000	.0000	.0000
	3	.0746	.0425	.0212	.0090	.0031	.0008	.0001	.0000	.0000
	4	.1596	.1115	.0689	.0368	.0162	.0055	.0012	.0001	.0000
	5	.2340	.2007	.1536	.1029	.0584	.0264	.0085	.0015	.0001
	6	.2384	.2508	.2377	.2001	.1460	.0881	.0401	.0112	.0010
	7	.1665	.2150	.2522	.2668	.2503	.2013	.1298	.0574	.0105
	8	.0763	.1209	.1757	.2335	.2816	.3020	.2759	.1937	.0746
	9	.0207	.0403	.0725	.1211	.1877	.2684	.3474	.3874	.3151
	10	.0025	.0060	.0135	.0282	.0563	.1074	.1969	.3487	.5987
12	0	.0001	.0000	.0000	.0000	.0000	.0000	.0000	.0000	.0000
	1	.0010	.0003	.0001	.0000	.0000	.0000	.0000	.0000	.0000
	2	.0068	.0025	.0008	.0002	.0000	.0000	.0000	.0000	.0000
	3	.0277	.0125	.0048	.0015	.0004	.0001	.0000	.0000	.0000
	4	.0762	.0420	.0199	.0078	.0024	.0005	.0001	.0000	.0000
	5	.1489	.1009	.0591	.0291	.0115	.0033	.0006	.0005	.0000
	6	.2124	.1766	.1281	.0792	.0401	.0155	.0040	.0005	.0000
	7	.2225	.2270	.2039	.1585	.1032	.0532	.0193	.0038	.0002
	8	.1700	.2128	.2367	.2311	.1936	.1329	.0683	.0213	.0021
	9	.0923	.1419	.1954	.2397	.2581	.2362	.1720	.0852	.0713
	10	.0339	.0639	.1088	.1678	.2323	.2835	.2924	.2301	.0988
	11	.0075	.0174	.0368	.0712	.1267	.2062	.3012	.3766	.3413
	12	.0008	.0022	.0057	.0138	.0317	.0687	.1422	.2824	.5404
15	0	.0000	.0000	.0000	.0000	.0000	.0000	.0000	.0000	.0000
	1	.0001	.0000	.0000	.0000	.0000	.0000	.0000	.0000	.0000
	2	.0010	.0003	.0001	.0000	.0000	.0000	.0000	.0000	.0000
	3	.0052	.0016	.0004	.0001	.0000	.0000	.0000	.0000	.0000
	4	.0191	.0074	.0024	.0006	.0001	.0000	.0000	.0000	.0000
	5	.0515	.0245	.0096	.0030	.0007	.0001	.0000	.0000	.0000
	6	.1048	.0612	.0298	.0116	.0034	.0007	.0001	.0000	.0000
	7	.1647	.1181	.0710	.0348	.0131	.0035	.0005	.0000	.0000
	8	.2013	.1771	.1319	.0811	.0393	.0138	.0030	.0003	.0000
	9	.1914	.2066	.1906	.1472	.0917	.0430	.0132	.0019	.0000
	10	.1404	.1859	.2123	.2061	.1651	.1032	.0449	.0105	.0006
	11	.0780	.1268	.1792	.2186	.2252	.1876	.1156	.0428	.0049
	12	.0318	.0634	.1110	.1700	.2252	.2501	.2184	.1285	.0307
	13	.0090	.0219	.0476	.0916	.1559	.2309	.2856	.2669	.1348
	14	.0016	.0047	.0126	.0305	.0668	.1319	.2312	.3432	.3658
	15	.0001	.0005	.0016	.0047	.0134	.0352	.0874	.2059	.4633

TABLE 5   Binomial Probabilities (*Continued*)

		p								
n	*x*	.55	.60	.65	.70	.75	.80	.85	.90	.95
18	0	.0000	.0000	.0000	.0000	.0000	.0000	.0000	.0000	.0000
	1	.0000	.0000	.0000	.0000	.0000	.0000	.0000	.0000	.0000
	2	.0001	.0000	.0000	.0000	.0000	.0000	.0000	.0000	.0000
	3	.0009	.0002	.0000	.0000	.0000	.0000	.0000	.0000	.0000
	4	.0039	.0011	.0002	.0000	.0000	.0000	.0000	.0000	.0000
	5	.0134	.0045	.0012	.0002	.0000	.0000	.0000	.0000	.0000
	6	.0354	.0145	.0047	.0012	.0002	.0000	.0000	.0000	.0000
	7	.0742	.0374	.0151	.0046	.0010	.0001	.0000	.0000	.0000
	8	.1248	.0771	.0385	.0149	.0042	.0008	.0001	.0000	.0000
	9	.1694	.1284	.0794	.0386	.0139	.0033	.0004	.0000	.0000
	10	.1864	.1734	.1327	.0811	.0376	.0120	.0022	.0002	.0000
	11	.1657	.1892	.1792	.1376	.0820	.0350	.0091	.0010	.0000
	12	.1181	.1655	.1941	.1873	.1436	.0816	.0301	.0052	.0002
	13	.0666	.1146	.1664	.2017	.1988	.1507	.0787	.0218	.0014
	14	.0291	.0614	.1104	.1681	.2130	.2153	.1592	.0700	.0093
	15	.0095	.0246	.0547	.1046	.1704	.2297	.2406	.1680	.0473
	16	.0022	.0069	.0190	.0458	.0958	.1723	.2556	.2835	.1683
	17	.0003	.0012	.0042	.0126	.0338	.0811	.1704	.3002	.3763
	18	.0000	.0001	.0004	.0016	.0056	.0180	.0536	.1501	.3972
20	0	.0000	.0000	.0000	.0000	.0000	.0000	.0000	.0000	.0000
	1	.0000	.0000	.0000	.0000	.0000	.0000	.0000	.0000	.0000
	2	.0000	.0000	.0000	.0000	.0000	.0000	.0000	.0000	.0000
	3	.0002	.0000	.0000	.0000	.0000	.0000	.0000	.0000	.0000
	4	.0013	.0003	.0000	.0000	.0000	.0000	.0000	.0000	.0000
	5	.0049	.0013	.0003	.0000	.0000	.0000	.0000	.0000	.0000
	6	.0150	.0049	.0012	.0002	.0000	.0000	.0000	.0000	.0000
	7	.0366	.0146	.0045	.0010	.0002	.0000	.0000	.0000	.0000
	8	.0727	.0355	.0136	.0039	.0008	.0001	.0000	.0000	.0000
	9	.1185	.0710	.0336	.0120	.0030	.0005	.0000	.0000	.0000
	10	.1593	.1171	.0686	.0308	.0099	.0020	.0002	.0000	.0000
	11	.1771	.1597	.1158	.0654	.0271	.0074	.0011	.0001	.0000
	12	.1623	.1797	.1614	.1144	.0609	.0222	.0046	.0004	.0000
	13	.1221	.1659	.1844	.1643	.1124	.0545	.0160	.0020	.0000
	14	.0746	.1244	.1712	.1916	.1686	.1091	.0454	.0089	.0003
	15	.0365	.0746	.1272	.1789	.2023	.1746	.1028	.0319	.0022
	16	.0139	.0350	.0738	.1304	.1897	.2182	.1821	.0898	.0133
	17	.0040	.0123	.0323	.0716	.1339	.2054	.2428	.1901	.0596
	18	.0008	.0031	.0100	.0278	.0669	.1369	.2293	.2852	.1887
	19	.0001	.0005	.0020	.0068	.0211	.0576	.1368	.2702	.3774
	20	.0000	.0000	.0002	.0008	.0032	.0115	.0388	.1216	.3585

TABLE 6   Values of $e^{-\mu}$

μ	$e^{-\mu}$	μ	$e^{-\mu}$	μ	$e^{-\mu}$
.00	1.0000				
.05	.9512	2.05	.1287	4.05	.0174
.10	.9048	2.10	.1225	4.10	.0166
.15	.8607	2.15	.1165	4.15	.0158
.20	.8187	2.20	.1108	4.20	.0150
.25	.7788	2.25	.1054	4.25	.0143
.30	.7408	2.30	.1003	4.30	.0136
.35	.7047	2.35	.0954	4.35	.0129
.40	.6703	2.40	.0907	4.40	.0123
.45	.6376	2.45	.0863	4.45	.0117
.50	.6065	2.50	.0821	4.50	.0111
.55	.5769	2.55	.0781	4.55	.0106
.60	.5488	2.60	.0743	4.60	.0101
.65	.5220	2.65	.0707	4.65	.0096
.70	.4966	2.70	.0672	4.70	.0091
.75	.4724	2.75	.0639	4.75	.0087
.80	.4493	2.80	.0608	4.80	.0082
.85	.4274	2.85	.0578	4.85	.0078
.90	.4066	2.90	.0550	4.90	.0074
.95	.3867	2.95	.0523	4.95	.0071
1.00	.3679	3.00	.0498	5.00	.0067
1.05	.3499	3.05	.0474	5.05	.0064
1.10	.3329	3.10	.0450	5.10	.0061
1.15	.3166	3.15	.0429	5.15	.0058
1.20	.3012	3.20	.0408	5.20	.0055
1.25	.2865	3.25	.0388	5.25	.0052
1.30	.2725	3.30	.0369	5.30	.0050
1.35	.2592	3.35	.0351	5.35	.0047
1.40	.2466	3.40	.0334	5.40	.0045
1.45	.2346	3.45	.0317	5.45	.0043
1.50	.2231	3.50	.0302	5.50	.0041
1.55	.2122	3.55	.0287	5.55	.0039
1.60	.2019	3.60	.0273	5.60	.0037
1.65	.1920	3.65	.0260	5.65	.0035
1.70	.1827	3.70	.0247	5.70	.0033
1.75	.1738	3.75	.0235	5.75	.0032
1.80	.1653	3.80	.0224	5.80	.0030
1.85	.1572	3.85	.0213	5.85	.0029
1.90	.1496	3.90	.0202	5.90	.0027
1.95	.1423	3.95	.0193	5.95	.0026
2.00	.1353	4.00	.0183	6.00	.0025
				7.00	.0009
				8.00	.000335
				9.00	.000123
				10.00	.000045

TABLE 7   Poisson Probabilities

Entries in the table give the probability of x occurrences for a Poisson process with a mean μ. For example, when $\mu = 2.5$, the probability of four occurrences is .1336.

					μ					
x	0.1	0.2	0.3	0.4	0.5	0.6	0.7	0.8	0.9	1.0
0	.9048	.8187	.7408	.6703	.6065	.5488	.4966	.4493	.4066	.3679
1	.0905	.1637	.2222	.2681	.3033	.3293	.3476	.3595	.3659	.3679
2	.0045	.0164	.0333	.0536	.0758	.0988	.1217	.1438	.1647	.1839
3	.0002	.0011	.0033	.0072	.0126	.0198	.0284	.0383	.0494	.0613
4	.0000	.0001	.0002	.0007	.0016	.0030	.0050	.0077	.0111	.0153
5	.0000	.0000	.0000	.0001	.0002	.0004	.0007	.0012	.0020	.0031
6	.0000	.0000	.0000	.0000	.0000	.0000	.0001	.0002	.0003	.0005
7	.0000	.0000	.0000	.0000	.0000	.0000	.0000	.0000	.0000	.0001

					μ					
x	1.1	1.2	1.3	1.4	1.5	1.6	1.7	1.8	1.9	2.0
0	.3329	.3012	.2725	.2466	.2231	.2019	.1827	.1653	.1496	.1353
1	.3662	.3614	.3543	.3452	.3347	.3230	.3106	.2975	.2842	.2707
2	.2014	.2169	.2303	.2417	.2510	.2584	.2640	.2678	.2700	.2707
3	.0738	.0867	.0998	.1128	.1255	.1378	.1496	.1607	.1710	.1804
4	.0203	.0260	.0324	.0395	.0471	.0551	.0636	.0723	.0812	.0902
5	.0045	.0062	.0084	.0111	.0141	.0176	.0216	.0260	.0309	.0361
6	.0008	.0012	.0018	.0026	.0035	.0047	.0061	.0078	.0098	.0120
7	.0001	.0002	.0003	.0005	.0008	.0011	.0015	.0020	.0027	.0034
8	.0000	.0000	.0001	.0001	.0001	.0002	.0003	.0005	.0006	.0009
9	.0000	.0000	.0000	.0000	.0000	.0000	.0001	.0001	.0001	.0002

					μ					
x	2.1	2.2	2.3	2.4	2.5	2.6	2.7	2.8	2.9	3.0
0	.1225	.1108	.1003	.0907	.0821	.0743	.0672	.0608	.0550	.0498
1	.2572	.2438	.2306	.2177	.2052	.1931	.1815	.1703	.1596	.1494
2	.2700	.2681	.2652	.2613	.2565	.2510	.2450	.2384	.2314	.2240
3	.1890	.1966	.2033	.2090	.2138	.2176	.2205	.2225	.2237	.2240
4	.0992	.1082	.1169	.1254	.1336	.1414	.1488	.1557	.1622	.1680
5	.0417	.0476	.0538	.0602	.0668	.0735	.0804	.0872	.0940	.1008
6	.0146	.0174	.0206	.0241	.0278	.0319	.0362	.0407	.0455	.0504
7	.0044	.0055	.0068	.0083	.0099	.0118	.0139	.0163	.0188	.0216
8	.0011	.0015	.0019	.0025	.0031	.0038	.0047	.0057	.0068	.0081
9	.0003	.0004	.0005	.0007	.0009	.0011	.0014	.0018	.0022	.0027
10	.0001	.0001	.0001	.0002	.0002	.0003	.0004	.0005	.0006	.0008
11	.0000	.0000	.0000	.0000	.0000	.0001	.0001	.0001	.0002	.0002
12	.0000	.0000	.0000	.0000	.0000	.0000	.0000	.0000	.0000	.0001

TABLE 7   Poisson Probabilities (*Continued*)

					μ					
x	3.1	3.2	3.3	3.4	3.5	3.6	3.7	3.8	3.9	4.0
0	.0450	.0408	.0369	.0344	.0302	.0273	.0247	.0224	.0202	.0183
1	.1397	.1304	.1217	.1135	.1057	.0984	.0915	.0850	.0789	.0733
2	.2165	.2087	.2008	.1929	.1850	.1771	.1692	.1615	.1539	.1465
3	.2237	.2226	.2209	.2186	.2158	.2125	.2087	.2046	.2001	.1954
4	.1734	.1781	.1823	.1858	.1888	.1912	.1931	.1944	.1951	.1954
5	.1075	.1140	.1203	.1264	.1322	.1377	.1429	.1477	.1522	.1563
6	.0555	.0608	.0662	.0716	.0771	.0826	.0881	.0936	.0989	.1042
7	.0246	.0278	.0312	.0348	.0385	.0425	.0466	.0508	.0551	.0595
8	.0095	.0111	.0129	.0148	.0169	.0191	.0215	.0241	.0269	.0298
9	.0033	.0040	.0047	.0056	.0066	.0076	.0089	.0102	.0116	.0132
10	.0010	.0013	.0016	.0019	.0023	.0028	.0033	.0039	.0045	.0053
11	.0003	.0004	.0005	.0006	.0007	.0009	.0011	.0013	.0016	.0019
12	.0001	.0001	.0001	.0002	.0002	.0003	.0003	.0004	.0005	.0006
13	.0000	.0000	.0000	.0000	.0001	.0001	.0001	.0001	.0002	.0002
14	.0000	.0000	.0000	.0000	.0000	.0000	.0000	.0000	.0000	.0001

					μ					
x	4.1	4.2	4.3	4.4	4.5	4.6	4.7	4.8	4.9	5.0
0	.0166	.0150	.0136	.0123	.0111	.0101	.0091	.0082	.0074	.0067
1	.0679	.0630	.0583	.0540	.0500	.0462	.0427	.0395	.0365	.0337
2	.1393	.1323	.1254	.1188	.1125	.1063	.1005	.0948	.0894	.0842
3	.1904	.1852	.1798	.1743	.1687	.1631	.1574	.1517	.1460	.1404
4	.1951	.1944	.1933	.1917	.1898	.1875	.1849	.1820	.1789	.1755
5	.1600	.1633	.1662	.1687	.1708	.1725	.1738	.1747	.1753	.1755
6	.1093	.1143	.1191	.1237	.1281	.1323	.1362	.1398	.1432	.1462
7	.0640	.0686	.0732	.0778	.0824	.0869	.0914	.0959	.1002	.1044
8	.0328	.0360	.0393	.0428	.0463	.0500	.0537	.0575	.0614	.0653
9	.0150	.0168	.0188	.0209	.0232	.0255	.0280	.0307	.0334	.0363
10	.0061	.0071	.0081	.0092	.0104	.0118	.0132	.0147	.0164	.0181
11	.0023	.0027	.0032	.0037	.0043	.0049	.0056	.0064	.0073	.0082
12	.0008	.0009	.0011	.0014	.0016	.0019	.0022	.0026	.0030	.0034
13	.0002	.0003	.0004	.0005	.0006	.0007	.0008	.0009	.0011	.0013
14	.0001	.0001	.0001	.0001	.0002	.0002	.0003	.0003	.0004	.0005
15	.0000	.0000	.0000	.0000	.0001	.0001	.0001	.0001	.0001	.0002

					μ					
x	5.1	5.2	5.3	5.4	5.5	5.6	5.7	5.8	5.9	6.0
0	.0061	.0055	.0050	.0045	.0041	.0037	.0033	.0030	.0027	.0025
1	.0311	.0287	.0265	.0244	.0225	.0207	.0191	.0176	.0162	.0149
2	.0793	.0746	.0701	.0659	.0618	.0580	.0544	.0509	.0477	.0446
3	.1348	.1293	.1239	.1185	.1133	.1082	.1033	.0985	.0938	.0892
4	.1719	.1681	.1641	.1600	.1558	.1515	.1472	.1428	.1383	.1339

TABLE 7   Poisson Probabilities (*Continued*)

5	.1753	.1748	.1740	.1728	.1714	.1697	.1678	.1656	.1632	.1606
6	.1490	.1515	.1537	.1555	.1571	.1587	.1594	.1601	.1605	.1606
7	.1086	.1125	.1163	.1200	.1234	.1267	.1298	.1326	.1353	.1377
8	.0692	.0731	.0771	.0810	.0849	.0887	.0925	.0962	.0998	.1033
9	.0392	.0423	.0454	.0486	.0519	.0552	.0586	.0620	.0654	.0688
10	.0200	.0220	.0241	.0262	.0285	.0309	.0334	.0359	.0386	.0413
11	.0093	.0104	.0116	.0129	.0143	.0157	.0173	.0190	.0207	.0225
12	.0039	.0045	.0051	.0058	.0065	.0073	.0082	.0092	.0102	.0113
13	.0015	.0018	.0021	.0024	.0028	.0032	.0036	.0041	.0046	.0052
14	.0006	.0007	.0008	.0009	.0011	.0013	.0015	.0017	.0019	.0022
15	.0002	.0002	.0003	.0003	.0004	.0005	.0006	.0007	.0008	.0009
16	.0001	.0001	.0001	.0001	.0001	.0002	.0002	.0002	.0003	.0003
17	.0000	.0000	.0000	.0000	.0000	.0001	.0001	.0001	.0001	.0001

μ

x	6.1	6.2	6.3	6.4	6.5	6.6	6.7	6.8	6.9	7.0
0	.0022	.0020	.0018	.0017	.0015	.0014	.0012	.0011	.0010	.0009
1	.0137	.0126	.0116	.0106	.0098	.0090	.0082	.0076	.0070	.0064
2	.0417	.0390	.0364	.0340	.0318	.0296	.0276	.0258	.0240	.0223
3	.0848	.0806	.0765	.0726	.0688	.0652	.0617	.0584	.0552	.0521
4	.1294	.1249	.1205	.1162	.1118	.1076	.1034	.0992	.0952	.0912
5	.1579	.1549	.1519	.1487	.1454	.1420	.1385	.1349	.1314	.1277
6	.1605	.1601	.1595	.1586	.1575	.1562	.1546	.1529	.1511	.1490
7	.1399	.1418	.1435	.1450	.1462	.1472	.1480	.1486	.1489	.1490
8	.1066	.1099	.1130	.1160	.1188	.1215	.1240	.1263	.1284	.1304
9	.0723	.0757	.0791	.0825	.0858	.0891	.0923	.0954	.0985	.1014
10	.0441	.0469	.0498	.0528	.0558	.0588	.0618	.0649	.0679	.0710
11	.0245	.0265	.0285	.0307	.0330	.0353	.0377	.0401	.0426	.0452
12	.0124	.0137	.0150	.0164	.0179	.0194	.0210	.0227	.0245	.0264
13	.0058	.0065	.0073	.0081	.0089	.0098	.0108	.0119	.0130	.0142
14	.0025	.0029	.0033	.0037	.0041	.0046	.0052	.0058	.0064	.0071
15	.0010	.0012	.0014	.0016	.0018	.0020	.0023	.0026	.0029	.0033
16	.0004	.0005	.0005	.0006	.0007	.0008	.0010	.0011	.0013	.0014
17	.0001	.0002	.0002	.0002	.0003	.0003	.0004	.0004	.0005	.0006
18	.0000	.0001	.0001	.0001	.0001	.0001	.0001	.0002	.0002	.0002
19	.0000	.0000	.0000	.0000	.0000	.0000	.0000	.0001	.0001	.0001

μ

x	7.1	7.2	7.3	7.4	7.5	7.6	7.7	7.8	7.9	8.0
0	.0008	.0007	.0007	.0006	.0006	.0005	.0005	.0004	.0004	.0003
1	.0059	.0054	.0049	.0045	.0041	.0038	.0035	.0032	.0029	.0027
2	.0208	.0194	.0180	.0167	.0156	.0145	.0134	.0125	.0116	.0107
3	.0492	.0464	.0438	.0413	.0389	.0366	.0345	.0324	.0305	.0286
4	.0874	.0836	.0799	.0764	.0729	.0696	.0663	.0632	.0602	.0573

TABLE 7   Poisson Probabilities (*Continued*)

					μ					
x	7.1	7.2	7.3	7.4	7.5	7.6	7.7	7.8	7.9	8.0
5	.1241	.1204	.1167	.1130	.1094	.1057	.1021	.0986	.0951	.0916
6	.1468	.1445	.1420	.1394	.1367	.1339	.1311	.1282	.1252	.1221
7	.1489	.1486	.1481	.1474	.1465	.1454	.1442	.1428	.1413	.1396
8	.1321	.1337	.1351	.1363	.1373	.1382	.1388	.1392	.1395	.1396
9	.1042	.1070	.1096	.1121	.1144	.1167	.1187	.1207	.1224	.1241
10	.0740	.0770	.0800	.0829	.0858	.0887	.0914	.0941	.0967	.0993
11	.0478	.0504	.0531	.0558	.0585	.0613	.0640	.0667	.0695	.0722
12	.0283	.0303	.0323	.0344	.0366	.0388	.0411	.0434	.0457	.0481
13	.0154	.0168	.0181	.0196	.0211	.0227	.0243	.0260	.0278	.0296
14	.0078	.0086	.0095	.0104	.0113	.0123	.0134	.0145	.0157	.0169
15	.0037	.0041	.0046	.0051	.0057	.0062	.0069	.0075	.0083	.0090
16	.0016	.0019	.0021	.0024	.0026	.0030	.0033	.0037	.0041	.0045
17	.0007	.0008	.0009	.0010	.0012	.0013	.0015	.0017	.0019	.0021
18	.0003	.0003	.0004	.0004	.0005	.0006	.0006	.0007	.0008	.0009
19	.0001	.0001	.0001	.0002	.0002	.0002	.0003	.0003	.0003	.0004
20	.0000	.0000	.0001	.0001	.0001	.0001	.0001	.0001	.0001	.0002
21	.0000	.0000	.0000	.0000	.0000	.0000	.0000	.0000	.0001	.0001

					μ					
x	8.1	8.2	8.3	8.4	8.5	8.6	8.7	8.8	8.9	9.0
0	.0003	.0003	.0002	.0002	.0002	.0002	.0002	.0002	.0001	.0001
1	.0025	.0023	.0021	.0019	.0017	.0016	.0014	.0013	.0012	.0011
2	.0100	.0092	.0086	.0079	.0074	.0068	.0063	.0058	.0054	.0050
3	.0269	.0252	.0237	.0222	.0208	.0195	.0183	.0171	.0160	.0150
4	.0544	.0517	.0491	.0466	.0443	.0420	.0398	.0377	.0357	.0337
5	.0882	.0849	.0816	.0784	.0752	.0722	.0692	.0663	.0635	.0607
6	.1191	.1160	.1128	.1097	.1066	.1034	.1003	.0972	.0941	.0911
7	.1378	.1358	.1338	.1317	.1294	.1271	.1247	.1222	.1197	.1171
8	.1395	.1392	.1388	.1382	.1375	.1366	.1356	.1344	.1332	.1318
9	.1256	.1269	.1280	.1290	.1299	.1306	.1311	.1315	.1317	.1318
10	.1017	.1040	.1063	.1084	.1104	.1123	.1140	.1157	.1172	.1186
11	.0749	.0776	.0802	.0828	.0853	.0878	.0902	.0925	.0948	.0970
12	.0505	.0530	.0555	.0579	.0604	.0629	.0654	.0679	.0703	.0728
13	.0315	.0334	.0354	.0374	.0395	.0416	.0438	.0459	.0481	.0504
14	.0182	.0196	.0210	.0225	.0240	.0256	.0272	.0289	.0306	.0324
15	.0098	.0107	.0116	.0126	.0136	.0147	.0158	.0169	.0182	.1094
16	.0050	.0055	.0060	.0066	.0072	.0079	.0086	.0093	.0101	.0109
17	.0024	.0026	.0029	.0033	.0036	.0040	.0044	.0048	.0053	.0058
18	.0011	.0012	.0014	.0015	.0017	.0019	.0021	.0024	.0026	.0029
19	.0005	.0005	.0006	.0007	.0008	.0009	.0010	.0011	.0012	.0014
20	.0002	.0002	.0002	.0003	.0003	.0004	.0004	.0005	.0005	.0006
21	.0001	.0001	.0001	.0001	.0001	.0002	.0002	.0002	.0002	.0003
22	.0000	.0000	.0000	.0000	.0001	.0001	.0001	.0001	.0001	.0001

TABLE 7   Poisson Probabilities (*Continued*)

					μ					
x	9.1	9.2	9.3	9.4	9.5	9.6	9.7	9.8	9.9	10
0	.0001	.0001	.0001	.0001	.0001	.0001	.0001	.0001	.0001	.0000
1	.0010	.0009	.0009	.0008	.0007	.0007	.0006	.0005	.0005	.0005
2	.0046	.0043	.0040	.0037	.0034	.0031	.0029	.0027	.0025	.0023
3	.0140	.0131	.0123	.0115	.0107	.0100	.0093	.0087	.0081	.0076
4	.0319	.0302	.0285	.0269	.0254	.0240	.0226	.0213	.0201	.0189
5	.0581	.0555	.0530	.0506	.0483	.0460	.0439	.0418	.0398	.0378
6	.0881	.0851	.0822	.0793	.0764	.0736	.0709	.0682	.0656	.0631
7	.1145	.1118	.1091	.1064	.1037	.1010	.0982	.0955	.0928	.0901
8	.1302	.1286	.1269	.1251	.1232	.1212	.1191	.1170	.1148	.1126
9	.1317	.1315	.1311	.1306	.1300	.1293	.1284	.1274	.1263	.1251
10	.1198	.1210	.1219	.1228	.1235	.1241	.1245	.1249	.1250	.1251
11	.0991	.1012	.1031	.1049	.1067	.1083	.1098	.1112	.1125	.1137
12	.0752	.0776	.0799	.0822	.0844	.0866	.0888	.0908	.0928	.0948
13	.0526	.0549	.0572	.0594	.0617	.0640	.0662	.0685	.0707	.0729
14	.0342	.0361	.0380	.0399	.0419	.0439	.0459	.0479	.0500	.0521
15	.0208	.0221	.0235	.0250	.0265	.0281	.0297	.0313	.0330	.0347
16	.0118	.0127	.0137	.0147	.0157	.0168	.0180	.0192	.0204	.0217
17	.0063	.0069	.0075	.0081	.0088	.0095	.0103	.0111	.0119	.0128
18	.0032	.0035	.0039	.0042	.0046	.0051	.0055	.0060	.0065	.0071
19	.0015	.0017	.0019	.0021	.0023	.0026	.0028	.0031	.0034	.0037
20	.0007	.0008	.0009	.0010	.0011	.0012	.0014	.0015	.0017	.0019
21	.0003	.0003	.0004	.0004	.0005	.0006	.0006	.0007	.0008	.0009
22	.0001	.0001	.0002	.0002	.0002	.0002	.0003	.0003	.0004	.0004
23	.0000	.0001	.0001	.0001	.0001	.0001	.0001	.0001	.0002	.0002
24	.0000	.0000	.0000	.0000	.0000	.0000	.0000	.0001	.0001	.0001

					μ					
x	11	12	13	14	15	16	17	18	19	20
0	.0000	.0000	.0000	.0000	.0000	.0000	.0000	.0000	.0000	.0000
1	.0002	.0001	.0000	.0000	.0000	.0000	.0000	.0000	.0000	.0000
2	.0010	.0004	.0002	.0001	.0000	.0000	.0000	.0000	.0000	.0000
3	.0037	.0018	.0008	.0004	.0002	.0001	.0000	.0000	.0000	.0000
4	.0102	.0053	.0027	.0013	.0006	.0003	.0001	.0001	.0000	.0000
5	.0224	.0127	.0070	.0037	.0019	.0010	.0005	.0002	.0001	.0001
6	.0411	.0255	.0152	.0087	.0048	.0026	.0014	.0007	.0004	.0002
7	.0646	.0437	.0281	.0174	.0104	.0060	.0034	.0018	.0010	.0005
8	.0888	.0655	.0457	.0304	.0194	.0120	.0072	.0042	.0024	.0013
9	.1085	.0874	.0661	.0473	.0324	.0213	.0135	.0083	.0050	.0029
10	.1194	.1048	.0859	.0663	.0486	.0341	.0230	.0150	.0095	.0058
11	.1194	.1144	.1015	.0844	.0663	.0496	.0355	.0245	.0164	.0106
12	.1094	.1144	.1099	.0984	.0829	.0661	.0504	.0368	.0259	.0176
13	.0926	.1056	.1099	.1060	.0956	.0814	.0658	.0509	.0378	.0271
14	.0728	.0905	.1021	.1060	.1024	.0930	.0800	.0655	.0514	.0387

TABLE 7   Poisson Probabilities (*Continued*)

x	μ 11	12	13	14	15	16	17	18	19	20
15	.0534	.0724	.0885	.0989	.1024	.0992	.0906	.0786	.0650	.0516
16	.0367	.0543	.0719	.0866	.0960	.0992	.0963	.0884	.0772	.0646
17	.0237	.0383	.0550	.0713	.0847	.0934	.0963	.0936	.0863	.0760
18	.0145	.0256	.0397	.0554	.0706	.0830	.0909	.0936	.0911	.0844
19	.0084	.0161	.0272	.0409	.0557	.0699	.0814	.0887	.0911	.0888
20	.0046	.0097	.0177	.0286	.0418	.0559	.0692	.0798	.0866	.0888
21	.0024	.0055	.0109	.0191	.0299	.0426	.0560	.0684	.0783	.0846
22	.0012	.0030	.0065	.0121	.0204	.0310	.0433	.0560	.0676	.0769
23	.0006	.0016	.0037	.0074	.0133	.0216	.0320	.0438	.0559	.0669
24	.0003	.0008	.0020	.0043	.0083	.0144	.0226	.0328	.0442	.0557
25	.0001	.0004	.0010	.0024	.0050	.0092	.0154	.0237	.0336	.0446
26	.0000	.0002	.0005	.0013	.0029	.0057	.0101	.0164	.0246	.0343
27	.0000	.0001	.0002	.0007	.0016	.0034	.0063	.0109	.0173	.0254
28	.0000	.0000	.0001	.0003	.0009	.0019	.0038	.0070	.0117	.0181
29	.0000	.0000	.0001	.0002	.0004	.0011	.0023	.0044	.0077	.0125
30	.0000	.0000	.0000	.0001	.0002	.0006	.0013	.0026	.0049	.0083
31	.0000	.0000	.0000	.0000	.0001	.0003	.0007	.0015	.0030	.0054
32	.0000	.0000	.0000	.0000	.0001	.0001	.0004	.0009	.0018	.0034
33	.0000	.0000	.0000	.0000	.0000	.0001	.0002	.0005	.0010	.0020
34	.0000	.0000	.0000	.0000	.0000	.0000	.0001	.0002	.0006	.0012
35	.0000	.0000	.0000	.0000	.0000	.0000	.0000	.0001	.0003	.0007
36	.0000	.0000	.0000	.0000	.0000	.0000	.0000	.0001	.0002	.0004
37	.0000	.0000	.0000	.0000	.0000	.0000	.0000	.0000	.0001	.0002
38	.0000	.0000	.0000	.0000	.0000	.0000	.0000	.0000	.0000	.0001
39	.0000	.0000	.0000	.0000	.0000	.0000	.0000	.0000	.0000	.0001

TABLE 8   Random Numbers

63271	59986	71744	51102	15141	80714	58683	93108	13554	79945
88547	09896	95436	79115	08303	01041	20030	63754	08459	28364
55957	57243	83865	09911	19761	66535	40102	26646	60147	15702
46276	87453	44790	67122	45573	84358	21625	16999	13385	22782
55363	07449	34835	15290	76616	67191	12777	21861	68689	03263
69393	92785	49902	58447	42048	30378	87618	26933	40640	16281
13186	29431	88190	04588	38733	81290	89541	70290	40113	08243
17726	28652	56836	78351	47327	18518	92222	55201	27340	10493
36520	64465	05550	30157	82242	29520	69753	72602	23756	54935
81628	36100	39254	56835	37636	02421	98063	89641	64953	99337
84649	48968	75215	75498	49539	74240	03466	49292	36401	45525
63291	11618	12613	75055	43915	26488	41116	64531	56827	30825
70502	53225	03655	05915	37140	57051	48393	91322	25653	06543
06426	24771	59935	49801	11082	66762	94477	02494	88215	27191
20711	55609	29430	70165	45406	78484	31639	52009	18873	96927
41990	70538	77191	25860	55204	73417	83920	69468	74972	38712
72452	36618	76298	26678	89334	33938	95567	29380	75906	91807
37042	40318	57099	10528	09925	89773	41335	96244	29002	46453
53766	52875	15987	46962	67342	77592	57651	95508	80033	69828
90585	58955	53122	16025	84299	53310	67380	84249	25348	04332
32001	96293	37203	64516	51530	37069	40261	61374	05815	06714
62606	64324	46354	72157	67248	20135	49804	09226	64419	29457
10078	28073	85389	50324	14500	15562	64165	06125	71353	77669
91561	46145	24177	15294	10061	98124	75732	00815	83452	97355
13091	98112	53959	79607	52244	63303	10413	63839	74762	50289
73864	83014	72457	22682	03033	61714	88173	90835	00634	85169
66668	25467	48894	51043	02365	91726	09365	63167	95264	45643
84745	41042	29493	08136	09044	51926	43630	63470	76508	14194
48068	26805	94595	47907	13357	38412	33318	26098	82782	42851
54310	96175	97594	88616	42035	38093	36745	56702	40644	83514
14877	33095	10924	58013	61439	21882	42059	24177	58739	60170
78295	23179	02771	43464	59061	71411	05697	67194	30495	21157
67524	02865	39593	54278	04237	92441	26602	63835	38032	94770
58268	57219	68124	73455	83236	08710	04284	55005	84171	42596
97158	28672	50685	01181	24262	19427	52106	34308	73685	74246
04230	16831	69085	30802	65559	09205	71829	06489	85650	38707
94879	56606	30401	02602	57658	70091	54986	41394	60437	03195
71446	15232	66715	26385	91518	70566	02888	79941	39684	54315
32886	05644	79316	09819	00813	88407	17461	73925	53037	91904
62048	33711	25290	21526	02223	75947	66466	06232	10913	75336
84534	42351	21628	53669	81352	95152	08107	98814	72743	12849
84707	15885	84710	35866	06446	86311	32648	88141	73902	69981
19409	40868	64220	80861	13860	68493	52908	26374	63297	45052
57978	48015	25973	66777	45924	56144	24742	96702	88200	66162
57295	98298	11199	96510	75228	41600	47192	43267	35973	23152

TABLE 8   Random Numbers (Continued)

94044	83785	93388	07833	38216	31413	70555	03023	54147	06647
30014	25879	71763	96679	90603	99396	74557	74224	18211	91637
07265	69563	64268	88802	72264	66540	01782	08396	19251	83613
84404	88642	30263	80310	11522	57810	27627	78376	36240	48952
21778	02085	27762	46097	43324	34354	09369	14966	10158	76089

TABLE 9 Factors for $\bar{x}$ and R Control Charts

Observations in Sample, n	d_2	A_2	d_3	D_3	D_4
2	1.128	1.880	0.853	0	3.267
3	1.693	1.023	0.888	0	2.574
4	2.059	0.729	0.880	0	2.282
5	2.326	0.577	0.864	0	2.114
6	2.534	0.483	0.848	0	2.004
7	2.704	0.419	0.833	0.076	1.924
8	2.847	0.373	0.820	0.136	1.864
9	2.970	0.337	0.808	0.184	1.816
10	3.078	0.308	0.797	0.223	1.777
11	3.173	0.285	0.787	0.256	1.744
12	3.258	0.266	0.778	0.283	1.717
13	3.336	0.249	0.770	0.307	1.693
14	3.407	0.235	0.763	0.328	1.672
15	3.472	0.223	0.756	0.347	1.653
16	3.532	0.212	0.750	0.363	1.637
17	3.588	0.203	0.744	0.378	1.622
18	3.640	0.194	0.739	0.391	1.608
19	3.689	0.187	0.734	0.403	1.597
20	3.735	0.180	0.729	0.415	1.585
21	3.778	0.173	0.724	0.425	1.575
22	3.819	0.167	0.720	0.434	1.566
23	3.858	0.162	0.716	0.443	1.557
24	3.895	0.157	0.712	0.451	1.548
25	3.931	0.153	0.708	0.459	1.541

Adapted from Table 27 of ASTM STP 15D, *ASTM Manual on Presentation of Data and Control Chart Analysis.* Copyright 1976 American Society for Testing and Materials, Philadelphia, PA. Reprinted with permission.

Summations

Definition

$$\sum_{i=1}^{n} x_i = x_1 + x_2 + \cdots + x_n \tag{C.1}$$

Example for $x_1 = 5, x_2 = 8, x_3 = 14$:

$$\sum_{i=1}^{n} x_i = x_1 + x_2 + x_3$$
$$= 5 + 8 + 14$$
$$= 27$$

Result 1

For a constant c:

$$\sum_{i=1}^{n} c = \underbrace{(c + c + \cdots + c)}_{n \text{ times}} = nc \tag{C.2}$$

Example for $c = 5, n = 10$:

$$\sum_{i=1}^{10} 5 = 10(5) = 50$$

Example for $c = \bar{x}$:

$$\sum_{i=1}^{n} \bar{x} = n\bar{x}$$

Result 2

$$\sum_{i=1}^{n} cx_i = cx_1 + cx_2 + \cdots + cx_n$$
$$= c(x_1 + x_2 + \cdots + x_n) = c \sum_{i=1}^{n} x_i \tag{C.3}$$

Example for $x_1 = 5, x_2 = 8, x_3 = 14, c = 2$:

$$\sum_{i=1}^{3} 2x_i = 2 \sum_{i=1}^{3} x_i = 2(27) = 54$$

Result 3

$$\sum_{i=1}^{n} (ax_i + by_i) = a \sum_{i=1}^{n} x_i + b \sum_{i=1}^{n} y_i \tag{C.4}$$

Example for $x_1 = 5, x_2 = 8, x_3 = 14, a = 2, y_1 = 7, y_2 = 3, y_3 = 8, b = 4$:

$$\sum_{i=1}^{3} (2x_i + 4y_i) = 2 \sum_{i=1}^{3} x_i + 4 \sum_{i=1}^{3} y_i$$
$$= 2(27) + 4(18)$$
$$= 54 + 72$$
$$= 126$$

Double Summations

Consider the following data involving the variable x_{ij}, where i is the subscript denoting the row position and j is the subscript denoting the column position:

		Column		
		1	2	3
Row	1	$x_{11} = 10$	$x_{12} = 8$	$x_{13} = 6$
	2	$x_{21} = 7$	$x_{22} = 4$	$x_{23} = 12$

Definition

$$\sum_{i=1}^{n} \sum_{j=1}^{m} x_{ij} = (x_{11} + x_{12} + \cdots + x_{1m}) + (x_{21} + x_{22} + \cdots + x_{2m})$$
$$+ (x_{31} + x_{32} + \cdots + x_{3m}) + \cdots + (x_{n1} + x_{n2} + \cdots + x_{nm}) \tag{C.5}$$

Example:

$$\sum_{i=1}^{2} \sum_{j=1}^{3} x_{ij} = x_{11} + x_{12} + x_{13} + x_{21} + x_{22} + x_{23}$$
$$= 10 + 8 + 6 + 7 + 4 + 12$$
$$= 47$$

Definition

$$\sum_{i=1}^{n} x_{ij} = x_{1j} + x_{2j} + \cdots + x_{nj} \tag{C.6}$$

Example:

$$\sum_{i=1}^{2} x_{i2} = x_{12} + x_{22}$$
$$= 8 + 4$$
$$= 12$$

Shorthand Notation

Sometimes when a summation is for all values of the subscript, we use the following shorthand notations:

$$\sum_{i=1}^{n} x_i = \sum x_i \tag{C.7}$$

$$\sum_{i=1}^{n} \sum_{j=1}^{m} x_{ij} = \sum \sum x_{ij} \tag{C.8}$$

$$\sum_{i=1}^{n} x_{ij} = \sum_{i} x_{ij} \tag{C.9}$$

Chapter 1

2. a. 10
 b. 4
 c. Industry and Comp. vs. Shareholder Return qualitative
    CEO Compensation and Sales quantitative

4. a. 10
 b. *Fortune* 500 corporations, April 1997
 c. $12,003.4 million
 d. $12,003.4 million

6. a, c, and d are quantitative
   b and e are qualitative

8. a. 2013
 b. Qualitative
 c. Percentages
 d. 563 or 564

10. a and e are quantitative
    b, c, and d are qualitative

12. a. Visitors to Hawaii
 b. Yes; vast majority travel to Hawaii by air
 c. 1 and 4 are quantitative; 2 and 3 are qualitative

14. a. 4
 b. All variables are quantitative
 c. Times series for 1993 to 1996

16. a. Product taste and preference data
 b. Actual test data from young adults

18. a. 40% in the sample died of heart disease
 b. Qualitative

20. a. 56% of market belonged to A. C. Nielson; $387,325 is
    the average amount spent per category
 b. 3.73
 c. $387,325

22. a. All adult viewers reached by the television station
 b. The viewers contacted by the telephone survey
 c. A sample requires less time and a lower cost compared
    to contacting all viewers in the population

24. a and c are correct
    b, d and e should be challenged

Chapter 2

2. a. .20
 b. 40
 c/d.

Class	Frequency	Percent Frequency
A	44	22
B	36	18
C	80	40
D	40	20
Total	200	100

4. a. Qualitative; Names of TV Shows
 b.

TV Show	Frequency	Percent Frequency
ER	16	32
Frasier	13	26
Friends	11	22
Jesse	2	4
Veronica	8	16
Total	50	100

 d. ER, Frasier is second

6. a.

Book	Frequency	Percent Frequency
Paranoid	7	11.67
Dilbert	15	25.00
Forbes	9	15.00
Dogbert	12	20.00
Gods	11	18.33
Other	6	10.00
Total	60	100.0

 b. Dilbert, Dogbert, Gods, Forbes, and Paranoid
 c. Dilbert 25%; Dogbert 20%

8. a.

Position	Frequency	Relative Frequency
P	17	.309
H	4	.073
1	5	.091
2	4	.073
3	2	.036
S	5	.091
L	6	.109
C	5	.091
R	7	.127
Totals	55	1.000

b. Pitcher
c. 3rd base
d. Rightfield
e. Infielders 16 to outfielders 18

10. a. Quality classifications
b.

Rating	Frequency	Relative Frequency
Poor	2	.03
Fair	4	.07
Good	12	.20
Very good	24	.40
Excellent	18	.30
Totals	60	1.00

12.

Class	Cumulative Frequency	Cumulative Relative Frequency
≤ 19	10	.20
≤ 29	24	.48
≤ 39	41	.82
≤ 49	48	.96
≤ 59	50	1.00

14. b/c.

Class	Frequency	Percent Frequency
6.0–7.9	4	20
8.0–9.9	2	10
10.0–11.9	8	40
12.0–13.9	3	15
14.0–15.9	3	15
Totals	20	100

16. a.

Stock Price ($)	Frequency	Relative Frequency	Percent Frequency
10.00–19.99	10	.40	40
20.00–29.99	4	.16	16
30.00–39.99	6	.24	24
40.00–49.99	2	.08	8
50.00–59.99	1	.04	4
60.00–69.99	2	.08	8
Total	25	1.00	100

b.

Earnings per Share ($)	Frequency	Relative Frequency	Percent Frequency
−3.00 to −2.01	2	.08	8
−2.00 to −1.01	0	.00	0
−1.00 to −0.01	2	.08	8
0.00 to 0.99	9	.36	36
1.00 to 1.99	9	.36	36
2.00 to 2.99	3	.12	12
Total	25	1.00	100

18. a. $31,000, $57,000
b.

Salary	Frequency	Relative Frequency	Percent Frequency
31–35	2	.050	5.0
36–40	4	.100	10.0
41–45	13	.325	32.5
46–50	11	.275	27.5
51–55	8	.200	20.0
56–60	2	.050	5.0
Total	40	1.000	100.0

c. .05
d. 25%

20. a. 38%
b. 33%
c. 29%
d. 163
e. 310

22.

5	7 8
6	4 5 8
7	0 2 2 5 5 6 8
8	0 2 3 5

24.

11	6
12	0 2
13	0 6 7
14	2 2 7
15	5
16	0 2 8
17	0 2 3

26. Leaf Unit = .1

0	4 7 8 9 9
1	1 2 9
2	0 0 1 3 5 5 6 8
3	4 9
4	8
5	
6	
7	1

28. a.

0	8
1	0 1 2 3 3 3
1	5 5 6 6 6 7 7 7 8 8 8 8
2	0 0 1 1 3 4 4
2	6 7 7
3	
3	8

b.

1998 P/E Forecast	Frequency	Relative Frequency
5–9	1	3.4
10–14	6	20.0
15–19	12	40.0
20–24	7	23.3
25–29	3	10.0
30–34	0	0.0
35–39	1	3.3
Total	30	100.0

30. Negative relationship

32.

	Book Value/Share				
Earn/Share	0.00–4.99	5.00–9.99	10.00–14.99	15.00–19.99	Total
0.00–0.99	7	4	1	0	12
1.00–1.99	2	7	1	1	11
2.00–2.99	0	1	4	2	7
Total	9	12	6	3	30

Lower earnings per share tends to have a lower book value per share

34. Positive relationship

36. a/b.

Car Model	Frequency	Relative Frequency
Accord	10	.20
Cavalier	9	.18
Camry	12	.24
Civic	9	.18
Taurus	10	.20
Total	50	1.00

38. a.

Status	Frequency	Percent Frequency
Already certified (C)	20	40
Already pursuing (P)	16	32
Will pursue (W)	8	16
Will not pursue (N)	4	8
Uncertain (U)	2	4
	50	100

b.

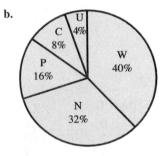

c. The trend appears to be toward obtaining ISO certification.

40.

Closing Price	Freq.	Rel. Freq.	Cum. Freq.	Cum. Rel. Freq.
0–9⅞	9	.225	9	.225
10–19⅞	10	.250	19	.475
20–29⅞	5	.125	24	.600
30–39⅞	11	.275	35	.875
40–49⅞	2	.050	37	.925
50–59⅞	2	.050	39	.975
60–69⅞	0	.000	39	.975
70–79⅞	1	.025	40	1.000
Totals	40	1.000		

42.

Income ($)	Frequency	Relative Frequency
25,000–29,999	9	.176
30,000–34,999	19	.372
35,000–39,999	15	.294
40,000–44,999	6	.118
45,000–49,999	1	.020
50,000–54,999	1	.020
Total	51	1.000

44. a.

```
1 |
2 | 8  9
3 | 2  3  5  7  7  8  8
4 | 1  1  2  3  3  6  6  8  8
5 |
6 | 1  3  3  3
7 | 8  9
```

b.

```
1 | 3  5  6  7
2 | 1  2  6  9  9
3 | 0  1  2  5  5  5  8
4 | 0  2  5  6
5 | 1  7
6 | 6
7 | 0
```

d. 12

e.

Temperature	High Temp	Low Temp
	Frequency	
10–19	0	4
20–29	2	5
30–39	7	7
40–49	9	4
50–59	0	2
60–69	4	1
70–79	2	1
Total	24	24

46. a.

		5–9	10–14	15–19	20–24	25–29	Total
				P/E Ratio			
Industry	Consumer	0	3	5	1	1	10
	Banking	4	4	2	0	0	10
	Total	4	7	7	1	1	20

b.

		5–9	10–14	15–19	20–24	25–29	Total
				P/E Ratio			
Industry	Consumer	0	30	50	10	10	100
	Banking	40	40	20	0	0	100

c. Consumer tends to have higher P/E ratios

50. b.

Year	Freq.	Fuel	Freq.
1973 or before	247	Elect.	149
1974–79	54	Nat. Gas	317
1980–86	82	Oil	17
1987–91	121	Propane	7
Total	504	Other	14
		Total	504

Chapter 3

2. 16, 16.5

4. 59.727, 57, 53

6. a. 91.45, 87.5, 120
   b. 66.3, 69.5, 70
   c. 500 @ $50
   d. Yes

8. a. 38.75, 29
   b. 38.5
   c. 29.5, 47.5
   d. 31

10. a. 48.33, 49; do not report a mode
   b. 45, 55

12. a. 4.44, 4.25, 4.20
   b. 4.10, 5.10
   c. 4.15, 4.80

14. 16, 4

16. a. Mainland
       115,130; 111,560
       Asia
       36,620; 36,695
   b. Mainland
       86,240; 26,820; 23.3%
       42,970; 11,400; 31.1%
   c. More visitors and more variation from Mainland

18. a. Range = 32, IQR = 10
   b. 92.75, 9.63

20. *Dawson:* range = 2, s = .67
      Clark: range = 8, s = 2.58

22. **a.** 170, 88; 85, 18
      b. 2545.84, 50.46; 447.69, 21.16
      c. 55.18, 31.9
      d. Greater for 500 @ $50

24. *Quarter-milers:* s = .056, Coef. of Var. = 5.8
      Milers: s = .130, Coef. of Var. = 2.9

26. .20, 1.50, 0, −.50, −2.20

28. **a.** 95%
      b. Almost all
      c. 68%

30. **a.** 96.7, 8.21
      b. $z = 2.84$, No
      c. 16%, 2.5%

32. **a.** 75%
      b. 77%
      c. 95%

34. 15, 22.5, 26, 29, 34

36. 5, 8, 10, 15, 18

38. **a.** 5, 9.6, 14.5, 19.2, 52.7
      b. Limits: −4.8, 33.6
      c. 41.6 is an outlier
          52.7 is an outlier

40. **a.** 79.31, 78.5
      b. 76.5, 80.5
      c. 72, 76.5, 78.5, 80.5, 90
      d. Camcorders have higher variation
      e. Yes; Hitachi and Mitsubishi are outliers

42. **a.** 37.48, 23.67
      b. 7.91, 51.92
      c. Limits: −58.11, 117.94
          Russia and Turkey are outliers

44. **b.** There appears to be a linear relationship between x
          and y
      c. $s_{xy} = 26.5$
      d. $r_{xy} = .69$

46. −.91; negative relationship

48. **b.** 4.14
      c. +.697

50. **a.** 3.69
      b. 3.175

52. **a.** 2.50
      b. Yes

54. 10.74, 25.63, 5.06

56. **a.** 138.52, 129, 0
      b. No, much more
      c. 95, 169

d. 467, 74
e. 9271.01, 96.29
f. Yes, the $467 value

58. **a.** 18.57, 16.5
      b. 53.49, 7.31
      c. Quantex
      d. 1.15
      e. −.90
      f. No, according to z-scores

60. **a.** Public: 32; auto: 32
      b. Public: 4.64; auto: 1.83
      c. Auto has less variability

62. .9856, strong positive relationship

64. **a.** 817
      b. 833

66. 51.50, 227.37, 15.08

Chapter 4

2. 20 ways

4. **b.** (H,H,H) (H,H,T) (H,T,H) (H,T,T)
          (T,H,H) (T,H,T) (T,T,H) (T,T,T)
      c. ⅛

6. .40, .26, .34; relative frequency method

8. **a.** 4; Commission Positive–Council Approves, Commission
          Positive–Council Disapproves
          Commission Negative–Council Approves, Commission
          Negative–Council Disapproves

10. **a.** .42
      b. .52
      c. .62
      d. .48

12. **a.** 1,906,884
      b. 1/1,906,884
      c. c.1/80,089,128

14. **a.** ¼
      b. ½
      c. ¾

16. **a.** 36
      c. ⅙
      d. ⁵⁄₁₈
      e. No; $P(\text{odd}) = P(\text{even}) = \dfrac{1}{2}$
      f. Classical

18. **a.** $P(0) = .05$
      b. $P(4 \text{ or } 5) = .20$
      c. $P(0, 1, \text{ or } 2) = .55$

20. **a.** .132
      b. .299
      c. .569

22. **a.** .40, .40, .60
    b. .80, yes
    c. $A^c = \{E_3, E_4, E_5\}$; $C^c = \{E_1, E_4\}$;
       $P(A^c) = .60$; $P(C^c) = .40$
    d. $\{E_1, E_2, E_5\}$; .60
    e. .80

24. .43

26. **a.** $P(V) = .7197$, $P(Q) = .4498$, $P(V \cap Q) = .2699$
    b. .8996
    c. .1004

28. **a.** .698
    b. .302

30. **a.** .67
    b. .80
    c. No

32. **a.**

	Single	Married	Total
Under 30	.55	.10	.65
30 or Over	.20	.15	.35
Total	.75	.25	1.0

   b. Higher probability of under 30
   c. Higher probability of single
   d. .55
   e. .8462
   f. No

34. **a.** .44
    b. .15
    c. .0225
    d. .0025
    e. .136
    f. .106

36. **a.**

East	NW	SW	West	Total
.010	.005	.004	.008	.028
.065	.058	.018	.057	.199
.299	.247	.060	.168	.774
.375	.310	.083	.233	1.000

   b. .028
   c. .083
   d. .048
   e. Southwest
   f. West

38. **a.** 52/1035
    b. .0004
    c. .0676

40. **a.** .10, .20, .09
    b. .51
    c. .26, .51, .23

42. **a.** 21
    b. Yes

44. .6754

46. **a.** .253
    b. .742

48. **a.** .61
    b. 18–34 and 65+
    c. .30

50. **a.** 76
    b. .24

52. **b.** .2022
    c. .4618
    d. .4005

54. **b.** $1 million–$2 million
    c. $P(2M) = .2286$, $P(2M \mid T) = .1556$, $P(2M \mid F) = .2833$
    d. No

56. **a.** .25, .40, .10
    b. .25
    c. B and S are independent; program appears to have no effect

58. 3.44%

60. **a.** .0625
    b. .0132
    c. Three

Chapter 5

2. **a.** x = time in minutes to assemble product
   b. Any positive value: $x > 0$
   c. Continuous

4. $x = 0, 1, 2, \ldots, 12$

6. **a.** 0, 1, 2, . . . , 20; discrete
   b. 0, 1, 2, . . . ; discrete
   c. 0, 1, 2, . . . , 50; discrete
   d. $0 \leq x \leq 8$; continuous
   e. $x > 0$; continuous

8. **a.**

x	1	2	3	4
$f(x)$	.15	.25	.40	.20

   c. $f(x) \geq 0$, $\Sigma f(x) = 1$

10. **a.**

x	1	2	3	4	5
$f(x)$	.05	.09	.03	.42	.41

   b.

x	1	2	3	4	5
$f(x)$	.04	.10	.12	.46	.28

   c. .83
   d. .28
   e. Senior executives more satisfied

12. a. Yes
   b. .65

14. a. .05
   b. .70
   c. .40

16. a. 5.20
   b. 4.56, 2.14

18. a. $E(x) = 2.2$, same
   b. $\text{Var}(x) = 1.16$, $\sigma = 1.08$

20. a. 166
   b. -94; concern is to protect against the expense of a big accident

22. a. 445
   b. 1250 loss

24. a. Medium: 145; large: 140
   b. Medium: 2725; large: 12,400

26. a. $f(0) = .3487$
   b. $f(2) = .1937$
   c. .9298
   d. .6513
   e. 1
   f. $\sigma^2 = .9000$, $\sigma = .9487$

28. a. .2301
   b. .3410
   c. .8784

30. a. Probability of a defective part must be .03 for each trial; trials must be independent
   c. 2
   d.

Number of defects	0	1	2
Probability	.9409	.0582	.0009

32. a. .90
   b. .99
   c. .999
   d. Yes

34. a. .2547
   b. .9566
   c. .8009

38. a. $f(x) = \dfrac{3^x e^{-3}}{x!}$
   b. .2241
   c. .1494
   d. .8008

40. a. .1952
   b. .1048
   c. .0183
   d. .0907

42. a. .1465
   b. 1
   c. .8647

44. a. $\mu = 1.25$
   b. .2865
   c. .3581
   d. .3554

46. a. 50
   b. .067
   c. .4667
   d. .30

48. a. .50
   b. .3333

50. a. .01
   b. .07
   c. .92
   d. .07

52. a. .5333
   b. .6667
   c. .7778
   d. $n = 7$

54. a. $f(x) \geq 0$ and $\Sigma f(x) = 1$
   b. 3.64, .6704
   c. Appears overvalued

56. a. .0364
   b. .4420
   c. 48
   d. 6.7882

58. a. .9510
   b. .0480
   c. .0490

60. a. .1912

62. a. .2240
   b. .5767

64. a. .5333
   b. .1333
   c. .3333

Chapter 6

2. b. .50
   c. .60
   d. 15
   e. 8.33

4. b. .50
   c. .30
   d. .40

6. a. .40
   b. .64
   c. .68

10. a. .3413
   b. .4332
   c. .4772
   d. .4938

12. a. .2967
 b. .4418
 c. .3300
 d. .5910
 e. .8849
 f. .2388

14. a. $z = 1.96$
 b. $z = .61$
 c. $z = 1.12$
 d. $z = .44$

16. a. $z = 2.33$
 b. $z = 1.96$
 c. $z = 1.645$
 d. $z = 1.28$

18. a. .2451
 b. .1170
 c. 69.48 minutes or more

20. a. .0069
 b. 6.18%
 c. A volume in excess of 810 million

22. a. .7295
 b. $19.49 per hour
 c. .0110

24. a. .2266
 b. .7745
 c. 31.12 years

26. a. $\mu = 20, \sigma = 4$
 b. yes
 c. .0602
 d. .4714
 e. .1292

28. a. .7910
 b. .9616
 c. .1066

30. a. 328
 b. .0239
 c. .9394

32. a. .8336
 b. .0049

34. a. $1 - e^{-x_0/3}$
 b. .4866
 c. .3679
 d. .8111
 e. .3245

36. b. .6321
 c. .3935
 d. .0821

38. a. .3935
 b. .5276
 c. .1353

40. b. .40
 c. .40

42. a. .3174, 317.4 defects
 b. .0028, 2.8 defects

44. a. .0918
 b. 12,468 tubes

46. a. .7229
 b. .0052
 c. 176,031

48. a. .4935
 b. .0618
 c. 3.59%
 d. $37,383

50. a. 5.16%
 b. 57.87%
 c. 99.55%
 d. Approximately 0

52. a. 300
 b. $\sigma^2 = 120, \sigma = 10.95$
 c. .8008
 d. .0125

54. a. 4 hours
 b. $1/4\, e^{-x/4}$
 c. .7788
 d. .1353

56. a. 2 minutes
 b. .2212
 c. .3935
 d. .0821

Chapter 7

2. 22, 147, 229, 289

4. a. JAL, Northwest, Delta, British Airlines, and Aeroflot
 b. 252

6. 2782, 493, 825, 1807, 289

8. New Mexico, Connecticut, Clemson, Cincinnati, Xavier, and Arizona

10. Finite, infinite, infinite, infinite, finite

12. a. .50
 b. .3667

14. a. .19
 b. .32
 c. .79

16. .80

18. a. 200
 b. 5
 c. Normal with $E(\bar{x}) = 200$ and $\sigma_{\bar{x}} = 5$
 d. The probability distribution of $\bar{x}$

20. 3.54, 2.50, 2.04, 1.77
    $\sigma_{\bar{x}}$ decreases as n increases

22. **a.** Only for $n = 30$ and $n = 40$
    b. $n = 30$; normal with $E(\bar{x}) = 400$
       and $\sigma_{\bar{x}} = 9.13$
       $n = 40$; normal with $E(\bar{x}) = 400$
       and $\sigma_{\bar{x}} = 7.91$

24. **a.** Normal with $E(\bar{x}) = 51,800$ and $\sigma_{\bar{x}} = 516.40$
    b. $\sigma_{\bar{x}}$ decreases to 365.15
    c. $\sigma_{\bar{x}}$ decreases as n increases

26. **a.** Normal with $E(\bar{x}) = 1.20$ and $\sigma_{\bar{x}} = .014$
    b. .8414
    c. .5224

28. **a.** .5036, .6212, .7888, .9232, .9876
    b. Smaller standard error

30. **a.** Normal with $E(\bar{x}) = 166,500$ and $\sigma_{\bar{x}} = 4200$
    b. .9826
    c. .7660, .4514, .1896
    d. Increase the sample size

32. **a.** No, $^{40}/_{4000} < .05$
    b. With: 1.2902
       Without: 1.2965
    c. .8764

34. **a.** .6156
    b. .8530

36. **a.** .6156
    b. .7814
    c. .9488
    d. .9942
    e. High probability with larger n

38. **a.** Normal with $E(\bar{p}) = .76$ and $\sigma_{\bar{p}} = .0214$
    b. .8384
    c. .9452

40. **a.** Normal with $E(\bar{p}) = .25$ and $\sigma_{\bar{p}} = .0306$
    b. .6730
    c. .8968

42. **a.** Normal with $E(\bar{p}) = .15$ and $\sigma_{\bar{p}} = .0505$
    b. .4448
    c. .8389

44. 4324, 2875, 318, 538, 4771

46. **a.** Normal with $E(\bar{x}) = 31.5$ and $\sigma_{\bar{x}} = 1.70$
    b. .4448
    c. .9232

48. **a.** 8.4853
    b. .50
    c. .4448
    d. .5934

50. **a.** 625
    b. .7888

52. **a.** Normal with $E(\bar{p}) = .74$ and $\sigma_{\bar{p}} = .031$
    b. .8030
    c. .4778

54. .9525

56. **a.** 48
    b. Normal, $E(\bar{p}) = .26$, $\sigma_{\bar{p}} = .0625$
    c. .2119

Chapter 8

2. **a.** 30.60 to 33.40
   b. 30.34 to 33.66
   c. 29.81 to 34.19

4. 62

6. 362.80 to 375.20

8. **a.** 12,003 to 12,333
   b. 11,971 to 12,365
   c. 11,909 to 12,427
   d. Width increases to be more confident

10. 279 to 321

12. 5.74 to 6.94

14. **a.** 1.734
    b. -1.321
    c. 3.365
    d. -1.761 and 1.761
    e. -2.048 and 2.048

16. **a.** 15.97 to 18.53
    b. 15.71 to 18.79
    c. 15.14 to 19.36

18. **a.** 13.2
    b. 7.8
    c. 7.62 to 18.78
    d. Wide interval; larger sample desirable

20. **a.** 21.15 to 23.65
    b. 21.12 to 23.68
    c. Intervals are essentially the same

22. **a.** 6.86
    b. 6.54 to 7.18

24. **a.** 9
    b. 35
    c. 78

26. **a.** 50, 89, 200
    b. Only if $E = 1$ is essential

28. 40, 110

30. 59

32. **a.** .6733 to .7267
    b. .6682 to .7318

34. 1068

36. a. .0908
   b. .0681 to .1134

38. a. .0430
   b. .2170 to .3030
   c. .822

40. a. .2505
   b. .0266

42. a. 85
   b. 340
   c. 2124
   d. 8494
   e. The sample size increases

44. 51.37 to 52.63

46. a. 49.8
   b. 15.99
   c. 47.58 to 52.02

48. 9.20 to 14.80

50. 37

52. 176

54. a. .5420
   b. .0508
   c. .4912 to .5928

56. a. 1267
   b. 1509

58. .2895 to .3718

60. a. .3101
   b. .2898 to .3304
   c. 8219; No, this sample size is unnecessarily large

Chapter 9

2. a. $H_0: \mu \leq 14$
       $H_a: \mu > 14$

4. a. $H_0: \mu \geq 220$
       $H_a: \mu < 220$

6. a. $H_0: \mu \leq 1$
       $H_a: \mu > 1$
   b. Claiming $\mu > 1$ when it is not true
   c. Claiming $\mu \leq 1$ when it not true

8. a. $H_0: \mu \geq 220$
       $H_a: \mu < 220$
   b. Claiming $\mu < 220$ when it is not true
   c. Claiming $\mu \geq 220$ when it is not true

10. a. Reject H_0 if $z > 2.05$
   b. 1.36
   c. .0869
   d. Do not reject H_0

12. a. .0344; reject H_0
   b. .3264; do not reject H_0
   c. .0668; do not reject H_0
   d. Approximately 0; reject H_0

14. $z = 3.11$; reject H_0

16. $z = -2.74$; reject H_0
   p-value $= .0031$

18. a. Reject H_0 if $z < -1.645$
   b. $z = -1.98$; reject H_0
   c. .0239

20. a. Reject H_0 if $z < -2.33$ or $z > 2.33$
   b. 1.13
   c. .2584
   d. Do not reject H_0

22. a. .0718; do not reject H_0
   b. .6528; do not reject H_0
   c. .0404; reject H_0
   d. Approximately 0; reject H_0
   e. .3174; do not reject H_0

24. a. $z = -1.06$; do not reject H_0
   b. .2892

26. a. $z = -1.71$; do not reject H_0
   b. .0872

28. a. 71,167 to 74,433
   b. Reject H_0 because 61,650 is not in the interval

30. a. 18
   b. 1.41
   c. Reject H_0 if $t < -2.571$ or $t > 2.571$
   d. -3.47
   e. Reject H_0

32. a. .01; reject H_0
   b. .10; do not reject H_0
   c. Between .025 and .05; reject H_0
   d. Greater than .10; do not reject H_0
   e. Approximately 0; reject H_0

34. a. $t = -1.33$; do not reject H_0
   b. Approximately .20

36. a. $t = -3.33$; reject H_0
   b. p-value is less than .005

38. $\bar{x} = 2.4$, $s = .52$, $t = 2.43$
   Reject H_0

40. a. Reject H_0 if $z < -1.96$ or $z > 1.96$
   b. -1.25
   c. .2112
   d. Do not reject H_0

42. .1118, do not reject H_0

44. a. .62
   b. $z = 3.13$; reject H_0
   c. Yes; it shows Burger King is preferred

46. a. $z = 1.38$; reject H_0
  b. .0838

48. $H_0: p \geq .91$
  $H_a: p < .91$
  $z = -5.44$; reject H_0

50. $z = -1.96$; do not reject H_0

52. a. $z = 1.80$; do not reject H_0
  b. .0718
  c. 349 to 375

54. $z = -3.84$; reject H_0

56. a. Show $p < .50$
  b. $z = -6.62$; reject H_0

Chapter 10

2. a. 2.4
  b. 5.27
  c. .09 to 4.71

4. a. 3.9
  b. 0.6 to 7.0

6. a. 125
  b. 36.82 to 213.18

8. a. Kitchens are less expensive by $1600
  b. -4.25 to 1.05

10. a. Reject H_0; $\mu_1 - \mu_2 > 0$
  b. .0212

12. Do not reject H_0

14. Reject H_0; mean ages differ

16. Reject H_0; wage discrimination exists

18. a. 1, 2, 0, 0, 2
  b. 1
  c. 1
  d. Reject H_0; $\mu_d > 0$

20. Do not reject H_0

22. 7.24 to 11.46

24. a. Do not reject H_0
  b. 6.45 to 11.27

26. a. SSTR = 570; MSTR = 285
  b. MSE = 5.5
  c. $F = 51.82 > F_{.05} = 3.89$; reject H_0

28. a. $F = 80$
  b. $F_{.05} = 2.76$; reject H_0

30. $F = 0.27 < F_{.05} = 3.47$; cannot reject H_0

32. Cannot reject H_0; p-valve = .403

34. Reject H_0

36. Reject H_0

38. a. Means are not significantly different
  b. Means are not significantly different

40. $F = 7.23 > F_{.05} = 4.26$; reject H_0

42. Reject H_0; p-value = 0.000

Chapter 11

2. a. $\bar{p} = .184$, $s_{\bar{p}_1 - \bar{p}_2} = .0354$, $z = 1.69$; reject H_0
  b. .0455

4. .04 to .14

6. a. .93, .85
  b. $z = 3.13$, reject H_0
  c. $.08 \pm .05$

8. a. $z = -3.42$; reject H_0
  b. .0637 to .2363

10. There is no significant difference; $z = 2.53 > 1.645$

12. $\chi^2 = 15.33$, $\chi^2_{.05} = 7.81473$; reject H_0

14. $\chi^2 = 29.51$, $\chi^2_{.05} = 11.07$; reject H_0
  Percentage figures have changed

16. $\chi^2 = 57.37$, $\chi^2_{.10} = 9.24$; reject H_0

18. $\chi^2 = 8.89$, $\chi^2_{.05} = 9.48773$; do not reject H_0

20. $\chi^2 = 19.78$, $\chi^2_{.05} = 9.48773$; reject H_0

22. $\chi^2 = 6.31$, $\chi^2_{.05} = 9.48773$; do not reject H_0

24. $\chi^2 = 13.43$, $\chi^2_{.05} = 12.59$; reject H_0

26. $\chi^2 = 37.17$, $\chi^2_{.01} = 9.21034$; reject H_0

28. $\chi^2 = 7.96$, $\chi^2_{.05} = 9.48773$; do not reject H_0

30. $\chi^2 = 45.36$, $\chi^2_{.01} = 13.28$; reject H_0
  Conclude ratings are not independent

32. a. $H_0: p_1 - p_2 \leq 0$
  $H_a: p_1 - p_2 > 0$
  b. $z = 1.80$; reject H_0
  p-value = .0359

34. .0174; reject H_0

36. $\chi^2 = 41.69$, $\chi^2_{.01} = 13.2767$; reject H_0
  Attitudes differ

38. $\chi^2 = 8.11$, $\chi^2_{.05} = 5.99$; do not reject H_0

40. $\chi^2 = 5.26$, $\chi^2_{.05} = 5.99147$; reject H_0

42. $\chi^2 = 59.41$, $\chi^2_{.025} = 23.3367$; reject H_0
  They are related

44. $\chi^2 = 6.20$, $\chi^2_{.05} = 12.5916$; do not reject H_0

Chapter 12

2. b. There appears to be a linear relationship between x and y
  d. $\hat{y} = 30.33 - 1.88x$
  e. 19.05

4. b. There appears to be a linear relationship between x and y
 d. $\hat{y} = -240.5 + 5.5x$
 e. 106 pounds

6. c. $\hat{y} = 6.02 - .07x$
 e. .42

8. a. $\hat{y} = 107.13 + 3.07x$
 c. 153.2

10. b. There appears to be a linear relationship between the variables
 c. $\hat{y} = 113.52 + 0.94x$
 d. 583.5

12. b. $\hat{y} = 43.40 + 1.11x$
 c. \$110,000

14. a. SSE = 12.40, SST = 80, SSR = 67.6
 b. .845
 c. SST = 80, SSR = 67.6
 d. +.9192

16. 52.7%, +.7259

18. a. SST = 335,000, SSR = 249,864.86, SSE = 85,135.14
 b. .746; good fit
 c. +.8637

20. a. $\hat{y} = 1246.67 + 7.6x$
 b. \$7.60
 c. .9587, 95.87%
 d. \$5046.67

22. a. 4.133
 b. 2.033
 c. .643
 d. Reject H_0
 e. $F = 16.36$

24. a. 1.33
 b. Cannot reject H_0: $\beta_1 = 0$
 c. $F = 3.33 < F_{.05} = 10.13$, cannot reject H_0: $\beta_1 = 0$

26. Years of experience and sales are related

28. Production volume and cost are related

30. a. 1.11
 b. 7.07 to 14.13
 c. 2.32
 d. 3.22 to 17.98

32. $-.40$ to 4.98, -2.27 to 7.31

34. a. \$11,740 to \$14,420
 b. \$9,300 to \$16,860
 c. Yes
 d. Any deductions exceeding \$16,860

36. a. $\hat{y} = 67.0476 + 5.8167x$
 b. $r^2 = .894$; good fit
 c. 250.59 to 290.67
 d. 215.39 to 325.87

38. a. $\hat{y} = 6.1092 + .8951x$
 b. Reject H_0: $\beta_1 = 0$
 c. \$28.49 per month

40. a. Price $= -11.8 + 2.18$ Income
 b. $r^2 = .861$; good fit
 c. \$70,290 to \$81,280
 d. \$60,010 to \$91,560

42. a. $\hat{y} = -7.02 + 1.59x$
 b. 3.48, -2.47, -4.83, -1.60, 5.22
 c. Difficult to tell with only 5 observations; plot does suggest curvature in the residuals, which would indicate that the error term assumptions are not satisfied

44. a. $\hat{y} = 29.40 + 1.55x$
 b. Significant relationship
 d. Question assumption of a linear relationship; dangerous to extrapolate beyond the range of the data

46. a. $\hat{y} = 343 + .051x$
 c. Assumptions should be questioned

48. a. $\hat{y} = 45.06 + 1.94x_1$; $\hat{y} = 132.36$
 b. $\hat{y} = 85.22 + 4.32x_2$; $\hat{y} = 150.02$
 c. $\hat{y} = -18.37 + 2.01x_1 + 4.74x_2$; $\hat{y} = 143.18$

50. a. REVENUE $= 88.6 + 1.60$ TVADV
 b. REVENUE $= 83.2 + 2.29$ TVADV + 1.30 NEWSADV
 c. No
 d. \$93,560

52. a. $\hat{y} = 66.5 + .414x_1 - .270x_2$
 c. 93,680

54. a. $\hat{y} = 9.265 + .7105x$
 b. Significant relationship
 c. $r^2 = .744$; good fit
 d. \$13.53

56. a. Market beta $= .95$
 b. Significant relationship
 c. $r^2 = .470$; not a very good fit
 d. Woolworth has a higher risk

58. a. Negative linear relationship
 b. $\hat{y} = 8.10 - .344x$
 c. Significant relationship; p-value $= .002$
 d. $r^2 = .711$; reasonably good fit
 e. 5.2 to 7.6 days

60. b. 3.19

62. a. 3.04, 3.61, 5.08
 b. Both are significant
 d. .91

64. b. Significant; $F = 22.79 > F_{.05} = 5.79$
 c. $R_a^2 = .861$; good fit
 d. Both are significant

66. a. Speed $= 97.6 + .0693$ Price $- .00082$ Weight $+ .0590$ Horsepower $- 2.48$ Zero60
  b. Significant relationship
  c. Price and Weight are not significant
  d. Speed $= 103 + .0558$ Horsepower $- 3.19$ Zero60

Chapter 13

2. a. 5.42
  b. UCL $= 6.09$, LCL $= 4.75$

4.

	R Chart	x̄ Chart
UCL	2.98	29.10
LCL	.22	27.90

6. 20.01, .082

8. a. .0470
  b. UCL $= .0989$, LCL $= -.0049$ (use LCL $= 0$)
  c. $\bar{p} = .08$; in control
  d. UCL $= 14.826$, LCL $= -0.726$
    Process is out of control if more than 14 defective
  e. In control, 12 defective
  f. np chart

10. $p = .02; f(0) = .6035$
  $p = .06; f(0) = .2129$

12. $p_0 = .02$; producer's risk $= .0599$
  $p_0 = .06$; producer's risk $= .3396$
  Producer's risk decreases as the acceptance number c is increased

14. $n = 20, c = 3$

16. a. 95.4
  b. UCL $= 96.07$, LCL $= 94.73$
  c. No

18.

	R Chart	x̄ Chart
UCL	4.23	6.57
LCL	0	4.27

Estimate of standard deviation $= .86$

20.

	R Chart	x̄ Chart
UCL	.1121	3.112
LCL	0	3.051

22. a. UCL $= .0817$, LCL $= -.0017$ (use LCL $= 0$)

24. a. .03
  b. $\beta = .0802$

26. a. Producer's risk $= .0064$
  b. Consumer's risk $= .0136$
  c. *Advantage:* excellent control
    Disadvantage: cost

Chapter 1

2. a. 10

b. 4

c. Industry and Compensation vs. Shareholder Return Rating are qualitative; compensation vs. Shareholder Return Rating, while numeric data, is a qualitative variable because the data are used to place the company into a class based on best to worst performance in terms of Compensation vs. Shareholder Return; CEO Compensation and Sales are quantitative variables

3. a. Average CEO compensation = $27,914/10 = $2791.4 or $2,791,400.

b. 2 of 10 are in the banking industry; 20%

c. 3 of 10 received a rating of 3; 30%

4. a. 10

b. *Fortune* 500 largest U.S. industrial corporations

c. Average sales = $120,034/10 = $12,003.4 million

d. Using the sample results, estimate the average sales for the population of corporations at $12,003.4 million

13. a. Quantitative

b. A time series with 7 observations

c. Number of riverboat casinos

d. Rapid increase but slowing recently

Chapter 2

3. a. 360° × 58/120 = 174°

b. 360° × 42/120 = 126°

c.

d.

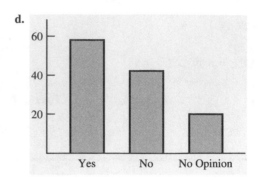

7.

Rating	Frequency	Relative Frequency
Outstanding	19	.38
Very good	13	.26
Good	10	.20
Average	6	.12
Poor	2	.04

Management should be pleased with these results: 64% of the ratings are very good to outstanding, and 84% of the ratings are good or better; comparing these ratings to previous results will show whether the restaurant is making improvements in its customers' ratings of food quality

12.

Class	Cumulative Frequency	Cumulative Relative Frequency
≤19	10	.20
≤29	24	.48
≤39	41	.82
≤49	48	.96
≤59	50	1.00

15. a/b.

Waiting Time	Frequency	Relative Frequency
0–4	4	.20
5–9	8	.40
10–14	5	.25
15–19	2	.10
20–24	1	.05
Totals	20	1.00

c/d.

Waiting Time	Cumulative Frequency	Cumulative Relative Frequency
≤4	4	.20
≤9	12	.60
≤14	17	.85
≤19	19	.95
≤24	20	1.00

e. $^{12}/_{20} = .60$

23. Leaf unit = .1

```
 6 | 3
 7 | 5  5  7
 8 | 1  3  4  8
 9 | 3  6
10 | 0  4  5
11 | 3
```

25.
```
 9 | 8  9
10 | 2  4  6  6
11 | 4  5  7  8  8  9
12 | 2  4  5  7
13 | 1  2
14 | 4
15 | 1
```

29. a.

			y	
		1	2	Total
	A	5	0	5
x	B	11	2	13
	C	2	10	12
	Total	18	12	30

b.

			y	
		1	2	Total
	A	100.0	0.0	100.0
x	B	84.6	15.4	100.0
	C	16.7	83.3	100.0

c.

		y	
		1	2
	A	27.8	0.0
x	B	61.1	16.7
	C	11.1	83.3
	Total	100.0	100.0

d. A values are always in $y = 1$
B values are most often in $y = 1$
C values are most often in $y = 2$

32. a.

		Book Value/Share				
		0.00–4.99	5.00–9.99	10.00–14.99	15.00–19.99	Total
Earnings per Share	0.00–0.99	7	4	1	0	12
	1.00–1.99	2	7	1	1	11
	2.00–2.99	0	1	4	2	7
	Total	9	12	6	3	30

b.

		Book Value/Share				
		0.00–4.99	5.00–9.99	10.00–14.99	15.00–19.99	Total
Earnings per Share	0.00–0.99	58.3	33.3	8.4	0.0	100.0
	1.00–1.99	18.2	63.6	9.1	9.1	100.0
	2.00–2.99	0.0	14.3	57.1	28.6	100.0

When book value is low, earnings per share tends to be low; when book value is high, earnings per share tends to be high

Chapter 3

3. Arrange data in order: 15, 20, 25, 25, 27, 28, 30, 34

$i = \dfrac{20}{100}(8) = 1.6$; round up to position 2

20th percentile = 20

$i = \dfrac{25}{100}(8) = 2$; use positions 2 and 3

25th percentile = $\dfrac{20 + 25}{2} = 22.5$

$i = \dfrac{65}{100}(8) = 5.2$; round up to position 6

65th percentile = 28

$i = \dfrac{75}{100}(8) = 6$; use positions 6 and 7

75th percentile = $\dfrac{28 + 30}{2} = 29$

8. a. $\bar{x} = \dfrac{\Sigma x_i}{n} = \dfrac{775}{20} = 38.75$

Mode = 29 (appears three times)

b. Data in order: 22, 24, 29, 29, 29, 30, 31, 31, 32, 37, 40, 41, 44, 44, 46, 49, 50, 52, 57, 58

Median (10th and 11th positions)

$\dfrac{37 + 40}{2} = 38.5$

At home workers are slightly younger

c. $i = \dfrac{25}{100}(20) = 5$; use positions 5 and 6

$Q_1 = \dfrac{29 + 30}{2} = 29.5$

$i = \dfrac{75}{100}(20) = 15$; use positions 15 and 16

$Q_3 = \dfrac{46 + 49}{2} = 47.5$

d. $i = \dfrac{32}{100}(20) = 6.4$; round up to position 7

32nd percentile = 31
At least 32% of the people are 31 or younger

15. Range = 34 − 15 = 19
Arrange data in order: 15, 20, 25, 25, 27, 28, 30, 34

$i = \dfrac{25}{100}(8) = 2$; $Q_1 = \dfrac{20 + 25}{2} = 22.5$

$i = \dfrac{75}{100}(8) = 6$; $Q_3 = \dfrac{28 + 30}{2} = 29$

IQR = $Q_3 - Q_1 = 29 - 22.5 = 6.5$

$\bar{x} = \dfrac{\Sigma x_i}{n} = \dfrac{204}{8} = 25.5$

x_i	$(x_i - \bar{x})$	$(x_i - \bar{x})^2$
27	1.5	2.25
25	−.5	.25
20	−5.5	30.25
15	−10.5	110.25
30	4.5	20.25
34	8.5	72.25
28	2.5	6.25
25	−.5	.25
		242.00

$s^2 = \dfrac{\Sigma(x_i - \bar{x})^2}{n - 1} = \dfrac{242}{8 - 1} = 34.57$

$s = \sqrt{34.57} = 5.88$

21. a. Range = 190 − 168 = 22

b. $\bar{x} = \dfrac{\Sigma x_i}{n} = \dfrac{1068}{6} = 178$

$s^2 = \dfrac{\Sigma(x_i - \bar{x})^2}{n - 1}$

$= \dfrac{4^2 + (-10)^2 + 6^2 + 12^2 + (-8)^2 + (-4)^2}{6 - 1}$

$= \dfrac{376}{5} = 75.2$

c. $s = \sqrt{75.2} = 8.67$

d. $\dfrac{s}{\bar{x}}(100) = \dfrac{8.67}{178}(100) = 4.87$

27. Chebyshev's theorem: *at least* $(1 - 1/z^2)$

a. $z = \dfrac{40 - 30}{5} = 2$; $(1 - \tfrac{1}{2^2}) = .75$

b. $z = \dfrac{45 - 30}{5} = 3$; $(1 - \tfrac{1}{3^2}) = .89$

c. $z = \dfrac{38 - 30}{5} = 1.6$; $(1 - \tfrac{1}{1.6^2}) = .61$

d. $z = \dfrac{42 - 30}{5} = 2.4$; $(1 - \tfrac{1}{2.4^2}) = .83$

e. $z = \dfrac{48 - 30}{5} = 3.6$; $(1 - \tfrac{1}{3.6^2}) = .92$

30. a.

Winner	Score (x_i)	$(x_i - \bar{x})$	$(x_i - \bar{x})^2$
Indiana	89	−7.7	59.29
San Antonio	84	−12.7	161.29
Cleveland	95	−1.7	2.89
New York	88	−8.7	75.69
Chicago	105	8.3	68.89
Minnesota	109	12.3	151.29
Portland	97	0.3	0.09
Utah	97	0.3	0.09
Boston	106	9.3	86.49
L.A. Clippers	97	0.3	0.09
Total	967	0.00	606.1

$$\text{mean} = \bar{x} = {}^{967}/_{10} = 96.7$$

$$s^2 = 606.1/9 = 67.3444$$

$$s = \sqrt{67.3444} = 8.2064$$

b. $z = \dfrac{120 - 96.7}{8.2064} = 2.84$; this z-score indicates that a score of 120 is 2.84 standard deviations above the mean; while large, we would not consider it an outlier since it is less than 3

c. $z = \dfrac{105 - 96.7}{8.2064} \approx 1.0$; approximately 16% of winning scores will be 105 or greater

$z = \dfrac{80 - 96.7}{8.2064} \approx -2.0$; approximately 2.5% of winning scores will be 80 or below

36. Arrange data in order: 5, 6, 8, 10, 10, 12, 15, 16, 18

$$i = \frac{25}{100}(9) = 2.25; \text{ round up to position 3}$$

$Q_1 = 8$

Median (5th position) = 10

$$i = \frac{75}{100}(9) = 6.75; \text{ round up to position 7}$$

$Q_3 = 15$

5-number summary: 5, 8, 10, 15, 18

39. a. Arrange data in order low to high.

$$i = \frac{25}{100}(21) = 5.25; \text{ round up to 6th position}$$

$Q_1 = 1872$

Median (11th position) = 4019

$$i = \frac{75}{100}(21) = 15.75; \text{ round up to 16th position}$$

$Q_3 = 8305$

5-number summary: 608, 1872, 4019, 8305, 14,138

b. IQR $= Q_3 - Q_1 = 8305 - 1872 = 6433$
Lower limit: $1872 - 1.5\,(6433) = -7777$
Upper limit: $8305 + 1.5\,(6433) = 17,955$

c. No; data are within limits

d. $41,138 > 27,604$. 41,138 would be an outlier; data value should be reviewed and corrected

e.

43. b. There appears to be a negative linear relationship between x and y

c.

x_i	y_i	$x_i - \bar{x}$	$y_i - \bar{y}$	$(x_i - \bar{x})(y_i - \bar{y})$
4	50	−4	4	−16
6	50	−2	4	−8
11	40	3	−6	−18
3	60	−5	14	−70
16	30	8	−16	−128
40	230	0	0	−240

$\bar{x} = 8; \bar{y} = 46$

$$s_{xy} = \frac{\Sigma(x_i - \bar{x})(y_i - \bar{y})}{n - 1} = \frac{-240}{4} = -60$$

The sample covariance indicates a negative linear association between x and y

d. $r_{xy} = \dfrac{s_{xy}}{s_x s_y} = \dfrac{-60}{(5.43)(11.40)} = -.97$

The sample correlation coefficient of $-.97$ is indicative of a strong negative linear relationship

51. a.

f_i	M_i	$f_i M_i$
4	5	20
7	10	70
9	15	135
5	20	100
25		325

$$\bar{x} = \frac{\Sigma f_i M_i}{n} = \frac{325}{25} = 13$$

b.

f_i	M_i	$(M_i - \bar{x})$	$(M_i - \bar{x})^2$	$f_i(M_i - \bar{x})^2$
4	5	-8	64	256
7	10	-3	9	63
9	15	2	4	36
5	20	7	49	245
25				600

$$s^2 = \frac{\Sigma f_i(M_i - \bar{x})^2}{n-1} = \frac{600}{25-1} = 25$$

$$s = \sqrt{25} = 5$$

52. a.

Grade x_i	Weight w_i
4(A)	9
3(B)	15
2(C)	33
1(D)	3
0(F)	0
	60 credit hours

$$\bar{x} = \frac{\Sigma w_i x_i}{\Sigma w_i} = \frac{9(4) + 15(3) + 33(2) + 3(1)}{9 + 15 + 33 + 3}$$

$$= \frac{150}{60} = 2.5$$

b. Yes

Chapter 4

2. $\binom{6}{3} = \frac{6!}{3!3!} = \frac{6 \cdot 5 \cdot 4 \cdot 3 \cdot 2 \cdot 1}{(3 \cdot 2 \cdot 1)(3 \cdot 2 \cdot 1)} = 20$

ABC	ACE	BCD	BEF
ABD	ACF	BCE	CDE
ABE	ADE	BCF	CDF
ABF	ADF	BDE	CEF
ACD	AEF	BDF	DEF

6. $P(E_1) = .40, P(E_2) = .26, P(E_3) = .34$
The relative frequency method was used

9. $\binom{50}{4} = \frac{50!}{4!46!} = \frac{50 \cdot 49 \cdot 48 \cdot 47}{4 \cdot 3 \cdot 2 \cdot 1} = 230{,}300$

10. a. P(Internet Access) = 21,733/51,745 = 0.42
   b. P(Internet Access) = 7,286/14,012 = 0.52
   c. Total number of Schools = 51,745 + 14,012 + 17,229 = 82,986
   P(Elementary) = 51,745/82,986 = 0.62
   d. Total number of schools with Internet Access = 21,733 + 7,286 + 10,682 = 39,701
   P(Internet Access) = 39,701/82,986 = 0.48

15. a. S = {ace of clubs, ace of diamonds, ace of hearts, ace of spades}
   b. S = {2 of clubs, 3 of clubs, . . . , 10 of clubs, J of clubs, Q of clubs, K of clubs, A of clubs}
   c. There are 12; jack, queen, or king in each of the four suits
   d. *For (a)*: 4/52 = 1/13 = .08
   For (b): 13/52 = 1/4 = .25
   For (c): 12/52 = .23

17. a. (4, 6), (4, 7), (4, 8)
   b. .05 + .10 + .15 = .30
   c. (2, 8), (3, 8), (4, 8)
   d. .05 + .05 + .15 = .25
   e. .15

23. a. $P(A) = P(E_1) + P(E_4) + P(E_6)$
   $= .05 + .25 + .10 = .40$

   $P(B) = P(E_2) + P(E_4) + P(E_7)$
   $= .20 + .25 + .05 = .50$

   $P(C) = P(E_2) + P(E_3) + P(E_5) + P(E_7)$
   $= .20 + .20 + .15 + .05 = .60$

   b. $A \cup B = \{E_1, E_2, E_4, E_6, E_7\}$
   $P(A \cup B) = P(E_1) + P(E_2) + P(E_4) + P(E_6) + P(E_7)$
   $= .05 + .20 + .25 + .10 + .05$
   $= .65$
   c. $A \cap B = \{E_4\}, P(A \cap B) = P(E_4) = .25$
   d. Yes, they are mutually exclusive
   e. $B^c = \{E_1, E_3, E_5, E_6\}$
   $P(B^c) = P(E_1) + P(E_3) + P(E_5) + P(E_6)$
   $= .05 + .20 + .15 + .10$
   $= .50$

28. Let B = rented a car for business reasons
   P = rented a car for personal reasons
   a. $P(B \cup P) = P(B) + P(P) - P(B \cap P)$
   $= .540 + .458 - .300$
   $= .698$
   b. $P(\text{Neither}) = 1 - .698 = .302$

30. a. $P(A \mid B) = \dfrac{P(A \cap B)}{P(B)} = \dfrac{.40}{.60} = .6667$

b. $P(B \mid A) = \dfrac{P(A \cap B)}{P(A)} = \dfrac{.40}{.50} = .80$

c. No, because $P(A \mid B) \neq P(A)$

33. a.

	Quality	Cost/ Convenience	Other	Total
	Reason for Applying			
Full-time	.218	.204	.039	.461
Part-time	.208	.307	.024	.539
Total	.426	.511	.063	1.000

b. A student is most likely to cite cost or convenience as the first reason (probability = .511); school quality is the first reason cited by the second largest number of students (probability = .426)

c. $P(\text{quality} \mid \text{full-time}) = .218/.461 = .473$

d. $P(\text{quality} \mid \text{part-time}) = .208/.539 = .386$

e. For independence, we must have $P(A)P(B) = P(A \cap B)$; from the table,

$P(A \cap B) = .218, P(A) = .461, P(B) = .426$
$P(A)P(B) = (.461)(.426) = .196$

Because $P(A)P(B) \neq P(A \cap B)$, the events are not independent

39. a. Yes, because $P(A_1 \cap A_2) = 0$

b. $P(A_1 \cap B) = P(A_1)P(B \mid A_1) = .40(.20) = .08$
$P(A_2 \cap B) = P(A_2)P(B \mid A_2) = .60(.05) = .03$

c. $P(B) = P(A_1 \cap B) + P(A_2 \cap B) = .08 + .03 = .11$

d. $P(A_1 \mid B) = \dfrac{.08}{.11} = .7273$

$P(A_2 \mid B) = \dfrac{.03}{.11} = .2727$

42. $M = $ missed payment
$D_1 = $ customer defaults
$D_2 = $ customer does not default
$P(D_1) = .05, P(D_2) = .95, P(M \mid D_2) = .2, P(M \mid D_1) = 1$

a. $P(D_1 \mid M) = \dfrac{P(D_1)P(M \mid D_1)}{P(D_1)P(M \mid D_1) + P(D_2)P(M \mid D_2)}$

$= \dfrac{(.05)(1)}{(.05)(1) + (.95)(.2)}$

$= \dfrac{.05}{.24} = .21$

b. Yes, the probability of default is greater than .20

Chapter 5

1. a. Head, Head (H, H)
Head, Tail (H, T)
Tail, Head (T, H)
Tail, Tail (T, T)

b. $x = $ number of heads on two coin tosses

c.

Outcome	Values of x
(H, H)	2
(H, T)	1
(T, H)	1
(T, T)	0

3. Let: $Y = $ position is offered

$N = $ position is not offered

a. $S = \{(Y, Y, Y), (Y, Y, N), (Y, N, Y), (Y, N, N), (N, Y, Y), (N, Y, N), (N, N, Y), (N, N, N)\}$

b. Let $N = $ number of offers made; N is a discrete random variable

c.

Experimental Outcome	(Y, Y, Y)	(Y, Y, N)	(Y, N, Y)	(Y, N, N)	(N, Y, Y)	(N, Y, N)	(N, N, Y)	(N, N, N)
Value of N	3	2	2	1	2	1	1	0

7. a. $f(x) \geq 0$ for all values of x
$\Sigma f(x) = 1$; therefore, it is a proper probability distribution

b. Probability $x = 30$ is $f(30) = .25$

c. Probability $x \leq 25$ is $f(20) + f(25) = .20 + .15 = .35$

d. Probability $x > 30$ is $f(35) = .40$

8. a.

x	$f(x)$
1	$3/20 = .15$
2	$5/20 = .25$
3	$8/20 = .40$
4	$4/20 = .20$
	Total 1.00

b.

c. $f(x) \geq 0$ for $x = 1, 2, 3, 4$
$\Sigma f(x) = 1$

16. a.

y	f(y)	yf(y)
2	.20	.40
4	.30	1.20
7	.40	2.80
8	.10	.80
Totals	1.00	5.20

$$E(y) = \mu = 5.20$$

b.

y	$y - \mu$	$(y - \mu)^2$	f(y)	$(y - \mu)^2 f(y)$
2	−3.20	10.24	.20	2.048
4	−1.20	1.44	.30	.432
7	1.80	3.24	.40	1.296
8	2.80	7.84	.10	.784
		Total		4.560

$$\text{Var}(y) = 4.56$$
$$\sigma = \sqrt{4.56} = 2.14$$

18. a/b

x	f(x)	xf(x)	$(x - \mu)$	$(x - \mu)^2$	$(x - \mu)^2 f(x)$
0	.01	.00	−2.3	5.29	.0529
1	.23	.23	−1.3	1.69	.3887
2	.41	.82	−0.3	0.09	.0369
3	.20	.60	0.7	0.49	.0980
4	.10	.40	1.7	2.89	.2890
5	.05	.25	2.7	7.29	.3645

$$E(x) = 2.30 \qquad \text{Var}(x) = 1.2300$$
$$\sigma = 1.11$$

The expected value, $E(x) = 2.3$, of the probability distribution is the same as the average reported in the *1997 Statistical Abstract of the United States*

$$\text{Var}(x) = 1.23 \text{ television sets squared}$$
$$\sigma = \sqrt{1.23} = 1.11 \text{ television sets}$$

25. a.

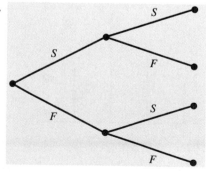

b. $f(1) = \binom{2}{1}(.4)^1(.6)^1 = \dfrac{2!}{1!1!}(.4)(.6) = .48$

c. $f(0) = \binom{2}{0}(.4)^0(.6)^2 = \dfrac{2!}{0!2!}(1)(.36) = .36$

d. $f(2) = \binom{2}{2}(.4)^2(.6)^0 = \dfrac{2!}{2!0!}(.16)(.1) = .16$

e. $P(x \geq 1) = f(1) + f(2) = .48 + .16 = .64$

f. $E(x) = np = 2(.4) = .8$
$\text{Var}(x) = np(1 - p) = 2(.4)(.6) = .48$
$\sigma = \sqrt{.48} = .6928$

30. a. Probability of a defective part being produced must be .03 for each trial; trials must be independent

b. Let D = defective
G = not defective

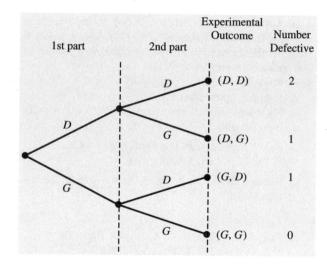

c. Two outcomes result in exactly one defect

d. $P(\text{no defects}) = (.97)(.97) = .9409$
$P(1 \text{ defect}) = 2(.03)(.97) = .0582$
$P(2 \text{ defects}) = (.03)(.03) = .0009$

39. a. $f(x) = \dfrac{2^x e^{-2}}{x!}$

b. $\mu = 6$ for 3 time periods

c. $f(x) = \dfrac{6^x e^{-6}}{x!}$

d. $f(2) = \dfrac{2^2 e^{-2}}{2!} = \dfrac{4(.1353)}{2} = .2706$

e. $f(6) = \dfrac{6^6 e^{-6}}{6!} = .1606$

f. $f(5) = \dfrac{4^5 e^{-4}}{5!} = .1563$

40. a. $\mu = 48(5/60) = 4$

$$f(3) = \frac{4^3 e^{-4}}{3!} = \frac{(64)(.0183)}{6} = .1952$$

b. $\mu = 48(15/60) = 12$

$$f(10) = \frac{12^{10} e^{-12}}{10!} = .1048$$

c. $\mu = 48(5/60) = 4$; one can expect 4 callers to be waiting after 5 minutes

$$f(0) = \frac{4^0 e^{-4}}{0!} = .0183;$$ the probability none will be waiting after 5 minutes is .0183

d. $\mu = 48(3/60) = 2.4$

$$f(0) = \frac{2.4^0 e^{-2.4}}{0!} = .0907;$$ the probability of no interruptions in 3 minutes is .0907

46. a. $f(1) = \dfrac{\dbinom{3}{1}\dbinom{10-3}{4-1}}{\dbinom{10}{4}} = \dfrac{\left(\dfrac{3!}{1!2!}\right)\left(\dfrac{7!}{3!4!}\right)}{\dfrac{10!}{4!6!}}$

$$= \frac{(3)(35)}{210} = .50$$

b. $f(2) = \dfrac{\dbinom{3}{2}\dbinom{10-3}{2-2}}{\dbinom{10}{2}} = \dfrac{(3)(1)}{45} = .067$

50. $N = 60, n = 10$

a. $r = 20, x = 0$

$$f(0) = \frac{\dbinom{20}{0}\dbinom{40}{10}}{\dbinom{60}{10}} = \frac{(1)\left(\dfrac{40!}{10!30!}\right)}{\dfrac{60!}{10!50!}}$$

$$= \left(\frac{40!}{10!30!}\right)\left(\frac{10!50!}{60!}\right)$$

$$= \frac{40\cdot39\cdot38\cdot37\cdot36\cdot35\cdot34\cdot33\cdot32\cdot31}{60\cdot59\cdot58\cdot57\cdot56\cdot55\cdot54\cdot53\cdot52\cdot51}$$

$$\approx .01$$

b. $r = 20, x = 1$

$$f(1) = \frac{\dbinom{20}{1}\dbinom{40}{9}}{\dbinom{60}{10}} = 20\left(\frac{40!}{9!31!}\right)\left(\frac{10!50!}{60!}\right)$$

$$\approx .07$$

c. $1 - f(0) - f(1) = 1 - .08 = .92$

d. Same as the probability one will be from Hawaii; in part (b) it was equal to approximately .07

Chapter 6

1. a.

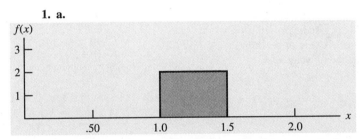

b. $P(x = 1.25) = 0$; the probability of any single point is zero because the area under the curve above any single point is zero

c. $P(1.0 \le x \le 1.25) = 2(.25) = .50$

d. $P(1.20 < x < 1.5) = 2(.30) = .60$

4. a.

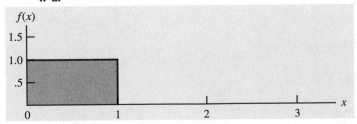

b. $P(.25 < x < .75) = 1(.50) = .50$
c. $P(x \le .30) = 1(.30) = .30$
d. $P(x > .60) = 1(.40) = .40$

13. a. $.4761 + .1879 = .6640$
b. $.3888 - .1985 = .1903$
c. $.4599 - .3508 = .1091$

15. a. Look in the table for an area of $.5000 - .2119 = .2881$; because the value we are seeking is below the mean, the z value must be negative; thus, for an area of $.2881$, $z = -.80$
b. Look in the table for an area of $.9030/2 = .4515$; $z = 1.66$
c. Look in the table for an area of $.2052/2 = .1026$; $z = .26$
d. Look in the table for an area of $.9948 - .5000 = .4948$; $z = 2.56$
e. Look in the table for an area of $.6915 - .5000 = .1915$; because the value we are seeking is below the mean, the z value must be negative; thus, $z = -.50$

18. a. Find $P(x \ge 60)$

At $x = 60$, $z = \dfrac{60 - 49}{16} = \dfrac{11}{16} = .69$

$P(x < 60) = .5000 + .2549 = .7549$

$P(x \ge 60) = 1 - P(x < 60) = 1 - .7549 = .2451$

b. Find $P(x \le 30)$

At $x = 30$, $z = \dfrac{30 - 49}{16} = -1.19$

$P(x \le 30) = .5000 - .3830$
$\qquad\qquad = .1170$

c. Find z-score so that $P(z \ge z\text{-score}) = .10$
A z-score of 1.28 cuts off 10% in upper tail
Now, solve for corresponding value of x

$1.28 = \dfrac{x - 49}{16}$

$x = 49 + (16)(1.28)$

$\quad = 69.48$

So, 10% of subscribers spend 69.48 minutes or more reading *The Wall Street Journal*

26. a. $\mu = np = 100(.20) = 20$
$\sigma^2 = np(1 - p) = 100(.20)(.80) = 16$
$\sigma = \sqrt{16} = 4$
b. Yes, because $np = 20$ and $n(1 - p) = 80$
c. Compute $P(23.5 \le x \le 24.5)$

$z = \dfrac{24.5 - 20}{4} = 1.13 \rightarrow \text{Area} = .3708$

$z = \dfrac{23.5 - 20}{4} = .88 \rightarrow \text{Area} = .3106$

$P(23.5 \le x \le 24.5) = .3708 - .3106 = .0602$

d. Compute $P(17.5 \le x \le 22.5)$

$z = \dfrac{17.5 - 20}{4} = -.63 \rightarrow \text{Area} = .2357$

$z = \dfrac{22.5 - 20}{4} = .63 \rightarrow \text{Area} = .2357$

$P(17.5 \le x \le 22.5) = .2357 + .2357 = .4714$

e. Compute $P(x \le 15.5)$

$z = \dfrac{15.5 - 20}{4} = -1.13 \rightarrow \text{Area} = .3708$

$P(x \le 15.5) = .5000 - .3708 = .1292$

28. Use the normal approximation of binomial probabilities with $\mu = np = 250(.04) = 10$ and
$\sigma = \sqrt{np(1 - p)} = \sqrt{250(.04)(.96)} = 3.1$
a. Compute $P(x \le 12.5)$

$z = \dfrac{12.5 - 10}{3.1} = .81 \rightarrow \text{Area} = .2910$

$P(x \le 12.5) = .5000 + .2910 = .7910$

b. Compute $P(x \ge 4.5)$

$z = \dfrac{4.5 - 10}{3.1} = -1.77 \rightarrow \text{Area} = .4616$

$P(x \ge 4.5) = .5000 + .4616 = .9616$

c. Compute $P(7.5 \le x \le 8.5)$

$z = \dfrac{7.5 - 10}{3.1} = -.81 \rightarrow \text{Area} = .2910$

$z = \dfrac{8.5 - 10}{3.1} = -.48 \rightarrow \text{Area} = .1844$

$P(7.5 \le x \le 8.5) = .2910 - .1844 = .1066$

34. a. $P(x \le x_0) = 1 - e^{-x_0/3}$
b. $P(x \le 2) = 1 - e^{-2/3} = 1 - .5134 = .4866$
c. $P(x \ge 3) = 1 - P(x \le 3) = 1 - (1 - e^{-3/3})$
$\qquad\qquad = e^{-1} = .3679$
d. $P(x \le 5) = 1 - e^{-5/3} = 1 - .1889 = .8111$
e. $P(2 \le x \le 5) = P(x \le 5) - P(x \le 2)$
$\qquad\qquad = .8111 - .4866 = .3245$

36. a.

b. $P(x \le 12) = 1 - e^{-12/12} = 1 - .3679 = .6321$
c. $P(x \le 6) = 1 - e^{-6/12} = 1 - .6065 = .3935$
d. $P(x \ge 30) = 1 - P(x < 30)$
$$= 1 - (1 - e^{-30/12})$$
$$= .0821$$

Chapter 7

1. a. AB, AC, AD, AE, BC, BD, BE, CD, CE, DE
  b. With 10 samples, each has a $\frac{1}{10}$ probability
  c. E and C because 8 and 0 do not apply; 5 identifies E; 7 does not apply; 5 is skipped because E is already in the sample; 3 identifies C; 2 is not needed because the sample of size 2 is complete

3. 459, 147, 385, 113, 340, 401, 215, 2, 33, 348

11. a. $\bar{x} = \dfrac{\Sigma x_i}{n} = \dfrac{54}{6} = 9$

  b. $s^2 = \sqrt{\dfrac{\Sigma(x_i - \bar{x})^2}{n-1}}$

    $\Sigma(x_i - \bar{x})^2 = (-4)^2 + (-1)^2 + 1^2 + (-2)^2 + 1^2 + 5^2$
    $= 48$

    $s = \sqrt{\dfrac{48}{6-1}} = 3.1$

13. a. $\bar{x} = \dfrac{\Sigma x_i}{n} = \dfrac{465}{5} = 93$

  b.

x_i	$(x_i - \bar{x})$	$(x_i - \bar{x})^2$
94	+1	1
100	+7	49
85	-8	64
94	+1	1
92	-1	1
Totals 465	0	116

    $s = \sqrt{\dfrac{\Sigma(x_i - \bar{x})^2}{n-1}} = \sqrt{\dfrac{116}{4}} = 5.39$

19. a. The sampling distribution is normal with
$$E(\bar{x}) = \mu = 200$$
$$\sigma_{\bar{x}} = \frac{\sigma}{\sqrt{n}} = \frac{50}{\sqrt{100}} = 5$$
For ± 5, $(\bar{x} - \mu) = 5$,
$$z = \frac{\bar{x} - \mu}{\sigma_{\bar{x}}} = \frac{5}{5} = 1$$
$$\text{Area} = .3413 \times 2 = .6826$$
b. For ± 10, $(\bar{x} - \mu) = 10$,
$$z = \frac{\bar{x} - \mu}{\sigma_{\bar{x}}} = \frac{10}{5} = 2$$
$$\text{Area} = .4772 \times 2 = .9544$$

25. a.

51,300 51,800 52,300

$$\sigma_{\bar{x}} = \frac{\sigma}{\sqrt{n}} = \frac{4000}{\sqrt{60}} = 516.40$$
$$z = \frac{52,300 - 51,800}{516.40} = +.97$$
$$\text{Area} = .3340 \times 2 = .6680$$

b. $\sigma_{\bar{x}} = \dfrac{\sigma}{\sqrt{n}} = \dfrac{4000}{\sqrt{120}} = 365.15$

    $z = \dfrac{52,300 - 51,800}{365.15} = +1.37$
    $\text{Area} = .4147 \times 2 = .8294$

34. a. $E(\bar{p}) = .40$

    $\sigma_{\bar{p}} = \sqrt{\dfrac{p(1-p)}{n}} = \sqrt{\dfrac{(.40)(.60)}{200}} = .0346$

    $z = \dfrac{\bar{p} - p}{\sigma_{\bar{p}}} = \dfrac{.03}{.0346} = .87$
    $\text{Area} = .3078 \times 2 = .6156$

b. $z = \dfrac{\bar{p} - p}{\sigma_{\bar{p}}} = \dfrac{.05}{.0346} = 1.45$
    $\text{Area} = .4265 \times 2 = .8530$

37. a.

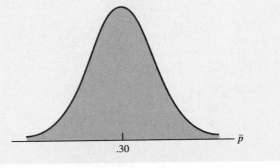

.30

$$\sigma_{\bar{p}} = \sqrt{\frac{p(1-p)}{n}} = \sqrt{\frac{.30(.70)}{100}} = .0458$$

The normal distribution is appropriate because $np = 100(.30) = 30$ and $n(1 - p) = 100(.70) = 70$ are both greater than 5

b. $P(.20 \le \bar{p} \le .40) = ?$

$$z = \frac{.40 - .30}{.0458} = 2.18$$

Area $= .4854 \times 2 = .9708$

c. $P(.25 \le \bar{p} \le .35) = ?$

$$z = \frac{.35 - .30}{.0458} = 1.09$$

Area $= .3621 \times 2 = .7242$

Chapter 8

2. Use $\bar{x} \pm z_{\alpha/2}(\sigma/\sqrt{n})$ with the sample standard deviation s used to estimate σ
  a. $32 \pm 1.645 (6/\sqrt{50})$
    32 ± 1.4; (30.6 to 33.4)
  b. $32 \pm 1.96(6/\sqrt{50})$
    32 ± 1.66; (30.34 to 33.66)
  c. $32 \pm 2.576(6/\sqrt{50})$
    32 ± 2.19; (29.81 to 34.19)

5. a. $\sigma_{\bar{x}} = \sigma/\sqrt{n} = 2.50/\sqrt{49} = .36$
  b. $1.96\sigma/\sqrt{n} = 1.96 (2.50/\sqrt{49}) = .70$
  c. $22.60 \pm .70$ or (21.90 to 23.30)

15. a. $\bar{x} = \dfrac{\Sigma x_i}{n} = \dfrac{80}{8} = 10$

  b. $s = \sqrt{\dfrac{\Sigma(x_i - \bar{x})^2}{n - 1}} = \sqrt{\dfrac{84}{8 - 1}} = 3.46$

  c. With 7 degrees of freedom, $t_{.025} = 2.365$

$$\bar{x} \pm t_{.025}\frac{s}{\sqrt{n}}$$

$$10 \pm 2.365\frac{3.46}{\sqrt{8}}$$

$$10 \pm 2.90; (7.10 \text{ to } 12.90)$$

17. At 90%, $80 \pm t_{.05}(s/\sqrt{n})$ with degrees of freedom $= 17$
    $t_{.05} = 1.740$
    $80 \pm 1.740(10/\sqrt{18})$
    80 ± 4.10; (75.90 to 84.10)

  At 95%, $80 \pm t_{.025}(10/\sqrt{18})$ with degrees of freedom $= 17$
    $t_{.025} = 2.110$
    $80 \pm 2.110 (10/\sqrt{18})$
    80 ± 4.97; (75.03 to 84.97)

24. a. Planning value of $\sigma = \dfrac{\text{Range}}{4} = \dfrac{36}{4} = 9$

  b. $n = \dfrac{z_{.025}^2\sigma^2}{E^2} = \dfrac{(1.96)^2(9)^2}{(3)^2} = 34.57$; Use $n = 35$

  c. $n = \dfrac{(1.96)^2(9)^2}{(3)^2} = 77.79$; Use $n = 78$

25. Use $n = \dfrac{z_{\alpha/2}^2\sigma^2}{E^2}$

$$n = \frac{(1.96)^2(6.82)^2}{(1.5)^2} = 79.41; \text{ use } n = 80$$

$$n = \frac{(1.645)^2(6.82)^2}{(2)^2} = 31.47; \text{ use } n = 32$$

31. a. $\bar{p} = \dfrac{100}{400} = .25$

  b. $\sqrt{\dfrac{\bar{p}(1 - \bar{p})}{n}} = \sqrt{\dfrac{.25(.75)}{400}} = .0217$

  c. $\bar{p} \pm z_{.025}\sqrt{\dfrac{\bar{p}(1 - \bar{p})}{n}}$
    $.25 \pm 1.96(.0217)$
    $.25 \pm .0424$; (.2076 to .2924)

35. a. $\bar{p} = 562/814 = .6904$

  b. $1.645\sqrt{\dfrac{.6904(1 - .6904)}{814}} = .0267$

  c. $.6904 \pm .0267$; (.6637 to .7171)

39. a. $n = \dfrac{1.96^2 p(1 - p)}{E^2}$

$$n = \frac{1.96^2(.55)(.45)}{(.03)^2} = 1056.44; \text{ use } n = 1057$$

  b. $n = \dfrac{1.96^2(.55)(.45)}{(.06)^2} = 264.11$; use $n = 265$

Chapter 9

2. a. $H_0: \mu \le 14$
    $H_a: \mu > 14$
  b. No evidence that the new plan increases sales
  c. The research hypothesis $\mu > 14$ is supported; the new plan increases sales

5. a. Rejecting $H_0: \mu \le 8.6$ when it is true
  b. Accepting $H_0: \mu \le 8.6$ when it is false

10. a. $z = 2.05$
    Reject H_0 if $z > 2.05$
  b. $z = \dfrac{x - \mu}{s/\sqrt{n}} = \dfrac{16.5 - 15}{7/\sqrt{40}} = 1.36$
  c. Area for $z = 1.36 = .4131$
    p-value $= .5000 - .4131 = .0869$
  d. Do not reject H_0

13. a. $H_0: \mu \ge 1056$
    $H_a: \mu < 1056$
  b. Reject H_0 if $z < -1.645$

$$z = \frac{\bar{x} - \mu}{s/\sqrt{n}} = \frac{910 - 1056}{1600/\sqrt{400}} = -1.83$$

    Reject H_0
  c. p-value $= .5000 - .4664 = .0336$

20. a. Reject H_0 if $z < -2.33$ or $z > 2.33$

  b. $z = \dfrac{\bar{x} - \mu}{\sigma/\sqrt{n}} = \dfrac{14.2 - 15}{5/\sqrt{50}} = 1.13$

  c. p-value $= 2(.5000 - .3708) = .2584$

  d. Do not reject H_0

23. a. $H_0: \mu = 18{,}688$

  $H_a: \mu \neq 18{,}688$

  Reject H_0 if $z < -1.96$ or $z > 1.96$

  $z = \dfrac{\bar{x} - \mu_0}{s/\sqrt{n}} = \dfrac{16{,}860 - 18{,}688}{14{,}624/\sqrt{400}} = -2.50$

  Reject H_0 and conclude $\mu \neq 18{,}688$

  b. p-value $= 2(.5000 - .4938) = .0124$

30. a. $\bar{x} = \dfrac{\Sigma x_i}{n} = \dfrac{108}{6} = 18$

  b. $s = \sqrt{\dfrac{\Sigma(x_i - \bar{x})}{n-1}} = \sqrt{\dfrac{10}{6-1}} = 1.41$

  c. Reject H_0 if $t < -2.571$ or $t > 2.571$

  d. $t = \dfrac{\bar{x} - \mu}{s/\sqrt{n}} = \dfrac{18 - 20}{1.41/\sqrt{6}} = -3.47$

  e. Reject H_0; conclude H_a is true

33. a. $\bar{x} = \dfrac{\Sigma x_i}{n} = 270$

  b. $s = \sqrt{\dfrac{\Sigma(x_i - \bar{x})^2}{n-1}} = 24.78$

  c. $H_0: \mu \leq 258$

  $H_a: \mu > 258$

  Reject H_0 if $t > 1.761$

  $t = \dfrac{\bar{x} - \mu_0}{s/\sqrt{n}} = \dfrac{270 - 258}{24.78/\sqrt{15}} = 1.88$

  Reject H_0; mean has increased

  d. Between .05 and .025

40. a. Reject H_0 if $z < -1.96$ or $z > 1.96$

  b. $\sigma_{\bar{p}} = \sqrt{\dfrac{.20(.80)}{400}} = .02$

  $z = \dfrac{\bar{p} - p}{\sigma_{\bar{p}}} = \dfrac{.175 - .20}{.02} = -1.25$

  c. p-value $= 2(.5000 - .3944) = .2112$

  d. Do not reject H_0

43. $H_0: p \geq .64$

  $H_a: p < .64$

  Reject H_0 if $z < -1.645$

  $\bar{p} = {}^{52}\!/_{100} = .52$

  $z = \dfrac{.52 - .64}{\sqrt{\dfrac{.64(.36)}{100}}} = -2.5$

  Reject H_0

Chapter 10

1. a. $\bar{x}_1 - \bar{x}_2 = 13.6 - 11.6 = 2$

  b. $s_{\bar{x}_1 - \bar{x}_2} = \sqrt{\dfrac{s_1^2}{n_1} + \dfrac{s_2^2}{n_2}} = \sqrt{\dfrac{(2.2)^2}{50} + \dfrac{3^2}{35}} = .595$

  $2 \pm 1.645(.595)$

  $2 \pm .98$ or 1.02 to 2.98

  c. $2 \pm 1.96(.595)$

  2 ± 1.17 or $.83$ to 3.17

7. a. $\bar{x}_1 - \bar{x}_2 = 15{,}700 - 14{,}500 = 1200$

  b. Pooled variance

  $s^2 = \dfrac{7(700)^2 + 11(850)^2}{18} = 632{,}083$

  $s_{\bar{x}_1 - \bar{x}_2} = \sqrt{632{,}083\left(\dfrac{1}{8} + \dfrac{1}{12}\right)} = 362.88$

  With 18 degrees of freedom $t_{.025} = 2.101$

  $1200 \pm 2.101(362.88)$

  1200 ± 762, or 438 to 1962

  c. Populations are normally distributed with equal variances

10. a. $s_{\bar{x}_1 - \bar{x}_2} = \sqrt{\dfrac{s_1^2}{n_1} + \dfrac{s_2^2}{n_2}} = \sqrt{\dfrac{(5.2)^2}{40} + \dfrac{6^2}{50}} = 1.18$

  $z = \dfrac{(\bar{x}_1 - \bar{x}_2) - (\mu_1 - \mu_2)}{s_{\bar{x}_1 - \bar{x}_2}}$

  $= \dfrac{(25.2 - 22.8)}{1.18} = 2.03$

  Reject H_0 if $z > 1.645$; therefore reject H_0; conclude H_a is true and $\mu_1 > \mu_2$

  b. p-value $= .5000 - .4788 = .0212$

14. $H_0: \mu_1 - \mu_2 = 0$

  $H_a: \mu_1 - \mu_2 \neq 0$

  Reject H_0 if $z < -1.96$ or if $z > 1.96$

  $z = \dfrac{(\bar{x}_1 - \bar{x}_2) - 0}{\sqrt{\sigma_1^2/n_1 + \sigma_2^2/n_2}} = \dfrac{40 - 35}{\sqrt{(9)^2/36 + (10)^2/49}}$

  $= 2.41$

  Reject H_0; customers at the two stores differ in terms of mean ages

18. a. $1, 2, 0, 0, 2$

  b. $\bar{d} = \dfrac{\Sigma d_i}{n} = \dfrac{5}{5} = 1$

  c. $s_d = \sqrt{\dfrac{\Sigma(d_i - \bar{d})^2}{n-1}} = \sqrt{\dfrac{4}{5-1}} = 1$

  d. With 4 degrees of freedom, $t_{.05} = 2.132$; reject H_0 if $t > 2.132$

  $t = \dfrac{\bar{d} - \mu_d}{s_d/\sqrt{n}} = \dfrac{1 - 0}{1/\sqrt{5}} = 2.24$

  Reject H_0; conclude $\mu_d > 0$

20. $d =$ rating after $-$ rating before

  $H_0: \mu_d \leq 0$

  $H_a: \mu_d > 0$

With 7 degrees of freedom, reject H_0 if $t > 1.895$; when $\bar{d} = .63$ and $s_d = 1.3025$,

$$t = \frac{\bar{d} - \mu_d}{s_d/\sqrt{n}} = \frac{.63 - 0}{1.3025/\sqrt{8}} = 1.36$$

Do not reject H_0; we cannot conclude that seeing the commercial improves the potential to purchase

26. a. $\bar{\bar{x}} = (30 + 45 + 36)/3 = 37$

$$SSTR = \sum_{j=1}^{k} n_j(\bar{x}_j - \bar{\bar{x}})^2$$

$$= 5(30 - 37)^2 + 5(45 - 37)^2 + 5(36 - 37)^2$$

$$= 570$$

$$MSTR = \frac{SSTR}{k - 1} = \frac{570}{2} = 285$$

b. $SSE = \sum_{j=1}^{k} (n_j - 1)s_j^2$

$$= 4(6) + 4(4) + 4(6.5) = 66$$

$$MSE = \frac{SSE}{n_T - k} = \frac{66}{15 - 3} = 5.5$$

c. $F = \frac{MSTR}{MSE} = \frac{285}{5.5} = 51.82$

$F_{.05} = 3.89$ (2 degrees of freedom numerator and 12 denominator

Because $F = 51.82 > F_{.05} = 3.89$, we reject the null hypothesis that the means of the three populations are equal

d.

Source of Variation	Sum of Squares	Degrees of Freedom	Mean Square	F
Treatments	570	2	285	51.82
Error	66	12	5.5	
Total	636	14		

29.

	Manufacturer 1	Manufacturer 2	Manufacturer 3
Sample mean	23	28	21
Sample variance	6.67	4.67	3.33

$$\bar{\bar{x}} = (23 + 28 + 21)/3 = 24$$

$$SSTR = \sum_{j=1}^{k} n_j(\bar{x}_j - \bar{\bar{x}})^2$$

$$= 4(23 - 24)^2 + 4(28 - 24)^2$$

$$+ 4(21 - 24)^2 = 104$$

$$MSTR = \frac{SSTR}{k - 1} = \frac{104}{2} = 52$$

$$SSE = \sum_{j=1}^{k} (n_j - 1)s_j^2$$

$$= 3(6.67) + 3(4.67) + 3(3.33) = 44.01$$

$$MSE = \frac{SSE}{n_T - k} = \frac{44.01}{12 - 3} = 4.89$$

$$F = \frac{MSTR}{MSE} = \frac{52}{4.89} = 10.63$$

$F_{.05} = 4.26$ (2 degrees of freedom numerator and 9 denominator)

Because $F = 10.63 > F_{.05} = 4.26$, we reject the null hypothesis that the mean time needed to mix a batch of material is the same for each manufacturer

Chapter 11

2. a. $\bar{p} = \dfrac{n_1\bar{p}_1 + n_2\bar{p}_2}{n_1 + n_2} = \dfrac{200(.22) + 300(.16)}{200 + 300} = .184$

$$s_{\bar{p}_1 - \bar{p}_2} = \sqrt{(.184)(.816)\left(\frac{1}{200} + \frac{1}{300}\right)} = .0354$$

Reject H_0 if $z > 1.645$

$$z = \frac{(.22 - .16) - 0}{.0354} = 1.69$$

Reject H_0

b. p-value $= (.5000 - .4545) = .0455$

11. Expected frequencies: $e_1 = 200(.40) = 80$
$\qquad\qquad\qquad\qquad e_2 = 200(.40) = 80$
$\qquad\qquad\qquad\qquad e_3 = 200(.20) = 40$

Actual frequencies: $f_1 = 60, f_2 = 120, f_3 = 20$

$$\chi^2 = \frac{(60 - 80)^2}{80} + \frac{(120 - 80)^2}{80} + \frac{(20 - 40)^2}{40}$$

$$= \frac{400}{80} + \frac{1600}{80} + \frac{400}{40}$$

$$= 5 + 20 + 10 = 35$$

$\chi^2_{.01} = 9.21034$, with $k - 1 = 3 - 1 = 2$ degrees of freedom

Because $\chi^2 = 35 > 9.21034$, reject the null hypothesis; that is, the population proportions are not as stated in the null hypothesis

13. H_0: $p_{ABC} = .29, p_{CBS} = .28, p_{NBC} = .25, p_{IND} = .18$
H_a: The proportions are not
$\qquad p_{ABC} = .29, p_{CBS} = .28, p_{NBC} = .25, p_{IND} = .18$
Expected frequencies: $300(.29) = 87, 300(.28) = 84$
$\qquad\qquad\qquad\qquad 300(.25) = 75, 300(.18) = 54$
$\qquad\qquad e_1 = 87, e_2 = 84, e_3 = 75, e_4 = 54$

Actual frequencies: $f_1 = 95, f_2 = 70, f_3 = 89, f_4 = 46$

$\chi^2_{.05} = 7.81$ (3 degrees of freedom)

$$\chi^2 = \frac{(95 - 87)^2}{87} + \frac{(70 - 84)^2}{84} + \frac{(89 - 75)^2}{75}$$

$$+ \frac{(46 - 54)^2}{54} = 6.87$$

Do not reject H_0; there is no significant change in the viewing audience proportions

19. H_0: The column variable is independent of the row variable

H_a: The column variable is not independent of the row variable

Expected frequencies:

	A	B	C
P	28.5	39.9	45.6
Q	21.5	30.1	34.4

$$\chi^2 = \frac{(20 - 28.5)^2}{28.5} + \frac{(44 - 39.9)^2}{39.9} + \frac{(50 - 45.6)^2}{45.6}$$

$$+ \frac{(30 - 21.5)^2}{21.5} + \frac{(26 - 30.1)^2}{30.1} + \frac{(30 - 34.4)^2}{34.4}$$

$$= 7.86$$

$\chi^2_{.025} = 7.37776$, with $(2 - 1)(3 - 1) = 2$ degrees of freedom

Because $\chi^2 = 7.86 > 7.37776$, reject H_0; that is, conclude that the column variable is not independent of the row variable

21. H_0: Type of ticket purchased is independent of the type of flight

H_a: Type of ticket purchased is not independent of the type of flight

Expected Frequencies:

$e_{11} = 35.59 \qquad e_{12} = 15.41$

$e_{21} = 150.73 \qquad e_{22} = 65.27$

$e_{31} = 455.68 \qquad e_{32} = 197.32$

Ticket	Flight	Observed Frequency (f_i)	Expected Frequency (e_i)	$(f_i - e_i)^2/e_i$
First	Domestic	29	35.59	1.22
First	International	22	15.41	2.82
Business	Domestic	95	150.73	20.61
Business	International	121	65.27	47.59
Full-fare	Domestic	518	455.68	8.52
Full-fare	International	135	197.32	19.68
Totals		920		100.43

$\chi^2_{.05} = 5.99$ with $(3 - 1)(2 - 1) = 2$ degrees of freedom

Because $100.43 > 5.99$, we reject H_0; type of ticket purchased is not independent of the type of flight

Chapter 12

1. a.

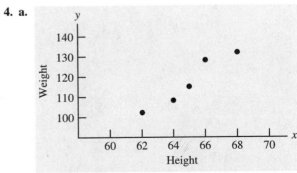

b. There appears to be a linear relationship between x and y

c. Many different straight lines can be drawn to provide a linear approximation of the relationship between x and y; in part (d) we will determine the equation of a straight line that "best" represents the relationship according to the least squares criterion

d. $\Sigma x_i = 15, \Sigma y_i = 40, \Sigma x_i y_i = 146, \Sigma x_i^2 = 55$

$$b_1 = \frac{\Sigma x_i y_i - (\Sigma x_i \Sigma y_i)/n}{\Sigma x_i^2 - (\Sigma x_i)^2/n}$$

$$= \frac{146 - (15)(40)/5}{55 - (15)^2/5} = 2.6$$

$$b_0 = \bar{y} - b_1 \bar{x}$$

$$= 8 - 2.6(3) = .2$$

$$\hat{y} = .2 + 2.6x$$

e. $\hat{y} = .2 + 2.6x = .2 + 2.6(4) = 10.6$

4. a.

b. It indicates a possible linear relationship between the variables

c. Many different straight lines can be drawn to provide a linear approximation of the relationship between x and y; in part (d) we will determine the equation of a straight line that "best" represents the relationship according to the least squares criterion

d. $\Sigma x_i = 325$, $\Sigma y_i = 585$; $\Sigma x_i y_i = 38{,}135$, $\Sigma x_i^2 = 21{,}145$

$$b_1 = \frac{\Sigma x_i y_i - (\Sigma x_i \Sigma y_i)/n}{\Sigma x_i^2 - (\Sigma x_i)^2/n}$$

$$= \frac{38{,}135 - (325)(585)/5}{21{,}145 - (325)^2/5} = 5.5$$

$$b_0 = \bar{y} - b_1 \bar{x}$$
$$= 117 - 5.5(65) = -240.5$$
$$\hat{y} = -240.5 + 5.5x$$

e. $\hat{y} = -240.5 + 5.5(63) = 106$
The estimate of weight is 106 pounds

14. a. $\hat{y}_i = .2 + 2.6x_i$ and $\bar{y} = 8$

x_i	y_i	$\hat{y}_i$	$y_i - \hat{y}_i$	$(y_i - \hat{y}_i)^2$	$y_i - \bar{y}$	$(y_i - \bar{y})^2$
1	3	2.8	.2	.04	−5	25
2	7	5.4	1.6	2.56	−1	1
3	5	8.0	−3.0	9.00	−3	9
4	11	10.6	.4	.16	3	9
5	14	13.2	.8	.64	6	36
				SSE = 12.40		SST = 80

SSR = SST − SSE = 80 − 12.4 = 67.6

b. $r^2 = \dfrac{SSR}{SST} = \dfrac{67.6}{80} = .845$

The least squares line provided a good fit; 84.5% of the variability in y has been explained by the least squares line

c. $\Sigma x_i = 15$, $\Sigma y_i = 40$, $\Sigma x_i y_i = 146$,
$\Sigma x_i^2 = 55$, $\Sigma y_i^2 = 400$

$$SSR = \frac{[\Sigma x_i y_i - (\Sigma x_i \Sigma y_i)/n]^2}{\Sigma x_i^2 - (\Sigma x_i)^2/n}$$

$$= \frac{[146 - (15)(40)/5]^2}{55 - (15)^2/5} = 67.6$$

$$SST = \Sigma y_i^2 - \frac{(\Sigma y_i)^2}{n}$$

$$= 400 - \frac{(40)^2}{5} = 80$$

Note that these are the same values shown in part (a)
d. $r = \sqrt{.845} = +.9192$

17. a. $\Sigma x_i = 19.2$, $\Sigma y_i = 18{,}900$, $\Sigma x_i y_i = 60{,}910$
$\Sigma x_i^2 = 62.18$, $\Sigma y_i^2 = 59{,}870{,}000$

$$SST = \Sigma y_i^2 - \frac{(\Sigma y_i)^2}{n}$$

$$= 59{,}870{,}000 - \frac{(18{,}900)^2}{6} = 335{,}000$$

$$SSR = \frac{[\Sigma x_i y_i - (\Sigma x_i \Sigma y_i)/n]^2}{\Sigma x_i^2 - (\Sigma x_i)^2/n}$$

$$= \frac{[60{,}910 - (19.2)(18{,}900)/6]^2}{62.18 - (19.2)^2/6} = 249{,}864.86$$

SSE = SST − SSR = 335,000 − 249,864.86
$= 85{,}135.14$

b. $r^2 = \dfrac{SSR}{SST} = \dfrac{249{,}864.86}{335{,}000} = .746$

The least squares line accounted for 74.6% of the total sum of squares

c. $r = \sqrt{.746} = +.8637$

22. a. $s^2 = MSE = \dfrac{SSE}{n-2} = \dfrac{12.4}{3} = 4.133$

b. $s = \sqrt{MSE} = \sqrt{4.133} = 2.033$
c. $\Sigma x_i = 15$, $\Sigma x_i^2 = 55$

$$s_{b_1} = \frac{s}{\sqrt{\Sigma x_i^2 - (\Sigma x_i)^2/n}}$$

$$= \frac{2.033}{\sqrt{55 - (15)^2/5}} = .643$$

d. $t = \dfrac{b_1 - \beta_1}{s_{b_1}} = \dfrac{2.6 - 0}{.643} = 4.04$

$t_{.025} = 3.182$ (3 degrees of freedom)
Because $t = 4.04 > t_{.05} = 3.182$, we reject $H_0: \beta_1 = 0$

e. $MSR = \dfrac{SSR}{1} = 67.6$

$$F = \frac{MSR}{MSE} = \frac{67.6}{4.133} = 16.36$$

$F_{.05} = 10.13$ (1 degree of freedom numerator and 3 denominator)
Because $F = 16.36 > F_{.05} = 10.13$, we reject $H_0: \beta_1 = 0$

Source of Variation	Sum of Squares	Degrees of Freedom	Mean Square	F
Regression	67.6	1	67.6	16.36
Error	12.4	3	4.133	
Total	80	4		

25. a. $s^2 = MSE = \dfrac{SSE}{n-2} = \dfrac{85{,}135.14}{4} = 21{,}283.79$

$s = \sqrt{MSE} = \sqrt{21{,}283.79} = 145.89$
$\Sigma x_i = 19.2$, $\Sigma x_i^2 = 62.18$

$$s_{b_1} = \frac{s}{\sqrt{\Sigma x_i^2 - (\Sigma x_i)^2/n}}$$

$$= \frac{145.89}{\sqrt{62.18 - (19.2)^2/6}} = 169.59$$

$$t = \frac{b_1 - \beta_1}{s_{b_1}} = \frac{581.08 - 0}{169.59} = 3.43$$

$t_{.025} = 2.776$ (4 degrees of freedom)

Because $t = 3.43 > t_{.025} = 2.776$, we reject $H_0: \beta_1 = 0$

b. $\text{MSR} = \dfrac{\text{SSR}}{1} = \dfrac{249,864.86}{1} = 249,864.86$

$$F = \frac{\text{MSR}}{\text{MSE}} = \frac{249,864.86}{21,283.79} = 11.74$$

$F_{.05} = 7.71$ (1 degree of freedom numerator and 4 denominator)

Because $F = 11.74 > F_{.05} = 7.71$, we reject $H_0: \beta_1 = 0$

c.

Source of Variation	Sum of Squares	Degrees of Freedom	Mean Square	F
Regression	29,864.86	1	29,864.86	11.74
Error	85,135.14	4	21,283.79	
Total	335,000	5		

30. a. $s = 2.033$

$\Sigma x_i = 15, \Sigma x_i^2 = 55$

$$s_{\hat{y}_p} = s\sqrt{\frac{1}{n} + \frac{(x_p - \bar{x})^2}{\Sigma x_i^2 - (\Sigma x_i)^2/n}}$$

$$= 2.033\sqrt{\frac{1}{5} + \frac{(4 - 3)^2}{55 - (15)^2/5}} = 1.11$$

b. $\hat{y} = .2 + 2.6x = .2 + 2.6(4) = 10.6$

$\hat{y}_p \pm t_{\alpha/2}s_{\hat{y}_p}$

$10.6 \pm 3.182(1.11)$

10.6 ± 3.53 or 7.07 to 14.13

c. $s_{\text{ind}} = s\sqrt{1 + \frac{1}{n} + \frac{(x_p - \bar{x})^2}{\Sigma x_i^2 - (\Sigma x_i)^2/n}}$

$$= 2.033\sqrt{1 + \frac{1}{5} + \frac{(4 - 3)^2}{55 - (15)^2/5}} = 2.32$$

d. $\hat{y}_p \pm t_{\alpha/2}s_{\text{ind}}$

$10.6 \pm 3.182(2.32)$

10.6 ± 7.38 or 3.22 to 17.98

33. a. $s = 145.89, \Sigma x_i = 19.2, \Sigma x_i^2 = 62.18$

$\hat{y} = 290.54 + 581.08x = 290.54 + 581.08(3)$

$= 2033.78$

$$s_{\hat{y}_p} = s\sqrt{\frac{1}{n} + \frac{(x_p - \bar{x})^2}{\Sigma x_i^2 - (\Sigma x_i)^2/n}}$$

$$= 145.89\sqrt{\frac{1}{6} + \frac{(3 - 3.2)^2}{62.18 - (19.2)^2/6}} = 68.54$$

$\hat{y}_p \pm t_{\alpha/2}s_{\hat{y}_p}$

$2033.78 \pm 2.776(68.54)$

2033.78 ± 190.27 or $1843.51 to $2224.05

b. $\hat{y} = 290.54 + 581.08x = 290.54 + 581.08(3)$

$= 2033.78$

$$s_{\text{ind}} = s\sqrt{1 + \frac{1}{n} + \frac{(x_p - \bar{x})^2}{\Sigma x_i^2 - (\Sigma x_i)^2/n}}$$

$$= 145.89\sqrt{1 + \frac{1}{6} + \frac{(3 - 3.2)^2}{62.18 - (19.2)^2/6}} = 161.19$$

$\hat{y}_p \pm t_{\alpha/2}s_{\text{ind}}$

$2033.78 \pm 2.776(161.19)$

2033.78 ± 447.46 or $1586.32 to $2481.24

37. a. 9

b. $\hat{y} = 20.0 + 7.21x$

c. 1.3626

d. $\text{SSE} = \text{SST} - \text{SSR} = 51,984.1 - 41,587.3 = 10,396.8$

$\text{MSE} = 10,396.8/7 = 1485.3$

$$F = \frac{\text{MSR}}{\text{MSE}} = \frac{41,587.3}{1485.3} = 28.0$$

$F_{.05} = 5.59$ (1 degree of freedom numerator and 7 denominator)

Because $F = 28 > F_{.05} = 5.59$, we reject $H_0: \beta_1 = 0$

e. $\hat{y} = 20.0 + 7.21(50) = 380.5$ or $380,500

42. a. $\Sigma x_i = 70, \Sigma y_i = 76, \Sigma x_i y_i = 1264, \Sigma x_i^2 = 1106$

$$b_1 = \frac{\Sigma x_i y_i - (\Sigma x_i \Sigma y_i)/n}{\Sigma x_i^2 - (\Sigma x_i)^2/n}$$

$$= \frac{1264 - (70)(65)/5}{1106 - (70)^2/5} = 1.5873$$

$b_0 = \bar{y} - b_1\bar{x}$

$= 15.2 - 1.5873(14) = -7.0222$

$\hat{y} = -7.02 + 1.59x$

b.

x_i	y_i	$\hat{y}_i$	$y_i - \hat{y}_i$
6	6	2.52	3.48
11	8	10.47	-2.47
15	12	16.83	-4.83
18	20	21.60	-1.60
20	30	24.78	5.22

c.

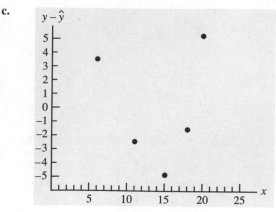

With only five observations, it is difficult to determine whether the assumptions are satisfied; however, the plot does suggest curvature in the residuals, which would indicate that the error term assumptions are not satisfied; the scatter diagram for these data also indicates that the underlying relationship between x and y may be curvilinear

44. $\Sigma x_i = 57$, $\Sigma y_i = 294$, $\Sigma x_i y_i = 2841$,

$\Sigma x_i^2 = 753$, $\Sigma y_i^2 = 13{,}350$

$$b_1 = \frac{\Sigma x_i y_i - (\Sigma x_i \Sigma y_i)/n}{\Sigma x_i^2 - (\Sigma x_i)^2/n}$$

$$= \frac{2841 - (57)(294)/7}{753 - (57)^2/7} = 1.5475$$

$$b_0 = \bar{y} - b_1 \bar{x}$$

$$= 42 - (1.5475)(8.1492) = 29.3989$$

$\hat{y} = 29.40 + 1.55x$

b. SSR = 691.72 and SST = 1002; therefore SSE = 1002 − 691.72 = 310.28

$$F = \frac{MSR}{MSE} = \frac{691.72}{310.28/5} = 11.15$$

$F_{.05} = 6.61$ (1 degree of freedom numerator and 5 denominator)

Because $F = 11.47 > F_{.05} = 6.61$, we reject $H_0: \beta_1 = 0$; the relationship is significant at the .05 level

c.

x_i	y_i	$\hat{y}_i = 29.40 + 1.55x_i$	$y_i - \hat{y}_i$
1	19	30.95	−11.95
2	32	32.50	−.50
4	44	35.60	8.40
6	40	38.70	1.30
10	52	44.90	7.10
14	53	51.10	1.90
20	54	60.40	−6.40

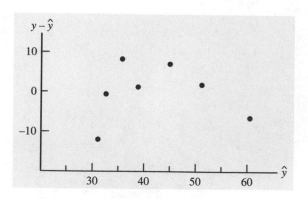

d. The residual plot leads us to question the assumption of a linear relationship between x and y; even though the relationship is significant at the $\alpha = .05$ level, it would be extremely dangerous to extrapolate beyond the range of the data (e.g., $x > 20$)

48. a. The estimated regression equation is
$\hat{y} = 45.06 + 1.94x_1$
An estimate of y when $x_1 = 45$ is
$\hat{y} = 45.06 + 1.94(45) = 132.36$
b. The estimated regression equation is
$\hat{y} = 85.22 + 4.32x_2$
An estimate of y when $x_2 = 15$ is
$\hat{y} = 85.22 + 4.32(15) = 150.02$
c. The estimated regression equation is
$\hat{y} = -18.37 + 2.01x_1 + 4.74x_2$
An estimate of y when $x_1 = 45$ and $x_2 = 15$ is
$\hat{y} = -18.37 + 2.01(45) + 4.74(15) = 143.18$

50. a. The Minitab output is shown in Figure E12.50a
b. The Minitab output is shown in Figure E12.50b
c. It is 1.60 in (a) and 2.29 in (b). In (a) the coefficient is an estimate of the change in revenue due to a one-unit change in television advertising expenditures; in (b) it represents an estimate of the change in revenue due to a one-unit change in television advertising expenditures when the amount of newspaper advertising is held constant
d. Revenue = 83.2 + 2.29(3.5) + 1.30(1.8) = 93.56 or $93,560

Chapter 13

4. *R chart:*
UCL = $\bar{R}D_4$ = 1.6(1.864) = 2.98
LCL = $\bar{R}D_3$ = 1.6(.136) = .22
$\bar{x}$ *chart:*
UCL = $\bar{\bar{x}} + A_2\bar{R}$ = 28.5 + .373(1.6) = 29.10
LCL = $\bar{\bar{x}} - A_2\bar{R}$ = 28.5 − .373(1.6) = 27.90

10. $f(x) = \dfrac{n!}{x!(n-x)!} p^x (1-p)^{n-x}$

FIGURE E12.50a

```
The regression equation is
REVENUE = 88.6 + 1.60 TVADV
```

Predictor	Coef	Stdev	T	P
Constant	88.638	1.582	56.02	0.000
TVADV	1.6039	0.4778	3.36	0.015

```
S = 1.215      R-sq = 65.3%    R-sq(adj) = 59.5%
```

Analysis of Variance

SOURCE	DF	SS	MS	F	P
Regression	1	16.640	16.640	11.27	0.015
Residual Error	6	8.860	1.477		
Total	7	25.500			

FIGURE E12.50b

```
The regression equation is
REVENUE = 83.2 + 2.29 TVADV + 1.30 NEWSADV
```

Predictor	Coef	Stdev	T	P
Constant	83.230	1.574	52.88	0.000
TVADV	2.2902	0.3041	7.53	0.001
NEWSADV	1.3010	0.3207	4.06	0.010

```
S = 0.6426    R-sq = 91.9%    R-sq(adj) = 88.7%
```

Analysis of Variance

SOURCE	DF	SS	MS	F	P
Regression	2	23.435	11.718	28.38	0.002
Residual Error	5	2.065	0.413		
Total	7	25.500			

When $p = .02$, the probability of accepting the lot is

$$f(0) = \frac{25!}{0!(25 - 0)!}(.02)^0(1 - .02)^{25} = .6035$$

When $p = .06$, the probability of accepting the lot is

$$f(0) = \frac{25!}{0!(25 - 0)!}(.06)^0(1 - .06)^{25} = .2129$$

INDEX